D0550195

# A Sociology of Ireland

Hilary Tovey & Perry Share

GILL & MACMILLAN

Gill & Macmillan Ltd
Hume Avenue Park West
Dublin 12
with associated companies throughout the world
www.gillmacmillan.ie

© 2000 Hilary Tovey and Perry Share
0 7171 2512 2
Index compiled by John Loftus
Print origination by
Carrigboy Typesetting Services, Co. Cork

A catalogue record is available for this book from the British Library.

3 5 4 2

# *Frontispiece*

It is a definition of a sociologist that he/she is someone who analyses his/her own society. There are no sociologists who do not also live through the complexities and incoherencies of a concrete historical situation and who do not try at the same time to bring out and define general processes of functioning or transformation. I claim for all sociologists not only the right but the duty to be both committed and uncommitted, partisan and independent, realistic and prophetic. How could we set apart the unity of our thought from the history of our personal lives and the experience of profound historical transformations? We not only work on our societies; we work on ourselves.

Alain Touraine
'A sociology of the subject' in J. Clark and M. Diani (eds)
*Alain Touraine*. (1996, p.326).

# Abbreviations

| | |
|---|---|
| AIM | Action, Information, Motivation |
| AP | Associated Press |
| BTSB | Blood Transfusion Service Board |
| CAP | Common Agricultural Policy |
| CEO | Chief Executive Officer |
| CEP | Community enterprise programme |
| CORI | Conference of Religious in Ireland |
| CSO | Central Statistics Office |
| CWC | Community Workers' Co-operative |
| DTEDG | Dublin Travellers' Education and Development Group |
| ENFO | Environment Information Service |
| ERI | Economic Research Institute |
| ESR | *Economic and Social Review* |
| ESRI | Economic and Social Research Institute |
| EU | European Union |
| FGM | Female genital mutilation |
| GAA | Gaelic Athletic Association |
| GNP | Gross national product |
| GRS | *Gerry Ryan Show* |
| HEA | Higher Educational Authority |
| IDA | Industrial Development Authority |
| IJS | *Irish Journal of Sociology* |
| IT | information technologies |
| IUCN | International Union for the Conservation of Nature |
| MAI | Multilateral Agreement on Investment |
| MRBI | Market Research Bureau of Ireland |
| NAFTA | North Atlantic Free Trade Area |
| NAPS | National Anti-Poverty Strategy |
| NATO | North Atlantic Treaty Organisation |
| NESC | National Economic and Social Council |
| NIC | Newly industrialising countries |
| NSM | New social movement |

| OECD | Organisation for Economic Co-operation and Development |
| PLAC | Pro-Life Amendment Campaign |
| REPS | Rural Environment Protection Scheme |
| RMT | *Resource mobilisation theory* |
| RSE | Relationships and Sexuality Education |
| RTC | Regional Technical Colleges |
| RTÉ | Radio Telefís Éireann |
| SAI | Sociological Association of Ireland |
| SPUC | Society for the Protection of the Unborn Child |
| SSIS | Statistical and Social Inquiry Society |
| TCD | Trinity College, Dublin |
| TD | Teachta Dála (Member of Parliament) |
| TNC | Transnational corporations |
| TWG | Technical Working Group |
| UCD | University College, Dublin |
| UCG | University College, Galway |
| UN | United Nations |
| UNEP | United Nations Environmental Programme |
| VAT | Value-added tax |
| VEC | Vocational Education Committees |

# Contents

# Part I

## Sociology in Ireland

# Introduction

This is a book about Irish society from a sociological perspective.

What exactly do we mean by this?

First, we offer an interpretation of aspects of Irish society that we hope will illuminate and resonate with the experiences of those living in, or connected with, or curious about, contemporary Ireland. You may already be expert in the analysis and practice of living in Irish society but we may perhaps add some unexpected, neglected or half-forgotten insights to that expertise. Second, we provide an introduction to the discipline of sociology itself, as a system of thought and a form of imagination that aims to make sense of our everyday life experiences and to place them in the context of their social surroundings. The sociological perspective (in contrast to historical, aesthetic, psychological or even philosophical approaches to reality) is often ignored and under-utilised in Irish social, cultural and intellectual life. We aim to show something of its strength and fascination while also recognising its limitations.

With these two elements together, then, this book is intended as an introduction to Irish sociology: it tries to convey a sense of how Irish sociologists and sociologists in Ireland have thought about, researched and interpreted their society. The idea that Irish sociology could be a valid topic for investigation may seem surprising. After all, sociology generally presents itself as the 'scientific study of society'; it claims to study social life in general: social groups, relationships and social activities wherever they occur. But in practice there is a close connection between the discipline of sociology and the idea of the bounded and unique nation state. Each emerged and was consolidated within the same milieu — the overlapping intellectual networks of nineteenth-century Europe. Sociological accounts of 'society', as a result, are usually those of the social institutions and practices found within the boundaries of specific national societies (especially the United States, Germany, France and Britain), though they are presented as if universal.

Teachers and students of sociology in smaller countries such as the Irish Republic, New Zealand or Finland may read about 'society' only to find that the texts are in reality accounts of British or North American society. Readers may find that the occupational structure of their own country, its political or educational systems or how it organises relations between the genders are not those

3

described. But because such structures and systems are presented as those of 'society' in the abstract, readers may learn little of the specificities of their own society and be unable to ask significant questions about it. They may even come to see their own society, with its different institutional forms and practices, as inferior or uninteresting, since it does not correspond to the 'norm' for a modern society.

In effect, all sociologies are 'national' sociologies. While they share common frameworks of analysis and guiding ideas, they are marked by specific historical and social circumstances. We must read them, not as innocent descriptions of 'reality', but as being deeply influenced by where and how they have developed. Irish sociology has been shaped by our incorporation into an English-speaking intellectual world dominated comprehensively by British and American participants. As a product of recent history and 'modern' ways of thinking, the sociological perspective is associated with a secularised self-consciousness characteristic of 'modern' actors. If we fail to recognise its national origins, it can become a vehicle for cultural dependency, promoting cultural change that imagines a particular and limited form of modernity, that ignores the specificities of space, time and power.

We thus address the sociology of Ireland in a deliberately *reflexive* way. Neither the discipline itself nor its application to Irish society is transparent or unproblematic. In Part I of the book we briefly sketch the historical background from which the discipline of sociology emerged and which shaped its subsequent development. We take Irish society as a case study to demonstrate and to reflect upon the questions that sociologists ask about society and the interpretations and explanations they offer.

The chapters of Part I are linked by the idea of 'modernity'. In Chapter 1 we argue that for the past 150 years sociology has developed specifically as the study of modern — effectively industrial — society. This does not mean that sociologists have no interest in the study of other sorts of societies, but that much sociology assumes modern industrial society to be the typical or normal case that the discipline should seek to analyse and explain. However, Irish students may find that many claims in typical sociology textbooks about 'modern industrial society' do not adequately reflect Irish experience. For example, Irish society has industrialised only recently; agriculture still occupies a sizeable minority of the workforce; nearly half of the Irish population lives outside large cities and towns; and religion remains a strong, if currently contested, force in Irish social life. In a number of ways Irish society seems to be distinctive or exceptional, even though it shares many features with other contemporary societies. Irish society today is certainly modern but it may also reveal that the conception of modernity that underpins much sociology is rather narrow and limiting. We need to query these conceptions and expose the assumptions that influence how we understand our own historical experiences and how we anticipate our future development.

In Part I and indeed throughout this book we argue that there is more than one way to be modern. The more sociology identifies 'society' with the social arrangements found in specific, usually advanced and powerful, states, the more this impoverishes the discipline, as it prevents us from recognising the open-endedness of all social development. In Chapters 3 and 4 we discuss the Irish experience of development and modernisation in the light of an analysis of the normative assumptions of core sociology. We suggest in Chapter 3 that to understand Irish economic and social development it is crucial to address the transformations in agriculture as well as in industry. The significance of agriculture and food production is not an indication that we are somehow 'less than modern', but emphasises the importance of recognising the variant pathways into modernity.

In Chapter 4 we pay particular attention to the state as an agent of modernisation in Ireland. We suggest that how the Irish state has managed the process of economic development has been fundamental in the production of modern Ireland, particularly in terms of its power and class structures. Other agencies, internal and external, including transnational corporations (TNCs) and the European Union (EU), have also been very important; the contemporary world is one where societies are interdependent and no society develops alone. The significant contribution of the state to the shaping of contemporary Ireland distinguishes our experience of modernity from that of many societies referred to as 'typically modern'.

Our analysis of the dynamics of Irish development is preceded by a discussion of the development of sociology in Ireland. Chapter 2 is central to our attempt at an element of reflexivity in this book. We argue that, while sociology sets out to provide interpretations of reality that are in some sense objective, it remains relative to the cultural and social/institutional context in which it is produced. To 'do sociology' in Ireland is not necessarily the same as in other countries: Irish sociology may emerge from a unique constellation of values and aims and may address different audiences and publics. This of course is true of this book as of any other sociological work; we encourage the reader to treat it as a small part of an unfolding 'national tradition' of Irish sociology that, we hope, will itself become an object of sociological analysis and reflection.

# 1
# *Sociology and modernity*

This chapter is a brief and selective introduction to sociology in general and contains little specifically Irish material, except for some illustrative examples. We sketch the historical context in which the study of social matters was first formalised into the discipline of sociology and outline some of the key ideas that emerged during that formative period. These ideas remain central to sociological thought today. We aim to connect with 'the high tradition' in sociology that can be traced back to the revolutionary discoveries about society by thinkers such as Karl Marx, Max Weber and Émile Durkheim in the period from 1850 to 1920.

The nature of Irish modernity is a key theme of this book and in this chapter we focus in particular on how sociology has interpreted this concept. The classic sociological debates about modernity offer a degree of intellectual vigour, emotional depth and engagement rarely found in Irish discussions of the topic. Sociology has also contributed to a specific conception of 'modern society' that can marginalise or confuse the experience of modernity in societies like Ireland. Our brief discussion of the classic sociological theorists, and how their ideas related to particular issues of social change, form the basis of this opening chapter.

## THE ORIGINS OF SOCIOLOGY

Sociology, as a distinct form of enquiry, is a product of the nineteenth century. The term itself was coined around 1838 by the French writer Auguste Comte. A long tradition of thought about the nature of society and social change can be traced back to the Ancient Greeks and to Islamic culture but most of this earlier thinking was philosophical (depending on reasoning from basic assumptions); theological (drawing from divine revelation); or psychological (in the sense that it started with some first principles about human nature and argued from these to an account of society). Writers like Comte sought a new approach with its own distinctive label that took society rather than human nature as its starting point and that used systematic methods to collect empirical evidence. But why did this new approach emerge in this particular historical period?

Two features of the time help us to understand the emergence of sociology, its subsequent development and the central issues that remain of concern to sociologists. The nineteenth century was the age of industrial and political revolution. It was also the age of science. Together, we could say these made it the age of control. The application of science, particularly through industrial technology, enormously increased the scope of human control over the natural environment and its resources. In politics, radical thinkers similarly tried to bring the institutions of the state under the control of human reason. Inevitably the desire to control through the accumulation and application of knowledge would be extended into the field of society.

The British sociologist Brian Turner (1996, p.3) suggests that it was then that the idea of 'the social' as a human creation separate from 'nature' became widely accepted:

> Modern industrial society was not a natural community . . . it dealt with needs and the satisfaction of wants in a wholly revolutionary and unique fashion. Natural communities were bound by tradition and by the traditional or conventional satisfaction of wants and needs.

The discipline of sociology, he suggests, developed in order to analyse this new concept of a 'separate and autonomous world of the social'; indeed the ideas of society, modernity and sociology emerged together. For some, sociology was a science that could be used to control both human behaviour and the development of societies. For others it appeared to offer a form of reasoning that could emancipate humans from external control and, by helping them to understand their own social situation and circumstances, increase their autonomy. These dual — and often competing — views of sociology persist. They often meet in debates over whether sociology is a science and, if so, what sort of science it should be.

The growth of sociology was part of the formation of modernity. By the early nineteenth century the conviction was widespread in Europe and North America that the most profound changes yet experienced by humanity were under way. The industrial revolution, first in Britain and later in France, Germany and the United States, precipitated new economic processes that seemed likely to alter for ever the organisation of societies and social relationships. The 'democratic revolutions' in the United States (1776) and France (1789) provoked intense debates about human nature, legitimate authority and the proper relationship between the individual and society. The speed of social change seemed to have accelerated tremendously and social thinkers became preoccupied with trying to identify modernity and to chart its likely future path. Contemporary sociology has inherited a view of itself not just as the study of society, but of *modern* society. By contrast the cognate discipline of anthropology is often defined as the study of pre-modern, or traditional, social forms, though many anthropologists would challenge this distinction.

Nineteenth-century social thinkers disagreed over how to characterise and evaluate modern society. They differed in their emotional and moral responses to social change. Some feared that the modern world posed a threat to social order; their aim was to discover how social stability could be restored and secured. This preoccupation has developed within contemporary sociology as *the problem of social order*: the attempt to explain how the organisation of society is maintained and reproduced over time. Other thinkers were far more excited by the potential of modernity to expand human control over social arrangements and to overcome existing constraints on human freedom. Their response shaped contemporary sociology's second core preoccupation: *the problem of social inequality*.

Most sociologists today see both these concerns as central to sociological inquiry. We may understand better what is common to all in a society (such as beliefs, values, shared identity and social consensus) when we recognise what divides individuals and social groups (unequal access to power and social respect, conflict over beliefs and values). We cannot explain social order in any society unless we can show how social inequality is managed within it; equally, the type and experience of social inequality is deeply influenced by how the society is ordered and organised.

We have considered above the emotional and moral responses to modernity of the social thinkers of the nineteenth century and their intellectual or analytic responses. However, we shall now see how the ideas and interpretations of modernity of some major sociological theorists of the period have influenced the way all of us today, sociologists or not, think about and interpret the world in which we live.

## SOCIOLOGY AS THE STUDY OF MODERN SOCIETY

The nineteenth-century writers who tried to interpret the changing world around them agreed on one thing — it was new and unique in historical experience — but they differed as to how to describe and characterise it. As a result their writings offer at least four distinct themes for characterising modern society. Three derive from attempts to identify the most important effects of the economic transformation introduced by the Industrial Revolution; the fourth is more concerned with tracing the social effects of cultural change. We might summarise them as follows:

- modern society as *industrial* society
- modern society as *capitalist* society
- modern society as *urban* society
- modern society as *rational* society.

## Modern society as industrial society

The Industrial Revolution is normally understood to be the transformation of an economy dominated by agriculture to one based on manufacturing that spread from eighteenth-century Britain to the rest of the Western world. The techno-logical changes involved, such as the invention of new machines and new ways of harnessing power for the production and transport of goods, had far-reaching effects on people's livelihoods and on the social organisation of work. In the early nineteenth-century British cotton industry, for example, the introduction of power looms brought weavers out of their cottages and small workshops and into factories where they experienced new work routines (the 'tyranny of the clock') and new work relationships of authority and control.

The French thinker Émile Durkheim interpreted the social changes that accompanied industrialisation as an increase in the *division of labour* in society. This refers to how work tasks are divided and shared among the working population. Durkheim argued that in pre-industrial societies, one worker or workgroup (such as a family) did a range of different work tasks necessary to meet survival needs and work was organised sequentially so that each stage in the production process was completed before the next was begun. This allowed a single worker to see the whole process through from beginning to end and to have a wide range of skills with limited specialisation.

In contrast, each worker now specialises in a single activity that has to be complemented by other specialised workers. With the shift from handicraft to machine production and from the workshop to the factory, all the processes necessary to produce a given item can be carried out simultaneously. The indus-trialisation of agriculture and food provides a good example of Durkheim's thesis. In Ireland, in the earlier part of the twentieth century, butter was produced manually by farm families who also tended, fed and milked the cows. Today the labour of producing butter is divided between the farmer who produces the raw milk; the factory that processes it into butter; the factory that produces feed for the cows; the factory that produces the computer programmes to regulate the timing and content of the cows' meals; and so on. We can see the same process in other areas of society. The job of 'teacher' has become divided into first-, second- or third-level teacher; and into educator, career guidance advisor, counsellor or youth worker. The role of 'enterprise boss' is now divided into financial controller, production manager, sales manager, personnel manager and so on. The outcome is a much more complex and detailed system of occupational divisions and identities in modern industrial society.

A question that preoccupied Durkheim was how a society with an advanced division of labour could retain the social bonds between individuals that he thought necessary for social order. Such societies tend to be very individualistic, with a danger that those within them may lose a sense of social connectedness or obligation to others. Pre-industrial societies were unified on the basis of similarities — most people shared the same sorts of skills, responsibilities, values and life experiences. This unity is destroyed by industrialisation. For Durkheim, an answer could be found in the fact that as people become more specialised occupationally, they become more dependent on their fellow citizens. As each of us provides only a specialised service to others, we rely on them to provide us with their services and skills. In a modern, industrialised society collective social order depends more on the acceptance of difference and on co-operation between individuals and groups than on feelings of sameness and collective identity.

Durkheim sometimes went so far as to suggest that industrial society is synonymous with 'civilisation' because of the new order of *moral individualism* that a highly developed division of labour can create. This moral code reverses earlier understandings of the proper relationship between the individual and society. It shifts the emphasis from the duties the individual owes to society to the duties society owes to the individual. Moral individualism treats the individual as the source of all ethical value and encourages the organisation of society to ensure maximisation of individual rights.

Durkheim realised that individualism could sometimes be amoral rather than moral. He argued that modern society constituted an abnormal form of the division of labour and a breeding ground for amoral individualism. The industrial society that emerged at the end of nineteenth-century Europe did not extend equal rights to all of its citizens. It was full of arbitrary inequalities and severely restricted the opportunity for an acceptable lifestyle for some social groups. Instead of generating feelings of solidarity and mutual respect between specialised and differentiated individuals, it tended to encourage either unbridled egoism (selfishness) or what Durkheim termed *anomie*.

This concept is one of Durkheim's most significant contributions to sociology. He used it to identify a condition of society that arises when the rules by which social life is organised are incoherent, incomplete or widely disregarded. Examples might include a society that publicly prides itself on its impartial exercise of justice but where everyone knows that in practice there is one law for the rich and another for the poor; or a society that legitimises divisions between rich and poor on the grounds that anyone can succeed if they work hard enough, yet systematically discriminates against some groups so they can never succeed no matter how hard they try. The result of living in an anomic society is that people may suffer a deep sense of isolation and meaninglessness in their lives and work. In certain social conditions anomie can, as Durkheim argued, lead to suicide, the ultimate statement of the collapse of the bond between the individual and society.

## Modern society as capitalist society

The society that has emerged over the past two centuries is often described as industrial capitalist society. Though the terms 'industrial' and 'capitalist' are often used in tandem in this way, they are not synonymous. Instances of capitalism can be found prior to the development of modern industry. Some forms of agricultural production in eighteenth-century Britain were capitalist, as were many business enterprises in fifteenth-century Italian city states. Similarly, the twentieth century has seen the development of industrial societies that were not capitalist, such as the former Soviet Union. Sociologists generally use the term 'capitalist' to describe a particular way that economic production is organised: it is oriented to exchange on markets; we produce things in order to sell them; the wealth or resources used in production are held in private ownership; and these resources are invested and reinvested to produce the greatest possible profit. Capitalist societies are those where this type of economic organisation predominates.

The major interpreter of modern society as capitalist society was Karl Marx. Marx understood capitalism very specifically as an economic system in which profit is made by those who own the means of production (land, money or credit, machinery, buildings) through exploiting the labour of those who do not. Owners, or 'capitalists', realise a profit when they can sell products on the market for more than they cost to produce. This is possible mainly through paying those who labour to create the product less than the true value of their contribution to its final market price. But how could they achieve that? It is only possible in a society where private ownership of wealth is concentrated in the hands of a minority and the rest of the population, reduced to owning nothing but their own capacity to work (their labour power), have to sell this to the capitalists in order to survive. Capitalism as an economic system, Marx argued, both produces and depends upon a particular type of social structure peculiar to capitalist societies — division into two major and opposed classes, the capitalist class or *bourgeoisie*, and the working class or *proletariat*.

While the concept of industrial society led Durkheim to ask questions about social order and stability, the concept of capitalist society enabled Marx to focus on questions of inequality and conflict. In his view, it is the relationship between the two major classes — a relationship of conflict — that determines the form and development of modern society. Capitalist economies are very dynamic and characterised by continual technological innovation as capitalists strive to reduce production costs, increase profits and diminish their dependence on human labour. But capitalist society is also a society that alienates human beings from each other and its structures reduce human freedom.

The Marxist concept of *alienation* is as significant to sociologists as Durkheim's notion of anomie. Marx used the term to attack what he saw as the profoundly dehumanising effects of capitalism. Under capitalist conditions, workers become alienated — separated — from the products of their work. What they produce does not belong to them but to the capitalist, the owner of the means of production who has bought their labour. Instead of being a recognisable outcome of their own human creativity, what they produce appears foreign to them, disconnected from their identity and lives. But alienation does not stop here, on the production line. The result of a capitalist division of labour is that people become alienated from work itself as work is subdivided into fragmented tasks, mechanised and managed from above, thus denying workers the use of their own skills and knowledge or control over the timing and sequence of their work. In these conditions work becomes a meaningless activity undertaken for purely instrumental reasons — to make money to survive. Inevitably, workers also become alienated from each other. They no longer see themselves as engaged in a joint productive task but merely as atomised individuals. Ultimately, since Marx believed that it is creative interaction with the environment through meaningful work that makes us human, this means that capitalism alienates people from their own essential humanity. Finding no meaning in their working lives, they become obsessed with material possessions and work harder and harder in order to acquire more and more, whether or not the possessions have any intrinsic value. They learn to see themselves as no more than consumers. It is inevitable that capitalist societies are dominated by an ideology that glorifies material possessions unless the working class can find the means to mobilise against it and regain humanity for modern human beings.

Marx's analysis of social change is often described as *materialist*. He understood the development of modern capitalism to be the result primarily of changes in economic organisation. While not denying the key role of the economy, Max Weber stressed that ideas and values also influence social change. Weber thought it important to ask how people could come to accept the new economic relations and behaviour that capitalism demands. In particular, he asked how they could accept that the search for profit should be the central, overriding goal of life, when in previous 'traditional' societies work was more often simply a means to achieve an acceptable standard of living, only to be abandoned once that was reached. How do we explain this change in people's values?

Weber argued that a key influence here was religion. He focused in particular on the religious changes that took place in the seventeenth and eighteenth centuries in Western Europe, especially the emergence of a puritan type of Protestantism (most clearly seen in Calvinism) whose followers came to believe that an austere, self-denying life of unremitting work was the best way to glorify God and to calm anxieties over whether they were one of the 'saved' who would find a place in heaven. Weber's sociology is laced with irony. The materialism of modern capitalist society can be traced back to the 'work ethic' of an ascetic religious world view.

Weber, like Marx, saw modern capitalist society as characterised by inequality. But whereas Marx's focus was on the material bases of inequality, Weber was more interested in the ideas that are used in modern society to explain and to justify inequality. Weber's view of sociology as the study of human action and of the meanings that actors give to their world has been of great influence on sociologists since.

## Modern society as urban society

As we have seen, industrialisation is widely associated with a switch from an agricultural to a manufacturing economy. It is also associated with urbanisation — the growth of towns and cities and the depopulation and decline of rural areas. Of course, cities existed in pre-industrial societies (for example, Alexandria or Lima) but industrialisation boosted and accelerated their development as well as transforming their character in important ways. The concentration of factories in urban areas attracted immigrants pushed out of the countryside by the commercialisation of agriculture, and the numbers of working class inhabitants in cities swelled enormously. Rapidly expanding, badly built and overcrowded working-class housing areas were prone to epidemics and seen by many upper- and middle-class urban people as symbolic of the threat to social order posed by a chaotic and uncontrolled poor.

Urbanisation was perhaps the most visible of the massive changes that modernity brought to society. It attracted the attention of many social commentators, including some sociologists who saw it as evidence of regress rather than progress. They mourned what was being lost with the passing of 'traditional' rural society. The influential German sociologist Ferdinand Tönnies, for example, wrote that urban industrial society was characterised by a loss of community. He argued that industrialisation increases the scale and thus the impersonality of society and with urbanisation the close personal relationships of small-scale pre-industrial local societies are replaced by impersonal calculative relationships where others may be seen as no more than a way to achieve one's own aims. Though Tönnies did not explicitly identify 'community' *Gemeinschaft* with rural areas or a rural way of life, nor 'impersonal association' *Gesellschaft* with urban areas, many writers subsequently did, with the result that 'rural society' is often confused with 'traditional' or 'pre-industrial' society, while the urban is inevitably linked to modernity.

Another important German social theorist, Georg Simmel, wrote about the city as the key location of the everyday experience of modernity. For him modern individuals are formed within and by an urban or metropolitan world. In cities people are constantly involved in interactions with strangers that engage only fragments of the individual personality, leaving most of it unknown. On the city streets people are bombarded by a constant stream of impressions and are brought into contact continuously with anonymous others. City dwellers typically respond to this by developing stratagems of defence such as inward retreat, social distance and an attitude of blasé indifference towards everything they encounter (Simmel 1971, p.326):

The metropolitan type of man . . . develops an organ protecting him against the threatening currents and discrepancies of his external environment which would uproot him. He reacts with his head instead of his heart . . . Metropolitan life, thus, underlies a heightened awareness and a predominance of intelligence in metropolitan man.

But if city living is associated with intelligence and heightened self-consciousness in a way that rural living is not, Simmel (1971, p.326) also emphasised that the city is the seat and the visual representation of the modern money economy:

> The metropolis has always been the seat of the money economy . . . money economy and the dominance of the intellect are intrinsically connected. They share a matter-of-fact attitude in dealing with men and with things; and in this attitude, a formal justice is often coupled with an inconsiderate hardness. . . . Money . . . reduces all quality and individuality to the question: How much?'

While Simmel's fascination with the metropolis was tempered with ambivalence, subsequent sociological characterisations of the urban way of life were far more positive. The American sociologist Louis Wirth, writing in 1938, claims the city to be the source of innovation in the modern world and the dominant, controlling centre of modern society. For him modern culture is virtually identical with urban culture. At the same time, the supposed absence from urban life of community was and is used to explain the high rates of crime and other social problems that seem to be a feature of modern society.

There is in fact little evidence to support the idea that settlement patterns, whether concentrated and large-scale as in urban settings, or dispersed and small-scale as in rural ones, determine either social relationships or psychological characteristics. The belief that there is a characteristically 'urban way of life' to be contrasted with the 'rural way of life' has come to hinder sociologists when investigating the very different ways that different social groups experience life. Nevertheless, the modern city distinguishes our world from that of earlier periods in history and the experience of modernity in the urban setting remains a focus of research for contemporary sociologists.

## Modern society as rational society

Political revolutionaries in late eighteenth-century Europe tried to replace tradition with reason and law as the basis for societal organisation. They claimed, for example, that rulers should no longer govern by inheritance or divine right, but should be selected in accordance with clear, formal and universally acceptable procedures. Behind this lay the belief that human beings are naturally sociable, co-operative and reasonable; if they often appeared to be the opposite, this was due to the distorting effects of oppressive and unreasonable forms of social organisation. With the removal of these distortions, people would be freed to create the type of society in which these natural qualities would gain full expression. The spread of democracy, universal education and beliefs in individual rights seemed to indicate the benign progress of reason in society, as did the development of law, science and, as suggested earlier, sociology itself. Nevertheless, not all sociologists were convinced that the increasing rationalisation of social life equated to undiluted progress nor that it necessarily advanced human happiness.

Simmel, as we have already noted, connected the hard-headed rationality of the inhabitants of large cities with the colonisation of all areas of urban life and experience by the money economy and monetary values. Weber argued that one important form of rationalisation in modern society was the development of bureaucracy as a way to administer and control large organisations. Modern bureaucracies are organisations whose official functions are set out in writing (for example, in 'rules and procedures') and are divided into sets of distinct tasks allocated to specific officials. These officials are given the necessary authority and resources to carry out these tasks, but no more; they do not 'own' their positions within the organisation but are selected for them on the basis of explicitly specified qualifications. Positions within the bureaucracy are organised in a hierarchical way with each position being under the control and supervision of a higher one; administrative actions, decisions and rules are recorded in writing and organisational records provide the basis for continual review and improvement of the organisation's performance. This type of administrative apparatus is quite different from any found in earlier societies and is above all a rational way to organise administration. Though today we often use the term 'bureaucratic' to mean 'inefficient', Weber at the time believed this type of rational administrative system to be extremely efficient.

For Weber, rationality refers primarily to a way of acting. *Rational action* is taken on the basis of a calculation of the relationship between means and ends: 'I choose to do x because I want to achieve y, and doing x is the most effective way to achieve y.' This contrasts with *customary action*: 'I'll do x because this is what people in my group have always done.' Modern society, according to Weber, is one where rational action, involving the application of knowledge, calculation and rules, increasingly replaces customary action. This spread of instrumental rationality undermines religious belief and fundamental values. A rationalised world thus threatens to become secularised, 'disenchanted' and, ultimately, meaningless.

Weber associated the growth of rational systems of administration with the development of large-scale capitalist enterprises but linked it in particular to the state. Modern capitalist society characteristically involves an expanded bureaucratic state which, in Weber's view, means that modern states possess the power to supervise, assemble information on, monitor and organise citizens to a degree unprecedented in the pre-capitalist world. Bureaucracy and democracy are in conflict, since the former centralises power and concentrates it in the hands of those who control the bureaucratic organisation. Ironically, therefore, the very advance of reason may lead to a reduction in human freedom and happiness.

Sociological theorising did not, of course, end in the 1920s. Later in this book you will encounter further references to Weber, Durkheim, Marx and Simmel and also modern theorists such as Habermas, Bourdieu, Giddens and Parsons and many Irish authors whose work is cited and discussed. They continue to carry forward the task of understanding the world in which they live, if not always by building on, at least in dialogue with, the ideas of the classic social theorists.

## SOCIOLOGY AS A SCIENCE OF SOCIETY

Restivo (1991, p.4) describes sociology as 'a field of inquiry simultaneously concerned with understanding, explaining, criticising and improving the human condition'. We have already devoted some attention to the 'understanding', 'criticising' and 'improving' aspects of sociological work, but not much to 'explaining'. Sociological inquiries are not only about exploring theories and ideas. Theories and ideas must be tested against reality if they are to be any use as explanations. Sociology is an empirical discipline that makes discoveries about social reality through the application of theoretical ideas and methods of research. Here we discuss briefly the practices and status of sociology as a research-based discipline or what many would call a (social) science.

There are many ways to research social life, such as large-scale questionnaire surveys; structured or unstructured interviews; ethnographic observation; or the collection and analysis of documents. For most sociologists, research is not just a matter of choosing a technique — it involves reflection on the fundamental issues of how we 'gain our knowledge of the social world, the relationships that are held to exist between theory and research, and the place of values and ethics in research practice' (May 1997, p.1). The attention paid to these issues makes sociology somewhat unique as a research discipline.

The technicist assumption that doing sociological research is just a matter of selecting appropriate tools implies an unproblematic relationship between researcher and social reality. Early sociologists such as Comte or Durkheim may have held such a view, but it is not easily accepted by contemporary sociology, with decades of reflection on the difficulty of trying to do good social research. Durkheim, who in 1895 authored one of the first textbooks of sociological research (*The rules of sociological method*), said that the social researcher should study social phenomena 'in the same state of mind as the physicist, chemist or physiologist when he probes into a still unexplored region of the scientific domain' (1964, p.xiv). Here he was following Comte, who believed that sociology could and should be modelled closely on the methods and procedures of the natural sciences to produce similar systematic knowledge of and control over the social world. Comte thought the social world could be explained as could the natural world — by deriving objective laws or generalisations about the behaviour of phenomena (in the case of sociology, people and groups) that would allow us to predict their future behaviour patterns. Prediction was important to him because the capacity to predict enhances the potential for control. In reality since then, sociologists have rarely been interested in prediction (now more a concern of economists) and have tended to concentrate on close description and interpretation of what has already occurred.

There are major difficulties with any attempt to treat the social and natural worlds identically or to argue that sociology can only be scientific if it models itself on the natural sciences. Indeed it has become increasingly clear (see Woolgar, 1988) that there is no single model of natural scientific inquiry that all scientists agree on and follow. As suggested above, it is also important for social researchers to be reflexive, that is, *critical of their own methods of generating knowledge*. As a result, sociology has had to devise its own distinctive methods and procedures for research.

A number of key considerations govern the practice of sociological research. First, people within the social world already understand to some degree how their world operates. As a consequence they cannot be treated as would the elements that make up the natural world. Objects in the natural world such as atoms, molecules or ecological systems 'behave' — they are governed by the laws of cause and effect. Humans 'act' — they have reason and purpose, they make choices and they confer meaning on their world. They have their own theories about why their world is as it is and these are also empirical facts for the sociologist to study. Second, sociologists are members of the world they research. Indeed without access to the social world as participants as well as researchers, it would be extremely difficult, if not impossible, for sociologists to understand anything about it. Social reality is a product of people's ideas and interpretations and is not automatically accessible to the senses or to measuring tools in the way that natural phenomena are. To grasp someone's interpretation of reality we need to participate, even in a minimal way, in their culture.

Sociologists differ in their responses to these difficulties. We can distinguish three main positions. *Positivism* refers to those who, in the tradition of Comte, hold the view that for the purposes of research people can be seen to react to their environment as molecules react to heat — without conscious knowledge of what they are doing. Positivism implies that we do not need to ask people *why* they do what they do but we can learn this from our own observation of them. Thus, for example, we need not ask heroin users why they take the drug since we can see that they are 'addicted' to it. More broadly, positivism assumes that there are 'facts' about the social world that are independent of how people define them. It may deduce, for example, that Irish society is class-divided, though most people in Ireland would claim that class is irrelevant and that people rise or fall largely on their own merits. Such facts can be revealed to us by research and it is possible to generate an 'objective' knowledge of social reality. This does not depend on the researcher's feelings about or interpretations of that reality but is produced by detached and impartial observation and measurement.

*Subjectivism* insists that 'the only thing we can know with certainty is how people interpret the world around them' (May, 1997, p.13). It rejects the positivist claim that research can provide privileged access to 'facts' that people in the social world are not themselves aware of. Extreme versions of subjectivism abandon the idea that there are such facts, indeed that there is *any* external reality beyond people's ideas and definitions of it. Less extreme versions redefine the goal of sociological research as description — it should reveal how interpretations are constructed and how people reach mutual agreements on working definitions of reality. A subjectivist approach to environmental problems, for example, might focus on how the idea that we are threatened by global catastrophe in the form of global warming, has come to dominate contemporary environmental politics, rather than on how the 'fact' of global warming is a result of collective human behaviour.

Subjectivist positions have been boosted by feminist critiques of conventional or positivist research. Feminists have revealed, in particular, how much supposedly objective and impartial knowledge generated by sociological research has been gender-blind or gender-biased. It has produced accounts of the social world that are only 'real' from a male point of view. Feminist sociologists have forcefully challenged the positivist claim that the good researcher is disengaged from the subject they study. They argue that research is in fact a two-way process where the findings are as influenced by the social identity, status and biographical experiences of the researcher as those of the 'researched'. Research knowledge is always the product of collaboration between researcher and researched and is thus relative to the conditions under which it was generated. There is no detached vantage point from which the absolute truth can be discerned.

A third position, *critical realism* or, as it is often called, *critical theory*, is mainly associated with Marxist sociologists, though it also shares elements with Freudian approaches to researching human behaviour. Both take as a starting point the idea that there are underlying mechanisms in society or in people's subconscious that operate outside consciousness and generate surface phenomena (losing your job; a 'Freudian slip') that we cannot fully explain just by looking at the surface. Critical theorists share with positivists the idea that research should do more than just describe how people act towards each other and how they develop shared ideas about reality. Research should go beyond description to explanation and try to identify the conditions that allow such interaction and interpretation to happen. This does not mean we should ignore the sense that people make of their world but we should recognise that it is often distorted or incomplete. Critical theorists part company both with positivists and subjectivists over the issue of detachment and disengagement in research. For them, the purpose of research is to reveal what needs to be criticised in contemporary society, for example, oppression and inequality. Their standpoint is engaged and passionate, not detached. They do ultimately accept, with caution, the notion that ordinary people can sometimes be wrong about how they understand and evaluate their own social world. The insights of critical research can help to illuminate more adequately the 'true' nature of the world.

Apart from the issues raised above, others that sociological researchers face include the place of ethics and values in research and the relation between theory and research. It was held as orthodoxy for many years that 'objective' research, in the social as in the natural sphere, does not allow an attachment to values to bias the gathering and interpretation of data. We have seen that there is now far less consensus among social researchers that this is possible or even desirable. The emphasis has shifted from trying to keep values out of research to developing codes of *research ethics*.

Ethical research is honest and avoids manipulating or exploiting subjects, readers, sponsors or funders unless there are, in rare cases, compelling reasons for deception. Reflection on ethics encourages researchers to examine the research process as a whole, in particular the values and interests, often unanticipated or unconscious, that shape it. Also of importance are the circumstances under which the research is being carried out: who has funded it; to what end; who has defined the core 'research problem'; and what is to happen to research findings. The fact that a government department, for example, has funded a piece of research and has an interest in how it is done and what it discovers does not necessarily make the research invalid, but it is important for researchers to keep in mind that they are operating in a world where there is unequal power, both in the definition of 'a problem suitable for researching' and in avoiding the intrusions of the researcher. The rich and powerful are far less often the subject of social research than the poor and marginalised. Social scientists are encouraged, with promises of funding, media attention and participation in policy-making spheres, to do research that is 'relevant'. For the sociologist, the construction of a relevant research topic is itself a social phenomenon that can be researched.

The sociologist of education Kathleen Lynch (1999a; 1999b) has argued strongly that even critical models of sociological research typically exclude the 'researched', who usually have no control over the research project and may never see the final product. Successful instances of genuinely participatory research are rare and if those researched have some control over the research methodology, this seldom extends to participation in the development of theory or analysis. The lack of any real engagement with those who experience inequality means, for Lynch, that sociologists are debarred from moving beyond a critique of existing systems towards any truly transformative or emancipatory practice.

Much social research is done without reference to theory — C. Wright Mills (1961) described this as 'abstracted empiricism' and Restivo calls it the 'low tradition' in sociology. The career world of the modern sociologist is organised so as to widen the gap between research and theorising. There are strong pressures to specialise in one or the other and those whose areas of competence are the most specialised tend to receive the highest rewards. Publication outlets such as journals and books are divided according to the specialised markets they serve. A widening gap between research and theorising leaves sociology vulnerable to a process whereby its research problems are determined by others. A sense of development or cumulation of knowledge about social reality becomes difficult to achieve. The discipline tends to fragment into a series of disconnected sub-fields of research that lack interconnection or possibilities for dialogue, for example, the sociology of childhood, urban life, economic development, food, religion, management, health and illness and so on. But research *can* draw on theory and contribute to the rebuilding and refinement of theoretical frameworks in many different ways. There is no single right way of relating the two, yet some mutual engagement appears to be essential to a dynamic and coherent sociology.

## SOCIOLOGY, MODERNITY AND POST-MODERNITY

Our brief review of the early sociological responses to the massive social changes of the eighteenth and nineteenth centuries showed how the experience of these changes led to interpretations of modern society that are still potent and continue to largely define what sociology is about. Sociologists are now aware that the development of modernity is not only a series of historical changes or processes in the material world, but also involves intellectual assumptions that legitimate and sanction these changes. They are captured particularly in the taken-for-granted identification of modernity and progress.

It is part of the modern attitude to assume that human history has a meaning and a destiny and that it consists of a sequence of movements towards a higher, more civilised, more orderly, more humanly satisfying way of organising social and individual life. It is characteristic of modernity to assume that people have developed ways to research reality that allow them to arrive at truth, and that the uncovering of truth aids and expands the realisation of human freedom. It is part of modernity to take for granted that revolutionary changes in society — political (the French Revolution) and technical (the Industrial Revolution) — are incremental advances in the unfettering of human reason so that it can be put to use to improve the world. It is, finally, a quintessentially modern belief that the development of science and its application in the empirical world through industrial technology enhances human control over and capacity to manage the natural environment for the greater benefit of all.

Such assumptions are so ingrained in modern thinking about the world, including sociological thinking, that we have come to accept them as largely unquestioned. Sociologists have begun to draw attention to the novelty of such ideas, in historical terms, and what we might call their fragility. Kumar (1995) points out that to seventeenth-century Europeans the very idea of historical change would have been strange as most believed that human life was fundamentally unchanging. For them the object of studying history was primarily to discover, as the Scottish philosopher David Hume put it, 'the constant and universal principles of human nature' under varying sets of circumstances. The idea of progress — that human history could be thought of as, in effect, a movement towards the realisation of Heaven on Earth — would have struck them as downright blasphemous. Similarly the idea that underlay the advance of science, that nature is made up of inert matter that can be partitioned, manipulated, combined and recombined to realise human ends, contrasts markedly with earlier understandings of nature as an unpredictable and explosive living system to be placated through ritual or co-operated with through long experience and observation (Merchant 1980).

Ironically, perhaps, the excavation of intellectual history in the period before modernity has helped the emergence of what is widely today referred to as *post-modernity*. Post-modern thinking contextualises and relativises modernity. Instead of believing, with the modernisers, that the intellectual assumptions of modernity are objectively true and absolute in all historical eras, it emphasises how they are historically quite novel, unique and contingent. The concept of post-modernity is notoriously difficult and we do not propose to go into it in great depth here. We will simply try to disentangle some of the different ways that it has been understood, in order to indicate some of its impacts on contemporary sociology.

It is most common to understand post-modernity as a historical period that comes *after* modernity. Thus, if we are now post-modern, it is because we have moved into an era characterised by new social, economic, political and intellectual conditions. Thus, while existing sociological analyses may not be entirely out of date in post-modern society, they may fail in some crucial ways to capture its core experiences. Ulrich Beck (1992), for example, argues that societies today are increasingly organised around struggles to escape from 'bads' (such as threatened environmental disasters) instead of struggles for access to 'goods' (social equality, well-paid work, education, housing). In the 'risk society' that is now replacing industrial society, your position in relation to environmental risks is more significant than your position in relation to the class structure. Class analysis, central to modern sociology, no longer tells the full story of how people's 'life-chances' are shaped. Zygmunt Bauman (1992) suggests that contemporary society has shifted from a society organised centrally around work to a society organised around consumption. In modern society work provided people with their core identities and the important relationships that tied them to the larger society. In post-modern society, we locate our identities and social ties in our patterns of consumption — what we acquire and how we display it. While much classical sociological theorising about modernity emphasises shifts in the world of work as basic to social change, we need to move beyond this to develop new theories for post-modern society. Sociologists do not necessarily agree on these points, in particular on whether contemporary society is so fundamentally different that it needs a radical revision of existing theories.

According to a second interpretation, post-modernity is about the aban-donment of the intellectual assumptions of modernity, especially the notions that human history has a discoverable meaning and that science can uncover absolute truth. While modernity took it for granted that we can establish 'overarching narratives' of history and progress, post-modernity involves turning our backs on any such attempt since all truth is relative and thus no interpretation of the course of history can ever claim absolute correctness. While the idea that truth is relative is perhaps hard for some scientists to accept, it may be easier for sociologists, especially those who work in the Weberian tradition. They are interested in the meanings that people use to guide their actions rather than in establishing whether those meanings are correct or incorrect. But the call to abandon *all* overarching narratives is rather more difficult. The impetus to do sociology reflects a desire to interpret the world in ways that make it meaningful, even if these are only fragmentary and partial interpretations. Sociology involves the construction of narratives and depends upon a belief that these narratives are more than just 'stories', that they have some scientific basis. Many sociologists, faced with this way of understanding the concept of post-modernity, deny that it makes any sense or has any relevance for their discipline.

A third approach to post-modernity sees it not as a historical successor to modernity nor as a rejection of its intellectual assumptions but as an occasion to reflect on the experience of modernity (Kumar 1995, p.67) or, in Bauman's words, 'as modernity conscious of its true nature — *modernity for itself*' (1992, p.187). Bauman argues that, while modernity struggled to order and organise the world, much of the time this struggle gave rise to chaos, to 'variety, contingency and ambivalence'. Instead of trying to repress these outcomes as evidence of the failure of modernity, we should embrace and reflect on them in order to develop new sociological understandings of the contemporary human condition. From this point of view, post-modernity is best understood as a *stance* adopted by the sociologist. It involves an acceptance of social and cultural difference, a readiness to revise interpretations and an openness to competing perspectives. Above all it implies a willingness to stand back and rethink the bases on which judgements and interpretations are made and the fundamental ideas that the discipline has developed. This approach is often called *reflexive sociology*. It is one that, as far as we can, we try to maintain throughout this book.

# 2
# *Irish sociology*

The dominant view of sociology in Ireland is that it is an applied social science. Governments, funders of research, media commentators and publishers expect sociology, like other social sciences such as demography, economics and political science, to provide empirical data by which public policy can be guided. Its task is to analyse patterns and predict trends and to help the powerful to manage society, solve social problems and bring about desired forms of social change. Of all the social sciences, however, sociology is probably regarded as the least satisfactory and reliable public servant. It is often seen to be less serious than other more 'scientific' disciplines, particularly economics. Kane suggests that, for both the public and the policy-makers, 'social scientists are seen to be, at best, jaywalkers, losing fact to science and meaning to literature' (1996, p.133).

For many sociologists, this understanding of the discipline is one-sided, 'slighting both the nature and potential of public life and the importance of other, more critical and theoretically informed versions of sociology' (Calhoun, 1996, p.429). For Calhoun sociology can do a lot more than provide the data needed to carry out the 'technical activities' of ruling elites. It can also generate and inform public debate on the important issues of the day and subject 'the concepts, received understandings and cultural categories constitutive of everyday life and public discourse to critical theoretical reconsideration' (1996, p.429).

In her analysis of the role of social scientists in Irish public life, Kane (1996, p.136) distinguishes between 'intellectuals' and 'the intelligentsia'. The former provide independent critical commentary on the state of the world, while the latter produce knowledge that tends to be 'market-driven [and] readily identifiable, particularly to other "intelligentsias" in management and public administration'. Such knowledge is used to produce, evaluate and extend existing modes of knowing in specific, well-defined areas of inquiry. As it works within established ways of conceptualising the world, it tends to be 'less threatening than the free-floating interpretation of intellectuals'. Lynch (1999b, p.53) is sceptical even about this role, arguing that the 'free-floating intellectual' is a myth. As she points out, 'even radical intellectuals are culturally and relatively financially privileged' and are part of the structures of power within Irish society.

Such analyses suggest there can be a variety of reasons for 'doing sociology'. These include a *managerial* objective to make government more effective and rational; a *democratic* objective to inform and develop individuals so they can participate more fully in society and its government; and an *intellectual* objective to critically examine the social world and better understand it. In Figure 2.1 we can see the connection between these objectives and the four 'founding theorists' of sociology whose ideas about modernity and its development we outlined briefly in Chapter 1.

## Figure 2.1 Sociological approaches of the 'founding theorists'

| *Playful/intellectual* | *Managerial* | *Critical/democratic* |
|---|---|---|
| Simmel | Weber, Durkheim | Weber, Marx |

Durkheim's writings reflect an instrumental and positivistic approach to sociology: it can provide the state with diagnoses of social trends that help it to manage society in a more rational and progressive and less conflictual manner. Marx offers a very different model: the sociologist as politically engaged critic who seeks to awaken and shape the consciousness of the public, in particular that part of it — the working class — that can bring about revolutionary social change. Simmel offers a third model. He was the first theorist to suggest that sociology should examine and analyse society at play as well as at work. It is possible to see his sociological work as a form of 'play' — a disengaged intellectual activity that recognises no external rules and sees playing the game as its own reward. The hardest person to locate in this simplified scheme is Weber. Less optimistic than Durkheim about the benefits of rationality and rational social management, Weber is closer to Marx in his attempts to develop sociology as a critical reflection on the long-term processes of social 'modernisation', but Weber, unlike Marx, had no alternative vision to capitalist modernity. His work often seems, like Simmel's, to provide only its own reward in the intellectual pleasures of understanding and creative interpretation.

From its earliest days, then, sociology has been characterised by disagreement over its nature, purpose and social role. When we look at the history of the discipline in Ireland, we may expect to find similarly competing views as to what it is or should be about. This chapter is an attempt to sketch that history. It argues that sociology in Ireland has tended most often to reflect the Durkheimian managerial model. Its desired contribution has been to help improve, reform and rationalise how Irish society is governed, but there have been occasional flights from this position towards the critical/democratic stance, particularly in the late 1970s, and towards the playful/intellectual approach, particularly in the late 1990s. We will try to explain, sociologically, why this has been the case.

# EARLY FORMS OF SOCIAL INQUIRY IN IRELAND

Social inquiry has a long history in Ireland. The first population census was attempted in 1821. This was followed in 1824 by a detailed educational census and in 1847 by the first agricultural census. In 1854 there was an exhaustive census of landholding throughout the country (Griffin's Valuation). In 1847, the first association in the country devoted to empirical social inquiry, the Dublin Statistical Society, was formed. Fifteen years later it was renamed the Statistical and Social Inquiry Society (SSIS). It celebrated its 150th anniversary in 1997 and continues its work to the present day (Daly, 1997; 1998).

Sociologists of science, in particular those who study the social construction of knowledge (for example, Woolgar, 1988), point out that science, like all knowledge systems, arises from social activity. With regard to the social sciences, Wagner (1994, pp.xiv–xv) argues that we should not take at face value the categorisation of modes of inquiry such as 'social science', 'political science', 'natural science' and so on, but should investigate the historical circumstances under which the discourses now known as the 'social sciences' were constructed. He suggests that they have tended to be closely interwoven with the practices they have claimed to observe, particularly the activities of the state and the market. This means that we must treat the writings of social inquirers 'in a double way' — not just as a source of information about society, but also as an indicator of the 'ways of seeing society' available to people at the time. So what were the historical circumstances relating to the establishment of the Statistical and Social Inquiry Society? Who were its members and how did they see Irish society?

Two circumstances, one external and one internal to Ireland, are worth noting. First, an interest in statistics, and the formation of 'statistical societies', was not unique to Ireland. It was a feature of nineteenth-century European society generally and was linked to the emergence and development of the modern nation state (see Chapter 4). The word 'statistics' originally related to the study of how a state should be organised, and embraced the legal, educational, public health, welfare, criminal and economic aspects of society. It gradually came to mean, more narrowly, quantitative information or 'figures' as states began to collect more and more numerical data as a way of monitoring and regulating populations.

The development of 'modern statistics' was founded on an assumption that, through the collection of objective information about social conditions and behaviour, states could find solutions to the major social problems confronting them. As Daly notes (1997, pp.19–28) it was no coincidence that the Dublin Statistical Society was founded at the height of the Great Famine in Ireland. The discourse of social inquiry in Ireland was shaped early on by the assumption that better information about the major problems and trends in society would produce better government by the state. This implies a belief that the state acts in response to appeals to rationality rather than, as a Marxist view might emphasise, in the interest of powerful groups in society.

This 'rationalist' view of the state, and of what social inquiry is about, would have been widely shared across nineteenth-century Europe. But for Ireland there was an additional factor. At this time Ireland was a colony of Britain and was, moreover, disruptive and difficult to control. As with military technology, the technology of social inquiry found colonial Ireland a good terrain on which to experiment. The early formation of the discourse of social inquiry in Ireland occurred in circumstances where it was deemed important not only to increase the rationality of the state but also to increase its control over society. This may help to explain the underdevelopment of a 'democratic' objective for sociology in Ireland until quite recent times.

The early membership of the Dublin Statistical Society was, as we might expect, drawn from the city's affluent male professional and intellectual elite — lawyers, Trinity College academics, some businessmen, senior Dublin Castle officials and leading members of the Church of Ireland (Daly, 1998, p.2). Few members of the Society were interested in statistical techniques as such. Rather, they believed that some sort of systematic and objective, or 'scientific', information would help to answer the great social questions of the day and suggest a direction for reformative action on the part of the state. Daly describes them as people who were generally optimistic about how Ireland was progressing economically in the wake of the Famine and who tended to share the 'assimilationist' view that 'the best recipe for further prosperity was to bring Irish laws and administrative practices into line with those in England and Wales'. For Boylan and Foley (1992) the social scientific inquiry that the Society helped to popularise was not a 'value-free universalistic science', but a key part of the 'civilising' project launched by a colonial elite that aimed to transform Ireland into, as Archbishop Whateley put it, 'a "really valuable portion of the British Empire" rather than a sort of "morbid excrescence"' (O'Dowd, 1992).

During the first twenty-five years of its existence the SSIS had a considerable impact on the United Kingdom's Irish legislation, and on other matters such as the management of poverty and of children in need. From the 1870s, however, its influence was undermined by the rise of nationalist politics. None of those actively involved in the new social movements such as Sinn Féin or Labour, or even in the Irish Parliamentary Party, were members of the Society. Yet, remarkably, within a few years of the establishment of the Irish Free State, the SSIS had become a highly significant political arena once again. It was able to establish close links with the new civil service — perhaps even closer than those it had enjoyed with Dublin Castle — and a large number of senior public officials became active members (Daly, 1998, p.4). The new Irish state continued to measure, count and analyse its population as part of its system of government. It found in the Society an appropriate forum for the generation of data and advice on the direction of policy. In turn, members of the Society appeared to have no difficulty in redefining the object of their research — 'Irish society' — to reflect the territorial boundaries of the new state, illustrating how, as Wagner notes, discourses of inquiry and the social practices of the state tend to be interwoven.

By the 1950s the SSIS had become a prominent advocate of 'economic planning', particularly through the papers read to it and published in its *Journal* by T.K. Whitaker. By the 1960s, it was entering into 'a golden age . . . Many views first aired at its meetings had now been accepted as official policy. Economics and statistics appeared to offer a blueprint for a modern and prosperous Ireland, precisely as the Society's founders had hoped in 1847' (Daly, 1998, p.7). In the process, however, 'social inquiry' had become very largely redefined as economic and statistical inquiry. A large proportion of the papers presented to the SSIS came from economists and statisticians, especially those employed by government departments and semi-state bodies; also, the Central Bank and the Central Statistics Office (Daly, 1997, p.165). The marginalisation of sociology within the SSIS foreshadowed the marginal position it would occupy within the larger society but it was also set free to begin to develop different understandings of its role and purpose over time.

## THE SHAPING OF IRISH SOCIOLOGY

The SSIS's understanding of the purpose and conduct of social inquiry strongly influenced the shaping of Irish sociology, in particular through its links to the Economic and Social Research Institute (ESRI), the major source of sociological research in Ireland and chief employer of professional sociologists. In 1959 the SSIS was instrumental, with funding assistance from the American Ford Foundation, in the establishment of the Economic Research Institute (ERI). Relations continued to be close between the SSIS and the Institute, with broadly overlapping memberships and similar intellectual concerns. The foundation of the ERI was directly linked to the economic and social development in Ireland that was taking place under the 1960s Programmes for Economic Expansion. The ERI's early concerns — European integration, productivity and tariff protection — mirrored the concerns of the government of the day (Daly, 1997, p.161). Despite this congruence, the ERI was explicitly 'non-political'. It had 'social' added to its remit, and became the ESRI, in 1966. Over the following three decades, it was to become a key location for sociological research in the country.

The ESRI has specialised in conducting large-scale social research that is numerical or quantitative in form. Research is addressed to issues seen as significant social or policy problems by the state or other elite groups (business or employers' associations, for example) and is undertaken with a view to making public policy and action more rational and effective. ESRI research has contributed in particular to our knowledge of class structure and mobility patterns in Ireland and of, in particular gender-related, inequalities in access to education. The influence of the ESRI in defining what constitutes useful sociological knowledge has been felt in other research institutions such as the Agricultural Institute/Teagasc, the Medical Research Board, the Educational Research Centre, the Linguistics Institute of Ireland and the National Economic and Social Council (NESC). Sociology has over time acquired a footing in all these sites but what constitutes the discipline is fairly tightly defined.

In addition to the state-centred sociology practised by the ESRI and other official research bodies, Irish sociology has been shaped by two other key influences with rather different impacts. The first is Catholic social teaching and the involvement of the Catholic Church generally in the early promotion of sociology in Ireland. The second is research by 'foreign', predominantly American, sociologists and anthropologists. The combination of these three powerful influences has produced a sociology in Ireland that is distinctive and not easily assimilated into just a regional variant of, for example, British or American sociologies.

In an analysis of the emergence of sociology in the West, Langer suggests that Catholicism has been less than helpful to the development of sociology, drawing attention to the comparative lack of development of the discipline in countries such as Austria and Spain. He argues (1992, p.5) that:

> Catholicism always generated its own 'social theories' which are usually less individualistic and less complex than the dominating theories of sociology. On the other hand they have more normative implications . . . when sociology developed in a Catholic milieu it was either occupied with the question of 'social order' (especially how to stabilise the state) or strongly empirically oriented (usually in a later stage). Sociology as the secularised self-consciousness of modern society did not flourish on Catholic foundations.

The development of a Catholic-influenced sociology in Ireland reflected aspects of the experience elsewhere. Sociology made sporadic appearances in academic circles in Ireland from as early as 1910, when it was taught in University College, Dublin, under the name of 'social philosophy'. Its adoption in the National University of Ireland reflected the interest in social ethics stimulated by the Papal Encyclical *Rerum Novarum* (1891) and later by the Encyclical *Quadragesimo Anno* (1931) 'with its concern for a counter to the trades unions and what was perceived as a drift on the part of the working class towards socialism and communism' (Jackson, 1998, p.1). By the 1950s, the Catholic Church's interest in pastoral and community issues and its strong involvement in voluntary associations and voluntary service provision (see Chapter 12) had led a number of its members to take an interest in the discipline of sociology being formed in post-Second World War Europe and America. The Christus Rex Society organised the teaching of sociology to selected groups of religious in the late 1950s. It also published a journal, *Christus Rex* (renamed *Social Studies* in 1973) that became an important outlet for Irish sociological writing during the 1970s and 1980s. As in Spain (Langer, 1992, p.12), clerics and former clerics were prominent as early sociologists in Ireland. The first Chairs in university sociology departments were held by Catholic priests, at University College, Dublin (where James Kavanagh, later Archbishop of Dublin, was appointed in 1966), University College, Galway, and St. Patrick's College, Maynooth. The first lay professor of sociology in the Republic of Ireland, Prof. Damian Hannan, was appointed to University College Cork in 1971 and the second, Prof. John A. Jackson, came to Trinity College, Dublin, in 1974.

In the universities, then — in contrast to the research institutions — Irish sociology was, from the outset, heavily influenced by Catholic social teaching and philosophy, particularly by the 'Catholic corporatism' that had developed in other European societies such as Belgium, Italy and the Netherlands. Whereas the positivist tradition in sociology inherited from the SSIS and similar organisations emphasised a social research that served the state, the Catholic corporatist tradition focused on what is often called 'civil society'. This referred to core institutions 'outside the state', for example, the family, the community and the parish, that, through a supposed better grasp of the dynamics of social processes, could be assisted and encouraged to take control of and manage their own affairs.

The relationship between the 'Catholic' and the 'official' elements in Irish sociology is interesting. Both discourses tended to be positivistic and rather uninterested in theoretical issues and debates. Each took for granted that they could easily identify the proper objects of sociological research in the 'real world' (social problems) and tended to encourage empirical research rather than theoretical or conceptual development. Lynch (1987, p.117), talking about the sociology of education though her remarks can be applied to the discipline as a whole, suggests that 'the Catholic view of the good — in terms of social order — has been transformed from being a religious ideal into a conceptual model of the world that purports to represent empirical reality.' O'Dowd (1988, p.9) has suggested that the empiricist emphasis of 1950s Catholic social philosophy explains why sociological research developed earlier in the Republic of Ireland than it did in the North. Yet the perceived consumers of 'official' and 'Catholic' research were quite different in each case: for the former, the state and its agents; for the latter 'the people', variously defined.

The extent to which early Irish sociology approached any form of social critique, or defined social problems independently of a statist perspective, was due to the influence of the Catholic tradition. It is a tradition carried forward today in the work of the Conference of Religious in Ireland (CORI) and Trócaire, for example, and is a discernible influence on the research of bodies like the Combat Poverty Agency and Focus Ireland. Catholic social teaching, on the other hand, had provided considerable opposition to the enthusiasm among members of the SSIS during the 1940s for the introduction into Ireland of a British-style welfare state (Daly, 1998, p.6). There is also no doubt that some Catholic clergy sought to appropriate Irish sociology so as to prevent it from becoming a vehicle for the importation of socialist or Marxist ideas into Irish society.

A third important influence on the early formation of Irish sociology has been that of 'foreign' sociologists and anthropologists, particularly the latter. Anthropology normally deals with 'other' societies perceived to be very different to our own. Thus, we are familiar with the idea of anthropologists leaving the western world to go and inquire into the 'primitive' peoples of Africa or the South Pacific but, for anthropologists in Britain, Europe, the United States and Australia, Ireland itself often provided a suitably exotic, or even 'primitive' location for research, made even more attractive by the fact that the society was English-speaking. This generated a steady stream of anthropological researchers, from Browne and Haddon in the 1890s (Curtin and Wilson, 1989, p.ix) to Eipper, Wilson, Peace and others in the 1980s and 1990s, seeking to understand our mysterious ways.

The most influential piece of anthropological research carried out in Ireland remains that by two American social anthropologists, Conrad Arensberg and Solon Kimball, in a farming locality in north Co. Clare in the early 1930s (for a more detailed discussion of this study, see Chapter 15). The most striking feature of Arensberg and Kimball's work, compared to other social research carried out in Ireland at that time or in the following forty years, was that it addressed a problem set not by the state, the church or any other 'external' body, but from within the discipline of anthropology itself. Arensberg and Kimball, following the research practices developed in America by Lloyd Warner (in his 'Yankee City' studies) and Robert and Helen Lynd (*Middletown*, 1929), wanted to discover how communities work — how do people who live in communities behave towards each other? And how does this behaviour add up to a set of patterns or a 'social system' that can reproduce itself over long periods of time, even when the individuals involved have gone and been replaced by new ones? Warner and others had developed the idea that communities (or micro-societies) can be analysed as integrated systems made up of interrelated parts that are 'functionally interdependent'. They had tested this theory through research into American, largely urban, communities. Arensberg and Kimball wanted to see if the theory held true in a remote and isolated rural community. Their interest was not initially in Irish society at all but in testing and developing a theoretical idea about how societies should be understood.

We could locate Arensberg and Kimball towards the 'playful/intellectual' end of the spectrum outlined in Figure 2.1 but it was their detailed observations about rural Ireland that made the greatest impact on Irish social researchers. Almost inevitably, given how social inquiry has been understood in Ireland, they were seen to be writing about a 'social problem': small or marginal farming in the underdeveloped western periphery. Arensberg and Kimball's work set the agenda for sociological research into urban (Humphreys, 1966) as well as rural Ireland and the context for analyses of the 'modernisation' of Irish social and cultural development for much of the next 40 years. It was only in the 1970s that critical assessment and discussion of their approach began to take place, marking a watershed in the development of sociology as a discipline in Ireland (Tovey, 1992a).

By the 1970s sociology was finally becoming consolidated in Ireland as a distinct discipline. Sociology departments were established in all of the universities of the Republic that did not already have them and new professors were appointed in two of these. Many of the staff that still work in university sociology departments today were appointed during this decade. By 1975, there were four or five sociologists in each of the departments in University College, Dublin, University College, Cork, and Trinity College, Dublin (TCD), and two in the Department of Political Science and Sociology at University College, Galway (UCG) (Jackson, 1998). Similarly, lecturers in sociology began to be appointed within the teacher training colleges and the Regional Technical Colleges (RTCs). Publication outlets for sociological work were increasing. The *Economic and Social Review* (ESR), a journal produced under the auspices of the ESRI, was first published in 1970. Though it published more papers from economists than from any other discipline (O'Dowd, 1988, p.20) it did publish an increasing number of sociological papers over time. In 1973 *Social Studies* rose out of the ashes of the previous *Christus Rex* journal.

Moreover, new perspectives and influences were coming in to Irish sociology as more appointments were made within universities and research institutions. The ESRI employed a significant number of researchers, both Irish and foreign, who had received their sociological training abroad, especially in the United States. Within the university sector, while many staff had taken a first degree in Ireland, virtually all had received postgraduate sociology training abroad. Staff employed in the National University colleges had generally trained in America — strong links existed with certain American universities such as Southern Illinois and St. Louis. In TCD the links were predominantly with Britain. All university sociology departments contained at least one staff member who was not Irish; in TCD from the mid-1970s until 1991, four out of five staff were recruits from Britain. The RTCs were more likely to employ Irish-born lecturers.

Both foreign and foreign-trained sociologists were instrumental in carrying out a form of 'technology transfer' in the importation to Ireland of British and American models of sociological theorising and research. A more critical analysis might depict the development of sociology in Ireland as dependent, in a similar way that the sociology of most smaller western countries was, for example, in Australia, Scandinavia and Canada. Berger (1992, p.4) makes the point that the sociology of the core countries, in particular the United States, the UK, Germany and France, has long dominated the development of the discipline in smaller peripheral countries. He argues that in the latter the resources devoted to sociology are comparatively small and that these countries rely heavily on their 'big brothers'. This is especially the case when, as with Ireland and Britain, the similarities between the countries appear at least on the surface to be substantial. This may explain why Irish sociologists have long drawn on the work of those in the core economies, rather than in countries that may have more in common economically, politically and perhaps socially, such as Finland, Austria or New Zealand.

American-trained sociologists working in Ireland largely adhered to structural functionalist theoretical models (see Chapter 3), while staff from Britain were largely followers of one or other variant of Marxism, which enjoyed a revival in Britain and Europe in the late 1960s and 1970s. During the following decade the study and debate of a wide range of other, imported, theoretical perspectives also began within Ireland. The social constructivist perspectives of symbolic interactionism, phenomenology and ethnomethodology, for example, confronted both Marxist and functionalist realist world views, while a growing interest in researching language and meaning, using qualitative rather than quantitative methods, challenged the dominance of positivist orientations in research. The growth of theoretical and methodological pluralism in Irish sociology during this time stimulated the opening up of new topics for research and new issues for debate. O'Dowd notes (1988, p.4) that some sociologists feared that such pluralism 'hindered the development of the discipline' and, in particular, 'undermined its potential contribution to policy-making'. It seemed likely to alienate prospective funders who were unable to take seriously a discipline riven with internal controversies and arguments about its own theoretical assumptions and research practices.

One of the most significant events in the development of sociology in this period was the establishment in 1973 of the Sociological Association of Ireland (SAI). The Association was organised on a 32-county basis and welcomed as members both practising and non-practising sociologists and graduates of some cognate disciplines. From 1973 to the present it has had an unbroken record of annual conferences, has organised occasional mid-year meetings and has published a *Bulletin* for members. The impact of the SAI as a forum for debate and self-recognition has been invaluable. During its first decade, its conferences were the site of lively arguments that pitted Marxism against functionalism; modernisation theory against dependency theory; revisited Arensberg and Kimball and the conception of Irish 'peasant' society; or disagreed over how to interpret the place of 'community' in Irish life. Irish sociology was beginning to understand itself and to recognise its distinctive approach to reality with its own particular issues and concerns. The process was, however, a rather halting and insecure one and continued to be dominated by the idea that the prestige of the discipline depended on its 'relevance' to society, defined in quite narrow statist/social-problems terms.

As the 1970s came to an end, it looked as though sociology might be able to secure for itself a place within Irish cultural and literary life that could offer an alternative model. Sociologists at TCD were invited to create a sociological exhibition on contemporary Ireland to form part of the Irish government-sponsored festival 'A Sense of Ireland' at the Institute of Contemporary Arts in London in 1980, which also included living art performances, poetry readings and concerts. The sociology section of the exhibition, 'No Country for Old Men', used text, photographs, graphs and cartoons to represent and celebrate the demographic, economic, social and cultural transformations of Ireland in the 1970s. However, the invitation was not repeated at later international festivals on Ireland, and the idea that sociology could be presented in a cultural rather than 'scientific' milieu was largely forgotten for another one and a half decades.

## CONTEMPORARY IRISH SOCIOLOGY

The 1980s were a time both of stagnation and consolidation for Irish sociology. During this decade sociology increased steadily in popularity as a university subject in Ireland, in contrast to the experience of decline in other countries such as Britain; but the possibilities for graduates of gaining employment in Ireland as a sociologist declined substantially. There was very little recruitment to permanent posts in sociology in the universities, where most of those recruited in the 1970s were still in place and no expansion in positions had occurred (O'Dowd, 1988). The situation in the research institutions and RTCs was only slightly better. Increasing numbers of sociology graduates who left Ireland to get postgraduate qualifications found themselves unable to return to employment while many of those who completed PhDs in Ireland subsequently had to go abroad to work. A study of sociology graduates of TCD between 1974 and 1996 (Jackson, 1998) located around 16 per cent who were pursuing a professional career in sociology; half were doing so outside Ireland. Irish sociology was successfully integrated into an international labour market but, consequentially, with the of loss of new voices and of critical mass at home.

The SAI continued to perform a key role providing a place to discuss and reflect on how Irish sociology was developing but it also became a force for the professionalisation of sociologists. It began to address such issues as the establishment of a set of principles of employment for people working in research, who were often temporary or contract appointees with few rights over how they conducted research or what happened to their findings; and the development of a code of ethics to guide research practice. At one point the Association appeared to be moving towards becoming a professional body that would seek to defend practitioners and monitor and regulate the right to practise. Understandable as a largely defensive response to the employment constraints of the 1980s, this trend created difficulties over the Association's generous rules on eligibility for membership and provoked some stormy debates about the purpose of the SAI and, more broadly, of sociology itself.

A very positive contribution by the SAI during the 1980s was its role in sponsoring the publication of sociology texts, including a series of readers, 'Studies in Irish Society'. The first, *Power, conflict and inequality*, was published in 1982, followed by *Culture and ideology in Ireland* (1984), *Gender in Irish society* (1986) and *Whose law and order? Aspects of crime and social control in Ireland* (1988). The SAI also commissioned chapters for a text on Irish society: *Ireland — a sociological profile* (1986; a second edition, with entirely new chapters, appeared as *Irish society: Sociological perspectives* in 1995). This was not the first attempt at a comprehensive integrated text on Irish society — Michel Peillon's *Contemporary Irish society* (see Chapter 4) was published in 1982 — but it was the first to target the growing interest in sociology among Irish third-level students.

The ESRI also contributed significantly to Irish sociological output, publishing throughout the 1980s reports based on its research into educational access and performance; education and gender; distribution of income; employment; social class and social mobility; and social change in rural Ireland. At the end of the decade it published *Understanding contemporary Ireland* (Breen et al., 1990), an analysis of social change since the 1950s that focused almost exclusively on social structural trends, integrated through the concept of social class.

The 1990s seemed to open up a range of new development possibilities. The Irish government's decision in 1991 to make funds available for a programme of university expansion in response to demographic and social pressures on third-level places brought a number of new staff into existing sociology departments. The teaching of sociology increased in the two new universities, in Dublin and in Limerick, and in the RTCs. Postgraduate teaching also expanded, as a range of taught Masters and diploma courses supplemented the traditional postgraduate degrees by research. In the 1990s, sociology departments across the Republic contributed to Masters courses in communications and cultural studies; European social policy analysis; peace studies; women's studies; the sociology of development; equality studies; community development; rural development; social research methodology; and racial and ethnic studies.

New sources of funds for research became available, particularly from the EU. This expanded the resources available to the ESRI and for the first time made large-scale research a real possibility for some academic sociologists. Government departments such as the Department of Health became more interested in funding research either through the employment of researchers or commissioning research from the universities and research institutes. Small, independent research consultancies were set up by sociology graduates and flourished in the new research climate. The Royal Irish Academy's National Committee for Economic and Social Sciences lobbied for funding for social science research and, in 1995, was able to set up a Social Science Research Council with a small fund, disbursed annually on a competitive basis, to support research projects and postgraduate training and to reward high achievement by postgraduate students. In 1998 the

Higher Educational Authority (HEA) made scholarships available to social science postgraduates and, in 1999, state funding for third-level research, via the HEA, included for the first time the Humanities and Social Sciences. At the same time the narrowness of the funding base has meant that research has tended to be very closely tied to specific policy issues (Lynch, 1999b, pp.44–46). This has meant a lack of research in some areas and the majority of funded research carried out has reflected a highly positivist approach aimed at producing 'useful results'.

In 1993 the SAI celebrated its twentieth anniversary with an Annual Conference on 'Irish Sociology — Themes and Tensions'. It then had a membership of some 180 of whom 10 per cent were based outside Ireland, about 14 per cent in Northern Ireland and about 7 per cent in non-university research institutions in the Republic of Ireland. The other two-thirds were predominantly third-level teachers and postgraduate students from the Republic. By 1996, membership had risen to 226. Two key developments in Irish sociology took place around 1990. The first was the introduction by the SAI of the annual *Irish Journal of Sociology* (*IJS*), to replace the now defunct *Social Studies*. The first three issues were edited from the sociology department at NUI Maynooth; the next three from UCG; and in 1997 it moved to Queen's University Belfast. The *IJS* showed itself to be distinct from both *Social Studies* and the *ESR* right from the first issue which included papers on cultural studies and post-modernism, ideas scarcely mentioned in public in sociological writings before this point. It also reviewed eighteen books, mainly about aspects of Irish society, reflecting the growth of publishing in the field. The journal's commitment to providing a forum for lively and rigorous critique of developments in both Irish sociological writing and sociology in general, established in this first issue, has remained a significant feature of all issues since. The interest in topics ignored in more statist versions of sociology has also persisted, with later issues carrying papers, for example, on the sociology of landscape; the relations between sociology and history; the mass media in Ireland; the Irish language in the North of Ireland; Irish football culture; and the entrance policies operated by gay and lesbian discos.

The second important development is the growth of feminist sociology. This took place in close liaison with the rise of the Irish women's movement. Writing in 1988, O'Dowd could still comment on the need for Irish sociology to address 'the perspective of gender'. He noted 'the extent to which all social science has been shaped by male perspectives' and, in particular, that 'Irish intellectual life, especially higher education, has been male-dominated. It is only very recently that social and historical research has sought to take full account of Irish women' (1988, p.16). Yet one might argue that sociology has been the *least* male-dominated among Irish social sciences. The SAI was chaired by women within the first decade of its establishment. Sociologists pioneered research on gender issues both in institutional and academic circles, for example, the ESRI study, *Schooling and sex roles* (1983) and *Gender and Irish society* (1986), respectively. In 1992, the first issue of the UCG *Women's Studies Review* appeared, edited by, among others, a UCG sociologist. In 1993/4 the *IJS* carried a debate between Ronit Lentin and Evelyn Mahon over the possibility of a feminist research methodology (see Chapter 8). Interest in and debates about feminist sociology continued during the second half of the 1990s with the establishment of the Cork-based *Irish Feminist Studies Review*; major studies of the gender aspects of areas such as health, education and rural life; and the publication of *Women and Irish society: A sociological reader* (Byrne and Leonard, 1997) and *Emerging voices: Women in contemporary Irish society* (O'Connor, 1998). Women were appointed professors of sociology in the Universities of Ulster and Limerick but the proportion of women at senior academic level does not yet reflect the dominance of women in sociology undergraduate and postgraduate courses, nor their increasing equality among the teaching staff of sociology departments. It is sometimes suggested that the feminisation of Irish sociology is related to its marginalisation within Irish public life, but whether sociology, of all the social sciences, has been most open to women's voices and concerns because it has been more marginalised, or the other way round, is open to speculation.

Over the past decade the number of sociology books published in Ireland has increased and the range of topics covered has continually widened. Subjects have included relations between family, society and the Catholic Church; language and ethnic identity; the lives and careers of illegal emigrants in America; urban cultures in Ireland; rural poverty and rural development; Travellers and schooling; a critical analysis of Irish tourism; media audiences and the formation of cultural identity; media representations of poverty; the management of health in Ireland; masculinity, fatherhood and sexuality in Ireland; the social construction of childbirth — this is just a selection. Other topics remain comparatively neglected, such as suburbia and suburbanisation; cultural identity (from a sociological rather than a literary perspective); sport and leisure, including pubs, clubs and drinking; popular culture and the music industry; food, eating and the food industry; and many other issues that relate to 'everyday' life experiences and concerns.

Despite this expansion of output, it is perhaps surprising that sociology has not really managed to establish itself within Irish life as a significant or stimulating guide to how that life is changing. While Langer (1992, p.1) suggests that in western society as a whole 'sociology has become the most popular way for society to interpret itself . . . firmly integrated into . . . everyday communication', in Ireland such influence seems to rest more clearly with historians, literary critics and, increasingly, psychologists. Sociologists rarely appear in the mass media as interpreters of everyday life. Compared to economists, sociologists are seldom called upon to discuss or determine policy matters in the public sphere. How then, with its history to date, should we evaluate the contribution that Irish sociology, has made to Irish society? Does Irish society need Irish sociology at all?

Reviewing *Irish society: Sociological perspectives* in the *IJS* in 1996, Kieran Bonner clearly regards this as open to question. He contends (1996, p.219) that the 'domain assumptions' of much of the sociology displayed in the text and elsewhere:

> are very much intertwined with the modernist project. The reflexive turn which emerged in sociology as a consequence of the influence of phenomenology provides the tools for a self-conscious reflection about the philosophical and political implications and meanings of these domain assumptions. Yet . . . one gets the sense from this book that Anglo-American empiricism (which is embedded in the modern project) rather than European continental theorising (which seeks to move some distance from the project) dominates Irish sociology.

Bonner suggests that Irish sociology has been good at producing a great deal of factual knowledge about Irish society but it has left questions of sociological theory largely unexplored. In this respect, it reflects the underdevelopment, as identified by historian J.J. Lee (1989, pp.562–643), of an intellectual tradition of philosophy or theorising in contemporary Irish life compared to our much stronger aesthetic and literary traditions. History and psychology are thus very popular ways to interpret reality, given their emphasis on the narrative and on the individual.

Anthropologist Eileen Kane (1996, pp.139–145) provides a similar, perhaps harsher, critique. She distinguishes three paradigms, or dominant approaches, that have shaped Irish social science. These are similar to those we have identified in this chapter and Chapter 1 — a dominant positivism/post-positivism; an emergent body of critical theory; and an essentially absent phenomenology or interpretative sociology. As social scientists in Ireland have drawn almost entirely from a post-positivist paradigm, they have been led into the production of 'facts, albeit second-class ones, rather than interpretation and . . . an emphasis on refinements of methodology, usually quantitative'. Positivistic thinking has been endemic within Irish society. It has 'shaped not only the social sciences, but official and public expectations about the nature of reality and what constitutes credible evidence as a basis for action'. The result is a 'stultifying empiricism'; a sociology oriented towards 'social engineering' that sees its primary audience as the state and the Catholic Church. As a result, Kane argues, Irish sociology has emphasised pathology, crime and deviance; poverty and unemployment; violence, drugs and alcohol; the conditions of some minorities; and the problems of rural areas. These are all fields that 'have symbolic and political resonance for both church and state'. A further consequence for Kane is that Irish sociology (like most others) studies 'down, in class and power terms, rather than up', with very little if any research being done on the powerful social groups in society. That is left to (a few) investigative journalists.

Kane contrasts this type of sociology with critical theory, which sees research as part of an attempt 'to facilitate transformation towards a desired end' (1996, p.140). For critical theorists, knowledge is always embedded in its socio-historical context. They ask 'knowledge for whom?'; 'knowledge for what?' Inquiry is thus 'a political act'. Kane remarks that critical theory can also produce a top-down or paternalistic perspective on the subjects studied. It sees others as in need of truth and empowerment, not the theorists themselves. It 'seeks to transform the world view of others, while failing to seek the insights of those whose thinking we are liberating to liberate our own' (1996, p.141). Thus, it can become a form of Western cultural imperialism. It is interesting that, while Kane mentions feminism, Marxism and neo-Marxism, liberation theology and participatory research as versions of critical theory, she does not name any Irish sociologists as examples of critical theorists nor does she discuss their work. We might question how well her comments apply to, for example, Drudy and Lynch's *Schools and society in Ireland* (1993) or Lynch and McLaughlin's 'Caring labour and love labour' (1995). Indeed Kathleen Lynch has been a major critic of contemporary Irish sociology from within the discipline and has recently (1999b) urged sociologists to adopt an approach to research that empowers those researched and overtly addresses issues of power within the research process.

For Kane, as for Bonner, it is ultimately the absence of a strong phenomenological or interpretative strand in Irish sociology that is most problematic and puzzling. It is easy enough to find explanations, Kane suggests, for the growing appeal of critical theory in Ireland's 'post-colonial marginal position, historical missionary association with the Third World, notional subscription to socialism, and exposure by some to liberation theory', but it is harder to understand why a discipline that could have had 'an interpretative brief' has been 'so bogged down in emphases on positivistic, "quantitative" methodologies' (1996, pp.142–3). Kane calls for more interpretative work in Irish sociology: research that recognises multiple realities and the multiplicity of alternative theories that can explain a given body of material. As facts are value- and theory-laden, research becomes a process of interpretation, and its product a narrative rather than a report. She argues that an interpretative approach is particularly germane to rapidly changing Irish society, with its significant levels of inequality and division and increasing uncertainty about its identity — where 'some speak of one nation, of two traditions, of the 'fifth province', of a unique perspective', we have to ask 'how many voices does Ireland have and how many perspectives?'. Within such a context the essential task of an interpretative sociology is 'to discover the diversity and commonality of Irish meanings and experiences, and what the lived life is like' (1996, p.151).

To what extent do Kane's and Bonner's criticisms remain justified? It may be that the wheel has come full circle and that positivism has been displaced in Irish sociology by interpretative or constructivist approaches. It may also be the case that critical approaches remain as poorly developed as ever or they may even, with the widespread rejection of modernist assumptions and forms of research practice, have retreated further. We end with a brief comparison of two recent Institute of

Public Administration books that might be taken as emblematic of the current state of the discipline.

*From famine to feast: Economic and social change in Ireland 1847–1997* (Kennedy, 1998) is a collection of papers based on a Thomas Davis lecture series broadcast on RTE radio during 1997 and 1998 to celebrate the 150th anniversary of the Social and Statistical Inquiry Society. The first paper (cited earlier) deals with the SSIS itself; others deal with the key areas that a sociology of Ireland might tackle, such as demographic trends; changing rural life; housing, health and social welfare; and education and the economy. The book has been listed in *Books Ireland* and elsewhere as a new sociological text — although it does not present itself as such. It seems to exemplify the accounts of Irish sociology given by Kane and Bonner — a heavy reliance on producing 'the facts' with a minimum of theoretical interference and a largely unquestioning, top-down and social-problems-oriented understanding of what the important facts are. It is interesting to note, therefore, that not one of the fourteen contributors to the book is a sociologist. Most are economists with the next biggest group being historians and the third, barristers. Not only did this important book on social and economic change in Ireland omit a sociological perspective but this appears to reflect a public assumption that such a perspective would generate nothing very different from what other social scientists say.

By contrast, all twelve contributors to *Encounters with modern Ireland* (Peillon and Slater, 1998) are sociologists and all come from academic settings rather than research institutions. Where the previous book is determined to be 'relevant', this slim volume attempts to be playful or intellectual. It follows Simmel in deliberately setting out to address 'trivial' topics, many of which have no immediate bearing on public policy, such as *Riverdance*, rugby and New Age Travellers, and some that are recognised as important public issues but tend to be ignored in conventional discussions of policy, for example, blood donation and the activities of the Blood Transfusion Service Board; the development of Temple Bar; and rubbish.

Slater's introduction to the book contrasts 'strolling' and 'walking with a purpose' as a metaphor for the reorientation of Irish sociology that the fundamental transformation of contemporary Irish society demands. The contemporary sociologist is a city stroller or *flâneur*, whose job it is to point things out to the rest of us and help us enjoy the many diverse encounters and experiences that living in a modern urban society offers (a role in marked contrast to the negative connotations of Kane's sociologist as 'jaywalker' cited at the beginning of this chapter). The sociologist who still thinks that they are 'walking to work' — carrying out research to inform the state or ruling elites and to advance the rational organisation of society — suddenly seems like a figure from the past, almost an urban monument to be paused by, fleetingly comprehended and then dismissed by the *flâneur*. The sociologist as Irish intellectual has become, as Bauman (1992) puts it, an interpreter instead of a judge: someone who no longer tries to set standards but who mediates between the standards set within diverse traditions, explaining each to the other and revealing all to be relative.

A senior Irish sociologist (Torode, 1999) has responded to *Encounters with modern Ireland* in the following terms:

> Stylistically [it] locates itself in the genre of the literary pub-crawl: an analysis of popular culture which is itself popular. Is this a viable project in its own terms, and if successful what does it do to the science of sociology, which has striven so hard in recent decades to achieve serious academic recognition from its colleagues in economics, political science, and psychology?

Torode's discussion in the *ESR* concludes that, despite many attractive features, *Encounters* is not viable as a piece of popular sociology. He argues that while the book presents itself as 'down-market and easily approachable' it actually comes across as 'an elite product: you have to be one of the *cognoscenti* to understand and appreciate it'. It is best seen as an invitation to 'insiders' or existing sociologists 'to consider a new style . . . and a new direction . . . and thereby to relaunch their discipline in the public arena'. However, public reception of the book suggests that the 'statist' view of sociology embedded in the public arena may be extremely difficult to shift. Moreover, that view, as much as can be judged from these cases, does not seem to consider sociology merely a second-class version of economics but still wants and expects it to be a critical discipline that tries to go behind the political and the mass media representations of Irish society to uncover 'how things really are'. There seems to be developing in Ireland an audience for a sociology that sets out to 'inform the democratic consciousness', as Calhoun puts it (1996, p.429), but this may not — at present — be what Irish sociologists want to do with their discipline.

# 3
# The dynamics of Irish development

In Chapter 1 we introduced sociology as *the study of modernity*. We suggested that to sociologists a 'modern' society is one that is rational, industrial, urban and, usually, capitalist. But is Irish society modern? An industrial society, for example, is often defined as one where most people live in urban areas and very few — perhaps one in fifty — work in agriculture. In the Republic of Ireland just a generation ago, as late as 1971, nearly a third of employed men worked in agriculture, either as farmers, as relatives assisting on the farm or as agricultural labourers, while over a third of the population lived in the countryside or in rural settlements of fewer than 200 people. Of those who lived in urban areas over half lived in just one city, Dublin.

Clearly, Irish society has become more urbanised and more industrialised in the past thirty years. But in comparison to other European states like Britain, Germany or France, it is doing so considerably later. As a consequence, Ireland is often described as a 'late moderniser', a latecomer to modernity. Much debate about Irish society and how it is changing still uses this notion. It assumes that there is a condition called 'being modern' or 'modernity' and that change in Irish society represents a shift towards this condition. But when we consider this further, some interesting questions are raised. If we say Ireland is becoming modern, what are we comparing it to? Are we implying it has become more like those societies that industrialised early? Or is there a different, specific way of 'being modern' that characterises late modernisers like Ireland? And if we say that Ireland is modern now, what are we implying about the past and about the processes of change that have occurred?

We begin this chapter, therefore, with a brief overview of sociological accounts of how societies 'become modern'. These are usually referred to as theories of social change or theories of development. Two general points can be made about these before we go on to look at specific examples. First, the question of how to explain change or development has been central to the growth of sociology as a discipline. It has produced much disagreement between sociologists, not just about details of the theory but about the theories themselves as broad perspectives or paradigms for understanding social life. They are also more than just academic disagreements. As we see in Chapter 4, states and other powerful actors in society have, for at least the last century, been preoccupied with achieving social change, particularly progressive change or *development*. In the contest between sociological theories of change we find resonances of the clash of ideas between elites in Irish society about how to understand our past history and how to locate Ireland as part of the contemporary world. Sociological theories both influence and are influenced by the ideas held by important social groups in society. Nowhere is this more obvious than in relation to social change since interpretations of the past are often used to explain and justify movements towards a particular sort of future.

The second point relates to the concept of development itself. Until recently much sociology identified 'development' with 'becoming modern' but this is increasingly seen as simplistic. As sociologists become more reflexive in thinking about society, they correspondingly become less certain that modernity is the most 'developed' condition to which societies can or should aspire. The values that underpin the ideal of modernity, discussed in Chapter 1, no longer command automatic allegiance as the problems generated by the continuous pursuit of 'progress' threaten to outweigh its benefits.

The sociological debate over development is itself, in a sense, characteristic of modernity and may lose its rationale as ideas about history as progress are abandoned or eroded. The debate has not become irrelevant but we should approach it in a more questioning and critical way than before. In particular, we should recognise that there is more than one way for a society to be modern. This is especially helpful to a society such as ours, that has for so long felt the pressure to see itself as 'unmodern', or backward, compared to the rest of the world and as a society that has only recently begun to 'catch up'. The idea that there are *varieties of modernity* liberates the potential for making choices about how we want to develop in future. It also lets us rediscover the value of our past instead of downgrading it as 'less than modern'. Sociological theorising helps us to examine not only how the world is but also how we think about the world.

## THEORIES OF DEVELOPMENT

In this section we outline the three dominant ways of thinking about social change and development: the theories of *modernisation*, *dependency* and *globalisation*. We will not discuss them in great detail, as we are mainly interested in providing a context within which to examine recent change in Irish society.

Sociological studies of development long assumed the best way to understand social change was to take a single society, analyse it in detail and then compare it with others to see what resemblances could be found on selected dimensions. This seemed a natural way to proceed as theorists took for granted that the societies of the world could be ranked on a *continuum* of development, from the most developed or 'modern' (say, Southern California) to the least (say, Chad). It was suggested that if we knew the main structural or cultural features of the most modern societies, we could interpret change in other societies as evolution towards these. This approach underpins modernisation theory. It has shaped the ideas of elite social groups, academics such as sociologists and historians, policy-makers and ordinary people, in Ireland and in many other countries, during much of the period since the Second World War.

In the 1980s and 1990s a very different perspective on development emerged in sociology. It argues that to understand the changes taking place in particular societies, we must start with an examination of the relationships that connect countries and regions into an international 'system'. It implies that no society exists in isolation. All are influenced in very significant ways by international trends and relationships. This approach underpins both dependency and globalisation theory. Below we note some contrasts in how these theories explain social change in general, before going on to look specifically at Irish society.

## Modernisation theory

Modernisation theory is used in sociology to mean a complex set of interconnected ideas, but two of its key features are:

- an evolutionary account of social change
- the belief that all societies in the world are converging at different speeds and from different starting points, towards the same point — modern industrial society.

Many nineteenth-century social thinkers (including Comte, Tönnies and Durkheim, see Chapter 1) were much influenced by Charles Darwin's ideas about evolutionary change in nature. They sought to apply these ideas to an understanding of social change, suggesting that we could treat societies as analogous to natural species that developed through the process of 'survival of the fittest'. More complex forms of social organisation are better adapted to survival within their environment and thus replace simpler forms. Therefore nation states replace tribal societies; factory production replaces the individual craft-worker; the supermarket replaces the local grocery.

Evolutionary interpretations of social change encouraged the assumption that change is unidirectional — that there is but one pattern of change, from primitive (simple, 'traditional') to modern (highly complex, highly adapted to survival) — and that all societies must eventually follow this pattern. They also encouraged the belief that development is 'an imitative process, in which the less developed countries gradually assumed the qualities of the industrialised nations' (Hettne, 1990, p.60). Ultimately they reflected a belief that change is the same as progress, so establishing the most 'modern' societies as the model that developing societies should try to emulate. Since the social theorists involved were all from the West and took for granted that that was where the most 'advanced' countries were found, this approach also encouraged an ethnocentric vision of development that saw 'modernisation' as identical to 'westernisation'. Thus, modernisation theory defined a clear task for development analysts (including sociologists, economists and political theorists) — to identify the qualities of modern societies that are to be imitated and to suggest ways to facilitate their imitation.

Rostow (1960) argued that as societies converge towards modernity, they pass through a sequence of distinct stages of development ('traditional', 'pre-modern', 'modernisation take-off' and so on). We can take a society and, by looking at specific features within it (does it have a mass education system? how developed is its banking system? how urbanised is it?), can say what stage of modernisation it has reached. We can then use this finding to explain other features such as its type of family structure or the extent of secularisation. This indicates further changes needed to move the society to the next development stage. We can see that modernisation theory is often used not just as an explanation for social changes but also as a set of prescriptions for putting directed social changes into practice. Its influence on leaders of both modern and modernising societies has made it something of a self-fulfilling prophecy.

If societies change by evolving through particular development stages into the 'modern' form, what starts the process off? Some modernisation theorists see *technological innovation*, perhaps imported into the society by a modernising elite, as the starting point. Technological change in agriculture, such as the introduction of mechanical harvesters or tractors, may set off a process in which large numbers of agricultural workers become redundant, move to urban centres and contribute to the development of urban industry. Modernisation theorists argue that social change follows a 'logic of industrialisation' — once the technology is present, industrialisation and its accompanying social changes inevitably follow. In turn, the division of labour becomes more complex as large-scale industrial production requires a wide range of specialised and technical skills. The society becomes more 'open' or meritocratic as jobs need to be assigned to people on the basis of their skills and talents, rather than any inherited social position. There is increased equality of opportunity and social mobility and reduced social conflict as different class, ethnic or regional groups come to share the same goals of further development and higher standards of living. Other cultural changes follow, for example, secularisation (see Chapter 12). In short, once the technological changes occur that allow industry to 'take off', social changes follow the same logic in all industrialising societies — they become more and more alike.

For other modernisation theorists social change is driven by cultural change, especially changes in *social values*, and it is the values and attitudes of the developed West, rather than its technology, that must be implanted into more traditional societies before industrial development can begin (Kirby, 1997). There is a parallel here with Weber's theories (see Chapter 1) about the relationship between particular sets of ideas and capitalist development. Cultural modernisa-tionists brought the term 'traditional' into widespread use to describe societies that not only lacked the science and technology of the advanced world but were still trapped within traditional values or culture. For example, they valued people more for their 'ascribed' than their 'achieved' characteristics; they preferred face-to face, personalised relationships to impersonal, detached ones; and social interaction was influenced more by kinship or familiarity than by universal rules. Modernisation theory implies that such values are an obstacle to cultural and, ultimately, economic development.

In summary, modernisation theory suggests that the social organisation and cultural features of a society can largely be explained by identifying the 'stage of development' it has reached on the path towards modernity. It seems to offer a very powerful analysis of change, because it treats societies as integrated systems where change in one part (for example, the organisation of work) leads to changes in almost every other part. While its roots go far back into the thinking of the 'classical' social theorists, particularly Durkheim and Weber, in the hands of later theorists discussions of modernity have often narrowed into checklists of technical and cultural criteria.

A major concern of the classical theorists had been to understand specific historical patterns of change in the countries of early Europe but theorists subsequently universalised these analyses into an account of global evolution. Modernisation theorists gave up the strong sense of ambivalence towards modernity that had characterised the classical theorists' discussions, such as Weber's concerns about the effect of increasing bureaucratisation and rational-isation on the human spirit, Durkheim's analysis of anomie or Marx's scathing analysis of the roots of alienation. Hettne (1990, p.72) concludes that:

> On the winding road towards a theory of social change there are many mistakes, both magnificent and more trivial. Modernisation theory certainly belongs to the first category. . . . It had a long tradition in Western social thought. . . . It had a great appeal to a wider public due to the paternalistic attitude towards other non-European cultures . . . [and] it is probably correct to say that the general outlook of modernisation theory still constitutes the popular image of developing countries.

The most damaging legacy of modernisation theory may be the simplistic conception of change as a transition from 'traditional' to 'modern'. The term 'traditional' took on pejorative overtones. It no longer simply referred to societies whose culture and ways of organising political, social or economic life were different from those of the most powerful European societies but suggests they were inferior — they lacked or had failed to develop modern forms. This position of innate superiority became a particular target in the critique of modernisation theory launched by dependency theorists.

## Dependency theory

Modernisation theory treats traditional societies as unchanging and isolated from contact with the outside world and, once technological or cultural change is introduced, the process of differentiation and evolution towards higher stages of development unfolds according to its own logic, independent of relationships with other societies. On both counts the theory has been heavily criticised, particularly by dependency theorists.

The first to outline dependency theory was a German-born economist working in South America, André Gunder Frank. It is significant that he came from Latin America, a part of the world that has had long experience of colonial domination. To Frank it was inconceivable that the pattern of social change in any single society could be explained without reference to its past and present relationships with others. Moreover, by the late 1960s when he put forward his theory, Latin American countries were no longer colonies. Most had been politically independent since the nineteenth century and had been trying to develop and modernise themselves, yet most remained economically underdeveloped. To Frank it was clear that there was no universal, linear pattern of change by which less developed countries 'converged' with more developed ones. He argued (1967) that all countries are part of an international system that affects societies in different ways. Some, mainly early-industrialising Western countries that had been colonisers, have been able to establish relationships with others, particularly those that had been colonised. These are essentially relationships of exploitation. Through these relationships the dominant or core countries systematically funnel out the wealth created in the underdeveloped countries. The wealth accumulates in the developed countries, both as capital and as 'human capital'. Frank argued, therefore, that it was wrong to see underdeveloped societies as being behind or outside the development process; rather, both developed and underdeveloped societies are part of a single international system. Underdeveloped societies have been underdeveloped and are maintained in a state of underdevelopment by the core countries that have developed at their expense. Lack of development is therefore not the result of the value systems or technologies of the underdeveloped countries but lies with the core countries and the resultant relationships.

Frank refused to label less developed societies 'traditional'. For him this was a term that 'denies all history' to the society concerned. Developed societies do not have a monopoly on history. Underdeveloped ones also have a history, usually one of colonisation where the economy and social institutions were restructured to suit the colonisers. Their agriculture was reorganised, for example, to produce cash crops such as coffee, soybeans or rubber for export as industrial raw materials rather than food for home consumption. Thus, Brazil became a major exporter of coffee; the Middle East of oil; Malaysia of rubber. Irish agriculture under colonial rule specialised in the production of live beef cattle for export and processing in

Britain. The history of colonised countries was therefore one of restructuring resulting in dependency. For the sale of their agricultural exports and the import of industrial products they became increasingly dependent on the core countries that profited from their underdevelopment. For Frank this was 'the development of underdevelopment'. He argued that even when such countries gained political independence they remained locked into international relationships that promoted the process of underdevelopment.

Modernisation theory saw world development as a process where modern societies helped traditional societies to develop through the transfer of new technology, values or capital. Dependency theory challenged that account. It argued that the transfers were primarily in the opposite direction, from the poor countries to the rich. This generated much debate on whether it was ever possible for underdeveloped countries to break free from underdevelopment. But in the 1970s and 1980s it became apparent that many previously underdeveloped countries *were* experiencing social change in the form of industrialisation. By the late 1970s, for example, there were nearly a million workers employed in industrial production, including car-making, in Brazil, many earning well above the minimum wage. The term 'newly industrialising countries' (NICs) was coined to mark this new phenomenon that seemed to contradict the claim that development was impossible in dependent societies. But what sort of development was it?

Dependency theorists point out that TNCs — companies that operate across national boundaries rather than within several or many nations — have played a significant part in the new industrialisation process. TNCs do not just replicate their firms in different countries. Their operations are underpinned by a structured division of labour: the production process is broken down into more and less skilled parts; or into stages further from and nearer to the finished product. These component parts of the process are located in different parts of the world depending on what a region has to offer. There may be a large unemployed or underemployed workforce, cheap to employ or docile to manage, or raw materials or resources and access to markets may be readily available. TNCs engender a new *international* division of labour that operates on a global level and shapes the possibilities for development of both the industrialised and the newly industrialising societies.

TNCs operate on a huge scale, with annual turnover often equal to or greater than the total gross national product (GNP) of the country in which they locate branch plants. They can influence government policies on trade unionism or prevent the introduction of controls on environmental degradation if these are likely to push up production costs. Many sociologists therefore refer to the industrial development occurring in NICs as *dependent development*. They argue that the social structure of NICs is not converging with that of early industrialising societies. Their place in the new international division of labour means that the social structure of NICs *remains* different to that of the core countries.

In summary, dependency theorists put forward a number of theses that contrast sharply with the modernisation paradigm. The most important obstacles to development are *not* internal characteristics such as lack of technology, capital or an entrepreneurial culture, but are external to the underdeveloped society and relate to its position in the international division of labour. In the international system, value is transferred mainly from the peripheral and underdeveloped societies to the core or developed societies. Thus, peripheral societies are deprived of a surplus that they *could* invest in development and at the same time are providing a surplus to the already developed societies. In this way, development in the core *produces* underdevelopment in the periphery. Development and underdevelopment, taking place in different regions or spaces of the world, are parts of the same single process. Relations with core countries severely constrain the capacity of peripheral countries to develop. Their best prospects would seem to lie in detaching themselves from core — periphery relations or from the world market through some form of protectionism and by working towards national self-sufficiency.

## From dependency to globalisation

During the 1970s and 1980s, dependency theory was exposed to intensive discussion and debate. Critics asked whether it was really possible to distinguish between dependent and independent economies and to allocate existing societies unequivocally to one category or the other. The problems experienced by peripheral economies, explained by Frank as the outcome of a process of underdevelopment, were said to be the product of a particular — and temporary — stage in global capitalist development and did not represent a permanent relationship of exploitation. Furthermore it was argued that the focus on external relationships encouraged dependency theorists to ignore social or cultural features *internal* to dependent societies that could be very relevant to understanding their situation. In particular, dependency theory was criticised for its lack of analysis of the class and power structures within dependent societies that could explain why they remained underdeveloped.

So intensive was the criticism of dependency theory that by the 1990s it was seen by many to be no longer relevant. However, if few theorists of change currently support it at least in its original version, it has had major impacts on social theorising. Chief among these must be the decline of the modernisation paradigm itself and the growing resistance to all theories of development that simplistically equate modernisation with westernisation, or that equate 'traditional' societies with societies that are non-western in practices and culture. Dependency theory opened up the possibility of 'indigenising' development and allowed people in the peripheral countries to think about the process of social change needed in their own countries based on their own cultural traditions and sense of history. The clash between modernisationists and supporters of dependency theory was experienced by sociologists and other intellectuals in many countries, not least in Ireland, as a sort of intellectual revolution or declaration of independence.

As a thesis about social change, the dependency approach has now evolved into theories of globalisation that shift the focus of analysis from dependence to interdependence. They recognise that no countries can exercise wholly autonomous control over their economies and societies and that development cannot be said to result purely from internal factors. To understand change in any society or region we must start from an overview of the world system at a given point in time and work back to locate the networks of cross-national relations in which a particular country is enmeshed.

Globalisation theory remains theoretically eclectic and relatively under-developed. It can generate exciting and illuminating descriptive accounts but offers few clear guidelines about how to interpret such descriptions. It is to some extent a new battleground for the protagonists of modernisation versus dependency theorists, though there are those (for example, Scott, 1997) who argue that it goes beyond the limitations of these approaches. Thus, in a reformulation of dependency theory, some versions of globalisation theory suggest that while all countries are interdependent, the type and extent of dependency varies from case to case. This argument recognises that the global system has a more complicated structure than a simple dichotomy between 'core' and 'periphery' can account for (we at least need a further distinction between peripheries and semi-peripheries).

O'Hearn (1998, p.14) argues that the concept of *interlinking commodity chains* is useful, where 'a global division of labour spans distinct core, semi-peripheral and peripheral regions'. World regions are thus organised into a hierarchy in terms of what they can offer to the commodity chain of a TNC, for example, different forms of 'human capital'. In this context, 'economic development' relates to how able a country or region is to improve its level of participation towards higher-value, more sophisticated and skilled and more profitable activities. Globalisation theory also recognises tensions and competition *within* the core (for example, between the United States and Europe or between different regions within each of these) and that processes of global change continuously give rise to the peripheralisation of some core areas and the development of some peripheries (for example, on one hand the de-industrialisation of Britain and, on the other, the industrialisation of regions of Asia such as South Korea).

Whilst this approach to globalisation emphasises inequality, exploitation and control as the fundamental elements of the new world system, other versions use the concepts of globalisation and interdependence to emphasise the growing similarities and equalities for people across the world. Here, as in modernisation theory, the similarities identified and celebrated are often those that re-emphasise the superiority of western values and ways of thought. The focus is on an emerging consensus across the world about what economic, cultural or political forms are valuable, and conflicts over the distribution of power or of material resources between different societies are played down.

## DEVELOPMENT IN IRELAND

Few sociologists today use modernisation theory to explain the Irish experience of development but, as a set of implicit, common-sense assumptions about what has happened to Irish society in the past and how it is likely to develop in the future, modernisation theory has been remarkably influential. It is widely assumed, for example, that the lifestyles, values, occupational structure and political concerns of Irish people are becoming more like those of the 'modern' countries of Europe and North America. This is often linked to industrialisation — as industry becomes more important in the Irish economy, it is argued, our way of life changes to that of a developed and modern society.

Ireland is often described as a 'late industrialising society'. This version of modernisation theory assumes that industrialisation is the universal end-point of social change, but that some societies reach it more quickly than others. The term 'newly industrialising country' or NIC is another variant of the same idea — it allows that societies can industrialise in different ways but assumes that industrialisation is the prime indicator of advancing modernity.

O'Hearn (1998, p.34) notes that the connection between industrialisation and modernity has a long history in Ireland; Marx remarked that 'every time Ireland was about to develop industrially, she was crushed and reconverted into a purely agricultural land.' This pattern became a powerful element in Irish nationalist mythology: if Ireland was ever to compete as a nation on equal terms with Britain, industrialisation was essential. For Sinn Féin leader Arthur Griffiths, speaking in 1918, 'a nation [could not] promote and further its civilisation, its prosperity and its social progress equally as well by exchanging agricultural products for manufactured goods as by establishing a manufacturing power of its own' (cited in O'Hearn 1998, p.36).

The struggle of the independent Irish state to develop an industrial economy may have been as much an expression of modernity as a response to material conditions. It is thus quite ironic to find O'Hearn reproducing such ideas in his discussion of the 'Celtic Tiger'. Agriculture is never included in O'Hearn's narrative about Irish economic development and the fact that the main industries left in the Republic of Ireland after partition were all agriculture-based (brewing, distilling and food processing) is offered as evidence of industrial *weakness*. By the 1990s, neither the food and drink industries nor rural-based tourism appeared to play any significant role in Ireland's 'economic miracle'. In O'Hearn's account, rural Ireland features only in the context of a discussion of poverty and inequality in modern Irish society.

In contrast, we could think of Irish society not as 'late industrialising' but as 'early agriculturalising' and it can then be characterised in terms of its achievements rather than its failings. This may not be the form of modernity enjoyed by all 'advanced' European countries but it is still an important variant. To be agricultural is not the same as to be traditional in the sense of 'backward' and so, as we discuss the Irish experience of development, we start, not as is conventional with an account of industrial development, but with one of agriculture and agricultural change.

## Agricultural development

### The agrarianisation of Ireland

The society that gained political independence in 1922 was highly specialised in agriculture. Some 58 per cent of the male labour force at the time worked in agriculture. Agricultural commodities made up the bulk of Irish exports and, as an earner of foreign currency and a source of livelihood for many Irish families (outside as well as inside farming), agriculture was a key sector both economically and politically. In this respect, Ireland was not unique in Europe. Denmark and Finland had similar economic profiles. Moreover, despite the reliance on agriculture, Ireland was by world standards at this time a comparatively wealthy country.

Ireland was not 'naturally' agricultural, but became so as a result of historical processes, in particular its long relationship with Britain. In the eighteenth century, British rule contributed to the spread of the industrial revolution throughout Ireland, with the development of rural industries such as linen and milling and of the urban-based woollen and food-processing industries (Cullen, L., 1987). By 1821 there were reported to be more people engaged in 'manufacture, trade and handicrafts' than in agriculture in one-third of Irish counties (Haughton, 1995) but this blossoming of 'proto-industrialisation' rapidly reversed outside the north-east of the country during the nineteenth century. A key factor was the incorporation of Ireland as a region of the British economy following the Act of Union. As a result, for a century prior to political independence Ireland, along with Scotland and Wales, was part of a 'common market' centred on England. In this context Irish society underwent specific processes of de-industrialisation and agrarianisation.

Ireland's agricultural economy was not a traditional economy if, by that, we mean one that was uncommercialised and isolated from markets. From the seventeenth-century Irish farmers were integrated into global food markets through their incorporation into British colonial and imperial trade relations. Irish farm products were exported to countries on the European continent, particularly France, Spain and Portugal (Cullen, L., 1987) and to French colonial markets in the West Indies. By the end of the seventeenth century almost half Irish agricultural exports went to Europe, especially to France (Haughton, 1995). Over the next 200 years exports became more focused on Britain and Ireland became an important source, especially of labour and food, for British industrial expansion.

Irish agriculture therefore has a long history of commercialisation and of integration into international markets. Much of what happened in Irish social and economic history can be explained only in terms of this external integration. Sociology in Ireland has generally been slow to recognise this and its implications for theories of development. This is partly because of the frequent dismissal of agrarian or rural Ireland as 'traditional' as a result of over-enthusiastic use of modernisation theory and partly because the form of farming that was inherited by the Irish state and that persisted largely unchanged for decades afterwards was family-based. Family-based forms of production tend wrongly to be linked with 'subsistence' agriculture, regarded as non-capitalist and remote from the modern, urban, capitalist and rationalised economy.

## Irish farming in the early twentieth century

This does not mean, of course, that Irish agriculture at the point of political independence was entirely commercialised or that all Irish farmers were equally involved in market relationships. On the contrary, what the new state inherited was a *dualistic* agrarian economy, characterised by wide gaps in wealth, income and political power between large and small farmers and between different farming regions. Smaller, poorer farm households were concentrated in the north and north-west of the country and the midlands; larger, richer farmers were found predominantly in the east and south.

While this dualism has persisted and strengthened up to the present (Commins, 1996), in the early part of the century it was less obviously a problem. Though there were extremes of size at each end of the scale, overall, Irish farms tended to be small, at least compared to those in Britain. Thus, in 1926, 57 per cent of farmers had less than 30 acres and less than a tenth owned 100 acres or more (Breen et al., 1990, Chapter 9). They were also less specialised than today in terms of output. Despite the massive dominance of cattle production, most farms operated a mixed production regime with some tillage, some dairying, pigs and poultry, either for consumption by the farm family and farm animals, or for sale, or both. They mostly had the same tenure conditions and organisation of farm production. It was therefore easy to categorise them as all belonging to the same social class and, by the 1920s, the great majority of farmers owned their land rather than renting it. Most worked it with family labour or, on larger farms mainly in the east, with the addition of just one or two hired labourers.

Arensberg and Kimball (1940) show how familial relations, on family farms, were shaped by the fact that they were also relations within a farm business. The father of the family was also boss of an enterprise in which the main workers were his wife and sons. This led to complex and often tense relationships between family members. For example, the marriage of a son had major implications for the continuity of the farm enterprise and so involved business considerations as much as personal choices in terms of timing, choice of partner and the nature of the contract between the new couple. Similarly, family needs influenced the form of farming. In particular, it encouraged the type of mixed farming outlined above. Arensberg and Kimball's account is based on relatively small farms in the west of Ireland. We have little comparable information about family relationships in large-farm, commercialised areas but it seems likely that they did not differ greatly. If anything, the greater value of the property to be managed and passed on to the next generation tended to intensify the patriarchal nature of family relationships on such farms. Gender inequalities on large farms were greater and farm wives and daughters were more actively excluded from a say in the business.

Though commonalities across Irish farming helped to obscure its dualistic structure, class differentiation between farmers was already marked by 1900 and became more pronounced over the course of the century. But it would be wrong to assume that the smaller, more westerly farmers existed independently and in isolation from larger farmers and the national and international markets in which they participated. Much Irish rural sociology implies this and suggests that the small-farm areas of the west were traditional in the sense that they remained outside the modernising capitalist farm economy. In fact, such dualism is more typical *of contemporary* Irish farming, as we see below, than it was in the early 1900s.

A brief sketch of the organisation of cattle production in Ireland illustrates this point. Calves born on dairy enterprises in the south and south-west were transferred to small farms in the west to be reared, 'brought on' for a year or two on small to medium farms in the midlands, then fattened and 'finished' on the large farms of the east (in Co. Meath in particular). From there they were sold for the market, primarily for export to Britain. This regime meant that small westerly farms, for whom rearing and selling on young cattle was a crucial source of household income, were the most vulnerable to fluctuations in international market conditions. In adverse conditions the dairy farmers, or the finishers and exporters, could defray their costs in the form of increased calf prices, or lower prices for young cattle (Crotty, 1974). Thus, the dualism that was apparent in Irish farming existed within a larger, globalised, capitalist agricultural economy and there was no division between those inside and outside this economy. We can see this cattle regime as a microcosmic example of dependency where the smaller farmers in the west were the least powerful and most dependent players in an Irish agrarian economy that was itself in a position of dependency and relative powerlessness within a larger agricultural world system.

**Figure 3.1 Policy aims of the Irish state in relation to agricultural and rural development**

|  | Policy aim(s) | Response(s) |
|---|---|---|
| 1920s | Maximise agriculture's capacity to earn foreign exchange. | Remove rates from agricultural land. |
|  | Reduce costs of production, such as land and capital. | Provide low-interest loans via the state-owned Agricultural Credit Corporation. |
| 1930s 1940s | Restructure agricultural production and employment to make economy and society more self-sufficient. | Encourage farmers to switch from extensive, export-oriented cattle production to tillage — more labour-intensive and oriented to domestic markets. |
| 1950s 1960s | 'Modernise' Irish farm production and responsiveness to markets. | Provide technical assistance and grants for modernisation of facilities. |
|  | Maintain and modernise smaller as well as larger farmers to reduce rural depopulation. |  |
| 1970s | Remove smaller and 'less efficient' producers. | Target agricultural development resources towards larger farmers. |
|  |  | Provide alternative livelihood for small farmers through rural industrialisation. |
| 1980s | Transform Irish farming to meet the needs of growing food-processing industry. | Provide technical assistance and grants. |
| 1990s | Further develop commercial agriculture and food processing | Provide technical assistance and grants |
|  | Respond to increasingly urbanised society and service-oriented economy. | Manage demands for rural space for tourism, recreation, heritage conservation, environmental protection, access to 'nature'. |

## Agriculture in Ireland: the 'development problem'

Our earlier outline of how the economy became agrarianised prior to independence suggests a third challenge to assumptions about the 'naturalness' or 'traditionality' of Irish agriculture which relates to the role of the British, and then the Irish, state (for more on the state in Irish sociology, see Chapter 4). Food security has always been an issue of concern to rulers as has the problem of how to pacify and control the inhabitants of open countryside outside easy reach of armies, tax inspectors, census takers and other agents of the state. State intervention in agriculture therefore has a very long history and generally tends to remain an issue even when governments are committed to non-interventionist, *laissez-faire* orientations to the economy. The British government, for example, made a range of interventions into Irish agriculture in the decades after the Famine, including the passing of the Land Acts and the establishment of the Congested Districts Board. Of key importance was the setting up of a Department of Agriculture and Technical Instruction which subsequently became the first government department of the newly independent state.

The role of the state is highly relevant for two reasons. First, the definition of the Irish 'development problem' — how the state could intervene in and change agricultural and rural Ireland — has gone through a number of shifts (see Figure 3.1). These have profoundly affected the living standards and life chances of different groups of Irish farmers. They also remind us that our definitions of 'development' and 'modernisation' are shaped by the economic opportunities made available by a dynamic global economic system and the political and ideological orientations of those in power.

Second, the state is important in how it has actively facilitated the global diffusion of ideas and assumptions, derived mainly from North America, about 'modern farming'. In modern farming, for example:

- There is the maximum possible distance between farm and family so economic decision-making is not clouded by irrational or emotional attachments.
- Farm women are encouraged to withdraw from farm work into domesticity and to leave the business to their husbands and sons.
- Farmers should respond actively to market trends and changes and should be guided by agricultural scientists and professional farm advisors rather than kinsmen, neighbours and other holders of 'local knowledge'.

This approach to agriculture coincided with the interests of the food industry and agribusiness which, since the 1960s, have become increasingly powerful actors in world agriculture. For example, the Kellogg food company has been an important agent in the global diffusion of these concepts, through the funding of research centres. But these are powerful ideas in their own right, forming part of a complex of beliefs about modern, rational economic behaviour whose adoption was fostered by the close relationships that grew up between American and Irish agricultural professionals in the post-war period. Indeed a number of Irish agricultural scientists received postgraduate training in American universities during the 1960s (Tovey, 1992a). Subsequently, as part of the Irish state's interventions into agriculture, they helped to introduce the new sets of beliefs and practices associated with 'modern farming'.

These processes fed into a policy orientation, now termed 'productionism', that concerned itself in an increasingly narrow way with the productive function of agriculture — its capacity to produce food or raw materials for a food-processing industry — and disregarded other important functions such as the provision of employment, the underpinning of a vibrant rural community, or the care and management of the environment. Productionism reflects a particular conception of modernity. It has not been peculiar to Irish agricultural policy but has dominated agricultural thinking in most parts of the 'developed' world since the late 1950s. It underpinned the EU's Common Agricultural Policy (CAP) for some two decades, from around the time of Ireland's accession to the EEC in the early 1970s to the so-called McSharry reforms of the late 1980s and early 1990s. Irish membership of the EU strengthened and consolidated existing productionist tendencies in Irish agricultural policy and it is only in recent years that its dominance as a discourse shaping Irish agriculture has waned.

## Changes in social structure

In this section we focus on two processes: the decline in the proportion of rural people who are farmers and consequently in the political power and dominance of agriculture in local country areas; and the transformation of 'family farming'.

Employment in agriculture in Ireland has declined sharply. The proportion of the labour force engaged in agriculture fell from around half in the 1920s to less than an eighth in the mid-1990s (Commins, 1995). Up to the late 1980s the number leaving agriculture in each intercensal period roughly equalled that of new jobs created (Commins and Keane, 1994) but many of the new jobs were created in urban areas and in the east of the country while most of those lost from agriculture were in the midlands and the west. As a result of the decline in agricultural employment many rural areas are no longer primarily made up of farm households, but of those dependent on other forms of work. This has had important effects on rural politics and on state policy.

Until the early 1980s the fall in agricultural employment was primarily among farm labourers and 'relatives assisting' (family members who lived and worked, often unpaid, on the farm) rather than among farmers themselves, but since then there has also been a marked decline in the number of farmers. This raises critical questions about the long-term future of farming, at least in certain parts of the country. However, it is not simple to identify who is a farmer and who is not: does it depend on owning farm land, or on working that land, or both? Irish Farm Survey figures show that a reduction in the number of farmers does not necessarily mean fewer farms. In fact, the number of farms has not markedly decreased. Many people apparently continue to hold land but have ceased to identify themselves as farmers, possibly due to rental of land to a farming neighbour; it does appear that renting of land is on the increase in Ireland again after nearly a century of pressure to convert tenants into owners. Owners of smaller farms appear most likely to rent out land rather than work it themselves. This may reflect the availability of off-farm income from employment or state benefits or a decline in the perceived status of farming as an occupation (an unpublished study of a rural area in the west of Ireland in the late 1980s suggested that local men who were regarded as farmers — rather than as, for example, factory workers or fishermen — found it much more difficult to find women willing to marry them). In addition, widespread ownership of land among non-farming people in Ireland distinguishes the Irish class structure from many other 'modern' societies and appears to have quite distinctive effects on the patterns of social mobility and class politics in contemporary Ireland (Hannan and Commins, 1992). It is perhaps one way that Irish society is more usefully compared with French rather than British society.

The demographic patterns noted above have changed the nature of family farming in some interesting ways. Formally, there appears to be continuity in the type of farming that predominates in Ireland — there has been very little movement, for example, towards large capitalist companies taking over farming and using entirely hired labour to work the land, in a similar way to industrial production. But even if Irish farming remains in some sense 'family farming', it is a different situation when the farm is operated individually by the male 'head of household' rather than with the labour and commitment of a number of family members. But we must take care not to overemphasise what may be unreliable data. The claim that 'relatives assisting' have virtually disappeared from Irish farming is based on what farm people report as their occupation, rather than on the contribution they may make, in terms of time or specific tasks, to farm work. The figures may, in particular, underestimate the work of farm wives, who are more likely to report themselves, or be reported in official surveys, as 'engaged in home duties' rather than as farm workers. The solitariness of contemporary farming may therefore be exaggerated. It may also be that the extent and nature of farm women's contribution — managerial and secretarial, for example, as opposed to manual — varies between large and small farms and in different parts of the country. Gender relations in farming is an area that Irish sociologists have only begun to study in any depth (see O'Hara, 1998; Shortall, 1997).

The withdrawal of farm sons and daughters from farm work is better documented. The main reason for declining numbers of farmers is not that farmers are moving into other jobs, but that those who retire are not being replaced by a member of the next generation. Increasingly, farm sons (this was always true of daughters — see Chapter 8) aim to secure educational certification and a place in a broader labour market rather than leave school early, go through an agricultural apprenticeship under their father, and in time succeed to the farm. Farm heirs who are already in work outside farming when their father retires or dies are increasingly likely to continue their existing job and work the holding part-time, if at all. This depends on the size and value of the farm and the region in which it is located.

## Changes in farming practices

A few key changes will be discussed here. First, and most striking, is how far Irish agriculture has moved away from a mainly mixed type of farming to one that is typified by *specialisation*. When Ireland joined the EEC in 1973, dairying was still carried out on almost two-thirds of farms. Today this has fallen to just over one-third. The average size of dairy herds increased over the same period from around 10 to around 27 cows per farm, suggesting that specialisation is accompanied by increasing scale and intensity of production. The most striking example is probably in pig production. Once widely dispersed on Irish farms, and small in scale, by the 1990s pig-keeping had become an enterprise concentrated on a small number of holdings — 2,900 in 1991 — and the average herd size — 29 in 1973 — was more than 450 animals (Commins and Keane, 1994, p.44).

Specialists in the more profitable types of farming, such as cattle fattening, dairying and cereals, tend to be large farms in the east and south-east while specialisation on the small farms of the north-west and west is in virtual monocrop production of 'drystock' (young beef cattle raised for selling on). The latter form of specialisation provides one of the lowest incomes in Irish farming and appears to be less the deliberate choice of farmers in these areas (though in some cases it may be chosen for its compatibility with off-farm employment) than the outcome of a continuous, decades-long process of exclusion and marginalisation from more profitable types of farming (Tovey, 1982).

A second important change is the *commoditisation* of farming — how farmers become increasingly involved in and dependent on markets, not just to sell what they produce, but also to obtain the resources or inputs they need to complete each round of production. This is generally regarded as the most critical form of change because it means that farmers lose skills and substantial amounts of control over the farm production process through dependency on the manufacturers whose resources or commodities they now buy rather than self-produce on the farm. An example is the switch in Irish farming in the 1960s and 1970s from the production of fertiliser on the farm itself from the previous year's round of animal production to buying in bags of industrially produced chemical fertiliser. Other examples include no longer keeping seeds from previous crops but buying them in from seed companies and suppliers; using the 'government bull' (artificial insemination) to inseminate one's cows instead of keeping one's own bull; and buying in young dairy calves or lambs instead of raising replacements on the farm itself.

Irish agriculture, we argued earlier, has been commoditised for centuries through the sale of its output on domestic and international markets. But input commoditisation has developed into the norm only in the period since the 1960s. It is linked to processes of increasing specialisation on farms and to the trend away from mixed farming. It appears to have been very deliberately encouraged by the state through the agricultural advisory service (Leeuwis, 1989). Agricultural economists and other specialists argued that a core problem in Irish farming was the fact that it generated quite low incomes compared, for example, to industrial wages in the 1970s. They believed that the best way to solve this problem was to increase the level of farm output (an example of 'productionism') and that this could be best done by moving farmers towards a 'high-input/high-output' regime that required extensive use of bought-in inputs. Farmers who resisted this approach were labelled and stigmatised, according to Leeuwis, as irrational, traditional or even stupid — ironic perhaps in the light of contemporary concerns about the environmental impacts of 'modern' farming.

Commoditisation of agriculture, especially of inputs, exposes farmers to external influence and control. The most crucial influences are agribusiness and science. Commoditisation is accompanied by a third key process: *scientisation*. This refers to a process of technological intensification where tasks once carried out by farm family members, perhaps using farm animals, such as ploughing, are taken off-farm, mechanised, made amenable to industrial production and sold back to the farmer in the form of new tools such as tractors. Such technological intensification has been a marked feature of Irish farming since the 1950s, particularly on larger farms. Scientisation also refers to how the knowledge needed to carry out farm tasks is removed from farmers and farming communities and brought under the control of scientific 'experts', from where it is returned to farmers in the form of state regulations or industrially produced 'technological packages'. State regulations, for example, have pushed farmers to change how they manage milk storage and milking parlour hygiene; these processes must conform to scientific norms rather than to local culture and practices. With technological packages the farmer's work is reorganised according to rules laid down in scientific laboratories rather than those derived from years of local practice, for example, using a laboratory-produced hybrid seed to grow winter wheat, which necessitates the application of certain levels of specific fertilisers, herbicides and pesticides at specific points in the growing process. The most recent and far-reaching scientific intervention into farm work is embodied in the technological packages associated with genetic engineering.

What are the implications of these changes? An obvious one is that dualism and inequality have intensified. Farmers are increasingly polarised between those who can survive and make a good living under these new conditions of production and those who cannot. In Irish farming such polarisation does not manifest itself in the concentration of land into fewer hands but in the concentration of capital and production. About one-third of all farms (about 50,000 holdings) now account for about two-thirds of all farm output; they receive about 70 per cent of all the income generated in Irish farming, and between them hold about two-thirds of all tillage acreage in the country, about 70 per cent of all dairy cows and about half of all grazing livestock (Power and Roche, 1993). Increasingly, farmers outside this elite are categorised as 'part-time farmers' even if they do not receive any earnings from off-farm work nor have any other occupation to put time into. They are, essentially, those who lack capital or access to educational and informational opportunities needed to adopt scientised, commoditised, specialised forms of farming. They are increasingly seen as surplus to the requirements of an efficient food industry and thus as available to be diverted into other, non-competing farm activities such as farm tourism or non-intensive, environmentally friendly types of agriculture like organic farming.

## From co-ops to capitalism: the rise of the Irish food industry

The dominance of the trends outlined above means that agriculture can no longer be thought of as a set of independent, separate farming units but instead as part of an extensive, even globalised, food system. Links, direct and indirect, are growing between farmers and the food industry as well as between farmers and manufacturers of farm inputs. This process of *integration* is encouraged by state policy where increasingly food industry interests, particularly those of the large food processors, transport companies and retailers, take precedence over those of farmers. The food industry also targets and seeks to bring particular sorts of farmers under its control. An important strategy is *contract farming* where farmers are engaged on contract to supply a specified quantity of farm produce, of a specified quality, at a specified time and price, to a processing company. In Ireland contract farming is less common than in the United States or the UK, but is found in some areas of agriculture, such as sugar beet, barley for brewing and peas for freezing or canning (Hoggart *et al.*, 1995, p.148).

In Ireland the farmers' co-operatives (co-ops) have historically played an important role as food processors or as intermediaries between farmers and food-processing companies. Since co-ops are legally made up of their farmer members, it is inappropriate for them to engage in contracts with farmers, but they have been able to use other strategies to achieve integration and control over selected producers, such as giving them privileged access to professional farm development advice or to the purchase of inputs for the farm on credit from the co-op, as well as paying bonuses to farmers who meet particular requirements of quality or timing of supply. Use of such practices is a sign of transformation within the co-ops from social organisations to increasingly capitalistically oriented enterprises.

Development of this increasingly integrated food system also reflects consumers' changing food preferences or, perhaps more accurately, changes in the sorts of food made available to them by retailers. Chief among these is the change from relatively unprocessed to highly processed foods. Although this is not as advanced in Ireland as in, for example, North America (particularly in relation to meat where Irish consumers still buy much of their meat butchered and otherwise relatively unprocessed), it is still quite developed in some food lines, such as dairy-based foodstuffs like yoghurts, dairy spreads and milk-based drinks. Growth in the extent of food processing means that the share of the price of food that goes to the farmer steadily declines: it has been estimated that 60 per cent (Europe) and up to 90 per cent (North America) of the price paid by consumers for food now goes to the companies that process, package, transport, advertise and market the food, rather than to farmers. In an integrated food system that links agribusiness, agriculture and the food industry, farmers appear to occupy an increasingly powerless, dependent position.

This position is exacerbated by the fact that the global food industry is exceptional compared to most other industrial chains in the extent to which it is dominated by a very small number of very large TNCs — Cargill, Grand Metropolitan, Nestlé and Unilever are probably some of the better known. It is a very highly concentrated branch of the global economy in which a small number of companies that have multiple interests in different foods or food-related activities command enormous power. These TNCs try to develop controlling positions within each of the different stages of a given food line, through what is known as 'vertical integration'. For example, some American corporations started as grain exporters and shippers, then expanded into supplying feed for chicken farms, then bought up and operated day-old-chick enterprises, established relations of contract with chicken farmers to whom they sold the chicks and the feed and from which they bought the finished birds, and finally bought into or set up outlets for the processed chicken in supermarkets or in fast-food chains. But food TNCs also invest in other areas of production that may not be closely related to food at all. Some move into food while retaining their original base in a quite different area — tobacco companies, for example, have been prominent investors in salmon farming in Ireland and vineyards in Australia. This diversity of interests enables TNCs to manipulate food prices and markets, sometimes making food available at below cost in the interests of removing competitors and to achieve long-term control over the sector (Bonanno *et al.*, 1994).

To some extent Irish farmers have, until recently, been protected from direct manipulation by such powerful companies by the strength of the co-ops. As long as, legally, only co-ops could do the initial stage of milk processing in Ireland, foreign companies could not easily penetrate the dairy food system, although the beef system was more open to them. But the co-ops have since the early 1970s become increasingly concentrated. The emergence of a small number of large co-ops coincides with the concentration of dairy farming in Ireland (fewer farms, larger herd sizes) noted earlier. A new stage in this concentration process was reached with the 1997 merger of Waterford and Avonmore Foods to form GlanBia, claimed to be the fourth largest dairy food company in the world. Over the same period the co-ops have been increasingly transforming themselves into conventional companies quoted on the Stock Exchange, thereby opening themselves up to influence from a growing number of non-farmer shareholders. Though still nominally farmer-controlled, the extent to which they can or wish to act on behalf of local farmers is doubtful. These co-ops have been the basis for the development in recent years of an indigenous group of Irish TNCs (Tovey, 1991). Whether the international division of labour in food production that they promote is good for either Irish farmers or Irish food-industry workers is open to question. In a sense, both farmers and industrial workers have become 'employees' of food-industry companies, though there are interesting social reasons why both groups find it hard to recognise any shared status.

## From agricultural to rural: a post-productionist regime?

We frequently hear the claim that, since the early 1990s, agriculture in Ireland and Europe has moved into a 'post-productionist' phase. European policy, it is said, is no longer narrowly concerned with agriculture simply as a means to produce food, but now recognises its other important dimensions as well, particularly environmental considerations in how we use the countryside and the importance of finding a way to maintain a rural, as well as an urban, society within an increasingly urbanised Europe. Some try to capture this change by suggesting that European, and by inference Irish, policy has switched from a policy for agriculture to a *policy for rural development*.

In the 1980s, growing European enthusiasm for a post-productionist rural policy coincided closely with a realisation that the CAP was leading to problems of overproduction that could financially cripple the EU. It was given a new boost in the late 1990s by pressures on the EU to enlarge and incorporate eastern and central European countries that have large numbers of farmers. It has become important to find ways of supporting farmers that do not necessarily translate into the production of more food or, at least, not food already in oversupply. But other factors have influenced policy changes:

- the creation, as outlined above, of a category of 'surplus' farmers that followed from the development of a streamlined food industry
- the urbanisation of European life, leading to new demands on rural areas such as leisure and housing
- growing concerns about the nature of food produced under the intensive, scientised methods promoted by the CAP in terms of the environment, animal welfare and food quality and safety.

While these concerns have shifted thinking about rural and agricultural areas towards post-productionism, they have not succeeded in moving policy decisively away from the ideal of 'the modern farm'. Rather, they have tended to reinforce support for polarisation and dualism, for it is only as long as we have — somewhere — highly efficient, intensive, technologically advanced farms that produce as much food as we need, as cheaply as possible, that we can enjoy the luxury of allowing large tracts of the countryside to be given over to non-productionist concerns, such as National Parks. The outcome is an increase in regional differences within Europe, and within Ireland, of which the social and environmental impacts have yet to be meaningfully evaluated (Hoggart *et al.*, 1995, pp.21–75).

## INDUSTRIAL DEVELOPMENT

It is easier to write more briefly about Irish industrial development, given the body of excellent analysis that already exists (Allen, 1997; Jacobson, 1989; Kirby, 1997; O'Hearn, 1992, 1998; Wickham, 1983, 1986, 1997), and we offer only a summary account here. Breen *et al.* (1990, p.5) suggest 1960 as an initial vantage point from which to survey earlier and more recent developments. This was a time when Ireland:

> could be characterised economically as one of the peripheral regions of the United Kingdom. British capital was the major source of foreign investment. Two-thirds of all exports went to the British market. Entry into the labour market for each new generation often meant emigration to Britain.

At a time when most of the developed industrial economies in Europe were experiencing economic growth, the Irish economy was stagnant and emigration rates were very high (see Chapter 5).

During the 1930s the Fianna Fáil government had tried to reduce economic dependency by protecting Irish industry against foreign competition and by encouraging domestic production in both agriculture and industry to replace imported goods. This period of protectionism and import substitution could be interpreted as an early attempt by the Irish state (anticipating dependency theory by some thirty years) to achieve 'independent development' by disengaging the Irish economy from the international exchange relations in which colonialism had entangled it. Allen describes Fianna Fáil's strategy as 'building native capitalism' and compares it to the later *populist development strategies* of countries such as Mexico, Argentina and Brazil (1997, pp.33–4):

> All these movements were concerned with national development and opposed the dominant agro-export model whereby their countries were reduced to supplying primary produce for metropolitan countries. Populist movements

became the political instruments by which a shift was made from agricultural interests to the promotion of manufacturing interests.

Similar protectionist barriers were erected by Australia and New Zealand as they sought to develop indigenous manufacturing industries while maintaining an export-oriented agriculture.

Protectionism sought to construct a 'tariff wall' inside which Irish indigenous industries could be nurtured. In an attempt to reduce the influence of foreign capital, the Control of Manufacturers Acts of 1932 and 1934 prohibited such investors from holding more than a 50 per cent stake in Irish companies. It also stipulated that a majority of a company's directors had to be Irish. Special tax and credit arrangements were made available to Irish firms, particularly in commodity lines that did not require much start-up capital such as hosiery or boot and shoe manufacturing. In terms of its own objectives the strategy was quite successful: between 1932 and 1935 nearly 900 new companies were registered; employment in a range of industries doubled or trebled; and output rose by large amounts (Allen, 1997, pp.40–41). But government intervention in the economy did not go far enough to be entirely successful: it 'never induced new producers to step in and produce things that were needed by existing companies' nor did it 'induce domestic capitalists to reinvest after they exploited the profitability of a few "easy" sectors' (O'Hearn, 1998, pp.36–37). In the 1940s growth slowed considerably and the level of imports, particularly from the United States, soared.

In 1958 protectionism was abandoned and a decision made to 'open up' the economy to foreign investment and promote export-oriented industrialisation. Barriers to foreign firms selling goods on the Irish market were also dismantled, especially with membership of the EEC in 1973. The impact of the new strategy was quickly visible: manufacturing output grew by 5 to 6 per cent per annum in the twenty years from the end of the 1950s, and employment in industry increased from 179,000 people in 1961 to 237,000 in 1981. Manufactured goods as a proportion of exports rose dramatically, from less than one-fifth in 1958 to nearly two-thirds in the early 1980s, while exports of live animals and other foodstuffs fell equally dramatically. By 1984, one-third of exports were going to EC countries other than Britain, with only 28 per cent going to Britain (Wickham, 1986).

The main contributors to this industrialisation process were foreign-owned companies and TNCs. Who were the main beneficiaries? Allen (1997, p.108) argues that the '1958 turn' to an 'open economy' was undertaken by Fianna Fáil governments who still pursued the goal of 'building native capital'. Grant aid and subsidies for foreign firms went to those that were export-oriented and did not compete with native capitalists in the home market. TNCs were perceived as bringing a new dynamism into the economy that could 'revive the Irish business class'. O'Hearn disagrees: he suggests that Irish companies selling in the home market lost out to foreign competitors and were unable to compensate through expansion into exporting (though some, such as food processors, did develop into major exporters). By the mid-1980s employment in Irish-owned manufacturing companies was at its lowest since the 1940s. By 1987, foreign firms accounted for 43 per cent of manufacturing employment, 52 per cent of manufacturing output and 74 per cent of manufactured exports (O'Malley, 1992, p.111). The Irish industrial economy had become heavily dependent on foreign investment for development. The main beneficiary, according to O'Hearn, has been global capital.

Ireland was more successful than any other peripheral area of Europe during this time in attracting foreign investment. This was partly due to the generous packages of tax waivers and grants offered by the Irish government. But there were also social and political reasons for success. Competing peripheral regions, such as Northern Ireland, Scotland and Wales or underdeveloped regions in England, did not possess their own state institutions that could pursue this type of development (see Chapter 4). Moreover, Ireland was attractive to outside investors because there was no internal social or economic group — not even radical left-wing political groups like the Workers' Party — that would oppose the TNC industrialisation strategy. Indigenous Irish entrepreneurs were too few in number and politically too weak to challenge the policy even if they had wished to. Farmers, led by the Irish Farmers' Association, did resist briefly but were mollified by government promises that the new policy of industry support would not divert resources from agriculture.

The Irish trade unions were still a significant political force in the 1970s and early 1980s and might have been expected to protest strongly about the anti-union or single-union-only policies of the incoming TNCs. But their objections were muted by the usually substantially higher wages that TNCs offered to their workers compared to native Irish employers and by the 'sweetheart deals' that some individual unions secured with some incoming firms. Many foreign companies set up their branch plants in rural areas that had no living memory of industrial employment and it is often claimed that they were therefore dealing with a workforce that had no interest in or commitment to trade union ideals, though Allen notes that the Italian experience indicates that 'rural workers who have no trade union traditions can also be less hidebound by some of the more conservative habits that grow up with more bureaucratised structures' (1997, p.126).

## Impacts of TNC-led industrialisation

The spatial and social impacts of the industrialisation strategy of the 1970s and 1980s have been the subject of debate. On the spatial side, the regional distribution of growth has attracted considerable attention. During the protectionist period, industrial growth took place mainly in larger urban centres and its distribution was largely unplanned or uncontrolled, despite de Valera's 'ideology of ruralism' (Breathnach, 1985). For a brief period in the 1950s (following the Undeveloped Areas Act 1952) regional development was encouraged through dispersal of industry to the least industrially developed areas of the country, but it was not until the early 1970s that regional planning became an overt part of development policy.

The pattern of regional growth then began to change markedly. In the early 1970s the eastern 'core' regions of the country had been the most attractive to new manufacturing firms, both foreign and indigenous. But the Regional Industrial Plans of the Industrial Development Authority (IDA) spurred on manufacturing employment in the other regions, particularly the west and mid-west, in rapidly expanding industries such as electronics and chemicals. Thus, by 1990, the highest proportion of hi-tech firms was in the mid-west region, followed by the Dublin area and the western region (Boylan, 1996, p.186). Foreign companies contributed most to the change. By the late 1980s they accounted for almost half of total employment in the 'western periphery of Ireland', that is, in all regions outside the three 'core' eastern ones, compared with about a third in 1973 (Drudy, 1991, p.166). In the period 1973 to 1989, these regions had a net gain of almost 30,000 jobs (98 per cent of the national net gain in foreign jobs).

Regions that had consistently lost population since the 1950s (or indeed 1850s) began to experience population growth, particularly through immigration or return migration. But, while the more peripheral areas of the country clearly needed the additional employment, the regional policy left the core areas, particularly Dublin, 'in serious difficulty in relation to manufacturing employment' (Drudy, 1991, p.167). Even within the peripheral regions the success of the policy is debated. According to Boylan, for example, rather than promoting rural development, industrialisation policy exacerbated growth disparities between rural and urban settlements, with manufacturing employment concentrated in the larger towns while smaller settlements and rural hinterlands were drained of population, jobs and services. This has borne particularly heavily on the rural poor who are excluded from participation in urban-centred regional growth by their limited access to transport (private or public) and a low level of technological skills.

The social impact of industrialisation on the Irish countryside has been much discussed. International research on the effects of 'industrialisation by invitation' has stressed its gendered nature and addressed in particular the significant part played by women in the process. O'Donovan and Curtin (1991) note that in Ireland during the 1960s and 1970s the IDA publicly stressed that jobs in the new factories were for adult males, suggesting that they would be high-quality, full-time, well-paid and highly skilled. In practice, many of the workers recruited were women, particularly rural women. Breathnach (1993) notes that in the 25 years after 1961 women's employment in manufacturing outside of Dublin, Cork, Limerick and Waterford increased by 139 per cent (it decreased by 35 per cent in these urban centres) and concludes that 'access to female labour from a rural/small town background has been a locational determinant of considerable significance to foreign firms investing in Ireland' (1993, p.23). Others (Harris, 1983, 1989; Jackson and Barry, 1989; Owens, 1992), have been less interested in the availability of cheap labour for incoming industry than in how the new work opportunities affected the lives of rural women. This research has revealed much about the position of women in Irish rural communities and 'the inequality in gender terms that rural women have encountered in the local development process' (Boylan, 1996, p.189).

Breathnach argues that TNCs employ women as part of their broader strategy: to locate the lower-skilled assembly stages of the production process in Ireland. The result has been to produce in Ireland 'a truncated and inferior form of development and therefore a dependent and subordinate position within the New International Division of Labour that emerged in the 1960s and 1970s' (1993, p.27). Dependency theorists generally believe that industrialisation in Ireland has contributed more to the growth of skilled and semi-skilled manual jobs than to managerial and industrial research positions. They also argue that the expansion of foreign-owned industries has not led to a corresponding growth in indigenous Irish industry or in industry-related services. Foreign industries remain an enclave within the Irish economy, importing most of what they need for production and exporting most of the products (Kirby, 1997; O'Hearn, 1998). Within the new international division of labour, TNCs organise production across national boundaries, keeping the most highly skilled work and most of the profits in core countries and distributing the less-skilled parts to the periphery. While this interpretation has dominated Irish sociological writing about the experience of 'industrialisation by invitation' since the 1960s, it is interesting to note that some of those who, earlier, were committed to a dependency position have now become more detached from it.

During the 1980s James Wickham (1986) focused on the Irish activities of United States-based TNCs in the high-technology sector (computers, pharmaceuticals and electronics). These firms located in Ireland largely to access the EC market. Their activities were mainly in the 'finishing' area, assembling and/or distributing goods largely developed in the core economies. The research and development activities of these science-based industries were rarely carried out in Ireland. As a result, in the 1980s, over half of the people working in the electronics industry in Ireland were semi-skilled assemblers and operatives but these made up only one-third of the workers in the US electronics industry; managers and professionals constituted 28 per cent of the American workforce but only 12 per cent of those working in the electronics industry in Ireland (Wickham, 1986, p.76). Wickham concluded that in terms of the development of the workforce Ireland was diverging from, rather than converging with, advanced industrial countries.

This situation now appears to have changed, at least in some branches of TNC activity. In a more recent study Wickham (1997, p.279) notes that by the end of the 1980s the occupational profile of electronics manufacturing had changed:

The relative weight of qualified employees within the workforces increased as firms automated production processes and took on more ancillary activities that required more skilled labour than production itself. At the same time, new entrants tended to have a relatively higher skill profile than existing firms.

At the beginning of the 1980s electronics companies were looking for technicians and by the end of the decade they sought graduates in electronic engineering and in computer science. According to Wickham the substantial software industry in Ireland that has emerged as a result of such developments appears to contain a much larger number of indigenous companies than the hardware industry does (for a more sceptical view, see O'Hearn, 1998, pp.74–8).

We noted above that the contribution of TNC industrialisation to economic development in Ireland has been seen as disappointing. TNCs are said to import a high proportion of their inputs and to withdraw substantial profits from the country. Relative to their total output they spend less money in Ireland on goods and services for production and on wages and taxes than Irish-owned companies do. Wickham questions this conclusion, arguing that foreign-owned industry has had a strong impact, particularly in the expansion of opportunities for Irish managers and in expanding ideologies of management in Irish society. He notes that, with the exception of Japanese-owned companies, TNC branch plants tend to be run with Irish management personnel as soon as possible after establishment. The indigenous management skills thus created became rooted in the local economy over time (Wickham, 1997; Sweeney, 1998).

TNCs are relatively mobile and respond quickly to changes in world economic conditions. Many of the more labour-intensive industries that came to Ireland in the early 1960s, in textiles, footwear, light engineering, for example, had by the end of that decade moved on to poorer countries with lower wages, such as Morocco or Malaysia. Increasing unemployment throughout Europe in recent years has increased competition between European governments to attract TNC investment and some companies have moved out of Ireland in response. Recession in America during the 1980s meant fewer new TNC plants were located here and those already established reduced their workforces. Kirby points out that, although over 390,000 new industrial jobs were created in Ireland between 1973 and 1994, over 400,000 were lost in the same period leaving the country with a net reduction in industrial employment despite two decades of huge expenditure of taxpayers' money on job creation (1997, p.131). Alternatively one could argue that the investment had improved the 'quality' of the jobs, and that shoe-manufacturers and biscuit-bakers had been replaced by 'modern' personnel, engaged in computing and the manufacture of health care devices.

It is clear that industrial development strategies have significantly changed Irish society. The economy has become less dependent on a single external 'core' — Britain — and a single type of export — agricultural commodities (though food-based exports remain highly significant). The occupational structure has become much more diversified: white-collar work in industry, services and the professions has grown, as has skilled or semi-skilled manual work, while agricultural employment has diminished. The class structure has also changed. In the 1950s about half of each new generation of young people who remained in the country and found work found it in family-owned businesses, particularly farming. Today the jobs people move into are related more to their educational qualifications than to their family connections. In many respects, then, we could argue that the Irish occupational structure and society more broadly, has been 'modernised' by the process of state-led industrial development.

Two aspects of current occupational and sectoral structures may help us to evaluate this conclusion. First, consider the position that service employment now holds in Ireland. The record growth in employment since the mid-1990s has been primarily in service rather than manufacturing jobs. The expansion of employment in service work during the 1990s accounted for 102 per cent of total employment growth, with around half categorised as 'routine clerical workers' and a tenth working in tourism (O'Hearn, 1998, p.97). Much of this new service employment is low paid and casualised. This may make us sceptical of claims that we are moving towards a post-industrial 'information society'. Second, the sectoral organisation of the economy has changed greatly since the early attempts at industrialisation under protectionism. Economic growth and exports have become increasingly concentrated in a small number of economic sectors dominated by TNCs: the so-called '3Cs' — computers (electronics and engineering), chemicals and cola concentrates. These account for around one third of *all* value-added in Irish manufacturing (O'Hearn, 1998, p.73).

The dominance of economic sectors that are not deeply embedded in their host society is of concern to both O'Hearn and Kirby. Kirby favours an industrialisation process that involves increasingly sophisticated value-adding to indigenous raw materials. He holds up Denmark as the ideal, where agricultural processing contributed to the development of a high-quality food-processing industry and associated engineering, mechanical and high-tech manufacturing. He argues that such a process 'is far more embedded in that country's social structure than an industrialisation process largely dependent on multinational companies setting up plants' (1997, p.142). It is remarkable that neither Kirby nor O'Hearn pay any attention to the Irish food industry, a sector that has provided 20 to 25 per cent of manufacturing employment in Ireland since the 1970s, has some history of product innovation, is 'one of the country's largest indigenous industries', has displayed phenomenal growth in turnover and exports since the 1970s and accounts for some 20 of the 'top 100 companies' in Ireland (*Irish Times*, 23 February 1998).

## IRELAND: WHERE IN THE WORLD?

Globalisation theorists suggest that Ireland occupies a 'semi-peripheral position' in the world economic system. The features that justify such a location are (Breen *et al.*, 1990, p.9):

- the key role of TNCs in the economy
- the continuing presence of unemployment (particularly long-term unemployment) and self-employment
- the recent experience of heavy emigration despite high educational standards
- the widening gap between the living standards of rich and poor despite decades of 'development'
- the still substantial agricultural sector
- the increasing dependence on tourism and other service industries.

The term 'semi-periphery', however, remains somewhat undefined in globalisation theory. It can mean that Irish society combines features of both developed capitalist and underdeveloped societies (Kirby, 1997). At one level, we are an integral part of the advanced capitalist world. The major processes that have shaped social change in Ireland reflect those in the core countries. At another level, we share characteristics with underdeveloped countries, such as a history of colonialism and continuing economic dependence. This could explain why industrialisation and capitalist development take different forms and produce different outcomes in Ireland compared with core societies. Whether or not we accept that argument, it is clear that Ireland belongs to a rather special group of 'semi-peripheral' societies. In particular, it is a member of the EU and our recent economic and social development has taken place under its influence. This raises another important question: where is Europe in the contemporary world system?

Globalisation theorists argue that we cannot understand the pattern of change in Irish society unless we use a 'global' approach. We must discuss Ireland not as a locally boundaried society but as an increasingly integrated element of a global capitalist system. Global processes lead to the incorporation, peripheralisation and re-incorporation of different zones within the global economy and, by placing Irish experience in relation to these trends, we can better understand our own recent history. O'Hearn, (1992, 1998) argues that the global system is dominated by the United States; Irish history has been shaped, far more than we realise, by changes in the US society and economy and in America's understanding of how the global system should be managed.

According to O'Hearn (1992, pp.22–8) the United States began to consolidate its position as a world power in the 1950s as the British empire declined. American interests required the expansion of a world order based on interdependence through trade and backed by American military might. The global system was to be maintained through a triangular system of trade wherein the United States would sell industrial products to Europe and modernise parts of Asia; the Europeans would sell their own industrial output to their former colonies who would supply raw materials to the United States. This centred the whole system on America and was actively pursued through the Marshall Aid plan for European restructuring. The Irish state, far from choosing to participate in free trade within the system, was unable to remain outside even if it wished to.

Over the following thirty years this regime proved remarkably tenacious, despite its failure to resolve unemployment, stagnation and poverty in Ireland and other incorporated countries. But there is evidence that, more recently, changes are occurring though they are 'hard to characterise because we are still living through the process' (O'Hearn, 1992, p.28). Challenges to the global dominance of the United States are increasing but O'Hearn believes that neither of the leading contenders, Japan or a German-led Europe, are willing to take on the essential role of military enforcer of the new world order. From the Irish point of view, O'Hearn suggests, the most important change is in European integration strategies. These have shifted in intent from 'a primarily United States-inspired plan to reintegrate Europe' into a project by the European core itself to increase its economic and military power. Significant trends here include:

- a decline in the US proportion of foreign capital invested in Ireland compared to European and Asian inflows
- a general reduction in investment from abroad since 1980
- increased reliance on 'handouts' from Europe
- significant changes in the 'institutional infrastructure' through which Ireland is incorporated into the EU (in particular the Single European Act and the Maastricht Treaty).

These represent steps towards the achievement of a unified European economic field that is now being complemented by the nascent development of a European military structure. The European periphery, including Ireland, is being reoriented towards the European core and away from the United States. O'Hearn argues that the most likely outcome of this for Ireland (and the rest of the European periphery) is 're-peripheralisation'. We can argue the details of this portrayal of the recent period in Ireland and we might question the one-dimensional view of change it offers, where the impact of globalisation on Ireland is confined to the economic level, with politics and culture essentially ignored (we return to the issue of globalisation, including its 'cultural' dimensions, in more detail in Chapter 18). But O'Hearn illustrates how a 'globalised dependency perspective' can be both narrow and powerful at the same time.

The debate between versions of modernisation theory and versions of dependency theory as contrasting ways to understand societal change is clearly not settled. We have argued that modernisation theory provides only a partial, and in some respects distorted, understanding of social change in Ireland as it overlooks the external relationships that have so strongly influenced how we have developed. At the same time, it is not helpful to assume that Irish social change has been totally externally imposed either: powerful groups within Irish society and particularly the Irish state have also shaped our development experience. It is to these 'internal' processes that we turn in Chapter 4.

# 4
# *The modernising state*

In Chapter 3 we examined some features of Ireland's agricultural and industrial development over the past fifty years and explored theoretical explanations of change and development. Now we ask not what happened or why, but who — who oversaw and managed development, took the decisions and influenced the policies adopted and implemented? The usual response to such questions is 'the state'. After all, for many the rationale for an independent Ireland is that we ourselves (Sinn Féin) can, through our own government, control and manage Irish affairs. Thus, we open this chapter with a discussion of the state:

- as a concept
- as a focus for sociological theorising
- as an actor in Irish affairs.

We conclude with the suggestion that the state is not the only power-holder and, in considering who the others may be, we raise questions about the meaning and nature of power itself.

## THE STATE: AGENT OF CHANGE OR REACTIVE FORCE?

In a survey of Irish state research, O'Dowd (1991, p.98) cautions against taking for granted that the state is, or can be, the author of development. Instead we should ask whether the state is an agent of social transformation in society or is best seen in a reactive and intervening capacity — as a response to other agents that initiate social change. The theories of development considered in Chapter 3 generate different answers to this question. For modernisation theorists the state does have a major role to play in transforming 'traditional' societies into 'modern' ones, but only in late modernising societies. In those that modernised early, the transition to modernity was stimulated by the bourgeoisie following their own class interests and aspirations. In late modernising societies, this class is not fully developed and its work falls to the state. A key role is played by intellectuals and professionals, often educated or trained in an 'advanced' society, who express ideas about becoming 'modern' that support and amplify state efforts. In peripheral or post-colonial societies, modernity can be 'a deliberately embraced project, a consciously pursued goal' (Bauman, 1995, p.228) and the intelligentsia takes on a transformative mission, often as part of the project of nationalism. Ironically, the result may be to *imitate* the colonial state, as much as to withdraw from it.

If the modernising state is the main actor in modernisation theory, the picture presented by dependency theory stands in sharp contrast. It argues that in a dependent society *under*development results from incorporation into trade and other relationships with a powerful core society or the broader world capitalist system. The drivers of change are external to the society and the role of the state in a dependent society is to act on behalf of the external power, to facilitate the restructuring of the economy in the desired direction and to persuade or even coerce the indigenous population to accept the changes involved.

Some dependency theorists have argued that at least some 'dependent states' are more autonomous than this account allows; they have been able to develop economically and raise living standards for *some* in society, if not all. This recognition has led to a reconsideration within dependency theory of the role of the state. It has been argued that possession of an autonomous state *can* confer benefits on a dependent society. For Wickham (1997) this is reflected in the advantage that Ireland has enjoyed as a peripheral region of Europe when compared to Scotland and Wales in competition for TNC investment. The Irish state has been able to take its own initiatives to make Ireland an attractive location for investment. Such a pattern of development remains rather different to that of powerful, core societies and is termed 'dependent development'. For most *dependent development theorists*, therefore, the state is not merely a passive recipient of external commands but does have the capacity to secure national interests, albeit within the context of unequal economic and political relationships.

What of globalisation theory — how does it understand the state? This is an ongoing debate that we explore at length in Chapter 18. Briefly, globalisation theorists share a view of the state with dependent development theorists, but have broadened the analysis in a number of useful ways. They talk of the contemporary world as a globalised economy shaped primarily by the activities of transnational capital but recognise that the capitalist world system is *also* a system of separate states. Considerable tension results within this system between 'footloose' capital, organising new international divisions of labour as it seeks out economic opportunities across the world, and 'immobile' states, trying to attract capital investment to their territories while dealing with the impact on their own populations of international economic developments.

A key issue for globalisation theorists is whether the rise of transnational capital means the end of the nation state as the basis of world political organisation. With highly mobile capital that see trillions of US dollars circulating daily in the world money markets, the power of any single state — even a superpower like the United States or Japan — to control and direct economic affairs has seriously diminished. But economic globalisation has also helped in some ways to enhance the importance of nation states. State institutions such as Ireland's IDA and its global competitors struggle to offer transnational corporations the most attractive infrastructure and taxation regimes, even as they try to manage the fallout or 'the local consequences of global restructuring'. People increasingly look to the state to organise the conditions that will create and sustain jobs. The state becomes involved in providing education and training for the workforce, advanced telecommunication facilities and joint enterprises in natural resource exploitation. People also now demand protection against the harm caused by international movements of capital, through unemployment benefits, retraining programmes and programmes to stimulate alternative industries.

Thus, it seems that the state has become a central institution in all contemporary societies whatever their position within the world system. But some globalisation theorists argue that in semi-peripheral and developing societies the state plays a particularly pivotal role. It is often the only 'actor' that can make and implement major decisions about development strategies and mobilise the support of the population behind these. Semi-peripheral societies are particularly vulnerable to changes in the international division of labour and as a result rely particularly heavily on state intervention.

We can find examples of all of these views of the state in Irish sociology. The dominant view corresponds closely to that of modernisation theory — hardly surprising, given the influence of this theory on Irish intellectual life over many decades. Such analyses assume that the Irish state has been, and remains, the pre-eminent agent in the transformation and modernisation of Irish society. Studies in this vein sometimes raise questions about how far other groups have challenged or eroded the independence of the state — the Roman Catholic Church, for example, or employers' organisations or trade unions. But they do so in the context of assuming that the state should be the primary initiator of development, even if in practice it is not in sole control.

A sharp contrast can be found in the work of O'Hearn, a globalisation/dependency theorist, whom we discussed in Chapter 3. He is highly critical of those who suggest that the Irish economic take-off in the late 1950s was a result of the deliberate actions of the Irish state or of specific individuals such as Taoiseach Seán Lemass or modernising professionals and civil servants. O'Hearn (1992, p.23) asserts that when we place Ireland in the context of the global economy, many shibboleths of Irish history dissolve, in particular:

the great myth that an officer from the Department of Finance named Whitaker wrote a monograph, started a planning bureaucracy, and transformed the nation. The Irish economic regime was transformed by the global economy long before Whitaker wrote *Economic Development* in 1958.

For O'Hearn, changes in the Irish economy since the late 1950s reflect shifts in the world economy, and in particular the strategies adopted by the United States in the post-war period in order to consolidate its position within the global core. The Irish state may have welcomed, even facilitated, the resulting incursion of TNC capital into Ireland, but cannot be considered the initiator of this change.

Between the modernisation theorists and the work of O'Hearn we can locate the analyses of writers like Breen *et al.* (1990) who see Ireland as a semi-peripheral country within a global system. The country's possibilities for development are deeply shaped and limited by that position and in particular by the fact that, along with Spain, Portugal and Greece, Ireland is on the EU periphery. This global position constrains but does not determine the policies adopted by the Irish state. In turn, its policies have major impact on internal social structure, especially in producing certain patterns of class difference and class inequality that are thought to be typical of the EU periphery. The choices open to the state may be limited by external factors but it would be impossible to understand contemporary Irish society without examining the part played by the Irish state in shaping social change. This is largely the position we adopt in this book. It is, indeed, part of the reason why we have confined ourselves to writing only of society in the Republic of Ireland, excluding the North. To the extent that different states shape and produce different societies, it is not possible to take 'Ireland' as meaning both Northern Ireland and the Republic of Ireland, nor to treat of both of them coherently within the confines of this text.

## DEFINING 'THE STATE'

Before we take our discussion further, we need to clarify how we understand 'the state'. Discussions of the topic can confuse, as sociologists tend to use the term 'state' in two senses. First, as a way to refer to *countries* in the world system — territorially bounded social systems that possess their own institutions of government. In this sense, 'Ireland', 'Irish society' and 'the Irish state' are often used interchangeably (as we have done in many cases ourselves). Second, 'state' refers to a *set of institutions* within a society that have some distinctive characteristics. These include:

- the political institutions of government
- administrative institutions such as the civil service and local government agencies
- discursive institutions such as the mass media and health promotion agencies
- institutions of control such as the courts and prisons
- institutions of coercion, including the army and the police.

Indeed what is *not* part of the state (that is, what sociologists call 'civil society') is not easy to determine. In each of its two senses 'the state' is a difficult concept to define and as a result it is the focus of much debate and disagreement.

But are all societies 'states' and all states 'nation states'? When sociologists talk of particular societies, rather than of society in general, they often equate 'society' and 'country' (thus Ireland = Irish society). They treat the boundaries of the society as congruent with the territorial borders of the state. But such relationships may be hard to establish in practice, as the case of Scotland illustrates. Many people would agree that Scotland is the name of a country — different to Wales, England or Northern Ireland. But Scotland remains part of the United Kingdom; it does not fully possess its own state, despite its distinctive legal and education systems and some devolution of government within the UK. So is Scotland a *society*, separate from other societies in the UK? Or, to put it another way, is the culture and social life of Scotland different? If we answer yes, we imply that what makes Scotland a separate society is that it is a nation. A society must have boundaries, so if the boundaries of Scottish society are not provided by a Scottish state they must be provided by a Scottish *nation*; but if it is state territorial borders that define a society, then Scotland must be part of UK society (McCrone, 1992).

To complicate matters further, sociologists often write as if the contemporary state means 'nation state' and Giddens asserts that 'all modern states are nation states' (1993, p.113). This view assumes that nation boundaries and state borders are the same, reflecting the influence on sociology of nineteenth-century nationalist ideas (see Chapter 13) that said the boundaries of the nation and the borders of the state *should* coincide. Every nation should have its own state — so every legitimate state today belongs to a particular nation. But if the case of Scotland questions the assumption that 'state', 'nation' and 'nation state' are identical, the Irish case makes it even harder to sustain. The *country* of Ireland is divided between two states, neither of which is co-terminous with 'the Irish nation'. Indeed the *nation* may include, not just the population of the Republic of Ireland and at least some groups in Northern Ireland, but also the almost one million Irish-born people living in Britain, first-generation emigrants in America, and perhaps even second- and third-generation Irish-Americans and Irish-Britons (not to mention those members of the 'Irish diaspora' in Australia, Germany, and so on). From another perspective, sometimes 'the Irish nation' does not embrace the whole population of the Republic of Ireland. Particular social groups, though subjects of the Irish *state*, may on occasion be defined, or define themselves, as outside the Irish *nation* (Protestants, non-Irish speakers, gays and lesbians and Travellers provide historical and contemporary examples).

O'Dowd notes that the lack of coincidence between state and nation is not at all peculiar to Ireland but is 'the empirical reality in much of Europe and the Third World' (1991, p.97). The Irish diaspora is mirrored by others, such as the Chinese, Jewish, Armenian, Indian, to list but a few. In fact, though it is part of the ideology of modernity that each state represents and manages its own nation, countries where this is the case would seem to be the exception rather than the rule. For purposes of clarity, then, it is best to describe the modern international political order as made up of 'states' rather than 'nation states', and to treat the relationship between 'state', 'nation' and 'society' as a matter for empirical investigation in each individual case.

The second use of the term 'state' in sociology has to do with the presence of particular types of institution within a given society. But how to identify state institutions and distinguish them from others? Weber defined the state as that agency within society that has a monopoly on legitimate violence. He suggested that in orderly societies private violence is not acceptable as a way to settle disputes. Rather, violence may be used legitimately only by the central political authority and by those to whom it delegates that right: these authorities and agencies constitute the state. Contemporary sociologists have broadened Weber's approach to include another element — territoriality. Thus, the state as an institution or set of institutions has three distinctive characteristics (and no other institutions within society possess these):

- It claims sovereignty over a specific *territory*.
- It holds the sole right to organised use of *violence* within that territory.
- It possesses *legitimacy* — the consent of the citizens to be governed by it.

There is continuing disagreement over whether legitimacy, or the control of the use of force, is the more basic source of state power. States that lose their legitimacy, such as the ex-communist states of Eastern Europe, lose much of their power. In stable societies most people obey the state because they accept its authority rather than from fear of its violence. Nevertheless the state's capacity to coerce has been seen by many sociologists as its ultimate 'power resource'.

In practice, of course, we can find examples of states that lack these distinctive characteristics. One state's claim to sovereignty over a territory may be disputed by another state (Taiwan is a good example); organised violence may occur outside state control (as in Colombia); two sets of institutions may contest each other's right to be the sovereign authority within the same territory (as has occurred in many post-colonial African states); or citizens may withdraw their consent to be ruled (again, as in the post-communist states). Irish history also provides examples of all of these situations. In practice too, the institutional form of 'the state' may vary considerably between societies or in a single society over time. States may be more or less interventionist. In some circumstances the state may undertake tasks that are otherwise left to society, such as industrial production as in 'semi-state companies', or the socialisation of young people through state education systems or youth organisations. The range of institutions that make up 'the state' is potentially very broad and it is therefore difficult to draw an absolute boundary between 'the state' and civil society.

These criteria do not always help us decide whether the institutions we are dealing with constitute a state or not. Is the EU a state? According to our three criteria there seems to be good reason for saying it is not. First, the EU does not clearly possess its own territory; although the Maastricht agreement defines the territorial borders of free movement of people, goods and capital, the territories involved are ruled directly by the member states and only indirectly by the EU. Second, the sovereignty claimed by the EU is problematic; while it can override specific laws of its member states, it has few means to enforce its decisions. Third, no EU agency yet has a monopoly on the organised use of violence across member states. Fourth, the legitimacy of its decision-making processes is frequently called into question given the low level of power accorded to the European Parliament and the 'democratic deficit' apparent in its political institutions. However, while we may agree that the EU is not a conventional nation state, it arguably has institutions (the European Commission, in particular) that operate in 'state-like' ways. Conversely, the EU may also be evidence for the decline of nation states, and the rise of supra-states, as the key players in the global political system.

There is a third, perhaps easier, way to define the modern state: to examine what it does, rather than try to list the institutions and agencies of which it consists. Breen et al. (1990, p.13) suggest, rather cynically, that the modern state is at base an administrative and military organisation that takes resources from a society and uses them to 'maintain order at home and to compete against other states abroad'. This view reveals something about the two key problems that confront the modern state: maintaining order and managing the economy. On one hand, it must ensure that the conditions for capitalist economic development continue. This may involve a defence of private property rights; the introduction of taxation measures to stimulate business expansion; or the provision of a healthy, well-trained and willing labour force. Such challenges relate to the problem of accumulation: the need to secure the profitability of capitalist businesses and thus the financial basis of the state itself. Simultaneously the state has to maintain the consent of those it governs and ensure that they support its economic development strategy, even when they derive little benefit from it. This is the problem of legitimation.

As the state seeks to resolve one of these problems it may exacerbate the other. For example, a move to control wages to improve business profits can lead to protests from workers; or provision of unemployment benefits for the victims of economic restructuring may mean higher taxes that deter investment in the economy. A particularly difficult problem for the modern capitalist state is the management of social inequality. As it strives to improve the possibilities for capitalist accumulation, it tends to increase inequality and divisions in society and obvious social inequality may put severe strains on the state's legitimacy.

## THE STATE IN IRISH SOCIETY

As it has sought to manage the economy and maintain social order, the state has contributed significantly to the formation of contemporary Irish society. To develop this point we focus on inequality to see if the ideas of accumulation and legitimation help us to understand how the state has responded to this issue. We discuss here the historical construction of inequality only; Part II addresses its more contemporary dimensions in some detail.

How has the Irish state responded to social inequality in Irish society? First, it can affect the life chances of individuals and families in two main ways. As an employer and facilitator of job creation and economic activity generally, it influences the occupational positions available and the incomes earned by different occupational groups. Second, the state influences incomes indirectly through its taxation policies and its policies for redistributing state resources across different groups in society.

The development strategy adopted since 1958 has used incentives to attract foreign capital and to develop an export-oriented industrial base in Ireland. Tax reliefs on export profits, accelerated depreciation and other tax allowances were made available to those who located in particular areas of the country. In agriculture, grants and subsidies for farm development were increased to encourage farmers to raise their output and agricultural exports were directed away from the 'cheap-food' British market to higher-priced European markets.

We can see these measures as an attempt by the Irish state to tackle its accumulation problem. They particularly benefited the owners of foreign capital, larger farmers, and those, for example, in the food industry, who set up export-oriented enterprises. The state itself became a major employer between 1960 and 1980. Most of the new public sector jobs were in white-collar, secure employment, located in Dublin, though much of the state-generated industrial employment was located outside the capital. One group strongly disadvantaged by the state strategy was the existing working class of Dublin and other east-coast centres such as Drogheda and Waterford. Many indigenous companies, in areas such as textiles, engineering and food processing, closed during this period and those made redundant were unable to compete for the new public sector jobs against better-educated immigrants to the city. Rural areas also experienced increasing inequality (see Chapter 3). While larger farmers expanded their businesses, smaller farmers, unable to take advantage of state development aids, were pushed into less lucrative types of farming such as rearing young cattle.

The new development strategy was primarily directed towards increasing wealth. It was argued that more wealth would translate over time into extra jobs and rising living standards for everyone — *the trickle down effect*. Initially this seemed to be the case as industrial employment increased and emigration declined but, by the late 1980s, unemployment rose to 18 per cent of the workforce and up to 15,000 people per annum were leaving the country (see Chapter 5). How the state raised resources through taxation and the way it redistributed these across different social groups contributed to this growing inequality. Between 1965 and 1984 state revenue from taxes on property, inheritance and corporate income fell while indirect taxation (VAT), personal income tax and social insurance contributions increased. Personal taxation increased at a higher rate than increases in earnings so people on low incomes experienced a *decline* in their real income. In 1980, large proprietors with an average income of £197 a week had the same average tax rate (16 per cent) as unskilled manual workers whose average weekly income was just £63 (Breen *et al.*, 1990, p.92). The tax system benefited owners of capital. The additional existence of secret overseas bank holdings, bogus non-resident accounts and further mechanisms for avoiding and evading tax was revealed in the many tribunals of enquiry that were a feature of the political life of the late 1990s.

Industrialisation was accompanied by the adoption of a version of the 'welfare state', the rationale here being that it would reduce inequality of access to basic services such as education and medical care and to basic needs for food, clothing, and housing. If we examine the effect on Irish households of state transfers, through taxation, unemployment benefits, free medical services and education, we find that middle- and upper-middle-class groups in 1980 ended up with 'final incomes' that were slightly less than their direct incomes while most working-class households ended with slightly more. But large proprietors and professionals still had around twice the final income of unskilled manual worker households. Despite expanded state services and increased expenditure on income-maintenance programmes over the period, the Irish welfare state failed to 'significantly reduce income inequality and certainly failed to abate the importance of class in determining life chances' (Breen *et al.*, 1990, p.97).

Taxation and state services have helped to ensure the survival of two vulnerable groups in the class structure: farmers with very small holdings; and/or poor quality land and low-skilled, urban, working-class people. Breen *et al.* suggest that in the absence of state intervention these groups would probably not exist today in Irish society but, they note, there is also a group at the top of the class structure — large proprietors — whose existence has depended equally on massive state subsidies. State intervention has provided a 'safety net' that ensured their continued profitability and made it possible for them to continue to hold this class position and to pass it on to their children (1990, Chapter 4). Middle-class families benefit disproportionately from free education and tax relief on mortgages; to that extent they too depend on the state to maintain their position in the class hierarchy. Irish class structure is thus a product, to a large extent, of the interventionist state and the development strategy it has pursued since 1958.

This suggests that whatever its response to its accumulation problem, the Irish state has not dealt adequately with its legitimation problem. Or has it? Despite occasional protests (the tax marches of the early 1980s, for example) persistent social inequality has not yet produced widespread and sustained protest or withdrawal of consent to be governed, even among the most disadvantaged groups. Why this is so is a very complex issue to address. It involves, among other things, examining the nature and use of power in Irish society.

## STATE, STATE POWER AND SOCIETY

As a small open economy on the European semi-periphery, Irish possibilities for development are constrained by international economic conditions and processes. But the course on which the Irish state embarked in 1958 was not predetermined. Industrialising countries in the European fringe, from Scandinavia to the Mediterranean, have exhibited a variety of ways to manage their development; the strategy adopted in Ireland was not the only one open to us. Earlier we suggested that state development policy has helped to perpetuate social inequality in Irish society. This was presumably an unintended, though perhaps not entirely unforeseen, consequence of policy. But it suggests we need to ask why states adopt the policies they do. On whose behalf do they act?

To take this question further, we must revise and problematise our understanding of the state. So far we have discussed it as something apart from and acting upon society, outside of and relatively untouched by the course of social change. But if the state acts on and influences society, society must act on and influence the state (Peillon, 1995). There are at least two ways that society can influence the state. First, as a set of social institutions the state reflects and is shaped by the power hierarchies and social divisions that exist in society. Over a period of time we find that some social groups have been better able to access state positions and to mould the understanding of, for example, 'the national interest'. Irish society contains different (and competing) social classes, genders, regions, religious and cultural groups, and we could expect the Irish state to recognise and represent the values and interests of some of these more than others. This view of the state still sees the state as being able to take independent action on society but suggests that how the state defines and selects its favoured projects is strongly influenced by its own history and by the various groups that played a part in its construction. A second, alternative viewpoint queries whether the state is a significant actor at all. It suggests that far from being an autonomous agent for change, the state is controlled by more powerful and less obvious interest groups within society. Variations on these views produce four main types of argument in sociology about the nature of state rule and about who the 'real power-holders' in society are.

The first can be called the *ruling class thesis*. This derives directly from Marx's analysis (see Chapter 1) that portrays capitalist society as sharply polarised between two opposed social classes: capitalist/bourgeoisie and working class.

Ruling class theorists contend that capitalist society is ultimately ruled by the capitalist class — the owners of capital and of large productive property. Though the state may appear to be independent, in practice it always acts in the interests of capital, being, as Marx put it, the capitalists' 'executive committee'. Despite occasional apparent conflict, the state has no goals of its own separate from those of the capitalist class. It may pursue goals that appear to militate against ruling class interests, such as certain taxation measures, but these are ultimately in the long-term interest of capital, for example, in development of the labour force.

This approach is resisted by many state theorists. Peillon (1995, p.363) remarks that while the state may emphasise 'the project of the bourgeoisie' this does not automatically make it 'an instrument of this particular class. The conflicts of interest that erupt from time to time between state and bourgeoisie simply rule out such a possibility'. While Peillon agrees that the state does generally privilege the interests of the capitalist class, in his view this is because the capitalist class controls a scarce resource required for economic growth, not because the state is merely its agent or mouthpiece.

A second argument is the *power elite thesis*. This maintains that society is ruled not by a ruling class but by a coalition of elites that includes owners of capital or their representatives. This group, termed the 'power elite' after a 1956 book of the same title by American sociologist C. Wright Mills, may include top financial advisors, employer association lobbyists, military leaders and major formers of public opinion such as politicians, journalists and even academics. The precise make-up of this group varies from society to society: Mills's original analysis was based on America during the Cold War when, he believed, business and military leaders dominated state policy, with government and state executives as junior partners. In contemporary Ireland, we might see military leaders as relatively unimportant but church leaders as a key element of the power elite.

The power elite differs from the ruling class: a class consists of people who share the same economic position and economic interests but who may have few social contacts with each other; an elite is a social group whose members share similar backgrounds, educational experiences and lifestyles. They move in the same social circles, often intermarry and share a common sense of group identity and a belief in their right to lead society. Not surprisingly, it is very hard to prove the existence of such a ruling elite (or 'golden circle') through research, even when one strongly suspects that it exists and exercises considerable power.

Both ruling class and power elite theorists see power as being sharply divided in society: the rulers have all or most of the power while the rest of society has little or none. A third approach rejects this view of power and argues that modern societies contain a plurality of relatively equal interest groups who compete with each other to influence the state. If ruling class theories have their roots in a Marxist analysis of capitalist society, *pluralist theories* owe much to Durkheim's argument that the transition to modernity involves a process of increased differentiation and specialisation of social and occupational roles. According to this view modern society is highly complex and diverse, made up of many pressure groups and associations that represent the outlooks and interests of people in different positions within the division of labour. Pluralist theorists regard the state as outside and above this interplay of interests. The state is a neutral referee that oversees the competition and decides which demands to favour at any given time. The state is portrayed as a rational actor responding primarily to the reasonableness of the case made by an interest group rather than to traditional loyalties or to threats. The rational state thus reflects the general *rationalisation* of society that accompanies modernisation.

The fourth analysis of power in modern society is often called the *corporatist approach*. This suggests that society is ruled by the state acting in conjunction with a small number of specific interest groups that it has taken into a privileged form of 'partnership'. Employer groups, farmers' associations and trade unions are allowed to participate with the state in the process of policy formation and implementation while this is denied to other interest groups such as the unemployed, consumers or the voluntary sector. In return, the privileged organisations guarantee to secure the support of their own members for state policies and this benefits the state by reducing the level of social conflict.

## WHO RULES IRELAND?

Do any of these theories help us to answer the question 'who rules Ireland?'. Do they assist in our understanding of the persistent direction taken by Irish state policy in relation, for example, to social inequality? The taxation policies followed in recent decades might suggest to us that power in Irish society is held by a ruling class. Research on the redistributive effect of taxation in Ireland in the 1970s and early 1980s (Rottman *et al.*, 1982; Peillon, 1995) shows that redistribution occurred primarily among people who lived from income: professionals on high incomes, for example, lost substantial amounts of their income in tax that was redistributed, in the form of state services and welfare payments, to those on very low incomes. But virtually no redistribution at all occurred from those who owned property (large business owners, large farmers) to those without property.

This seems to be evidence of a bias in state policy towards owners of capital but it does not necessarily show that Irish capitalists constitute a ruling class. Furthermore, indigenous industrialists and some large farmers feared that the development strategy adopted by the state in the late 1950s would adversely affect them but were unable to prevent its adoption. Much of the capital subsequently invested in Ireland has been foreign-owned. Does this fact then force us to conclude that the class that rules Ireland is located *outside* the country and that capitalists within Ireland are not a ruling class but merely the local representatives of an international capitalist class? Dependency theorists argue that this is a feature of semi-peripheral societies in general and term the local capitalists a *Lumpenbourgeoisie* to indicate their dependent and controlled position. Others argue that this does not sufficiently recognise the power that local capitalists possess, even in dependent or dependently developing societies. The pluralist thesis offers a less conspiratorial account of who rules Ireland but does not fully explain why some interest groups, even when organised into formal associations, obtain little effective recognition in state policy-making. These tend to be the groups already most disadvantaged — the unemployed, small or part-time fishermen and farmers or tenants of under-resourced public housing complexes.

A corporatist analysis may better explain the mechanisms at work. Corporatism in one version or another has a long history in Ireland. It was experienced first in the form of Catholic corporatism: a programme that sought to minimise state intervention in civil society so that people could express their Christianity through the voluntary organisation of their own economic and social lives. It was popular across much of Europe at the beginning of the twentieth century and reached its zenith in the 1930s to 1950s. Catholic corporatism encouraged people to form local or sectoral organisations to take over the management of their daily lives and saw these also as natural units through which people could participate in the political process. The impact of this teaching in Ireland is evident in the Constitution of Ireland drawn up under de Valera's leadership in 1937 and has left a residue in the contemporary make-up of the Irish senate. However, it failed to make any other significant impact on the Irish social or political system, a fact that Whyte (1979, pp.74–6) attributes to the influence of entrenched political and civil service structures. Corporatism was revitalised, in a secular mode, in the late 1950s as a way to organise development planning and to provide a system of consultation and conciliation between the state and major interest groups. It has been extensively used since then as a means to secure industrial peace (through national wage agreements, for example) and to ensure that state development goals are widely disseminated and promoted among significant social groups.

The effect of corporatism in Ireland is that a small group of peak organisations have come to exert particular influence. According to Peillon (1992, p.22) they have 'been co-opted as privileged partners in the dialogue between state and society. Trade unions, employers' associations, [some] farmers' organisations and some professional bodies have come to enjoy privileged access to the state'. This tells us little about the relative power of the groups that are admitted to partnership with the state. Are trade unions, for example, given the same privileged access as business or employers' representatives? If not, this may suggest that behind the corporatist state there *is* a ruling class of capitalists that holds the real power.

Corporatist accounts of the state help to explain how it can maintain social order in an unequal society — in other words, how the state solves the legitimation problem. To involve the main, and often opposed, interest groups in society in the process of policy formation ensures that both will ultimately accept state policy. On the other hand, the more interventionist a state becomes, the more it gets entangled in social conflict. Before the late 1950s the Irish state intervened in civil society in a quite limited way. In many spheres of life (education, the family, health care) it restricted its role to that of support for non-state institutions, in particular the churches, that claimed the main responsibility for organising affairs relevant to themselves. Indeed, Irish society in the 1930s and 1940s was marked by a strong resistance to state interference that emanated largely from the social teachings of the Catholic Church (Whyte, 1980). In recent decades the Irish state has, like most other western states, become progressively more interventionist. It now seeks to undertake the leading role in modernising not only the economy, but other institutions, such as education and welfare, that can influence economic performance. Thus, it has become an increasing target for its citizens' demands and aspirations; it is expected not only to organise economic growth but also, for example, to prevent environmental pollution that results from industrial production. Incidents of environmental damage can draw the state itself into the conflict between polluting companies and the affected population. This widens the arena of conflict and makes corporatist strategies more difficult to maintain.

So far we have said nothing about Irish politics. Where do they fit into theories of state power? If we take the view that Irish society is ruled by a ruling class or power elite, party politics and electoral processes effectively become irrelevant. The only function of the political process is to provide an appearance of democratic control that masks where the real power resides. Even corporatist theories may support that conclusion. But in Irish politics there are some features that may help to explain how the society has developed in recent decades and why there has been little opposition to the form of that development. Political scientists have suggested that the structure of political parties in Ireland during this period has been unusual when seen from the perspective of core societies. Parties have divided, not along a left/right axis like those in most European or Australasian countries, but around a nationalist cleavage inherited from the early years of the state's foundation (Garvin, 1998). Furthermore, Irish parliamentary processes are thought to be particularly influenced by clientelist relationships between politicians and citizens where electoral support is traded for the real or apparent granting of favours or assistance by politicians (see Sacks (1976) for a classic analysis; Komito (1984) for an alternative view). Whether either of these features is peculiar to Irish politics, or is common to semi-peripheral societies, is open to debate but both processes arguably help to prevent people from recognising or organising themselves in opposition to social inequality.

What remains is the power elite analysis, but this has been little researched in Ireland. On the basis of extant research, it is often claimed that the theory has little application. Peillon argues that there are few links between Irish social elites and thus it is not possible to see them as forming a single ruling group. He argues (1992, p.20) that:

> In the sense that the boundaries of each particular elite are clearly drawn . . . we observe little overlap in their membership and rather limited exchange between them. Higher civil servants rarely retire to high positions in the corporate private sector, and very few politicians transfer to the economic elite. In a similar way, owners or managers of large firms do not belong in a significant way to the political class.

One criterion for the existence of a power elite — overlapping career paths — seems to be absent. But Peillon does go on to warn that there may be other ways elites are interconnected. Members can 'develop close relations and even produce a high level of integration on a totally different basis: a similar background, school networks . . . close social interaction [and] a significant cultural closeness'. Without more research it is difficult to judge how much Irish elites share these characteristics. Furthermore, to establish that they added up to a power elite in the sense meant by Mills, we would need to show not only a social and cultural overlap but also that those involved *saw* themselves as members of a distinct, bounded group that had a legitimate right to rule Irish society.

Nevertheless the power elite thesis is rich in the possibilities it brings to a discussion of power in Irish society. It focuses less on structures than on processes. The power elite is understood as a collective agent and what is of interest are the processes through which this agent assembles, manages and exercises power in particular situations (Weber's influence, as a sociologist of social action, is especially marked in elite theories of power). An implication of the ruling elite thesis is that we must look at the intelligentsia in Ireland as a powerful group. For Mills this sector played primarily a legitimating role within the power elite. Their job was to show that rule by the elite over the masses is right and natural. Is this how the Irish intelligentsia has acted?

Before we consider this question, we need to discuss one final perspective on the state. Much of our discussion has drawn upon the work of Michel Peillon and we should look more directly at how he approaches the question of state – society relations. This was first spelt out in his book *Contemporary Irish society: An introduction* (1982) and was revisited briefly in a more recent (1995) paper on interest groups and the state. Peillon regards the state as a social force, a collective actor, and one of a number that exert a significant influence on Irish society. Others include the business class, the Irish Farmers' Association, the Roman Catholic Church and to a lesser extent the Gaelic League. Social forces, Peillon says, have *projects* — collective understandings about the future state of affairs that they would like to see realised in society; and the state in no exception. Peillon argues that the state must be seen as an initiator of action in its own right, not merely a mouthpiece for another social force (as ruling class theory suggests), nor as a neutral arbiter between the projects of a number of other social forces (as in pluralist theory). While the state project reflects the power structure of Irish society and seeks to promote private enterprise development, it remains an autonomous project that is never identical with that of any other social force. Rather, it seeks to manage the others by integrating or discarding elements of them from time to time and by playing them off against one another when it suits (Peillon, 1995, p.362).

Peillon's approach is in many respects similar to a power elite theory. He too tries to construct a view of the state that emphasises process over structure; for him, the state is a type of actor, with its own goals, principles of action and orientations to the future. However, compared to power elite theory, Peillon's analysis remains abstract. We remain ignorant of who constructs the state's project and who are its main intellectual architects and maintenance workers. As we noted above, power elite theory sees this as an important task of the intelligentsia. These are the people who translate the sectional interests of other members of the elite coalition — the military or big business — into a project for society that appeals to and appears to embrace the interests of all the people. The role of the intelligentsia is to legitimate the elite's hold over power by providing it with ideas and concepts to help mobilise the support of the people it rules. We briefly consider some sociological work on the intelligentsia to conclude our current discussion.

## THE INTELLIGENTSIA IN IRISH SOCIETY

Like most of the terms we have encountered in this chapter, the term 'intelligentsia' covers a complex reality. At its broadest it includes the increasing number of workers who create and communicate knowledge rather than material goods and resources and are often referred to as the (new) 'knowledge class'. Here, however, we are using the term much more narrowly, to refer to those often called *intellectuals* (this distinction was first discussed in Chapter 2). Intellectuals are arguably a particularly important group in peripheral and dependently developing societies. Earlier we quoted Bauman's suggestion that in such societies modernity is taken on self-consciously by the state as a deliberate project. Intellectuals participate significantly in this process and contribute importantly to the process of state-building that post-colonial countries like Ireland go through in the early decades of independence, as they try to transfer the allegiance of their populations to the new state institutions that replace those of the ousted colonial rulers.

O'Dowd (1996, p.19) summarises the work of intellectuals in such countries as including the:

- protection of national or religious identity

- modernisation of institutions and building of a 'welfare state'
- introduction of cosmopolitan thinking or the avant-garde into the national stasis.

We could see these three tasks not so much as things that all peripheral-society intellectuals do but as three different roles or self-images adopted by groups of intellectuals in various periods. In that sense, they correspond rather well to some features of Irish intellectual life.

At the time of political independence the main intellectuals influencing Irish life came from the nationalist movement and the Roman Catholic Church (there was also a significant tradition of Anglo-Irish or Church of Ireland intellectuals, but their influence on society was limited and oppositional). In the following three decades or so, up to the 1950s, the values and goals of this group dominated Irish life: a vision of a social order organised around small to medium property (farms and manufacturing concerns), distinctively Irish in language and values, with a dominant voice for the church in education, health and welfare and a limited role for the state (O'Dowd, 1992).

From the late 1940s, however, a new intelligentsia was developing — senior civil servants, professional economists and other government advisors, journalists — who gradually replaced the established intellectual elite of nationalists and clerics. This 'modernising elite', as it saw itself, believed that the state could play a much greater role in achieving development and it gave significant support to the state when it adopted the strategy of industrialisation through foreign investment in the late 1950s. In turn, these intellectuals benefited from the expansion of state and semi-state activities that accompanied modernisation in the subsequent decades. A considerable proportion of the almost exclusively male (O'Connor, 1998, p.83) intellectual elite was to be found in some form of state employment: as university teachers, members of the judiciary or as managers and scientists in semi-state organisations like Bord na Móna and the Office of Public Works. With the advent of RTÉ in 1961 and the general expansion of media and cultural activities in the 1960s and beyond, the composition and orientation of the intellectual elite changed again. Encouraged by Ireland's membership of 'Europe', the focus of younger intellectuals and media personalities increasingly came to match the third task outlined above: to 'open up' the local society to cosmopolitan values and ideas. After the nation-building intellectuals and the modernising intellectuals came the globalising intellectuals.

Much of the power exercised by intellectuals and the respect they command derives from their claim that the knowledge they produce is 'free-floating', that is, unbiased by any particular social memberships (class, gender, local community, age group or generation) that the intellectual may have. Intellectuals, when speaking as such, claim to be able to transcend social positions, political affiliations and socialisation and produce ideas that are universal and timeless. Intellectuals present themselves as non-partisan and therefore take for granted that their efforts to shape state policy are made in the public interest and not in their own.

Much of the sociology of intellectuals has involved a critical investigation of this self-image. This has taken two main forms. The first argues that intellectuals come from a specific class position that shapes the ideas and knowledge they promulgate. International research suggests, for example, that intellectuals tend to be drawn overwhelmingly from middle- or upper middle-class families of the sort where education is highly valued and where there are plenty of resources available to obtain it. In Ireland, the picture appears a little different since both the strength of the Catholic and nationalist intelligentsia in the early years of the state and the expansion of technical and professionalised intelligentsia in more recent decades has meant that many Irish intellectuals came from a lower middle-class background. But the argument that their class background makes their world views less than 'universal' and non-partisan still stands.

A second sociological position argues that class of origin is less important in terms of explaining the particular values and orientations that intellectuals articulate than class of orientation — that is, the class they move into as adults or the class they would like to be part of and identify with in terms of culture and economic interests. The French sociologist Bourdieu, on the basis of research into intellectual and academic life in France, argues that intellectuals should be seen as part of the bourgeoisie, the dominant class in capitalist society, albeit a rather 'dominated' part of that class. They may own little material capital but do possess 'cultural capital' and this encourages them to see their interests and those of the bourgeoisie as intertwined. This class position, in Bourdieu's view, profoundly shapes intellectuals' judgements about what is to be regarded as genuine intellectual activity; what political ideas, artistic products, and so on, should be given serious critical consideration and which should be simply ignored, ridiculed or marginalised.

Our emphasis on the class position of intellectuals, as part of and dependent on an expanded state apparatus, may surprise those who hold rather different views of what 'an intellectual' is. Such views may be shaped by knowledge of the great intellectuals thrown up by the Soviet regime such as Solzhenitsyn or Pasternak, or North Americans like Martin Luther King, Susan Sontag or Noam Chomsky. Some sociologists suggest we need to distinguish between two sorts of intellectual:

- the thinker who finds him or herself at odds with society and who responds intellectually as social critic or alienated outsider
- the thinker who is firmly tied into the existing social order, credentialised by the formal education system, employed in an institution controlled or funded by the state, and certified and approved by a professional organisation to practice their skills.

The first is the more popular image of the intellectual and associates intellectual work with great writing or art; the second is more often simply called 'a professional'. In modern society the latter seem to predominate: the typical 'intellectual' now is a professionalised expert, trained to work with a specific and narrowly delimited body of knowledge but who claims to be able when required to rise above this narrow specialism and address issues to do with the well-being of society as a whole. Many Irish historians, psychologists and economists recognised as intellectuals or 'opinion-formers' would fit this second category.

There is thus some basis for the claim by power elite theorists that intellectuals' main contribution to society is to legitimate the activities of those in power. A number of studies (for example, O'Dowd, 1996; Lynch, 1999b) suggest that Irish intellectual life has been characterised by a lack of significant criticism of or dissent from existing social arrangements. We can explain this by reference to the class background of Irish intellectuals or to their links with the modernising state, or both. But this is not a criticism that Irish sociologists can make of other Irish intellectuals without being willing to turn it on themselves. In Chapter 2 we suggested that Irish sociology has avoided an investigation of its biases, including its avoidance of the more critical traditions in the discipline, and has committed itself to a rhetoric of 'objective knowledge' and 'research expertise'. Sociology in Ireland is remarkable for the slight influence it has had on mainstream intellectual life in comparison with that of other academic disciplines or of artists and writers. But whatever influence it *has* achieved has failed to significantly expand the role of intellectual as alienated outsider or as protagonist of human emancipation.

## POSTSCRIPT: SOME COMMENTS ON POWER

Finally we need to critique the idea of 'power' itself. Power has always been a central concept in sociology and many sociologists would say that theories of society stand or fall, ultimately, on the basis of how well or how interestingly they are able to deal with this phenomenon. An early but still influential discussion of power was that of Max Weber and we draw briefly again on his ideas to end this chapter.

In our discussion we have associated power with the capacity to initiate action. We suggested that the state can be considered the real power-holder only if it has the capacity to take autonomous action to modernise or develop Irish society. If the state cannot act autonomously in this way, then power may lie elsewhere, perhaps in a ruling class. But, for Weber, power is best defined by the *outcomes* of action rather than its initiation. The powerful person or group is the one who ultimately manages to get what he/she/they want, particularly in the face of opposition from others. This suggests that, in the end, to identify who really holds power we must discover who consistently and over a period of time achieves the outcomes they want and that benefit them most.

Once we have an idea of how to begin researching power, we can go on to ask other questions about it. A central question for Weber was: if an actor or group of actors tries to achieve their goals against resistance from others, what are the main 'resources of power' available to them? One is the capacity to exercise coercion: to force other people — by physical force if necessary — to do what you want. Weber saw that this capacity was such an important power resource that states always try to monopolise it. But coercion is not restricted to physical force; it is possible to speak of economic coercion, for example. If one group in society controls the means of livelihood and others are dependent on them for the necessities of life, then they possess an economic power resource. A key feature of a class-divided society, according to Weber, is that power is unequally distributed within it, largely for this reason.

Threats of violence and of economic damage are very effective ways to ensure compliance with one's wishes but Weber suggested that ultimately they are rather unstable and easily open to challenge. A more effective method is to persuade people that they should obey you and that you have a right to command them and ensure your wishes take precedence; this, as we have seen, was Weber's problem of legitimation. We have devoted considerable space to discussing this and in particular how the state can enlist the services of the intelligentsia to represent its development projects as the legitimate way forward for the whole of Irish society.

Weber's discussion of power led him into a rich historical analysis of the different types of legitimation. We have no space to develop this here but end simply by suggesting that the alternation and tension between coercion and legitimation to which Weber draws our attention is a core feature of all kinds of power, and a core management problem for all power-holders, whether agents of the state or groups in civil society. A significant feature of state power is that most of the time, in most societies, the state can take its legitimacy for granted; other groups and organisations have to achieve legitimacy to secure their power. Holding *legitimate* power is part of what it means to be a state. Legitimacy is such an important resource for the state because it must face deep and pervasive inequality in society. In Part II we look in more detail at the extent and types of inequality found in Irish society.

# Part II

---

## Irish society

# Introduction

In Part I we have tried to show something of the development of sociology as a discipline: internationally and in its Irish manifestations. We have emphasised the connection between the birth and subsequent growth of sociology and the development of modernity itself. Thus, we have paid considerable attention first to the concept of *development* and second to the question of the *state* and where it sits in relation to civil society.

This discussion provides us with a good launching pad for an examination of Irish society. In the next section of the book we deal with some of the key aspects of Irish social life. Inevitably, for practical reasons, we have had to be selective and our choice of topics — population, class and inequality, education, gender, health, crime and deviance — is driven largely by our own fascinations, experience, and judgements as to what others may see as crucial objects of analysis.

We cannot claim that these topics are necessarily the most important. They may not even reflect how people spend their time. There is evidence that people spend a large proportion of their lives in routinised activities such as watching TV, eating, sleeping, socialising with friends, relatives and neighbours, commuting and working inside and outside the home. Except for perhaps the last of these to some extent, all these aspects of life have been virtually ignored by sociologists across the world. It is only very recently, for example, that a sociology of food and eating has developed or that researchers have begun to pay any attention to how people watch television. As in literature and film, the mundane aspects of everyday reality tend to get short shrift in sociology.

We may speculate as to why this is so. Much of the reason may lie in the powerful influence that a concern with 'social problems' has had over sociology. Sociologists have tended to reflect those areas of life that have generated public discourses of concern, for example, health, the family, poverty and class conflict. As we have seen, this has been cemented by sociology's strong links with the concerns of the state. The modern state is pre-eminently concerned with the management of the economy, and of key aspects of society — often those that take an *institutional* form; the state is intimately involved in the running of prisons, schools, hospitals, sometimes churches. It is inclined to intervene in matters of population, of social conflict, of sexual morality and of gender relationships. Thus, the ubiquity and pervasiveness of the state has helped to generate many of the key areas of interest for sociologists. State intervention also helps to produce voluminous documentation in the form of statistics, reports, enquiries and procedures which in itself makes these aspects of society highly visible to the sociologist. It also provides research funding and supports publication in these fields, again helping to stimulate interest.

It would be too cynical to suggest that it is only the supportive role of the state and its institutions that has contributed to a sociological interest in the matters we address in Part II. The labour movement and the women's movement have been two of the most powerful generators of social change in the modern world. The struggles of workers and of women against the status quo have contributed to the emergence of distinctive sociologies of class and gender. Each area embraces a vast range of human activity, has ramifications into all aspects of human behaviour and has generated a rich body of research and theory. No sociology could ignore these aspects of life.

Similarly sociologists have long been involved in, and frequently passionate about, education. In particular, they are concerned with the relationships between education and inequality, emphasised by Durkheim and especially Weber and still of major interest to sociologists, not least in Ireland. Interest in health reflects similar concerns. Some of the earliest empirical research in the social sciences was focused on the issues of public health and the connections between health, power and inequality remain of key interest to sociologists. In addition, the human interactions that take place in the arena of health, for example, between doctors and patients, or doctors and nurses, are of considerable fascination to sociologists, revealing as they do taboos, vulnerabilities, sometimes huge inequalities of status and abnormal social situations. It is of no surprise that the medical drama has long been a staple of popular TV programming and similarly of no surprise that it has attracted social researchers.

Finally, crime and deviance have fascinated sociologists from the earliest days of the discipline. Here the sociologist has the capacity to focus on an area of social life that is often hidden and rarely treated dispassionately in popular culture or everyday discourse. The sociologist has a number of possible roles here: to carefully sift the evidence and provide a more 'objective' picture of the incidence and effects of crime; to question the whole notion of crime itself, at times asking the awkward question as to why the petty thief receives a three-month jail sentence while the corporate criminal or corrupt politician escapes without a conviction; and perhaps, though not very commonly, to penetrate the hidden world of crime and to reveal to us 'outsiders' how it operates, how it is socially structured and how it has meanings for those involved.

We trace here a line through these topics and, though we leave much unexplored and unsaid in the hope of stimulating the reader to extend their own investigations, we maintain our primary concerns with the nature of modernity as it is experienced in Ireland and with how Irish sociologists have struggled to respond to Irish experience within a largely imported theoretical framework. We focus on issues of inequality, questioning the current practices and perceptions that help to maintain Ireland as an unequal society, one that continues to deprive many of its people of full citizenship. And we draw attention to how people make their own accommodations and live their own lives within the dominant structures, for it is important that sociologists, while stressing the determining influence of social institutions and structures, never lose sight of the agency that people bring to social processes.

# 5
# *Population and migration*

If you see a country as its people rather than its territory then, far from being small and well-defined, Ireland has been, for at least 150 years, scattered, splintered, atomised like the windscreen of a crashed car. (O'Toole, 1998, p.12.)

What we have now is a very literate emigrant who thinks nothing of coming to the United States and going back to Ireland and maybe on to Germany and back to Ireland again . . . the world is now one world and they can always return to Ireland with the skills they have developed. We regard them as part of a global generation of Irish people. We shouldn't be defeatist or pessimistic about it. We should be proud of it. After all, we can't all live on a small island. (Brian Lenihan TD, cited in Hazelkorn, 1991, p.135.)

Population is one of today's most pressing concerns. The relationship between the number of people living on the planet and the resources to support their continued existence and welfare is a complex and dynamic one. We are all familiar with media images of global starvation and famine, of teeming cities and shanty towns, of fleeing refugees and conflicts over resources and territory. Similarly, there is much debate over issues such as the 'greying' of society, family structure, abortion and divorce, all of which are related to population. In Ireland, no less than elsewhere, population has been a perennial social, personal and political concern.

Of particular concern to Irish society has been emigration and the demographic and economic effects that the long-term haemorrhage of people from the country has created. Half a century ago, Geary pointed out that 'of no country in the world is it more true to say that the political and economic boundaries do not coincide' (1951, p.400). It is true that for much of its history, a large proportion of Irish-born people have chosen or have been forced to live outside the geographical confines of the island. Even today up to a quarter of all Irish-born people live outside the country (Courtney, 1997, p.26). The continuous movement of people from the country to all ends of the earth raises questions about national, cultural and personal identity. As the poet Seamus Heaney says (cited in Hayes, 1990, p.14):

we are a dispersed people, whose history
is a sensation of opaque fidelity.

It is impossible to talk about Irish population and demography without talking about emigration and it is a major focus of this chapter.

Population is ultimately about birth and death and movement; aspects of every individual's life story that combine together to produce the story of a society. At times the patterns of natality and mortality can be almost static; at others they change with amazing rapidity. Even over the last fifty years the behaviour of Irish people in relation to birth, marriage and family formation has changed quite dramatically. Conversely, trends in mortality appear to have stabilised. Nowadays Ireland seems to present a picture that is in many ways less notable for its exceptionality and more in line with that of our European neighbours, but previous experience shows us that this may change again in the future.

As in much of Europe and the world, *immigration* has now become an issue for Irish people, particularly in relation to refugees and foreign workers. We may now need to address the reality of a multicultural Ireland, what that might mean for our personal and social identities and for social policy and practice. In this time of globalisation, population issues have never been more important.

## POPULATION AND SOCIOLOGY

Population is a social phenomenon. Changes in population not only reflect individual decisions about family size, place of living and lifestyle, but are structured by broader societal patterns. In particular, population may be related to historical development, economic activity, value and belief structures and environmental constraints, and in turn it has a structuring effect on these aspects of social life. In other words population patterns and changes have consequences for society. They can create increased demand for resources and changes in the political, social or economic organisation of society and can shape opportunities for mobility and relationships.

Population phenomena, as they relate to the totality of people's experiences, are necessarily complex. Though they can be reduced to series of discrete figures about births, marriages and deaths, and mathematical formulae for fertility and mortality that can be applied over space and time, the reality behind people's decisions about, literally, life and death matters is inevitably complicated and open to many interpretations and explanations. As a result, in studies of demography and population matters, there is a constant tension between 'objective' analyses that tend to focus on the macro-level and often appear to be highly determinist; and 'subjective', micro-level accounts that try to 'get behind' the figures to probe the personal motivations and experiences of people as they give birth, emigrate or make decisions about familial matters and relationships.

Analysts of Irish population frequently remind us how difficult it can be to understand what is happening. For sociologist Ryan, 'Irish twentieth-century emigration is an extremely complex phenomenon' (1990, p.49) while Hazelkorn suggests (1991, p.135) that the experience of emigration can only be understood as 'a complex process, structured by class and gender inequality'. Historian Guinnane (1997, p.283) says that institutional and economic factors, rather than cultural ones, are the key factors affecting demographic change, but also suggests that 'from a slightly more distant perspective . . . Ireland's demographic history suggests that . . . the distinction between culture or institutions or economics is a bit artificial'. In summary, migration is an outcome of multiple and intertwining social factors.

Sociologists have long had an interest in population matters, an interest shared with economists, historians, and the specialists in the population field: demographers. In Ireland the SSIS (see Chapter 2) had a 'perennial interest' in the area (Daly, 1997, p.141) as have more recently founded research and statistical bodies such as the ESRI, NESC and the Central Statistics Office (CSO). However, there has been little active interest in demography within modern Irish sociology, with the work being left to a small number of individuals such as Courtney (1995; 1997) and to official bodies such as the CSO. Commentary on emigration has largely been left to historians, geographers and cultural practitioners and critics.

The key concerns of demographers are the identification and measurement of those factors that help determine the size and structure of the population, namely, fertility, mortality and migration. Demographic data on Ireland has been poor (Coleman, 1992, p.53), with problems in relation both to the adequacy of census data and the registration of births, marriages and deaths. It was not until the twentieth century that the data began to improve and this makes historical analysis, so crucial to understanding long-run trends such as population change, difficult to carry out. The data sources that demographers use tend to be those produced by official bodies. Of particular importance in Ireland are the national censuses, registries of vital statistics (births, marriages and deaths) and sample surveys such as the Labour Force Survey (now the Quarterly National Household Survey) (Courtney, 1995, pp.43–7). Increasingly such surveys are being coordinated across the EU, thus allowing for more effective generation of comparative data. Ireland does not provide for local registration of population (unlike say Japan or the Scandinavian countries) and therefore it can be difficult to obtain accurate data at the local level on an ongoing basis. Even the level of migration is difficult to determine as it is not easy to interpret the nature of movement into and out of the country.

## THEORIES OF POPULATION

### Conventional approaches

The theoretical basis of demography has been shaped around responses to the eighteenth-century writer Thomas Malthus. Malthus was most renowned for his prediction that, unless checked (for example, by war, famine, birth control or delayed marriage), population would increase more rapidly than food production. He argued that the obstacles presented by the natural environment would thwart attempts to improve the position of humanity (Furedi, 1997, p.14). Ireland's Great Famine was interpreted by many, including the British administration and parts of the Irish middle class, as empirical proof for Malthus's predictions. Despite the many subsequent criticisms of Malthus's theories, from religious, political, scientific and other quarters, he can be said to have made a significant contribution to the development of demography. In particular, he drew attention to the *social* nature of population, showing that it was linked to economic, environmental, social and political factors. Demography as practised in western societies has subsequently come to be strongly shaped by functionalist sociology and modernisation theory. Courtney (1995, p.40) suggests that as a result there has been an overemphasis on empirical analysis, with far less attention paid to theoretical development.

*Demographic transition theory* emerged in the 1920s as a response to the apparent stabilisation of population patterns in twentieth-century Europe. The situation where many European governments were expressing concern about low birth rates and slowing population growth was in marked contrast to the rapid expansion in population seen by most European countries during the preceding century. The theory of demographic transition suggests that societies move through five demographic phases as they develop towards modernity. In other words, following Malthus, demographic change is seen to be closely related to economic and technological development (Courtney, 1995, p.41). The stages have been identified as follows:

1  *Static phase* — poor standards of living and lack of education, medical knowledge and facilities result in high mortality and fertility rates (as in some developing countries today).
2  *Early expanding phase* — better living conditions, especially improved diet and sanitation, mean the mortality rate declines while the fertility rate remains high (for example, Ireland in the years preceding the Famine).
3  *Late expanding phase* — increased knowledge of contraceptive practices, improved status of women and higher living standards cause the fertility rate to start to decline (Ireland in the 1970s).
4  *Low static phase* — mortality and fertility rates are both at a relatively low level (the UK after the Second World War).
5  *Diminishing phase* — fertility dips below mortality: the population ages and diminishes as there are not enough people being born to replace those that die (for example, West Germany in the 1980s).

The theory of demographic transition is firmly linked to that of *modernisation* and similar criticisms have been made of it: it is teleological and unidirectional; it does not allow for the influence of cultural and social diversity. More recently, demographers have spoken of the 'second demographic transition' (Courtney, 1995, p.42) which we discuss later in this chapter.

## Critical approaches

As mentioned above, demography has tended to strongly reflect a functionalist approach to sociology. More critical approaches to population issues have derived from Weberian and Marxist positions. From a Weberian perspective, sociologists have focused on how population has increasingly become an object of control for states and elite groups such as the medical profession. Such control has been exercised, for example, in the twentieth-century rationalisation of childbirth and in the eugenics movement. Movements that have attempted to control the growth and nature of the population have operated both within countries and at the global level, for example, the International Planned Parenthood Federation. The Weberian concern with rationalisation has been developed by sociologists who, drawing on the insights of the French writer Foucault, have brought to our attention how populations are increasingly monitored in time and space. For Foucauldians the surveillance and monitoring of the populations of modern states and societies has acquired central importance and it is here that sociological concerns with population overlap with health concerns (see Chapter 9).

Marxist sociologists have paid little attention to issues of demography or family structure. They have been more interested in the topic of migration, particularly as it relates to the development of global capitalism. Marx was an early analyst of globalisation, arguing that the development of global capitalism divided the world into core industrial areas and peripheral agricultural areas that supplied the former with raw materials and labour power (Mac Laughlin, 1994, p.8). Ireland and other areas like the Scottish Highlands were for Marx, 'emigrant nurseries' that provided such labour. Thus, as outlined by Hazelkorn (1991, p.124):

> Whether permanent, casual or seasonal, Irish emigration [to Britain] provided a large reserve army of labour; its desirability was its mobility and willingness to enter employment, often unacceptable to British workers, and usually of an unskilled, low-paid nature

In this sense the Irish and British economies were integrated into a single labour market, to the benefit of the latter economy.

Within the Marxist tradition Mac Laughlin (1994; 1997a) is a social geographer who has perhaps made the most significant analysis of Irish emigration from the standpoint of social theory. He adopts a world systems theory approach to explaining emigration, arguing that 'persistent and widespread Irish emigration is indicative of the peripheral *status* and not just the peripheral *location* of the Irish state in the world economy'. It can therefore only be understood by an analysis of the broader structural developments of global capitalism and the specific development of capitalist social relations within the country itself. 'It is . . . an intrinsically geographical and social class phenomenon in that it had clear geographical causes and social consequences which in turn structured and were structured by the regions which emigrants left behind and by the regions where they settled' (Mac Laughlin, 1994, p.45). World systems theory, according to Mac Laughlin, allows us to see emigration as a complex historical, geographical and social process that links the peripheralisation of Ireland to the development of industrial cores in the international economy.

Despite his global perspective, Mac Laughlin advocates that the best way to study emigration is at the local, community level and not on the more 'abstract national plains inhabited by statisticians, demographers and economists' (1994, p.54). This allows us to study the personal and social effects of emigration in detail. At the same time, Mac Laughlin is critical of behaviourist explanations — presumably those of historians such as Akenson and Guinnane, or of many popular commentators who focus on individuals' motives for emigration — which he sees as 'sanitised' and 'voluntaristic'. This point is echoed by Corcoran (1998, pp.137–8) and by Castles and Miller (1993, p.20) who see such accounts of migration as individualistic and ahistorical. This reminds us of the tension noted earlier between different approaches to explaining the migration phenomenon. A complete account would need to look both at the structural imperatives that drive migration and the meanings that individuals bring to their experiences.

## Post-modern approaches

Post-modernist analyses of globalisation have shown a considerable interest in population and migration. The language of post-modern theory is replete with references to space and movement, and to concepts such as 'nomadism', 'fluidity of boundaries' and 'border-crossings' (Featherstone, 1997, p.240). It is an approach that celebrates movement, diversity, cross-pollination and multiplicity of identities. The effect of the vastly increased mobility of modern populations is to break down traditional social categorisations. Featherstone (1997, p.241) suggests:

> The numbers of sojourners, refugees, and migrant workers means that 'the other' is no longer something to be searched out in exotic locations in the distant parts of the world by adventurers, literary travelers and tourists. The others work and live alongside us in the metropolitan areas. In effect, 'the rest is in the west'.

Furthermore, an appreciation of the issues of migrancy and mobility challenges the frameworks of sociology itself. As we have already seen, the discipline of sociology emerged as part of the project that saw the establishment of nation states and societies with(in) clearly drawn boundaries. The notions of 'society' and 'community' conjure up images of entities that are tied to location and where there is a strong connection between people and a particular space (country, town, suburb, street, and so on). An appreciation of the extent to which populations have always involved migrants, nomads and sojourners calls into question the perceived coherence of sociological and social categories. Writers on the Irish experience of migration have also begun to frame the analysis in terms of the fluidity and complexity of identity, space and everyday life (Kearney, 1990; Mac Laughlin, 1997a).

Post-modern analyses extend the world systems approach into an analysis of globalisation. British sociologists Lash and Urry have shown how the experience of migration is part of the process of reflexive post-industrial development that is taking place in the western world. Their analysis (1994, p.173) of migration into the United States shows how immigrants 'are concentrated in manufacturing, retail and low value-added consumer services in the information and control economies of the global cities' such as Los Angeles, Miami and New York. However, Lash and Urry point out that despite the globalisation of the migrant experience, the particular patterns across specific societies are highly variable.

Much recent analysis of global population flows tends to focus on issues of networks and clusters. For example, based on an analysis of emigration from Hong Kong, Wong and Salaff (1998) highlight the importance of how emigrants and potential emigrants draw on social networks as a form of capital. This reflects what Irish people have long known about the emigration process: that human networks, based on kin, previous residence, occupation or education, are of key importance in shaping the decision to emigrate and the life chances of the new immigrant. Corcoran's (1991; 1993) analysis of Irish illegal immigrants in the New York construction industry reveals key aspects of this process.

## POPULATION IN IRELAND

Ryan (1990, p.45) has argued that 'emigration is at the centre of the Irish experience of modernity'. It has been part of the process by which Ireland has been able to move from being a predominantly rural-based, agrarian society to an industrial state. Certainly the period of modernisation in Ireland has been accompanied by a constant stream of people leaving (and in many cases returning to) the country. The question is whether continual migration sustained or constrained the process or even had no effect on it at all.

Emigration has been closely related to other population patterns; indeed it is inseparable from them. The forces that have led so many people to leave the country are derived from how families and communities have translated economic opportunities, property relations and religious and social attitudes into individual behaviour. The limits of economic opportunity available to, mainly, young people have led them to make decisions that have been shaped by the experiences of those that have gone before them. Others have felt compelled to escape the dominant frameworks of attitudes and behaviour that have governed religious, moral and social behaviour. The structures of families, the links that families have to property and opportunity and the patterns of birth and marriage: all have fed into people's decisions about where they can and should live.

Ireland's population pattern is often seen to be unusual or even unique in global terms. But how singular has Ireland been in its demographic experience? Not very, according to historian Guinnane. While pointing out (1997, p.272) that the demographic history of the country 'elicits an odd fascination from both contemporaries and historians', he suggests that 'claims about Irish exceptionalism usually fly in the face of similar institutions, problems and population developments in other regions of Europe'. He argues that it was the specific *combination* of elements in Ireland that was unusual.

On the other hand, there are those that argue that Ireland's experience was, and remains, truly exceptional. Fahey (1998a, p.52) suggests that it had 'a pathological quality'. Coleman (1992, p.53) suggests that the demography of Ireland has been unique since the nineteenth century and is a 'challenge [to] demographic theory'. There are certainly a number of remarkable features. For example, in the first half of the 1900s, it was the only country in the world whose population *declined* (Geary, 1951, p.401), with its excess of emigration over natural increase. Furthermore, it was unusual in that more women emigrated than men. This combined with women's higher death rate (also unique) to produce a country with an unusual sex ratio of more men than women.

Though Ireland's fertility was unusually low by European standards in the latter half of the nineteenth century, it changed little during the subsequent century, while fertility rates in Europe plummeted. As a result, by the 1920s Ireland's fertility rates were, in the European context, unusually high. Even as late as 1987 Ireland's fertility rate was the highest of any developed country with the exception of the former Soviet Union (Coleman, 1992, p.56). It had the lowest proportion of first births and the highest proportion of births that were the fourth or subsequent child of the same mother. As a consequence the proportion of births to women over thirty was twice the western norm. Ireland became the most 'youthful' country in the industrialised world, with almost a third of the population under fifteen. At that time it was the only developed industrial country that had net emigration. By the late twentieth century, Ireland was also unique in the western world in prohibiting both divorce and abortion, though marriages were dissolved through legal separation and women did travel to Britain to procure abortions. One can conclude that, while individual aspects of Irish demographic history have been found in other regions of the world (Quebec, Bavaria, Puerto Rico, Spain), the specific constellation of features experienced in Irish society *has* been unusual, especially by European standards (Figure 5.1). The difficulty has been in explaining why this has been the case.

Whatever the past has held, in many respects the demography of Ireland is now rapidly converging with other European countries. Since the late 1970s there has

# Figure 5.1 Ireland demographic indicators compared

36 Industrial countries *circa* 1987

| Variable | Ireland | Mean | Coefficient of variation *100 | Median | N |
|---|---|---|---|---|---|
| Population (millions) | 3.6 | 35.3 | 177.8 | 12.7 | 36 |
| Density (per sq kilometre) | 52.0 | 416.8 | 267.0 | 116.5 | 34 |
| Population growth rate/000 | –0.9 | 6.2 | 73.0 | 5.2 | 36 |
| Natural increase/000 | 8.1 | 4.7 | 86.0 | 3.8 | 36 |
| Proportion aged <15/000 | 289.0 | 215.9 | 15.7 | 213.0 | 36 |
| Proportion aged ≥65/000 | 109.0 | 116.6 | 26.2 | 122.0 | 36 |
| Total fertility rate | 234.0 | 179.0 | 16.3 | 173.5 | 36 |
| Completed family size | 265.0 | 197.1 | 8.8 | 192.0 | 15 |
| Age at first birth | 25.8 | 25.6 | 4.4 | 25.8 | 19 |
| Proportion 1st births/000 | 313.0 | 430.9 | 8.6 | 438.5 | 28 |
| Proportion 2nd births/000 | 258.0 | 353.5 | 6.5 | 357.0 | 28 |
| Proportion 3rd births/000 | 185.0 | 142.5 | 17.0 | 137.0 | 28 |
| Proportion 4th+ births/000 | 243.0 | 66.5 | 34.8 | 64.5 | 28 |
| Illegitimacy ratio | 126.0 | 176.7 | 83.7 | 133.0 | 25 |
| Age at first marriage bachelors | 27.9 | 27.0 | 4.5 | 27.0 | 17 |
| Age at first marriage spinsters | 25.8 | 24.7 | 5.2 | 24.6 | 25 |
| Births to mothers aged >30/000 | 458.0 | 275.9 | 34.4 | 262.5 | 12 |
| Abortion ratio/000 live births | 69.0 | 281.8 | 66.0 | 221.0 | 16 |
| Divorces/10,000 married | 0.0 | 82.8 | 52.0 | 85.0 | 17 |
| Infant mortality rate/000 | 7.8 | 11.2 | 53.8 | 9.0 | 36 |
| Expectation of life at birth (m) | 70.1 | 71.0 | 3.8 | 71.5 | 35 |
| Expectation of life at birth (f) | 75.6 | 77.3 | 3.1 | 77.6 | 35 |
| Expectation of life age 65 (m) | 12.6 | 14.1 | 7.4 | 14.3 | 27 |
| Expectation of life age 65 (f) | 15.7 | 17.7 | 7.4 | 17.6 | 27 |

(*Source*: Coleman, 1992, p.55)

been a marked decline in the fertility rate and in completed family size (Coleman, 1992, p.64). For example, Ireland's birth rate now approaches that of countries like Italy, Spain and Portugal, while mortality rates, though still slightly higher than in most EU countries, are also much closer to the European norm than they have ever been. Furthermore, Ireland's pattern of very late marriage has changed considerably. The age of marriage is now gradually increasing again and this is in line with western trends more generally.

Coleman attributes the dramatic decline in fertility rates in Ireland to the widespread adoption of contraceptive practices, as Irish behaviour converges with that of the rest of the western world (1992, p.73). This is seen by Coleman as evidence that Irish women are becoming more *modern* in their behaviour. Overall, he concludes that 'it looks as though the distinctive Irish fertility regime is finally over, and will join those of Quebec, Spain, Portugal and other Catholic countries as problems of recent history rather than those of the contemporary world' (1992, p.76).

Population patterns in Ireland have been affected historically by a number of factors, including:

- emigration
- the dominance of rural livelihoods and private property relations
- low levels of urbanisation
- low incomes
- the influence of the Roman Catholic Church.

Now the patterns may be being affected by trends such as higher educational levels, increasing costs of raising children for longer periods of time and the widespread entry of married women into the workforce. This shift can be seen to be explicitly linked to processes of modernisation and to reflect 'a modernised, literate, mobile, open society with a modern economy offering rewards to skills and education' (Coleman, 1992, p.74). But international comparisons suggest that there is no simple link between modernisation measures such as levels of workforce participation by married women and levels of fertility.

Emigration renders the Irish demographic picture more complex. It has allowed high fertility to coexist with a relatively stable or even declining population size. Coleman (1992, p.76) suggests a direct connection between emigration and reproductive activity; the former has 'destroyed demographic feedbacks' and has thereby delayed the 'modernisation' of fertility. This reflects the unitary and teleological nature of much demographic writing. We would argue, with Gungwu (1997, p.8), that rather than following a single pattern the history of population across the world is one of variation:

> The patterns all suggest that global history is not a teacher of the directions of change. Instead it focuses and sharpens our awareness of variation and flux by turning more lights on to the past and opening more windows to a possible global future.

Nevertheless, the social impact of emigration has been profound. It has been argued that it facilitated the commercialisation of Irish agriculture; contributed to Ireland's de-industrialisation; and intensified Anglicisation and the eastward drift of political power (Mac Laughlin, 1994, pp.5–11). It has also been said to have altered power relations by removing young people from the society, so reducing the possibility of social or political change (Guiomard, 1995, p.190; Mac Laughlin, 1997, p.13). It placed power firmly in the hands of property owners but also consolidated the power of organised labour by removing much of the 'reserve army' of labour to elsewhere. Crotty (1986, p.79) argues that emigration gave Ireland:

> higher living standards than any other former capitalist economy. It gave it an unparalleled record of political stability and public finance rectitude. It created an intellectual and political void wherein policies are cursorily or superficially examined; and wherein governments, accustomed to act regardless of the interests of the emigrant half of the population, have had no difficulty in neglecting the consequences of their actions for future generations, who are as powerless as the emigrants to effect [sic] the present course of Irish politics.

The changing patterns of Irish migration are discussed in more detail in the sections to follow.

## ORIGINS OF IRELAND'S POPULATION PATTERNS

Though it has been a matter of great historical controversy, there now appears to be agreement that the distinctive features of Ireland's demography were established prior to the Famine, in the early nineteenth century. They included:

- late age of marriage
- high fertility within marriage
- a low level of births outside marriage
- an overall low rate of fertility across the population as a whole
- high levels of emigration.

Mortality rates, apart from the exceptional time of the Famine itself, were comparatively low, possibly, as Coleman (1992, p.57) suggests, through low levels of urban living and the 'safety valve' of emigration. After the Famine, the social reality of emigration tended to overshadow all other aspects of Irish demographic experience (Figure 5.2).

As the nineteenth century progressed, the demography of Ireland increasingly diverged from European patterns. In particular, it did not experience the same decline in fertility rates, partly because Irish couples, unlike most other Europeans, did not practice birth control. While, from the 1870s, most European populations began to practice contraception within marriage, the Irish generally did not, except to some extent in urban areas (Coleman, 1992, pp.59–61; Guinnane, 1997, p.273).

According to Akenson (1991, p.3), from the nineteenth century, the Irish became the 'most internationally dispersed of the European national cultures'.

## Figure 5.2  Ireland: natural increase and net migration 1880–1980

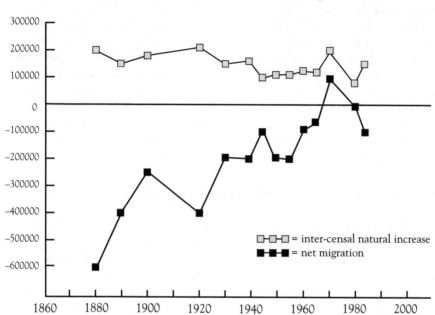

(*Source*: Coleman, 1992, p.58)

Post-Famine emigration was built upon a history of movement — especially among Ulster Presbyterians — that stretched back to the early seventeenth century when the 'Atlantic economy' began to emerge (Kirkham, 1990). Even before that there was a long tradition of Irish people leaving the country's shores to found monasteries, fight in foreign armies, or take up seasonal work. While the numbers of Irish people leaving the country prior to the nineteenth century did not approach the levels of subsequent times (not least because transport technology was less advanced) those that left did help to set the trend for migration on a mass scale from the 1820s onwards.

It is estimated that 7 million people left Ireland for North America alone between 1600 and 1922 (Mac Laughlin, 1994, p.4), 4 million of those in the years from 1846 to 1925. Ireland was thus, along with countries like Russia, Italy and the Scandinavian countries, a 'leading European exporter of labour'. Emigration was at such a high rate in the wake of the Famine that it cancelled out natural increase and, as a result, Ireland was the only country in western Europe to experience a decline in population throughout the second half of the nineteenth century.

The demography of nineteenth-century Ireland was shaped by the patterns of livelihood and property, in particular landholding (Guinnane, 1997, p.284). Of special importance was the dominance of small farmers and peasants, enhanced through the land purchase legislation enacted by the British government in the late nineteenth and early twentieth centuries. Demographic patterns were also, as Guinnane reminds us (1997, p.252), a reflection of world economic conditions and Ireland's place in the British Empire and the world economy. Ireland was a major provider of labour and personnel for both the British imperial system and the emergent societies of North America. In return, emigration provided an important input to the home economy, especially through the earnings of seasonal labourers. For example, Mac Laughlin (1994, p.16) reports that 'Scottish money' — remittances sent back from Scotland by young Irish emigrants — accounted for up to a quarter of the cash income of poor families in the west in the period prior to the First World War.

## POPULATION IN INDEPENDENT IRELAND

Overall the population of the island of Ireland as a whole shrunk from 8.2 million in 1840s to 4.2 million in 1926, a decline of 48 per cent (Courtney, 1995, p.48). But Irish independence did not bring an end to emigration as had been hoped. Indeed after the effects of the Great Depression and the Second World War had passed, the stream of people leaving the country returned to nineteenth-century levels. The population continued to decline until 1961 apart from a small increase in the post-war years of 1946 to 1951. This decline can be clearly related to the failure of the country to economically develop in such as way as to provide a livelihood for its inhabitants. In the period 1926 to 1961, numbers of those in agricultural employment fell by over 272,300. As only 101,800 non-agricultural jobs were created in this period, there was a net loss of jobs of the order of 170,500.

Levels of emigration in the 1950s approached those of the 1880s: from a level of 16,600 per year in the period 1926 to 1936 to 42,400 per year in the 1950s (Drudy, 1995, p.75). With fourteen in every thousand people emigrating every year, more than half those that left school in the early 1950s had emigrated by 1961 (Guinnane, 1997, p.279). For Hazelkorn (1991, p.125) such people were 'reacting rationally to severe economic decline and labour surplus at home as well as widening differentials in welfare payments' between Ireland and Britain.

In Ireland itself fertility rates diverged increasingly from the European norm, with only the Netherlands and Iceland — and in North America, Quebec — approaching Irish levels. This was a reflection of the fact that Irish levels fell very slowly during the twentieth century while those of other Western countries fell sharply. At the end of the 1950s the Irish pattern of late marriage began to break down and this inevitably impacted on fertility rates. By the 1960s Ireland's fertility rate was the highest in Europe. Despite its already high levels of fertility, Ireland, like other western countries, experienced a baby boom in this decade, though the boom reflected more the levels of earlier births than increased fertility. It was not until the early 1970s that fertility in Ireland began to drop sharply towards

European levels; a fact reflected in the sharply declining proportion of fourth and higher order births (Coleman, 1992, pp.61–7).

A number of reasons have been suggested for the demographic change that appears to have brought Ireland 'into line' with the core European societies. These include, not surprisingly, the increased availability and use of contraception and (via the Irish Sea) abortion. The 1970s saw a high level of political and legal action (spearheaded by women's groups and individuals including, later, President, Mary Robinson) aimed at removing the legal impediments to the availability of contraceptives. The demand for contraceptives was probably the result of a complex set of factors but research in the European context suggests that these include the increased costs of having children, improved education, the erosion of traditional moral and religious strictures, increased female workforce participation, and the political and social liberation of women (Coleman, 1992, p.75).

While emigration continued in independent Ireland, there was a marked change in the destination of emigrants. From the mid-1930s, Britain became the main destination as opposed to the United States, partly following a tightening of entry regulations there. While 1876 to 1921 saw 84 per cent of emigrants go to the United States and only 8 per cent to Britain, by the period 1946 to 1951, four-fifths were emigrating to Britain (Hazelkorn, 1991, p.125). It is estimated that, in the period 1890 to 1990, over 2 million Irish people emigrated to Britain, two-thirds of whom stayed (Ryan, 1990, p.46). In the 1960s there were over a million Irish-born people there, making the Irish the largest ethnic minority group in Britain. The destinations within Britain changed during that period, with a substantial shift southwards. Scotland and the north of England no longer attracted substantial numbers. Emigrants followed the shift of economic balance to the south-east of the country, particularly London: by 1971, the Irish-born made up nearly 4 per cent of London's population (Ryan, 1990, p.48). The shift to Britain, being more easily accessible to Ireland, meant for many a change in the *experience* of emigration as pointed out by Geary in the early 1950s: 'very large numbers now return on holidays and a considerable proportion of those who go come back after a year or two' (1951, p.402).

The immigration of large numbers of Irish provided Britain with a convenient labour pool, thus reducing its dependence on workers from ex-colonies or the developing world. Britain has never had to develop a 'guest worker' system like that in Germany, France or other European countries. Those who emigrated from Ireland were largely unskilled, often from rural backgrounds. The 1954 *Commission on Emigration* revealed that three-quarters of male emigrants were of this category while 90 per cent of women were classed as domestic labourers or other service workers, though were more likely to work in bars, restaurants and hotels than in private homes. There was also a small but significant number of skilled professionals, doctors and engineers, for example, who could not secure employment in Ireland and constituted a 'brain drain' (Hazelkorn, 1991, p.128). Mac Laughlin suggests that, by the 1960s, 'Irish graduates with qualifications in engineering, medicine and law were probably regarding Britain and Ireland as an integrated labour market' (1994, p.28). The growth in the service industries in the 1960s saw an increase in the number of Irish emigrants moving into white-collar work such as nursing, teaching and office work. This coincided with the shift in focus towards the south of England and away from the more traditional industrial areas of the midlands and the north.

## IRISH POPULATION IN THE AGE OF GLOBALISATION

As suggested earlier in this chapter, Ireland has long been recognised as part of a global economy and culture and this has been a central element of 'Irish identity'. In recent years there has been an intensification of this discourse. From cultural theorists to media personalities, all have a view about how the particular development of Irish population patterns has reflected our increasing integration into a global society.

In some ways, contemporary demographic patterns in Ireland are becoming increasingly similar to those of western Europe and countries like Australia. Since the 1980s a number of distinctive patterns have emerged in the majority of western countries and the *second demographic transition* (Courtney, 1995, p.42) describes this emergence. Ireland has been seen as a late entry to this transition, as have been other essentially Catholic countries such as Spain and Portugal. The trends related to the second demographic transition include:

1   *marriage*
    fewer legal marriages
    a rise in cohabitation
    later age of marriage
    higher rates of separation and divorce
    higher rates of second and subsequent marriages
    more homosexual unions.

2   *fertility*
    smaller families
    later motherhood
    more voluntary childlessness
    more single-parent families
    more 'only children'
    more children born outside legal marriage.

3   *ageing*
   people living longer
   better health in later years
   more 'old elderly' (those over 75)
   later retirement (for some)
   longer periods of retirement.

While Irish society appears at last to be converging with western trends, in other ways the country's demographic profile remains exceptional. For example, while most other European countries are faced with the challenge of an ageing and increasingly dependent population over the next thirty years, the opposite is true in Ireland. Indeed Fahey and Fitzgerald (1997) argue that the country is now entering an unprecedented period of 'demographic advantage'. This is a result of a further baby boom in Ireland in the 1970s and early 1980s and the combined impact of reduced emigration and increased return migration. Thus, while the number of people dependent on the active workforce is set to rapidly increase in Europe, especially in countries like Italy and Greece, Ireland's dependency peaked in the mid-1980s and the situation is becoming increasingly favourable. The country is now moving from a high fertility/high emigration regime to low fertility/low emigration. Thus, Fahey and Fitzgerald (1997, p.111) are able to conclude that:

> The new demographic era may have its problematic aspects, but the contrast with the past is likely to be striking. The demographic prospect in Ireland is also in contrast with that of most western countries. For the most part they are now entering the downside of what has been a long period of upward movement, while Ireland is just emerging from a long trough.

Many of the demographic changes now taking place reflect the changing position of women in Irish society which has been expressed in legislation, social attitudes, economic activity and sexual behaviour. The number and proportion of births outside marriage has risen considerably. While the rate of around 20 per cent is lower than that of the Scandinavian countries (where over half of births are outside of formal marriage), the UK or Australia, it is now higher than in many European states, such as Italy, Switzerland and Cyprus. This may reflect an increase in the Irish social acceptance of unmarried mothers (Mac Gréil, 1996). The dramatic increase in the number of married women in the workforce has probably contributed to an increase in delayed childbearing, a further decline in completed family size (the process commenced in the 1960s) and an overall decrease in fertility in recent years.

   Emigration continues to shape Ireland's population experience and remains a fertile topic for political and academic commentary and debate. In the late 1980s the net emigration rate was higher at over 70,000 per annum than in the first decade of the century — high enough to lead to a return of population decline. The increased flow reflected the parlous state of the Irish economy in the 1980s, in particular the contraction in employment in indigenous manufacturing industries such as textiles and engineering and the inability to convert new investment into jobs. Despite a considerable expansion in the developing service industries (109,000 new jobs from 1981 to 1993) the period saw a surge in unemployment in Ireland with the rate doubling from 10 per cent (126,000) in 1981 to 17 per cent (230,000) in 1993 (Hazelkorn, 1991, p.126; Drudy, 1995, p.75). The situation did not improve in the early 1990s as 175,000 left the country's shores (about 33–35,000 per annum) between 1991 and 1996, two-thirds of them aged 15 to 24 (Corcoran, 1998, p.140). In 1997 the levels of emigration began to decline again. In that year 29,000 people left the country and the figure further decreased to an estimated 21,000 by 1998 (Courtney, 2000). Unemployment and poor economic conditions at home were a significant 'push' factor in emigration while 'pull' factors related to the strength of host-country economies and the nature of their regulation of immigration.

For Hazelkorn the continuation of the emigration flow accorded with the globalisation of the Irish economy. Drawing parallels with the government of Turkey in the 1960s and 1970s, she suggests (1991, p.131) that 'Irish governments facilitated emigration as a means of alleviating social and political tension, a possible means of providing additional skills and experience, and as a source of income through remittances and tourism'. Skill shortages in host countries such as the United States, UK and Germany continued to provide a market for the export of Irish workers (Figure 5.3). As the nature of economic activity has changed — from labour intensive to capital intensive to knowledge intensive — so the demand for labour has changed. The development of 'global cities' as powerhouses of economic activity (for example, London, an increasingly important emigrant destination) has also helped to shape the decisions of intending migrants (Skeldon, 1997, p.187; Lash and Urry, 1994).

As noted earlier, Geary had already identified in 1951 that the nature of the Irish emigration experience was changing. Return migration, probably helped by cheaper and easier transport links, was increasing. Hazelkorn (1991, p.129) suggests it may now generally be more useful to use the term 'migration' rather than 'emigration', signifying the casual and transient nature of much of this mobile workforce. Mac Laughlin refers to it punningly as 'seasonal migration', the emigrants returning for seasonal holidays like Christmas as reflected in the well-reported crowds travelling through Dublin airport and other travel nodes at these times. His West of Ireland survey found that almost a third of the emigrants to Britain had been home on at least three occasions in the previous twelve months (1994, p.66). It may now make sense to think of Britain and Ireland as a single

# Figure 5.3 Ireland: gross migratory outflows 1852–1990

| | | Destination | | Gross |
| Period | UK | US | Other overseas | outflow ('000) |
|---|---|---|---|---|
| 1852–1861 | — | — | — | 792 |
| 1861–1871 | — | — | — | 697 |
| 1871–1881 | — | — | — | 446 |
| 1881–1891 | 41 | 514 | 62 | 617 |
| 1891–1901 | 17 | 347 | 13 | 377 |
| 1901–1911 | 14 | 240 | 12 | 266 |
| 1911–1922 | 9 | 97 | 10 | 116 |
| 1926–1931 | n/a | 104 | 15 | n/a |
| 1931–1936 | n/a | 2 | 2 | n/a |
| 1936–1941 | n/a | 3 | 2 | n/a |
| 1941–1946 | 173 | — | — | 173 |
| 1946–1951 | 119 | 17 | 8 | 114 |
| 1951–1961 | n/a | —— 68 —— | | n/a |
| 1961–1971 | n/a | —— 49 —— | | n/a |
| 1971–1981 | 155 | —— 21 —— | | 176 |
| 1981–1990 | 245 | 49 | 64 | 358 |

(*Source*: Mac Laughlin, 1994, p.13)

labour market with people travelling from Ireland to London and south-east England as they would from other parts of England, Scotland or Wales.

Changes in the nature of labour demand mean that emigrants may now be more skilled than previously. According to Hanlon (1991, p.53), who has studied the emigration of Irish accountants, the 'upwardly mobile middle class were the most likely emigrants'. The NESC report of 1991 showed that a third of emigrants in the 1980s and 1990s were already employed full-time prior to departure. Hazelkorn (1992, p.128) similarly argues that, compared with those of the 1950s, more recent emigrants tend to be better educated, more urban, increasingly male and 'predominantly young, single and mobile'. A large proportion of graduates from the third-level education sector emigrated during the 1980s — up to two-thirds for some courses. Many subsequently returned during the 1990s, including a high proportion of those with third-level education (Sweeney, 1998, p.105).

As Lash and Urry (1994) point out, the development of the post-modern economy has seen expansion of demand for labour at both the top and bottom ends of the market. Accordingly, Irish emigrants are now a diverse group. Between 1980 and 1983 a fifth of Irish immigrants to Britain held university degrees yet the number lacking qualifications also increased. In Britain, as in other western economies, the expansion in professional and technical jobs has been accompanied by a boom in employment in relatively menial and insecure service work in hotels, shops and restaurants, and in the lower ends of the clerical and construction fields. These jobs have continued to provide a market for the more 'traditional' unskilled and semi-skilled emigrants — so much so that Mac Laughlin (1994, p.69) remarks: 'while a minority of Irish male emigrants are climbing social ladders abroad, many more are still climbing ladders'.

For Corcoran, Irish emigration is best understood within a global context where (1998, p.139):

> For those whose decision to leave is dictated by the increasing flexibilisation of the international labour market, emigration can and does involve dislocation, exploitation and marginalisation.

This is especially the case for the undocumented or illegal Irish workers in America that are the focus of her study. On the one hand their 'official' identity is tenuous and may be fictional, perhaps expressed through the national insurance number of a long-dead person; on the other hand, they continually create and re-create a strong 'Irish identity' based on travel, media and the language of home.

## INTERPRETING POPULATION

Given the centrality of population to social change (and stasis) in Ireland, it is hardly surprising that it has generated numerous and complex interpretative discourses. As in other countries, population has been the object of political debate and intervention. The debate around population is closely related to other social topics such as the rural-urban divide, changes in family structure and the growth of suburbia.

Since the nineteenth century, emigration has been seen as an Irish 'problem' (Delaney, 1998, p.25), but the nature of the problem has varied considerably over the years. Within nationalist discourse, emigration was seen as a problem caused by an external force: British colonialism. Nationalists ignored the role of indigenous property and placed the blame for emigration at the hands of the English and the 'ranchers'. According to this 'narrow nationalist' viewpoint, landlordism was the sole cause of emigration and emigrants were victims of alien oppression by 'tyrants' who drove the Irish as exiles from their 'happy home' (Mac Laughlin, 1994, p.21). Contemporary nationalist literature portrayed emigration as the product of 'alien' rule and suggested that self-government would solve Ireland's social and economic problems and thus lead to the end of emigration. As a result, the issue of emigration was a key part of the campaigns of Irish political leaders such as O'Connell, Parnell and Pearse (Delaney, 1998, p.25).

Attitudes to Irish emigration have been shaped not only by ideas of nationhood, but also by ideas of social class. Ryan (1990, p.50) makes the point that emigration was seen negatively by the rural petty bourgeoisie, where ideologies about land and 'blood' were perhaps strongest (Mac Laughlin, 1997a, p.22). Amongst other groups emigration was strongly linked to notions of nation-building and bourgeois respectability. Counter to the popular nationalist argument, Irish and British Malthusians saw emigration as a natural and rational response to overpopulation in Ireland, and as a facilitator of rural modernisation. By the middle of the nineteenth century such an approach had become part of bourgeois Irish nationalist ideology. Emigration was seen as a way of removing the 'weaker' elements of the population (ideally far away to America) and thereby strengthening the stronger and more 'manly' indigenous population.

After independence, and a recognition that the problem had not gone away with the British, the discourse on emigration had to change. A contradiction emerged between the private-property-oriented policies of successive governments since independence, and their condemnations of emigration (Delaney, 1998, p.28). Fianna Fáil was the most vocal of the political parties in its opposition to emigration, making heard the concerns of its western and small-farmer constituency. This was also reflected in its 'self-sufficiency' economic policy of the 1930s and 1940s. For its leader, de Valera (Dáil debate 17 February 1937, cited in Delaney, 1998, p.30):

The aim of the Irish government [was] not to provide facilities for the emigration of our people to the states of the British Commonwealth or elsewhere. Its aim is to concentrate on utilizing the resources of this country and so improving the conditions of life here that our people will not have to emigrate, but will be able to find a livelihood in our country.

Emigration became increasingly important as a political issue during the 1930s and in the wake of the Second World War, becoming a key feature of the Dáil campaign of 1948. That year the widespread concern about the issue saw the establishment of the statistics-oriented *Commission on Emigration and Other Population Problems*. There was much concern about emigration of young women and there were even proposals put forward for a ban on the emigration of females under twenty-two.

The most recent changes in Irish demographic experience have, not surprisingly, further influenced the political discourse around population. As Fahey (1998a, p.51) suggests, the 'normalisation' and 'convergence of Irish demography towards European patterns . . . has lent substance to the image of Ireland as a modernising, developing nation . . . the demographic recovery . . . has signalled a new vibrancy and has helped justify the positive rhetoric which now dominates political discourse'. In contrast to the image of an ageing Europe, Ireland's nation of 'Young Europeans' (a popular slogan used by the IDA to attract TNCs to the country) is perceived as active and dynamic.

But the modernisation of the Irish population as expressed in our participation in the second demographic transition has also been seen to present threats. In particular:

- the dramatic changes in the nature of family structure
- the volatile discourse around sexuality
- the shifts in the role and status of young people
- the intense debates around reproductive rights.

These have generated a powerful conservative reaction (see Chapter 15) that perceives demographic change and the associated attitudinal shifts not as progress but as decline.

The issue of migration is very much tied into globalisation and the emergence of communications and transport technologies such as the Internet and air travel. It is suggested that there is now an interpenetration of Irish and world cultures. For Kearney (1990, p.110):

The internationalisation of the Irish community is not only a matter of the extended Irish family abroad, it also bears on our political and cultural understandings of ourselves as an island nation. . . . [Thus,] . . . we are rediscovering ourselves through our encounters with others, reclaiming our voice through our migrations through other cultures and continents.

Against this somewhat utopian view of contemporary migration, Mac Laughlin (1994, p.1) suggests that we are perhaps better informed of the experiences of nineteenth-century emigration than we are of its most recent manifestations. He suggests that the treatment of emigration as a cultural and historical phenomenon rather than as a key issue for contemporary society has served to sanitise it as an issue. In a period of economic growth, or boom, even, it has to a certain extent lost its position on the political and social agenda. Mac Laughlin argues that since the 1960s emigration has been sanitised and de-nationalised, now seen in technocratic and administrative terms and not as a national political issue. Indeed, in many quarters it is now regarded as 'a socially progressive response to the modernisation of an island economy on the periphery of Europe' (1994, p.31). No longer an unfortunate destiny visited upon the less favoured in Irish society, emigration is now an *option* for well-educated, autonomous, rational individuals. 'There is an increasing tendency today to treat emigration as a cultural tradition and a voluntary activity which attracts upwardly mobile individuals who are assumed to be leaving Ireland to climb social ladders abroad' (Mac Laughlin, 1994, p.31). It has become a lifestyle- and career-related issue: the 'perception that

Europe is an untilled field of opportunity is deeply embedded in contemporary Irish youth enterprise culture' (Mac Laughlin, 1994, p.39).

The notion of the 'diasporic hero' (Gray, 1997, p.228; Corcoran, 1998: 136) has emerged: those elite individuals, often tied into the global media industries (Frank McCourt, the Corrs, Terry Wogan, Roy Keane, Gloria Hunniford, and so on) who are able to 'sustain their own unique biographical narratives in the context of a myriad of possibilities and choices'. As Corcoran suggests, we are encouraged to accept and celebrate the successful emigrant or agent while we fail to acknowledge the existence of the other, the marginalised, less successful emigrant. 'Such a characterisation of emigration as a beneficial experience for the best and brightest functions as a soothing anodyne, assuaging any doubts we may have about the fate of those who leave Ireland without credentials, prospects, or marketable skills' (Corcoran, 1998, p.138).

## A MULTICULTURAL IRELAND?

Multiculturalism has become a familiar term in the discussion of societies such as Canada, Australia, the United States and Britain, but it can have very different meanings and resonances. In Canada and Australia it tends to have positive overtones and reflects official discourses about the need for those societies to recognise the cultural diversity brought about by long histories of immigration. In the United States and Britain, the term tends to be far more politically charged and tends to refer to the struggles of minority groups (most specifically Black, and, in Britain, Asian) in conflict with a majority white culture. In Ireland it is not clear what people are referring to when they are talking about multi-culturalism, though generally the term seems to embrace elements of both of these meanings.

In recent years Ireland has had to face a phenomenon that has been largely absent for most of its recent history: substantial *immigration*. According to the Central Statistics Office, in 1997 over 44,000 people came to live in the country. Returned emigrants, 'returnees', especially from the UK, are estimated to have made up half of this number (Cullen, 1997). Before that, the last period of high inward flow was in the late 1970s, also a period of economic expansion. The surplus of immigration over emigration was 15,000 in 1997 and 23,000 in 1998 (Courtney, 1997, Table 8). As a result, immigration is now as important a factor as natural increase in determining the growth in population.

The origin of the immigrants to Ireland, which includes both returnees and those coming to live in Ireland for the first time, is increasingly diverse. The majority of the 44,000 in 1997 were from the United Kingdom (20,000); 8,000 came from other EU countries; 6,000 from the United States; and 9,000 from the rest of the world. Over 4,600 people applied for political asylum in Ireland in 1998. However, the population of Ireland remains 93 per cent Irish-born with many of the residual 7 per cent being the children of Irish-born parents that have returned (Courtney, 1997, Table 8).

The responses to this new demographic reality have also been diverse and are still developing. For example, there has been some debate as to whether Ireland is a racist culture. Mac Laughlin (1994, p.35) suggests the export of the urban and rural working class has meant that there has not been the development of racist 'blood and soil' type social movements or political parties, as we find in, say, Germany and France. However there is strong evidence of racism in Ireland and among Irish people (Mac Gréil, 1996). Aniagolu (1997) reminds us that the Irish were heavily implicated in the British imperial project and supplied many of the (frequently overtly racist) rulers and administrators of the British Empire in Africa, India and elsewhere. Ó'Drisceoil (1997) has pointed out that there was a considerable level of anti-semitism in Ireland during the Second World War. There is also evidence that racist activity and discourse is intensifying in Ireland as the number of immigrants increases, though, as Aniagolu (1997, p.50) argues, it is not necessarily contact with increasing numbers of immigrants that is the cause of racism:

> In most multicultural societies contact between the races is minimal and attitudes towards racial minorities is generally formed through media contact, not through contact with actual people. This is also the case in Ireland.

## CONCLUSION

In this chapter we have attempted to explore some aspects of Ireland's rather exceptional demographic experience. In many ways it forms one of the more atypical aspects of Irish society and it is perhaps surprising that, apart from some interest in emigration issues, Irish sociologists have not paid more attention to population. Furthermore, in a context where population profiles tend to be fairly stable (at least in the developed world) Ireland is perhaps unusual in the volatility of its demographic experience. Recently Fahey (1998a, p.64) was able to remark that 'it seems possible that all those young people who want to stay in Ireland will have jobs and earnings prospects to enable them to do so.' Such a statement would have been greeted with incredulity only five years before.

So, does Ireland's convergence with the rest of Europe, its 'coming of age' in the demographic stakes, signify the arrival of a truly 'modern' society as is often suggested? Guinnane, from the more measured perspective of history, draws our attention to how some features of Ireland's nineteenth-century demographic experience are re-emerging in contemporary demographic trends across the western world; for example, late age of marriage, delayed childbirth, high rates of non-married people. He concludes (1997, pp.282, 283) that:

The Irish grew increasingly to organise and to conduct their lives in household units that were not centred on a married couple. The same is increasingly common in the modern world. Why? .... increasingly men and women seem to think marriage is not worth the sacrifices it entails. In this respect the post-Famine Irish were very modern.

This telling passage indicates not only the importance of determining the social bases of people's population experiences but also the complexity of the links between them. While Ireland's demographic profile may be increasingly conventional in comparative terms, what is certain is that it will continue to retain the capacity to surprise.

# 6

# *Class, inequality and poverty*

Irish society is often thought of as a classless society. Irish people tend to treat one another fairly informally, preferring, for example, to use first names even with relative strangers rather than titles and surnames. Holding a certain job or speaking with a particular accent is not widely regarded as entitling a person to special respect. Irish social life is characterised by an egalitarian ethic that rejects attempts by some groups to claim social honour from others. There is also a widespread belief that opportunities for social betterment have increased and that anyone can study hard, get good educational qualifications and move into a better position in society if they want to.

This does not mean that people have no sense of inequality as a part of Irish society; rather, inequality tends to be understood in terms of a gross differentiation between the majority — the 'more or less middle classes' — and an 'underclass' made up of the poor, the long-term unemployed, substance abusers and marginalised groups such as Travellers. Kieran Allen (1999, p.39) has described this picture as 'the duality of a contented majority versus a socially excluded minority'. He argues that inequality is ideologically articulated by key opinion-forming groups as 'a residual category' — a feature of life that applies only to the socially excluded, to 'them', not to 'us', the included, no matter how unequal the terms of our inclusion may be. Public discussions of class inequality in Ireland tend to be framed overwhelmingly in terms of the 'social problems' of poverty and social exclusion.

Thus, while the issue of social class has been central to European sociology and its analysis of capitalist modernity, we cannot take for granted that it is as important in Ireland or that it operates in the same ways. We therefore open this chapter with two questions:

- What place, if any, does class occupy in the self-understanding of Irish society?
- How has class been understood and researched through Irish sociological analysis?

Irish sociology has made some major contributions to the *empirical* uncovering of inequality in Irish society, most notably through ESRI-based research, but also in the work of individual researchers such as Hout and Jackson (1986) and Millar (1998). Strongly influenced by the work of British class analysts such as Goldthorpe, this research has interpreted questions of class and inequality in very specific terms, suggesting that they are best addressed through a focus on *occupational stratification* and *social mobility*. These researchers see the task of class analysis essentially as describing the patterned stratification of the occupational structure and inter-generational movement across it and identifying the individual and social-structural factors that can explain these patterns. Using this approach, they have been able to show that despite common-sense assumptions to the contrary class inequality is and has been a highly significant feature of Irish social organisation. While class boundaries may be somewhat less ritualised and less marked in Ireland, and therefore may appear to be less constraining, the reality is that they are more rigid and harder to penetrate than in many other societies. Breen and Whelan (1999, p.322) argue that:

> Class inequalities in educational attainment are substantially less in Northern Ireland than in the Republic. In the latter such class differences are particularly marked and notably persistent over time. . . . In addition, it is well known that inequalities of income and wealth are particularly great in the Republic of Ireland and are larger than in the UK.

## SOCIAL MOBILITY AND INEQUALITY IN IRELAND

Analysis of class and inequality in Ireland has taken place against a background of significant and rapid social change — especially occupational and locational change. Breen and Whelan (1996, p.4) suggest that, when asked to think of their society as a class society, the discomfort that many Irish people experience derives at least in part from a belief that the large-scale economic change of the past four decades has destroyed the 'old order' organised around inequality and has ushered in a new order in which equality of opportunity has greatly expanded. They note that many sociologists across the world have thought about inequality in the same way and have taken for granted that economic growth, especially industrialisation, has inevitably been accompanied by increased social mobility.

It was widely argued that high levels of mobility in industrial societies were a consequence of a shift towards *universalism*. Where universalistic criteria were used to assess and value individuals, the social position that a person attained over the life course would be based not on their ascribed or innate characteristics but on their own achievements. This is a core belief within the ideology of modernisation whose impact on Ireland is discussed in Chapter 3 and elsewhere in this book. Societies that have greater mobility may not be more equal overall, but they are thought to have greater *equality of opportunity*. Modernisation theorists expect industrialised societies to be more open, socially fluid places where talent and performance, not inherited advantage, determines people's life chances. A key aim of the class analysis carried out by ESRI and related researchers since the 1970s has been to test, question and, increasingly, to challenge such assumptions.

The approach to class that they have developed is often labelled 'neo-Weberian' but this is a misleading and perhaps inaccurate description. In many ways it would be more appropriate to call it 'neo-Durkheimian'. The influence of Durkheimian thought on this body of research is revealed in a number of ways, from the researchers' commitment to the ideal of an 'open', meritocratic society to their understanding of 'equality' as meaning equal opportunities rather than equal rewards (Baker, 1997). We find in their work neither the sense of tragic irony that runs through Weber's analysis of struggles over power, nor the radical democracy of Marx's conception of a classless society as one organised around the principles of 'from each according to capacity, to each according to need'.

The ESRI research has concerned itself particularly with the study of social mobility. It rests on a key distinction between:

- *absolute social mobility* — a consequence of changes in the class or occupational structure itself, and
- *relative social mobility* — an individual's chances of moving, as an adult, into a different social class from the one into which they were born.

Absolute mobility may be linked, for example, to expansion in service-sector jobs as a result of developments in technology and the labour process in industrialising societies, or to a decline in the numbers of small-scale family businesses and thus of occupational positions inheritable through the family. Both processes increase the importance of education as a means of competing successfully in the job and livelihood market.

In the first half of the twentieth century, opportunities open to Irish people depended heavily on whether their family owned property such as a farm or small business. Those set to inherit a position in a family enterprise could stay in Ireland. The rest generally had to emigrate or enter the religious life or, if they found work in Ireland at all, it was often as a result of family contacts and connections; not many positions were available to those who had only educational qualifications to rely on. By the mid-1980s the pattern had changed dramatically. Nearly three-quarters of males at work were employees in businesses owned by others, that is, non-family ownership. There was an increase in the numbers of men in the managerial, skilled manual and white-collar areas, with marked declines in unskilled and semi-skilled occupations.

Thus, the shift out of agriculture has been central to changes in class structure and to absolute social mobility rates in Ireland. In 1961 half the gainfully employed men in Ireland worked in farming; this had decreased to a fifth by 1981 (Whelan 1995, p.332). Late and rapid industrialisation meant that the transition from agricultural to industrial and service employment did not follow that of the core capitalist economies. Whereas societies such as the United States and Britain saw a shift of workers from agriculture to industry and then to service occupations, the weak development of industrial employment in Ireland saw those displaced from agriculture leaving the country — and exiting the class structure — through emigration. In other words, those displaced by modernisation in Ireland came to make up a significant, and largely subordinated, element of the British class structure (Hazelkorn, 1991).

Over a period of fifty years the occupational structure in Ireland has changed from one dominated by self-employment and small family enterprises to one dominated by employee status in larger enterprises. Recruitment is now based primarily not on family sponsorship but on educational credentials, though kinship connections often remain crucial in finding out about available jobs (Allen, 1998, p.193). Since the 1960s, cross-generational social mobility has not been an unusual experience for Irish men. A study conducted in the late 1980s found that almost two-fifths of men aged between 20 and 64 had moved into a class position that was different from the one they had been born into. But Breen and Whelan (1996, p.170) suggest this is related 'not to economic growth *per se* but to restructuring of the occupational structure, in particular the decline of agricultural employment, and the expansion of the professional and managerial class'.

As a result of the shift in the structure of the Irish economy towards one based on industry and service provision and the decline in agricultural employment, enough room opened up at the 'top' to allow considerable mobility into the professional and managerial class from other classes, including farming and urban

## Figure 6.1 Working males: changes in class categories 1951–1990 [percentages rounded up]

|  | 1951 % | 1961 % | 1971 % | 1981 % | 1990 % |
|---|---|---|---|---|---|
| Employers and self-employed | 38 | 36 | 28 | 19 | 18 |
| Employees |  |  |  |  |  |
| • upper middle class | 5 | 8 | 11 | 16 | 18 |
| • lower middle class | 14 | 16 | 18 | 20 | 20 |
| • skilled manual | 10 | 12 | 17 | 20 | 18 |
| • semi-/unskilled manual |  |  |  |  |  |
| – agricultural | 11 | 8 | 5 | 3 | 3 |
| – non-agricultural | 14 | 13 | 14 | 11 | 9 |
| Total at work | 100 | 100 | 100 | 100 | 100 |
| Total unemployed | 4 | 6 | 7 | 10 | 16 |

(Source: Breen and Whelan, 1996, p.17)

working classes. This is also true of intermediate white-collar groups. But this does not mean that the relative advantages enjoyed by families with privileged positions in the earlier class structure have disappeared. In Ireland, absolute mobility rates (measuring the 'inflow' into given classes) may have increased substantially, but relative mobility rates (measuring 'outflow' from class of origin or the extent to which individuals are able to move up or down the class ladder) have remained remarkably unchanged over time (Breen and Whelan, 1996, p.171). It is *relative* social mobility — discovered, for example, by comparing the occupational level attained by a son with that of his father (more recent work has included daughters, but not mothers) — in which mobility analysts in Ireland have been particularly interested.

This relationship is of interest to mobility analysts because the degree of association between a person's class of origin and their current class position contributes to the measure of social fluidity in a society. If there was no association, this would represent the 'perfect mobility' of a completely open society but this is only ever hypothetical. What mobility research seeks to uncover is how much social fluidity exists in one society in comparison to another. Measuring mobility is important, according to Breen and Whelan (1996, p.169), as 'restrictions on mobility opportunities are a crucial mechanism by which resource and constraint differences between families become perpetuated across generations'. In other words, when mobility opportunities are blocked or constrained, what might otherwise remain simply economic differences between individuals are transformed into membership of identifiable *social classes* with distinctive lifestyles and unequal life chances.

In the late 1980s, 'outflow' from class of origin remained surprisingly limited. Over half the children of managerial and professional fathers were themselves in the managerial and professional class; among working-class men, 70 per cent were themselves the children of working-class men. In comparison to other western European countries, the Irish figure for immobility is comparatively high but what further marks out the Irish experience is the 'extremely low level of upward mobility from the working class to the professional and managerial class' (Breen and Whelan, 1996, p.169). While, in terms of the types of people that become professionals and managers, Ireland *appears* quite an 'open' society, this appearance 'turns out to be consistent with very substantial inequalities of opportunity associated with a persistence of the underlying pattern of relative advantages' (Breen and Whelan, 1996, p.172). In other words, the 'classlessness' of Irish society is, in this respect anyway, something of a myth.

Those born into the upper class enjoy a number of advantages — ownership of property or capital, social status or prestige and access to influential social networks, the opportunity to obtain educational credentials — that allow them to avoid downward social mobility. The distribution of these 'class resources', Breen and Whelan (1996, p.174) note, 'shows virtually no change over time'. As Clancy (1995a, p.487) devastatingly remarks:

It would appear that, since social destinations are so closely related to social origins, the middle classes have perfected the process of passing on their 'achieved status' from one generation to the next. The reproduction of achieved status in an apparently meritocratic society seems to have replaced the inherited privileges of an ascriptive society.

Our discussion has concentrated on social mobility among Irish men, but what about Irish women? Whether their positions in the occupational structure are influenced more by their social class background or their gender is a highly controversial issue. Crompton (1998, p.19) suggests that it is very hard to combine both class and gender in a single analysis of inequality, as 'the persistence of the gendered division of labour . . . continues to create apparently insuperable obstacles to the development of a single classification which would encompass both men and women'.

Mobility analysis in Ireland suggests that while class of origin strongly influences the occupational achievements of women as well as men, class and gender also interact to produce some distinctive outcomes for women. Women working outside the home still tend to be found in a restricted range of occupations, primarily professional and managerial, white-collar and semi-skilled manual classes; they are largely excluded from farming, petit bourgeois, technician and skilled manual occupations (see Chapter 8). Women remain largely excluded from the inheritance of productive property, such as agricultural land (O'Hara, 1998). Such exclusion means that 'women experience more mobility than men and, in particular, are a good deal more likely to experience downward mobility' (Breen and Whelan, 1996, p.175). Women also change class through marriage and are more likely, though not by much, to do so than men are to change class through employment. Overall, Breen and Whelan conclude, what most determines one's life chances or eventual position in society is not one's gender but the class or occupational position of the *family* into which one is born.

The work of the ESRI researchers has been of great importance in challenging assumptions complacently made about the decline of inequality as Irish society 'modernises'. Increasingly this research has turned its attention away from a simple focus on father–son occupational mobility to address more problematic issues in the study of inequality, such as:

- gender differences in mobility
- the emergence of the two-career family and the problems it raises for analysis
- how far the problems of a socially-detached underclass can be understood through measures of inequality based on positions within the labour market.

Nevertheless, the empirical perspective on class inequality remains rather narrow. It has little to say about social or cultural dimensions of class, nor about classes as historical agents of social change.

Rather, Breen and Whelan (1996, p.2) think of 'class' primarily as 'sets of structural positions' within the economic structure. While in theory, understanding how these structural positions may form into groups that possess a distinctive socio-cultural identity is important, how this might happen is hardly addressed in this research. And despite their challenges to the underlying assumptions of modernisation or industrialisation theory, they replicate some of them. For example, the analyses produced from this research tend to have a strong 'meritocratic' bent. The distribution of class positions within Irish society, while noted, is taken to be a less interesting phenomenon than relative mobility between these positions. This is because the latter is 'taken as an indicator of the degree of equality of opportunity or "openness" in a particular society' (Breen and Whelan, 1999, p.329). The implication is that inequality in occupational positions is in itself acceptable. What is unacceptable is for access to higher or better rewarded positions not to be 'open' to everyone (see also Lynch and O'Riordan, 1999, for a strong critique of a similar approach to meritocracy in education).

For Breen and Whelan, relative social mobility is the most useful measure of the level of inequality in Irish society. Other ESRI-linked work considers inequality in other terms, such as 'income inequality', the distribution of income across families and social groups in Ireland. This issue is central to much of the work done by both Nolan and Callan on levels of poverty in Ireland, where the measure used to estimate rates of poverty is in fact a measure of income inequality. For example, this is the basis for the three 'poverty lines' developed by Callan and Nolan (1988), where households are defined as being 'in poverty' when in receipt of an income that is either 60 per cent, 50 per cent or 40 per cent below the average household income in the state. (A commonly used poverty line in Ireland, also adopted by EU bodies such as Eurostat, is based on a figure of 50 per cent of average weekly industrial earnings. Other poverty lines may be based on the level of payments for various social welfare benefits, such as Social Welfare Allowance). The existence of large numbers of households whose income falls so far below the average indicates substantial inequality in the distribution of income across society.

Hardiman (1998, p.130) argues that the distribution of wealth in Ireland is highly skewed. She ranks Ireland among countries like the United States, the UK and Switzerland in the extent to which wealth is concentrated in the hands of a small minority of the population. On the other hand, Nolan (1999) notes that the marked growth in inequality in household incomes in the UK and the United States in recent decades has not been paralleled in other Organisation for Economic Co-operation and Development (OECD) countries. On this measure, inequality is now less severe in Ireland than in the UK, he argues, and Ireland 'is certainly still among the more unequal, but is broadly similar to Greece, Spain and the UK and much less unequal than Portugal' (1999, p.85). But any improvement in the Irish picture is not due to a reduction in inequality in this country, but as the consequence of a deterioration in some other places. Thus, 'while Ireland appeared as something of an outlier in 1987, by 1993 this was no longer the case.'

## Poverty

Poverty, class and social inequality are closely linked issues. Indeed, the early sociologists were drawn to the question of class partly as a desire to explain the incidence and persistence of poverty in industrial society. But there is much debate about how to define poverty and how this is done can have significant effects on how it is perceived and managed in society. Callan and Nolan (1998, p.147) point out that 'no single measure of poverty commands universal acceptance or is appropriate for all purposes', but the most common perception of poverty in Ireland, both from 'common-sense' and sociological perspectives, is that of *relative poverty*. This conceptualisation of poverty relates to the acceptable social standards within a society. Ireland contains few people living in the *absolute poverty* experienced at times in some developing countries, but much of the population remains in situations where they are denied many of the attributes of an acceptable social life. This is expressed clearly in the Irish government's National Anti-Poverty Strategy (NAPS), outlined in 1997 (NAPS, cited in Callan and Nolan, 1998, p.147):

> People are living in poverty if their income and resources (material, cultural and social) are so inadequate as to preclude them from having a standard of living which is regarded as acceptable by Irish society generally. As a result of inadequate income and resources people may be excluded and marginalised from participating in activities which are considered the norm for other people in society.

It is this understanding of poverty that underpins the establishment of the poverty lines (see above) as a means of measuring the phenomenon. Equally important, suggest Callan and Nolan (1998, p.148), is the distance by which people are located below the poverty line, that is, the *depth of poverty*. Both measures conceptualise poverty in terms of a lack of money and wealth — 'economic poverty' (Atkinson, 1997, p.10) — but more recently the concepts of *deprivation* and, in particular, *social exclusion* have come to the fore both in sociological thinking and policy debates. Each of these terms attempts to capture how deficiencies and inequalities of wealth and income combine with other aspects of power and social interaction.

Deprivation can include other deficiencies in people's lives, such as the lack of a cooked meal each day or a warm coat in the winter. The notion of 'exclusion' may relate to broader deficiencies, for example, an individual or household's inability to socially interact; to exercise political power; or to access services and facilities, perhaps because they cannot afford a telephone or they have no access to transport. A person may be poor but not deprived or excluded, and vice versa, though in practice there is usually considerable overlap between the two. 'Social exclusion' often serves as no more than a convenient euphemism for 'poverty', being a term that is less politically charged than the latter.

Overall there is much debate about how to measure poverty. Poverty statistics, like those for unemployment (Allen, 1998) are politically sensitive: a government may choose one set of figures, interpreting them in a certain way, while a lobby group may derive a completely different picture using a different measurement, or even draw opposite conclusions from the same set of figures. Atkinson (1997, pp.16–17), for example, has demonstrated how 'optimists' and 'pessimists' can each draw solace from the figures that relate to the decline (or growth) in poverty in Ireland during the 1990s, depending on whether ESRI or EU measurements are adopted. Furthermore, the picture can be changed quite considerably depending on whether households or individuals are taken as the unit of analysis. The main source of recent research data in Ireland is the Living in Ireland survey (Callan et al., 1996), which has been in progress since 1994 and is based on information derived from interviews with 4000 households. This has provided ammunition both to those who assert that poverty in Ireland has increased and those who see an improvement in the situation. But it has made available a wealth of data about patterns of income and expenditure in the population that expands our understanding of the forms of inequality found in Irish society.

There has been little change in the overall incidence of income inequality in Ireland during the period 1973 to 1994 (Atkinson, 1997, p.18). Substantial numbers of people in Ireland continue to experience deprivation and exclusion as a result of inadequate financial resources, but there has been a marked shift in the types of individuals and groups that experience poverty. Poverty in Ireland is found decreasingly among the retired or elderly and increasingly among the unemployed (and consequently families with children). A remarkable one-third of children under fourteen lived in households that were below the 50 per cent poverty line in 1994 (Callan et al., 1996, p.92). This contrasts with the situation in some other EU countries where the retired make up a much larger proportion of those in poverty, as do those in work — the 'working poor'. In Italy and France in the late 1980s, this group made up nearly a third of those in poverty (Atkinson, 1997, p.15). Factors such as disability and changes to family structures also have the capacity to significantly affect the incidence and experience of poverty. Ireland now fares worse in relation to overall levels of poverty than some of our EU partners, such as Denmark and the Netherlands, but better than others such as Greece, the UK and, especially, Portugal (Atkinson, 1997, p.13).

Changes in the groups experiencing poverty reflected increases in unemployment up to the late 1990s, and changes in social welfare and superannuation (pension) policies and levels of payment. Long-term unemployment has been a particular problem in Ireland, with a greater proportion of the unemployed falling into this category — without a job for over a year — than in other EU or OECD countries. A significant proportion of the long-term unemployed have been out of a job for over three years. Such people typically lack educational qualifications or marketable skills. This would suggest that poverty is clearly linked to class; yet class theory has been rarely used to explore poverty in Irish sociology.

In summary, the work of the empirical class researchers has been very significant in challenging facile assumptions about the disappearance of 'class divisions' in Irish society. The painstaking research of Whelan, Breen, Nolan and others has provided extensive quantitative data about the extent of persistent social inequality in Ireland, though we have already seen that such data is open to differing interpretations and 'spins'. But the dominant themes that contextualise the research — the treatment of inequality as a poverty issue and the identification of class inequality with occupational inequality — has meant that many other important questions to do with class in Irish society have hardly been raised, let alone answered. To counter the narrow focus of much Irish work on class, we now illustrate some of the diverse ways that sociology has addressed and discussed the idea of class, before returning at the end of the chapter to look at some less well-known, but often most illuminating, accounts of class and class processes in Irish society.

## WHAT IS 'CLASS'?

All known societies are characterised by forms of social inequality and by sets of meanings that seek to explain, justify or obscure such inequality. There are many ways to explain, even to justify, inequalities of opportunity and outcome. Age, gender and, at times, ethnicity, are important factors. But in all modern societies, wealth, income, education and social esteem or status are always of key importance. 'Class' is widely used by sociologists in discussion of these kinds of inequality.

Despite some suggestions that, both as a social issue and as a useful sociological category, class is no longer relevant (Crompton, 1998, p.9; Lee and Turner, 1996), most sociologists agree that the texture of people's lives, the shape of society and the essence of social inequality continue to be determined to a considerable extent by the ownership of property, the distribution of power and rewards and the nature of people's livelihoods. Furthermore, as Savage (1995, p.16) points out, it is only in recent times that the methodological and theoretical sophistication of sociology has begun to provide high-quality substantive information about class inequalities in modern societies, not least, as we have seen, in Ireland. But if we argue that class difference remains central to understanding society, what do we mean by class?

Class carries a number of broadly accepted separate meanings:

- It can refer to a system whereby people are grouped according to their common economic position, especially as those positions give access to differential rewards in the shape of wealth, property, income or power.
- It is widely understood as an expression of people's lifestyles, in particular how they consume and how they express themselves through certain styles of consumption.
- It is seen by many as a matter of social esteem, prestige or status — a measure of social standing within a particular society.

These three sets of meanings obviously overlap to an extent but they also give rise to differing implications and understandings. Given its centrality to an understanding of society, the definition and analysis of class has been a highly contentious issue within sociology. Not least, there is a complex interrelationship between class and other social and analytical categories such as gender and ethnicity.

Class can be understood on a number of different levels. At the *macrosociological level* sociologists may analyse the structural features of inequality. Why and how is it that societies continue to manifest broad patterns of inequality? How are these structures of inequality reproduced over time and how is this related to the activities of broad social groups and interests? What are the implications for macrosocial outcomes such as health, welfare or development? At the *microsociological level* of analysis, sociologists may ask questions about how class is experienced, for example, within the workplace or the household; how do attitudes and values relate to class and how are these expressed through social interaction? A focus on the broad social structure may help to delineate consistencies and patterns that endure over time and set limits to social action, consciousness and change. An analysis of the minutiae of everyday activities and relationships may allow us to focus on the dynamic living out of social structures, in other words, to capture something of the 'lived experience' of class. The greatest challenge for class theorists and analysts is to combine the two levels of understanding: to show how people's everyday lives and experiences are tied into, or appear to be disconnected from, the broader structures that shape societies.

Is 'class' merely a descriptive category and a way to categorise certain aspects of social experience? Or should classes be seen themselves as social actors, as a motive force in history? This has been a central issue in debates between different sociological perspectives on class and it raises questions about the importance of a temporal or historical dimension in class analysis. Sociologists who think of classes as social movements that can shape historical outcomes generally emphasise an understanding of the particular class formation as a key element in the class analysis of a society. To understand *class formation* means to grasp how the class structure has been shaped by and has emerged from a history of relationships between classes. In contrast, positivist (see Chapter 1), or what are often misleadingly called 'neo-Weberian', approaches to researching class tend to be *categorical* or *taxonomic*: they slot people into positions or 'boxes' and then locate these positions in relation to a social hierarchy, such as a hierarchy of occupations. Like analysts of class formation, positivists think of classes as having an objective reality — they are empirically observable and measurable — but their reality is as a social category rather than a historically acting collective subject. Those who adopt a more interpretative approach in sociology are more likely to define class as a set of meanings that structure individual actions and social space, the complex but invisible patterns of relationships between groups and individuals.

We can conclude then that 'class' contains a very complex set of ideas. It can embrace many aspects of social life, from inequalities of wealth, property and income to the work people do, the education they receive and the housing they occupy, their values, attitudes and political beliefs and practices and even the art, literature and mass media that they produce or consume. Furthermore, these dimensions overlap and interact. As Breen and Whelan suggest, 'If we are to develop an appreciation of the pervasive nature of class differences it is necessary to take into account the manner in which class differences feed off each other' (1996, p.2). How we understand class is also fundamentally determined by the particular theoretical lens that we use to examine the phenomenon.

## THEORIES OF CLASS

It is common for introductory presentations of class theory to begin with a contrast between three broad perspectives:

- functionalist
- Marxist
- Weberian.

Functionalist analyses can be described as basically 'common-sense' understandings of inequality. They see inequality as normal, indeed functional, for society. Thus, 'inequality in complex societies [is] rendered legitimate via an emerging consensus of values relating to the societal importance of particular functions . . . such theories incorporate a moral justification of economic inequality' (Crompton, 1998, p.7). In other words, social inequality is not only inevitable but morally defensible (traces of this functionalist position can be seen in the meritocratic tone of much Irish social mobility analysis, as noted earlier). The existence of unequal material rewards provides incentives for socially desirable behaviour such as innovation, business development and the creation of wealth; and it is further claimed that there is a consensus across society that disproportionate rewards for such innovators and wealth creators are justified and legitimate. Simply put, functionalists argue that it is both necessary *and* desirable that surgeons and company directors have greater wealth and income than cleaners and bus drivers.

Marxist analyses of class, on the other hand, are sharply critical both of the basis of the class system and its social effects. For Marx, productive activity or work was central to human experience and society. The central division in all societies is based on people's relationship to the material basis of production. In capitalist society this is highly unequal. Productive property like land, railways or factories is held and controlled by a small group of owners — the bourgeoisie — while the vast bulk of the population owns no capital assets and has only their labour power to sell — the proletariat. These two classes have diametrically opposed interests: the bourgeoisie in maximising the profit they can make from the labour of the proletariat; the workers in maximising the return to themselves on their labour. The struggle over these interests is termed 'class conflict'. It is on the basis of this inequitable system of organising production that, for Marxist sociologists, social inequality is founded. For Marxists, the wealth of company directors is directly at the expense of their employees.

The nature of capitalist society has changed considerably since Marx was writing in the nineteenth century and, accordingly, Marxist sociologists have developed more complex and sophisticated analyses of class while retaining the fundamental elements identified by Marx. Theorists such as the American sociologist Erik Olin Wright have expanded Marx's analysis of work-based inequality to embrace other dimensions of the productive process, for example, the power to control others through the organisation and management of work; access to specific types of skills or credentials that workers can use to bargain for a bigger slice of the cake. There is little Marxist-influenced class research in Irish sociology. Most Irish class analysts understand themselves to be Weberian or neo-Weberian in their theoretical perspective but this is achieved largely by selectively emphasising some aspects of Weber's theory at the expense of others.

Weberian approaches to social inequality have focused very much on the issue of status but, for Weber, the key struggles in society were over the issue of *power*. These struggles were not limited to the economic realm and could include struggles in relation to authority, political influence or the determination of social standing and respect. The three key aspects of power identified by Weber were economic power, prestige and political power. They are summed up in the trio: *class*, *status* and *party*.

Like Marx, Weber related class to the distribution of the means of production and to the economic market. He too emphasised how the majority of people have only their labour to sell on the market — whether that labour equates to manual strength, dexterity or the intellectual and organisational abilities that were gaining importance at the time Weber was writing — and how this placed them in a very unequal position compared to those who owned capital. For Weber, however, classes were not self-conscious groups with a specific political interest as they were for Marx; rather, they were categories or collections of workers of a given type (it is this aspect that may lead people to label stratification research as 'neo-Weberian'). Self-consciously organised groups with political goals fell more in line with Weber's second category, *status groups*.

For Weber, status is based on social prestige. A status group has been defined as follows (Cuff et al., 1998, p.51):

> a collection of people who recognise themselves as equals, who look upon one another as equally worthy, and who look up to and down on other social groups. A status group involves shared understandings, mutual recognition among its members and, of course, acknowledgement from its superiors and inferiors of its standing in the general scale of social position.

Status groups are characterised by a shared culture or belief in cultural distinctiveness: Weber was particularly interested in religious or ethnic divisions in a society as a basis for their formation. More recently, status has been linked to the consumption of particular sorts of goods. Indeed, class theory has come to be differentiated between Marxists, seen to be interested in *production* (and associated issues such as work and the organisation of the labour process), and Weberians, associated with an emphasis on *consumption* (and related issues such as culture, education, housing and so on). In this sense, status represents the ability of those who share a similar class position to convert their economic (or political) advantage into symbolic markers of cultural superiority: having the right sort of house, car or fashion clothing (see Chapter 16).

Finally, *party* is the term used by Weber to denote the role of political (with a small 'p') power in shaping social inequality. In other words it concerns the ability of groups to organise for their own ends. Much status group activity characteristically takes the form of *social closure*, attempting to limit access by outsiders to the cultural characteristics that form the basis of a claim for superior status. This might mean a refusal to accept people of certain religious beliefs; to prevent outsiders from becoming proficient in the language of the high status group; or to impose quotas to restrict access to high status educational qualifications such as in law or social work. The success of social closure practices is influenced by the relationship that the group has to political power structures. Like Marx, then, Weber understands inequality as being significantly shaped by the nature of the formal political system in a given society and by relations to the state. Weber's ideas cannot be reduced to a simple hierarchy of occupational positions but, unfortunately, in the guise of 'neo-Weberian stratification theory', this is how they are often presented.

Class theory has always been difficult to pin down because of extensive debates in social theory and rapid change in the contours of western society (Crompton, 1998, p.13). There are numerous varieties of class theory and analysis and not enough space here to explore even a fraction of them (see Crompton, 1998; Devine, 1997; Lee and Turner, 1996, for comprehensive and up-to-date discussions). In talking about the analysis of class in contemporary societies, it is important to be aware of the changes taking place in the nature of global society: shifts that have variously been described as the movement towards a post-modern world of 'disorganised capitalism' (Lash and Urry, 1994). In particular, the perceived decline of class politics, the break-up of traditional social divisions and categories and the emergence (at least in popular discourse) of groups such as yuppies, slackers and downshifters have provided challenges for class analysis. Yet the analyses of the classical social theorists, developed during the triumph of modernity and subsequently elaborated by generations of sociologists, retain a great deal of relevance in understanding today's societies.

Combining in particular Marx's and Weber's ideas, we argue, following Wright (1989) that the explanatory and theoretical power of class analysis can be found in how it links three key elements of social life:

- *material interests* — the means of maximising economic welfare; in our type of society this relates very much to power, wealth, property, income, education and work.
- *the lived experience of everyday life* — a very broad term that may embrace numerous aspects of people's existence; of particular relevance, perhaps, in the study of class, are aspects of life such as work, family, values and consumption.
- *the capacity for collective action* — how people may act together in the world based on their membership of a broader social entity; once again, this is a very broad set of ideas. Collective action may take the form of gang warfare, social movements or a range of activities related to people's material and social circumstances, perhaps based on what they perceive to be 'class' issues. Examples may include industrial action, political behaviour or forms of social protest.

Theories of class, then, can be said to operate on at least three levels:

- as a theoretical understanding of how social structures operate to constrain the possibilities of social action
- as an understanding of the nature of everyday life in terms of how its practices and patterns reflect and are constrained/endowed by social structures
- as an understanding of the strategies and organisational arrangements that groups use to represent themselves and to establish their symbolic boundaries and vision of the world.

However, these analytical ideas have some complex implications in terms of sociological understanding and analysis.

## Structure and agency and the class debate

Arguments about social class in sociology have been very much influenced by ongoing debates in social theory, in particular, that known as the structure and agency debate. This debate contrasts theories that suggest that social structures determine human action with those that focus more on the potential of individuals and groups to shape their own destinies. Like most perennial debates, this one is never likely to be resolved but the debate remains essential to understanding much about how social class has been, and continues to be, used within sociological analysis.

The 'structure' side of the debate owes much to the influence of Marx. It is undeniable that Marx stressed the key role of the economic dimension in shaping human history and contemporary society. Many readings of Marx deduced that cultural and social phenomena could in effect be read off from an understanding of the economic and production relationships within society, including the class structure. As a result, many Marxist theorists, in particular those calling themselves 'scientific Marxists' (for example, the writers Althusser and Poulantzas, prominent in the 1970s), paid a great deal of attention to the theoretical definition of class groupings within capitalism but they did not devote similar attention to how people actually experienced (or did not experience) class in everyday life.

Structuralist approaches to class have much in common with functionalism, despite their very different pedigrees. They tend to emphasise the power of society and to underplay the ability of human actors to influence events. Both approaches also tend to be teleological, in other words, they assume a particular end-point in advance. Not surprisingly many sociologists of class have been highly critical of structuralist accounts. Interestingly these critics also draw on the Marxist legacy but have tended to emphasise the humanist side of Marx's writings (especially those that he completed earlier in his life which were in fact published after his death) rather than the more materialist analysis found in later works such as the celebrated work *Capital*.

Writers in the humanist Marxist tradition included the Hungarian, Lukács, and the Italian, Gramsci. Each of these was to have a very significant influence on thinking about capitalist society and class, particularly in Europe. Each stressed the importance of politics and ideas in the formation of class. In many ways they attempted to address the question that had haunted Marxism: if it was in the interests of the workers to overthrow the capitalist system, why did this not occur? Lukács stressed the role of *reification* — a concept drawn from Marx. This is the process by which people see the world as an independent object rather than an outcome of their own actions. At its most extreme, reification results in fatalism and a belief that nothing can be changed via human action; more generally it means that people tend to accept the world as it is, not believing that they can effect a difference.

Gramsci is best known for his concept of *hegemony*. This notion builds on Marx's ideas about the role and nature of ideas in class society. For Marx, as famously stated in his book *The German ideology*, written in 1846, the dominant ideas in society are the ideas of the ruling class. Gramsci devoted much of his writings to trying to explain how this process took place, focusing in particular on

Italian society. The struggle for hegemony in society, the intellectual domination of debate and interpretation, is a key element in the class struggle. We can see in the work of both Lukács and Gramsci part of a larger debate about how the struggles for power and influence between competing class groups are experienced, at least partly, as battles over meaning, understanding and the nature of social reality.

A number of social historians, investigating the historical development of such struggles and how they related to economic and political conflicts, have made a significant contribution to our understanding of how class has developed in western society. A particularly important figure is the English Marxist historian Edward (E.P.) Thompson who argued that historical classes can 'be recognised only in the cultural activities and beliefs of social agents' (Savage, 1995, p.21). Thompson (1968) argued strongly against determinist and structuralist views of class. His work has had widespread influence (see, for example the work of Australian historian and sociologist Bob Connell in Connell and Irving, 1980) within historical and sociological thinking about class and within the field of cultural studies. Thompson's focus was very much on the question of how classes are brought into being and reproduced through time. In other words, how are classes *made*?

The ideas of Bourdieu are increasingly influential among researchers on class. Like many modern social theorists, Bourdieu has attempted to reconcile the objective and the subjective sides of human societies (Cuff *et al.*, 1998, pp.322–7). This has led him to devote considerable study to cultural phenomena and to attempt to combine an analysis of the production and consumption of culture (in education, the mass media and in high and popular culture) with an understanding of class that draws heavily on the work of both Weber and Marx.

Bourdieu's writings try to link issues of consumption with economic and social power (see Chapter 16 for more detail). A key concept that Bourdieu has developed is that of *cultural capital*. This refers to the existence of dominant and socially legitimated ideas about what is culturally valued and desirable in our society, for example, art house cinema (as opposed to *Die Hard*), literary fiction (as opposed to the works of Maeve Binchy), fine art exhibitions (as opposed to greyhound racing) and gourmet food (as opposed to spiceburgers and chips). Bourdieu believes that the power of the bourgeoisie is based both on economic wealth and income *and* on possession of 'cultural capital, the forms of cultural distinction that privileged middle-class groups can embrace and pass on to their children by giving them the right "disposition" to perform well in the educational system' (Heath and Savage, 1995, p.278). Thus, the privilege of middle-class groups is maintained partly through the passing on of property (housing, shares, money); their greater access to success in the education system; and their ability to engage in exclusionary and valued forms of cultural activity. Of course access to all three types of scarce resources is often overlapping and mutually reinforcing.

As class theorists have attempted to address the issues raised by the structure and agency debate, we see that they are also led to raise questions about how people actually experience and 'live' class. But success in integrating questions of culture and lifestyle into class theory can bring its own problems. Too great a focus on issues of lifestyle can cloud an awareness of how class is structured by unequal access to resources, power and control. The challenge for a sociological analysis of class is to incorporate both aspects of the phenomenon.

## Material interests

The notion of 'material interests' is important as it enables us to understand class divisions as growing out of the structure of society itself. Some treatments of class as occupational stratification, particularly if stratification is regarded as an outcome of prejudices about different types of work, tend to suggest that class is an *epiphenomenon*, relatively detached from the basic workings of society. In contrast, class theorists who understand class as being linked to the unequal distribution of material resources argue, following Marx, that the class division found in any society constitutes its *central* structural characteristic. Analysing the class structure enables us to understand how a society is organised in order to meet the key material needs of the people within it — food, shelter, health, rest, and so on. In capitalist society, economic organisation places people in competitive relations with each other on terms of inequality. Those whose access to key resources is constrained or limited have an interest in trying to alter that situation; those whose profits come from restricting the access of others have an interest in maintaining the status quo.

If classes are organised around opposed interests in the distribution of material resources, it becomes possible to see them as engaged in social struggle. The focus then shifts from classes as static entities to class struggle as a continuous process. A Marxist approach to class is distinguished by a view of classes as relational, that is, formed out of and only intelligible in terms of their relations to other classes. Even if one does not accept, with Marx, that class struggle in capitalist society is the struggle between capitalists and workers, it is still always important to identify with whom a given class is in conflict at any particular time. Allen (1999) notes that much discussion of inequality and poverty in Ireland talks of groups as 'marginalised' or 'excluded' but it never asks *who* is doing the marginalising or excluding. This makes consignment to the marginalised appear almost natural for those concerned, not needing any further explanation.

But the argument that classes have and pursue material interests needs to be treated with some sophistication. As E.P. Thompson argued, it is a mistake to think of classes as collectivities that pre-exist, fully formed, and with a conscious sense of where their own interests lie and clearly articulated strategies for pursuing these. It is only in the experience of struggle against opposed interest groups that classes become aware of their own identity and needs. Classes, Thompson argued, are formed in, through and out of the process of class struggle itself. Thus, the problem of material interests brings us back to the debates around structure and agency, but it also raises questions about the relationship between social experience and self-consciousness in everyday life (see further discussion below).

The material resources in which we develop an interest cover quite a wide range since they are linked to the meeting of essential human needs; thus, one could treat, for example, access to affordable and good quality housing as a material resource, the unequal distribution of which gives rise to classes in conflict with each other (sometimes called 'housing classes'). But sociologists, in understanding people's material interests, have tended to attribute particular importance to two issues:

- the concept of *property*
- the domain of *work*.

'Upon the different forms of property, upon the social conditions of existence, rises an entire superstructure of distinct and peculiarly formed sentiments, illusions, modes of thought and views of life', according to Marx (cited in Newby *et al.*, 1978, p.24). While research into social inequality has tended to focus on the variables of occupation and income, transmission of property is crucial to the reproduction of social structure and relations and may have important ideological, economic and political effects. The central place of property in class relationships is succinctly described by Saunders and Harris (1990, p.66):

We generally think of property as defining our relationship to things. . . . It is, however, more accurate to think of property as defining sets of power relationships between people. . . . Encoded and enforced through law, it specifies rights and duties governing the behaviour of those with title and those without and these rights and duties both enable and constrain our actions in respect of one another.

Most analysts of class follow Marx in emphasising the importance for class analysis of the ownership of productive property, in Marx's terms the 'means of production', or property used in work rather than in other areas of social life, such as consumption. The social relations of work appear in concrete form in the labour process: how production and other work activities are organised, the relationship of work practices to ownership of the means of production and how these help shape workers' consciousness.

The emphasis on class relations as an expression and response to opposed interests in the organisation, control and profits of work is characteristic of many contemporary Marxist class theorists. For example, Erik Olin Wright argues that people's common interests emerge as they become involved in 'similar dilemmas and trade-offs' (1989, p.286), in their pursuit of economic welfare and social power at work. Collective as well as individual action is needed to maximise these. Wright is well known for his attempts to develop Marxist theories of class, both theoretically and methodologically, in ways that would make them more applicable to the United States and other late capitalist societies. But his analyses of class have been criticised for their rather narrow focus on the formal, paid workplace. Struggles over opposed interests can occur in other sites besides that of work.

Many feminist theorists in particular argue that a comprehensive analysis of class requires attention to the household as an important site of consumption, production (especially in the case of farmers and other small business families) and reproduction. Individuals experience exploitation and domination not only in the workplace and in public affairs but also within the household and in what are conventionally seen as 'domestic' relations. Theorists such as Bauman (1991) go so far as to argue that the world of work is no longer the defining social reality for people living in an increasingly post-modern society, though many would agree with Jamrozik (1991, p.84) when he says that:

> Work is still the most important, some would say, fundamental activity in contemporary industrial society. Apart from providing the means of livelihood for the majority of the population, it also confers a social identity on the incumbent and a place in the occupational as well as in the social structure.

Breen and Whelan (1996, p.2) show how work 'spills over' into other aspects of life. Thus, a lifelong experience of dehumanising and alienating work can lead people to reduce their 'capabilities to be flexible, sensitive and creative in other areas of their lives'. New forms of work, such as 'telework', may see a literal shift of work back into the domestic environment and the effects of these are only beginning to be analysed from a sociological perspective.

## SYMBOLS AND STRATEGIES OF CLASS

As Thompson argues, classes are formed *within* and as a result of class struggle. The third aspect of class is class consciousness and collective action. A key debate in class theory and analysis has been the extent to which classes 'act' in their own interests (Crompton, 1998, p.16). For some Marxist theorists, a class will, by definition, act to defend its own interests within the realm of class struggle. From a Weberian viewpoint such action is possible, even likely, but not inevitable.

Either theoretically or empirically, it is very difficult to establish relationships between class position, class consciousness and class action or social mobilisation (Marshall and Rose, 1990; Baxter *et al.*, 1991). It is untenable to simply read off observed behaviour from a theoretically specified 'base': for as Cloke and Thrift (1990, p.169) point out, 'people whose earnings and relations with capital production are similar will not necessarily share a corporate consciousness, interest or inclination for action.' To analyse collective action requires an understanding of how issues and projects are collectively articulated and expressed and how groups are mobilised as a result.

Bourdieu draws our attention to how classes are, through action and language, *discursively* produced (in other words, how class-based groups talk about and explain and defend their positions). Through a process of 'classmaking', class groupings are formed or called into existence. In this process (1987, p.9):

> Collectives having an economic and social base, be they occupational groups or 'classes', are symbolic constructions oriented by the pursuit of individual and collective interests.

These may be called into existence through strategies of discursive identification and mobilisation, particularly through organisations (1987, p.7):

> A theoretical class, or a 'class on paper' might be considered as a probable real class, or as the probability of a real class, whose constituents are likely to be brought closer and mobilised (but are not actually mobilised) on the basis of their similarities (of interest and dispositions).

Many class analysts make a distinction between class awareness and class consciousness. *Class awareness* refers to the extent that people identify with a particular class grouping in terms of lifestyle, attitudes, patterns of consumption and so on. It does not mean recognising the group as a class; indeed for middle-class people it may require a belief that class itself does not exist and that it 'is all down to the individual'. In other words (Breen and Whelan, 1996, p.3):

> Class awareness involves a shared awareness and acceptance of a common style of life among the members of a class; it does not imply recognition that the attitude, beliefs and styles of life that members of this class have in common signify a class affiliation, that there are other classes with different attitudes, beliefs and patterns of behaviours.

*Class consciousness* thus means a recognition that classes exist and that one is a member of a particular class distinct from other classes.

While much class theory is concerned with macrosociological issues of social structure, mass political and industrial movements, historical development and large-scale social change, it is clear that class analysis also applies to the level of 'everyday life'. How people daily live out class relationships is of importance for at least two reasons. Class concepts can help us to better understand people's day-to-day experiences of inequality and powerlessness; similarly, an insight into people's everyday lives can contribute to an understanding of how class groupings are produced and reproduced and how class consciousness, ideologies and class-related attitudes are sustained.

To an extent we all live in what Mike Allen (1998, p.11) terms the 'partitioned society'. 'What defines us' in the class sense, he suggests, is 'the total segregation of all life's hopes, chances and experiences.' He is indicating how modern (especially urban) life allows us to circumscribe our experience so that it obscures our direct experience of inequality. This provides us with a feeling of control over our own lives, or self-determination. But the capacity to feel in control of one's life is itself unequally distributed. For example, it is frequently dependent on access to privacy. As Allen (1998, p.32) says, there is a sharp contrast between the lack of basic privacy accorded to recipients of state benefits (for example, queueing for the dole) and the privacy demanded by the wealthy and powerful when tribunals of enquiry or the Inland Revenue are attempting to investigate their financial affairs. He suggests (1998, p.43):

> To be unemployed is to live without enough money to meet your needs or your family's; it means to look for work in the constant face of failure and rejection, it means to be subject to casual humiliations and slights, to have more time than you can possibly fill. Mostly it means to be in a negative, incomplete state.

Everyday experiences of class awareness or of social inequality may also be shaped by relationships to space. Class and inequality are often related to neighbourhood and 'community'; territory, residence, distance, space and movement help to shape people's experiences of class, inequality and poverty. In larger urban settlements, neighbourhood segregation may render social relationships and groups more homogenous and class and status more clearly delineated. In other words, people are 'sorted' by class, wealth and income into particular neighbourhoods and suburbs (Fahey, 1998b). Once there, they tend to interact to a large extent with others of similar background and class identity. In smaller rural settlements, despite substantial material inequalities and social exclusiveness, there may be more informal and friendly contact between relatively wealthy and poorer people. People of different classes may interact as neighbours or be linked by personal ties of work, kinship or friendship. Indeed, regular interaction in a variety of institutional contexts may lead to a social and psychological desire to ignore or deny social inequality. Residence in a smaller community may increase the likelihood of class mobility, affect class solidarity and consciousness and lead to a more flexible set of class distinctions.

## CLASS FORMATION, CLASS CONFLICT, AND THE LIVED EXPERIENCE OF CLASS IN IRELAND

We have argued that the interest, usefulness and explanatory power — indeed, the value of class analysis — depends on how well it links three key elements of social life: the structured distribution of material resources; the lived experience of everyday life; and the capacity for collective action that groups exercise. We conclude this chapter by asking how well Irish sociology has succeeded in addressing these dimensions. We focus briefly on some Irish studies of class that differ in approach to those of occupational stratification or income inequality initially discussed. These studies attempt to capture some of the broader dimensions of class outlined in our discussion, though most do not capture all of them.

We look first at attempts to relate *class formation* and *class mobilisation* to Irish material or cultural conditions in order to understand how these processes are shaped by the distinctive history and economic and political location of a given society. We understand class formation to refer not only to the emergence of new classes in a society but also to how existing classes are reproduced or indeed change over time. Crotty (1983) argues that the 'capitalist colonial' relationship between Ireland and Britain in the late nineteenth century, in encouraging the development of a particular sort of small-scale agrarian-based economy, contributed to 'the embourgeoisement of the periphery and the proletarianisation of the core'. Those Irish who emigrated to Britain because they were surplus to the requirements of agriculture in Ireland became landless and propertyless labourers, while those, often from the same family, who stayed to work in Ireland became owners of small property.

The importance of property is stressed in a more recent study. Hannan and Commins (1992) emphasise the persistence of a 'vibrant, small-scale landholding sector' in Irish society right into modern times. They point out (1992, p.90) that, though only a seventh of the workforce is employed in agriculture, almost a quarter of all households in Ireland own land. To them this represents a major challenge to the position of convergence theorists who maintain that industrialisation tends to make all developing societies more alike (see Chapter 3). They argue that the remarkable endurance of such a 'pre-industrial' property-holding class into the 1990s has been ignored in most analyses of contemporary Irish society (1992, p.87). The dispersion of small property ownership across a substantial section of the population renders the Irish class structure and experience quite different to that of many other modern societies.

Hannan and Commins are interested in this class of small property owners for two reasons. First, they want to understand why this class has adapted so successfully to 'the modernisation of the country's economic and social structure' (1992, p.79). Second, they want to contrast it with the fate of the urban working class which, they say, has been far less successful in this regard. To explain the success of the small property owner involves an examination of both the individual and collective strategies used by this group. Individually, households with land have been able to work out a range of 'survival strategies' that in many cases allowed them to move out of full-time farming into multiple sources of income generation, which has often provided a better gross household income. This class has also been adept at taking advantage of opportunities for social mobility, particularly through education, for their children (see Chapter 7 and O'Hara, 1998). Collectively, it has not only enjoyed considerable favouritism from the Irish and EU states (in relation to state industrialisation strategies, as agricultural producers and as land-owners) but has also displayed a remarkable capacity to organise politically in pursuit of its own interests. In nearly all these ways, there is a strong contrast with the urban working class whose members' chances of employment and upward mobility have been consistently much poorer over recent decades.

Hannan and Commins's treatment of class in this analysis is quite limited. Though directed towards small property owners, their analysis largely equates these with farm households or households that have recently ceased farming. They do not discuss whether it makes sense to speak of these as being in 'the same class' as other petit bourgeois, that is, property owning, groups. In general the authors have little to say about class consciousness or even class awareness among this social grouping. They do not locate the small property owning class clearly in any relationships with other classes in Irish society, preferring to focus on contrasts between classes, nor is the formation of this class explained through tracing its position in the class structure overall. Small property owners are presented as competing for state benefits with the urban working class, but independently of them. Despite these omissions Hannan and Commins's analysis remains interesting as it shows how the dynamics of Irish societal development have been shaped by historically distinctive processes of class formation.

An earlier work (Hannan and Tovey, 1978) pursues a similar argument but draws attention to the impact of cultural rather than material capital in shaping class processes. It examined the relationships between social and occupational status and people's sense of 'ethnocultural identity' as measured by the answers they gave to a set of questions on attitudes towards the Irish language (the survey data came from the Committee on Language Attitudes Research survey of 1973 and from earlier national census data). The occupational data was detailed enough to allow people to be categorised according to the sector they worked in (state or public service, commercial, agricultural and so on) as well as by the status of the occupation they held. The groups most supportive of the survival of Irish were those working in professional and particularly public sector employment, whose interests and commitments were closely tied to the maintenance of a separate Irish state and whose career prospects were based closely on their educational qualifications. People in private business or commercial employment, where educational credentials generally held little relevance for career mobility and those whose work involved transactions across national boundaries were generally least supportive of the Irish language. The findings suggested that, over a long historical period, class formation processes in Ireland have been shaped by conflict over the issue of whether competence in or commitment to Irish constitutes legitimate 'cultural capital'. This is symbolic of broader cleavages around the legitimacy or desirability of an independent state in Ireland. Ideologies of class and ideologies of nationalism or supra-nationalism have been and remain closely interwoven in Irish society (Tovey et al., 1989).

While this study did not make explicit mention of Bourdieu's ideas, later work on language issues has done so. Ó Riagáin (1997, p.80), for example, argues that what Bourdieu calls 'strategies of language assimilation and dissimilation':

> are inevitably and unavoidably linked to the more general strategies of social reproduction adopted by groups and individuals (ie the strategies by which each generation endeavours to transmit to the following generations the advantages it holds). Thus, strategies of social mobility . . . are all likely to have linguistic consequences.

Equally, strategies for linguistic reproduction or change generally have major consequences for processes of class formation and social mobility.

A second way to look at class formation and mobilisation in Ireland has used an approach that emphasises classes as formed in and through their relations with other classes, usually, though not always, in relations of struggle and conflict. This is the *political economy approach* (Tovey, 1982; Curtin et al., 1996; Tovey, 1999) and has been applied in particular to the issues of rural development (and underdevelopment) and rural poverty. It offers a strong contrast to the dominant spatial approach to these topics, that treats poor people essentially as 'people who live in poor places' (Pringle et al., 1999). While not wanting to deny that where people live can bear upon their social and economic opportunities, the political economy approach tries to understand poverty as 'a dynamic condition, that is, produced out of, maintained and/or changed by dynamic processes in society in general' (Tovey, 1999, p.97). Thus, to understand rural poverty, 'we must start from an analysis of the processes of change and restructuring which are working through rural societies . . . and try to achieve some insight into the differing effects which these have on the situation and life chances of different groups of rural people'.

The political economy approach argues that the situation of disadvantaged groups is best analysed through an examination of their relations with other classes or groups. In the case of rural poverty, for example, the disadvantage of small farmers or landless labourers has been produced by how *other* classes have pursued their own interests. The progressive marginalisation of smaller producers since the 1850s has occurred not as an accident of location but as the outcome of strategies used by larger farmers (Crotty, 1974) and the food industry (Tovey, 1982) to secure and increase their own profits and place in society. Curtin et al. (1996) argue that the class position of 'family farmers' across the developed world must be understood in terms of their relationships with an increasingly globalised and integrated food industry, control of which (even in Ireland where it has historically been dominated by farmer co-ops) has progressively shifted away from primary producers towards the distribution and retailing end of the chain. Thus, rural social classes can be seen, like urban industrial ones, to be formed in their relations with other classes and, in particular, in relation to the owners and managers of industrial capital. At this point, from a political economy perspective, the understanding of rural poverty intersects with and becomes part of the understanding of poverty and exploitation among urban industrial workers.

The Marxist or materialist theme that underpins the political economy approach contrasts markedly with the 'neo-Weberian' orientation of most Irish class analysis. Marxist concepts, approaches and positions have also influenced ethnographic accounts of the *lived experience of class* in Irish society. Apart from research sponsored by the Combat Poverty Agency (for example, O'Neill, 1992), nearly all research in Ireland that has addressed how it feels to live in a class-divided world or to live through the construction of a sense of class identity has been produced by anthropologists. For example, Silverman (1989; 1993) has sought to uncover 'the notions of locality, class and personhood' that permeate the life stories constructed by ordinary people; she sees this as a way 'to understand how individuals manage their lives and present their selves in the society and culture in which they live' (1989, p.111). In her research (1989), she draws on a biographical account collected over a lengthy period of conversation with Aggie, a 'labouring man's daughter' from Thomastown in Co. Kilkenny, to construct a picture of local class relationships. The 'central idiom' of the labouring class from which Aggie comes that gives meaning both to the social world that she inhabits and to her reconstruction of her life experiences is 'respectability'. This shapes her interaction with others whether 'above' or 'below' her in the local class hierarchy.

In research carried out in the town of Ennis, Curtin and Ryan (1989) examine the relationships between class, occupation, lifestyle, leisure and social interaction in an attempt to provide a more holistic account of the lived experience of class. They compare, in particular, the periods of the 1930s and the 1980s. In the former, class difference was clearly marked in a number of ways that were immediately intelligible to Ennis residents: 'on the streets one could judge with some accuracy a person's occupation by his style of dress, and from his occupation determine the type of house he lived in and in which quarter of the town it stood' (1989, p.129). Clearly demarcated class positions were reinforced through everyday activity and, of particular interest to Curtin and Ryan, the social clubs to which Ennis men typically belonged. Ranging from elite clubs for the bourgeoisie to labour clubs for the working class, these institutions provided both a location for leisure activity (most working-class houses were too small to allow for this) and, on occasion, for class-based political activity. In the 1980s most of the town's 'clubs' had disappeared and leisure activity had shifted towards, on the one hand, the domestic space (that is, in front of the television) and, on the other, to pubs in the town, which reflected to some extent the class and gender-based divisions previously provided by the exclusive clubs. The changes in everyday life, structured by employment, education and place of residence, were implicated in many complex ways with issues of class, gender and age. While inevitably partial and impressionistic, this research provides an important parallel to the empiricist investigations of the occupational stratificationist approach outlined at the start of this chapter.

Perhaps the most detailed and theoretically developed analysis of class from an ethnographic perspective is that of Australian anthropologist, Chris Eipper (1986). His study focused on the town of Bantry in Co. Cork in the light of the impact of Gulf Oil, a multinational oil company that had established an oil refinery in Bantry in the mid-1960s. Eipper's analysis of local community interaction sought to examine the changing nature of class domination in Irish society in its local, national and international forms (see also Chapter 13). Although he treats the lived experience of class as a key issue for understanding local social life, Eipper does not believe that class and class processes can ever be fully understood if they are treated as purely local. At the same time, he argues, class cannot be treated, as has sometimes been the case in locally based studies, as no more than 'external factors' that provide a 'context' for local experience. Rather, what Eipper calls the 'nexus between church, state and business' (the 'ruling trinity' that provides the title for his study) is forged and operates *simultaneously* at the local and national level (1986, p.3). We can only understand 'how class worked in Bantry' if we link this up to 'how it worked in a number of other places too'. Eipper's approach is ambitious in that it tries to look at the macro and the micro at the same time, unusual in sociological analyses of class. It also tries to keep in sight both issues of structure and of agency. As a result, Eipper has perhaps been the most successful at constructing a theoretical perspective on class in Ireland that integrates the three key dimensions of class analysis: interests, cultural meanings, and political action.

To develop this perspective, Eipper makes an essential distinction between two ways that people can act in their relations with others: as 'acting subjects' and as 'social agents'. 'Class', he argues, 'has to be analytically grasped as both an ideological encounter and as a material condition' (1986, p.12). Class is understood as a material condition when we treat people's behaviour as a result of the material constraints under which they operate; or the economic location they occupy; or as an expression of their pursuit of material self-interest. But the problem is how to translate abstract categories of class, such as capital or wage labour, into substantive classes that have cultural and political histories, such as the bourgeoisie or the working class. To understand social experiences 'in all their lived complexity' we cannot 'satisfactorily treat people as merely personifications of economic relations . . . the actual flesh and blood people who empirically relate to one another in real life' relate to one another 'as persons' (1986, p.12). They are formed by social and cultural experiences as well as by economic position. Their interaction is shaped by notions of status and social honour, in turn expressions of the dominant ideological beliefs about the types of persons and ideas that are entitled to respect and deference. Eipper, then, argues that class analysis has to combine the analysis of two forms of class relationship:

1 People act as the 'social agents' or representatives of economic class locations, for example, as the representative of the interests of owners of capital.
2 They are acting subjects, real people living a distinctive way of life within a given social habitat.

Both ways of acting involve struggles for power and control, particularly for control of people's class consciousness 'which is the acme of class struggle, of class formation' (1986, p.14).

Eipper uses these theoretical concepts to produce an analysis of class and power relationships in Bantry before and after the arrival of multinational capital in the area. As we have already suggested, he sees Irish society as dominated by a ruling bloc comprising church, state and business. He examines closely both the personal power exercised by each of these groups in Bantry life, historically and contemporaneously, through the clergy, politicians and local business elites, and, at a national level, the relationships between the church 'as a corporate body', the state and business institutions, particularly as these involve the control of 'development' and its ideologies. But spanning both these levels is a third form of class power: 'the impersonally instituted authority of corporate property, of capital accumulated and organised on a world scale, as a more imperious version of class domination than that confronted in the analysis of the ruling bloc dominating Irish society' (1986, p.203). This is the class power of multinational corporations. The penetration of this global form of class power into Irish society, Eipper argues, leads to the subordination of local and national class processes to international ones (1986, p.203):

> At Bantry, Gulf Oil was able to subordinate all other objectives to its pursuit of profit. If it enhanced the profits and the power of the local business people it did so only by creating an affluent and assertive industrial proletariat, and if it enhanced the wealth, privilege and prestige of the local bourgeoisie, it did so only by making a vassal of it. And . . . nationally, it does seem reasonable to suggest that the growing penetration of the national economy by foreign capital will have analogous consequences.

The arrival of Gulf Oil in Bantry not only signalled a realignment of class forces, locally and nationally, but also a reconstruction of the dynamics of social change in Irish society. In future, the capacity of classes to reproduce themselves and their relationships with other classes would increasingly be mediated by and dependent upon the class interests of global capital.

## CONCLUSION

The work of Eipper and other researchers discussed in the last section reminds us that class analysis is not only about uncovering the extent and distribution of inequality or poverty (or even wealth) in society, but is also an attempt to understand social dynamics, and the emergence and trajectories of distinctive cultural worlds of being. As Eipper argues, following Thompson, class is not a static category, but an historical one. It is linked inevitably to social change: classes change society and social change alters classes and their relations. As Eipper (1986, p.11) points out: 'it is not the evolution of classes as such, which explains change, but the evolution of the processes forming classes; it is the processes which create classes more than the classes themselves which are important.'

The primary emphasis of class analysis, from this point of view, should be on processes of class formation. The key to understanding class formation is class struggle. But the ultimate goal of class struggle is to control class consciousness or, more broadly, those cultural understandings that help either to reproduce or to suppress class formation and mobilisation. Class analysis must then also concern itself with the cultural realm and how it shapes the experience both of individuals and collectivities. Irish sociology has gone a long way in addressing and explaining the sources of inequality in Irish society, but the analysis of social processes as class dynamics is still in its infancy.

# 7
# *Education*

Education stands at a central point in our discussion. On the one hand it is about the creation of particular forms of knowledge, and how certain understandings of life and society are generated, transmitted and debated in Irish society. On the other hand education is intricately bound up with questions about modernity: it is seen as a key to modernisation and as a key driver of social, economic and personal change.

Any sociological analysis of education faces an institution of great complexity. The activity of formal education involves a huge proportion of Ireland's population — an estimated one third of the people (Drudy and Lynch, 1993, p.ix). 'Education' is an umbrella term that covers a broad range of activities and sites from pre-school to primary and post-primary, through to third-level and adult education. It can also include public- and private-sector training and even extend to processes of self-education that take place outside of any formal structure. Furthermore, many other activities, from tourism to sport to the mass media, also have a significant, and sometimes quite self-conscious, 'educational' component.

The range of actors and institutions involved in education is similarly broad and includes children and parents; students and lecturers; pupils and teachers. Of major importance are also the personnel and institutions within the state — in the bureaucracy of the Department of Education and Science and of the numerous official bodies involved in education, from the school inspectorate to parents' groups and third-level accreditation bodies. Education is intricately connected to other institutions such as the world of employment, law, the mass media and social administration. Like many of the aspects of society discussed in this book, 'education' as a separate field of analysis is constituted at an abstract level while the social reality of education is in many ways inseparable from the totality of the fabric of social life.

Education is also closely connected to the concept and the project of *modernity*. As Clancy (1995a, p.467) points out, this is for at least two reasons. First, education stands for our ability to develop society in ways that can lead to the betterment of populations: through economic growth; spiritual enlightenment; aesthetic appreciation; and social progress. As a consequence the measurement of educational development, in terms of, for example, levels of literacy, numbers of schools or the output of scholarly articles, is often used as a way to measure social development more generally. In Ireland our success as a western European economy is often linked with our 'educated workforce' and high levels of cultural achievement. Second, education reflects modern humanity's urge to shape nature through the application of rational knowledge: through learning about and knowing the world we can better control it. Education can thus contribute to a more efficient use of physical resources, for example, through better farming practice, and can also help in the creation of a more ordered and rational society, through consumer education, civics and so on.

In this chapter we examine some key aspects of education that have been of interest to Irish sociologists. First we examine some of the mythology that has grown up around education. On the one hand, state institutions and the popular media trumpet our levels of educational achievement while, on the other, a range of international statistics indicate that Ireland compares quite poorly on a number of indices. We then provide a brief overview of the main sectors of education, focusing in particular on issues of management and control. The content of education is discussed: what is taught in schools and other educational sites, and why? We may be better able to answer these questions by exploring how educational outcomes and processes are related to issues of social inequality, of gender, class and ethnicity. And finally we look to the future and pose some of the questions that Irish sociologists will need to ask as the shape of education changes, or indeed does not change, in response to broader trends in work, technology and other social institutions.

## EDUCATION IN IRELAND: MYTH AND REALITY

Ireland presents itself, for example, in IDA advertisements, as a modern (even post-modern) country with a highly educated and literate population. Yet even a brief survey of some of the relevant statistics reveals a very different picture.

Figure 7.1 indicates the proportion of the population with upper secondary education (post-Junior Certificate or equivalent) within the OECD countries. We can see that Ireland scores within the lower end of the range of all age levels, together with the countries of Southern Europe. Ireland also has poorly resourced primary education, with large class sizes and often poor facilities. There are also major problems with literacy (see below) and few resources have until very recently been dedicated to tackling this issue. If Ireland does have a reputation for high-quality education it may be despite, not because of, the resources allocated to it.

Wickham (1998) criticises aspects of Ireland's educational performance from another perspective, throwing cold water on the notion of the 'intelligent island'. He argues that though in Ireland 'we have a lot of education', we are far from being a 'learning society' (1998, p.82). In particular, the links and networks

# Figure 7.1 Proportion of the population who have completed secondary education

| | Age 25–34 | Age 35–44 | [1995] Age 45–54 | Age 55–64 | Age 25–64 | 2005 Age 25–64 | 2015 Age 25–64 |
|---|---|---|---|---|---|---|---|
| **North America** | | | | | | | |
| Canada | 84 | 80 | 71 | 54 | 75 | 81 | 84 |
| United States | 87 | — | — | — | 86 | 88 | 88 |
| **Pacific Area** | | | | | | | |
| Australia | 57 | 54 | 51 | 43 | 53 | 58 | 62 |
| Korea | 86 | 61 | 39 | 23 | 60 | — | — |
| New Zealand | 64 | 64 | 55 | 47 | 59 | 64 | 68 |
| **European Union** | | | | | | | |
| Austria | 81 | 73 | 66 | 50 | 69 | 76 | 79 |
| Belgium | 70 | 58 | 47 | 31 | 53 | 64 | 70 |
| Denmark | 69 | 65 | 61 | 47 | 62 | 66 | 69 |
| Finland | 83 | 74 | 59 | 37 | 65 | 74 | 81 |
| France | 86 | 74 | 62 | 42 | 68 | 79 | 84 |
| Germany | 89 | 88 | 84 | 72 | 84 | 88 | 89 |
| Greece | 64 | 50 | 34 | 21 | 43 | 57 | 66 |
| *Ireland* | 64 | *51* | 36 | 27 | 47 | 58 | 66 |
| Italy | 49 | 43 | 28 | 15 | 35 | 48 | 57 |
| Luxembourg | 32 | 33 | 28 | 20 | 29 | — | — |
| Netherlands | 70 | 65 | 56 | 46 | 61 | 66 | 70 |
| Portugal | 31 | 24 | 16 | 9 | 20 | 30 | 36 |
| Spain | 47 | 32 | 18 | 10 | 28 | 41 | 49 |
| Sweden | 88 | 81 | 69 | 52 | 75 | 82 | 87 |
| United Kingdom | 86 | 80 | 72 | 59 | 76 | 82 | 86 |
| **Other OECD countries** | | | | | | | |
| Czech Republic | 91 | 86 | 83 | 70 | 83 | — | — |
| Norway | 88 | 86 | 79 | 65 | 81 | 86 | 89 |
| Poland | 88 | 82 | 68 | 47 | 74 | — | — |
| Switzerland | 88 | 85 | 79 | 73 | 82 | 86 | 88 |
| Turkey | 26 | 23 | 20 | 14 | 23 | — | — |
| **Country mean** | 71 | 63 | 53 | 41 | 60 | 69 | 73 |

— = no data available

(*Source*: OECD, 1997, p.39)

between education and industry need to be much better developed. In this criticism he is carrying on the long tradition that has existed since the late nineteenth century of calling for more 'technology' in Irish education (Drudy and Lynch, 1993, p.217). Ireland suffers, according to Wickham, from a highly academic approach to teaching and learning, as reflected in the focus of our secondary schools, exam system and universities. In contrast, our vocational education is too narrowly focused, aiming to meet the needs of firms and single industries like the computer industry, rather than the requirements of society as a whole. There is very little company-based training (unlike in Japan) and academic research is very poorly funded. All this adds up to a 'weak national system of innovation' and means that as a society and economy we are likely to remain dependent on others to do our thinking for us.

While Wickham is correct in highlighting the shortcomings of the Irish system, he also reflects a rather narrow view of education in Ireland. For example, he pays little attention to the range of courses offered in the non-university third-level sector. Though often vocationally oriented, they incorporate a broad range of employment options, from the training of make-up artists for the film and TV industries to multilingual secretaries for the financial sector as well as the more familiar education of computer programmers and laboratory technicians. Furthermore, while he acknowledges the importance of the cultural sector, he does not recognise the importance of 'academic' knowledge in the development of growth and investment in this field. Such 'non-instrumental' knowledge is crucial to the development of industries as diverse as computer games, tourism and teleservices. If technical, scientific and rational knowledge are the hallmarks of modernity, it may be that a post-modern society and economy demands more in the nature of critical thought, creativity and flexibility.

It is now commonplace for educationalists, sociologists and policy-makers to make explicit the connections between education and the information economy. In a related study within the Irish third-level environment McBrierty and Kinsella (1998, p.8) assert that 'knowledge, information and associated skills have displaced labour as the primary source of productivity and competitiveness.' A feature of recent Irish economic growth has been the rapid rise in industrial productivity (comparable to the 'Asian Tigers' of Taiwan and South Korea). While there is considerable disagreement over the causes for this phenomenon, a key role is attributed to the influence of expanded education (Haughton, 1998, p.32).

The arguments over the extent and nature of education give some indication of its centrality not only to economic growth and development but also to the creation of national identity, personal fulfilment and the institutionalisation of power. As a major institution in western societies, including Ireland, it will always be at the centre of emotive and extended debates. We examine some of these debates in this chapter but first we provide a brief sketch of the main contours of the Irish education system.

## THE IRISH EDUCATION SYSTEM

It is conventional to divide the provision of education into four stages:

- primary education
- post-primary education
- tertiary education
- adult education.

We will keep this convention though it omits consideration of important aspects of the educational process, as suggested above, such as pre-school education and vocational training. The Irish education system provides a unique amalgam of state, religious and other interests. It is also dynamic: responding in different ways to changes in social attitudes; the strength and influence of other institutions; industry-based pressure groups; and competing 'expert' discourses, including sociological and educational research. This section therefore can provide only snapshot views of the system.

## Primary education

The 1937 Constitution specifically acknowledges the role of parents in Irish education. It asserts that the family is the primary and natural educator of the child — Article 42.1 states that it is the inalienable right and duty of parents 'to provide, according to their means, for the religious and moral, intellectual, physical and social education of their children'. While a very small number of parents have claimed their rights under the Constitution and have opted for home-based education, virtually all children in Ireland are educated from an early age in national school; there are over 3000 national schools in the state and only 60 non-state-funded primary schools (Curry, 1998, p.76; p.79).

Despite the intention of those that developed the Irish national school system in the mid-nineteenth century, it rapidly became a *de facto* and *de jure* denominational system, with its denominational nature explicitly recognised and supported by the state (Curry, 1998, p.79). The churches secured the dominant position in the provision of primary education in the country and Ireland maintained a largely state-financed but religion-controlled system. This position of power has been actively protected by the churches and it is only since the 1970s that others, such as teachers and parents, have had any formal role in the management of national schools. Even this role remains heavily circumscribed, with effective power still in the hands of a heavily centralised government department, the patron of the schools (the local bishop) and industrial agreements between the teachers' unions and the state.

Church control of the primary school system only began to be challenged in the mid-1970s. In the face of both Catholic Church and state opposition, some parents sought to establish inter-denominational national schools. The first of these, the Dalkey School Project, opened in the late 1970s and it was followed by similar institutions, often having to operate out of unsuitable temporary premises, in towns like Sligo and Galway. A second challenge to church control has come from a perhaps unlikely source: the expansion of primary education through the medium of the Irish language, in the *gealscoileanna*. Like the multi-denominational 'project' schools, these are managed by boards of people committed to a specific educational and social objective, rather than by nominees of the local Catholic or Protestant bishop.

The impact of these developments is reflected in the recent pattern of school establishment. Between 1986 and 1997 a total of 72 new national schools were approved by the Department of Education and Science. Only two of the schools established in this period were traditional Catholic Church controlled institutions. The remainder comprised 56 gaelscoileanna; 13 multi-denominational schools and one Muslim national school (*Irish Times*, 21 September 1999). In 1999 the control of national schools shifted perceptibly away from church to state as the government announced that it was to fully fund capital development of primary schools, thus removing the reliance on church and parish funds. This will inevitably reduce the considerable influence of religious bodies in primary education and will help to reduce some of the discrimination that has existed against multi-denominational schools.

## Post-primary education

Historically post-primary education in Ireland has been provided by a mix of church, state and other private bodies, with the first of these agencies being dominant. Participation rates in post-primary education have risen markedly since the introduction of 'free' secondary education in 1967. The sector serves almost 370,000 students in a variety of school types: secondary, vocational, community and comprehensive. Though almost completely funded by the state, this level of education remains organisationally dominated by religious bodies, principally the Catholic religious orders. Of a total of 762 second-level schools, 435 are secondary; 246 are vocational; and 81 are community or comprehensive (Commission on the Points System, 1999). The four types of school differ mainly in their ownership, management structures and funding arrangements but offer a common curriculum determined by the Department of Education and Science.

Unlike most other European countries that have, or have had, a binary system of post-primary education, the greater proportion (around 60 per cent) of post-primary education in Ireland takes place in 'academically oriented' secondary schools. These are privately owned and managed institutions under the control of religious communities, boards of governors or individuals, but are formally recognised, funded and regulated by the Department of Education and Science. Vocational schools and community colleges educate just over a quarter of post-primary students. They are administered by and funded through the Vocational Education Committees (VECs) of local government. Community and comprehensive schools, containing about 14 per cent of post-primary students, are managed by boards of management of differing compositions: those of community schools are representative of the local VEC, religious communities, parents and teachers. Those of comprehensive schools represent the relevant diocesan religious authority, the local VEC and the Minister for Education and Science, with no input from the other partners in education, that is, students, parents or teachers.

There are significant differences between the privately owned secondary schools and the others in the sector. The former are far more likely to be denominational and single-sex while the latter are non-denominational (in the case of vocational schools) and coeducational (in the case of vocational, comprehensive and community schools and colleges). The secondary schools have a tradition of providing an 'academic' curriculum while the vocational schools have, in the past, had an explicit mission to offer 'technical' education. This distinction is overlaid by a class distinction: secondary schools (with a number of important exceptions) have been oriented towards a middle-class clientele with vocational schools being for working-class students. The more recently developed comprehensive and community schools and colleges aim explicitly to bridge this division — with varying degrees of success.

The 'points race' for access to third-level education has given rise to a significant private, unregulated post-primary education sector, as in countries like Japan and Italy. This manifests itself in private colleges catering to 'repeat' exam candidates (popularly known as 'cram schools') and in the provision of personal private tuition or 'grinds'. According to the Commission on the Points System (1998, p.100), 'a high number of students report attendance at grinds. This . . . raises very fundamental questions as to how students and their parents perceive the work of schools, particularly in fifth or sixth year.' Though small in comparison with the fee-paying sector in countries such as the UK, the United States and Australia, the emergence of private institutions at upper-second and third level is evidence of the incipient marketisation of Irish education.

As in the primary sector, the influence of the churches is starting to diminish in the post-primary sector, but for different reasons. The main causative factor is the decline in membership of the religious orders, such as the Christian Brothers and the Mercy Sisters, who had such a key role in the establishment and management of secondary schools and who also secured influence over community schools and colleges. Already a considerable number of Catholic secondary schools are under the direction of lay principals and this will increase greatly in the next two decades. The orders have begun to establish alternative structures that may permit them to retain a management role in such schools into the future.

## Tertiary education

The third-level education sector is made up of a number of different types of institution, funded directly by the state, and a small private sector. These include seven universities; thirteen Institutes of Technology; seven teacher training colleges (all effectively under religious control) and a small but growing number of privately funded colleges. As in a number of other countries, like the UK and Australia, a binary system of tertiary education has developed and, while these countries have at least formally abolished the binary divide, government policy in Ireland has been to maintain it. Rhetorically the universities and Institutes of Technology enjoy a 'parity of esteem'; in practice the provision of funding for teaching and, especially, research tends to strongly favour the former.

In 1995/6, 95,000 full-time students were enrolled in third-level courses aided by the Department of Education and Science: 55,850 were enrolled in universities and other institutions funded through the Higher Education Authority; 38,130 in the then Regional Technical Colleges and the Dublin Institute of Technology; and over 1,100 in teacher training colleges. These numbers reflect a huge expansion of participation in tertiary education since the 1960s: from 21,000 full-time students in 1965 to over 103,000 in 1997/98. Over half — about 56 per cent — of school leavers now enter third-level education, about half of whom take degree-level programmes; this compares with a figure of just 11 per cent of the age cohort in 1965. The *Report of the Steering Committee on the Future of Higher Education* (1995) predicted a further rise to around 61 per cent of the age cohort by 2002/3, representing a total of 117,000 students (a figure that will also include mature age students) (Commission on the Points System, 1999). Some thousands of students also study outside the state, particularly in the UK, though the numbers have declined since tuition charges for some students were introduced in Britain. Like most other western countries, Ireland is effectively moving towards a system of mass third-level education. This was stimulated in 1995 by the introduction of the 'free fees' initiative — tuition fees for third-level study in designated institutions were abolished completely from 1996/7 onwards. The state/European Social Fund also pays (small) grants on a means-tested basis to a small majority (52 per cent) of full-time students (Curry, 1998, p.97).

## Adult education

Adult learning has been one of the more neglected elements of educational provision in Ireland — not least by sociologists — but is now one of the most rapidly growing; it is estimated that in 1996 there were at least 1,000 community-based education initiatives or groups in the country (Department of Education and Science, 1998, p.21). In recent times it has begun to acquire a higher profile, particularly in relation to economic and community development. Lynch (1997, p.118) suggests that there are complex causes behind this expansion but 'the greatest of all is probably the changing trends in thinking among educationalists, a movement both physical and psychological . . . a movement for education to go out into the community, rather than the community coming to it'. Adult education is now seen as 'the route to empowerment for many marginalised groups in modern Irish society', including those in poverty, substance abusers and those suffering from educational disadvantage (Connolly, 1997, p.40). Women in particular are central to the provision and use of many aspects of adult education. Adult education is seen by many as an opportunity for people to make up for the poor educational provision of previous years, and to move beyond the considerable inflexibility of the Irish school system (Hannan et al., 1998, p.127). But the sector remains heavily underfunded and has a low political profile compared to other aspects of education.

As Slowey (1987, p.118) points out, the adult education sector is highly diverse and it may be misleading to talk about it as a 'system' at all. It continues to reflect its origins in 'the labour movement, church activities, university extension, women's associations, scientific and literary groups and community activities'. As a consequence the range of activities that fall under the rubric of 'adult education' is vast, from the person completing a PhD with the Open University to the community activist undertaking training in lobbying skills and the retired person learning how to make their own wine. The motivations for engaging in adult education may include social involvement and contact, acquisition of specific knowledge and skills, general self-development and a means of assessing one's potential (Slowey, 1987, pp.131–3). For women in particular adult education may also provide an opportunity to move out of a purely domestic role and to (re)enter the paid workforce.

Notwithstanding the extreme diversity of the adult education field, there is now greater interest in the concept of *lifelong learning*, where the process may be as important as the outcome. This is not a particularly new concept, and Ó Buachalla (1974) was talking about 'permanent education' nearly three decades ago. The Irish government has argued for support for lifelong learning on the basis that it can address poverty and disadvantage, promote equality, competitiveness and employment and support community advancement (Department of Education and Science, 1998, p.12). It has yet to be seen whether the policy rhetoric is accompanied by practical outcomes and whether there is a real appreciation of the barriers to access, including funding, accreditation and child care, that actively militate against wider participation in adult education.

A major problem that has emerged in Ireland in recent years, and that challenges dominant concepts of the modernity of Irish society, is that of literacy — or the ability to communicate adequately in certain situations. A 1995 OECD survey (the International Adult Literacy survey, cited in Department of Education and Science, 1998, pp.30–31) showed that Ireland had greater literacy problems than any other OECD country surveyed, with the exception of Poland. A quarter of Irish adults were restricted to the most basic literacy tasks (finding simple information in a text) compared with just 6 per cent in Sweden and 10 per cent in the Netherlands. The OECD survey showed that literacy barriers were closely linked to poverty, lack of educational qualifications, unemployment, older age and lack of participation in any form of adult education.

Lack of literacy skills may lead to reluctance to accept promotions at work or to fully access social welfare benefits. In addition, literacy problems in childhood, reinforced by negative educational experiences, often lead to a generalised lack of self-esteem and self-confidence. Literacy problems may also provide a very real barrier to the first steps of the adult education ladder, in particular for those already otherwise disadvantaged. As the Green Paper on Lifelong Learning (Department of Education and Science, 1998, p.32) points out:

> The relationship between low levels of initial education and low participation in Adult Education raises a number of issues. Firstly, it challenges any assumptions concerning the compensatory possibilities of Adult Education. Secondly, it raises the possibility of Adult Education as a force for further inequality, widening gaps rather than closing them. Lastly, it draws attention, in a lifelong learning context, to the quality of the early school experience and to the factors which underpin success and failure there.

Lynch (1997, p.119) remarks: it is ironic that 'those who lack the necessary literacy skills to get one foot on the first rung of the educational ladder are in fact amongst those who suffer most from marginalisation and exclusion.'

While it is difficult to obtain information specifically about mature students, there is evidence that participation rates of such students in Ireland is much lower than in the OECD as a whole. While about a fifth of entrants to universities in all OECD countries were aged twenty-six or over, the Irish figure is just 2 per cent; for non-university tertiary education programmes, such as those offered by the Institutes of Technology, the Irish figure is 1.1 per cent compared to an OECD average of 36.8 per cent (Commission on the Points System, 1999). Like other adult learners, mature students at universities, colleges or Institutes of Technology suffer from numerous barriers — financial, logistical, domestic and regulatory (Lynch, 1999a, pp.187–214).

## THEORETICAL BASES FOR THE STUDY OF EDUCATION

We have seen that the Irish education system is both large and complex. It involves a great proportion of the population and consumes vast resources. But what is it for? And how should we understand it? This is where the differing theoretical orientations towards education come into play. Reflecting as they do the broader shapes of sociological theorising (discussed in Chapter 1) they sometimes differ sharply as to how we should interpret the educational enterprise. There are also some important areas of commonality between them, as we shall see.

A *functionalist analysis* of education focuses on how it contributes to the stability of society. The education system, from primary school to third level is seen to have a range of functions. These include a socialisation and training function, providing people with the basic and more developed skills required to operate effectively within society (such as literacy) and more specialised skills that support the functioning of the economy (such as computing skills). Schools and other educational institutions are also a key location for the creation and maintenance of national and cultural identities. This function is perhaps most starkly illustrated in the US system, where the teaching of national symbols, songs and historical narratives is particularly overt, but this process is mirrored in all societies. Education also has a major allocative function, based on the notion of meritocracy: it functions to distribute jobs and social positions to individuals based on their capacity, abilities and performance. In this way the education system is an essential basis for social stratification in society. A further set of functions — the integrative functions of education — include the maintenance of language communities and the development of social networks.

Like most manifestations of functionalist thinking, its place in educational sociology has been sharply criticised from conflict and interpretative viewpoints. But, like other functionalist arguments, it continues to have great resonance with common-sense accounts of social life and, as it does not challenge to any extent the existing power relationships within society, it enjoys considerable support among governments, policy-makers and many researchers.

One of Max Weber's main concerns in the analysis of western society was the spread of *rationalisation* — the development of calculative and technical ways of thinking about the world that are most clearly expressed in science and economics (see Chapter 1). Though Weber did not deal at length with the issue of education in his work, it is clear that the themes underpinning his analyses of social life are of considerable relevance to an understanding of this topic. For example, his analysis of bureaucracy and bureaucratic systems of societal management stressed the importance of particular forms of rational, specialised and disinterested knowledge. This type of knowledge may be contrasted with 'magical' or religious knowledge, and with the notion of 'cultivation', whereby a person is socialised in a more general way for a particular station in life.

In modern societies the acquisition of specialised knowledge becomes a key to social standing and, increasingly, to wealth and power. Members of society are able to perceive the importance of such knowledge and to pursue it. Access to education becomes a crucial aspect of personal development and, inasmuch as resources are scarce, is of benefit to those individuals and groups that can gain access to specialised knowledge. In Ireland a *neo-Weberian approach* to education, which sees education very much as a resource that individuals and groups can access to varying degrees, has been influential. Drudy and Lynch (1993, p.39) argue that a neo-Weberian approach 'also draws our attention to concepts such as power, domination and authority; to the conflict over economic resources and rewards; to the competition for status and prestige; to the struggle for control; and to the role of bargaining, negotiation and compromise'.

Whereas a neo-Weberian approach stresses the choices and strategies that social groups may adopt, the *Marxist approach* to education reflects an economically determinist position. Clancy (1995a, p.469) points out that both functionalism and Marxism, as varieties of structuralism, share a determinist, macrosociological view of education. The main difference is in the normative assessment of the situation. The Marxist approach focuses on how the education system operates as an institution for the creation and transmission of social inequality and the maintenance of the class system. Schools are seen as a site for social control, both through the overt activities of reward and punishment and through the 'hidden curriculum' that stresses and rewards punctuality, obedience and respect for authority — the very attributes required of a productive workforce. The school, for Marxists, is also a site for the transmission of capitalist ideology, in particular, values related to private property, nationalism and individualism. Of those theorists operating within a Marxist or neo-Marxist paradigm, perhaps the most influential in the last two decades has been Pierre Bourdieu. Bourdieu moves away, to some extent, from the mechanistic determinism of more traditional Marxist arguments about education. He emphasises the cultural sphere and the notion of 'cultural capital' as a significant source of inequality.

A *feminist analysis* focuses on gender inequalities within education. The main issues for feminists here are the sexism of both the hidden and overt curricula; discrimination against girls and women within the education system; the male control of educational institutions and other aspects of gender inequality. Early feminists saw education as having the potential to radically transform the nature of gender relationships and to provide women in particular with a means to redress discrimination against them in public and private spheres. Later feminist research recognised that entering the institution of education was insufficient in itself to bring about wholesale social change. They argued that not only were girls and women disadvantaged in terms of access, but that the system was a key site for the creation of dominant ideologies about masculinity and femininity. The school was therefore not an arbiter and transmitter of neutral knowledge but a mechanism for the maintenance of patriarchal social relations. More recently feminists have enthusiastically adopted post-structuralist theories in an attempt to better understand the operation of discourse and the creation of subjectivities within the educational field. This has led to a fundamental critique of the philosophical basis of schooling and of knowledge, as well as analysis of educational processes and practices.

An *interactionist approach* to education is microsociological and focuses especially on what happens within the classroom or other educational sites. In other words, it emphasises the importance of the process of *schooling* itself. There is a concern with the meanings and interpretations that people bring to social situations, including those related to education. Interactionist and other interpretative approaches argue that structuralist approaches to education, whether functionalist or Marxist in nature, ignore the realities of teaching and learning. Post-structuralist approaches are also highly critical of the notion of the participants in education being viewed as fixed identities. They emphasise the processes of personal growth and development that occur within the system and point out that identities are multiple and dynamic, rather than singular and static. This approach pays a great deal of attention to issues of language and discourse. The overall thrust of these types of sociological approach is away from *determinism*. The experience of education can be neither read off from notions of ability or attitude nor deduced from class, gender or ethnic position. Rather it is something that needs to be examined in detail, in context and with an openness to its dynamism and capacity for change.

One influential approach is *rational action theory* that suggests that people make calculations about the value of education to themselves or their children. While this approach emphasises the capacity of people to make choices about the paths and options available to them, it can be said to largely ignore broader patterns of inequality and meaning that shape the choices that people face. Of greater importance since the late 1970s, especially within the British sociology of education, has been *resistance theory*. This approach suggests that oppositional behaviour of some within the education system (most importantly, working-class students, especially males) is a rational response to the situation in which they find themselves. It tries to combine the determinism of structuralist theories of education with the voluntarism of the more interpretative approaches. Resistance theory grew out of the work of ethnographers who closely studied everyday behaviour in schools — especially the work of writers at the University of Birmingham, such as Angela McRobbie and of Paul Willis, whose 1977 book *Learning to labour* has been one of the most cited books in British sociology and cultural studies. While resistance theory does help to make sense of the rejection of education by a significant minority of those within it, it does little to point towards an alternative. Fagan (1995, p.94) concludes that, '[while it] certainly draws a more politically enabling picture of early school leavers, and does not construct them in positions of subordination, it leaves them without a political strategy or political project for emancipatory social change'. Lynch and O'Riordan (1999, p.92) are more positive. They suggest that resistance theory:

> has identified spaces and places for challenging unequal social relations through education. It has enabled people to see beyond the limits of structures and to identify modes of thinking and analysing which can facilitate change. It has offered hope for change which is important in and of itself.

But they point out that most resistance theory is developed by middle-class people on behalf of marginalised groups and not *in conjunction with* such groups or individuals themselves.

*Post-structuralist approaches* focus very much on the role of language in the creation and power of definitions of educational reality. An early example in Ireland was the work of Denis O'Sullivan (1989; 1992) who examined how the American economist Dale Tussing helped to shape the discourse of Irish education in the late 1970s. A more recent and extensive analysis of Irish education that has consciously adopted a post-structuralist viewpoint has been that of Honor Fagan (1995). This study attempts to deconstruct the discourses that constitute the social category of 'early school leaver'. Fagan outlines and deconstructs the dominant discourses within education, including the sociology of education itself. Thus, the phenomenon of the 'early school leaver' is shown to be constructed within a range of powerful discourses, each of which seeks to explain the phenomenon and does so in a way that disempowers and oppresses its object — those that leave school 'early'. These discourses include the genetic, the 'cultural deprivation', the structuralist Marxist and what she defines as the 'political discourse' — one with a radical and emancipatory aim. It is within the last of these that she places her own intervention into the debate. The ultimate aim of a post-structuralist approach is to question the assumptions made of existing 'realities' and how sociology constructs the objects of its analysis. Its political aim is to open up alternatives to how issues are posed and the action that flows from the analysis.

The post-structuralist approach favoured by Fagan (see also Ryan, 1997) has a distinctive methodological approach. It combines extensive but selective use of the 'voices' of the researched, with a complex and dense theoretical exegesis that seeks to make sense of the phenomena being analysed. It is as if the complexity of the social world is reflected in the very language being used to talk about it. It is not surprising that it is a mode of discourse that is deeply unattractive to policy bodies and government agencies who seek clear, concise, information that appears to incorporate common sense with a scientific style of presentation. Thus, while a post-structuralist approach challenges the orthodoxies of education on many fronts, it has had as yet had little impact on the policy-making or management processes around Irish education.

## Education and modernity

Concluding a review of Irish educational development in the period 1945 to 1960, Sheehan (1979, p.70) suggested that it was 'part of the transformation of Irish society which began in the early 1960s'. In this he was reflecting the common view that ties the phenomenon of education ineluctably to the processes of development and modernisation. The project of modernity is, among other things, a project about changing knowledges and identities. It is about the population becoming 'modern' in its attitudes and values as much as in the country's economic growth or infrastructural development. The institution of education, along with that of the mass media, is seen as a key to this change process.

Fahey (1992b, p.386) points out that education was the largest single area of expenditure of the newly independent Irish state and that primary schooling in particular 'was a major instrument in the political consolidation and rejuvenation of independent Ireland . . . [state] influence was central, extensive and ambitious in at least some of its objectives'. The modernising effects of education were complex, however, and sometimes contradictory. Among other things they led to a significant reordering of the relationships between children, families and the state. One effect was that children were, rather than being seen as an immediate labour asset, more likely to be regarded as dependant and as an investment for the future.

A key moment in Irish education was the publication in 1965 of the *Investment in education* report (Department of Education, 1965). The product of OECD experts, this report, in the words of Luke Gibbons (1996, p.83), 'set out to remove the school from the sacristy and place it in line with the need for greater technological change in Irish society'. It was positioned very much against the background of the programme of industrialisation and the opening up of the Irish economy and was centred on the notion of manpower planning (Kelleghan, 1989, p.204). The report helped to shape the future of Irish education and, through giving greater impetus to nascent trends, contributed to an expansion of the system and to issues such as social inequality and educational effectiveness being placed on the political agenda. Overall, however, the report was part of a pragmatic rather than ideological response to the educational challenges raised by a modernising society. Even when potentially controversial initiatives such as comprehensive schools were mooted, they were discussed within existing political and social discourses of localism and control and not in the fiercely ideological context typical of many other western countries (O'Sullivan, 1989).

The influence of education in relation to modernity is seen as manifold. Curry (1998, p.74) points out that the Irish national school system was very important in the development of mass literacy — a literacy, it must be pointed out, that in many parts of the country entailed the replacement of the Irish language by English as a symbol of modernity. Education has also, more recently, been viewed as a key to change in political attitudes. Political scientist Tom Garvin (1998, p.154) suggests that 'mass education of a kind not available to previous generations has accelerated the detraditionalisation of Irish political culture.' This has seen a decline in traditional Catholicism and in militant republicanism, each commonly associated with the 'old' Ireland. Garvin further sees an effect on power relationships within Irish society: 'the old peasant deference to clerical authority, partly derived from a popular perception of priests as educated men who could be trusted because they were on your side, has faded' (1998, p.152). These examples reflect a very broad and influential discourse that explicitly links changes in Irish society and culture to the impact of education.

Drudy and Lynch (1993, p.85) suggest that 'having one of the highest retention rates in education in the EC [European Communities], Ireland is fast becoming a sophisticated, well-educated, industrialised society in which rational rather than traditional authority holds sway.' Within such a modernising society, expectations of teachers and of schools have steadily expanded: they should now play an explicit socialisation role in terms of assisting students' personal and social development and in implementing various community and health education projects. Schools have become a significant area for intervention through government programmes to combat social disadvantage, promote healthy lifestyles, prepare young people for a labour market that requires information-based skills and to promote values of citizenship and political responsibility. Schools have also been given the task of addressing broader patterns of inequality in society, including those of class and gender; these issues are discussed later in this chapter.

The changing roles of education and the demands placed on it by other societal institutions are reflected both in Irish government policies and in the broader approach of the EU to education. For example, the EU Commission's most recent White Paper on Education and Training underlined the role of schools in human resource development and recommended that the education system be viewed as a critical element of the economic infrastructure of member states (Commission on the Points System, 1999). Similarly, a Commission White Paper on teaching and learning explicitly links education to the development of modernity. It argues that education is wedded to the 'dawning of the information society and the relentless march of Science and Technology' (cited in Department of Education and Science, 1998, p.17). This is representative of a discourse that has permeated and shaped Irish education at least since the *Investment in education* report.

It would be a mistake, however, to assume a clear and unambiguous link between education and the project of modernisation. While education has been associated with the development of scientific rationality, specific types of interpersonal relationship, achievement orientation and a facility with technology, it has also provided an arena for the maintenance of attitudes, behaviour and relationships that have been seen as barriers to the development of a modern sensibility. Thus, Ó Buachalla (1974, p.355) has remarked that 'it often appears in educational systems as if the rate of change and innovation is frustratingly slow — education seems to follow a haphazard pattern of development — with huge inertial resistance within systems inhibiting long-term adaptation and reform.'

## THE SOCIOLOGY OF EDUCATION IN IRELAND

Though there has been some history of sociological research into education in Ireland, public debate in the area was until the 1990s largely the preserve of historians and economists. Sociological analyses tended to be rather narrow and instrumentalist and a review of the field by Drudy in 1991 identified the dominant approach as functionalist and positivist. Research tended to be very much shaped by the predominance of policy-related issues and there was a lack of independent research funding. This tended to severely circumscribe educational discourse and, in the vivid terminology of O'Sullivan (1992, p.434), alternative viewpoints were notable by their absence: 'to utter the unsayable is to invite marginalisation, exclusion or communicative dismissal.' This lack of theoretical diversity led, according to Drudy (1991, p.110), to 'considerable paradigmatic insulation and lack of debate on the nature of the educational system and its relation to other major social institutions'. In other words, there was little impact on educational sociology from the broader theoretical and methodological debates within the sociology discipline, in particular in relation to more interpretative and critical approaches. The dominant interest was very much in the relationship between socio-economic status and educational attainment. A more critical approach has since developed that has focused on the nature and role of the educational system and its relationship to the state (Drudy, 1991, p.112) and on people's attitudes about aspects of the system, but there is still a lack of research within the Irish sociology of education that can tie together the experiences of students, teachers, families and the broader community. Ireland has yet to produce a holistic sociology of education to match that of, for example, Bob Connell and his associates in Australia (Connell et al., 1982; Connell, 1985).

Despite the limitations of many sociological analyses, the discipline has been of major importance in exploring the relationship between education and society though, for a variety of reasons (Kelleghan, 1989, pp.202–5), it is difficult to directly relate research to policy outcomes. It has been crucial in expanding thought about education and schooling beyond the psychologistic interpretations that dominate much educational discourse (Lynch, 1999a, p.3). In Ireland it has provided comprehensive data with which activists and policy analysts can push for reforms to the provision of education, particularly for disadvantaged groups. It has provided educators with an alternative to individualistic and fatalistic accounts of school 'failure'. On the other hand it has done little to incorporate any input from the 'objects' of research. In this sense the sociology of education has, like much sociological discourse, been a 'colonising activity' (Lynch, 1999a, p.40). It has had little space for the voices or interests of children and young people, the main consumers of education. For example, research by Lynch (1999a, pp.217–59) has identified the lack of democracy *within* schools as a key issue for students but this has never been the focus of large-scale, government-funded research, nor is it likely to be.

The ESRI has been a major site of sociological research into Irish education. In common with its programme of research into socio-economic inequality (see Chapter 6), it has largely adopted a so-called 'neo-Weberian' focus (Drudy, 1991, p.112; Drudy and Lynch, 1993, p.39). It sees social inequality as an outcome of the skewed distribution of resources in Irish society such as property, skills and credentials and adopts a largely pluralist model of the state (see Chapter 4). The ESRI has focused on the two main issues that have dominated the international literature: the relationship between social inequality and education (especially as this relates to questions of intergenerational social mobility) and the links between gender and education, including such issues as subject choice, coeducation and exam performance. ESRI research tends to be highly quantitative (cf. Smyth, 1999) and policy-oriented; indeed it has contributed significantly to recent educational policy documents.

For critics such as Lynch the major shortcoming of Irish educational sociology is that it has failed to challenge the broader structural issues of poverty and class inequality. Research such as that carried out by the ESRI and the Education Research Centre at Drumcondra tends to focus on the distribution of chances within the existing, unequal and hierarchical, system. Within this dominant liberal model of meritocratic individualism (Drudy and Lynch, 1993, pp.49–50), issues of class or gender are not analysed as 'generative forces of action' within the education system but as attributes of individuals. This shortcoming has been replayed more recently in the shift of theoretical interest from issues of inequality to issues of 'difference', and a concern for other types of disadvantage based on ethnicity, culture and gender. Lynch (1999a, p.29) argues that this shift further marginalises fundamental issues of inequality.

The challenge of responding to these issues is taken up by Fagan who, as previously indicated, is one of the small number of Irish sociologists of education to adopt an overtly post-structuralist research strategy. Fagan's approach is to present a text based on interview material garnered from her subjects through what she terms (1995, p.95) 'a modernist social-research framework' and then to analyse it through alternative 'readings' or theoretical frameworks. The aim is twofold: to examine the usefulness of various widely-used theories, such as reproduction theory and resistance theory; and to provide a range of alternative ways to analyse the social reality in question. A major issue for Fagan is to move beyond theoretical analysis. For her, while the theoretical approaches discussed above do something to illuminate the experiences of early school leavers (her research focus) they are fatalistic with regard to outcome. They reflect 'a prevailing logic that shows *how it is* and gives us an understanding of *why it is* the way it is' (1995, p.121) — but go no further. Fagan's aim (like Lynch, 1999) is to develop an emancipatory politics out of her sociological analysis of education — a 'cultural and pedagogical politics of early school leaving'.

The move within the western sociology of education from 'class' to 'difference' may represent an avoidance of the most intractable issue in education, arising perhaps from a frustration with reformist approaches as well as reflecting a response to the demands of marginalised groups. In other words, three decades of educational reform, including the development of comprehensive education, widespread coeducation, extensive curriculum reform and changes in teaching practice have left patterns of class inequality in education largely unchanged. Therefore it is not entirely surprising that sociologists of education, in Ireland as elsewhere, have begun to enquire into the more fundamental levels of the philosophy of education, the microsociology of the teaching process and the discourses of power and language within which the educational subject is constituted. The danger is that, in shifting their focus to these areas, broader unresolved issues to do with poverty, class and exploitation may once more be left behind. It is fortunate that Irish sociologists of education are maintaining an interest in issues of class, power and inequality, as we will see below.

## DEFINING KNOWLEDGE: SHAPING THE CURRICULUM

The content of the curriculum — what is taught — is a key site of struggle in education. In Ireland this was particularly the case within the primary system. Historically the national schools were the locus of a battle over the hearts and minds of Irish children between the colonial state and the Catholic/nationalist opposition to it. According to Clancy (1995a, p.473) 'issues of moral socialisation took precedence over issues of technical socialisation', and the teaching of subjects such as Irish, history and religion assumed great importance in the independent state.

Many critics (though few sociologists) have drawn attention to the religious domination of the Irish education system. It is certainly true that Irish schools have to an extent been saturated with religion: religion may be 'fully integrated into the rest of the curriculum and . . . the ethos and "hidden curriculum" fully reflect the religious ideals of the school' (Clancy, 1995a, p.476). But the extent to which religion permeates the curriculum is variable. There is evidence (an Irish National Teachers' Organisation survey of 1996) that teachers are becoming resistant to their religious role in national schools, with a majority of 60 per cent wishing to relinquish it (Irish Times 21 September 1999). Similarly, religious ideas and ideals no longer permeate the content of what is taught. As Drudy and Lynch point out (1993, p.82), greater numbers of students now study:

scientific, commercial and technological subjects, which teach students to seek empirical proof for the existence of phenomena, to maximise profit, and to rely on technological solutions for human problems. Such principles are very much at variance with a faith based on dogma or belief in the efficacy of divine intervention for the resolution of human difficulties.

Apart from religious ideas, the education system seeks to inculcate a number of other qualities and values: key among these is that of achievement. As Clancy

(1995a, p.470) suggests, 'the differentiation which teachers make between students within the school prepares students for the differential allocation in the labour market.' The demands of the labour market are directly (in the gearing up of the Institutes of Technology to respond to 'skills shortages' identified by industry) or indirectly fed through to the education system. Through this process the value placed by the labour market on particular subjects reflected in the status or rewards accruing to different occupations shapes the evaluation of particular types of knowledge (Lynch, 1999a, p.284). The limited fields of endeavour that are recognised by the system are then further narrowed according to notions of ability. Ability is reduced to one's performance according to a set of standardised tests: ultimately the exam-based Leaving Certificate. There is little or no recognition that 'ability' is discursively created, dynamic, contingent and shaped by broader issues of class, ethnicity, age and gender.

Clancy alerts us (1995a, p.479) to the growing *instrumentalism* of the Irish education system. The official discourse on Irish education has come to be suffused with a concern for labour market issues and competitiveness to the detriment of more humanist concerns. Do business and industry have too much influence over what is taught and learnt through the Irish education system? Clancy suggests that it is not just a matter of successful interest groups but the discourse of education itself has shifted from its humanist base: 'the growth in provision and take-up of economically utilisable subjects on the post-primary school curriculum reflects the centrality of economic self-interest as a cultural value' (1995a, p.480). Similar trends exist in the tertiary sector where the language of 'total quality management', with its emphasis on 'benchmarking', 'best practice', 'stakeholders' and the student as customer, has come to dominate policy- and decision-making.

A Marxist approach to education looks critically at the content of the curriculum. It sees the focus on achievement as an ideological process that helps to underpin the logic of the capitalist system. There has been little such critical research examining the assumptions that underlie the curricula of Irish education or how they reflect the interests and views of the powerful in Irish society. This conclusion is hinted at by Clancy, very much a mainstream sociologist of education, though he does not mention capitalism *per se* when he says that the educational system is 'an instrument of cultural domination; its real function is best understood in terms of the need for social control in an unequal and rapidly changing social order' (1995a, p.471).

Lynch (1999a, p.260) argues more fundamentally that because of the power of ruling-class male social groups, 'only particular forms of knowledge have been legitimated within education.' These are forms of knowledge that are based on linguistic and, to a lesser extent, mathematical skills and abilities. Other competencies and qualities, such as artistic and creative ability, caring and empathetic skills, kinetic (movement) skills, lateral thinking and what Lynch terms 'personal intelligences' (1999a, p.275) are routinely neglected or ignored by the examination system that dominates Irish education. Lynch finds this deeply ironic (1999a, p.260) as:

> the educational institution has, in certain respects, become cut off from many of the lifeworlds and labour markets which it serves at the very time that educational credentials are being used more than ever to select and satisfy people within the labour market.

In other words, in a time when cultural diversity and creativity are becoming key economic resources in themselves, it can be said that education is in some ways becoming less functional for Irish society. This also applies to the skills required for 'love labour' — increasingly required activities of caring, nurturing and looking after others.

McSorley's (1997) Clondalkin study suggests that the content of the curriculum is unattractive and irrelevant to working-class students. Fagan's (1995) findings are very similar. She points out that the education system completely fails to reflect the reality of students from poor families. Thus, 'by not using the life experience of the young people as a basis from which to educate, and by not linking the background of the young people to the curriculum, the curriculum is irrelevant and meaningless' (1995, p.100). The result is a very high level of conflict between students and teachers and also between families and teachers.

## GENDER AND EDUCATION

Gender is central to the experience of education. People's experiences of 'being a boy' or 'being a girl' are shaped in many ways by the experience of schooling (Ryan, 1997). Here we indicate how the education process is crucial to the social construction of gender (itself discussed in some detail in Chapter 8). Drudy's (1991, p.115) review of Irish educational research suggests that gender has only become an issue since the 1980s. Since that time there has been a considerable amount of sociological research on gender and education in Ireland but this has tended to take place within a limited number of institutional contexts and from a rather narrow theoretical position. Lynch (1999a, p.135) points out that the dominant discourse in the Irish sociology of gender and education has been the liberal feminist discourse of *equality of opportunity*. In other words, it has been about identifying barriers to equality of opportunity within existing structures rather than challenging them in any fundamental way. Lynch suggests that there has been 'no substantive analysis of mainstream compulsory education in terms of its pedagogical, organisational or curriculum practices from a critical feminist standpoint' (1999a, p.134). Nor, it must be said, has there been any extensive analysis of the relationship between masculinity and education. Perhaps ironically this has only now started to occur as girls have begun to significantly outperform boys in public examinations. Overall, it can be said that the orthodoxy of hierarchical and meritocratic educational structures and discourses has not been effectively challenged.

Given that educational research has, as we have seen, tended to 'work within the system', there has been a tendency, reinforced by positivist models within social research, to measure 'equality' through indicators such as the number of women participating in particular educational courses; the number of men and, especially, women in non-traditional areas; or the number of images of men and women depicted in texts (Lynch, 1999a, p.135). Though we have an increasing quantity of information about gender in Irish education, this is rarely combined with a sensitivity to issues of class or ethnicity.

Historically Irish women have a history of higher participation in second-level education (partly due to a lack of alternative employment opportunities). Males and females are now equally represented in many aspects of education, with females now making up a slight majority (in the range 51 to 55 per cent) at post-primary level (Lynch, 1999a, p.141). Women have increased their level of participation in third-level study and now form the majority, rather than the minority, of students within Universities, teacher training colleges and even Institutes of Technology. Rates of participation across socio-economic groups are similar for males and females. Girls now outperform boys in the majority of subjects in second-level public examinations (Junior and Leaving Certificates), though the perception of 'male' subjects (such as technical drawing) and 'female' subjects (such as home economics) persists and is reflected in the distribution of exam candidates in these areas. (Lynch, 1999a, pp.142–3).

Notwithstanding a certain lack of theoretical adventurousness, a considerable range of sociological data on gender-related issues is now available. This includes social/historical analyses such as those collected in M. Cullen (1987), detailed statistical studies of gender-related issues (for example, Hannan et al., 1996) and significant overviews (for example, Lynch, 1999a, pp.134–161; O'Connor, 1998, pp.162–8; Drudy and Lynch, 1993, pp.167–205). We will now examine a small number of issues related to gender:

- the experience of one sector of the population — those on farms
- gender relationships in school, particularly in relation to coeducation
- sexuality within the school environment.

Finally in this section, we look briefly at the relative absence of sociological information in Ireland on boys and schooling.

One part of the Irish population that has been particularly successful at accessing education, especially third level, is the farming community, where participation rates are higher than for all other groups except for the managerial and professional class. Patricia O'Hara's research into the educational experiences of farm children, and the associated strategies of farm mothers, is an interesting illustration of how education intersects with broader gender, familial, demographic and economic processes.

Within the demographic and economic constraints of Irish farming, maternal support for children's education must be seen as a key element of the reproductive role of farm women. In an industry that promises only limited opportunities for economic survival, education is seen as a means to secure an off-farm livelihood. According to O'Hara (1998, p.136): 'farm women are the key architects of farm families' efforts to secure for their children desirable occupations outside of farming'. Women are the key influence over children in the goal of maximising educational opportunity.

In the period 1961 to 1971 the participation rate of farm children increased from 28 per cent to 55 per cent (O'Hara, 1998, p.137). By the early 1980s over two thirds of farmers' children were completing the Leaving Certificate, compared to little over half this for the children of the urban working class. By the late 1980s over three in ten of farmers' children that completed the Leaving Certificate went on to third level. Even on the smallest and poorest of agricultural holdings participation rates in third level were high. By 1992 very nearly half of farm children went on to full-time higher education, more than double that in 1980 (O'Hara, 1998, p.137). Farm children had the highest rate of participation in the then Regional Technical Colleges and the second highest rate (after professionals and managers) in universities.

Farm families were very adept at securing education grants: 'it seems that farm families, accustomed to dealing with eligibility criteria, form-filling and other bureaucratic procedures associated with EU and state aid to farming, have been quick to grasp the opportunities which state grants for third-level education, and latterly the EU Social Fund, afforded their children' (O'Hara, 1998, p.138). In addition, farm mothers actively support the education of their children in a number of important ways, for example, by supervising homework and attending parent–teacher meetings. There is evidence that on dairy farms the labour input of farm women generates crucial income for the support of children's education (O'Hara, 1998, p.146).

As previously mentioned, the proportion of farm *daughters* accessing third-level education is particularly high. As O'Hara remarks 'it is clear that farm families make exceptional efforts to educate their daughters' (1998, p.139). She argues that education was, and is, an important means of escape from the limited occupational opportunities offered by rural areas, and was also a way to avoid the patriarchal structures of Irish family farming. Educational success can offer rural women a measure of financial independence they could rarely achieve on the farm, given the male-dominated patterns of property transfer that persist in rural Ireland. O'Hara (1998, p.147) suggests that 'mothers' commitment to education for their children can be interpreted as a strategy of resistance to their own subordination within family farming and to farming as an occupation.' While clearly the specific experience of farm women cannot be extrapolated to all of Irish society, their experience reveals the importance of examining the mechanisms whereby educational choices are enacted and the specific cultural and economic contexts within which they are made.

Sociologists have demonstrated that educational institutions are key sites for the construction of gender identities. The work of researchers such as the Australian post-structuralist sociologist Bronwyn Davies (1990) has shown that gender is being formed from very early on in the education process, that is, in pre-school or play group. There is some evidence that, by the time they reach second-level school, girls have a poorer academic self-image (Lynch, 1999a, p.142). While high levels of stress have been identified in both male and female students, especially in exam classes (Hannan *et al.*, 1996, p.199), levels appear to be particularly high in all-girls secondary schools, perhaps related to the strongly academic focus combined with a strong emphasis on the personal formation of students in particular directions (Lynch, 1999a, p.229).

There has been considerable debate about the merits of coeducation in terms of its 'overall' benefits and whether it favours boys, or girls, or both. While Ireland has had a long history of segregated single-sex schooling at post-primary level, now the majority of pupils (about 60 per cent) are educated in coeducational environments (Smyth and Hannan, 1997, p.13). This applies particularly to those in the vocational, community and comprehensive school sectors. It has been argued that girls suffer from coeducational schooling, especially as they have been shown by some research to receive less attention and encouragement from teachers than do boys (Lynch, 1999a, p.143). A study carried out in Irish schools by Emer Smyth and Damien Hannan (1997) sought to examine the effects on girls of coeducation, in particular, whether a shift to non-segregated schooling adversely affects their educational and occupational achievements.

According to the authors of the study (1997, p.10), coeducation changes the patterns of interaction and the 'engenderment' of schools. International research remains inconclusive as to who benefits from coeducation; it is a very complex issue that requires careful disentanglement of the multitude of factors that shape students' school experiences. These include the social background and prior ability of students; school history, management, ethos and organisation; policies of selectivity of schools; and coeducation itself (Hannan *et al.*, 1996). The Irish research, which examined performance in Junior and Leaving Certificate examinations, showed that after other factors had been taken into consideration, the effects of coeducation on performance were minimal and were certainly less important than other factors such as social class and ability. One finding that did stand out was that girls in coeducational settings underperformed in the area of mathematics. While this finding will take further research in the Irish context to explain, it is suggested that this may be the outcome of dominant ideas among pupils, teachers and parents about the gender appropriateness of certain subjects.

There has been little research in Ireland that explores the nature of students' everyday school experience from a gender standpoint. Post-structuralist research methodology promises to uncover in detail how gender identities are created and sustained within the school context. Ryan (1997) examines how the discourse of 'essential' female sexuality has facilitated the regulation of girls in schools. Schools are often highly sexualised locations, though this is an aspect of education notable by its absence in nearly all educational research. The school is a site for the creation of all aspects of youth identity — including sexuality. Ryan (1997) is one of the few Irish sociologists to explore this field. Her small-scale study of girls attending six coeducational schools in the Dublin area sought to investigate youth sexuality as an aspect of the creation of gender identity in education. She remarks on the importance of 'reputation' and how it is understood in different ways for boys and for girls. Girls reported that they had to be seen to be attractive and interested in sex but not so interested that they could appear 'easy' or be branded a 'slut' — itself a complex and contradictory term. On the other hand, they could not appear too uninterested in sex and boys, for fear of being labelled 'frigid', 'stuck up' or 'lesbian'.

Other small-scale research carried out by Inglis of transition-year students (boys and girls) in a non-metropolitan school had similar findings, but they were presented in a more optimistic framework. Inglis (1998b, pp.145–6) concluded that 'pupils may be far more experienced and adventurous in their sexual attitudes and practices than either the teachers or the parents believe. Sex has become part of their lives. It is a central aspect of their everyday relations. . . . sexually active is seen as being the norm.' Information was obtained from the mass media and (occasionally) from parents but the main source was friends and siblings. Teachers and, especially, religious personnel were generally seen as being irrelevant. The key issues for students were related to what to do in situations like 'relationships, bad experiences, being drunk and having unprotected sex' (1998b, p.138). The main fears, especially for girls, were pregnancy and 'getting a reputation'. But Inglis found evidence of ultimate female control 'there was a sense that while avoiding pregnancy and a reputation was a girl's responsibility, girls ultimately had the final say as to what would and would not happen sexually' (1998b, p.143).

Both Ryan and Lynch, in separate research exercises, have observed behaviour in Irish schools that they would define as sexual harassment, including verbal denigration and unsolicited touching of female students and teachers. Ryan argues that there is no acceptable framework within schools for dealing with such abuse or harassment. Nor was there any discourse 'that supplied positive ways of thinking and talking about active adolescent female sexual desire and activity' (Ryan, 1997, p.32). Lynch (1999a, p.236) argues that 'gender inequality was not part of most students' daily vocabulary-of-analysis' and thus harassment was not identified or recognised within the institutions concerned.

We outline in Chapter 8 the neglect of issues of masculinity within Irish sociology. The same critique can be made in the area of education, for much the same reasons: there has been little examination of the specific experiences of boys or of the construction of masculinity through the practices and discourses of Irish education. Lynch (1999a, p.233) has suggested that in boys schools she studied, 'the equation of superior masculinity with physical prowess and sport was particularly evident in schools where sporting success was central to the school's sense of identity.' There is a perception that (especially working-class) male peer groups adopt a culture that is hostile to education. A cultural milieu of this type was described in Britain in Willis's *Learning to labour* (see above), but there has been no Irish equivalent study. A similar milieu is described in Fagan's analysis of early school leavers but this does not make any particular attempt to bring gender issues to the forefront. The gendered experiences of males at all levels of the education system is a rich area for future sociological research.

## EDUCATION AND CLASS INEQUALITY

As outlined in Chapter 6 there has been a major shift in the class basis of Irish society. Where formerly property was the main determinant of social wealth and position this has now been at least partly replaced by the ability to secure wages or salary in a competitive and dynamic labour market (Breen and Whelan, 1996, p.98). As a result there is now a closer link between educational attainment and labour market position. A key concern of sociologists of education, in Ireland as elsewhere, relates to how schools operate as a selection mechanism for future occupational positions: how do people acquire the qualifications that will provide them with the means to access scarce resources in the future?

There is now a considerable body of Irish sociological research that examines issues of educational opportunity and economic and class inequality. According to Lynch and O'Riordan (1999, p.93) this, as with other educational research, has been from within a positivist framework. They argue that the 'equality empiricists' have dominated the debate around educational inequality, framing it within a 'liberal political perspective and a broadly functionalist sociological tradition'. Within this approach the problem of class inequality in education is defined as a lack of opportunity to move upwards within an already class-stratified society. Lynch and O'Riordan conclude that, while this 'liberal model' helps to show how educational resources within the existing system are (mal)distributed, it does little to challenge the hierarchical nature of the system itself. It fails to critique the content and objectives of education and the broader systems of inequality that shape the nature and priorities of the system. For Lynch (1999a, p.252), 'while distributing more education to those groups who want it is crucial, it may also be necessary to change the education system itself to take account of the differences which various groups bring to that system. Schooling needs to recognise and respect difference if it is to treat all people with equality of respect. It cannot assume that all people will fit the one mould.'

As indicated by Lynch and O'Riordan, the Irish 'equality empiricists' (largely located within, or connected to, the ESRI) have produced a sizeable body of data in relation to the links between social inequality and educational participation and outcomes. This research continues a process of research that has been taking place in Ireland since the mid-1960s (Drudy and Lynch, 1993, p.141). The government-sponsored *Investment in education* report of 1966 (carried out by economists, not sociologists) revealed the links between educational and class inequality. The considerable investment in education that took place in the wake of this report (including the introduction of 'free' secondary education) led to a growth in educational participation, but this was not equitably distributed across the population. Research by Clancy (1982; 1988) during the 1980s showed that in terms of access to tertiary-level education, investment in secondary education had actually contributed to an *increase in inequality*: those favoured in class terms were better able to make use of the new educational opportunities that had been opened up.

Research into (male) social mobility in Ireland by Whelan and Whelan (1984) also demonstrated the links between education and class. It suggested that access to educational opportunity was a major factor in the 'inheritance' of class inequality and that this pattern was particularly marked in Ireland, at least during the 1970s. Subsequent research by Breen and Whelan on data from the late 1980s revealed that little had altered: a 'modest' change for men and none at all for women. They concluded (1996, p.126) that:

> Despite increasing overall levels of educational attainment the pattern of educational social fluidity has remained unaltered. There is a continuing strong link between class origins and educational attainment.

This can be seen clearly from the data presented in Figure 7.2. Over half the children of those in the 'higher professional' social group leave school with five or more Leaving Certificate honours; only 4 per cent of those with parents who are unskilled manual workers enjoy the same outcome. The implications for further study and employment are clear.

The relationship between educational attainment and subsequent labour force outcomes has also endured and exhibits, 'a relatively straightforward pattern . . . whereby class origins are largely translated into educational qualifications which then determine the distribution of relative chances of access to the more desirable classes' (Breen and Whelan, 1996, p.126). Overall, while investment in education in Ireland has led to an increase in educational attainment and performance at all levels, the differentials between classes have not diminished. Rather the increased emphasis on education as a mechanism for social advantage has seen the already advantaged groups in Irish society further secure their position.

An HEA report (Technical Working Group (TWG), 1995), drawing on the work of a number of sociological researchers, has identified three crucial schooling

## Figure 7.2 Educational performance and family background

| Family background | No qualifications % | Junior cycle % | Senior cycle | | |
| | | | Level 1 Pass LC % | Level 2 Up to 4 hons LC % | Level 3 5 hons or more LC % |
| --- | --- | --- | --- | --- | --- |
| Unskilled manual | 16.2 | 31.2 | 29.4 | 19.0 | 4.1 |
| Other agricultural | 12.3 | 24.7 | 27.9 | 22.2 | 10.7 |
| Semi-skilled manual | 9.9 | 28.4 | 33.9 | 22.4 | 7.1 |
| Other non-manual | 7.7 | 21.7 | 29.4 | 32.4 | 8.7 |
| Skilled manual | 5.9 | 18.1 | 30.6 | 35.9 | 9.4 |
| Intermediate non-manual | 3.5 | 11.9 | 20.2 | 46.2 | 17.9 |
| Farmers | 2.7 | 13.9 | 20.2 | 46.5 | 16.7 |
| Self-employed, managers | 1.8 | 7.8 | 17.0 | 46.7 | 27.2 |
| Salaried employees | 1.6 | 4.7 | 21.8 | 44.7 | 26.7 |
| Lower professional | 0.4 | 3.4 | 10.2 | 45.4 | 40.1 |
| Higher professional | 0.0 | 2.9 | 6.8 | 37.0 | 52.9 |
| Low status | 9.0 | 22.6 | 30.1 | 30.3 | 8.0 |
| Average | 5.7 | 16.3 | 24.0 | 37.4 | 16.7 |
| High status | 2.0 | 9.3 | 17.1 | 45.2 | 26.3 |

(*Source*: Department of Education and Science, 1998, p.27)

transition points at which the effects of socio-economic background are particularly significant. The first of these relates to whether a student continues in school long enough to take the Leaving Certificate or becomes an 'early school leaver'. While a fifth of all students left school without reaching Leaving Certificate level, only 3 per cent of those with higher professional backgrounds failed to make this transition compared with almost half of those from unskilled manual backgrounds. This pattern is long established. Research by Rudd on early school leavers in 1966/7 (cited in Clancy, 1995a, p.484) revealed that the 15 per cent of students who left after primary school (note the change in measurement) were predominantly from the unskilled/semi-skilled working-class and farming groups. One determinant of early leaving is reading ability, which has been shown to be linked to social class background. McSorley (1997, p.39) reports large differences between children who attended schools in outer-suburban Clondalkin and inner-city Dublin, where 19 to 35 per cent of children were two to three years behind in reading ability, and those at school in Rathgar, a wealthy suburb, where no children were below their expected ability for age. The implications of leaving school without qualifications are severe. There is a strong relationship between lack of qualifications and unemployment. In 1993, 78 per cent of those without a formal qualification remained unemployed after leaving school, this figure dropped to just 30 per cent for those with a Leaving Certificate (Allen, 1998, p.199). Of those unemployed in 1997, 63 per cent had not completed secondary education (Department of Education and Science, 1998, p.25).

A second key educational transition relates to the level of achievement of those who remain to complete the Leaving Certificate. Here the level of achievement varies widely according to socio-economic group. As Smyth and Hannan (1997, p.16) point out 'most of the difference between schools in average Leaving Certificate performance is due to differences in the social background and prior performance characteristics of their pupils'. While fewer than a third of those from unskilled and semi-skilled manual backgrounds attained at least two grade Cs at higher level, over three-quarters of those from the higher and lower professional groups did so. This raises many issues in relation to the 'neutrality' of the examination system as a measure of 'merit'. As Smyth and Hannan (1997, p.15) indicate (Figure 7.3) the constellation of factors shaping 'exam performance' is complex.

The third transition relates to the destinations of those who do successfully complete the Leaving Certificate. While overall participation in third-level education has increased dramatically since the 1970s, in Ireland as in most western countries, very significant differences in terms of social class persist. In an analysis

**Figure 7.3 Factors that may influence exam performance.**

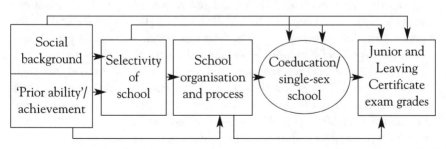

(*Source*: Smyth and Hannan, 1997, p.15)

of entrants to third-level education during the period 1980 to 1992, Clancy (1995b) found that while the participation rates of most groups had increased, with some reduction in social class disparities, very significant levels of inequality remained, particularly for those with more modest levels of educational achievement. For example, a young person whose father was a 'higher professional' was about six times more likely than the child of an unskilled or semi-skilled manual worker to enter a third-level institution. The children of unemployed fathers are also seriously under-represented among third-level entrants. Such differences may be expressed in spatial terms: admission to third level is just 4.5 per cent for young people from the working-class Dublin suburb of Clondalkin but it rises to 54 per cent for those from the wealthy area of Rathgar (McSorley, 1997, p.39). For those that make it to college, Clancy also found significant social class selectivity between different types of institution and, within institutions, between different fields of study.

A final set of barriers may exist for those who wish to engage in adult education. There is consistent evidence (Drudy and Lynch, 1993, pp.261–7; Department of Education and Science, 1998) that those already disadvantaged in the education process, such as early school leavers, are also excluded from adult education. Barriers to participation include financial constraints, lack of child care provision, entry requirements and lack of appropriate information and guidance. Thus, suggest Drudy and Lynch (1993, p.262) adult education has not become a viable 'second-chance' option for the majority of those that have already been let down by the education system.

Given that such disparities have been long recognised in Ireland and that the state has made some attempts to increase equality of opportunity through its funding mechanisms and policy decisions, why is it that access to education remains so skewed by social class background? There have been a number of explanations. Some of these locate the causes of inequality in cultural factors, others in the economic sphere, while others are more focused on the content and nature of the educational process itself.

In a study of young people who had dropped out of the primary and post-primary school systems in the outer Dublin suburb of Clondalkin, McSorley (1997, p.2) reports that home-based factors related to poverty, parental separation, unemployment, imprisonment, chronic illness and addiction are 'pivotal', as are parental attitudes and behaviour. McSorley suggests that parents in deprived areas such as parts of Clondalkin, who are socially and economically very disadvantaged, tend to 'lack the economic, academic and emotional resources to ensure their children are up, fed, dressed, with homework properly done and uniforms, books and lunch all ready in time for the school day'. Long-term and intergenerational unemployment, addiction problems and familial conflict each contribute to a breakdown in structure and routine that is inimical to academic success.

Many of the parents interviewed in the course of McSorley's research said they had 'hated' secondary school and had left as early as possible, without any qualifications. Of those interviewed, only 6 per cent had a qualification as high as the Intermediate Certificate and 59 per cent had left after primary school (the average age of respondents was thirty-three years so most of these parents would have had available to them the 'free' secondary education system introduced in the late 1960s). These parents now have far more positive views about primary school, seen as participatory and welcoming, than they do about secondary school, which remains an 'alien environment'. This may relate to the low levels of expectation that these parents have for their children: less than a third expect that their children will complete the Leaving Certificate (McSorley, 1997, p.27).

Many of McSorley's findings reflect earlier research carried out by Fagan (1995) who explored the lives of some inner-city 'school drop-outs'. Absenteeism was a major contributory factor to school failure — whether this was 'going on the hop', as described by Fagan's respondents, or missing school with parental knowledge and consent, as McSorley found to be widespread in her Clondalkin study. Parents sometimes actively encourage their children (especially girls) to stay away from school. Pupils often have to look after ill parents or siblings and may miss large amounts of school at times of family bereavement. Fagan (1995, p.48) argues that school drop-outs are typically 'surrounded by a community of early school leavers', including their peers, parents and others. There is little positive orientation to education; rather, an instrumental approach to work. The opportunity to gain an independent income is highly valued, both by school students and their families.

There has been considerable resistance to culturally based analyses such as those sketched above. It has been suggested that they do no more than reflect the particular sets of assumptions and values that (almost universally middle-class) researchers bring to the research process (Drudy and Lynch, 1993, pp.149–51). Lynch (1999a, p.112) offers evidence, provided by community activists, that working-class communities and parents do value education highly. Fagan (1995, p.83) remarks that a deficit account assumes a deficiency on the part of the individual, family and community. Clancy (1995a, p.489) argues that there is a need to move away from such culturalist accounts: for him it is more important to examine the class-based nature of the education system itself: 'instead of focusing on the class characteristics of those who succeed and those who fail it is appropriate to examine the class characteristics of the educational experience at which they succeed or fail. This reorientation in approach represents an important development within the sociology of education'. The implication of this approach is that if there is large-scale failure within a system, it pays to look at features of that system itself.

Bourdieu's theory of *cultural capital* places a discussion of cultural factors within the broader context of the class-based nature of the education system. For Bourdieu cultural capital refers to the ideas, practices and artefacts that are highly valued in our society (see Chapters 6 and 11). There is some evidence that particular forms of cultural expression are favoured in schools and that more advantaged students have greater cultural capital through access to resources like private tuition, books, computers, leisure activities and travel (Drudy and Lynch, 1993, pp.156–7). Though Bourdieu's theories have had some impact on Irish educational research there has been much debate over their usefulness. In particular, it is argued that such an approach can divert attention back to the cultural aspects of students and families and away from the broader question of economic inequality.

Critical researchers argue that such economic barriers remain the most important determinants of educational success. Drudy and Lynch (1993, p.161) suggest that poverty is an educational issue that has been neglected. The voice of the poor is effectively excluded from debates about educational inequality. Poverty makes it more difficult for working-class students to maximise any advantages that the system can offer. Furthermore, parents experiencing poverty find it difficult to experience a positive relationship with the education system. For Lynch (1999a, p.240) the persistence of poverty challenges the notion of choice in relation to access to education: 'those who have resources can exercise choices and those without resources generally cannot, or have relatively restricted choices depending on the area they live in.' McSorley's research (1997) indicates that teachers in Clondalkin schools perceive the problems of early school leaving as being connected with poverty and related social factors. The unemployment rate in the local authority housing estates in the Clondalkin areas studied can be as high as 73 per cent.

In addition to culturalist and economic accounts, a third set of arguments relates to the organisation of schools themselves: the *school effects approach* (Smyth, 1999). This involves the study of a variety of schools to determine whether, and how, the organisation of the school as an institution has an important impact on the academic and social development of its pupils. The issue of 'school effectiveness' is a controversial and complex one, brought into focus through the activity of governments, particularly that of the UK, where school performance has become a contentious political issue and there is an increasing marketisation of education. Rigorous and regular school inspections, the compilation of performance indicators and the newspaper publication of 'league tables' for British schools has helped to generate a climate for a considerable academic 'school effects' literature (Smyth, 1999, pp.1–11). But it is very difficult to say what makes an effective school. A school that is effective in one area, may not be in others. The criteria for measurement are highly contentious.

Smyth (1999, p.215) reports that gender, class and age remain as key predictors of pupil performance in Irish schools. But aspects of the organisation of schools are important: 'school matters'. For example, the practice of 'streaming' students according to a measure of ability is shown by Smyth (1999, pp.31–6) to have an overall negative effect. It increases the inequality of outcomes and reduces overall average marks, particularly at Junior Certificate level. Restriction of subject choice also has negative effects. It is better to allow students to sample the maximum number of subjects and to optimise the possibility that they will choose subjects they like. Smyth also reports that an enhanced level of participation in school management by the various groups — students, parents and teachers — involved in the schooling process leads to increased school effectiveness. The benefits of a clear and consistent disciplinary environment are demonstrated, as are those of positive teacher/pupil interaction and provision of feedback by teachers to students.

McSorley (1997, p.1) reports that in north and south-west Clondalkin over a third of the school-going population is absent on any given day and more than half the population leave school by age fifteen. Part of the reason, she suggests, is that 'the academic content and organisational structures of school do not meet the needs of poor and disadvantaged pupils.' Many early school leavers come into direct and frequent conflict with the structures, ethos and everyday practices of school. They have discipline problems, poor relationships with teachers, experience of bullying, a perception that there are 'too many subjects' of limited relevance, too much homework, and a view that school is 'too hard' and 'boring' (McSorley, 1997, p.31). Clondalkin parents report that the middle-class value system that typified schools was a major contributory factor to poor teacher/pupil and teacher/parent relations. Parents questioned the purpose of the education their children were receiving and wanted them to do more practical subjects such as typing and car mechanics. Fagan (1995, p.103) suggests that the education system actively colludes in absenteeism by not dealing effectively with the issue. She argues that a genuine response would entail a radical examination of the aims and objectives of education: 'obviously the problem is so pervasive, indeed structural, that to tackle it would be to call the whole educational system into question.'

The milieu of the working-class school itself is a cause of educational inequality. Research by McSorley and Fagan shows that there is an institutional devaluation of working-class culture within educational institutions. We have seen Fagan's remarks about the gulf that exists between the conventional academic curriculum and the reality of life for poor and many working-class pupils. The lack of respect for the culture of students was reflected in a lack of respect by teachers for pupils (which was reciprocated). According to Fagan (1995, p.19) for some of her respondents, ongoing psychological battle and psychological torture occurred in the classroom. As a consequence, for the pupils placed in the lowest-grade class and where there is no hope of them progressing at school, no respect is felt for any teachers whatsoever, and so indiscipline reigns and the teacher is the enemy (Fagan, 1995, p.19). The outcome was a repertoire of resistance that spanned 'bunking off', 'messing' in class, through to open violence against teachers and school property. Ultimately, concluded Fagan, the response available to pupils alienated from the system was 'extremely destructive as opposed to culturally creative' (1995, p.119).

Issues related to ethnicity have yet to receive much prominence in sociological analyses of Irish education, though there has been some concern with the (negative) experience of Travellers. According to Kenny (1997) one-third of primary-school-aged Travellers are 'fully integrated' into primary schools, one-third have specialised support or classes and a third remain outside the formal educational system. For Kenny, improvement of the educational experience for Travellers depends on proactive change within schools: 'if education provision, from the central policy-makers through to the local classrooms, were informed by principles of anti-racism and inter-culturalism, the need for special support for Travellers would be pared back to its true extent, because at least an alien school programme would not be confounding the difficulties confronting Traveller children' (1997, p.66). There is still little enthusiasm among the Travelling community for second-level education and there is a major challenge in reconciling a nomadic and culturally distinct lifestyle with an increasingly credentialised society.

Lynch and O'Riordan (1999, p.122) point out the important fact that educational disadvantage within Irish society can only be fully understood in terms of the *advantages* enjoyed by others. They argue that:

> The financial, cultural and educational experiences of working-class students need not, in and of themselves, create educational inequality; what creates inequality is the fact that others have differential access to resources, incomes wealth and power which enables them to avail of opportunities presented in education in a relatively more successful manner.

In very many ways the education system has been structured by the advantaged in order to maintain their position. As well as operating within a system that reflects their economic and cultural interests, wealthier students are able to purchase on the private market goods and services (grinds, computers, books, foreign travel) that give them an educational advantage. They enjoy better study conditions and experience fewer pressures to take up part-time or full-time work.

The facilities and opportunities available to more advantaged groups in education relate to how the process itself is perceived. Allen (1998, p.202) makes the point, for example, that whereas training for the long-term unemployed is seen as a 'social cost', similar education provided for graduates is defined as an 'investment'. Such analysis may help to explain the consistent enactment of education policies (such as 'free fees' in secondary and more recently third-level education) that disproportionately benefit the already well-off (Clancy, 1995a, p.485); and the neglect of areas (in particular, primary and adult education) that have a greater capacity to lead to social equality.

Lynch and O'Riordan (1999, p.122) argue, 'those whose own class are the definers of what is culturally and educationally valuable in the first instance, are strongly positioned to be the major beneficiaries of educational investment'. Historically in Ireland there is a strong discourse, supported by church and state, that favours academic education. Academic education, translated into high

Leaving Certificate honours, can be used by the advantaged to gain access to prestigious third-level and professional courses in fields such as law, medicine and dentistry; thus, social and economic power is maintained.

## POSTSCRIPT: EDUCATION IN THE AGE OF INFORMATION TECHNOLOGY

> Information technology is dramatically reshaping the classroom. As we enter the Digital Age, technology will become an integral part of the learning environment at every level of education — primary, secondary, and third level. Formal education will not be confined exclusively to the classroom: instead a major part of a child's learning experience will be in the home. Nor will education be something that is undertaken solely in the early part of one's life. In the Digital Age, people will be life-long learners, continually replenishing their knowledge-base and skills. (Forbairt, 1996, p.19)

This statement, taken from the publication, *Ireland: the digital age, the internet*, published by the industry development agency Forbairt, is reflective of much thinking about the future of education. Its unbounded faith in technology should make any sociologist prickle with suspicion. In view of our discussion of the various aspects of social inequality and education, there are important questions to be asked about the future direction of education in Ireland.

A remarkable thing about education is that despite the impact of technologies such as video and computers (and earlier the film strip and 'fuzzy felt'), the practice of school-based education has remained remarkably static (Lynch, 1999a, p.276). A teacher, popularly regarded as an 'expert' either in a particular field or in the practice of teaching, or both, instructs an individual or group and it is assumed, or hoped, that some type of knowledge transfer takes place. This remains the dominant model of teaching, even if 'chalk and talk' is replaced by video, satellite delivery or computer-aided assessment.

Over the last decade there has been great enthusiasm among some educationists, policy-makers and governments about the capacity for new information technologies (IT), in particular the Internet, to radically change the nature of the education system — an enthusiasm reflected in the extract above. There are at least two questions of interest here to sociologists:

- Will a change in technology really lead to the hoped-for changes in teaching and learning? In other words, to what extent is education technologically determined?
- If changes in teaching and learning do take place, what are the implications for the social structuring of education discussed in this chapter?

The incorporation of new technologies, from the fountain pen to the television, has always been a part of education. There is a long history of enthusiastic promotion of 'learning machines' that have promised to revolutionise the teaching process. But sociologists have generally expressed a scepticism that new technologies in general, and IT in particular, will lead to a radical change in the broader structures that shape the experience of education. For example, research by Baines focuses attention on the relations of inequality that are built into, and intensified by, the 'technologisation' of education. She points out (1992, p.79) that visions of technological change can be 'very powerful and may become hardened into policy decisions which materially affect the distribution of resources and the availability of options'. Her research casts doubt on any notion that educational technology of itself has the capacity to challenge social inequalities.

The current enthusiasm for IT is built upon a number of assumptions: that it is becoming ubiquitous; that it is neutral; and that it has the capacity to change the relationships of power in education, in particular, to shift power from the 'teacher' to the 'learner'. The ubiquity of new technologies is far from being the case. Despite quite extensive investment in IT only a minority of Irish homes have access to personal computers and still fewer are connected to the Internet. On a global scale, the vast majority of the world's population has no access to any telephone, let alone more sophisticated communications technologies. The processes of planned obsolescence built into computer products means that there will always be a majority whose hardware and/or software is out of date. IT usage is inevitably shaped by social inequality and therefore, within education, less-advantaged learners are less likely to own up-to-date computers, to have the privacy to use them effectively, to have computer-owning friends or to have parents with relevant computer skills.

If the ubiquity of IT is something of a myth, so too is the notion that the technology is somehow neutral. There is a considerable sociological literature that demonstrates how technology is always imbued with social relations: that it is a concrete manifestation of social values and relations of inequality. As Baines suggests (reflecting the view of many feminist researchers), 'technology , far from being a neutral backdrop to the play of gender relations, may be intimately entwined with the gender identity of human beings and a deadly weapon in the ever deeper entrenchment of gender practices' (1992, p.80). This is no less the case for educational technology. The blackboard, for example, is a technology that reflects a particular hierarchy between teacher and student; further reflected in the layout of the typical classroom. Similarly the PC, despite its recent domestication within the home, remains associated with technology, masculinity and instrumentality. This is not to suggest that the 'genderedness' of technologies are fixed. The telephone and the radio, for example, are two technologies that have largely escaped their hi-tech, masculine image and have been appropriated by women (though radio DJs and telecom engineers are still almost always male).

The final question is perhaps the most interesting: does IT have the capacity to alter the teaching/learning process and to shift the relationships of power and inequality that typify the institution of education? Certainly the rhetoric of educationalists suggests that it will. Almost any description of IT in education is accompanied by phrases like 'lifelong learning' and 'self-directed education'. It is argued that the teacher will shift from instructor to facilitator; will no longer be a fount of expert knowledge but an expert guide to the world of information and ideas available on-line and elsewhere. The roles of teacher and learner will blur and merge and the relationship between the two become one of shared excitement in discovery, rather than hostility and control.

What is missing from nearly all such images is any consideration of the social impacts of such shifts. When they are mentioned it is almost always in a positive tone. There is little serious consideration of how any fundamental change in the nature of educational practice may affect the broader institution; nor how those institutional constraints may impinge upon the direction and extent of change. In a discourse highly reminiscent of modernisation theory, the enthusiasts are apt to brand those that 'resist the inevitable' as Luddites, technophobes or just 'traditional'.

But we may well ask questions such as:

How will the existing powerful groups in education (teachers, the church, the state) respond to a process that places more power in the hands of the student?
What will be the response of teachers to the loss of control over what students can and do read, see and learn?
How will students' self-identity be shaped if the world of cyberspace becomes as important to them as that of the schoolyard?
How will the state address inequalities of access to sophisticated computing technology when it cannot even provide equality in terms of books, toilet facilities or sports equipment?
What is the role of a classroom, or a school building, or a school, if learners can gain direct access to any information, knowledge or guidance that they wish?

We do not suggest that the school is an outmoded institution. History demonstrates its remarkable durability. But education will certainly continue to provide difficult and interesting social and sociological challenges.

# 8

# Gender, sexuality and the family

The most significant development in the discipline of sociology in the last three decades has been the rise to prominence of gender issues. This is related to two key processes:

- the reconstruction of western (and also non-western) societies in terms of occupational structures, secularisation and demography as outlined elsewhere in this book
- the rise of the modern women's movement and the permeation of feminist and gender-oriented discourses into all aspects of social life.

Similarly, many of the major issues of public and private social and political debate in Ireland for the past thirty years have related to issues of gender, sexuality and the family. The country has been convulsed by a series of conflicts around the, often linked, issues of contraception, adoption, abortion, censorship, homosexuality, sex education and divorce. In addition, the abuse of children and women — physical, sexual and psychological — has come to prominence in the media and the legal and welfare systems. These revelations and debates have placed sex, gender, the body and the family at the centre of arguments that have also brought into play discussions of morality, freedom, personal integrity, authority and control. For many participants and observers these conflicts and exposés have been central to the question of modernity and Irish society. For many, the vigorous public arguments over issues of the family, sexuality and gender are indicative that, for better or for worse, Ireland is becoming an increasingly modern society.

There are at least three common viewpoints about how relationships between men and women have changed in Ireland over the last three decades. One view is that there has been a huge amount of positive change and progress. Commentators point to the election of Presidents Mary Robinson and Mary McAleese and the prominence of women politicians such as Mary Harney, Liz O'Donnell and Mary O'Rourke; female sportspeople such as Michelle de Bruin, Sonia O'Sullivan and Catherina McKiernan; and the appointment of women as pilots and High Court Judges. They may also cite the exposure of abuse against women and children, the conviction of the perpetrators and the calling to account of the institutions of church and state; the increasing involvement of men in housework and child care; the cultural prominence of women artists, writers and musicians; and the huge shift of women into the paid workforce and into formerly male-dominated occupations. They may draw attention to the achievement of legal equality for men and women; the gradual development of women's health services, child care services, coeducational schools and youth groups; and so on. To such commentators these factors are often seen as further indicators that Ireland is becoming a 'modern European state'.

A second view is essentially opposed to the first, stressing how *little* has changed in Ireland and how much gender inequality and differentiation remains. This view propounds the continued real discrimination against women in many areas of employment and social life; women's inferior position with regard to wealth, property and income; the continuing economic dependence of women and children on men; and the continued existence of widespread violence inflicted by men upon women and children. We may be reminded of the fact that Irish social institutions such as the law, medicine, the media, the churches, business and government continue to be dominated by males; of the persistence of stereotyped images of masculinity and femininity within our culture; and of the failure of society and government to respond to key issues such as child care, abortion, care of the elderly and other social concerns.

A third and developing view is that the nature of gender inequality is changing and that increasingly *men* are disadvantaged within Irish society. This argument points to men's poorer health status and shorter life expectancy; to the academic weakness of boys and suggestions that the educational environment has become 'feminised'. This approach can be summed up in the popular phrase: 'boys are the new girls'. There is concern over males' higher level of exposure to violence and to their high tendency towards suicide and road trauma. Men have campaigned against their perceived marginalisation within the new forms of family and over legal decisions in relation to custody of and access to children. Overall, there are concerns over the inability of men to adjust to changes in society, education and the workplace and to develop new models of masculinity. The existence of these three sets of views (and others) — which in turn may all overlap and coexist — indicates something of the complexities of the gender issue.

Despite the emergence of gender as a significant category of analysis in global sociology, and the importance of gender-related social issues in Irish society, it has tended to be played down in many texts dealing with Irish society (O'Connor, 1998, p.6). But, increasingly, gender issues have underpinned important areas of sociological research in Ireland including, for example, rural life, education and religion (discussed accordingly throughout this book).

The topic of gender is open to discussion and analysis from any number of vantage points. In recent decades important gender-based geographies, histories, cultural studies and psychologies have emerged, along with numerous studies from within other disciplinary areas, that have attempted to examine the position of women and men in the context of Irish society and its institutions. Of equal importance, there has been a concerted effort to change the paradigms within which we think about society, to move away from a male-centred or 'malestream' way of looking at the world and to adopt a view that reflects the experience of all people. We would argue that, within this re-thinking of the world, a sociological perspective is important and that the tools offered by sociology can provide us with useful knowledge about how society's structures, institutions, discourses and processes have helped to shape the relationships between men and women and how these relationships have been interpreted. Conversely, a focus on the experiences of commonality, difference and inequality within gender relationships is a crucial part of any thoroughgoing sociological analysis.

This chapter is not an attempt to produce a comprehensive sociology of gender in an Irish context. There are already excellent volumes that do that in far more detail than we can attempt here (see, especially, Byrne and Leonard, 1997; O'Connor, 1998; Galligan, 1998a) — though there is as yet little published work in Ireland on the nature of men and masculinity (an exception is McKeown *et al.*, 1999). Here, we limit ourselves to:

- outlining the conceptual basis for a sociological examination of gender
- providing an overview of how issues of gender have been related to Ireland's development and identity
- examining some issues in relation to gender and work, family and power
- exploring some aspects of the sociological study of sexuality in Ireland.

In summary, in other parts of this book, we discuss how gender relates to issues of:

- agriculture and industrial development (Chapter 3)
- education (Chapter 7)
- health (Chapter 9)
- crime (Chapter 10)
- consumption (Chapter 16)
- the emergence of the women's movement (Chapter 15).

Additionally, gender as an analytical category makes its presence felt in a more diffuse way throughout all chapters of the book.

## SEX AND GENDER

It is important, and useful, at this stage to address some questions of definition. In particular, the differentiation between the concepts of *sex* and *gender* is important in the development of a sociological understanding of the relationships between women and men. Sex is commonly held to refer to the differing physical attributes, genital arrangements, chromosomal structures, reproductive systems and secondary sexual characteristics such as distribution of body hair, breast development and so on. Sex gives rise to two categories: *female* and *male*. Gender refers to the *meanings* that arise out of sexual classification; and to the socially constructed experiences and identities that arise from assumed sexual differences. The clues to such gender identities are found in the physical attributes of sex and in a whole gamut of qualities and activities, ranging from social attitudes to style of dress, work performed, emotional make-up. The categories that gender gives rise to in western societies are *feminine* and *masculine*. The word 'gender' has in many situations become a euphemism for 'women': 'gender studies' has come to mean 'women's studies' and a politician may refer to 'gender equality' when what they mean is 'more opportunities for women'. However, it is important to emphasise that, in sociology, issues of gender are to do with all aspects of sexual difference and identity and relate to the experiences of men *and* women.

While the distinction between sex and gender has been very significant in emphasising the social constructedness of gender, it may not now be as useful as it once was (Oakley, 1998). In particular, there has been a tendency to link sex to the *natural* and gender to the *social*. In other words, sexual characteristics are those you are born with while gender attributes are developed after birth. A whole range of scientific research has now begun to challenge these assumptions and the distinction is becoming increasingly blurred. But this discussion is beyond the scope of this chapter; here we will maintain a focus on gender as it is the socially constructed categories of masculinity and femininity that concern us. For simplicity we will use the terms 'men' and 'women', and 'female' and 'male' — though we are aware that these tend to emphasise 'natural difference' more than we would like.

## THEORISING GENDER

## Sociobiology

There is a strong set of ideas, found both in common-sense and academic theories, that the differences between men and women are founded on a 'natural' basis. Writers point to *biological* differences such as those found in brain structure, hormones or body size, shape and strength. Men, for example, are typified as aggressive and goal-driven and women as submissive and emotional. It is argued that such differences provide an explanation, and often a justification, for differential outcomes in regard to sex roles, occupational segregation or inequality. The search for 'natural' explanations may be particularly intense at a time when the common assumptions about gender relationships are under threat.

It seems we have moved on from a time when women were seen to be naturally weak, emotionally unstable and believed to have smaller brains than men, but the belief in a direct biological basis for gender difference and inequality persists. The most recent research in this area tends to focus on genes (for example, a gene for 'aggressiveness') and on the nature of hormonal influences. But for sociologists there can never be a simple or automatic link between any biological basis and social outcomes: even the most extreme of biological variations must be mediated by social processes. Nevertheless, the interdisciplinary perspective known as sociobiology has sought to explain certain aspects of human social behaviour — including those aspects related to gender difference — in biological terms. Sociobiology has always been intensely controversial as there is a fine line between explaining differences in terms of a biological basis and *justifying* them in these terms. When the differences concerned are expressed as social inequalities, this becomes a highly emotive field.

## Patriarchy

The concept of patriarchy has come to refer to the systematic patterning of society in such a way that men dominate, exploit and oppress women (O'Connor, 1998, p.7). For O'Connor (1998, p.13) a variety of everyday taken-for-granted practices reflect and reinforce patriarchal control, including practices and processes within the family; in interpersonal relationships; within the paid and unpaid workforce; in consumption; and in the bureaucratic structures of the state and the economy. The problem with patriarchy is that it appears to be both universal and timeless. Though a number of matriarchal societies have been identified through anthropological studies and although some societies, such as hunter–gatherer societies, appear to display less gender inequality than our own, all known societies can be seen to be patriarchal to some extent. As patriarchy has been identified as a universal quality of extant human societies, it has been criticised as an essentialist and fatalistic concept, that adds little to our understanding. For sociologists it is a description rather than an explanation. It is certainly the case that all societies are differentiated by gender and have been dominated in various ways by men. The question is, *why?*

## Sociological theories

It can be argued that theories derived from sociobiology *and* theories of patriarchy are non-sociological, in that they are *essentialist*. In other words, they fail to examine how gender differences are created and expressed through social processes. Conversely, sociological theories attempt to trace how gender difference is constituted within particular types of social institutions, processes and historical contexts, and to explain why it is that gender inequality exists and is reproduced within society. There are many varied sociological theories of gender, including broad-brush theories in relation to the historical origins and global experience of gender inequality; middle-range theories about how gender is structured in and through social institutions like the family, the educational system and the state; and micro-level theories that seek to explain how gender is constructed through and shapes phenomena such as conversation and everyday social interaction. Furthermore, sociological theories reflect the full range of political positions that exists in relation to gender, from conservative and reactionary to radical and revolutionary. It is therefore very difficult to summarise and convey the diversity of sociological approaches to gender. Here we can only briefly mention the main theoretical stances that sociologists adopt in relation to gender issues.

For *functionalists* gender relationships and differences are seen as crucial to the effective functioning of society. Gender differences serve an integrative function in society: they help to bind members together. Thus, masculinity and femininity are seen as a complementary set of roles that span the family (in particular), the public sphere and the workplace. Women are responsible for the domestic arena, for the management of family life, and the socialisation of children; while men are to be found in the public sphere, the world of paid work and making connections to the broader world outside the family. Socialisation, for functionalists, is among other things the preparation of people for the 'proper' fulfilment of such sex roles. Males are brought up to be rational, competitive and instrumental; females to be affective, empathetic and co-operative. Subsequent social interaction reinforces these gender scripts and sanctions are brought to bear on those that do not clearly reflect the appropriate role. Society discriminates against 'masculine' women or 'feminine' men and those who step outside the proscribed gender-appropriate activities (a female boxer, for example).

While functionalist approaches (which share many assumptions with sociobiology) are little in favour with contemporary sociologists, they clearly continue to have resonances in everyday life and popular culture. Many jokes and throwaway remarks relate directly to the 'proper' roles of the sexes while, perhaps more seriously, stereotypes in relation to the appropriate behaviour of males and females may adversely affect individuals' progress through the education system, employment and in public life. The functionalist concept of 'sex role' continues to be very widely used, often in a non-critical way, in analyses of social phenomena.

Within Marxist thought the oppression of women is an aspect of class conflict and antagonism. Marxists point to the discrimination against women and the consequent low cost of female labour (for example, in the textiles or computer industries) as a means of further exploiting the working class. In addition, the unpaid work of women within the nuclear family allows the next generation of workers to be *reproduced* at a lower cost to the forces of capital. More broadly, the family is also a key site for the inculcation of ideologies favourable to capital: the family, and in particular women, who bear the brunt of this work, teaches children to be obedient, productive, healthy and communicative, the very values necessary for an efficient labour force. These sets of ideas have been brought together in sociology in *social reproduction theory* — an approach that argues for a systematic connection between the subordination of women and capitalist economic exploitation (Connell, 1987, p.43).

Whether such reproduction takes place in ways that 'suit' capital is always contingent: always open to question. The family equally has the capacity to become a site of *opposition* to capitalism, and the relationships between men and women are constantly reworked and redefined, not pre-set by the nature of the capitalist economy. Similarly, it is debatable whether gender inequality *does* favour capitalism. As we saw in Chapter 1, a key historical feature of capitalism has been that it breaks down what are seen as traditional relationships and structures and reconstitutes people as workers and consumers. In many respects the development of capitalist social relationships has seen a greater level of equality between men and women. If we think of how changes in the position of women have created new sources of educated workers and enthusiastic consumers, we can see how higher levels of gender equality can be of great service to capital.

Despite theoretical disagreements over the necessity of gender inequality for capitalism, it is important to emphasise that gender relationships remain a key aspect of class and production relations in modern societies. Research by writers such as Game and Pringle (1983 and subsequent works) in Australia and Cockburn (1983 and subsequent works) in Britain has demonstrated the existence of key relationships between inequality in the workplace, definitions and representations of gender, notions of 'skill' and exploitation.

*Feminist sociology* is usually associated with the second wave feminist movement. (The 'first wave' is usually taken to refer to the suffragist movements of the late nineteenth and early twentieth century, but of course this does not mean that organised women's movements or systematic feminist thought did not precede this.) While always being concerned with the issue of gender inequality and particularly its relation to women, there are many varieties of feminism: it is by no means a homogenous movement or system of thought.

It is common to divide modern feminist thinking into three main strands: liberal, socialist and radical feminism. Each overlaps with social theory in other fields: thus, socialist feminism shares many assumptions with Marxism; radical feminism with libertarian thinking. Similarly, intellectual currents in feminism are inextricably linked to competing political positions and strategies within the women's movement. For example, radical feminism is strongly connected to small-scale social movements and alternative lifestyles; socialist feminism to trade union activity; and liberal feminism to parliamentary politics and 'femocracy'.

*Liberal* feminists are concerned to uncover the immediate forms of discrimination against women and to fight for legal and other reforms to overcome them. They tend to focus on mainstream methods of bringing about social change, such as political lobbying, use of the media and working through existing political, business and bureaucratic structures. A good example in the Irish context would be the family law reform group AIM. *Socialist* feminists argue that women's oppression is both an aspect of capitalism and of patriarchy. An end to the current nature of capitalism does not in itself mean an end to the subordination of women, but is an essential part of it. The full liberation of women from oppression will also require a struggle against the control by men of private and public institutions. Socialist feminists often work through smaller left-wing political parties and groupings, trades unions, social movements and in academia and the media. *Radical* feminists see male control of all women through patriarchy as the main problem. They argue that women must struggle to free themselves from the control of male institutions. They are most likely to work through women-only groups. Forms of action may span conventional lobbying techniques to innovative forms of protest such as the long-running Greenham Common anti-nuclear weapons protest in 1980s Britain. Each of these approaches to feminism finds a reflection in the work of feminist sociologists.

In the 1990s a body of writing arose that challenges what it sees as the orthodoxies of western feminism, including the established divisions between the strands outlined above. Known as 'the new feminism' it rejects the oft-quoted precept that 'the personal is the political' and attempts to move feminism away from what it sees as 'lifestyle' politics and back into the public sphere. A key proponent of the 'new feminism', British writer Natasha Walter, suggests that the former approach has led feminism to a 'dead end'. Thus, she suggests, the feminist focus on women's cultural and sexual behaviour has not led to the expected radical changes. She argues (Walter, 1998, p.4) that:

> Feminism has enunciated many, too many, critiques of dress and pornography, of poetry and film-making, of language and physical behaviour. It has sought to direct our personal lives on every level. And yet women have still not achieved fundamental equality; they are still poorer and less powerful than men. Rather than concentrating its energy on the ways women dress and talk and make love, feminism now must attack the material basis of economic and social and political equality.

The rise of the 'new feminism' expresses the tensions of a movement that has achieved remarkable success but which has still to fully challenge the underlying realities of entrenched gender inequality. Thus, writers like Walter and the Australian feminist Catherine Lumby (1997) argue for a more pragmatic approach to political change and for a freeing up of the personal. For Walter (1998, p.6) the new feminism is, above all, materialist: 'it concentrates on the material reality of inequality, and allows women to live their personal lives without the constraints of rigid ideology.' As such it may represent a return to much of the style and substance of earlier models of feminism, particularly those found in the trade union movement and among socialist feminists.

Lumby argues (1997, p.169) that it is hard for young women in particular to find a place in the institutionalised feminist world, as it leaves no space for how women's experiences might differ along age, ethnic, class and cultural lines. She argues that, like traditional philosophy, institutionalised feminism 'relies on the strategies of saming (women are the same) and othering (women are different from men) to construct identity'. The new feminism aims to tap into the concerns of younger women (and men), to draw on the vibrancy of popular culture (including fashion and music) and to make use of the new communications technologies of a globalising world: 'riot grrrls, guerrilla girls, net chicks, cyber chix, geekgirls, tank girls, supergirl, action girls, deep girls — this is the era of DIY feminism' (Bail, 1996, p.3). Inevitably the new feminism has had to confront suggestions of a 'sell-out' to patriarchy and capitalism, and a lack of political purity. The debate between traditional and new feminists is a vigorous and challenging one for feminist thinking. Within sociology it may lead to a shift away from the concern with cultural issues of sexuality and representation and towards more mainstream sociological concerns with the structures of social inequality.

In response to the development of the women's movement and stimulated by the increased reflexivity of (post-)modern society, there has been a recent interest in the nature of *masculinity*. There has been a recognition that changing models of femininity may give rise to changes in the imagery or experience of masculinity. For a long time within society, and within sociology, masculinity has been 'invisible'. As British social psychologists Edley and Wetherell (1995, p.2) suggest, 'masculinity has been regarded as the standard case, the usual pattern, synonymous with humanity in general.' Historically men have had the capacity to define 'normality'; it is women who have been positioned as deviations from the norm and femininity that has required exploration and explanation. Thus, gender studies, as suggested earlier, have tended to focus very much on women's experience and studies of men *as men* have been until recently comparatively rare.

For Edley and Wetherell (1995, p.5) the new focus on masculinity and the experiences of men can be explained at least partly by the changes in the nature of economic relations and production, in particular the shift towards knowledge-based industries and new patterns of work. These have combined with changes in the structure of families (see below) to radically alter the position of men within society. The traditional image of the male breadwinner labouring in the male-dominated workplace of farm, factory or office now has a declining resonance in reality. Edley and Wetherell argue that a comprehensive understanding of contemporary masculinity requires an interdisciplinary approach, one that combines a sociology of men with a social psychological understanding of male subjectivity and an appreciation of the discourses within which masculinity is defined and framed within our culture. In reviewing how masculinity has been constructed over 2000 years of history, they conclude that it is 'a story, not of smooth transitions, but of struggle and bitter dispute' (1995, p.7).

The failure of sociologists to adequately analyse the nature of masculinity has impoverished our understanding of gender as a whole. Buckley (1997, p.105), in looking at the experiences of Irish women in Britain, suggests that, 'only when the real discourse of Irish male experience is released will our men cease to punitively project their repressed difficulties onto women.' In arguing that a fuller knowledge of masculinity will in itself lead to an emancipation both of men and women, she shares much with Kieran McKeown et al. (1999) as they seek to comprehend the nature and context of fatherhood in modern Ireland. For McKeown et al., a full understanding of Irish masculinity is necessary to trace out, and to intervene in, fathering practices in Ireland. Drawing on research within the feminist tradition and from the rapidly expanding body of international research into masculinity, they place the practice of fatherhood within the context of the law, the 1937 Irish Constitution, psychoanalysis, work and, perhaps most interestingly, the division of domestic labour within the home. While the analysis and conclusions that McKeown et al. arrive at are in some ways controversial (for example, in their call for a constitutional amendment to protect paternal rights), they have provided a useful contribution to the understanding of gender relationships in Ireland. Increasingly analyses such as these will be combined with feminist-derived work to provide a fuller picture of gender in Irish society.

## RESEARCHING GENDER

The emergence of the second wave women's movement and of feminist analysis has been instrumental to the development of an extensive sociology of gender. The research agenda has been extremely broad, as indicated above. But a gender-oriented sociology has not just been about opening up new or neglected areas of analysis; it is also about *doing* sociology differently. It has seen a concerted attempt to develop ways to generate sociological knowledge and understanding that lie outside of, and provide an alternative to, the 'malestream'. As a result there has been much debate within sociology as to whether such a thing as a feminist research methodology can exist: are there particular ways to do research, and to analyse the findings, that can avoid the biases identified in 'malestream' research? Taken further, are there ways of doing research that can reflect and develop the feminist ethos of gender equity?

There has been much debate over the possibility of a feminist research methodology. It has been suggested that feminist research should be reflexive, participatory, egalitarian, qualitative, action-oriented and critical of conventional methods and research tools. Millen (1997, p.15) suggests that feminist research is 'a politicised framework for the understanding of knowledge, and charges *all* researchers, male and female, to examine the role of sex and gender in society and to ensure that androcentric norms are not incorporated into their work'. The debate about feminist research methodology centres largely on whether it implies simply a particular focus on and sensitivity to gender issues — sometimes called (pejoratively) the 'add women' approach; or whether feminist research involves a wholly different paradigm — the development of a feminist epistemology or system of knowledge. This divergence of views is illustrated in a brief debate that took place in the pages of the *Irish Journal of Sociology* between two Irish feminist sociologists: Ronit Lentin and Evelyn Mahon.

For Lentin (1993, p.120), feminist research methodologies (for they are multiple) are those that '[make] visible the lived experiences of Irish women or which have included the researcher's lived experience and reflexivity as part of the research process and findings'. Feminist research can include any type of research method (interview, survey, discourse analysis and so on) but — for Lentin — to be feminist it must be *reflexive*. In her research into gendered responses to the Holocaust, this meant 'including [her] own intellectual and emotional autobiography' (1993, p.122). The aim of such a feminist methodology is the transformation of the discipline of sociology from the inside: by an outsider. The totality of such feminist interventions, suggests Lentin, has led to the creation of a new *feminist research paradigm* within sociology. Underpinning this paradigm are the following principles: 'feminist research draws on women's own interpretations of their own experience, relates them to the way in which the society in which we live is constructed and reflexively includes the researcher in all stages of data collection and data production' (1993, p.124). Feminist research, she claims, requires a shared experience of oppression between sociologist and subject; conversely, 'traditional research' involves and expresses an inequality of power between the researcher and researched. Ultimately, adoption of a feminist research paradigm means that the gap between 'academic feminists' and 'Irish women they seek to empower' is narrowed. A brief survey by Lentin of a selection of extant research reports assesses their feminist research credentials on the basis of whether they 'make visible real women'. She suggests that through either a lack of resources or a desire to be accepted by mainstream sociology and funding agencies, Irish feminist researchers have largely failed to adopt what she has defined as a feminist research paradigm.

This position is strongly rebutted by Mahon. While for Lentin feminist research is research carried out by avowed feminists, for Mahon it is research that is underpinned by a *feminist theoretical perspective*; it can thus be carried out by men as well as by women. She argues that feminist research is more than merely rendering women's lives 'visible' (after all, *Hello* magazine does this rather effectively); rather, it is a process whereby the sociologist depicts 'the social processes by which [women's] lives are constructed and reproduced in a way which has generally led to their oppression or unequal treatment in society' (1994, p.166). It is research that rejects the assumption that male experience is universal. For example, the feminist challenge to class theory has meant that sociologists of class can no longer define a woman's class position simply by reference to her husband's. In addition,

Mahon rejects Lentin's position that the feminist researcher must share in the oppression of the subject. She argues that an academic detachment *is* possible and that it is not necessary to have experienced a situation personally in order to be able to understand it. Overall, she is arguing for a more positivist and theoretically informed, and less emotive and grounded, approach to feminist research.

## GENDER, HISTORY, IDENTITY

So far in this chapter we have teased out some of the contours of the diverse sociological approaches to gender issues and have given an indication of the complexity and sophistication of these views; as already mentioned, it is impossible to condense this discussion into a simple outline of the 'sociology of gender'. We now examine some aspects of Irish society through the lens of a gender perspective. Topics have been selected that may help to illuminate some of the other concerns identified, in particular the nature of Irish 'modernity'. The changes that have taken place in Ireland, over at least the last three decades, have often been reflected in or shaped by the changing relationships between women and men.

An understanding of contemporary gender relationships in Ireland requires consideration of how such representations and identities have developed over time. In a sense, all history is a history of gender, in that gender is implicated in all human activity. But it is also the case that until comparatively recently historical writing tended to focus disproportionately on the experiences of men: women (and children) were marginalised or remained completely absent from written accounts (O'Dowd and Wichert, 1995). As a result, the lived, day-to-day experience of Irish women has been overlooked and its importance played down.

The writing of history is in many ways a search for identity, an attempt to develop a coherent narrative that embodies the character of a people. In turn, 'history' becomes part of the context within which gender relations are lived out in the contemporary world and is therefore crucial to a sociological understanding. A number of writers have attempted to trace the historical and discursive connections between gender, sexuality and 'Irishness'. In common with Nash (1997, p.108) they argue that different versions of Irish national identity have prescribed 'certain kinds of gender and sexual identities for Irish men and women. These gendered representations . . . impact upon the lives of women and men and influence their opportunities and constraints in work, education, political activity, personal relationships and senses of themselves.' One of the tasks of the sociologist is to try to interpret the nature and directions of such 'impacts' in contemporary Irish society.

For Ronit Lentin (1998, p.11; 1999) the construction of Irishness has been 'disturbingly gendered'; the definition of Irish citizenship that has emerged since independence has actively marginalised women and indeed has sought to erase all expressions of difference. Thus, for example the 1937 Irish Constitution has been labelled by Lentin and other analysts as a conservative document that assigns a subordinate role to women. It places women essentially as wives and mothers within the context of the family. The model of femininity it espouses is 'passive, private and domestic'. Most notoriously, Article 41.2.1 of the Constitution, which recognises the special contribution to Irish society of women 'within the home', has been identified as a patriarchal statement about the 'proper' place of women in Irish society. It closely reflected Catholic Church teaching at the time it was written but continues to exert an influence over policy and law.

A number of writers have argued that the *land* of Ireland — the central motif of our history — has been viewed historically in a gendered way: as a feminine entity (see Lentin, 1999, pp.5–7). Ireland is not unique in this regard. Similar arguments have been made for other national landscapes, including those of Australia (Schaffer, 1988) and of Sweden (Åberg, 1999). The geographer Catherine Nash suggests that the land of Ireland has been depicted as female in a number of traditions and contexts that range from old Gaelic representations to colonialist viewpoints to nationalist myths (such as Dark Rosaleen, Caitlín ní Houlihán and the *aisling*). To nineteenth-century English colonialists, Ireland (and its people) was typified by 'supposedly . . . feminine characteristics of sentimentality, ineffectuality, nervous excitability and unworldliness' that rendered it incapable of self-government; in contrast, for Irish–Ireland nationalists 'avowals of heroic masculinity were made alongside the celebration of dependent, passive, domestic and selfless Irish femininity' (Nash, 1997, p.114). In such discourses of nationhood 'Ireland is raped, seduced or married and in turn features alternatively as virgin, wanton woman, bride, mother or old woman' (1997, p.116). For O'Connor (1998, p.84) the images of 'Mother Ireland' and 'the self-sacrificing Irish mother' — dominant images within Irish nationalist discourse — 'reflect and reinforce men's fear and loathing of women', though this provocative point is not developed any further.

Nash goes further and argues that the historical perception of the land as feminine, especially within Irish nationalism, is linked to how the femininity of Irish women has been constructed. She suggests that there are 'traditional associations between nature, land, fertility and femininity' (1997, p.110) and that these are reflected in women's legal, social and ideological position. For example, beliefs about the sanctity of Irish womanhood were converted into the regulation of cultural forms such as fashion, film, literature, music and dance. 'Foreign notions' of sexual equality, it was said, undermined the home and native honour towards women and degraded Irish women (Nash, 1997, p.115). The idea that the gendered imagery of Ireland as a country is linked to the formation of gendered identities among its people is an intriguing one, but it needs to be further understood through research. One of the problems with such analyses, from a sociological point of view, is that they tend to essentialise both femininity and masculinity.

Much of the historical analysis of gender relations in Ireland focuses on the country's colonial position. Carol Coulter (1993, p.7) suggests that within colonial societies, such as Ireland, there was a particularly strong link between religion and the family: 'religion sanctifies the moments of significance in human lives — birth, passage to adulthood, marriage and death'. She, more controversially, links the incidence of domestic violence to the colonial position of the state (1993, p.11):

> In a colonised society the father or husband, treated as inferior at work and in the public world where the model of maleness offered was authoritarian and often brutal, often found that the only place he could play this proscribed role was within the family, with the resulting brutalisation of his wife and children.

Such a position, which other feminists may interpret as 'letting men off the hook', has also been expressed in relation to other anti-colonialist struggles, for example, those of Australian Aboriginal populations and the African-American population of the United States. Once again, it is difficult to trace the sociological connections between feelings of national identity and particular patterns of social behaviour (an interesting attempt may be found in Theweleit's (1987; 1989) studies of gender in Nazi Germany).

It is only recently in Ireland that sociologists have begun explicitly to grasp the relationships between gender and *ethnicity*, though this has been a key issue for the study of gender in the United States, Britain and Australia. Studies (for example, Lennon *et al.*, 1988; Buckley, 1997) of Irish women in Britain have led the way, bringing attention to the ethnic minority status of Irish people in Britain and drawing out some of the implications of this in terms of inequality, racism and the complexities of personal and social identity. Ronit Lentin has sought to focus on the inherent racism of the dominant constructions of 'Irishness', such as that expressed in the 1937 Constitution, and, closer to home, within Irish sociology and women's studies. For her, 'the assumption that to be Irish is to be Roman Catholic (or, in a very limited sense also Protestant) settled and White, has not been adequately challenged by politicians, social scientists or the media' (Lentin, 1999, p.9). Lentin mounts a strong argument that narrowly defined conceptions of 'Irishness', for example, as expressed in the Constitution, serve to deny full citizenship to ethnic minority women, such as refugees and asylum seekers, Travellers, Muslim and Jewish people, and Black-Irish people.

Lentin has focused in particular on the issues of minority ethnic groups, including the Travellers (the issue of whether Travellers constitute a separate ethnic group is a highly controversial one: see Chapter 15). For Lentin Travelling women have been 'occluded in Irish sociological and feminist studies of women and citizenship, which often do not problematise the term 'Irish women' and tend not to engage with the thorny question of difference' (Lentin, 1998, p.13). She points out that in Ireland Traveller women are 'excluded from full access to political, but mostly civil and social citizenship' (1998, p.14) — this includes feminist political and academic projects. Lentin is highly critical of Irish feminism in this regard: 'at worst, "white" sedentary Irish feminism discusses racism as if it is the problem of the racially excluded' . . . 'at best [it] tends to "speak for" racialized Irish women' (1998, p.18). Tannam (1999, p.31) points out that policy and academic texts on gender in Ireland tend to ignore the experiences of migrant women and those of minority ethnic groups. The rapid change that Ireland is now undergoing, particularly its transition to a multi-ethnic state, means that analysis of gender in Ireland needs to examine the specificity of Irish women — and men — of varying ethnic identifications and, inseparable from this, the nature and practice of racism in Ireland.

The issue of gender is inextricably tied up with questions of identity and difference. In Ireland, as elsewhere, the constitution of personal and social identity is a complex and highly dynamic process. It is suggested by many that in Ireland key components of our identity can find their explanation in our colonial history, the nature of our land(scape) and how we conceptualise others. It is further suggested that ideas about identity are translated into specific forms of social practice. We have outlined some of the arguments that have been put forward to link these questions in an Irish context but would suggest that, while the arguments are fascinating, there remains much work to be done within the Irish sociology of gender to explore such connections.

## THE FAMILY

The family, in Ireland as elsewhere, has been identified as 'an important symbol of collective identity, unity and security' (O'Connor, 1998, p.89). It is seen by many — including many social scientists — as the 'natural' basis for society. It has also risen to prominence in commercial, political and social policy rhetoric, with much attention being given to 'the family' in political campaigns, media advertising and social policy initiatives, where it stands for themes such as 'parental care, wholesome meals and morals, conjugal eroticism and sibling responsibility' (Robertson, 1991, p.166). An understanding of the family is also central to any discussion of gender relationships, for it is through this institution, and others, that our experiences and understandings of gender and of sexuality are formed and mediated.

As the term 'family' has risen to prominence in public discourse, however, it has become more problematic and opaque. While for marketers of cars or breakfast cereals it has positive connotations of nostalgia and emotion, for economists and bureaucrats it may give rise to negative perceptions of 'tradition'. The rationalist economic discourse of modernity tends to focus very much on the *individual* as worker and as consumer, and perhaps as citizen. There is much focus on individual rights and actions in 'the market' and the family is seen within this context as somewhat anachronistic and limiting: as in 'family business', 'family farm' or 'family obligations'. As Robertson (1991, p.157) suggests:

The analytical assumption that modernization has atomized society into a mass of individual 'rational actors' has fostered the notion that the western democracies are composed of socially featureless decision-makers, devoid even of age or gender.

Such a focus on the, implicitly male, individual has allowed questions of oppression and inequality of, and within, families to be largely ignored. But as Robertson (1991, p.158) further points out we need to understand the family as the locus of much of what we define as social behaviour. Thus, 'if we are interested in such things as economic performance and social status, the interaction of life-cycles within the domestic group is much more informative than the life-cycle of each individual.' An understanding of the family is basic to a sociological understanding.

In western societies there has been much debate over competing definitions of 'the family'. It is now widely accepted that there are many variations from 'the norm' of the nuclear family of married heterosexual couple plus children. For example, Irish social welfare policy and practice has now begun to recognise the validity of families based on cohabiting (not married) couples or lone parents (O'Connor, 1998, p.90). There is far less agreement — in Ireland and elsewhere — over the possibility of families based on homosexual unions, for example, such arrangements have no validity under Irish legislation governing inheritance. In Ireland and other western countries, the range of family types is becoming increasingly diverse, including 'blended families' that result from a number of relationships involving different partners; single-parent families; and groups of unrelated people living together in 'family-like' arrangements. There is also an increasing number of people living alone.

While diversity of family types is not new (Irish history speaks of a number of types of domestic arrangement), the challenge to traditional conceptions is seen by many as further evidence of modernity. For example, the trends around single parenthood, where increasingly women choose to bring up children without a permanent male partner, have been said by Irish sociologist Pat O'Connor (1998, p.122) to suggest a new 'marginalisation of men within the family'. For O'Connor this trend implies a 'radical challenge to our ideas about the family and to the cultural and social construction of heterosexuality'. Similarly, the greater acceptance of divorce and remarriage in Ireland signals a change in what can constitute a valid family arrangement. At the same time the more limited notions of the 'traditional' family continue to receive active support from many, if not the majority, in Irish society. In particular, most men, and women that are not working outside the home, tend to have more traditional views in relation to the family (Galligan, 1998b, p.118). Such views are often expressed in self-conscious opposition to perceived changes in Irish society. Defence of a particular view of 'the family' is central to conservative thinking everywhere.

Crucially, the family is implicated in relationships of power and inequality in Irish society. It is an important mechanism through which economic inequality is maintained and property rights are transmitted. It also provides a basis for access to, and success within, the education system. The family as a set of relationships is a major conduit for the transfer of property, particularly through the inheritance of farm businesses and residential property. But property rights are unevenly distributed *within* families: many forms of property are male-dominated and owned. O'Connor, pointing out, for example, that in Ireland three quarters of farms are registered in male names only, suggests that 'at the level of ownership, women's economic power basis within the family is limited' (1998, p.115). Similarly, property rights within marriage continue to disadvantage women.

The experiences of women and men in Irish families may be shaped in important ways by the broader social relationships within which a family is located. Involvement in paid work, for example, may help to determine who has the 'power' within families while at the same time women *and* men tend to underestimate and devalue the importance of unpaid work both 'inside' and 'outside' the family (O'Hara, 1998, p.87). There has been a considerable body of research in Ireland into the decision-making processes within family units, particularly in relation to farm families. A seminal work in this area was Hannan and Katsiaouni's (1977) analysis of farm families 'in transition'. This work was overtly informed by modernisation theory and sought to examine how traditional patriarchal structures within Irish farm families were being replaced by more modern negotiated roles, as rural families increasingly converged with urban ones.

Recent research into the lives of rural women by O'Hara (1998) places such decision-making more specifically within the economic and gender-based power structures within which farm women find themselves. Thus, 'the weight of culture, tradition and family ideology in rural Ireland clearly identifies the farm family as a patriarchal structure where the interests of men (fathers and sons) supersede those of women and daughters' (1998, p.114). Male power is significantly reinforced by men's legally supported domination of property ownership. In O'Hara's study fewer than a fifth of farms were jointly owned by husband and wife and this usually only happened where a woman brought land to the relationship. As has been found in Britain (Symes and Marsden, 1983), the more 'modern' or commercially oriented a farm business is, the more likely it is to be structured along 'traditional' gender lines. However, in terms of house ownership on farms, there appears to be a move towards a more gender-equitable relationship, with family homes being placed in both names. According to O'Hara (1998, p.118) this reflects 'more egalitarian ideologies of marriage' and the financial resources that a woman working off-farm can bring to the family.

Like Australia and Britain, and in contrast to countries like Sweden and Denmark, Irish society is built on a strong male breadwinner model. This helps to account not only for unequal domestic power relationships but also for the lack of support for women in the public sphere, such as the comparative lack of maternity entitlements; poor child care provision (though this has improved markedly in Australia since the early 1980s); and high involvement in part-time work (except in the Republic of Ireland where levels of part-time employment are relatively low). Within such a model women are perceived primarily as potential mothers. Motherhood exists between the areas of health, labour and welfare (Kennedy, 1997). Mothers have roles as carers, earners and lifegivers, the last of these being exclusively the domain of women (1997, p.314):

> It is only woman who can conceive, lactate and give birth. It is only the biological mother who is caught in the grips of labour pain. It is only the biological mother who experiences abortion, suffers the pain of miscarriage or the experience of childbirth. It is only the biological mother who lactates. These are the very basic elements which the mother has to balance with her role as carer and earner and these are the most prudent issues ignored by social policy analysts.

On the other hand, many of these areas (for example, childbirth, the abortion debate) have been commandeered by the male dominated institutions of church, law and medicine.

Demographic trends are both a reflection and a determinant of ideas about gender and family. Ireland like many other western countries has seen a major change in the nature and structure of the family unit in recent times. This set of changes has been referred to as the 'second demographic transition' (see Chapter 5). Key trends include: a marked decline in marriage, birth and fertility rates; later age of marriage and first childbirth; increased ex-nuptial births; smaller completed family size and an increase in the number of people remaining single. For writers such as Galligan (1998a, p.27) such changes reflect the modernisation of Irish society, a growing level of secularisation and a more assertive attitude among women in relation to family planning. Though Ireland reflects the broad trends of demographic change found in Europe as a whole, important differences remain. For example, the ideal family size (that desired by couples) and actual family size remain larger in Ireland than in most countries of the EU (Whelan and Fahy, 1994, p.61), while the fertility rate in Ireland is at the higher end of the EU scale (with the Nordic countries). In an apparent contradiction, Ireland in 1994 had the lowest marriage rate in Europe and, outside the Nordic countries, the latest age of marriage (26.3 years for brides) (O'Connor, 1998, p.110). Ireland's population also has the lowest proportion of elderly people in the EU (11.5 per cent compared to EU average of 16 per cent) (Silke and Whyte, 1999, p.167).

By 1996 births outside marriage made up a quarter of all births in Ireland and lone parents (including separated and divorced parents) now head one in five of families (O'Connor, 1998, p.119). There is evidence (O'Connor, 1998, p.120) that the majority of lone parents have to an extent chosen their situation and, overall, enjoy routine parenting tasks and the independence of single parenthood. At the same time, lone parents form a significant proportion of those in poverty, they continue to face discrimination and face particularly high barriers when it comes to (re)entering the labour market, for example, poor transport and child care facilities and the poverty traps created by the social welfare system (Leane and Kiely, 1997).

Family relationships represented a key issue for the women's movement that emerged in Ireland in the 1970s. In particular, many feminist activists, as in other parts of Europe, especially the Mediterranean countries, focused on family law reform. Such challenges took place in a society that had developed a highly conservative view of the family and gender, buttressed by the institutions of church and state (Galligan, 1998a, p.91): the role for women as spelled out in the Irish Constitution of 1937 has already been mentioned. There had been minimal legal reform in Ireland in relation to the family prior to the early 1970s. Feminist pressure groups such as AIM focused on (Galligan, 1998a, p.95):

- the protection of married women's property and other interests within the family
- opposition to discrimination against married women
- changes in the legal machinery of family law
- the legal status of separation and divorce.

For Galligan, voluntary groups such as AIM brought Irish family policy 'out of the Victorian age to a respectable stage of enlightenment comparable to similar policies in most European states in the late twentieth century' (1998a, p.105). Overall, while family policy in Ireland has not seen a fundamental restructuring of the family, it has seen an incremental improvement in the human rights of women and children within marriage.

It is very important for sociologists to remember that the family is a *dynamic* concept. In Ireland we have seen within a relatively short time a considerable shift in the nature and understanding of the family unit. There is evidence that the extended family was the norm within Irish rural society. Movement to urban and suburban areas does not necessarily mean that the extended family unit has disappeared, but it may be experienced in different ways, perhaps facilitated by the telephone and the car. In looking to the future we can begin to discern some important changes, for example, a rise in numbers of single people; considerably smaller families; the rise of the one-child family; increasing levels of lone parenthood; more gay and lesbian couples; and more voluntarily childfree people. What will the broader social effects of these changes be? and of other shifts in our society, such as the changes in the nature of jobs and careers? and what of the possibility of an extended lifespan and more 'active ageing'?

## GENDER AND WORK

The last three decades of the twentieth century saw significant changes in the relationship of Irish women and men towards the labour market (see Chapter 6). But the world of work remains a key site for the expression of gender difference and the positions that men and women hold in the labour market are a major determinant of wealth, income, power and status. Work itself is a major element of personal identity and influence over well-being and is a complex and contentious concept. Common-sense understandings, reflected in many public discourses, assume that work means 'paid work'. Such conceptions underpin, for example, the statistical measurement of work; social welfare policies and procedures; child care provision; and employment policy. Furthermore, the notion of paid work in Ireland is further narrowed to 'full-time paid work' and there has been little recognition of part-time, casual or seasonal work. O'Connor (1998, p.191) argues that 'male work norms' have been taken as typical. But it is clear that what we think of as work has the potential to embrace a much wider range of human endeavour: all the work arrangements listed above, as well as unpaid work of various sorts — caring for others, voluntary work, domestic labour (housework) — and work carried out on a reciprocal basis (such as repairing a neighbour's car). Such is the gendered nature of work that we often associate men with paid work in the public sphere and women with unpaid work in the home; but it should be obvious that such a distinction holds little meaning, and says more about dominant ideologies in Irish society than about how people spend their time and energy.

While work is difficult to define, it is apparent that at least paid work is changing quite radically in its forms. Thus, O'Hearn (1998, p.103) points to the following trends:

> Irish work has undoubtedly become more casual and less secure since 1985. In industry and services alike, more and more employees have flexible status like part-time, temporary and fixed-contract work. This is partly a result of newly created jobs that are on flexible terms. But it is also the result of large numbers of employees who have been shifted from full-time permanent status to more flexible terms.

The types of work relationships listed by O'Hearn are sometimes termed 'atypical' in relation to the traditional norm of a full-time, life-long job. But such forms of flexible, casual, part-time, contract-based and insecure work are becoming more widespread. Historically, women have been more likely to be involved in these atypical arrangements, which now account for between a fifth and a quarter of all jobs in Ireland (O'Hearn, 1998, p.105).

The contemporary nature of work in Ireland has inevitably been shaped by the patterns of economic development that have taken place since the late 1950s, as discussed in some detail in Chapter 3. The Irish economy has seen a rapid and large-scale expansion of the service industries, ranging from financial services to tourism and catering, and there has been extensive inward investment by TNCs and other 'foreign' firms. This economic change has influenced the development of the Irish labour market, not least in relation to gender. For example, Crowley (1997, p.81) suggests that how TNCs operate in Ireland 'maintains both Ireland's dependent status in the international economy and the increasing feminisation of that dependency'. In particular she highlights how the bulk of work for women in TNCs has been low paid and low skilled. This situation is perpetuated by no-union policies or 'sweetheart deals' with unions which do little to challenge gender inequality in the workplace. Crowley argues that as the TNCs have 'capitalised upon the already existing patriarchal order within Irish industry' (1997, p.86) they have done little or nothing to raise the status of women in Ireland. Such a position assumes, of course, that employment in the paid workforce in itself brings no benefit to women — a highly debatable position. Furthermore, things may be changing: while the employment of young women in unskilled jobs was certainly the strategy for TNCs that came to Ireland during the 1970s and 1980s, the nature of TNC operations in Ireland since the 1990s may have led them to focus more on skilled labour and on 'pink-collar' information-based jobs.

The factors that shape the involvement of men and women in the labour market reflect both 'supply side' and 'demand' factors (Smyth, 1997, p.63). Changes in the nature of the family; in social attitudes; in educational participation; and in social infrastructure have helped to make more labour of particular types available. At the same time, changes in the economy and in the productive sector have led to demands for new kinds of worker and different skills and attributes.

In 1926, 60 per cent of women who were gainfully employed worked either in agriculture or in domestic service (Beale, 1986, p.140). Just one in ten worked in industry. Women who had paid jobs were predominantly young and single, though there was a significant proportion of women within the urban workforce who were never-married. From 1932 to 1973 married women were formally and legally excluded from the public service and system of administration through the so-called 'marriage bar'. From the 1930s to 1961, as emigration took its toll, the paid female workforce in Ireland actually diminished. Many women left the country to take up service sector and industrial jobs in Britain and elsewhere.

As indicated in Figure 8.1 the labour force participation of males declined from 82 per cent in 1971 to 69 per cent in 1996. This was largely due to greater involvement in education and also perhaps due to earlier retirement. Conversely, women's participation rate increased from 28 per cent in 1971 to 39 per cent in 1994. This comparatively slow rate of change hides the fact that while the participation rate of single women declined (again largely due to involvement in education) that for married women increased quite considerably. The period 1951 to 1991 saw a seven-fold increase in the number of married women in the paid

# Figure 8.1 Work, unemployment and labour force participation 1971–1996

| | At work '000 | Unemployed '000 | Labour force '000 | Labour force participation rate % |
|---|---|---|---|---|
| **Women** | | | | |
| 1971 | 276 | 14 | 290 | 28 |
| 1981 | 329 | 30 | 359 | 30 |
| 1991 | 386 | 53 | 439 | 33 |
| 1996 | 488 | 52 | 540 | 39 |
| **Men** | | | | |
| 1971 | 774 | 62 | 836 | 82 |
| 1981 | 809 | 104 | 913 | 77 |
| 1991 | 747 | 156 | 903 | 71 |
| 1996 | 797 | 138 | 935 | 69 |
| **Total** | | | | |
| 1971 | 1050 | 76 | 1126 | 55 |
| 1981 | 1138 | 134 | 1272 | 53 |
| 1991 | 1133 | 209 | 1342 | 52 |
| 1996 | 1285 | 190 | 1475 | 54 |

(*Source*: O'Connor, 1998, p.191)

workforce. For O'Connor (1998, p.188) this is 'one of the most dramatic changes to have taken place in Irish society over the past twenty-five years'. Indeed, by 1994 married women made up half the female labour force (Smyth, 1997, p.64) and by 1996 they outnumbered single women (Galligan, 1998a, p.32). So marked has been the shift of women into the labour market that sociologists in Ireland and elsewhere now talk about the 'feminisation' of the workforce; 90 per cent of the increase in employment in the EU since 1971 has been in women's employment (O'Connor, 1998, p.214), particularly in the burgeoning service sector.

Factors that increase the 'supply' of women's labour and which have been seen by many to underpin their increased participation in the workforce include better education, declining fertility rates, and the capacity to earn higher wages. The 'opportunity costs' of staying at home to mind children or do housework (in other words, the income foregone) have greatly increased, especially as education levels have risen (Smyth, 1997, p.65–6). Other factors that have increased the supply of female labour have been the removal of many of the social and legal barriers to women's employment, for example, the elimination of the public sector marriage bar. Married women's work has also become more visible. Often it was hidden in the overall labour of a small family business or farm but now it is more likely to be in the paid workforce as an employee. The result of such changes, as we have seen, has been a significant increase in the number of married women in the Irish labour market. This has paralleled the comparative reduction in availability of single women. But despite the reduction in completed family size in Ireland to a position much closer to the EU average, participation rates by married women in the labour market are still considerably lower than in most other European countries. Indeed, given the abject failure of the Irish state and society to support women's participation in the labour market, such as an almost total lack of child care provision, very low participation by men in household labour and discriminatory tax policies, the increase is quite remarkable.

It is not enough to focus on the factors that have increase the 'supply' of female workers; we must also look at factors that have shaped the demand both for women's and men's labour. These factors are inextricably bound up with the change in the Irish economy since the late 1950s. The expansion of manufacturing and service industries within the Irish economy as part of broader global trends has contributed to the expansion in women's employment opportunities. Many of the jobs in the new electronic, light engineering, pharmaceutical and manufacturing industries attracted to the country were taken up by women. The huge growth in the service industries, in particular, retail, tourism, financial services and community and personal services, has also been a stimulus to the expansion of female employment. Conversely, the manufacturing and agricultural industries that traditionally employed mainly men have declined. These facts challenge the way that the Marxist 'reserve army of labour' thesis has been applied to women. Marx argued that there are groups of workers who have a marginal attachment to the labour force and who can be drawn in or driven out of employment as the economy expands or contracts. Thus, it has been suggested that women (especially married women) are brought into the labour force as necessary and can be easily dispensed with in times of restructuring or recession. However, this theory was not borne out in the Irish recession of the 1980s, when female employment continued to increase (Smyth, 1997, p.71).

As noted above, the workforce participation rate of Irish women remains low by EU standards and compares with countries such as Spain, Italy and Greece. There remain significant barriers to women's equal participation in the labour force. These include 'the absence of flexible working hours, the virtual non-existence of child care facilities and lack of appropriate training due largely to the negative attitudes of employers' (Galligan, 1998a, pp.34–5). This reflects dominant discourses within Irish society in relation to women's work (O'Connor, 1998, p.21):

> Concepts of womanhood continue to revolve around caring, familism, repro-duction, love, sexual attraction and gendered paid employment, preferably in a 'little job' which is part-time, low paid, and undertaken for the 'good of the family'.

The 'traditional' attitudes that help to prevent the development of appropriate supports and facilities are changing very slowly, and issues such as child care promise to gain a higher public profile as changes in the nature of the labour market continue to take place.

Of key importance in understanding issues related to gender and work is the concept of *labour market segmentation*. Sociologists argue that there is not a single labour market; rather, the demand for labour is segmented in a variety of ways. Most simplistically, there is a primary or 'core' labour market of relatively highly paid, secure, skilled jobs that offer promotional opportunities and other benefits (for example, teaching); and a secondary or 'peripheral' labour market that, conversely, offers low security, demands flexibility, has low pay and benefits and little or no career structure (for example, restaurant work). There is also segregation *within* industries. There is much debate about the extent to which employers and employees (particularly through unions) can shape these differentiated labour markets.

There has been no systematic study of labour market segmentation in Ireland and it is therefore difficult to gauge how men's and women's workforce experiences are determined by this process. There is some evidence that women are more likely to work in peripheral industries, such as textiles and the clothing sector, while men are more likely to be found in core industries such as printing and brewing (Smyth, 1997, p.73). But the location of specific industries within the 'core' or 'periphery' in this way is highly problematic. It is perhaps more useful to examine *occupational*

## Figure 8.2 Female occupational segregation in Ireland 1996

|  | 1996 | | |
|---|---|---|---|
|  | '000 | % of female labour force | % of total employed in group |
| Agricultural workers | 14.4 | 2.9 | 10.3 |
| Producers, makers and repairers | 44.2 | 9.1 | 16.9 |
| Labourers and unskilled workers | 2.8 | 0.6 | 7.2 |
| Clerical workers | 125.2 | 25.7 | 77.4 |
| Commerce, insurance and finance workers | 64.4 | 13.2 | 42.7 |
| Service workers | 85.8 | 17.6 | 60.9 |
| Professional and technical workers | 125.5 | 25.7 | 53.0 |
| Others | 16.7 | 3.4 | 22.1 |
| **Total** | **488.0** | **100** | **38.0** |

(*Source*: Department of Equality, Justice and Law Reform, 1997, p.99)

*segregation*: the extent to which men and women are concentrated within particular sorts of occupation and whether the labour market is effectively divided up into 'men's jobs' and 'women's jobs' (see Figure 8.2).

Occupational segregation in Ireland is very marked. Thus, in 1992, 77 per cent of working women were to be found in the services sector (EU average 71 per cent). They were further concentrated in four occupational groups:

- commerce and finance
- professional and technical
- services
- clerical.

A number of occupations are highly feminised: including child care, primary education, health care, clerical work and personal and domestic services. Over half the female workforce is found to occupy just two occupational groups: clerical (around 25 per cent) and professional/technical (around 25 per cent) while only 18 per cent of men occupy these areas combined (Smyth, 1997, p.73). Women remain concentrated in low-pay sectors of the economy and are frequently found in low-paid, part-time, insecure and 'low-skilled' occupations.

While equal pay has been an Irish industrial issue since it was first debated by the Irish Trade Union Congress in 1917 (Beale, 1986, p.145), it has yet to become a reality. Women's hourly earnings across all types of industry are still only four-fifths of men's (O'Connor, 1998, p.198). Many women are trapped in low-pay industries like catering or cleaning or are concentrated at the bottom of hierarchies in higher paying industries like law. At the same time, women are over-represented in the professional/technical area, partly reflecting their major role in the health care and education industries. While the extent of occupational segregation has diminished somewhat over the past three decades, the process is complex. Some areas have become more homogenous (for example, primary teaching, banking) whereas others have become more diverse (for example, law, accountancy). Why have these patterns persisted? It is certainly the case that stereotypes about certain kinds of occupation remain: 'male' occupations are seen as dirty, physical, to do with power and strength (Carey, 1997) while women's occupations express aspects of femininity such as 'caring', dexterity, communication skills. These clearly relate to broader gender stereotypes.

It is still the case that very few women are found in senior management. For example, in 1993 women made up 1.6 per cent of the boards of the top ten companies in the country and in 1994 there was no female Chief Executive Officer (CEO) in the country's top 100 companies. This imbalance is reflected in the public service, with only one Secretary, 6 per cent Assistant Secretaries and 13 per cent of Principal Officers, despite the female domination of the civil service workforce as a whole. There are practically no women at all at senior management level within local government, the health boards or the Institutes of Technology. Women are also badly represented at higher levels of trade unions, even those that have high female membership, and are very badly represented in employers' and farmers' organisations (Galligan, 1998a, p.44). The glass ceiling, or perhaps more appropriately the 'concrete ceiling', is still very much part of the Irish business and administrative worlds.

The links between paid and unpaid work are important: both in how unpaid work obligations (like looking after children or elderly relatives) can impact on availability for paid work; and how the experience of paid work is shaped by parallel non-paid work obligations (from delivering children to school to minding children when they are ill). Leonard (1997, p.120) says that 'because of modern industrial society's preoccupation with formal paid labour as the purest form of economic activity, the economic value of forms of labour which exist outside this limited definition tend to be underrated.' Leonard argues that unpaid 'caring' work is differentially valued along gender lines. Thus, cooking a meal for an elderly relative (typically done by a woman) is virtually 'invisible' and is rarely seen as work whereas servicing a car for the same relative (typically done by a man) is far more easily identified as such. Informal work is carried out within a gendered network of expectations and obligations. Therefore, 'women's motivations for engaging in informal helping networks [are] closely bound to culturally defined rules regarding gender specific obligations both within and outside the household' (Leonard, 1997, p.122). While Leonard cautions against a romanticising of 'love labour' she points out (1997, p.123) that 'caring and loving others is for many women much more life enhancing than the mundane badly paid formal work carried out under the exploitative conditions which most women have to endure.' Such work remains undervalued by men and by society.

In some similar ways, other areas of women's work are structured by the relationships with unpaid work. Daly's study of women cleaners (cited in O'Connor, 1998, p.204) showed that respondents' attitudes to work were based on their identities as housewives rather than employees. O'Connor concluded that this identification was of disadvantage to the women concerned: 'they saw themselves basically as housewives, and saw their skills as personal, indeed often female characteristics. They effectively colluded with the devaluation of their work' (1998, p.205).

In recent years there has been considerable public interest in the areas of homeworking (or outworking) and teleworking, two forms of work where the workplace and the home coincide. The former is a very old method of work organisation whereby firms contract out work to people (usually women) to be carried out at home. Outwork has often involved trades such as sewing, knitting and other manual work and also certain forms of clerical work. Teleworking represents a new twist to the same concept, based on new forms of information technology such as computers and the Internet. Telework is usually of a clerical, administrative or occasionally creative nature. There has been much debate as to whether these new forms of 'high-tech' outwork are in essence any different to the more traditional forms.

Research in the UK has indicated that homeworking is on the increase, but the study of it is bedevilled by measurement and definitional problems. There is very little research on homeworking in Ireland. Richards (1997) in the late 1980s focused on hand and machine knitters. They earned from just 25p to 75p an hour. A major problem was their 'invisibility' within the labour force, for example, they were not unionised and did not pay income tax or PRSI. In fact they were not seen as 'real workers'. Based on her limited research, Richards (1997, p.138) was forced to conclude that homeworking was 'a form of employment which is almost exclusively female, it is very badly paid, completely unregulated, and fraught with health and safety dangers'. There has been much concern that telework is likely to share the same features. Some unions, in particular, have pointed out the dangers inherent in working at home and the likelihood of exploitation of workers (Bibby, 1996; Huws et al., 1999). Like the more traditional forms of homeworking, teleworking seems to largely involve women. When men are identified as teleworkers it is often in high status occupations such as author, graphic designer or software programmer. Women are more likely to engage in lower status and less well-paid occupations such as proofreading, processing insurance claims or teleservice work such as directory enquiries. There is little to suggest that technology has the ability in itself to change the gendered patterns of occupational segregation.

## GENDER AND THE PUBLIC SPHERE

> When we talk about women's power we are still talking about potential rather than reality. (Walter, 1998, p.3)

As we said earlier, conflicts over gender, sexuality and the family have been a significant part of the Irish political and public discursive landscape for at least the last thirty years. For many people the shift towards modernity in Ireland is symbolised not only by the development of the economy and the physical infrastructure, but also by how people think, talk and act in relation to moral issues. Often, in Ireland, this means issues related to gender. Thus, as Jenny Beale argued (1986, p.184): 'as Irish society has industrialised and urbanised, and as traditional values and ways have been challenged and questioned, every aspect of women's lives has been subject to scrutiny and change.' For Beale the image was one of progress, of overcoming the barriers to women's full equality in Irish society. A decade and a half later, the picture is perhaps more complex. While many of the challenges faced by the women's movement have been addressed, the more intractable issues related to gender remain. Galligan, in an analysis of women's political mobilisation in Ireland, points to an apparent contradiction: 'there is little doubt that the role of women in Ireland today is very different to the social role and function assigned to their mothers, even if attitudes towards that new role remain staunchly traditional' (1998b, p.106). This is a contradiction that we may perhaps more usefully call a particularly Irish model of feminism, lived out in the stances of Ireland's two women Presidents, Robinson and McAleese.

Furthermore, in Ireland as elsewhere, the direction of change is being questioned. Is 'having it all' in a consumer heaven the aim of Irish people — particularly women — or does a more equal opportunity to work and to consume only serve to paper over the deeper layers of inequality within Irish society, such as occupational segregation, family violence and the unequal burden of domestic labour and child care? Discussion of gender and family issues in the public sphere continues to reflect the long-term issues of gender inequality, and the unresolved uncertainties of moving rapidly towards a post-modern society. It is often around gender- and family-related issues that the tensions and connections between the personal and the political are made most apparent, whether in relation to, for example, state support for home births; responses to male youth suicide; or the policing of domestic violence.

The cacophony of debate is summed up by Bradley and Valiulis (1997, p.1) in their introduction to a collection of articles on gender and sexuality in Ireland:

> Reform of laws affecting divorce, the availability of contraception, the decriminalisation of homosexuality, the sensational events around what has become known as the X case, the fall of an Irish government over the extradition of a pedophile priest, the revelation of a bishop's and priests' actual rather than figurative paternities, and the various pathologies of misogyny that have come to light — all these, whether progressive social changes or disturbing revelations, have given an urgency to issues of gender and sexuality.

It would be superfluous here to list the many public debates — usually heated, often sensationalised — that have taken place over such issues. They are very well known to all people in Ireland through saturation media coverage and continual public and private debate. The very frequency and ubiquity of such debates, scandals and revelations are evidence to many people of the speed and depth of the processes of modernisation within Irish society. Peillon (1998, p.117) suggests that 'through these crises Ireland is being propelled, at an incredible pace, into what Anthony Giddens has called *high modernity*.' Irish people are being forced, through the sheer speed and depth of change, to adopt a thoroughly modern stance of reflexivity, to be increasingly self-conscious about the sort of changing society they inhabit. It is thus hardly surprising that, as suggested by Foucault, our society has become highly involved in perpetual talk of gender, sexuality and morality.

From the 1930s to the 1960s women in Ireland suffered from legal discrimination in a broad range of areas, including employment, property rights, family law, inheritance, social welfare, taxation and access to, and protection of, the law (Galligan, 1998a, p.30). The legal system explicitly and implicitly favoured men. As a consequence the key issues for the Irish women's movement (and for supportive males) have been equal pay; the reform of family law; issues in relation to contraception and divorce; male violence; and child care — items on the agenda of most western feminist movements.

The early second wave feminist movement in Ireland was not particularly radical in its challenge to prevailing social and political values compared to the women's movement of many other countries of the West. But given the conservative nature of Irish society, the limited liberal agenda of the majority of Irish feminists was seen by both public and politicians to be a radical challenge to established tenets of public policy. The strategies and outcomes of the Irish women's movement had less in common with the more advanced movements of northern Europe and Britain and much similarity with those of countries such as Greece and Italy (economies with a strong agricultural sector and powerful institutionalised churches) and the United States (with a comparatively small public sector) (Galligan, 1998a, p.54). As a result, according to Galligan (1998a, p.29), 'women's public participation [was] clearly predicated on traditional social attitudes reinforced by the ideology, institutions and structures of an authoritarian Roman Catholic Church and a conservative, nationalist State.'

While women make up a significant proportion of the ordinary membership of the Republic's political parties (about 40 per cent), this is not reflected up the scale. The percentage of women in local government stood at 11.4 per cent in 1991. As exposure and success at the local level is the key to success in Irish politics it is not surprising that the comparatively low measure of participation at council level is reflected in the national political institutions. Thus, in the 1997 election, men made up 80 per cent of candidates and 88 per cent of those elected as Dáil deputies. On the other hand, those women who do make it into the Dáil are more successful, perhaps as they have to be of a particularly high calibre to gain election in the first place. From 1992 to 1996 women held a greater number of government ministries than their proportion in the Dáil would imply (Galligan, 1998a, p.35). The reasons for women's comparative lack of success in the political sphere (a feature by no means unique to Irish society) are complex and not easily explained or remedied. They may include direct political party discrimination against female candidates; timing of political meetings that pay little attention to women's domestic obligations; male networks of political power and influence; women's lack of power in other fields that 'produce' politicians such as business, law and the unions; and male-dominated political agendas that may be of little interest to women.

While women's success in Irish party politics may be limited (though still highly significant) they may have a more enduring level within local, grass-roots and community-based politics, the emergence of which has been an important part of the Irish political scene over the last decade. While Galligan suggests that 'the nature, quantity and outcomes of women's public activities at grass-roots level have yet to be analysed in any form' (1998a, p.58) she points out that the experience in Ireland parallels that of other European countries. Such involvement tends to be 'specific and issue-driven', for example, in the areas of adult education and drugs issues. 'It is seen as an end in itself, not necessarily the start of a broader level of political involvement, as the dearth of women in local politics does not reflect the extent of women's participation in local political activities' (Galligan, 1998a, p.59). This also suggests that the highly adversarial and ritualised nature of local politics may have little attraction for publicly minded women.

While local government yet fails to be attractive, across the EU women are actively becoming involved in locally oriented bodies such as the area-based partnerships. But even here they may find that they are marginalised by men, especially when it comes to formally powerful roles within such organisations. Geddes (1998, p.106), in a recent study of such partnership bodies across the EU, reports that 'women play active and prominent roles in many local partnerships, but are much more likely to be community representatives, and project leaders than partner representatives on partnership boards or management committees where policy decisions are made . . . in most local partnerships formal and active equal opportunity policies are conspicuous by their absence.' He suggests that even when a partnership is focused on issues related to women, women are not necessarily dominant in the decision-making process. In Ireland there has been an attempt to address the gender inequality in partnership organisations. Local partnerships have been directed by the government to have at least 40 per cent female representation on management boards. This requirement may be difficult to meet due to a lack of women in senior positions in partner organisations (health boards, farmer organisations and so on) but in the Tallaght Partnership, for example, 41 per cent of board members are women, an outcome aided by the presence of strong, local women's networks (Geddes, 1998, p.106).

Despite the barriers facing women within both the formal and informal political processes, it is apparent that the specific raising of gender issues and input by women have had significant effects on the form and the content of political debate and policy-making. Thus, suggests Galligan (1998a, p.21), the 'mainstreaming of feminist priorities has made a significant contribution to the increased output of public policies with a women-centred focus in modern times.' If nowhere else, this is reflected in the support that women's groups have received from the state. For example, by 1993, 600 groups were receiving financial support from the Department of Social Welfare alone (Galligan, 1998a, p.60). At the same time, as Coulter shows (reflecting a global reality), the women's movement is experienced and expressed very differently within groups that are experiencing racism, poverty and social exclusion. Movements around gender, despite the sometimes universalising nature of their object, can be as exclusive and divisive as any social or political movement. Lentin, among others, has argued (1998, pp.6–7) that:

> Most studies addressing citizenship and Irish women . . . presume a homo-
> geneity of 'Irish women' and of feminist struggle, and fail to address the impact
> of both racist discourses and the multi-tiered access to citizenship on women of
> ethnic minorities.

In other words, mobilisation around the categories of gender can occlude other
important divisions and differences in Irish society.

## SEXUALITY

In the words of Oliver J. Flanagan TD: there was 'no sex in Ireland before
television' (Tobin, 1996, p.68). Similarly, sexuality is a topic that has been
virtually ignored within Irish sociology (Inglis, 1998d). This neglect is unfortunate
because, since at least the early 1960s, debates over a range of issues linked to
human sexuality have formed a key element of Irish society and of gender
relationships. There is a commonly held perception that attitudes towards
sexuality have seen a marked change in Ireland in recent years and, as Beale
(1986, p.87) argues: 'it is over issues to do with sexuality that the conflict between
traditional and progressive forces in Irish society can be seen most clearly.' As with
constructions of gender more generally, our understandings, experiences and
attitudes about sexuality are socially shaped — by the media, the education
system, religious institutions, the family and social interaction with others.

'Sexuality' is not an unproblematic term. Like 'gender' it is a social construction.
We find not only one sexuality but multifarious sexualities, discussion of which
could fill a whole chapter of this book and more. In many ways sexuality permeates
every aspect of our lives, though often in a subconscious or unremarked manner.
It is built into how we experience aspects of life such as education, work, leisure
and the media. Inasmuch as we can perceive it as a unified field of practices,
attitudes and institutions it is, as British social historian (or historical sociologist)
Jeffrey Weeks points out, 'an *historical* unity which has been shaped by a
multiplicity of forces, and which has undergone complex historical transformations'
(1989, p.ix). In other words 'sexuality' is a diverse field of experience and
behaviour that is brought together at certain times through a common body of
language or discourse. There are many such discourses that help to mould our
understandings of sexuality. Among the most powerful are those generated from
within the family, the education system, medicine, popular culture and the
churches. In Ireland the legal and political systems have also been very important
as debates about various aspects of sexuality have irrupted into the public sphere.

One of the few Irish sociologists to have looked in any detail at the issues
around sexuality is Tom Inglis of UCD. He has discussed the nature of Irish gender
and sexual relationships within the context of the sociology of the Catholic
Church in Ireland (see Chapter 12) and in relation to the development of (and

reaction to) sex education programmes (see, in particular, Inglis, 1998b). A key aim of Inglis's research is to 'break the silence' in relation to Irish sexuality and to question our assumptions. He is especially concerned (1998b, p.3) about the ignorance of many Irish people on the topic and suggests that the failure of Irish people to confront the issue of sex leaves them lacking in confidence and competence.

Inglis's theoretical approach to the analysis of sexuality is founded in the work of French writers Michel Foucault and Pierre Bourdieu. The former theorist has been particularly influential in the development of analyses of the relationship between sexuality and modernity. Sexuality, for Foucault, is not a 'natural' or timeless universal expression of human desire. Rather, it is actively created through *discourses* derived from professional knowledge, social institutions and everyday understandings. Such discourses shape how we think and talk about sex and this, according to Foucault, is something that people in modern societies do all the time. He argues in the first volume of *The history of sexuality* (1980, p.35) that 'what is peculiar to modern societies . . . is not that they consigned sex to a shadow existence, but that they dedicated themselves to speaking about it *ad infinitum*, while exploiting it as the secret.' Knowledge about sex, as about other things, is for Foucault a *site* of struggle, power and control. It is indeed the case that in Ireland the link between sexuality and the desire to control others has been very strong, whether expressed in the realm of family relationships, in the school or in the public sphere.

Contrary to Oliver J. Flanagan's belief, talk about sex did not emerge in Ireland only in the time of modern communications technology. Foucault points out to us that sexuality in the past was not so much hidden or repressed, but talked about in a different sort of way. As Inglis suggests (1998e, p.102) in 'traditional' Ireland 'sex was real and demanding and it was rigorously inculcated in every church, school, hospital and home in the country.' This was a discourse that linked sex to ideas of sin, control, danger and regulation. As constituted by the churches (especially, but not only, the Catholic Church) and the state, sex was a powerful force that needed to be curtailed, particularly within the institution of marriage.

In a fascinating discussion, Inglis has analysed the historical role and influence of the 'Irish mother', in particular how this has helped to shape attitudes to sexuality in Ireland. The basis of this process was laid in the nineteenth century with the restructuring of the rural economy towards pastoral farming (see Chapter 3). As women lost their productive role — for example, as weavers and spinners — they were increasingly confined to a powerless domestic position. A new basis of power was built through an 'alliance' between Irish rural mothers and the modernising Catholic Church, which was worked out as follows (Inglis, 1998e, pp.198–9):

The domination and control of women by the Church, and the necessity for women to ally themselves with that dominating power if they themselves were to have any power, led to their high level of marital fertility which, in turn, created the need for postponed marriage, permanent celibacy and emigration among their children. These practices were encouraged by the mother in the home through a devotion to the Church, a rigorous sexual morality, and a physical and emotional distance from her children. It is this scenario, re-enacted over the generations, that is the essence of the dialectical relationship of power between Church and family in modern Ireland.

The implications of this 'alliance' for the shaping of sexuality in Ireland were manifold. Inglis suggests that priests gained control of the sexual life of mothers by their portrayal of women as 'weak, fragile beings who must be protected (by the priest) from the sexual viper that lurked within them'. The church imposed a strict discipline of sexual morality. Women were encouraged to feel ashamed of their bodies. The discourse of the church penetrated their everyday lives as the Catholic confessional became a site for the interrogation of women about their sexual feelings, desires and activities. Inglis suggests (1998e, p.188) that 'sex became the most abhorrent sin'. Indeed, it came to dominate the notion of sin itself. On a broader plane, Inglis sees mothers as having an essential role in the 'civilizing process' (as defined by German sociologist Norbert Elias). The modernisation of Irish society was reflected in the extension of disciplines of cleanliness, control and obedience into the Irish family and the key instruments of this process were the church, the school and the mother. The home, along with the school, became a site for supervision and surveillance by the church. The mores of the church and the practices of priests provided a powerful model for child rearing, as mothers imitated the social and moral perspective of the religious. 'Through an imitation of their celibate lifestyle, their body discipline and morality [mothers] inculcated a sexual and emotional repression which was crucial to the attainment of postponed marriages, permanent celibacy and emigration' (1998e, p.193).

In modern Ireland we now talk about sex in very different ways, with a complex range of public and private discourses that embrace 'news reports, feature articles, documentaries, panel discussions and talk radio' (Inglis, 1998b, p.148). The nexus of sex and religion has been at least partly broken and 'desire and fantasy [have been] liberated from the cells of sin' (Inglis, 1998e, p.103). The church itself has also learnt how to talk about sex in the new language of 'relationships', if not yet of pleasure. There is now a multiplicity of competing discourses that relate to issues of modernity, the public sphere and sexuality. For Inglis (1998b, p.150) modern Ireland is now witnessing a conflict between two main opposing belief systems. One set of beliefs is based on traditional Catholicism and links contemporary manifestations of sexuality to materialism, consumerism and liberalism. Such a view sees modern expressions of sexuality as being intricately linked to the process of producing, buying and exchanging commodities. The other discourse of sexuality reflects 'a modern, or indeed post-modern, secular society based on liberal individualism'. It claims to be open about sexuality and to be non-judgemental about people's private and intimate behaviour or about depictions of sexuality in the media. The existence of these two powerful and competing discourses can, as Inglis (1998b, p.150) says, give rise to a particular contradictoriness in Irish experience. He remarks:

> It may well be that a characteristic of our open, democratic, pluralist society is that children are expected to be able to reconcile these contradictory images and, on a Sunday morning, move from watching Madonna on MTV to praying in church to images of Our Lady.

Overall, Inglis argues that Irish attitudes to sexuality have changed for the better, with an increased self-confidence about sexuality (1998b, p.146):

> There is no longer the same shyness, embarrassment, guilt and shame about being sexual. There is not the same sense of fear that used to be a characteristic of Catholic Ireland. Sin and damnation seem to be a thing of the past. Being sexually active is the norm.

Inglis identifies himself with a liberal discourse that stresses responsibility, individualism, maturity and critical reflection and welcomes the critical debate and discussion of sexuality. This extends to revelations about his own sexual development which he relates in a (fortunately) humorous tone (see, for example, Inglis, 1998e). While the liberal discourse has certainly increased the quantity and range of talk about sexuality, there are those who are more sceptical about whether this in itself will change dominant structures and discourses. Thus, Ryan (1997, p.33), in a discussion of how adolescent sexuality is formed in schools, argues that 'such talk can reproduce sexuality according to dominant discourses and continue to structure it in ways that reinforce women's essential sexuality and passivity.'

Inglis does point to a major issue when discussing sexuality, one that applies to any attempt at discovering sociological knowledge: he reminds us that most individuals are skilled social actors and know how to talk about sexuality (or any other topic) in terms of what is deemed appropriate in any social situation. Thus, 'how young people talk about sexuality varies according to whether they are a couple being intimate, in a group, in a classroom or with their parents'. Thus, in a sense, people's sexual identities are *plastic*. They are, to an extent, shaped by social situations and by competing definitions. Similarly, a man who has sex with another man may not identify himself as 'gay' but he may be labelled so by powerful discourses of the law, medicine or popular culture.

Inglis's most recent (1998b) research focuses on the attempts to introduce systematic sex education (the Relationships and Sexuality Education programme or RSE) into Irish primary schools. This has been a long and very divisive struggle

— one that has not yet been resolved. For Inglis it represents another episode in the struggle between the (Catholic) Church and state over sexuality and the regulation of bodies. He argues that it can be seen as an aspect of the secularisation of Irish society (see Chapter 12): 'part of a slow, steady, but ongoing struggle by the state to take ownership and control of education away from the churches, particularly the Catholic Church, and to assume authority for shaping the minds, hearts and bodies of Irish children' (1998b, p.6). Inglis sees the response of the Irish government to sexuality education as 'an Irish solution to an Irish problem': one that carries an implicit recognition by the state of the 'special position' of the Catholic Church in Irish society and, in particular, the field of education.

*Inter alia* Inglis's analysis reflects the dearth of concrete information on Irish sexual behaviour and attitudes. For example, the survey material he reports on in relation to the sexual activity of Irish young people (1998b, p.10) was commissioned by the condom manufacturer Durex, so may not be as disinterested and objective as we might want. Furthermore, his own research findings (1998b, Chapter 7) on attitudes to the RSE programme are based on focus group interviews carried out with small groups of parents, teachers and children in a small Irish country town and may not be very representative of broader opinions. Irish sociology has yet to produce a comprehensive account of sexual behaviour.

While Inglis reflects a liberal optimism about sexuality, some Irish feminists have stressed the complexities and contradictions inherent in its practices, especially where it concerns women. O'Connor (1998, p.177), for example, indicates the distinguishing features of sexuality as experienced by young Irish women: an emphasis on active heterosexuality; continuing problems over the availability of contraception; the tangled concept of 'love'; the experience of sexual harassment; the stigmatisation of abortion; powerful and contradictory messages around body imagery; an emphasis on sex as a consumer product; and the pressures against 'saying no'. She points out (1998, p.180) that 'there is considerable pressure on young women to be sexually active but little acceptance of the need to locate the conception in the wider context of social responsibility.' For women, 'love' can be a source of both power and vulnerability — a veil that hides the power within a relationship or a means of achieving a measure of equality. Unfortunately, the slowly developing sociology of masculinity in Ireland has yet to provide a similar critical analysis of the challenges that modern patterns and discourses of sexuality provide for Irish men.

## Homosexuality

One of the more rapidly changing discussions around sexuality in Ireland relates to the experiences of lesbians and gay men. While there has been major change in how lesbians and gay men have been viewed in Irish society it is far from the case that alternative sexualities are broadly accepted or encouraged. Moane suggests that despite the perception of rapid social change in Ireland in recent times, 'psychological change' has not followed suit. She argues (1997, p.431) that, despite important legislative changes in the 1990s and an unprecedented level of inclusion in public life, 'fear and prejudice is alive and well in Irish psyches and society.' In a review of Irish gay and lesbian film-making, Petitt (1999, p.62) describes the 'audible groans of disgust' he witnessed in a Dublin cinema on the occasion of Irish film's 'first gay kiss' in the movie *Reefer and the Model*. There is also evidence that attitudes are slow to change. In discussing the issue of homosexuality with secondary school students, Lynch (1999a, p.245) reported the following:

> Students were generally not accustomed to addressing the subject of sexual orientation, so they literally did not know what to say or how to say what they did feel or know . . . most students displayed visible discomfort and unease if the subject arose . . . many students seemed to lack a vocabulary to name their feelings and views on the subject of sexual differences. The only view which boys especially felt comfortable expressing were those of hostility and derision.

At least partly as a consequence of continued hostility to homosexuality within the Irish population, much of gay and lesbian experience in Ireland is still hidden, not least to sociologists. Similarly, the nature and processes of homophobia as a key element of dominant gender identities — masculinity in particular — is a much neglected topic. As Petitt (1999, p.63) reminds us, 'teenage gays are disproportionately represented in Irish suicide figures . . . men still get assaulted by homophobes, and . . . many gay men still feel compelled to emigrate despite law reforms, some shifts in social attitudes and increased prosperity.' Discrimination against gay and lesbian people, extending to physical violence, remains an important aspect of social inequality in Ireland. While sociological research into the lives of Irish gays and lesbians is very sparse, there is some evidence (reported in Moane, 1997, pp.437–8) that they suffer higher levels of poverty and social exclusion than the community as a whole.

It is also important to realise that there are many contradictions and complexities in relation to gay and lesbian experience in Ireland. For example, gay and lesbian issues are often lumped together, without recognition of important gender differences. As McVeigh (1997, p.80) points out, 'any label applied to a body of people as diverse as those in the gay and lesbian community, can ultimately only offer a fairly crude and functional blanket description of the many sexual practices and lifestyles experienced by members of that community.' Thus, for example, the experiences of bisexual men and women and transgendered individuals are often overlooked. The connections between sexual behaviour and social and personal identity are not direct and not always predictable. There may be those who engage in sexual activity with a member of the same sex who do not identify as gay or lesbian; at the same time a homosexual identity is no more dependent on physical sexual activity than is a 'straight' one.

Within social sciences such as sociology and psychology homosexuality and other 'alternative sexualities' have tended to be discussed within the context of the sociology of 'deviance'. According to Moane (1997, p.432) such an approach has posed considerable problems for lesbians and gay men and, along with religious views, has been a significant source of prejudice and discrimination. The most recent conceptualisations of homosexuality, and indeed of sexuality more generally, have been within the perspective of *queer theory*, which, following writers such as Foucault, challenges all gender categories, including 'gay' and 'lesbian'. Queer theorists emphasise the diversity of sexualities and their social and cultural constructedness and stress the fluidity of categorisations. Sexual orientation and identity need not be fixed, but may be more fluid and contextually determined. Moane cites the work of feminist Adrienne Rich who posited the notion of the 'lesbian continuum' as a 'range of . . . woman-centred experience'. Similarly, there has been the development of the 'men who have sex with men' category — a definition that attempts to include those who identify as gay, bisexual and those men who may occasionally experience sex with other men, such as prisoners, in what is termed by Weeks (1989, p.109) as 'situational homosexuality'. The theoretical perspective reflects the practical need within discourses of public health, generated by the spread of AIDS and other sexually transmitted diseases, to reflect the diversity of sexual identity and behaviours that men (and women) may engage in.

How society responds to, and shapes, homosexuality is of importance not only for gays and lesbians, but is crucial to the formation of sexualities more generally. Homophobia, or fear of homosexuality, is a potent force in the development of dominant modes of masculinity and femininity. McKeown *et al.* (1999, p.223) show how *hegemonic masculinity* (a term derived from the work of Australian sociologist Bob Connell) is created and at least partly sustained through homophobia:

> At a public level the hegemonic definition of masculinity still values power which is exercised — mostly by men — in such a way that alternative ways of being and viewing men are closed off. Within this exemplary form of masculinity, qualities and practices of care and nurture are subordinated and associated not merely with femininity but, at worst, with gayness — a form of masculinity which is constructed as the worst thing a man can be.

Indeed, gayness is seen as a negation of manhood and this is translated into anything that can be seized upon as evidence of feminine behaviour: involvement in domestic work, particular popular cultural choices or ways of walking, talking or dressing. Similarly, homophobic responses to lesbianism help to shape dominant notions of femininity. Moane (1997, p.88) argues that:

[Homophobia] is damaging to all women because [it] involves extreme negative images and views of women, and induces fear in heterosexual women about their own feelings of affection for other women. The label 'lesbian' has been used as a weapon to silence and intimidate women who speak out assertively or defiantly, and as a label to express an anti-feminist position.

It is not surprising then that Inglis (1998b, p.98) links Irish gays and lesbians to a 'radical attitude to sexuality': one that challenges existing conceptions of gender, family and sexuality. The emergence of gay and lesbian sexualities into Irish public life has served to disrupt traditional patterns of sexuality and gender relationships that have developed since the famine period. Similarly, lesbian and gay activism has challenged dominant discourses of national and cultural identity. Perhaps the most celebrated and high profile example has been the ongoing debate around the participation of Irish gays and lesbians in St Patrick's Day parades in the United States. This conflict involves a 'redefinition of Irishness' (O'Carroll and Collins, 1995, p.5) and directly challenges dominant images of ethnic identity (Maguire, 1995, p.207):

The St Patrick's Day parade symbolizes more than the coming of age of Irish-identified lesbians and gay men in the United States. It represents a constant reference point regarding issues of ethnic and racial identity, constitutional questions and the separation of church and state, lesbian and gay community politics, matters concerning Catholicism and other religious doctrines, homophobia and other parades.

In Ireland, as elsewhere, gays and lesbians have been very much involved in the processes of building a community. While we discuss some of the problematic issues around the concept of 'community' elsewhere (see Chapter 13), it is notable that, particularly since the foundation of the Irish Gay Rights Movement in 1974 and the formation of separate lesbian organisations in 1978, Irish gays and lesbians have sought to develop a way to express and celebrate their sexuality — and to defend their rights — that is specifically Irish while also having a global context. Like other aspects of Irish cultural identity, such a process entails a negotiation of the local and the global. Kieran Rose indicates some of the tensions involved (1995, p.72):

While the lesbian and gay movement is quintessentially an international movement it tends, because of the unequal world we live in, to be dominated by the politics, culture and priorities of advanced capitalist countries and, in particular, of their metropolitan centres such as New York and London.

The challenge and the achievement has been to develop an indigenous Irish gay and lesbian movement and community that reflects the nature and history of the society. According to Rose this has been achieved through the linkage of gay and lesbian issues to broader social movements such as the labour movement and with state agencies such as the Combat Poverty Agency.

## Contraception

If homosexuality has been one of the main sites of struggle over sexuality in modern Ireland, of similar importance has been the issue of contraception. Galligan (1998a, p.142) suggests that the conflict over the right to birth control reflects the modernisation of Irish society and represents 'a visible weakening of restrictive social norms and religious orthodoxy and . . . a focus for liberal voices in parliament and public life. Significantly, it mirrored a silent revolution on the part of women, changing in a fundamental way the nature of women's relationship with society.'

The demand for the legalisation and provision of contraception was a key plank of the Irish women's movement. Indeed, the conflict around the issue helped to define the forces that were subsequently to contend over the issues of divorce and abortion. The sale, importation, advertising and public discussion of contraceptives and birth control were proscribed by the Irish state in a series of legislative acts from 1929. In its bans on contraception Ireland was not alone. Other Catholic countries such as France, Italy and Spain had similar laws, though they were changed earlier than in Ireland. Other states such as Chile and the Philippines maintain restrictions in the area (Galligan, 1998a, p.143). Demographic patterns indicate that the practice of contraception was developing in Irish society from the early 1960s. People smuggled contraceptives into the country and doctors were able to prescribe the contraceptive pill as a 'cycle regulator'. By the early 1970s there was considerable public debate on the issue, yet the (Fianna Fáil) government of the time was implacably opposed to attempts to legalise contraception. Despite the failure to legislate, illegal family-planning clinics were established, including one in a state-funded maternity hospital. At this stage, about a third of the population supported a change in the law to make the supply of contraceptives legal (Galligan, 1998a, p.149).

In 1973 Mary McGee (with the assistance of many others, including Mary Robinson) successfully challenged the state's prohibition on the importation of contraceptives. Mary Robinson introduced a total of seven private members bills into the Seanad in her attempts to secure the legalisation of contraception. It was not until 1994 that all prohibitions on the sale and distribution of contraceptives were lifted (Galligan, 1998a, p.142). According to Galligan (1998a, p.155), 'the contraceptive issue is an interesting example of a feminist issue being main-streamed and in the process being redefined by feminist legislators.' The concerns of the women's movement were subsumed into a general liberal campaign. The specific needs of women to control their fertility were largely ignored and the even more inflammatory topic of abortion constantly impinged upon the debate.

## POSTSCRIPT: GLOBAL SEX?

The Australian writer and gay activist Denis Altman (1999) has remarked on the impact of 'the globalisation of sex'. He argues that, while sex and sexuality remain central to much political discourse, on a global level they are increasingly used by 'reactionary forces' to mobilise against social and cultural change, as reflected, for example, in the Western pro-life movement and in the tenets of fundamentalist Islam (finding its most extreme and horrific expression in the Taliban regime in Afghanistan). For Altman sexuality has become the arena around which human rights are disputed in the name of 'traditional morality'. The forces of globalisation have led to a convergence of sexual mores across the world but they have also had contradictory social effects with regard to sexuality:

> The incorporation of the world within the dominant capitalist order undermines 'traditional' ways of understanding and regulating the personal, and, as it does so, leaves open the possibility for both greater freedom and greater suffering. In destroying traditional pre-capitalist economies and ways of life, globalisation breaks down existing assumptions of order and tradition and incorporates sex into the market economy.

The contradictory effects of such change may include, for example, the breakdown of extended families and the growth of self-conscious gay and lesbian identities and communities. Such changes are, as we have sought to demonstrate, apparent in Ireland. Whether such changes can be described as a 'good thing' or a 'bad thing' in the Irish context remain very much open to debate, research and analysis.

# 9

# *The body, health and illness*

Our everyday understanding of the body is that it is an organic entity, or perhaps even a machine or system, that is subject to occasional breakdown and gradual deterioration. When we think of our own body, or of health and illness, we tend to think in individual, personal terms. The contribution that sociology makes is to emphasise the social nature of the body and of the processes and conditions that we call health and illness.

For example, our likelihood of contracting hepatitis is partly an effect of the robustness of our immune system and our exposure to a particular virus but it is also shaped by our:

- age
- sex
- gender
- occupation
- geographical location
- lifestyle, including our behaviours in relation to sex and drugs
- previous involvement with medical systems (especially blood transfusions)
- knowledge and attitudes.

The same applies to any other form of illness or wellness, from our chances of having a trim, taut and terrific body to our likelihood of developing malaria. All are the result of social processes.

This chapter commences with a brief discussion of the emergent discipline of the sociology of the body, for without human bodies there is no health or illness. It then outlines the main concerns of the sociology of health and illness, emphasising how the varying theoretical perspectives brought to bear influence the choice of object of study. We argue that the biomedical model of health remains dominant and in an Irish context continues to shape much of the sociological analysis of health and illness and the policy initiatives that are often based on such research. Finally, we look very briefly to the future, for ours is an era of dramatic change in the fields of medicine and the sciences of life and the body. What is the role for sociologists as society grapples with the social and ethical challenges of the Human Genome Project, cloning and transgenic transplants?

# THE BODY

Whilst sociologists often speak of individuals in abstract terms (agents, actors, role-players and so on) there has been a strong shift in recent years towards recognising the social importance of the body — hardly surprising in a culture seemingly obsessed with *physical* bodies — with interests ranging from dieting to working out, from fashion to cosmetic surgery. Furthermore, as society becomes increasingly interested in the possibilities of 'virtual' entities, there is also an increased focus on the corporeal, whether through technology, health or sport.

Sociological interest in the body is comparatively new. Sociological thinking has long emphasised the 'cultural' and consequently the 'natural' — including the body — has long been played down. There has even been considerable hostility towards approaches like sociobiology and genetics which have sought to incorporate biological processes into social analysis.

Recent sociological interest in the body has been stimulated by a number of factors (Nettleton and Watson, 1998, pp.4–7). First, recent times have seen a *politicisation* of the body. Two groups have been of particular importance here. Feminists have focused very much on how women's bodies have been controlled and abused in a range of cultures. Works such as *Our bodies, ourselves* (Boston Women's Health Book Collective, 1973) and analyses of childbirth and eating disorders have critically examined how women's bodies are shaped by social factors and practices such as the medical industries, advertising and the fitness industry. Similarly, disabled groups have focused on how society discriminates against those that stray in any way from the dominant view of the 'normal' body.

Second, *demographic change*, particularly in relation to the ageing or 'greying' of the population in Western societies, has led to new issues. Increased lifespan has led to the emergence of new sets of questions. The incidence of some diseases, such as cancer and stroke, has increased while there are important issues related to the quality of life in later years. Many of these are directly linked to the body and its functioning. Ultimately, there are social and sociological questions related to death and the issue of euthanasia.

Third is the rise in *consumer culture*. There is a hugely increased focus on the body as part of this development. On the one hand, the body is a staple of advertising imagery and questions are constantly raised about the effects of images portrayed in the media. On the other hand, the body itself has become a major site of consumption: from cosmetics, fashion, diet and fitness to plastic surgery, tattoos and body-piercing.

Fourth is the effect that the development of *new technologies* is having on our bodies and our experiences of them. Again there are many areas of change here. New surgical techniques, including organ transplants, artificial body parts and cosmetic surgery, lead us to question the boundaries between humans and technology. One writer (Hayles, 1995, p.321) suggests that up to 10 percent of the

American population may now be considered cyborgs — part human, part machine — in as much as their bodies are partly made up of pacemakers, plastic hips, penile implants, silicon breasts, artificial skin, stomach staples or transplanted corneas. There are other areas of technological development that can only be listed here but which may have as yet unforeseen impacts on our personal and social lives: smart drugs (to improve memory or intelligence); genetic manipulation; cloning; dietary supplements ('nutriceuticals') and transgenic implants (the use of animals' body parts).

Finally, the development of *communications technologies*, in particular the Internet, but also technologies such as digital cameras and computer viruses have helped to raise questions about the nature of the 'virtual' and the 'real'. In an age where a person can adopt multiple personas on the web or continuously retouch their own family photograph album, the physical body may become a touchstone of 'reality' and authenticity. This may increasingly be the case as other aspects of our identity — such as nation, class and religion — become less salient or defined.

Overall, we are now far more *reflexive* about our bodies. Rather than a vehicle (or encumbrance) for action that is taken for granted, our bodies are now sites of activity: always open to monitoring, improvement, alteration and concern (Jenkins, 1999). We no longer adopt a fatalistic approach to our bodies but expect to be able to assert a greater degree of control. This translates into a wide range of behaviour: from working-out and dieting, to yoga and aerobics, to cholesterol tests and pap smears. Our heightened consciousness of our bodies has undoubtedly driven the continual expansion in the field of 'health' described below.

There is now a considerable sociological industry that focuses on the body (Nettleton and Watson, 1998, p.2), much of it pitched at a very abstruse and abstract level and often with little analysis of how the body operates in everyday life. However, the renewed interest in the body and the self has stimulated new insights into the sociology of health and illness, calling into question particularly the assumptions made of many of its routine categories. The challenge for sociology now is to combine the new critical approach to the body with empirical analyses of how people view, use and feel about their bodies within a range of social settings and structural situations.

## THE SOCIOLOGY OF HEALTH AND ILLNESS

A major aspect of our embodied existence is the health or illness that we experience — individually and socially. Whereas the sociology of the body has tended to be neglected, there has long been an interest in medical sociology and in the sociology of health and illness. This can be traced back to Durkheim's work on suicide which in many ways provided a model for the sociological study of illness and became one of the bases for the specific social science discipline of epidemiology.

Medical sociology has given much in the way of support to the medical industry by supplying data about patterns of disease and in attempting to deduce causal relationships from such observations. It has also provided an interpretation of the 'sick role': the process whereby people adopt the role of 'patient'. Such a role requires the stripping away of many of our everyday beliefs and practices and allows us to expose ourselves to unquestioned subservience to professional instructions, outside observation of humiliating bodily practices and invasive medical examinations and procedures. In return we can claim the status of 'patient' and escape adherence to many of the norms of society, such as daily work, a cheerful countenance and appropriate dress. The sick role concept has been widely used in the training of doctors and other medical personnel.

The sociological analysis of health and illness has now moved beyond epidemiology and analysis of the sick role to embrace numerous aspects of social life. This reflects the increased interest in the body as well as the expansion of 'health' to embrace an ever increasing proportion of our everyday life and behaviour. According to Porter (1997, p.15), 'the rise of sociology in health care can largely be explained by the gradual demise of . . . the "biomedical model" of health and illness [see below] which saw health and illness as a purely mechanical, physical matter.' It is now recognised that issues of health and illness can not be reduced to malfunctions of the individual body or the prevalence of germs or other causes of disease (though these of course are and remain factors). Rather, there is now a recognition that health and illness are social entities — a sociology of health and illness is therefore necessary. Such a sociology can investigate many aspects of the medical field.

Sociology allows us to investigate patterns of health and illness. This embraces the branch of social research known as epidemiology. Epidemiology is the side of medical sociology that is closest to the medical professions themselves. It tends to use a positivist and highly quantitative approach focusing on rates of illness or other factors, attitudinal research and the use of control groups and other aspects of scientific research.

Sociology has much to contribute to an understanding of the experience of health and illness. Here both quantitative and qualitative techniques are used. How people define and experience pain, for example, has much to tell us about how they may or may not respond to the provision of health care services. Similarly, the exploration of how women have experienced childbirth and the medical interventions associated with it has helped to alter how maternity services are being provided.

The sociology of health and illness has also contributed a great deal to our understanding of the medical industries and the medical professionals and other workers that operate within them. It has often been critical of the professions, laying bare the ways that professional groups create and sustain relations of power and domination over others in society, particularly through legitimated monopolies of knowledge and practice such as the right to issue prescriptions or sign sickness certificates. Moreover, it can teach us a lot about how professional groups attain and maintain their privileged status.

Interpretative sociology has much of interest to say about how health care is provided, in particular how members of the various groups involved in the practice of health and illness, such as doctors, nurses, patients and administrators, interact in ways that help to define each others' roles and the nature of health and illness themselves. Discourse analysts, drawing on the work of writers such as Thomas Szasz (1961) and Michel Foucault (1973), have explored how the discourses of health are created and maintained through institutions such as hospitals, clinics, asylums and popular medical books. This approach emphasises the social constructedness of health and illness. Some of the most radical critiques of medical practice and medical knowledge stem from this approach. Categories such as 'health', 'madness' and 'sick' are called into question and revealed to be fully social in nature. Medical knowledge is shown to be a particularly powerful form of discourse, and this approach is critical to an analysis of the 'medicalisation' of modern social life.

## THE BIOMEDICAL MODEL

The most powerful discourse within the field of medicine remains the biomedical model of health. This model dominates current thinking about wellness and illness as it appears in people's everyday beliefs and attitudes, in the practices of most health workers and in medical research and policy-making. The model holds that health and illness are caused by identifiable factors such as bacteria, viruses, toxins, chemical imbalances, genetic disorders or physical accidents. These factors can be identified most effectively by trained and professional personnel according to standardised tests and diagnoses. They can then be treated to varying degrees of success by specific practices, drugs and techniques. Medical research is a process of cumulatively discovering more about the causes of disease and ill health and, as society develops, medicine will gradually identify and cure an increasing number of ailments and conditions. At the same time, 'folk' knowledge, traditional cures and superstitions will become increasingly less prevalent. As a result, the welfare of people in developed societies will gradually improve, longevity will increase and people will suffer less.

This is a very powerful discourse and one that appeals both to health consumers and to the medical industry. It supports the position of medical professionals, gives hope to patients and predictability to policy-makers. It justifies the activities of drug companies, medical researchers and builders of hospitals and other health facilities. It also aligns very well with the theories of modernisation. It is a discourse taken so much for granted that it is very difficult to challenge or subvert.

Tucker (1997, p.31) suggests that 'it is one of the characteristics of the modern biomedicine that it has hegemonic designs and it has consistently discredited, marginalised or suppressed other systems or practices.' These include 'folk' medicines, 'alternative' medicines and other approaches, some of which have nevertheless managed to become more 'respectable' and have been admitted to the field of 'real' medicine, for example, chiropractic, acupuncture and meditation.

Tucker reminds us that medical knowledge, like all knowledge, is socially constructed. The answers to health challenges are not just out there waiting to be discovered by scientists, doctors and researchers. Rather, medical knowledge is intrinsically tied up with social factors such as class, religion, gender difference and the interests and activities of commercial and political interest groups. This helps us to understand, at least partly, why so much money has been channelled into the development of drugs like Viagra, while across the world millions of children die every year from diarrhoea.

The biomedical model tends to be individualistic; thus, the Department of Health's women's health policy targets cigarette smoking as the greatest threat to women's health, rather than poverty, discrimination or the nature of the workplace (O'Donovan, 1997a, p.160). Similarly, dietary advice is applied to the individual patient, rather than being aimed at the food industry as a whole.

What might be the alternative to the biomedical model? *Holism* is often cited. This term can have various meanings, and the boundaries between 'biomedical' and 'holistic' medicine overlap and are hotly contested. An holistic approach can apply to the individual where a broader range of systems, including the 'biological, the energetic, the psychic, the interpersonal and the spiritual' (Tucker, 1997, p.42) are brought into view. More broadly holism encompasses economic and political as well as biological and environmental systems; it reflects the idea that health and illness are not simply biological phenomena but are socially produced. Tucker (1997, p.42) argues for a holistic medicine that does not privilege single explanations or therapies, which he contrasts with the 'reductionism' of the biomedical model. He suggests that:

> The emergence of a holistic paradigm will require not only a change in the practice of medicine and health care, but also in the knowledge system and the model of science on which it is based. It will also require changes in the institutional fabric of health care.

What might this mean in practice? Perhaps it might be to provide the consumers of health care with more information, thus leading to greater choice of therapies. Such an approach is advocated in policy documents such as the Irish Department of Health's *Shaping a healthier future* (1994, p.40). It may mean giving greater recognition and support to alternative medicine and therapies, such as homeopathy, herbalism or shiatsu. Or it may mean paying greater attention to social and environmental issues such as air pollution, workplace hazards or dietary intake. The spiritual dimension is also seen as important. This may mean providing ways for people to have more 'meaning' in their lives.

The end result of a holistic approach may be to enhance the health of the population, but it may also serve to increase the level of surveillance of people and to extend the reach of medical dominance into ever more areas of everyday life. This is suggested by O'Donovan (1997a, p.159), who argues that broader dissemination of medical information leads to an 'intensification of biomedical hegemony'. Similarly, the adoption of 'alternative' therapies may result in a replication of the biomedical model, particularly as practitioners strive to become 'professionals' (the case of chiropractic illustrates this).

The conflict between biomedicine and holism is intense, but also complex and dynamic. It is clear that one of the strategies used by professional medical groups has been the active exclusion of many forms of therapy and practice. In Ireland as elsewhere, the history of the medical profession as we know it today has been the marginalisation and negation of 'folk' practices such as bonesetting, herbalism and faith healing. The discourse of biomedicine has achieved great power, and its supporters can hold up great achievements and point to any number of 'medical marvels'. However, popular choices seem to favour an increasing number of 'alternative' therapies, and many medical problems are dealt with through a broad variety of means of self-medication (MacFarlane, 1997) or attendance with 'alternative' practitioners (Tucker, 1997, p.31). It seems clear that both models of health and illness will continue to contend for public and official support.

## DEFINING HEALTH AND ILLNESS

While we can usually say of ourselves that we are feeling well or sick, health itself is a difficult concept to define (Blaxter, 1995). In its 1946 Constitution, the World Health Organisation defined health as a 'state of complete physical, mental and social well-being', but this understanding poses as many questions as it answers and seems to set up an impossible ideal — few of us could claim such a state for ourselves. Indeed, survey research has revealed that up to 95 per cent of the population experiences some sort of ill health in any two-week period (MacFarlane, 1997, p.17).

In many respects health and illness are relative terms and thus very difficult to define. Furthermore, definitions are often dependent on the criteria and normative frameworks used by the observer. While the existence of a broken arm may be fairly unproblematic, conditions such as obesity, depression or hyperactivity are far more open to interpretation and, as Cleary (1997, p.195) suggests, even for the understanding of 'diagnosis-specific data', methodological and conceptual considerations are crucial. Post-modern theorists, building on the work of writers such as Foucault, further problematise the notion of health. As Fox (1998, p.11) suggests, 'all definitions [of health] have a politics associated with them; all try to persuade us to a particular perspective on the person who is healthy or ill.'

Medical policy-makers and epidemiologists use the term 'health status' to refer to the present state of illness or wellness in a community. It can be described in terms of 'rates of death and illness in a community, the prevalence of good and poor health practices, rates of death and disease (chronic and infectious) and the prevalence of symptoms/conditions of well-being' (Doorley, 1998, p.17). Health status can be defined and measured by an outside observer, perhaps an 'expert' such as a doctor or dietician, according to various criteria. Similarly, it can be based on the reported health-related perceptions of a person — physical functioning, emotional well-being, pain and so on. In reality it is difficult to combine both measures.

We have seen that it is very difficult to define health or well-being in any sort of holistic way. As a result, those that seek to measure such entities tend to use simpler indicators such as life expectancy; incidence of and/or death rates from specific diseases; availability and provision of specific health services. In terms of capturing the complex state that may constitute health these are obviously fairly crude and indirect measures. However, there is a strong desire to establish and measure health in terms of these sorts of indicators. These include the desire to compare countries according to their health status; the need to inform health policy and expenditure; the ability to measure progress in a certain direction; and a way to anticipate future health needs (Doorley, 1998, p.18).

The most common indicators of health status used are life expectancy; death rates; morbidity rates (that is, rates of incidence of certain diseases); patterns of lifestyle; and self-perceived health status. Ireland continues to lag behind many countries in the availability of such data, especially at the localised level. This has made it difficult to analyse health patterns in Ireland; to identify causal patterns (for example, links between pollution levels and health outcomes); or to inform policy-making in a critical way.

## Life expectancy

Life expectancy is seen as one of the most important of health measures. It is widely used to compare countries (for example, in United Nations (UN) reports) and to measure 'progress' in a country, especially in terms of its modernisation. It is calculated by applying the death rates within a five- or one-year age group, and within each sex from the population under study, to a hypothetical birth cohort of 100,000 individuals (Doorley, 1998, p.20). Compared to other European countries (Figure 9.1), life expectancy in Ireland (at age 40) is relatively low, but slowly improving. While the contributory factors are complex, it may be that our high incidence of cardiovascular disease and certain cancers is a cause (Doorley, 1998, p.20).

## Figure 9.1 Life expectancy for males and females, EU countries

| Country | Year | Sex | Life expectancy in years at ages: | | | | Excess of female life expectancy over male expectancy at age 0 |
|---------|------|-----|------|------|------|------|------|
| | | | 0 | 1 | 40 | 65 | |
| Austria | 1994 | M | 73.4 | 72.8 | 35.6 | 15.1 | 6.3 |
| | | F | 79.7 | 79.2 | 41.0 | 18.6 | |
| Belgium | 1994 | M | 73.4 | 72.9 | 35.7 | 14.8 | 6.7 |
| | | F | 80.1 | 79.5 | 41.4 | 19.1 | |
| Denmark | 1994 | M | 72.7 | 72.2 | 34.7 | 14.3 | 5.4 |
| | | F | 78.1 | 77.5 | 39.3 | 17.7 | |
| Finland | 1994 | M | 72.8 | 72.2 | 34.9 | 14.6 | 7.3 |
| | | F | 80.1 | 79.5 | 41.3 | 18.6 | |
| France* | 1994 | M | 73.8 | 73.2 | 36.3 | 16.2 | 8.1 |
| | | F | 81.9 | 81.3 | 43.2 | 20.6 | |
| Germany | 1994 | M | 73.1 | 72.5 | 35.1 | 14.7 | 6.5 |
| | | F | 79.6 | 78.9 | 40.8 | 18.4 | |
| Greece | 1994 | M | 75.2 | 74.8 | 37.4 | 16.1 | 5.0 |
| | | F | 80.2 | 79.8 | 41.5 | 18.4 | |
| **Ireland** | **1994** | **M** | **73.2** | **72.7** | **35.1** | **13.9** | **5.5** |
| | | **F** | **78.7** | **78.1** | **39.7** | **17.4** | |
| Italy | 1992 | M | 74.0 | 73.7 | 36.5 | 15.4 | 6.6 |
| | | F | 80.6 | 80.1 | 42.0 | 19.2 | |
| Luxembourg | 1994 | M | 73.2 | 72.5 | 35.4 | 14.6 | 6.5 |
| | | F | 79.7 | 79.2 | 41.1 | 18.7 | |
| Netherlands | 1994 | M | 74.6 | 74.1 | 36.2 | 14.8 | 5.7 |
| | | F | 80.3 | 79.7 | 41.5 | 19.1 | |
| Portugal | 1994 | M | 71.6 | 71.2 | 34.9 | 14.4 | 7.0 |
| | | F | 78.6 | 78.2 | 40.4 | 17.9 | |
| Spain | 1993 | M | 73.8 | 73.4 | 36.5 | 15.7 | 7.3 |
| | | F | 81.1 | 80.6 | 42.5 | 19.5 | |
| Sweden | 1994 | M | 76.1 | 75.4 | 37.6 | 16.0 | 5.3 |
| | | F | 81.4 | 80.7 | 42.3 | 19.7 | |
| UK | 1994 | M | 74.2 | 73.7 | 35.9 | 14.7 | 5.2 |
| | | F | 79.4 | 78.8 | 40.5 | 18.3 | |
| EU average | 1992 | M | 73.3 | 72.9 | 35.6 | 15.0 | 6.6 |
| | | F | 79.9 | 79.4 | 41.3 | 18.8 | |

* provisional data
(*Source*: Murray, 1999, p.268)

# Causes of death

Figures on the major causes of death are often used as an indicator of the health status of a society and even of its success in becoming developed. The reasons why people in a society die, and the stage of life at which they die, are determined by social factors. Thus, in 'less developed societies' major causes of death are likely to be infectious diseases (such as measles, typhoid, malaria) and malnutrition; in more 'advanced' societies wealth, improved diet and sanitation and access to medical treatment means that such causes of death are far less likely. People, living longer, then succumb to the 'diseases of modernity' such as heart disease, stroke and cancer.

In Ireland there have been major changes in the pattern of mortality in the past five decades. There has been a *decline* in deaths from infectious diseases such as influenza, measles and tuberculosis and an *increase* in deaths from cancer and cardiovascular disease (including heart disease and stroke) (Devlin, 1997, p.19). There has also been a decline in deaths attributed to 'senility' as the coding of causes of death has changed over the years (see Figure 9.2).

## Figure 9.2 Causes of death in Ireland 1947 and 1995

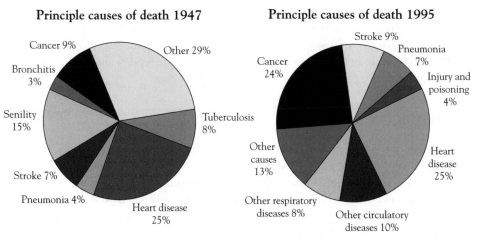

**Principle causes of death 1947**

Cancer 9%
Other 29%
Bronchitis 3%
Senility 15%
Tuberculosis 8%
Stroke 7%
Pneumonia 4%
Heart disease 25%

**Principle causes of death 1995**

Stroke 9%
Pneumonia 7%
Cancer 24%
Injury and poisoning 4%
Other causes 13%
Heart disease 25%
Other respiratory diseases 8%
Other circulatory diseases 10%

(*Source*: Devlin, 1997, pp.14 and 20)

## Morbidity

Morbidity data relates to the level of 'illness' in society. As we have seen, 'illness', unlike death, is open to interpretation and contestation, thus the data is far less reliable. Furthermore, the collection and collation of such data is dependent on cases coming to the attention of the formal health services, which occurs with only a minority of medical conditions. Some, such as cancer, almost inevitably involve contact with the health services, therefore data is quite good; others are legally notifiable (such as certain infectious diseases) and again, the information is relatively reliable; others, especially 'minor' ailments such as influenza or muscle sprains, are far less likely to be recorded or measured.

A more effective method of gathering data about morbidity is the health experience questionnaire, where people are asked about their health-related experience and activity over a defined period of time (for example, 'the last month'). A number of internationally recognised questionnaire instruments have been developed and these allow for international comparisons. One of these, used in the United States, UK, Scandinavia and Germany and to a limited extent in Ireland, is called SF36. It reflects once again the complexity of what we term 'health', and attempts to capture this by measuring eight health concepts that are relevant across all social groups, including (Doorley, 1998, pp.24–5):

- limitations in physical activities because of health problems
- limitations in usual role activities because of physical health
- bodily pain
- general health perceptions
- vitality (energy and fatigue)
- limitations in social activities because of physical and emotional problems
- limitations in usual role activities because of emotional problems
- mental health (psychological distress and well-being).

## PROVISION OF HEALTH SERVICES

As in relation to health and illness, data on the provision of health services is also highly complex, open to interpretation and contestation and difficult to gather. However, there has been a long tradition of comparing countries on the level of services provided. The level of provision, in terms of numbers such as total and per capita health spending, hospitals, hospital beds and doctors, is one of the key pieces of information that is commonly used to measure the 'development' of a country.

Figures in relation to health services need to be placed in context. For example, the period 1980 to 1991 saw a drop in the number of hospitals in Ireland from 157 to 105 and a reduction in the number of hospital beds from over 19,000 to under

14,000 (Curry, 1998, p.128). It would be a mistake to interpret such figures as merely an indication that the level of health service provision in the country had dropped. Rather, what occurred was, to an extent, a shift of resources into 'community-based' care, with an accompanying rationalisation of the hospital sector. The danger of relying on raw statistics, for Ireland as for any other society, is revealed.

The expansion of the health field over the years has meant that the health services provided by the public and private sectors have also developed. These range from the supply of drugs and medicines to the provision of many 'social services' such as care for children and the elderly, through to the delivery of acute hospital care. The range of services provided by a typical Health Board, the main public administrative structure in the field, is illustrated in Figure 9.3.

## Figure 9.3 Health Board functions

| Programme Area | Type of Service |
| --- | --- |
| Community Care | General Practitioner Services<br>Child Care and Family Support Services<br>Dental, Ophthalmic, Aural Services<br>Maternity and Infant Care Scheme<br>Supplementary Welfare Services<br>Services for the Elderly<br>Public Health Nursing Services:<br>    Family Planning/Pregnancy/Counselling/<br>    Women's Health Services/Hepatitis C<br>Environmental Health Services<br>Care of Deprived Children<br>Services for Travellers<br>Services for People with Physical/Sensory Disabilities<br>Community Drugs Schemes |
| Special Hospitals | Adult Psychiatric Services<br>Old Age Psychiatry Services<br>Mentally Handicapped Services<br>Alcoholism Services<br>Addiction Centres |
| General Hospitals | Medical, Surgical Hospitals<br>Maternity Hospitals<br>Out-patient Clinics<br>Ambulance and Transport Services<br>Pharmacy Services |

(*Source*: O'Hara, 1998, p.24)

# HEALTH, ILLNESS AND SOCIAL CHANGE IN IRELAND

The sociology of health and illness in Ireland needs to be understood against the background of the significant social changes discussed elsewhere in this book. For example, there have been significant changes in fertility patterns, family size and composition and marriage rates. There have been substantial changes in the relationships between women and men and between adults and children. The involvement of the state in people's everyday lives has greatly increased. There have been dramatic alterations in the nature of work people do and how they spend their leisure time. There have been changes in the food people eat, the drugs they use and the natural and built environment. All of these factors have at least the potential to significantly impact on how we see and use our bodies and how we experience health and illness.

There has also been a huge expansion in the health infrastructure. The Department of Health was established in 1947 and since then there has been a development of public and private health provision that has been broadly in line with that of other western countries. Ireland has developed a 'mixed' health system based on public and private funding; in this way it is similar to other European countries such as France and Austria.

As Robins (1997, p.5) reminds us, the changes in patterns of health in Ireland since the foundation of the Department have been striking. Life expectancy for females has increased from to 62 to 79 and for males from 61 to 73. Infant mortality has plummeted from 68/1000 to just 6, one of the lowest rates in the world, and maternal mortality, once frequent, is now a rare event. Beyond the statistics are the changes in attitudes, approaches, institutions and practices that have made for a greatly increased quality of life (Robins, 1997, pp.5–6):

> Fifty years ago many citizens with mental illness or mental handicap, elderly and infirm persons in need of care, unwanted and deprived children, outcast unmarried mothers, were being cared for en masse in large institutions of mainly nineteenth-century origin. Patients of little means needing basic medical care were subjected to the discriminating and restrictive requirements of the Victorian dispensary doctor system. Those of modest means requiring hospital treatment received no support from the state and often had to face intolerable financial burdens. Persons who were functionally, economically and socially disadvantaged by long-term disability were ignored, written off by society, with little effort made to integrate them in normal living activity.

By all these measures, the improvements in our health care system have been dramatic. For many analysts they are a clear reflection of the fact that Ireland has become a fully 'developed' society. The patterns of disease and mortality in Ireland resemble those of other western nations and are very different to those of the 'developing world' where mortality levels are higher and deaths from infectious diseases are the main cause of death.

More recent trends have started to reflect the significant changes that have taken place in Irish society and the broader international trends in how health care is delivered. Many of these reflect the pressures created by the expansion of the health field; the increased costs dictated by new medical technologies, procedures and drugs; the demographic challenge of the ageing of the population; and the increased incomes of an expanding range of health professionals and ancillary staff.

One response to increased costs that also reflects significant changes in the concepts underpinning suitable modes of care has been the shift from institutional to 'community' care. This trend has been particularly noticeable in those areas previously structured around large residential institutions, such as mental health and care for young people, but it has also begun to change the way that health care is delivered to the aged and to other groups. The change reflects many sets of ideas in the health care field and, according to Saris (1997, p.218), there exists:

a broad political consensus, encompassing such diverse elements as policy-makers interested in reducing the profile of 'big government' and utopian visionaries valorising the 'community' as a place of refuge from a heartless 'society', formed around the proposition that the time had come to close down these big institutions.

Community care is not without its controversies. Feminists, in particular, have pointed to the fact that 'care in the community' very often means care by women, whether family members or often very poorly paid female staff (earning as little as £1 an hour). In the area of aged care, for example, fewer than 1 per cent of home helps in Ireland are men (O' Donovan, 1997b, p.150). Community-based services are seriously under-resourced, patchily provided and of low status, often focused on the 'needy' and the 'down and out' (Edmondson, 1997, p.162). Much of the work is, like domestic labour, not seen by health care managers as 'real work'. Rather, 'care has been constructed . . . as charitable non-work provided by philanthropic women to their less fortunate neighbours' (O' Donovan, 1997b, p.153). Community care may be an opportunity to respond to health needs in a more holistic way but at present it remains very much the poor relation of institutionalised health care.

There has been an increase in the numbers and varieties of health professionals, paraprofessionals and 'wannabe' professionals. Doctors, surgeons and nurses have now been joined by dieticians, physiotherapists, chiropractors, acupuncturists and medical social workers, not to mention foot reflexologists, iridologists and a whole panoply of 'alternative' therapists. There is a burgeoning of specialists in all areas as medical knowledge becomes increasingly rationalised and fragmented.

The increasing rationalisation of medicine has seen a greater level of evaluation, performance measurement, research and monitoring built into the health care system. Increasing public and private resources are being channelled into health care and there are increasing demands for accountability within the system involving concepts such as 'casemix' and Diagnostic Related Groups whereby health systems are funded on the basis of identifiable and measurable conditions and practices. Moves in this direction may represent a shift in power from autonomous professionals to managers and bureaucrats, though there is a high level of collegiality and common purpose among management and practitioners within the Irish hospital system. Furthermore, the increasing attempt to rationalise medicine runs counter to the holistic philosophies that are becoming increasingly influential.

Worldwide, medicine is increasingly experienced as 'big business' — a highly profitable one at that. The United States represents one extreme and its largely private health care system consumes a greater proportion of financial resources than any other in the world. There are numerous opportunities for profit-making in health care:

- fees-for-services for private practitioners (often working in publicly funded hospitals)
- health screening and tests
- pathology services
- health insurance
- drug and appliance manufacture
- private hospitals, clinics and nursing homes.

Some have characterised this as the 'medical-industrial complex' (Davis and George, 1993, p.185). The medical industry provides significant employment in Ireland. Ten of the world's top fifteen health care product corporations are located in the country and the sector employs over 12,500 people through multinational corporations such as Abbott, Boston Scientific, American Home Products and CR Bard. The pharmaceutical industry is also large: over 120 overseas companies, including Pfizer, Rhone Poulenc Rorer and Smith Kline Beecham, employ over 15,000 people and export US$12 billion annually, making Ireland one of largest exporters of pharmaceuticals in the world (IDA, 1999).

## Social inequality and health care

Despite the continuing expansion of medical services and infrastructure and, at least in terms of the biomedical model, an improvement in average health status, health and illness in Ireland are still very much determined by inequalities of class, gender, ethnicity, wealth and power. Sociologists have long had an interest in such inequalities — and in seeking to explain them.

Our knowledge of how health and illness are related to social inequality is an outcome of social epidemiology. Such research has consistently indicated (for example, Davis and George, 1993, pp.70–91; Wilkinson, 1996; Collins and Shelley, 1997; Nolan and Whelan, 1997) that in advanced industrial economies like Ireland, the UK, Australia and the United States, poor health status is associated with variation in social class. Class difference has been shown to be related to overall mortality, infant mortality, disability and morbidity (Collins and Shelley, 1997, p.87; Doorley, 1998, p.37). Poorer than average health has also been shown to be strongly correlated with unemployment (Nolan and Whelan, 1997).

Negative health factors and indicators associated with poorer and less powerful social groups include higher levels of:

- peri-natal mortality
- admission to psychiatric hospitals
- standardised mortality rates
- incidence of diseases such as pneumonia, cancer and heart disease.

Economic inequality is also associated with lower incidences of breast-feeding and 'healthy lifestyles' (Collins and Shelley, 1997, p.88; Doorley, 1998, pp.37–8; *Irish Times*, 12 March 1999). Doorley reports that in Ireland 'there are indications that income is an important variable affecting health, with lower socio-economic status and unemployment being associated with higher mortality, morbidity and psychological stress.' This is supported by research carried out by Nolan and Whelan (1997) for the ESRI. The Kilkenny Health Project (Collins and Shelley, 1997, p.88) found that social class differences in health in Ireland are persisting despite improvements in the health of similar social groups in other similar countries like Finland and Australia and an overall improvement in the health of the Irish population (see Figure 9.4).

Other key axes of inequality that have been related to health care and health status are those of ethnicity and gender.

### Ethnicity

In many societies a correlation has been demonstrated between ethnicity and health status. Such relationships may be asserted to be biological (for example, sickle cell anaemia in African-Americans) or are recognised as the outcome of inequalities of wealth and power, discrimination and racism. The relationships are often complex. Ethnicity and class interact with each other as well as with other social factors such as age, gender and place of residence.

One group that has been identified in Ireland as having particularly poor health status is the Travelling community. According to the Department of Health (1994, p.60) life expectancy and general health status among Travellers are considerably lower than the population average:

## Figure 9.4 Socio-economic group related to standardised mortality rates

| Socio-economic Group | 15–24 | 25–34 | 35–44 | 45–54 | 55–64 | Standardised Mortality Rate |
|---|---|---|---|---|---|---|
| | | | Death rate per 1,000 | | | |
| Farmers | 0.9 | 0.8 | 1.4 | 5.6 | 14.8 | 79 |
| Farm labourers | 1.6 | 1.3 | 3.1 | 4.6 | 15.2 | 86 |
| Higher professional | 0.2 | 0.3 | 0.8 | 3.5 | 12.8 | 55 |
| Lower professional | 1.5 | 0.5 | 1.4 | 5.5 | 16.0 | 79 |
| Employers and managers | 0.9 | 0.5 | 1.2 | 4.5 | 11.6 | 62 |
| Salaried employees | 1.0 | 0.6 | 1.5 | 3.6 | 15.2 | 71 |
| Non-manual white collar | 1.0 | 1.1 | 2.4 | 7.8 | 20.2 | 105 |
| Non-manual other | 1.8 | 1.2 | 2.0 | 6.2 | 20.1 | 104 |
| Skilled manual | 0.9 | 0.7 | 1.9 | 6.2 | 18.7 | 91 |
| Semi-skilled manual | 1.7 | 1.1 | 3.0 | 7.2 | 22.1 | 117 |
| Unskilled manual | 1.9 | 1.5 | 3.4 | 10.7 | 31.6 | 163 |
| Unknown | 3.0 | 6.8 | 6.8 | 13.4 | 25.9 | 174 |

(*Source*: Cleary and Tracy, 1997, p.101)

> Factors such as transient lifestyle, poor sanitation and living conditions, high unemployment and generally poor health awareness continue to militate against real health improvements in the health of travellers.

There has been some recent interest in the health status of Irish people living abroad, particularly in Britain (Williams, 1996). It is only recently that the Irish have been recognised as an 'ethnic group' for the purposes of public policy in the UK. Williams reports that, though data on the Irish-born in Britain is very difficult to interpret, data on second and subsequent generations of the Irish community reveals higher than average mortality rates (1996, p.59). These are traced, at least tentatively, to the economic and cultural structures associated with migration. As migration is such an important aspect of Irish society, the implications may be profound.

## Gender

Health status is clearly patterned by gender, in Ireland as in most other countries. Gender issues in health remain controversial and cannot be separated from broader questions about gender, power and inequality. On nearly all indicators, the health status of men is worse than that of women. Men have higher death rates at all ages, from babyhood to older age groups; they are more likely to die in accidents, from suicide, and from diseases like heart disease and certain cancers, for example, lung cancer and cancer of the bowel (Doorley, 1998, p.37). Moreover, in recent times the male suicide rate, already higher than the female, has increased sharply in many western societies including Ireland.

However, the statistics do not necessarily reflect the whole picture. As Kelleher (1997, p.vii) points out:

> While women do live longer they also have a poorer quality of life as they age than men, bear the inequalities found in every society in the world more than men, carry the hidden un-prestigious and extensive responsibility for the iceberg of health need in every country, and strive throughout to bear and rear new generations of people in a complex and unjust world.

Furthermore, Irish women have rates of certain cancers (colon, breast, larynx and oesophagus) and ischaemic heart disease that are among the highest in the EU (Mahon, 1997, p.88). This may be attributed largely to 'lifestyle factors' (diet, smoking, lack of exercise) and inadequate screening and preventative health strategies.

Irish sociologists of health and illness have attempted to identify and account for gender-based disparities in health status. An extensive survey of women's health-related knowledge, attitudes and behaviour was carried out in 1993 by the ESRI (reported in Wiley and Merriman, 1996) Medical issues identified as especially germane to women appear to be limited to substance abuse (in particular during pregnancy) and reproductive health, and it may be that 'women's health' runs the risk of being 'ghettoised' into these areas. The ESRI study paid no attention, for example, to the important issues of occupational health and safety or environmental health. Women's health issues are very much constructed as a matter of *attitude*, rather than structural inequality.

Once again, we are confronted with the difficulty of defining health, especially as the biomedical model is increasingly open to critique. On the basis of the indicators used by health managers and policy-makers, men are more unhealthy, but feminists in particular have drawn attention to how women's experience of ill health is broader, more diffuse and more hidden. There is a message here: sociological analysis of health and illness needs to reflect the difficulty and complexity of the issues involved and avoid simplistic interpretation of statistics that may be misleading, or partial, or both.

Women have an important role as health care providers, particularly within the home, where much primary health care takes place. This is a dual role: maintaining good health of family members through, for example, food preparation and maintenance of hygiene standards; and direct provision through caring for others and mediation with health care services. Within Irish society, there is a strong expectation that women, especially female family members, will take responsibility for health care tasks. Further, the caring role is 'intricately bound up with definitions and conceptions of femininity' (Hodgins and Kelleher, 1997, p.43).

The unpaid (and low-paid) work of women as health care providers is reinforced by community care policies that have seen a shift in emphasis away from the institutional delivery of some forms of health care like psychiatric care and care of the chronically ill. It has been shown that 'care in the community' usually means care by families and more often than not care by women (MacFarlane, 1997, p.19). The assumptions made of this gender division of labour underpin the perception of the nursing profession. Conversely, women are under-represented in senior and well-paid positions within the health services: only 13 per cent of Health Board members and 16 per cent of hospital consultants are women. Remarkably, only 3 per cent of consultants in obstetrics and gynaecology are women (Mahon, 1997, p.95).

## Causes

It is one thing to say that social inequality and health are related. It is another to tease out the many factors that help to create and sustain this relationship. Thus, in relation to unemployment (Nolan and Whelan 1997, p.103):

> It is extremely difficult, with the types of data usually available, to distinguish the role of different factors, or to isolate the impact of unemployment *per se* from that of the broader socio-economic background from which those experiencing unemployment generally come.

In the UK, the wide-ranging *Black Report* of 1982 (Townsend and Davidson, 1982) offered four main explanations for the observed relationships between class and health:

- *artefactual data* — the findings were a result of how the data was collected and the limitations inherent in this
- *selection* — healthier people, as a result of their better health, were able to get better jobs or otherwise move into higher social class groups
- *materialist explanations* — health was affected by material deprivation, including poor housing, poverty, pollution, hazards at work
- *cultural explanations* — class shaped certain lifestyle factors such as alcohol and tobacco consumption, diet and exercise.

The conclusion was that the last two explanations were the most likely; similar conclusions have been reached in other studies. In Ireland, the Kilkenny Health

Project found that levels of smoking among unskilled and semi-skilled manual workers were almost twice those of non-manual workers. In general it found 'an association with social class for smoking prevalence, alcohol consumption, prevalence of obesity, [measurements of blood pressure] and [health] knowledge levels, but not for mean cholesterol levels or light leisure activity' (Collins and Shelley, 1997, p.92). There is some evidence that the health-related factors for manual workers are improving, albeit slowly, with slightly reduced levels of smoking and alcohol consumption and slowly increasing levels of exercise and knowledge about health issues.

It must be emphasised that the links between broader beliefs and attitudes, knowledge of health factors and everyday behaviour are very complex. Key sets of beliefs relate to whether or not one feels susceptible to particular conditions, in control in everyday situations and how one can reasonably behave in social settings. This may influence, for example, a person's decision whether or not to give up smoking, notwithstanding their knowledge that it is a health hazard (Jacobsen, 1988). It is important not to fall into a 'blame the victim' mentality when addressing the issue of 'lifestyles'. Morris (1995, p.136) reminds us:

> These behaviours plainly are embedded in the social structure. When questions are asked not merely how people behave but why they behave as they do, 'lifestyles' provide no release from the need to confront that structure — which also has so many other effects on health.

It has also been argued that the modernist concern with 'inequalities in health care' fails to reflect the diversity of post-modern society. Bunton proposes (1998, p.23):

> Social and welfare relations surrounding health care have undergone considerable transformation and reconceptualisation which render single guiding policy principles such as inequalities in health problematic. Moreover the importance of 'other' knowledges in the field of health and health policy have resulted in more diverse values guiding health policy.

We have seen that the health field has expanded greatly in recent times. The concerns of modernist reformers were with ameliorating the health impacts of industrialism as these related to the incidence of infectious diseases, workplace hazards, poor housing and other social factors associated with mass society. Post-modernism sees an interest, both among sociologists of health and policy-makers, in other issues, particularly those to do with identity, rights and culture. An example may be found in the response of activists, sociologists and policy-makers to the issue of female genital mutilation (FGM), a practice widely carried out by some of the peoples of Africa and the Middle East. While the standard western response to FGM has been one of horror and a 'high moral tone' (Shaughnessy, 1997, p.123) the issue is shown to be highly complex, involving a range of sexual, health-related, political, religious, economic and social factors. Any attempt to address the issue requires a sophisticated and multi-faceted social understanding. Once again, we see a tension between the rationalist, positivist approaches to social issues that tend to be favoured by policy-makers, and the more speculative, interpretative and complex approach of much of contemporary sociology.

## Policy responses to inequality

Hederman O'Brien reminds us that once a certain level of income is attained in a society, ill health is usually a reflection of economic and social inequalities (1998, p.81):

> Neither the total amount spent on health services nor the availability of sophisticated procedures will, of itself, offset the decreasing health standards and mortality rates of those at the bottom of widening differentials in a prosperous society.

The implication here, one that has been recognised in other societies (see Morris, 1995), is that any attempt to tackle the persistent links between health and inequality *must* include action on broader issues of social inequality such as poverty, unemployment and gender discrimination. Doorley (1998, p.38) concludes that a better distribution of economic resources would probably be the most effective way to reduce inequalities in health. The health sector thus needs to be more vocal in advocating stronger social policies to achieve this. However, these aspects of social inequality are deeply entrenched in Irish society.

One of the difficulties of responding to issues of social inequality is expressed in the paradox described by Bunton (1998, p.25):

> The analysis of social policy process has become increasingly important in contemporary health care, especially due to an increased emphasis on the enhancement or promotion of health rather than simply the treatment of illness. Yet at the same time the possibilities for coherent social policy are being increasingly restricted and our conceptions of social policy have undergone considerable change.

In other words, the extent to which the state can influence outcomes in society is increasingly open to challenge. 'Health policy' can be seen as a highly modernist notion — it is assumed that social life is predictable, rational and relatively homogenous (or predictably heterogeneous). All these assumptions are now called into question in Irish society.

Social policy is increasingly being determined by supranational bodies, in particular the agencies of the EU. Many of the factors that help to determine the notion of health are under the control of multinational corporations, for example, in the drug, tobacco, food, insurance and health care industries. There have been significant changes in the organisation of work and employment that have rendered problematic the way that health care is funded. There is an increased heterogeneity of population and behaviour: Ireland is witnessing increasing ethnic and cultural diversity and there has been a rise in 'alternative' lifestyles, medicines and therapies, many of which are widely dispersed (MacFarlane, 1997). Within consumer culture there is an increased emphasis on personal choice and the object of health care may now be seen as the 'customer', rather than the 'patient'.

It is also important to consider changes in the nature of the organisations and institutions that deliver health care. There has been much criticism of how Irish health care systems are managed. For example, McKevitt (1998, pp.44–5) argues that in Ireland the delivery of health services is typified by a 'strategic deficit' and by 'poor performance measurement systems, inadequate professional supervision and underdeveloped management capability'. Given the highly complex and conflicting nature of health care institutions, detailed and intrusive management and policy-making are indeed difficult. The model that appears to be emerging in Ireland as in other similar countries is one of facilitation and support for a range of diverse activities (McKevitt, 1998, p.60).

## Irish health care institutions

There is extensive evidence that most health care issues are dealt with by people themselves, without reference to formalised health care services such as doctors and hospitals (MacFarlane, 1997, p.18). Therefore health care institutions only come into play in relation to specific events, conditions and situations. It should therefore be remembered that health care institutions represent only one, albeit important, part of the health care story.

The Irish health care system is based on a mixture of private and public funding, with the latter accounting for about three-quarters of the expenditure (down from 85 per cent in the 1980s). This is similar to most other European countries but represents a much higher level than the United States where less than half of health expenditure comes from public funds (Macionis and Plummer, 1997, p.567). Health care is expensive and consumes about a fifth of all Irish government spending and approximately 9 per cent of GNP (O'Hara, 1998, p.4). Over a third of the population are entitled to free medical care under the medical card scheme while over 40 per cent are insured through the VHI or BUPA.

The period since the early nineteenth century has seen a continual expansion in the provision of institutionalised health services. The first institutions were the workhouses, established in 1703; county infirmaries followed in 1765 and these provided the basis on which the public health services were subsequently developed (O'Shea, 1998, p.55). Among the earliest country-wide systems was that of asylums for the insane, first developed in the early nineteenth century as part of the general process of 'civilising' the country (Saris, 1997, p.214). Voluntary hospitals date back to the early eighteenth century. Jervis Street Hospital, now part of the Beaumont Hospital in Dublin, opened in 1718 (O'Shea, 1998, p.54). The churches, especially the Roman Catholic Church, have been actively involved in the development of health services since the 1830s. Public health services in the community as we understand them today started in 1878 with the appointment of dispensary doctors and in 1925 county medical officers (O'Shea, 1998, p.55).

The Department of Health was established in 1947 and subsequently expenditure on health care expanded rapidly until the fiscal crisis of the 1980s. There was a sharp decline in spending in real terms during the 1980s but since then there has been a gradual shift back towards expansion, though spending on health has not kept pace with the expansion in the economy. Health policy and the structures that stem from it have increasingly been driven by expert groups within and outside government, in particular since 1995. There is now a highly technocratic approach to the development of health care services. The 1994 strategy document, *Shaping a healthier future*, has been particularly influential (McAuliffe and Joyce, 1998, p.1).

The public system now plays 'a major role in the provision and funding of services, the regulation and setting of standards for inputs to the health system and in recent times [there has been] an increasing emphasis on setting standards and objectives' (O'Hara, 1998, p.4). The management and planning of the health care system is not fully centralised, rather (O'Hara, 1998, p.5):

a combination of government, Department of Health and Children, advisory and executive agencies and voluntary organisations all play a role in service delivery and development, though their degree of power and influence varies.

## Medicalisation

One factor driving the global expansion of health services is medicalisation: the process by which an increasing range of events and conditions are defined as being of interest to medicine. Many conditions, previously taken to be non-medical, are now grounds for consulting a doctor. Forms of behaviour previously seen as deviant are now defined as medical problems: bad behaviour by children is now hyperactivity or attention deficit disorder; shoplifting is kleptomania. Occasionally the process can operate in reverse, for example, alcoholism is decreasingly likely to result in admission to psychiatric institutions in Ireland and more likely to be viewed as the result of personality or social factors.

The critique of medicalisation is most closely associated with the work of writers such as Thomas Szasz, Ivan Illich and Michel Foucault. Szasz (1961) was sharply critical of the regimes of psychiatry, in particular how psychiatric terminology and practice were being used to respond to social problems such as crime and poverty; Illich (1976) was critical of the whole medical industry/bureaucracy and highlighted the perverse role of medicine in *creating* illness and injury (iatrogenesis) through inappropriate and incompetent interventions; Foucault saw the institutions, techniques and discourses of medicine, along with the penal and other state systems, as a means of surveilling and controlling populations. The level and efficacy of such surveillance has only increased as holistic medicine has become more favoured. A whole range of lifestyle, social and even spiritual factors is now taken into account and subjected to comment, intervention and control. This has contributed to the expansion of medicalisation.

One part of life that has become increasingly medicalised and has attracted the attention of many sociologists is that of childbirth. The discipline of obstetrics excluded and marginalised traditional midwifery practices, in particular through the monopolisation of specific technologies such as forceps. In the process female practitioners were replaced by men (McDonnell, 1997, p.70). In an Irish study Hyde (1997) shows not only how medicine has 'taken over' the process of childbirth itself but argues that the medical profession also makes moral judgements on the circumstances of pregnancy, particularly in relation to 'unmarried mothers', and justifies these on medical grounds. This then affects the interpretation of events such as post-natal depression or whether or not a baby should be given up for adoption. In Hyde's study, women were seen to be unable to decide what was in their own best interests, so medical staff, particularly 'paternalistic' doctors, attempted to impose processes and activities (like seeing a social worker) upon them. This was related to class and age. Hyde concludes that, along with other discourses such as economics and religion, 'medicine at least plays a part in the maintenance of social order around social arrangements for childbearing' (1997, p.123).

## Professionalisation

The issue of the professionalisation of health care is very much linked to that of medicalisation. Professionalisation is the process whereby an occupational group is able to claim special status for itself, for example through access to special knowledge or training, a monopoly over certain practices and the ability to exclude competing groups. The outcome is a greater measure of prestige, power and income. By the early twentieth century medicine had achieved dominance of the health field in North America, most countries of Europe and Australia (Daniel, 1998, p.209).

Medicine has been able to create and sustain its professional status through a variety of strategies. The key process is that of *closure*: the ability to keep others out of the field of operation of the professional group. The most effective way to do this is through a process of registration, backed up by legislation. This requires the state to give legal backing to a range of occupational practices (Davis and George, 1993, p.209):

- access to restricted substances (for example, prescription drugs)
- direct access to clients (fees-for-services)
- control over content of education and training
- self-regulation
- control of all others in the field.

Strategies to secure public acquiescence with the claim for professional status have largely been made through appeals to science and reason, according to the biomedical model. At the same time, the knowledge must retain a level of opacity and mystique as to render it inaccessible to others.

The development of professional power does not rest only on securing rights over knowledge and practice — it is also crucially based on interactive relationships such as *trust*. As Daniel points out, if we do not accord a doctor or nurse trust, they have little power over us. Of course, the relationship of trust is built very much on the types of knowledge that are at stake (1998, p.212):

> The complexity with which the expert [doctor, specialist] deals is typically baffling and alarming in the risks it poses. Trust reduces the client's apprehension of external complexity and uncertainty by substituting an inner confidence in the simplification of control held out by the expert.

Many of the accoutrements of professional practice — the framed degree in the consultant's office, the letters after the name, the calm demeanour, the conservative dress — are props that aid in the building of a trusting relationship. At the same time, numerous distractions, such as disagreements over appropriate care, personal or social factors (such as ethnicity, dirty finger nails) or situational factors (a run-down office, a rude receptionist) can rapidly erode the relationships of trust that are so difficult to create. Access by clients to alternative sources of information, for example, health information on the Internet, can also threaten the trust relationship. Trust is also sustained by the discipline itself: our belief in medicine as a rigorous, *scientific* practice that strives for the most effective outcome; and its *ethical* basis, our belief that a doctor will not intentionally harm us.

## Nursing

In contemporary Ireland a particularly interesting site for the observation of professionalisation in medicine is the field of general nursing. The process of professionalisation has created an opportunity — and a dilemma — for this key group that accounts for 40 per cent of the Irish health workforce (Dwyer and Taaffe, 1998, p.237). Nursing is an almost exclusively female occupation — only 6 per cent of nurses are men. Indeed, it has been one of the few secure professional careers open to women until very recently. Irish nurses have historically been recruited from middle class and farming backgrounds and are well educated. Religious orders have played a very significant role in the development of nursing and in recruitment and training.

While medical practice has become the dominant profession within the health care system, nursing has historically been subordinated. Unlike most doctors, nurses work under supervision, for wages and for fixed hours, usually in a fixed location. They lack real autonomy. They have also faced considerable gender discrimination and stereotyping within the workplace and the industry. As Davis and George remark (1993, p.210): 'the emergence of nursing as a full-time occupation has occurred within a framework of gender inequality which has led to the subordination of nursing in the health care occupational hierarchy, and resistance to attempts to change it.' McCarthy (1997, p.176) reflects on how Irish nursing has been affected by the particular vision of femininity espoused by the founder of modern nursing, Florence Nightingale:

> It is true to say that Ms. Nightingale's ideas of vocation, discipline, diligence and obedience lived on in Irish nursing up to the 1970s and some remnants may still remain. They were perpetrated through an outdated method of education which included personal training and schools of nursing set within the hospital culture. The effects can be seen within the profession itself and in social appreciation and expectation. They have affected professional growth, and inhibited roles, education, accountability and management.

Historically, nurses have been largely excluded from management and policy-making positions but more recently have sought to escape such subordination by adopting a strategy of professionalisation.

The dramatic changes in recent times in the nature of nursing have contributed greatly to the thrust towards professional status. There has been considerable specialisation, with the emergence of numerous specialties within nursing, such as critical care, midwifery, oncology, anaesthetic and A and E (accident and emergency) nurses, to name just a few. Nurses now work with highly expensive and sophisticated technology, with complex medications and procedures and with a high level of autonomy and decision-making ability.

The changes in nursing have led to efforts to change the nature of nurse training, now increasingly carried out through the third-level education sector, and to develop an autonomous body of nursing knowledge, including a sociological component (Porter, 1997). This has not been without its difficulties, given the hostility of the existing medical professions and the lack of development in the field in the past. The shift towards the creation of a professional discourse for nursing has been accompanied by an increased use of industrial muscle. Unthinkable in the past, nurses have increasingly threatened and carried out industrial action, and have resolutely pursued their claims through the industrial relations systems.

There are signs that the professionalising efforts of nursing are beginning to pay dividends. This may mean an increasingly professional and managerial role for nurses and there is some evidence that this is taking place in the Irish health system (Dwyer and Taaffe, 1998, p.250):

> The first Chief Nurse was appointed to the Department of Health and Children in 1998 and hopefully will soon be followed by the appointment of nurses to the executive management structure of health boards. Nurses will also take their place on policy-making committees in hospitals and the community. They will participate in clinical units of management and at ward level be facilitated to become full managers with staff and budgetary control.

However, while there is evidence of some success in raising the power of nurses, the strategy has created some of its own difficulties. The change in the status of nurses may mean some dilemmas for the emerging profession. The shift in educational status may mean that the traditional hierarchies within medicine will need to be confronted. Will university-trained nurses be content to adopt the subordinate role of their hospital-trained predecessors, or will the improved status of nurses mean the emergence of additional levels of assistants and technicians, as is already the case in many countries? How will patients respond to nurses that may be more focused on technology and management than on the more traditional caring skills? Will the emerging discourse of professional nursing simply ape the biomedical model, or will it provide for a more holistic and patient-centred model of health care?

## FUTURE CHALLENGES

During the last fifty years the major social questions in relation to the body, health and illness in Ireland have changed dramatically. In the 1950s the issues were about the control and eradication of infectious diseases such as TB and polio. The major challenge was to build a modern public health infrastructure on the base of an often-despised system that had grown out of the workhouses of the eighteenth and nineteenth centuries. The major challenges for medicine in the years to come are posed by new medical technologies ranging from human genome marking to artificial body parts grown from embryonic stem cells (Connor, 1999). The challenges are financial and ethical and have the capacity to fundamentally alter our notions of the body, health and illness and the very nature of the self.

In the Irish context, particular ethical challenges have been raised by the way that technological advance has led to a redefinition of 'life' in the areas of the 'conceptive technologies' (for example, IVF) and the life-sustaining technologies (for example, life-support machines). Such technologies force us to consider issues about life, death and medicine that were formerly implicit. They 'reorder the boundaries between culture and nature and they raise fundamental philosophical questions about biological contingency. They alter the concept of the body itself' (McDonnell, 1997, pp.71–2). When life is dependent on a respirator, how then do we define death? Questions then arise about the right to die and the possibility of a 'good' death. Similarly, reproductive technologies raise legal, ethical and social dilemmas in relation to motherhood, the role of women and the nature of the human embryo.

Another major challenge relates to the management of the health care system. International trends reflect a tendency for the proportion of national resources consumed by health care to expand. In some ways Ireland benefits from this trend: the spectacular success of the impotency drug Viagra in 1998 (the main ingredient for which is manufactured in Ringaskiddy in Co. Cork) is but an indicator of the substantial income industries located in Ireland derive from global health care expenditure. But the spiralling costs of health care provision also place strains on the Irish exchequer and there are major challenges in delivering efficient and effective health care to an ageing population. Increased efficiency and rationalisation may lead to a depersonalisation of health care, with the emergence of what Ritzer (1996, pp.43–5) terms 'assembly line medicine' — offering 'Docs-in-a-box'.

The dual tendencies of holism and biomedicine will continue to contend for public acceptance and support. The acute hospital sector, increasingly sophisticated and high-tech, will demand a growing share of resources. At the same time, people are increasingly turning to alternative therapies and practitioners. There are demands for a community-based approach to health that embraces a more preventative role, focusing on health promotion rather than cure. There is also an increasing recognition that control of environmental factors, from noise pollution to farm chemicals, is crucial in the maintenance of health. Overall, shifts in public images of health will also provide challenges of shifting resources, and a threat to the entrenched power and status of some professional groups. Health, illness and the body will continue to provide a fascinating area of research for sociologists. And sociologists have the potential to shape a health care system that is of benefit to all.

# 10
# Crime and deviance

For many Irish people one of the most significant perceived social changes over the past thirty years or so has been in the extent and nature of crime. This chapter explores that perception. Discussing the topic from a sociological perspective allows us to raise some questions about change in Irish society, as well as about how sociologists and others more directly concerned with problems of order and social control, think about and define crime. A sociological approach challenges much of the received wisdom in this field, especially in relation to the apparent increase in crime rates. It also questions the very definition of crime and raises issues about the links between crime and social inequality.

Crime has long been of interest to sociologists, not only because it is recognised as a major social issue, but also because it reflects much about the condition of society itself. This insight goes back at least to Durkheim, who was particularly interested in examining rates of crime and how they varied between different societies or in the same society at different times. He argued that the rate of crime in any society reflected the balance it had managed to achieve between *individualism* (encouragement and approval of efforts towards individual self-realisation) and *social regulation* (the imposition on the individual of group rules and values). In theory, a society that has got the balance right would display a 'normal' rate of crime. In practice, however, most societies have abnormal levels of crime — either too low, when there is too much regulation of the individual by society, or (something we are probably more familiar with) too high, when individualism becomes uncontrolled.

Durkheim's ideas remain very influential in the sociology of crime. He reversed the common assumption of criminologists, that we need only study 'social factors' as part of the 'explanation' of crime; he stressed that crime itself was profoundly social. He also demolished the idea that societies can ever be crime-free or that this is even a meaningful aspiration to have. He introduced the counter-intuitive idea that it is just as important to study a very low crime rate in a society as it is a very high one. We suggest that this is a very useful insight if we are trying to understand recent patterns of crime in Irish society.

Durkheim's interpretation of crime rates is queried by many other sociologists even when they accept his core idea that the nature and extent of crime in society is a good indicator of social, cultural and economic conditions. Many suggest that crime rates are best seen as an indicator of social inequality, where high crime levels reflect high levels of inequality. This is not to suggest that there is a simple relationship between the two variables: as we show below, the links between crime rates and social inequality are complex and sometimes contradictory.

Sociological research on crime in Ireland has to date been quite limited. Most takes the form of analysis of official crime statistics and is mainly concerned to establish levels of crime and how they change over time. To a lesser extent, researchers have also tried to show how crime is socially distributed in Ireland in terms of both criminal actors and victims of crime. Very little research has been published on other dimensions of the crime issue, such as the operation of the Irish criminal justice system, the routine policing practices of the Gardaí, the operations of the courts or the social processes of imprisonment. This situation seems likely to change for the better as there now appears to be a greater willingness of such institutions to facilitate research and to open themselves up to public enquiry and debate. O'Donnell (1999, p.175) notes that 'after years of public and political disinterest, 1998 was a time of wide-ranging consultation and review.' A National Crime Forum was established, for example, and the Department of Justice Equality and Law Reform, for the first time published an annual report and set out a three-year strategic plan.

These developments may indicate some profound changes in the beliefs in contemporary Irish society about the nature of authority and how it should be exercised. In this chapter we address a more limited set of issues to do with crime, primarily relating to crime rates. These are used as a basis to examine some aspects both of Irish society and of how sociologists study crime. We have stressed at a number of points in this book that, given Ireland's position as a culturally and economically dependent society, it is important for Irish sociologists to deconstruct or reflect upon the practice of sociology itself. Thus, much of our discussion deals with the complexity of the notion of crime and the various ways that it has been researched and studied.

## CRIME IN IRISH SOCIETY

We open with a fairly straightforward discussion of the extent of crime and of recent trends in relation to crime in Irish society. It is often said that crime is a serious social problem in Ireland — is this claim accurate, or is it more true that it is the *fear of crime* that is a serious and increasing social problem? Questions like these are difficult to answer, a task not made any easier by the fact that virtually the only available data is the *Annual report on crime* compiled by An Garda Siochána. Like all official statistics on crime, this is subject to a number of ambiguities (see below) that make its interpretation quite problematic. However, the official crime statistics are exhaustively discussed in McCullagh (1996) and O'Mahony (1993), who draw some guarded conclusions.

In recent years around half a million offences per annum have been 'known to the Gardaí'. Over 80 per cent of these are 'non-indictable offences' — misdemeanours not thought to be serious enough to warrant trial by jury but which can be summarily dealt with by a district court. Of approximately 100,000 'indictable offences' recorded annually since the early 1980s, over 95 per cent have been property crimes. Some of these 'offences against property with violence', such as burglary, robbery or arson, might be regarded as relatively more serious but still did not include violence against people. No more than 2 per cent of all crimes recorded were 'crimes against the person' — murder, manslaughter, rape, wounding and assault. The official statistics thus suggest that violent crime is at a very low level in Ireland. This is broadly similar to levels found elsewhere in Europe and Australasia, but is very different from the pattern in America where 'crimes against the person' are four times more frequent than they are here.

We might conclude that, contrary to the impression given by much public and political commentary, Irish crime statistics do not give great cause for alarm but it is noticeable that when experts on crime make that sort of claim in public, they are generally received with hostility. Most Irish people appear to be committed to the idea that to have any crime at all is a cause for alarm. The widespread expectation that we should be trying to, and could, achieve a crime-free society can itself be treated as an appropriate object of research. It seems plausible to suggest that the genuine indignation many Irish people express over the level of crime is linked to the powerful view of Irish society as a *community*, or 'community of communities' (see Chapter 13). Thus, to rob or steal from others is an offence against neighbourliness that threatens collective solidarity and undermines our self-construction as a homogeneous cultural group (Irish media focus on the alleged criminality of refugees reflects this, as pointed out by Pollack, 1999). But there has been very little research carried out into the beliefs and interpretations about crime held by ordinary Irish people, so this argument must remain somewhat speculative.

To return to our focus on official statistics, it might be argued that a real justification for public concern about crime is afforded by the observable trends. These indicate that in a thirty-year period, from the early 1960s to the early 1990s, the official crime rate in Ireland rose dramatically. In 1961 the Gardaí recorded only about 15,000 indictable offences, a figure that had been more or less stable for several decades; but in 1971 they recorded some 38,000 indictable offences, in 1981 some 89,000 and in 1991 nearly 95,000. The main period of increase was between 1961 and 1983, when, with 102,000 offences recorded, Irish crime rates were nearly seven times higher than they had been twenty years earlier. From that peak they dropped back steadily every year until 1987, when they started to rise gradually again; most recently, however, they have again been declining.

According to the 1996 *Annual report on crime* (1997, p.29), 'a period of relatively stable recorded crimes can be seen' in the past 15 years, contrasting markedly with the twenty-year period before 1981, and 'annual crime rates are now similar to what they were in the early 1980s.'

Many people argue that even if crime itself has not been increasing greatly in the last ten years the real problem and cause for concern is the growth in *violent* crime. O'Donnell (1999, p.177) notes the near doubling in the number of murders in the state (from an annual average of 23 in 1990 to 1994 up to 43 in 1995 to 1996) that occurred at a time when crime rates in general were declining. The high profile murders of investigative journalist Veronica Guerin and of Garda detective Gerry McCabe in 1996 appeared to many commentators to confirm the claim that Irish society was becoming increasingly violent. Both O'Mahony and McCullagh, however, looking at trends in violent crime over a longer time period, argue that the claim is unfounded. Describing the pattern of trends in 'crimes against the person' from 1973 to 1991, O'Mahony (1993, p.36) points out that it would be more accurate to say that levels of violent crime in Ireland prior to 1995 had been very low:

> The graph has the rough shape of a hump-backed bridge, indicating that the number of such crimes climbed steadily for the first half of this period and then as steadily declined in the second half. The total of such crimes was 1,655 in 1973 and rose to a maximum of 2,478, almost exactly 50 per cent more, in 1981, but then progressively declined to a figure of only 1,435 in 1991. Astoundingly and totally contrary to the current public perception of crime and views on the prevalence of violence and brutality, the figure for 1991 is the lowest for any year in the whole study period. According to these figures there appears to be less violent crime against the person today than for a long period past.

It is also misleading to focus on the murder rate. The 1996 *Annual report on crime* shows that there was a 7 per cent drop in the total number of 'crimes against the person' in 1996 compared to 1995, while armed robberies and aggravated burglaries fell by over one-third in the four years after 1993.

Further evidence that Irish crime rates do not reflect a major social problem might be found in comparisons with other societies in Europe. Cross-cultural or comparative analyses of crime patterns, pioneered by Durkheim at the end of the nineteenth century, were relatively neglected during most of the twentieth century and have only recently begun to command attention and support again (Downes, 1992). Comparative researchers nowadays are much more aware than Durkheim was of the difficulties attached to official statistics in general and the particular problems of trying to compare statistics across countries that have different ways of counting, categorising and recording crimes. Nevertheless, it is fairly safe to conclude that from 1950 on, and particularly since around the mid-1960s, most

European countries experienced a steady increase in the level of crime. Ireland is not in any way exceptional in this. In 1950, Sweden and the Federal Republic of Germany, for example, already had official annual crime rates of around 2,000 reported crimes for every 100,000 in the population, while England and Wales, France and the Netherlands had rates of around 1,000 per 100,000 population. By 1988, Sweden's crime rate had risen to around 11,000 per 100,000 population and in the other four countries the rate was around 6–7,000 with France having the lowest rate (Heidensohn and Farrell, 1991). If we put the Irish crime figures into this context, it is clear that our rise in crime started from a much lower level (around 430 per 100,000 population in the 1950s) and — at around 2,500 offences per 100,000 people — is still much lower today than in many European countries. While most Irish sociological discussions of crime focus on explaining the rise in crime rates since the 1960s, perhaps what most needs to be explained, or what is most exceptional about the Irish case, is the comparatively *low* level of crime that has persisted throughout this period, despite an overall rise in European crime rates.

## Explaining trends in crime: modernisation or expanded capitalism?

The increase in crime in Ireland, which started around the early 1960s and soared dramatically during the 1970s, came just as Irish society was starting to modernise and, particularly, to industrialise. Sociologists argue that this is more than a coincidence, that modernisation inevitably brings a rise in crime. In a sense, increased crime is the price we have to pay for the affluence and individual freedom we enjoy in modern society. But sociologists vary considerably in how they explain the connection between modernisation and rising crime.

One argument is that it is the experience of change itself — especially when rapid and externally imposed as in many developing societies — that leads to increased crime. Change produces social disorganisation, with disruption of societal values and of the institutions and methods of social control. In the transition from a 'traditional' to a 'modern' society, the shared values that maintained order formerly are eroded but new values have not yet developed to replace them. As a consequence there is no consensus about how people should behave. As people become more mobile, especially as they migrate from rural areas into cities, the old institutions of family, church and local community lose their capacity to restrain behaviour while new institutions of control are not yet fully established. Social dislocation is widely experienced as old jobs disappear and people have to move in search of new ones. In other words, modernisation like any type of social change brings into being a temporary (though possibly quite long-lasting) period of social disorganisation when people are left without clear values or controls; it is therefore not surprising that during this time the crime rate soars.

Behind this account we can detect some interesting underlying assumptions. It assumes, for example, that people need to be closely guided and regulated by society if they are to behave in a moral or sociable way — left to themselves they are naturally anarchic and violent. This is a powerful argument that turns up very frequently in discussions about crime not just in sociology, but also in mass media treatments of crime. But does it really make much sense of either the European or the Irish experience? In Europe, as we have seen, rising crime rates occurred in most countries from the 1960s but they have been particularly marked in those that, from an Irish vantage point, we would regard as already modern, and advanced. This is odd, for if rises in crime are associated with the *transition to* *modernity*, the crime rates in these countries should be levelling off and stabilising, to reflect a new 'organisation' of values and a social control system that reinstates social regulation.

Moreover, the Irish experience of industrialisation and economic development in the last 30 years has not involved massive *social disorganisation* — certainly not in comparison to the experiences of many 'late industrialising' societies. In Ireland industrialisation was dispersed throughout the countryside rather than con- centrated in cities. Dublin's population did grow substantially but this was due more to indigenous growth than to massive immigration from rural areas; those who did in-migrate from the countryside were mainly educated people moving into secure middle-class jobs. Irish society did experience rapid social change, but not the social disorganisation or breakdown of 'the traditional social order' that could satisfactorily explain the rapid rise in crime. Only certain groups in the population did, perhaps, experience severe dislocation: those who emigrated (and who now make up a disproportionate number of prisoners in British jails) and the urban working class whose jobs disappeared as older industries declined, and who were moved out of the centre of Dublin as parts of the city were redeveloped during the 1970s economic boom. Disorganisation theories *may* help to explain the predominance of youths from new outer suburban estates who passed through the criminal justice system in the 1970s and 1980s, but they do little to explain general trends in crime over the period.

It is interesting in this context to compare Ireland and a number of post- Communist countries in Europe. These countries have also seen a recent surge in official crime rates — in a more compressed time period than was the case in Ireland — since the fall of Communism at the end of the 1980s. Attempts to explain this rise by sociologists and criminologists living in these countries, have also drawn heavily on theories of social and cultural disorganisation (Parker, 1993). While these experts are well aware of the oppressive nature of the state security apparatus during the Communist era, the restrictions on citizens' rights of movement within or across borders and the highly developed powers of sur- veillance, what comes through in their accounts is in many cases almost a nostalgia for the controlled and organised nature of social life in that earlier period, with its much lower rate of crime. Parker reports similar accounts from police and justice officials and from Czech politicians, people for whom the change in regime had in many cases meant a loss of security and certainty about their work, and often also a loss in social power or status. His study helps to remind us that explanations for crime often reflect the situation and concerns of the person doing the explaining as much as any objective features of the crime rate. Regret for the loss of some aspects of the past, or fears about the future, seem particularly likely to give rise to theories that treat change in itself as responsible for pathological rates of crime.

McCullagh (1986, 1996) discusses an alternative explanation of the connection between modernisation and rising crime rates (put forward originally by Rottman, 1984) that is concerned less with the fact of social change in itself and more with the type of society that we are changing into at the time. This has been called a *social structural explanation* (in contrast to a 'social disorganisation' one) as it emphasises that the modernisation of society brings into being a new social structure, one that is organised in particular around *property*: ownership of property, social status based on property and careers in relation to property. Modernisation in Ireland opened up a range of new, legitimate career opportunities in Irish society during the 1960s and 1970s based around the production, sale, advertising, management and protection of property. But it also opened up a range of *illegitimate* career opportunities to do with property. In modern, urban, industrial society, property has become more widespread, more visible, more transportable and more desirable, so that opportunities and motives for property crime inevitably increase. This explains why even in highly developed societies the crime rate continues to rise. Property keeps on expanding, taking on new forms and becoming more highly valued in these societies.

In addition to showing how the new society is structured around property, we need to address the issue of *inequality* in access to property. Modern capitalist society has been described as a society that systematically encourages every person within it to aspire to property ownership, to a higher standard of living and increased consumption; but at the same time, as it is so unequal, it systematically prevents certain groups within the society from realising these aspirations in legitimate ways. These conditions — which the American sociologist Robert Merton, following Durkheim, called 'anomic' — seem to provide the best possible chance of producing rates of property crime that are very high and that are particularly associated with the lower working class. Note that this way of explaining crime in society rests on rather different assumptions about human nature to those of the disorganisation thesis. It assumes that people are not naturally aggressive and selfish but that these qualities are fostered in them by an anomic society — one which encourages people to believe that only wealth and consumption can give their lives meaning and worth but which nonetheless denies many of them the chance to ever achieve these goals.

# The social distribution of crime in Ireland

Merton's *anomie theory* of crime rests on the claim that most crime is committed by the most marginalised and excluded people within the capitalist class system. It prompts us to ask how crime is socially distributed in Ireland, that is: what sort of people, typically, are victims of crime and what sort of people are perpetrators? The media often suggest that the main victims of crime in Ireland are the elderly and poor, perhaps particularly old people living in rural areas. We might think that crime is largely a matter of the disadvantaged preying on the disadvantaged as people in poor areas are attacked and robbed by their own neighbours or by those from a similarly deprived social background. However, if the findings of a victim survey carried out by the ESRI in the early 1980s (Breen and Rottman, 1985) remain valid, this is not an accurate picture of the situation. In their study of who among the general population had been a victim, they found crime to be very clearly an *urban* phenomenon, heavily concentrated in Dublin, and one most likely to be experienced by people in higher social categories (self-employed or white-collar employees), generally younger (young middle-aged) rather than older people, and living in fairly new middle-class housing estates.

It is less easy to describe the typical 'victimiser'. We have no 'self-report surveys' in Ireland that ask people to report if they have ever been involved in criminal behaviour; and the reports compiled by the Gardaí only give details on the minority (less than one-third) of crimes that result in detection and a conviction. A small number of studies exist that can shed some light on this, for example, Rottman's (1984) analysis of people 'apprehended' for indictable offences in the Dublin Metropolitan Area, while not fully generalisable, provides some striking information. Rottman found that most of these people were male (84 per cent), generally very young (one-quarter were under sixteen and a further half between seventeen and twenty), economically extremely marginal (80 per cent of the seventeen- to twenty-year-olds were unemployed and the rest were in unskilled or semi-skilled work) and drawn from very specific locations in Dublin that were at that time places of great physical and social deprivation.

More recently, O'Mahony (1993) carried out research on male prisoners in Mountjoy prison. This produced a picture of 'the typical Mountjoy male prisoner' that is quite similar to the above: he is a little older than Rottman's group of 'apprehended offenders' (early to mid-twenties), from a large family, an early school leaver (probably having dropped out of school before the legal minimum leaving age), who has been unemployed for most of the period since and, when employed, has had unskilled and poorly paid work. Typically, Mountjoy male prisoners come from urban areas, especially from the Dublin inner city or from one of the poorer outer suburban areas such as Crumlin or Ballymun. While we have to consider the possibility that some of these characteristics explain better why the person is in prison than why he broke the law (see below), it may be safe to conclude that typical offenders in Ireland come — or came, in the 1980s and early 1990s — from extremely disadvantaged and marginalised groups.

The picture that emerges from both the official statistics and the small amount of available research could be summarised as follows: the bulk of the crime committed in contemporary Ireland is still relatively small-scale property crime and the property attacked is mainly that of younger middle-class people, while those who attack it are very young males from working-class backgrounds who have little chance of integrating into stable and rewarding jobs and lives. We might be tempted to conclude that in a society where the state has generally intervened to redistribute resources from those with little to those with quite a lot, crime offers an alternative resource redistribution from those with quite a lot to those with very little.

## Explaining Ireland's low crime rate

To the social disorganisation and social structural theories outlined above, McCullagh (1996, pp.133–42) has added a third way to explain how crime is linked to processes of change and development. He argues that the pattern of change is best understood as a process not simply of the expansion and institutionalisation of capitalism but of dependent development (see Chapter 3). He argues that *dependent development* has influenced Irish crime patterns in a number of ways. First, it generated new levels of affluence in Irish society that in turn, as Rottman argued, produced new opportunities for crime. Second, it created a group in society who are prepared to take advantage of these new opportunities (1996, p.136):

> As development has proceeded, increasing numbers of young working-class people have been marginalised to positions of almost permanent unemployment and disadvantage. In such situations crime becomes a mode of economic and social survival.

McCullagh emphasises that the opportunities created were not only opportunities for 'conventional' working-class crime. The increase in business activity as a result of development also created new opportunities to engage in white-collar and business crime. The issue of white-collar crime is very important and is discussed further below. Here we note only that McCullagh sees the increase in commercial and business crime as related to a third characteristic of dependent development — the weakness of the state. McCullagh (1996, p.135) suggests that peripheral and dependent development turns the state into 'a broker for international capital' with 'a deferential stance towards multinational companies'. Such states adopt a relaxed attitude to the regulation and policing of incoming corporations, for example, in the area of environmental pollution. The Irish state, McCullagh argues, was already finding it difficult to regulate the behaviour of indigenous business, making it doubly weak in the face of commercial crime.

McCullagh recognises that this explanation has not been tested out in any detail by research. Nevertheless, compared with the modernisation perspective, and even the 'development of modern capitalism' perspective of Rottman and Merton, it does promise a better grasp of how features specific to the Irish experience of development may have shaped the nature of crime in Irish society in recent decades. But it remains rather unclear in McCullagh's discussion just what it is about Irish crime rates that can be explained by the dependent development theory — a rise in the rate of crime? or a low rate of crime compared to countries whose development has not been constrained or formed by dependency? Arguably, the concept of dependent development *can* explain rather well why the crime rate in Ireland, despite marked increases in recent decades, remains consistently *low* compared to many other developed societies.

For example, societies that have experienced dependent development are often characterised by high rates of emigration: they import capital from core societies but export labour to them. Irish emigration statistics vary inversely, in an almost perfect correlation, with Irish crime statistics. When emigration rates are high, as in the 1950s or the second half of the 1980s, crime rates fall; when emigration rates are low, as in the 1970s or the late 1980s/early 1990s, crime rates increase. An explanation may be that crime rates tend to be related to the proportion of the population that is under approximately twenty-five years of age: when this is high, for example, if emigration outlets are blocked, the crime rate increases. This again suggests that crime is largely something engaged in by the young (or at least, young men) and that most people, given reasonable opportunities in life, 'grow out of' crime as they age.

There is a second and rather different way that McCullagh's argument could be used to explain why Ireland has a low crime rate. The rule-breaking behaviours that he suggests are encouraged under dependent development, particularly given the presence of a weak state, include breaches of health and safety or environmental regulations; illegal or marginally legal business and banking schemes; and corporate and individual strategies for tax evasion. These have generally either not been treated as criminal offences or, if criminalised, have not been policed or prosecuted with the same vigour that is applied to 'ordinary' crime, even when practised on a fairly large scale and/or leading to considerable social harm. Thus, a rapid increase in these types of behaviour will not show up in official crime statistics and they will continue to reflect a society that appears much more consensual and orderly than it actually is.

This argument indicates the major problems that exist in how crime is defined and measured and casts doubt on whether crime rates, as measured by official statistics, are in any way meaningful phenomena for the sociologist to study. We explore some of the issues involved in the next section of this chapter but, before leaving this discussion, it may be worth considering a country that has attracted a good deal of attention from sociologists of crime in recent years, precisely because of its rather low official crime rate. If we wish to understand crime in Irish society, we might find it illuminating to draw comparisons not with America, or even with core countries in Europe, but with Japan. Though Japanese development history may not easily be summarised as dependent (Dore, 1987), many discussions of Japanese economic performance since the 1950s stress its distinctive cultural underpinnings. This distinctiveness is also widely seen as relevant to understanding its low levels of crime.

Bayley notes that the rate of serious crime in Japan is less than one-third that in America. For him this raises questions about how 'this orderliness has been achieved' (1991, p.169). Modernisation theory cannot explain it, for Japan is 'fully as modern as the United States, transformed equally during the last century by processes of urbanisation, industrialisation and technological development'. It has a similar, if more historically recent, democratic political structure; and its legal system, if generally more lenient than the American, is very similar to it in form, 'hardly surprising since the Japanese system is the product of American reform after World War II, overlaying earlier borrowings from Germany and France' (1991, p.170). So what might explain the different levels of crime in the two societies?

Bayley suggests two highly significant features. First, Japanese society is more egalitarian, at least in terms of the distribution of wealth. The average income per capita is about the same in both countries but there is a much greater gap between high and low incomes in America than in Japan. Second, Japanese culture is characterised by 'mechanisms that are peculiar to Japan in their strength and extensiveness' (1991, p.172) which inhibit the impulse to crime. Bayley summarises these as 'propriety' (the voluminous and detailed rules about what is proper behaviour in every social situation that make the Japanese 'compulsively watchful about decorum'), 'presumption' (by that he means the acceptance of the presumptive right of immediate social groups — particularly family, school and workplace — to tell the individual how to behave, with the result that 'fitting in is the ultimate discipline in Japan') and 'pride' ('discipline is maintained in Japan because people take enormous pride in performing well the roles demanded of them'). Ultimately it is the 'cultural dynamic' constituted from these three mechanisms that for Bayley provides the strongest explanation of Japan's low crime rate. He acknowledges that from an American point of view, the low level of crime may be achieved at too high a price: as Durkheim earlier suggested, crime rates may be seen as 'pathologically low' as well as 'pathologically high' in the sense that they are the outcome of a degree of collective regulation of the individual that would be unacceptable to Western observers socialised within a culture that values individual self-determination above all else.

Bayley's analysis of crime rates in Japan suggests that Irish crime researchers might usefully investigate what it was about Irish cultural arrangements in the

1950s and 1960s that so effectively inhibited the impulse to crime. Moreover, such an approach might still pay dividends in addressing and explaining our current crime situation. But it would be important to bear in mind, as Durkheim originally argued in developing his concept of anomie, that such inhibitions are likely to be experienced differently in different social groups and may well bear much more heavily on lower than on higher social strata.

## SOCIOLOGICAL APPROACHES TO CRIME

Of all the subjects that sociologists study, crime is particularly difficult to introduce in a simple way. It has generated much disagreement within sociology itself and with other disciplines with an interest in the area (like law, psychology, criminology) — not just about the empirical facts involved but about the concept of crime itself, how it should be defined and how it can be researched. Crime is also, as we noted above, an important political issue and there is always much public concern and talk about crime, which has helped to shape how sociologists have addressed it.

One way that sociologists have tried to clarify the topic, and to move away from a simple echoing of public concerns, has been to develop the concept of deviance. What is the relationship between *deviance* and crime? The former is a broader concept: it refers to behaviour that deviates from or breaks *any* social rule, whether of politeness (how close you should stand when having a conversation, not talking with your mouth full); of self-presentation (dress so that others can tell what gender you are); of property (do not take what does not belong to you); or of sexual orientation (do not become sexually involved with young children or with members of your own sex). It is obvious that deviance is an extremely wide concept — whenever we identify a social rule, we can identify behaviour that breaks that rule. Crime refers to a subcategory of deviance; it is behaviour that breaks a particular type of social rule, namely, those rules that in our society have been enshrined within and given the force of criminal law.

## Studying crime as a social problem

Until the 1950s most sociologists took for granted that what they should study was, simply, crime: all they had to do was discover what sort of behaviour was prohibited under the criminal law of their country, and that defined what they were studying. Moreover, most early researchers in the field were motivated by a desire to respond to public concern about crime. The public defined crime as a major social problem about which something should be done, so sociologists and criminologists set out to study this social problem in the hope that, if they could discover its causes, they could help society to control or even eliminate it.

Effectively, they allowed the public — or more accurately, the more powerful and vocal groups among the public — to define their topic and set their research agenda for them.

Much of this early work started from the assumption that crime is something done by *criminals*. As a result, what sociologists ended up studying was groups of convicted criminals, arguing that the cause of their criminal behaviour lay within the individuals themselves, something that made them different from other, law-abiding people. If they could find what it was that made criminals *different*, that would be the key step towards a solution to the problem of crime. The 'causes' that researchers looked for varied considerably and have been the subject of much lively debate. In the nineteenth century, it was common to look for *physical causes* of criminality. Thus, phrenologists argued that criminality could be detected in the shape of the skull or the size of the brain (Gould, 1997). This approach still manifests itself from time to time, for example, in the search for genetic differences between 'criminals' and 'normal people', such as the presence of extra chromosomes in the brain. Other researchers looked more for *psychological defects*: people who took illegal drugs were (and indeed still commonly are) thought to suffer from personality defects of various sorts, such as a poorly developed super-ego, or excessive narcissism; or were people with 'addictive personalities'. Sociologists were particularly likely to look for defects in the *socialisation* or childhood upbringing or environment of the criminal.

What is striking about these different approaches is that they all located the cause of crime as an individual defect or pathology within the individual criminal. They assumed a difference between people who break criminal laws and those who do not — or who have not been discovered to have done so. And it is in that simple point that the weakness of this approach to crime is revealed. People who break criminal laws do not equate with convicted criminals. Furthermore, it would be impossible to find any group of 'ordinary conformists' with whom we could compare convicted criminals because any selection from the general population is bound to include at least one person who has broken a criminal law but has not been charged with an offence. Nearly everybody in the ordinary law-abiding population has broken some law at some time in their lives.

Just as convicted criminals — that is, people with a *public identity* as a criminal — are not the same as 'all those in society who break the criminal law', we need also to note that official statistics on crime, such as those produced annually in Ireland by the Gardaí, do not include all crimes committed. The Gardaí can only report a crime that is known to them, which generally means that some member of the public has told them about it. But the public is much more likely to report some types of crime than others — victim surveys indicate that people are readier to report car-thefts, for example, than house burglaries, and that in general how likely they are to report any sort of theft depends on whether the objects stolen were insured and whether the insurance company insists that the police be informed. Also what people are prepared to report changes over time; rape and child sex abuse, for example, are much more likely to be reported nowadays than even ten years ago, while a couple of generations ago they were reported very rarely indeed.

Official statistics on crime, then, are not a simple snapshot of what is happening at a point in time, but are the outcome of a complex series of social interactions and processes. First, a member of the public has to report to the Gardaí that a crime has been committed or the Gardaí themselves need to detect the commission of a crime, a fairly rare event except for public order and traffic offences. Then the Gardaí have to record the crime as a crime, and in many cases this does not happen, for a number of reasons. For example, for a long period 'domestic violence' was not treated as a crime. The reported crime may for administrative reasons be aggregated with a number of others. A crime may be detected and recorded as 'cleared up' or it may be 'written off' when a suspect admits to a number of crimes. The Director of Public Prosecutions may decide not to bring a case to court or a judge may dismiss a case for lack of evidence or on a legal technicality. Given this complex set of processes, we may conclude that what official statistics measure is not the 'rate of crime' in society, but rather the outcomes of a complex process of reporting and recording of crime. They tell us more, perhaps, about what other people do in responding to a crime than about what criminals do.

If official statistics only include a selection of all 'crimes' committed (and we are taking the perhaps unjustifiable step here of assuming that 'crime' has an objective existence outside of the processes that define it), it seems that official statistics on *criminals* (which tell us things like their age, gender, social class, or place of origin) are even less reliable. To 'officially' become a criminal a person has to pass through a series of stages from arrest, to preparation of a case against them, to court appearances, and finally a guilty verdict and the recording of a conviction. At each stage there is a high drop-out rate which happens for a range of reasons that may have little to do with whether the person actually committed the offence or not. Moreover, those who come to the attention of the Gardaí or are arrested or convicted are not a random sample of all criminal law breakers but a specific select social group: generally young, male, unemployed and from particular locations within urban areas. The *social* characteristics that distinguish these people from the rest of the population are far more striking than any alleged physical or psychological 'defects' they might carry.

Other objections can be made to studies of crime that equate it simplistically with breaking the criminal law: crime is, as was suggested above, a social construct. Criminal laws are not fixed or static — they vary between societies and change, sometimes quite radically, over time in the same society. What counts as a crime is thus *relative* to a particular time, place and culture. If the assumption that criminals are different from conforming people is hard to sustain, so is the assumption that crimes (and criminals) resemble each other. Why should burglars have anything in common with those who live off immoral earnings, or illegal phone-tappers share anything with rapists, other than that they have all been found to have broken a law? Similarly, if our concern is with behaviour that does *harm* to society, there is little reason to confine ourselves to the study of crime since much harmful behaviour is not criminalised and, in addition, there are 'crimes' that most people would feel are not really very harmful (such as keeping a dog without a dog licence). The criminal law produces a very narrow and biased measure of 'harmful rule-breaking': it concerns itself primarily with the sort of harmful behaviour the poor or the powerless are likely to engage in (particularly rather petty property theft) but is much less concerned with the sort the rich and powerful engage in.

## Studying deviance as part of social order

For such reasons many sociologists largely abandoned the concept of crime and defined the object of their study as *deviance*. They set out to investigate any sort of rule-breaking that arouses public disapproval (for not all rule-breaking does) whether or not it was criminalised. The impetus for research was increasingly derived from within sociology rather than from the real or perceived demands of governments or policy-makers. The research effort was aimed at further understanding the problem of *social order*: how did people manage their social relationships; how did they make their social world meaningful and intelligible? In short, how was society organised in a routine, regular way so that we can usually explain what has taken place and what might happen next? Rule-*making* is obviously an important element in our attempts to make society 'orderly', but so is handling and dealing with rule-*breaking*, and the concept of deviance was a means towards researching these issues.

But the switch from 'crime' to 'deviance' did not deal with all the difficulties that faced those working in this area. Almost immediately they had to confront the issue of whose disapproval counts — if some members of society strongly disapprove of a certain type of behaviour (for example, sex before marriage) but others do not, should we regard the behaviour as deviant or not? Should sociologists simply endorse the view of the more 'respectable' and more powerful groups? It also became apparent that the same rule-breaking behaviour might be disapproved of and therefore deviant in one set of circumstances, but tolerated and therefore not deviant in another. For example, if you help yourself to stationery in a shop you are stealing, and deviant; but if you do so at work where such pilfering is seen as a perk of employment, you are not deviant. In grappling with such problems, sociologists of deviance, particularly those known as *labelling* theorists, made an interesting discovery: crime and deviance are not characteristics of individual rule-breakers, but result from the *reaction* of others to the rule-breaker. Whether they ignore, tolerate, disapprove or punish is crucial in determining whether someone achieves the social identity of a deviant, or criminal, or continues to live a life that is to all outward appearances one of conventional conformity.

This approach emphasises that deviance is *socially constructed* — partly from what the rule-breaker does (or is thought to have done) and partly from how others respond to that behaviour. There is no point then in searching for the causes of criminality *within* the individual. Personal characteristics might help to explain why a person broke a rule in the first place, but to explain how they went on to become a (labelled) criminal we must also investigate how society responds to and treats this sort of rule-breaking. This response, as noted earlier, can change over time and different subgroups may respond in different ways. If you smoke marijuana in one type of social setting, you may very quickly find yourself arrested and charged; in another type of setting you may be ignored. Deviance is the result of interaction between rule-breaker and witness and not merely the result of what the rule-breaker does.

## A new research agenda on crime

Thinking of deviance as socially constructed led sociologists to develop a new and interesting research agenda. They asked:

> *How are official crime statistics created?*
> How do police practices influence how levels of crime are measured and announced to the public?
> *How is a small group of 'criminals' produced from a much larger initial pool of rule-breakers?*
> Is there something about the social background of 'criminals', or about how they present themselves to others, that leads police to suspect and arrest them, a jury to convict them and a judge to imprison them when others may escape these processes?
> *Does it make a difference to their future career if a rule-breaker is dealt with by the police, or by another agency such as psychiatry or social work?*
> In the United States the problem of illegal drug use is regarded as primarily the property of the police and is dealt with by lawcourts and prisons; in The Netherlands, substance abuse falls in the field of the medical and welfare agencies and is dealt with in different ways. Do these variations make a difference to the rule-breaker in terms of the sort of commitment she or he may develop to a further career in crime?

Increasingly we can bring into the picture the whole issue of *social control* — how society handles and manages crime — as well as the issue of crime itself.

## CRIME AND INEQUALITY

Most research on crime, including much sociological research, takes for granted that crime is somehow connected with poverty, disadvantage or powerlessness. Some of the more interesting sociological theories of crime, such as Merton's reworking of Durkheim's anomie theory, provide us with convincing accounts of why criminals are drawn overwhelmingly from the most deprived groups in society. But sociologists of deviance have raised a number of questions about this presumed connection. Labelling theorists ask whether the poorest in society are the most prone to breaking the law, or whether they are the most prone to being *caught*: identified and publicly labelled as law-breakers. Marxists ask how we should understand the law in capitalist society: does it extend equal rights to all, or is it partisan and biased, primarily concerned to protect the interests of the powerful? Box (1983) and McCullagh (1995) suggest that sociology should ask not 'who commits most crime?' but 'who causes most social harm?' It may then find that much severely harmful behaviour is not even defined as crime or, if so defined, offenders are not subjected to criminal charges, proceedings or punishment. The behaviour that is most likely to escape the criminal justice system is white-collar crime.

## White-collar crime in Ireland

The term 'white-collar crime' was coined by American criminologist Edwin Sutherland (1949, p.9) to refer to 'a crime committed by a person of respectability in the course of his occupation' in order to make a profit for or otherwise benefit his company or employer. It is also referred to as occupational crime — to differentiate it from 'street' crime. It may take two forms: there are crimes committed for personal gain, which a person can only carry out because they hold a particular occupational position. A teller may defraud a bank; a dentist carry out unnecessary dental work; or a planning official may take a bribe from a property developer. A second form of occupational crime (that originally defined by Sutherland) is that committed in the course of an occupation in order to benefit or further the corporate goals of an employer; this is now often called corporate crime.

McCullagh (1995, 1996) suggests two reasons why sociologists should be particularly interested in white-collar crimes. First, they are primarily 'crimes of the middle class' — not usually committed by people in disadvantaged or socially excluded situations. Second, they are crimes that are mainly marginal to public consciousness — our imagery of typical crimes or criminals does not usually embrace respectable businessmen engaged in fraud, negligence or misleading practices. Societal response to harmful or criminal behaviour varies greatly, so that while certain types of property theft receive great public attention and disapprobation, others are hardly noticed.

This situation may be changing rapidly. In Ireland, as in other countries such as Australia, public awareness of political and police corruption, industrial negligence, commercial fraud and professional malpractice is growing rapidly. In Ireland, this new public consciousness dates back at least to the discoveries of the so-called Beef Tribunal, set up in May 1991 to investigate claims of malpractices within the Goodman Group of beef-processing companies. It was alleged that these companies enjoyed excessive favours from the government and state departments. The Tribunal found evidence of occupational crime: the group was found to have '[abused] public funds on a large scale' by 'systematically taking meat that it was deboning under contract for the EC intervention system, meat that belonged to the EC, and packing it for its own commercial contracts with, for instance, the Tesco supermarket chain in England' (O'Toole, 1995, p.264). It also discovered evidence of corporate crime: the group '[contrived] to cheat the public of taxes' (O'Toole, 1995, p.281). However, no member of the Group was convicted of any criminal offence. By 1999, the public proceedings of three further tribunals of enquiry, the McCracken, Moriarty and Flood tribunals, and the Dáil's Public Accounts Committee, had reinforced public concern and anger over white-collar crime. Yet crime continues to be routinely portrayed in the popular media, and even in much academic discussion, as intimately connected with, and explained in terms of, experiences of poverty, disadvantage and social marginalisation.

How does this happen? McCullagh identifies three processes that operate to emphasise working-class crime and conceal or play down middle-class crime. First, the process of *law-making*. How laws are made has the effect of sanctioning some kinds of harmful behaviour while ignoring others. For McCullagh (1995, p.412) 'in Ireland the law has been written in such a way that the anti-social behaviour of those in business, corporate and commercial positions is inadequately regulated, or where it is regulated, it is generally not done so through the criminal law.' He illustrates this through a discussion of the Bantry Bay disaster of 1979, when a tanker discharging oil blew up and fifty people were killed. The subsequent inquiry into the disaster showed that these deaths were 'avoidable' yet no related criminal prosecutions ever followed. More recent examples, such as the outcome of the Beef Tribunal, appear to support his case.

The second process is that of *law enforcement*. Even where white-collar crimes are defined in law as crimes, enforcement tends to be selective and considerably less energetic than in the case of 'street' crimes. McCullagh notes that while the average larceny recorded by Gardaí in 1993 involved less than £500, we find examples of corporate frauds that involve at least ten times that amount where criminal offences have been identified, but no prosecutions have followed. Tax evasion is a type of white-collar crime that is widespread among companies in Ireland but, though listed as a serious crime on the statute books, few resources are put into policing it. Criminal sanctions have been used extremely rarely against corporate tax evaders and no-one has yet been imprisoned. For McCullagh (1995, p.420) 'the situation with tax evasion can be summarised as being a common activity where the chances of non-detection are still significant and the risks of being criminally adjudicated are relatively minor.'

The third process is that of the *court system*. Research into the decision-making processes of Irish courts suggests that white-collar criminals, even in crimes aimed at personal benefit, such as embezzlement, are relatively unlikely to be convicted. If they are convicted, they are less likely to receive a prison sentence, or to have to serve it, than working-class 'professional' criminals are. Overall, McCullagh (1995, p.424) concludes, while there is 'compelling evidence that corporate and white-collar misbehaviour is a significant problem in Irish society', it can also be shown that it is systematically dealt with in a different way to working-class criminality. Middle-class crime largely escapes 'the stigma of criminality', and so has quite different effects on the future life of the offender and on the public perception of the seriousness of the offence. The production of working-class crime as the major social problem in Irish society is thus as much the achievement of the criminal justice system, and of those that create and sustain it, as it is of working-class criminals.

Earlier we suggested that, if we wish to develop a comparative perspective on Irish crime, useful comparisons could be made with Japan. Setting aside the complex statistical and definition problems alluded to above, Japan appears to have relatively low levels of conventional crime but quite high levels of white-collar crime. If Japan's low levels of conventional crime are the outcome of powerful cultural dynamics that inhibit deviance, how is it that middle- and upper-class groups can often escape their hold?

Kerbo and Inoue (1990) suggest that the explanation may lie in some aspects of Japanese social structure. They argue that the top of the Japanese power structure is occupied by a relatively closed, interlocking circle of three elites: the corporate elite, the national bureaucratic elite and (the weakest of the three) a political elite organised around the then ruling Liberal Democratic Party. The corporate elite consists of the most powerful business executives, who are closely linked, 'especially through intercorporate control of corporate stock' (1990, p.141) plus members of the big professional associations that, representing these businesses, 'organise business pressure and political activities to an extent probably considered illegal' elsewhere. The bureaucratic elite consists of career civil servants and administrators who, though relatively low paid, enjoy considerable power and respect; many retire early to top corporate executive positions. Kerbo and Inoue (1990, p.143) note that the ruling elites do not share a privileged class background and have little 'old upper class family wealth in Japan'; rather, they have 'come up from relatively humble origins' as a result of 'sponsored mobility that is channelled through elite universities. The "old school ties" are extensive'.

Can the existence of a group very like Mills's 'power elite' (see Chapter 4) explain the high levels of corporate crime in Japan? Kerbo and Inoue suggest that it can, for two reasons. First, the inner circle of power is very hard to break into: executives of smaller business are locked out of the big money deals and find themselves having to compete ruthlessly and often illegally if they want to break in. Second, the elite group is relatively free from formal pressures to make them accountable to other groups in the wider society. The importance of mobility through sponsorship means that white-collar crime in Japan is *collective* rather than individual in orientation. Corporate leaders who engage in illegal activities are often protected and their activities covered up or concealed by subordinates. Subordinate groups will make efforts, sometimes illegal, to enhance the position of their leaders as this enhances the position of the whole group. It can thus be argued that the same cultural dynamic that helps to reduce conventional crime levels in Japanese society operates, in the circumstances of the commercial upper and middle classes, to *increase* the likelihood of, and provide justifications for, white-collar crime. The power structure in Irish society is clearly not identical with the Japanese; yet there are enough similarities, perhaps, to make research into the nature and relationships of Irish business, administrative and political elites a useful way forward in understanding white-collar crime in Ireland.

## WOMEN AND CRIME

We noted earlier that much sociology of crime aims to identify and explain the links between criminality and social factors such as class, age or location. Yet as Heidensohn (1989) points out, if you wanted to find just one characteristic to predict which children were most likely to become criminals in adult life, you could not do better than to choose *gender* as your explanatory variable. Yet until the mid-1980s, gender issues in relation to crime were scarcely mentioned at all in sociology. The blind spot in relation to women probably had much to do with the fact that the sociology of deviance, like most sociology, was until very recently carried out almost entirely by men. But it also owed much to the fact (as we have seen) that crime was studied as a social problem. Since female criminals were few, they did not merit study. But the study of women and crime (within a context of greater sensitivity to gender issues in general) can reveal a great deal about the nature and operation of the criminal justice system. In particular it helps to develop our understanding of social control.

Women do feature quite rarely in official statistics on crime: in the early 1980s it was predominantly men (84 per cent) that were apprehended by Dublin Gardaí for indictable offences. The further we move on through the criminal justice system, the fewer women appear. For example, the *Annual reports on crime* show that around 10 to 15 per cent of those convicted of offences in any year are women. This varies by type of offence: about a quarter of those convicted of larceny are women but this falls to just 4 per cent for those convicted of 'offences against the person' or 'offences against property with violence'. Women are also most unlikely to be imprisoned for crime or to spend long periods of time in prison. As O'Mahony points out (1993, p.101), around 6 per cent of those committed to prison in recent years have been women; and women constitute around 2 per cent of the total daily average of people in prison, suggesting that on average they get shorter sentences than men.

Studies from elsewhere in Europe, where similar gender patterns have been found, show that, when charged by the police, women are more often first time offenders than men and that very few of them indeed could be called 'professional criminals'. One sociologist has remarked that the world of organised crime can hardly be described as an Equal Opportunities Employer, and another that in general crime is 'a field of endeavour in which women could be said to have underachieved'. More seriously, how might we explain the under-representation of women in official statistics on crime? Many of the classical explanations that were formulated to explain male involvement in crime become less convincing when we look at women. As we have seen, for example, there is often said to be a link between crime and poverty. But are women not poor? Is there something about how women respond to and manage poverty that is different from men and is less likely to lead into crime? High crime rates are also often associated with powerlessness, but women in general occupy positions in society of even less power than men.

There are two possible ways to respond to this problem. One takes the data at face value and tries to find differences in the social experiences and positions of men and women that would explain their very different patterns of involvement in crime. The other is more critical of the official statistics and suggests that perhaps they indicate not the 'real' extent of women's involvement in rule-breaking, but the interaction processes between women rule-breakers and those who witness and respond to their rule-breaking. Perhaps there is something about these processes that systematically leads to women's rule-breaking being less obvious; or more tolerated; or less likely to attract the attention of official agencies of control. Perhaps women are treated more leniently; are less likely to develop an official criminal record; or be sentenced to go to prison. If any or all of these were true, we might conclude that women engage in a lot more rule-breaking than official statistics reveal.

Labelling theory has been important in exploring the links between gender, crime and deviance. It argues that deviance is a *social role* imposed on some in society, often for reasons that have less to do with behaviour than the sort of person they are. For labelling theorists, the labelling of someone as deviant (thief, prostitute, drug abuser) is often precipitated by *contingencies* — aspects that are contingent (accidental) to the rule-breaking act, such as where it occurred, in front of what audience, or what sort of person the rule-breaker appears to be. Gender is a characteristic of people that is generally highly visible and socially significant, in the sense that we are always aware of, and respond to, the gender of a person we are interacting with. It seems most likely that gender will enter into the labelling process that leads to the social creation of criminals in our society.

Research on this topic does to some extent confirm that people who witness rule-breaking are influenced by the gender of the rule-breaker in framing their response (McCullagh, 1996, Chapter 4). Women are generally not seen as serious rule-breakers and are less likely to be reported to the police; the police are less likely to proceed to charge them; and there is less public fear of women criminals so police and judges can respond in a more lenient way. But this appears to be true only where the offence involved is fairly trivial; and there is considerable debate over whether we should summarise the treatment of women offenders in terms of leniency at all.

Some sociologists have argued that women offenders benefit from the fact that the criminal justice system tends to be staffed primarily by men who have been taught to take a chivalrous and protective attitude towards women; others interpret the situation very differently. For them, if women sometimes escape labelling for an offence that a man would have been labelled for, this is not evidence of a chivalrous attitude but shows that women, here as elsewhere in society, are not taken seriously by men. But what most women experience at the hands of the criminal justice system, it is argued, is not more lenient treatment but treatment that *differs* to that received by men. Sometimes it is less severe, but sometimes more so.

For example, in the case of juvenile offenders, British and Australian studies show that girls whose behaviour is 'unruly' are more likely to be put into institutional care than boys. This is usually justified by magistrates on the grounds that girls need 'care and protection'. This indicates that such girls are seen to be at risk of immorality as well as crime, whereas boys in the same situation are only seen as at risk of crime. Studies of adult criminals also suggest that the courts often respond on the basis of their gender role rather than or in addition to their actual offence. A woman offender who is a mother with dependent children, or who has a husband to be sent home to, may be given a non-custodial sentence where a male offender would have received a prison sentence. On the other hand, women whose lives do not accord with conventional gender roles, even those who are victims of rape, often experience harsh and punitive treatment by the police and the courts.

This suggests that the criminal justice system is a patriarchal institution that both acts on and helps to reproduce gender stereotypes that reinforce men's dominance over women in the society as a whole. A growing body of research (see Heidensohn, 1989; Walklate, 1995) reveals the existence of deeply rooted patriarchal assumptions and beliefs about women among British police officers, magistrates and judges. These include assumptions that women are emotional rather than rational; are unlikely to plan crimes but are easily led into supporting other criminals; and that what they say is unreliable or untrue. There is as yet no comparative research on the Irish criminal justice system, but we should not necessarily take for granted that similar attitudes exist here. Moreover, in most though by no means all cases the outcome for women of the operation of such assumptions does tend to be less punitive in conventional terms.

When we recognise how the criminal justice system may be biased in relation to gender, we can see how it may also be involved in the reproduction of class inequalities and in some contexts inequalities of national or ethnic difference. As we saw in our discussion of white-collar crime, so it is with crime and gender: we cannot treat the operation of the criminal justice system as if it were purely a reaction to crimes committed in society, but must recognise that it is involved in the creation of patterns and trends in relation to crime and in the social constitution of deviance.

This is a most important outcome of recent work on women and crime. But even allowing for the fact that women are less likely to be labelled as criminal than men, they do also appear to be less likely to break rules in the first place. That still needs explanation. One very promising line of argument here suggests that we should investigate the different patterns of informal social control to which men and women are subjected. Women and girls appear to be subjected to more extensive informal policing within the family, school, by neighbours, by colleagues at work and by strangers in public places. If, in everyday social life, men were treated the same way as women, the prisons would be virtually empty and the police and judiciary idle (Heidensohn, 1989). But what we learn from studies of women and informal social control might suggest that law and order achieved in this way could come at too high a price. It is useful to end as we began, by reminding ourselves of Durkheim's view that crime rates can be 'abnormally' low, as well as 'abnormally' high.

# Part III

---

## Cultural change

# Introduction

For Welsh writer Raymond Williams (1976, p.76), who has traced the history of the term 'culture', it is 'one of the two or three most complicated words in the English language'. In Part III we make an attempt to get to grips with this complex entity and to start to explore some aspects of Irish culture from a sociological perspective.

For sociologists, culture refers primarily to the way of life of a people, social group or historical period. It includes two main elements: *ideas*, for example, from philosophical systems, values and rules for behaviour through to concepts and perceptions in everyday use; and *material artefacts*, such as tools, works of art, furniture or food. Culture is often contrasted with *nature* — the progress of human civilisation is thought to involve a process of overcoming our natural instincts and replacing them by obedience to learnt rules. Williams shows how the concepts of culture and *civilisation* are linked, and that in everyday life 'culture' is most likely to be used in reference to intellectual and artistic activity.

But sociologists do not confine their understanding of culture to the so-called high culture of classical music, fine art and serious literature; they are as likely to study pop music, TV soaps, street murals or John Grisham novels — often referred to as popular culture. Increasingly the line between the two is becoming blurred through, for example, techno versions of Handel's *Messiah*, the annual media hype over the Booker Prize and blockbuster exhibitions in museums and galleries.

At its broadest, culture embraces the customary ways that people behave towards each other, This is the territory of everyday rituals, from religious wedding ceremonies to buying a round in the pub. It also includes the *meanings* and interpretations that people attach to social relationships and to the world in which they live. Material objects are part of culture insofar as they have been created for a purpose, or reflect a set of meanings, and they are meaningful to their makers and users.

Though sociologists usually separate structure and culture, as indeed we have in this book, in reality they are closely interrelated. The process of structural change we call industrialisation is as much about change in meanings and ideas as it is about technological change. Tools and technologies carry social meanings that help to shape the process of industrialisation. For example, many European farmers of the 1950s and 1960s bought tractors, even when their farms were too small or their land too mountainous to use them profitably, because they had been persuaded that the modern farm is a mechanised one.

The patterning of inequality in Irish society is also at least partly a product of ideas and meanings, for example, about how valuable to society different occupations are and what sort of rewards their holders deserve. To study society as culture, then, has always been a part of sociology, though often a rather peripheral and neglected part. This may be due to the sway of positivism — it is hard to capture meaning through quantitative or statistical methods. As a consequence, the sociology of culture has been seen as less than scientific, its findings less able to be generalised and of less social or political utility. Yet without a sociology of cultural meanings we cannot obtain a sense of *social process*. We may know how the social structure fits together but not how it works — how it comes into existence, how it shapes, constrains or facilitates particular sorts of action and interaction, or how it may be changed or discarded over time.

The influence of post- or late modernity and its analysis has led to a welcome surge in the sociological analysis of aspects of culture. The discipline has been strongly influenced by the currents running through cultural and media studies, feminism and literary theory: disciplines that all take culture seriously — perhaps sometimes *too* seriously. This also reflects the increasing social and economic importance accorded to culture. The period is witnessing the burgeoning of the 'culture industries' — tourism, media, retailing — and concomitant policies, and politics as culture becomes the field of real struggles over power and resources. Furthermore, there has been an explosion of 'identity politics', based on the cultural values of ethnicity, sexuality and lifestyle. It is no surprise that issues of culture threaten to edge out structural themes of inequality within international sociological thought.

Among Irish sociologists, however, research into culture has been fairly slow to develop (see Chapter 2). In the early 1990s, Bell (1991, p.88) could still complain that:

> We can, for instance, count the number of ethnographic studies of youth subcultures in Ireland on the fingers of one hand. . . . We still have only one major academic study of the history and politics of film in Ireland. The history of broadcasting over the last twenty-five years is yet to be written. No substantial studies of popular music, its production, exchange and consumption exist. . . . The study of sport as popular culture and its role in the formation and reproduction of national identity is in its infancy.

Although cultural studies was alive and vibrant in Ireland by 1991, it was mainly carried out by literary and to a lesser extent historical experts, with very little input from sociology. In the years since Bell made these comments the situation has changed. The *Irish Journal of Sociology* increasingly carries papers on the sociology of culture and in 1997 the Sociological Association of Ireland devoted its entire Annual Conference to the theme of culture and identity in Ireland. But published work in this area remains scarce and tends to be concentrated in a limited number of fields — media, nationalism, religion, community and, more recently, gender identities and cultures of nature, all of which we address here.

In Chapter 1 we argued that sociology has long been preoccupied with the analysis and interpretation of modernity. That modernity involves not just changes in social structure but also specific processes of cultural change was apparent in the work of the classic social theorists. As Durkheim drew attention to the emergence of individualism as the new morality, Marx predicted the growth of alienation and commodity fetishism. Theorists of urbanisation, from Tönnies to Simmel, understood the transition to urban life as a profound alteration in the meanings we attach to our relationships and our sense of self. Perhaps most famously, Weber envisaged modernity as deeply shaped by cultural processes of increasing rationalisation, secularisation and the loss of mystery and enchantment.

Weber, in particular, provides some guiding ideas with which to approach culture and cultural change. But we find again that the specificities of Irish experience are not always easily subsumed into dominant sociological interpretations. Bell (1991, p.90) remarks:

> European sociology developed historically alongside capitalist modernity as an attempt to grasp the dimensions of this emerging order. In a sense, classical sociological theory is a persuasive narrative about capitalist modernisation. As we know, this narrative has been less convincing when applied to the Irish experience.

Despite such divergences, we also discover that apparently unique Irish experiences have universal dimensions that may be illuminated by a broader sociological vision. Post-modernism has opened sociological awareness to the odd, the non-standard or deviant in human social experience so that these no longer have to be marked as 'failures of modernity'. In an Irish context, this perspective can be something of a liberation. But it needs always to be accompanied by sociological interest in the standard and the norm, in what is seen to be socially normative and legitimate.

We open Part III with a popular if perennial question: does Ireland have a distinctive, homogeneous culture? If so, has it been changing over time, perhaps becoming less distinctive? Development of this idea inevitably leads us into a discussion of nationalism itself as an ideology that has played a large part in shaping modern Ireland. The belief that Irish society is united around a single shared culture can also lead us to overlook cultural differences within the society. We introduce the idea of *cultural politics* to suggest that culture can be an arena of power struggles and conflict as well as a basis for social unity and cohesion. Our discussion moves from a concern with the content of culture at the start, to a concern with cultural practices and cultural processes. In our analyses of national culture, 'community', religion and media we hope to explore both these aspects and to raise some questions, at least, about what it means to be Irish today.

# 11

# *One nation, one culture?*

What makes a person Irish? Is it because they carry an Irish passport or because they were born in Ireland? Must they speak Irish, drink Guinness, be Catholic, or play camogie or hurling? Must they live in Ireland, or is it enough to be one of the 40 million across the globe that allegedly claim an 'Irish identity'. These are questions that have become both less and more important in late modernity. As the world dissolves into a single global culture and the cultural products of global capitalism pervade our daily lives, what continued relevance can specific national cultures retain? At the same time, as our economy increasingly turns on the production and consumption of meanings and images, possession of a national culture, if only to sell to tourists, film-goers or duty-free purchasers, may be of crucial importance.

In this chapter we explore aspects of Irish cultural and national identity. We open our analysis with a discussion of nationalism and the idea of nation: a topic often neglected in English-language sociology texts. We trace connections between modernisation, language, culture and nation and examine how these have worked themselves out in an Irish context. We then examine the importance of the state in relation to the nation, developing some of the points made in Chapter 4. Finally we look critically at various meanings of 'culture': one of the most complex in the lexicon of the social sciences. The chapters that immediately follow explore further aspects of cultural expression in the fields of religion, community and the media.

In his book *The nation state and violence* (1985) British sociologist Anthony Giddens argues that the emergence of the 'nation state' and of a world order founded on relations between nation states is one of the core characteristics of the modern world. He also points out that the dominant paradigms for understanding modernity — Marxism and theories of industrial society — lack a satisfactory account of the nation and nationalism. In these theoretical narratives it is the emergence of social class and societies structured around class divisions and relationships, that is central. Thus, when they describe nineteenth-century Europe, it is with an eye to the creation of group identities based on social class rather than on nation; and towards the activities of those involved in the labour movement rather than nationalist organisations. When they turn to the twentieth century it is to explain what happens to class identity as societies become more diversified and individualised and new forms of integration or social management are developed.

Giddens has sought to reinstate the centrality of the nation as part of modernity and, as we see below, other sociologists have developed interesting analyses of nationalism and the construction of nationhood. Yet it remains that sociology has problems with nationalism. It sits uneasily alongside the universalising, rationalising modes of thought that have long pervaded the discipline. As a result nationalism is often seen as a minor, peripheral or deviant element in the modern world: something of an embarrassment that can and should be disregarded or dismissed as no more than a defensive reaction to modernity. In contrast to this, here we hope to show that its analysis is a key towards understanding contemporary Irish society.

## CULTURE AND NATION IN IRELAND

To return then to our opening question: what is it that determines Irishness? In the twenty-first century we regard ourselves as living in a world of separate nations, each of which is marked out by its own distinctive culture, shared by the majority of its population. Thus, membership in the 'Irish nation' is often thought to mean displaying a culture that is recognisably Irish. But what are the particular cultural characteristics that give us our national identity? This is where the issue becomes far more complex. One feature is that such characteristics are quite malleable, according to the situation concerned. They may relate to quite minor aspects of interaction, such as how close a person stands to another, how they pitch their voice or the sort of jokes they make; at other times they may refer to the historical or cultural knowledge a person displays — a 'real Irish person' ought to recognise Cromwell's phrase 'to hell or to Connaught' or know who Dana is. The variability of shared culture is an issue that we return to later in this chapter.

Initially, we focus on two aspects of national culture that many would agree on. First, the cultural characteristics that underpin our national identity are usually thought of as basic, inherited characteristics that are ascribed rather than achieved. No matter how hard someone from outside the nation tries to 'become' Irish it is usually impossible for them to do so perfectly. Second, of the cultural attributes that may define nation and identity, the most important in the Irish case are commonly identified as language and religion. The Irish nation has often, at least until the last decade or so, been described as 'Catholic and Gaelic'. It is this particular religious inheritance and connectedness with a specific linguistic and cultural past that is believed to constitute us as a separate and distinctive nation.

Territoriality, or connection with a particular space and place, is also a key to defining national identity. The Irish historical experience of emigration and diaspora, as we saw in Chapter 5, has distinctively shaped our understandings of what it is to belong to the Irish nation but also makes it eminently possible to be Irish and to live outside of the territory of Ireland. Portable cultural attributes appear to be given more significance, in the Irish case, than spatial location and attachment; thus we are able to think of John F. Kennedy, Mick McCarthy or former Australian premier Paul Keating as in some way Irish even if they spent by far the greater part of their adult lives outside the country, or indeed even if they never visited Ireland at all.

## Modernisation and national culture

Those for whom a nation is defined by a shared and distinctive culture often argue that maintenance of national difference depends on a degree of isolation from, or a barrier against, intercultural contact. A distinctive language or to a lesser extent a separate religion, helps to provide such a barrier. This is based on the assumption that nations emerged through a process of separation and differentiation. It is often taken for granted that the absence of contact between social groups allowed distinct cultures to form and develop and, conversely, that the increased international contacts that typify the modern world threaten the survival of unique national cultures. For example, some of the concern currently being expressed about immigration to Ireland springs from a fear that this will dilute Irish cultural distinctiveness.

Interestingly, not only nationalists argue like this. Proponents of transnationalism often make similar claims: thus for Deutsch (1966) integration towards a transnational European identity results from increased transactions between previously non-communicating individuals and groups. He suggests that the more people communicate across national boundaries, the more likely they are to see themselves as part of a common 'European nation'. EU programmes such as Socrates which support international mobility of students and young people reflect similar assumptions about the significance of cross-cultural contact in the development of a supranational European culture and society.

Modernisation theorists like Deutsch generally welcome the merging of separate national cultures and identities into international and supranational ones, whereas this is generally a cause of regret for nationalists. For modernisation theorists the process of modernisation sees societies becoming more alike, structurally and culturally. The theory suggests that to develop economically, societies must first detach their populations from local, 'divisive' loyalties (to kinship, community or minority languages) in order to establish a shared national culture as the basis for the nation state. The values of this national culture then increasingly converge with those of the advanced societies and ultimately give rise to a shared 'world culture' in which nationalism and national cultural barriers are no longer significant (see Chapter 18 for further discussion).

How useful is this thesis as a way to understand Irish national culture? Has it become less distinctive as Irish society modernises? Earlier we suggested that two major cultural markers of the Irish nation have been the Roman Catholic religion and the Irish language. If the modernisation argument is correct, we might expect to find a pattern of decline in both in recent decades.

In the next chapter we examine in detail aspects of religion in Ireland. One issue we discuss is whether Irish society has become more secularised in recent decades: has the influence of religion declined? Modernisation theorists largely agreed with Weber that modernising and industrialising societies are also secularising ones. For Weber 'the disenchantment of the world' — the triumph of scientific and economic rationality over magic and mysticism — was a central feature of modernity. But at first sight Irish society appears to be an exception to the secularisation thesis. Religiosity is still a salient feature of Irish life and remains a key to our culture and behaviour. Fahey (1992) argues that if we locate its origins in the aftermath of the Famine, rather than in the late 1950s, the 'modern era' in Ireland has been marked by growing church power and influence. Inglis (1998a, pp.249–59) makes his point more explicitly: through its control of the institutions of education, health and welfare and its influence over family structure and interpersonal relationships, the Catholic Church has had a pivotal role in the process of modernisation of Irish society.

The complexities of secularisation are addressed further in the next chapter but here we focus now on the issue of language and modernisation. While sociological research on the Irish language has been ongoing for some time, it is rarely addressed in sociological debates nor accorded any relevance to an understanding of contemporary Ireland (an exception is O'Reilly, 1996). This neglect, we suggest, could profitably be reconsidered. It seems to be related to a general lack of interest within Irish sociology, until quite recently, in issues to do with culture, but may also be an indication of Irish sociology's commitment to modernism, which finds great difficulty in seeing minority languages and their speakers as other than deviant and exceptional.

## Language and modernisation

A modernisation perspective encourages a belief that modernising societies become linguistically homogeneous: within them everyone will eventually speak the same language or, at the very least, linguistic differences will decline as a significant source of division and conflict. If a minority language does, exceptionally, survive, it will be in those parts of the society that have been more isolated from cross-cultural contacts and have remained more traditional in their economic and social practices. But as soon as these areas modernise, the language will disappear there as well.

At first sight, this thesis might seem to adequately describe the fate of the Irish language. Since the middle of the nineteenth century, Irish culture has been transformed by an extraordinary language shift from Irish to English. By the 1960s Irish survived as an everyday language mainly in rural communities along the western seaboard that could easily, if inaccurately, be described as traditional and isolated. As these communities have been incorporated into modern Irish society (particularly its mass media) it is often argued that the language is now disappearing there (Hindley, 1990). Nevertheless, Irish is not dead. The number of families that use Irish as the main language in their family circle is roughly the same today outside as inside the Gaeltacht areas, with a particularly high proportion living in the greater Dublin region. The number of children receiving an education through Irish has increased noticeably in the last fifteen years. Most English speakers in Ireland today know some Irish, and like religious affiliation, the Irish language is still regarded as a central element in Irish national identity by a large majority of the population (Ó Riagáin, 1988; Language Planning Advisory Committee, 1988). Outside of Gaeltacht areas, and increasingly in some of the Gaeltachtaí as well, Irish tends to be used most by people in higher social class positions and with higher educational qualifications and Irish speakers tend to be most numerous in the larger cities and towns.

These points suggest little support for the modernisation theorists' argument that the culture of modernising societies becomes more homogeneous and that minority languages and other minority cultural elements fade away. Modern Irish society remains bilingual — a feature it shares with many other societies in Europe that contain two or more distinct language groups (such as France, Spain, the Netherlands, Belgium, Italy, Switzerland, Finland). Worldwide, bi- or multi-lingualism is the normal condition of social groups and societies, rather than the exception. Furthermore, the rise or decline of any language is not a 'natural' phenomenon that occurs without human or social agency, as the modernisation thesis tends to suggest. The relationship between a majority and a minority language is not one of modernity versus backwardness but one of power.

This is reinforced by a significant EU report on minority languages. It defines minority language groups as those (Euromosaic, 1996, p.1 [italics added]):

> marked by a specific language and culture, that exist within wider societies and states, but which lack the political, institutional and ideological structures which can *guarantee the relevance* of these languages for the everyday life of members of such groups.

The report indicates that the most enduring languages are those that have the support of a state, even if that state is located in another territory (thus Dutch/Flemish in Belgium benefits from the position of Dutch as the official language of The Netherlands) or have benefited from policies of decentralisation or regionalisation (for example, Catalan, in Spain). State support for Irish, though limited, is similarly a crucial factor in explaining the survival of Irish speakers as a social group. Its backing for the Irish language television station TG4 has been a major contribution towards 'guaranteeing the relevance' of the language.

Correspondingly, the lack of a genuine policy of supporting Irish language programmes on RTÉ over many years was a clear signal to the Irish people of the irrelevance of the language.

The Euromosaic report makes a key point about the salience of theories of social change like modernisation theory. It argues that conceptions of modernity, especially the assumption that cultural and linguistic homogeneity are essential for a nation to develop, have acted as significant factors in 'minoritising' certain European languages. This has particularly been the case for those languages that were not incorporated into the national discourse of economic development. In other words, those languages that did not find expression within the structures and processes of development lost out as they increasingly became perceived as being excluded from the project of modernity. The decline of linguistic diversity has been part of this project across most of Europe but it has failed, inasmuch as 'minority languages' survive. The twist now is that European governments and the EU are finding in such languages a resource for cultural diversity: increasingly they are recognised as part of Europe's 'cultural capital'.

We have suggested that the fate of a distinctive linguistic culture is shaped by the policies and practices of states but it is also important to recognise how they may be shaped by cultural processes. Speaking Irish appears to have gained a certain cachet among certain class and age groups in Irish society — the last time it was perhaps as fashionable was just prior to the establishment of the independent Irish state, though for rather different reasons. In late modernity, individuals appear to develop a heightened concern about self-realisation and identity; they pursue a 'project of the self' (Giddens, 1991) and look for distinctive ways to express and symbolise an authentic individuality. This creates new circumstances where choosing to speak Irish acquires a range of new cultural meanings; it might even be described as 'post-nationalist' (McCrone, 1992) in that it no longer articulates an identity based on membership in the collective Irish nation, but rather a highly individualised way to 'be Irish' where difference is as important as sameness in the elaboration of identity.

If Irish society is bilingual, what of the English language in Ireland? The modernisationist argument that cross-cultural contacts erode national cultural differences can be applied here too, and perhaps be seen to be a better fit. Some observers have argued that, in the past twenty years or so, English as spoken in Ireland, particularly by urban middle-class groups (as in the notorious 'DARTspeak', named after Dublin's suburban rail system), has become much less distinctively 'Irish' in both accent and idiom than it was in the past. Tovey et al. (1989) suggest that we have come to share the same standards for 'good English' as are used by the English themselves, and that middle-class Irish people can 'pass' very easily into English society as a result. Others see 'Hiberno-English' as developing into a 'mid-Atlantic' variety of English that is as easily assimilated into American as English ways of speaking.

Such trends, if real, could be interpreted as a shift from national distinctiveness towards a more modern, global culture — an issue we revisit in Chapter 18. But for now we must conclude that the question of whether Ireland is losing its national cultural distinctiveness is clearly not an easy one to answer. The example of language suggests, in fact, that the idea that the Irish people have a unitary national culture to 'lose' does not reflect the situation very well — we have at least two main linguistic cultures, one Irish-using and one English-using, and a growing number whose first language may be Romanian, German or Chinese. The barrier to analysis may be to assume that every nation must have a separate, shared culture that differentiates it from other nations, and that we should be able to identify and define this culture in an exact way. This assumption can be traced back to ideas about the nation that shaped the emergence of nationalism as an ideology in the nineteenth and early twentieth centuries.

## The idea of an Irish nation

If nations are based in separate cultures, then nationalism simply expresses pre-existing cultural differences between groups. Earlier we suggested that such differences are thought to have emerged from earlier periods of cultural isolation. Sociological studies of nationalism question these ideas. They ask how people could become aware of their own culture as something distinctive, if they had no contacts with other cultures. If people lived only within their own group and never encountered strangers, they would probably have no concept of 'a stranger' and, equally, no concept of 'ourselves' or 'my own people'. We only realise that we share a distinctive culture when we encounter people who have a different one.

This argument, first developed by the Norwegian anthropologist Barth (1969) has been applied by Tovey et al. (1989) to an analysis of Irish culture. Barth develops the argument that our sense of cultural or national identity develops largely through reference to others. In identifying what 'we' are, we contrast ourselves with what those in another group — 'they' — are like. In this process, selected aspects or symbols of our lives are positioned centrally to our cultural or national identity — usually those items that most clearly differentiate us from the group with whom we are making the comparison. Our national identity is thus constructed from cultural elements that we choose to treat as significant markers of difference. This process is often linked to social and political struggles, providing a way of drawing boundaries around the groups involved. Thus, an increase in cross-national contacts should lead to, if not increasing differences between cultures, at least an increasing belief in and emphasis on difference.

In applying this approach to Irish national identity, we note that the association of the Irish nation with Gaelic culture and Roman Catholicism occurred primarily in the nineteenth century in the context of increasing political and economic integration into the United Kingdom. We thus compared ourselves most directly with the British, especially the English. Religious affiliation was an obvious cultural marker, given the decline of linguistic difference. But Catholicism became a defining symbol of Irishness not just because a religious difference existed. In Ireland the Catholic Church was greatly expanding its role (for example, establishing a Catholic secondary school system) and, while distancing itself from nationalist politics, was very alert to any challenge to its authority from the colonial regime. But events in England were also relevant. In the second half of the century it experienced waves of anti-Catholicism. In the struggle between Ireland and England it was not only the Irish who were concerned to assert their national identity. The English nation was also being constructed, forged around the symbols of Empire, the Anglican Church and the English language and its 'glorious literature'. The nation in Ireland was defined by prioritising those elements of culture where the contrast with the emerging English nation was clearest. Inevitably, Irish nationalists would see the restoration of the Irish language and the celebration of Catholicism as essential to Irish nationhood.

Nations, therefore, are not derived from cultural essences but are the invention of nationalists. They are what Benedict Anderson (1983) in a celebrated phrase refers to as 'imagined communities': idealised visions of contemporary social relationships based on particular interpretations of the past. In imagining it as a community nationalists assert that those within the nation share a deep sense of solidarity with even those fellow-nationals they never meet, and with past generations from whom they claim biological or cultural descent. Nationalists imagine the nation as having distinct boundaries and that people belong clearly to a single nation and know which nation is their own. Nationalists also imagine the nation as having a right to self-determination, to independent self-government. In this view the nation is a set of ideas and beliefs and nationalism is an ideology. Nations are produced by 'thinking nationally'.

This argument contrasts sharply with the belief that nations existed prior to nationalists, whose role was to bring them to our attention. Early nationalists included scholars and antiquarians who saw themselves as uncovering and returning to public awareness a heritage that belonged to a particular people, or nation. Following Anderson, we can interpret such actions as the *invention of a past*, to provide a social group with a sense of pride in their identity and a feeling of collective solidarity. The Gaelic scholar Douglas Hyde, for example, argued that Irish men should stop wearing trousers (an English dress custom) and return to the 'traditional' Irish dress of knee-breeches. He saw himself as uncovering a forgotten national tradition in dress but could equally be said to have invented a traditional past or heritage in order to help realise a future Irish nation.

Anderson says that nations 'move up and down history'. They are not, as nationalists may claim, primordial 'givens' that have been in continuous existence since the beginning of history — this long historical existence is *also* imagined. In 'thinking nationally' we make connections with past events — the Great Famine, the Act of Union, the Flight of the Earls, the coming of St. Patrick — that seem to explain some feature of our present situation. Imagining the nation is to a large extent a matter of constructing myths: myths of origin, for example, that recount how the nation was founded. Even if revisionist historians point out that nationalist interpretations of history are 'mistaken', the myths generally survive as their task is to help us to make sense of the present and future, not the past. Dublin may or may not have been 'founded by Vikings', but the claim that it was helps to explain the feeling of many Dubliners that they are different from the rest of the Irish people.

## Nationalism as ideology: the nation and the state

What is an ideology, and how is it related to culture? At the most general level, an ideology is a set of beliefs, or a belief-system, that shapes how people understand their social world and how they organise it. Ideologies are often implicit and can only be discovered by careful analysis of what people say or write. They are part of what sociologists examine when they examine culture. But there are major philosophical differences between sociologists in how they use the term 'ideology' (Thompson, 1984). Marxists use it to describe what they see as false or 'mystificatory' beliefs: they might label the belief that we live in a democracy ideological, if in fact all the important political decisions in Ireland are made by a ruling class. Others use ideology to simply refer to a systematic set of ideas (or a 'world view') that is important in shaping social institutions: the belief that jobs should go to the best qualified (not 'who you know') is widely shared in Ireland and could be called 'an ideology of meritocracy'. Sociologists of education (for example, Lynch, 1999a) might ask how this ideology has influenced the organisation of the Irish education system.

Our discussion of the concept of nation suggests that it is constructed through an ideology of nationalism. Key analysts of the phenomenon (Anderson, 1983; Smith, 1986; Hobsbawm, 1990; Gellner, 1983) have argued that ideologies of nationalism are particularly associated with the nineteenth-century development of industrial society and the centralisation and consolidation of political power into the modern state. They focus particularly on how powerholders within a territory could assert their rule over other groups, dissolve existing cultural differences and divisions (especially through the establishment of a universal education system) and construct the image of a unified citizenship that consented to a single system of laws — a process referred to in one famous study as 'turning peasants into Frenchmen' (Weber, 1976).

A striking feature of nationalist ideology in this period, often contrasted with contemporary or 'new' nationalisms, was its inclusiveness (Delanty, 1996). The goal of nineteenth-century nationalists was to build a society in which citizenship would be available to all social categories and would transcend all 'partial' identities of class, ethnicity, religion or region (Rex, 1996). Successful construction of a nation in these terms, according to Gellner, required, more than anything else, the legitimation across the entire territory of a single language as that of state authority and civilised society. This ideal has turned out to be far more problematic than was expected: language conflicts have persisted or reappeared in virtually all modern nation states.

Nationalism has not just been an ideology used by existing territorial rulers to enhance their legitimacy. Many *new* states, including the Republic of Ireland, have come into existence as a result of the imaginings of nationalists. Here too, the state has played a large part in realising nationalist aspirations towards a shared national culture and solidarity. Nationalism has been a particularly useful ideology for new states. Their legitimacy is greatly enhanced if they can present themselves as 'nation states' — if their territorial borders appear to coincide with the cultural boundaries of the nation. Thus, new states commonly adopt the symbolism and mythologies forged by nationalists before independence and associate these with all possible state or public occasions. Indeed, in most contemporary societies, whether old or new, it is the state that creates the nation not, as nationalist ideology claims, the other way around.

Important tools for nation-building are mass education and the mass media. In a national education system, new generations of students can be socialised into a common culture, language and values and thus increase their sense of national belonging. The strong presence of the national flag and anthem in American schools can be seen as meeting the need of a federal state, built on continual immigration and with strong ethnic tensions, to constantly re-create a shared national identity. Irish language and history were used by the new Irish state in a similar way. In the first two decades after independence the state strongly supported the extension of schooling through Irish at both primary and post-primary levels: in 1930, twenty-four post-primary schools were teaching through Irish, with some 2,500 pupils, and by 1948 there were 102 such schools, with close to 11,000 pupils or around one in every four secondary school students (Language Planning Advisory Committee, 1986). While education through Irish has since declined, the rule that all Irish children must learn some Irish at school remains state educational policy. It is sometimes said that the place given to Irish within the education system reflects how a group of Irish linguistic nationalists captured and maintained control over the state after independence. But it can equally be argued that the Irish state captured (and some would say almost killed) the language, recognising its centrality to the creation of a new shared culture that would underpin loyalty to the new political regime.

The mass media has also played a key role in the construction of Irish national identity (see Chapter 14). When the Free State government first set up Radio Éireann in 1926 it was given a clear remit to 'contribute to the project of building the Irish state and nation' (Kelly and Rolston, 1995, p.565). The broadcasting service was put under the direct control of the Minister for Posts and Telegraphs and he took for granted, as evidenced in his reports to the Dáil, that it had a political, economic and in particular a cultural role: to confirm the separate identity of the new state by frequently broadcasting in Irish and by giving significant space to coverage of GAA All-Ireland finals. Its remit was also to contribute through its educational programs to agricultural, industrial and commercial development in the country. In later years the role of television was admitted to be far more ambiguous: a reality not lost on Eamon de Valera who, as he launched RTÉ television on New Year's Eve 1961, referred both to the power of the media to 'build up the character of a whole people' but also its capacity 'to lead through demoralisation to decadence and dissolution' (Savage, 1996, pp.xi–xii).

## Nation states and state nations

The problem of securing loyalty to a new set of state institutions has been experienced by all post-colonial states, but O'Dowd (1992) argues that relationships between nation and state are particularly problematical in Ireland. This is because, although the legitimacy of the Irish state rests on its claim to represent the historic Irish nation, the nation is not coterminous with the population of the Republic of Ireland, and the boundaries of the state arose out of struggle and coercion rather than as a 'natural' manifestation of a boundaried cultural unit. Not unexpectedly, then, in recent years there have been concerted attempts by elites in the Republic to redefine national identity and to construct a new national consensus that 'aims to have the state shape the "nation" rather than vice versa' (1992, p.35).

The 'new national consensus', according to O'Dowd, involves predominantly three elements. First, it implies a willingness to 'postpone indefinitely' any resolution of 'the national question', in effect to dismiss the claim of older nationalists that state and nation must coincide if the former is to have any legitimacy. Second, it switches the focus of political attention towards the EU, accepting that the nation state is no longer the only significant unit. And third, it seeks to build a consensus among Irish people around economic and social development rather than in terms of shared nationality. The development of a range of state institutions, including national media; professional and voluntary associations; and research bodies, has consolidated an Irish 'public' whose identity derives from membership within the Irish state. Thus, argues O'Dowd (1992, p.36), 'the Irish Republic is increasingly portrayed as a "state-nation" rather than as nation-state.'

As the Republic of Ireland state replaces the Irish nation as a source of identity for the population, the identification of peoplehood with a common culture undergoes some interesting changes. On one hand, it is now possible to exhibit cultural traits (an interest in soccer, or even in cricket) that would once have called into question one's 'Irishness'. On the other, new movements arise that try to re-create a sense of national identity outside the state. The move to identify and preserve items of 'national heritage' might be regarded as a new expression of nationalist ideology within Ireland but, according to McGrath (1996, p.41), this process can be problematic:

> How heritage constructs a particular identity in a country which does not have an agreed national history has generated considerable contention and criticism . . . the landscape is a product of history, a testimony to the work of successive generations of people and nature; but the process by which history is translated to people living in the present is not a neutral activity.

Slater (1993) has investigated how the landscape of Co. Wicklow, now widely regarded as an essential part of Irish heritage, derives its current form from the activities of eighteenth- and nineteenth-century landlords guided by a visual ideal of 'the picturesque'. This idea came originally from the Romantic movement in European painting, where landscapes earlier thought to be threatening and aw(e)ful were redefined as sublime, and painters sought to arrange their material so that they could incorporate a contrast between the sublime and the beautiful: high, rugged mountains against gentle harmonious, smoothly flowing foregrounds. The Wicklow landlords physically altered the landscape to accord with these ideas, going so far as to remove any signs of tenants' existence at strategic viewing points. Thus, 'picturesque' locations such as Lough Tay, that we now claim and value as part of Irish heritage, were constructed to literally erase from the image the human social relationships that constituted agrarian Ireland (Brett, 1996, pp.39–51). The translation of landscape into heritage may thus impose a constructed national identity on people without their realisation. And while the contemporary drive for the construction of heritage may have started out as a movement to re-create a sense of communal identity that had little to do with the state, it has now become part of state policy in terms of both economic development (particularly tourism) and education (discussed further in Chapters 13 and 17).

## SUBCULTURES, COUNTER-CULTURES AND 'CULTURAL POLITICS'

Many sociologists, particularly modernisation theorists, have shared with nationalists the belief that societies are or should be, broadly speaking, culturally homogeneous. They have assumed that societies cannot be integrated and orderly unless they are held together by consensus on some central values and ways of doing things. But sociological research consistently reveals cultural difference *within* society. So how can sociologists best understand and explain this apparent contradiction? Often they have recourse to the concept of subculture.

This concept implies the existence of a dominant or major culture. It suggests in effect that there is a set of values and beliefs that is shared by most people and which is essential to the harmonious working of society, but that some 'subgroups' may display a certain amount of variation from the cultural norms. For example, the dominant culture of modern industrial societies places particular emphasis on the values of achievement — hard work, long-term career planning, accumulation of material possessions — but we can find groups within these societies who behave in ways and hold views that do not conform to these values.

The American sociologist, Talcott Parsons, was one of the first sociologists to write about a distinctive 'youth culture'. He said that teenagers commonly develop ideas and ways of behaving that emphasise leisure and play over hard work, and hedonism and immediate gratification over long-term aspirations. Parsons saw youth culture as a *subculture*, in the sense that he thought it was a transient stage in the lives of young people that did not jeopardise the dominant culture. It was a subcultural element that society could accommodate and that even contributed to social order in the society as a whole. Parsons explained that modern societies develop youth subcultures because young people within them are required to go through an extended period of education and training. Adult status is deferred for much longer than in pre-industrial societies, and this creates tensions between young people and other adults (such as their parents and school teachers) on whom they are dependent. The youth subculture provides a way to deal with these tensions as well as a way that young adults can gradually separate from their families and move into the world of their peers.

Since Parsons's time, 'subculture' has been widely used to refer not only to transient groups but to culturally distinctive ones that are permanent features of society — religious or ethnic minorities, for example, or social class groups. In Ireland some research in relation to Travellers suggests that beliefs and customs that exist within that community — for example, in relation to marriage and the role of women — are a variation on those in mainstream Irish culture, but are not so different as to constitute a separate culture (they resemble, rather, an exaggerated version of the dominant culture of an earlier period). However, some (including some Travellers) contest the label 'subculture', claiming that Travelling People in Ireland are a distinct *ethnic group* (or 'nation') with a separate and distinctive culture of their own (see Chapter 15). This alerts us to some difficulties in the use of the term 'subculture': the decision to define a group in such a way is to an extent a political and ideological one.

As increasing numbers of subcultures were studied, sociologists began to make a distinction between a subculture and a *counter-culture*. If subcultures are variations on the dominant culture, we need a different term for groups that more completely oppose dominant societal values and meanings. The term 'counter-culture', introduced for this purpose, represented a first step in recognising that culture not only unites societies but can also divide them and be a source of conflict.

It is not always easy to decide if we are dealing with a subculture or a counter-culture. Youth culture at times appears subcultural — when, as Parsons suggested, it operates to relieve the tensions of adolescence and to give young people a space from which to integrate into an adult world. But at times youth culture appears to be counter-cultural, and to form a basis for the emergence of social movements that challenge the dominant values of society. Similarly, the distinctive culture of working-class groups can be seen as an adaptation of mainstream values and beliefs, or as a counter cultural expression of values that are opposed to those of the dominant classes.

Terms like subculture and counter-culture encourage us to assume that there is a normal or mainstream culture in society. Cultural difference can then be explained as an adaptation to this culture by people who live in specific and non-normal circumstances, such as those in very poor inner-city areas of Dublin with little access to conventional employment; or rural groups that have remained largely outside modern Irish life. But we should recognise that normal culture is often that of a particular group in society that has been able to establish its normality against attempts by other groups to have their culture regarded as legitimate or valuable. Sociologists who talk in terms of subculture have often implicitly regarded their own culture as the normal one.

Many sociologists have abandoned the assumption that a single dominant culture holds society together. They assume that societies are naturally diverse and ask instead *how* some groups can establish their own customs and values as normal, so that those of others are seen to be subcultural deviations from the norm, less worthy of respect. The diverse cultures found in a society tend to be placed in a hierarchy and to establish a high position for one's own culture is part of an ongoing struggle for power between different groups. Weber first referred to social groups whose power derives from the prestige accorded to their culture as *status groups*. In Irish society, the metaphorical 'Dublin 4' is a status group at the top of the cultural hierarchy, while refugees are a status group at the bottom; the Anglo-Irish Ascendancy is a status group that was once at the top but is now, perhaps, downwardly mobile. Weber believed that conflict between status groups is as important as class conflict. He was drawing our attention to the fact that it is not only the ownership of property that confers power, but also the possession of superior cultural credentials.

Pierre Bourdieu, whose work we discuss in more detail in Chapter 16, has combined Weber's ideas with insights from Marx to develop a theory of culture as a kind of economy or marketplace. It is a marketplace where people use cultural capital rather than economic capital. They bring to their exchanges with others certain cultural attributes — an upper-class accent; an Oxford degree; fluency in Italian; knowledge of W.B. Yeats; ability to dance the Macarena — that they know will secure the respect and admiration of others in a particular social context. Such respect and admiration can in many cases be converted into economic wealth or social power.

Bourdieu says people come to acquire cultural capital largely through their social class background and educational experiences. In general, the most valuable cultural capital is that associated with a high level of education and a cultivated upper-middle-class background. But there are 'cultural markets' where other sorts of cultural capital — such as dancing the Macarena — can command a high return. But Bourdieu recognises that the value of any cultural attribute is an outcome of social strategies to secure it. We can compare the ownership of cultural attributes here with the ownership of material possessions. Land, a form of material capital, is extremely valuable to its owner in a situation where land is needed and is in short supply, for example, a building site in Dublin's Grafton Street. But land may have very little value for its owner when it does not appear to be needed for anything and there is no demand by others to acquire it, for example, poor agricultural land in a remote and non-scenic area of Co. Roscommon. People who own land and want to increase its value will often engage in strategies to reduce supply or increase demand, through, say, securing a rezoning. In a similar way, Bourdieu suggests, those who possess cultural capital are also constantly manoeuvring to ensure that the price of their possession is kept as high as possible, for example, by ensuring that a particular accent or a particular educational qualification is handed on within an exclusive social circle.

## Cultural divisions: the rural and the urban

Following Weber and Bourdieu we can see the development of cultural patterns as a history of struggles over taste and 'distinction' (Bourdieu, 1984). A similar contest has taken place between urban and rural cultures in Irish society (see Chapter 13 for a full critical discussion). Rural–urban conflicts have been central to cultural politics in Ireland, but it is important to trace who evokes this distinction, under what circumstances, for what purposes and with what results. Such contrasts are often used by groups in pursuit of political or social campaigns. Movements to rescue rural society, or to stress the values of urban living, occur at particular points in time, and adherents select particular meanings for 'rural' and 'urban' which they promote to the powerholders in society.

Appeals to the rural–urban divide are a familiar part of Irish culture. On the one hand, the Irish Farmers' Association tries to engender a sense of threat from urban Ireland in order to maintain its members' solidarity in the face of increasing rural diversity and differentiation; on the other hand, urban trade union leaders and politicians in search of an easy target construct rural Ireland as a privileged receiver of EU and Irish state supports, thus making it in some way responsible for unemployment and poverty in Irish cities.

Political scientist Tom Garvin (1982) has developed the thesis that in the early decades of independence the new Irish society was rather exceptional, in European core terms, as it was dominated by an elite based in and oriented towards rural society. In the early Irish state the urban centre was unable to impose its interests and values on the society. The template for the new 'real Ireland' was constructed from elements that were not only rural, but based on western, small-scale, family farming, rural areas. For Lincoln (1993, p.206) the consequences were as follows:

> The reality is that Dublin has rarely featured in recent history as a place meriting special attention. Its role as capital has seldom counted as a matter of any material consequence, still less as a locus of Irish 'culture' in which people should have pride. Dublin has enjoyed an ambiguous relationship with the country of which it is capital and the urban culture which it represents has seldom been viewed as something of value.

This ambiguity was, for Lincoln, the outcome of colonialism. Dublin was the centre from which a colonial administrative class ruled the rest of Irish society, and it constructed the city to suit its own cultural conceptions. When colonialism ended it was inevitable that the colonised would respond by overthrowing all things urban. But Lincoln traces the 'anti-urban emotional thrust of Irish nationalism' even further back, to the work of Thomas Davis, himself a member of the colonising class. Davis probably learnt his anti-urban rhetoric from English culture rather than from the Irish dispossessed, since anti-urban sentiment and a romantic view of the rural as a 'green and pleasant land' was a strong element in English Victorian ideology (Offer, 1981). It seems unlikely that in Ireland this idealisation of the rural was accepted by everyone, even in the early years of the new state, in the uncontested way that Lincoln suggests. For example, emigration rates from rural areas, particularly among rural women, suggest that rural life was seen by many ordinary people as something to be escaped from at the earliest possible opportunity.

Contesting narratives about the contribution of rural life to 'making the nation' are found in many newly post-colonial societies with substantial rural populations. As Vandergeest (1996, pp.283–4) suggests:

> Because the national culture and history is invented, different nationalists may not agree on what constitutes the core culture. There are often important differences between groups of intellectuals and their selection and interpretation of traditions that they feel exemplify national culture.

For one group of intellectuals, national identity is associated with the continuity of urban culture or with central rule such as a monarchy, with the result that rural villages are seen as places that need to be modernised and civilised in order to become part of the nation. Others, in imagining the nation, 'look to a natural history based in the countryside and in tribal or rural cultures, as typified by the Romantic movement in Europe and more recently by oppositional movements in

Asia' (1996, p.284). Recovery of an authentic national identity requires recovery or re-invention, codification and defence (against modernisation or Westernisation) of the traditions of rural life. Vandergeest comments that 'both are descriptions of rural areas as seen by urban people, and they both simplify rural life by associating the village with a more primitive or pure past' (1996, p.280).

In the early decades of independence the culture of rural Ireland was elevated to a position of prestige and symbolic importance in the new society. Politicians, church leaders, writers, artists and film-makers agreed that the real Ireland was rural Ireland, while urban life and culture were often regarded with suspicion as 'foreign' to Irish ways. But since the 1960s it has been urban culture that has increasingly established itself as the expression of the real (modern) Ireland, while the rural has been labelled backward and traditional.

Urbanisation is more than a shift in regional population balance and the concentration of population around Dublin. It is a state of mind. It refers to how the political balance has tilted from the rural to the urban as urban areas increasingly attract infrastructural resources, gain access to the media and influence state policy and public debate. It reflects how Irish national identity is constructed and how we understand and represent ourselves. The 1970s and 1980s were marked in Ireland by a strong tendency towards historical, political and economic revisionism — perhaps the first manifestations in Ireland of a 'post-modern' sensibility — as sacred cows were slain and established myths were cast aside. Where the rural had been constructed as the revered heartland of the real Ireland, leading groups in the society began to promote the idea of a European Ireland. The features once valued as rural were recast as 'peasant', 'peripheral' and 'uncivilised' — summed up well, for example, by the slang term 'culchie'. Farmers in particular came to represent and stand for the traditional Ireland from which Europe would help us to escape (ironic, since Irish farmers were probably the most 'Europeanised' group in Irish society and gained disproportionately from EC membership).

With increasingly urban patterns of residence and occupation we would expect Irish culture to have changed since the 1960s. But what has changed is not just the culture but the prestige accorded to two different cultures in Irish society. Urban status groups have been able to claim for themselves much of the prestige — the 'cultural capital' — of modernity, despite the efforts of some rural status groups (for example, developed farmers) to contest this. In contemporary Ireland, to be urban has become the cultural norm, even if it is still not the material reality for much of the population. Struggles within the intelligentsia in Ireland (see Chapter 4) and the possible emergence of a new knowledge class, have played a significant part in this transformation (Doak, 1998).

For Bourdieu, cultural politics have material consequences. As urban Ireland has asserted its cultural dominance, beliefs about ownership of and rights to the rural countryside have changed. Rural land is no longer regarded solely as the private property of the farmer but also as part of the 'national heritage' to be conserved and enjoyed by an increasingly urban population (see Chapter 17). Ownership of rural land remains concentrated in the hands of farmers and continues to constitute a major form of wealth, but the conservation movement has helped to shift its control towards urban people. From this perspective, conservationism can be seen as an ideology that advances the interests of a particular status group in Irish society — a largely urban, well-educated, but property-less group. It advances a claim to power based on possession of scientific and technical knowledge, against the claims of rural property owners.

The rural has now become a strongly contested issue throughout Europe (Hoggart *et al.*, 1995). Disputes over the meaning of rurality can have important consequences for the groups involved. The current fashion for identifying rurality with nature is a reprise of nineteenth-century Romantic attitudes to the countryside, with contemporary effects. As long as the rural was defined primarily as the location of a special culture and way of life then rural groups, especially the more organised and vocal, could claim legitimate guardianship of that world and a right to determine its future. But as the rural–urban contrast is increasingly portrayed as one between *nature* and *society* (for example, in EU documents that stress the importance of rural places as 'lungs' or 'buffers' between built up areas), groups other than farmers and land-owners can lay claim to legitimate guardianship of rural Ireland. These are particularly likely to include people who have formal educational credentials in the management of nature, such as natural scientists or environmentalists (see Chapter 17). Inevitably, this creates conflicts between the new and the established claimants over appropriate use and future development of rural land.

## Creating the appearance of cultural unity

Classical social theorists were very much interested in the fate of cultural difference in modern societies. Generally, they were agreed in predicting that differentiated identities would diminish. Marx, for example, thought that the development of capitalism threatened to reduce human beings to little more than 'quantities of labour power' without social or personal identity; Weber feared that human beings might be allowed to be 'economic actors' only, in rationalised societies; while Durkheim, even though he recognised that modern society is distinctive in its 'cult of the individual', saw that a collapse of collective solidarity could leave individuals with no identity in common other than their essential humanity. But much recent sociological debate has been about, not the decline but the survival or revival of difference and division. For Floya Anthias (1999) the late modern world is one that has experienced both the proliferation of difference and its increasing celebration. She argues that concern with difference is not the same as concern with equality: whereas sociological theorising about class was founded on a modernist belief that inequality, social exclusion and marginalisation should and could be removed from society, contemporary theorising about difference is based on a post-modernist belief in the value of diversity for its own sake and as a necessary condition for authentic self-realisation.

This turn towards the analysis of difference has been powerfully encouraged by developments within feminist sociology, where there have been lively debates on the virtues of pursuing 'gender equality' for women as against trying to reconstruct social relations and institutions to better fit the 'different' life experiences and world views of women. Within feminist sociology also, the problems associated with essentialist use of the category 'women' to represent all women, have been widely debated. An interest in difference has also been encouraged by sociological recognition of contemporary ethnic conflicts and issues.

The arrival in Ireland in recent years of immigrants and refugees from non-Western societies, in greater numbers than has ever occurred before (see Chapter 5), has stimulated a renewed awareness of and interest in studying minorities, both old and new, in Irish society. This has re-opened debates on the impact of nationalism and the construction of national identity in Ireland. To allow minorities the power and the right to express their different identity, it has been argued, the identity system of the cultural majority must be deconstructed. Thus, Lentin (1998) argues that discourses of Irish national identity are racist in that they identify Irishness with ethnic homogeneity and thus exclude minority women from access to key dimensions of citizenship within Irish society. Discussing the 1937 Irish Constitution (1998, p.11), she states that 'the consequences of privileging a nationalist, Catholic, sedentary "we" in framing "Irishness" de-privileges sub-national ethnicities by its very definition, however unacknowledged and probably unintended by the authors of that "we".'

Our argument in this chapter has been that it is precisely the construction of such 'we's that sociological investigation can illuminate, by recognising their essentially contested and political character. While societies may be culturally diverse, there are strong forces within them that aim to sustain the appearance of cultural unity. Among these forces are nationalist ideologies and the activities of different status groups as they struggle to represent their own culture as *the* national or modern culture. But they are not the only relevant actors. The mass media, for example, is also credited with being a major force for cultural homogenisation, both within societies and between them (see Chapter 14). Modernisation theorists have seen the development of global mass media as reflecting the formation of a world culture as modernising societies converge in values and beliefs. Dependency theorists have been more likely to describe this development as a form of cultural imperialism where the core countries of the world impose their own culture on dependent peripheral societies. Either way, the mass media are a significant contributor to the establishment of norms that define the legitimate, standard culture within a society, and which treat other cultures as either absent or deviant.

## POSTSCRIPT: CULTURAL UNITY AND DIVERSITY;
## MODERNITY AND POST-MODERNITY

Much of this chapter has been preoccupied with teasing out the associations between national identity and shared culture, and with the connections made by sociologists, modernisation theorists and others, between increasing cultural homogeneity in society and the process of economic and political modernisation. We have put forward a number of ways of thinking about the concepts of nation and culture while trying to avoid the suggestion that they must somehow coincide. We pointed out, for example, that nations are culturally diverse and that uniformity is an ideal, or ideology, articulated by nationalists in their attempts to legitimise the nation state as the natural basis for an international political order. We suggested that ownership of the national (in the sense of the normal or legitimate) culture is a valuable asset that different groups in society struggle and compete with each other to achieve and retain, using various strategies to further their aims. In particular, we emphasised that cultural differences within a society are not neutral but are inevitably ranked in a hierarchy of social worth and prestige, where the capacity to represent one's own culture as the real or modern culture of the society as a whole can make a material difference to the situation of the group to which one belongs.

Behind much of the discussion is a further issue that struggles for recognition: the idea that achieving cultural homogeneity is not just evidence that a society is modernising, but is in fact part of the project of modernity itself. It is only with the development of theories of post-modernity that sociology has begun to take stock of modernity and to start to understand how deeply sociology itself has been imbued with the values, goals and world views that characterised a quite specific period in world history. The ideologues of modernity — not just nationalists, but other intellectual elites committed to the universalising values of democracy, meritocracy and science — believed that the way forward for the world was through the reduction of cultural difference and the gradual eradication of particularistic and divisive minority cultures. The rediscovery and re-evaluation of cultural pluralism, a central feature of post-modern thinking, is both a rejection of the project of modernity and a recognition that that project did not, and could not, succeed.

Theorists of post-modernity see in the pluralisation of cultures and meanings an image of the contemporary world. In everyday life, they argue, people encounter a range of cultures and must routinely deal with cultural difference as normal. This is part of our growing sense of living in a global society. Our everyday consumption — food, technology, fashion — is increasingly globalised: and more likely to originate outside of than inside Ireland. Yet our primary concerns — family, housing, work — remain rooted in our own local and national society. This may produce a peculiar combination of experience — simultaneously global and local — that distinguishes the contemporary era quite sharply from that of preceding generations. In this pluralistic world, post-modernists suggest, people have abandoned faith in overarching, comprehensive, *objective* explanations of their experience. The ideologies of the modern era — of social change as progress, so important to the early sociologists — can no longer explain the shape of history as we move into the post-modern world. The world has become *relativised*: all perspectives and cultural meanings are equally valid, and all have become interchangeable.

Durkheim suggested that modern societies differed from earlier ones in the value placed on individualism. In post-modern society, belief in individual self-realisation turns into a quest for personal identity. In a pluralistic world the question 'who am I?' becomes increasingly important, and increasingly difficult to answer. Some people turn to psychotherapy, looking for an answer in their own psychological biographies; others find an identity through consumer choices or in particular lifestyles. In recent years, as we noted earlier, there has been some increase in the use of the Irish language by urban people in Ireland; according to the post-modern thesis, they are adopting Irish not because they are convinced by a nationalist 'grand narrative' or perspective on history but because this lifestyle choice offers them a sense of personal identity.

Perhaps ironically, in a globalised world, attachment to local place and local culture offers a sense of personal rootedness. But it may be too soon to say if this is a new social phenomenon. Post-modernity as a perspective in sociology is still ambiguous (as it would be) as to whether it describes a new type of society, which comes *after* modern society, or whether it is describing a new state of mind where we can reflect on modernity and see it in a much clearer light. The rebirth of interest in minority languages (and other forms of ethno-cultural difference) is evident not only in some middle-class groups in Ireland, but right across Europe. It may be the end of nationalism as an ideology, and so the end of modernity; or it may be the start of a nationalist rebirth, in a new social context, and thus the next instalment of the modernist project. Watch this space!

# 12
# *Religion*

If religion be the opium of the people, the Irish were addicts.
(O'Farrell, cited in Akenson, 1991, p.139)

Religion can be difficult to analyse sociologically, due to the emotive nature of the concepts involved. At the same time, it is arguably one of the key factors that affect Irish social life. Any sociological study of Ireland must reflect the importance of religion in the shaping of our contemporary society, its continuing relevance in terms of everyday social life and the still central role of religious institutions.

Remarkably enough, given its centrality to Irish social life, Irish sociologists, with some key exceptions, have failed to produce much description or analysis of the power of the churches in contemporary Irish society. Much of the sociological research has been carried out by the churches themselves and not surprisingly turns out to be less than critical of the institutions. Most critical analysis of the churches, and of the role of religion in Irish social life, has come from the pens of historians, novelists or visiting anthropologists.

A major limitation of Irish sociological research into religion is that it has tended to be highly positivist. It has, according to Inglis (1987, p.2) 'concentrated on gathering facts and data, usually through social surveys, and has avoided dealing with the larger, more general questions about the position and influence of the Church'. Conversely, as Akenson (1991) has argued, much historical research on religion in Ireland has relied on anecdotal and skewed sources of evidence, and has lacked rigorous statistical or comparative analysis. Thus, our knowledge of many aspects of the role of religion in Irish social life remains less complete than it could — or should — be.

## WHAT IS RELIGION?

Irish author Mary Morrissy provocatively addressed this question in an *Irish Times* article (17 December 1996) as she drew parallels between shopping and religion:

It is the shopping mall that opens on a Sunday, at hours when most people in the 1950s would have been making holy the Sabbath day . . . in the next century — when surely most of our shopping will be done via a terminal from home — the shopping centre may well become the cathedral of its time. A place to be viewed as grandiose and lofty, impossibly old-fashioned and impractical and by then probably completely redundant.

These remarks are certainly thought-provoking and may force us to define what exactly we mean by 'religion'. This is also a question that many of the early sociologists, in particular Durkheim and Weber, were drawn to.

What then are the key aspects of religion? They include the following:

- *sacred symbols* — the crucifix, the star, holy statues, the sign of the cross, and often certain colours such as red, purple and gold
- *rituals and special behaviour* — pilgrimages, prayers, hand and body movements
- *a feeling of reverence* towards and awe, even fear, of sacred symbols, practices, personnel and places
- *a community of believers* — a parish, congregation, sect, cult, religious order or religious community.

Symbols provide a key to the development of religion and to an understanding of what it might mean. They carry with them the emotional charge that arises from feelings of belonging to a group — the excitement and fulfilment that comes from being part of a crowd or of an intimate group. Symbols and the rituals associated with them emphasise and develop group solidarity.

The distinctive contribution of sociologists has been to move beyond the common-sense understanding of religion as dealing with mystery and the supernatural and to emphasise its social nature. Thus, as Émile Durkheim pointed out in his 1915 work *The elementary forms of religious life*, one of the first sociological studies of religion, 'if in the midst of these mythologies and theologies we see reality clearly appearing, it is none the less true that it is found there in an enlarged, transformed and idealised form' (cited in Bocock and Thompson, 1985, p.1). Religious belief has a special nature and language but is clearly linked to underlying social patterns and structures.

The complexity of the religious symbolic universe may reflect the complexity of the society of which it is part. Functionalist sociologists stress how religious symbols (heaven and hell, good and evil) help to delineate the norms and values of society and how religious institutions and practices help to ensure adherence to those norms and values. They also show how religious symbols, and others including ethnic, 'racial' and linguistic ones, can be used to establish the boundaries of a society, thus helping to define who is 'in' and 'out'.

For Durkheim, a common feature of all religious systems is that they divide the symbolic world into the *profane* and the *sacred*. The profane is the matter-of-fact, everyday world that can be dealt with pragmatically, for example, the supermarket bread and wine that we may consume with our dinner. The sacred refers to aspects of the world that must be approached in a special, controlled and self-conscious way, with special sorts of behaviour and attitude, rituals and language — the bread and wine that appears and is consumed during a Christian communion ceremony. It is the meanings, actions and language that communities of believers enact around sacred objects, texts and places that helps to constitute religion.

Religions in modern societies, including Ireland, are the long-term outcome of historical processes that have seen the development of specialised and limited rites and cults into larger and more organised and institutionalised bodies of knowledge and practice. These processes include generalisation, abstraction, symbolisation and reification — all ways of organising knowledge about the cosmos — together with the development of specialised organisational and institutional structures such as churches, bodies of religious law, religious orders, seminaries and sacred works (Restivo, 1991, p.151).

## THE SOCIOLOGICAL ANALYSIS OF RELIGION

The analysis of religion was of key importance to the early sociologists, both in terms of the influence and impact of forms of religious beliefs on society as a whole and in terms of the power and role of religious institutions in everyday social life. Restivo (1991, p.150) draws our attention to the important point that, from a comparative sociological perspective, religions reflect much about the nature of the societies where they are found. He suggests that the sacred realm is:

> a sort of map of the social geomorphology, and the correlations between types of societies and types of religions illustrate the relationship between technological and economic development on the one hand and religious beliefs and institutions on the other.

Furthermore, religions are *active* instruments in the creation of societies. This approach to the relationship between belief systems and other aspects of social life can be found in particular in the works of Durkheim, Weber and Marx in relation to the development and evolution of religious belief.

Durkheim pioneered the functionalist analysis of religion as part of his broader attempt to develop a systematic sociology of modern society. For him the *functions* of religion include social cohesion, social control and providing meaning and purpose. Religion helps to maintain the boundaries of society and creates a sense of belonging, especially through shared participation in religious rituals and recognition of shared symbols. Religious bodies typically lay down standards of acceptable behaviour, of good and evil, and these operate to govern the behaviour of populations. Religions also tell stories that relate to the origins, history and purpose of peoples, and often speak of an afterlife. This helps to provide meaning and purpose for people over and above the mundane.

While Weber was not the first to connect religion and economic and social activity, his study of the links between Protestantism and capitalism was one of the most systematic. His work on the influence of religion, initially published in essay form in 1905 as *The Protestant ethic and the spirit of capitalism* and later expanded into a comparative historical sociology of world religions, was an attempt to study the development of religion from a historical viewpoint and to methodically explore its sociological fundamentals through the application of 'ideal types' to a mass of complex empirical material on religious belief and practice (Swingewood, 1984, p.151).

Weber did not posit a simplistic link between religion and economic activity; rather, he wanted to show that religious ideas were not mechanically linked to the economic structure but actively shaped how individuals lived out their day-to-day lives. His main concern was to explore how a set of beliefs about the world and the afterworld was linked to specific sorts of individual and group behaviour — beliefs that would ultimately underpin the development of the Western European capitalist economic system. The kernel of his analysis was how adherence to an ascetic form of Protestantism, specifically, Calvinism, led people towards a particular way of thinking about work, social values and social action.

Weber was moved to describe this particular form of Protestantism as it developed in Western Europe in the sixteenth and seventeenth centuries as 'the spirit of capitalism'. For here was found an emphasis on the deferral of gratification; on self-control; and on efficiency as a way towards salvation and away from eternal damnation. As it happened, these qualities were also those necessary for effective strategies of financial investment and capital accumulation (Swingewood, 1984, p.155):

> The spirit of capitalism is expressed in the rationalising attitude to life, in such maxims of conduct as be prudent, diligent, punctilious in repayment of debts and loans, avoid idleness since time is money, be frugal in consumption and so on. The spirit of capitalism is a social ethic, a structure of attitudes and behaviour closely identified with ascetic Protestantism and its associated religious sects such as the Puritans and the Calvinists.

Weber went on to carry out wide-ranging comparative studies of world religions in order to explore how religion, as one of the many factors that shaped societies, operated in a range of settings.

Weber's analysis has been much criticised, not least for its empirical shortcomings (see Swingewood, 1984, p.158). However, inasmuch as it emphasises religion as a crucial element in the development of society, it clearly has great relevance to Ireland for, as the historian Donald Akenson (1991, p.16) points out, during the last two centuries, it has been 'one of the most religiously sensitised nations in the western world'. Arguments similar to those of Weber have been mobilised from time to time in Ireland, especially in trying to explain why the (Protestant) north-east of the country industrialised while the (Catholic) remainder did not (see Akenson, 1991, p.18; Keating and Desmond, 1993; Fahey, 1994).

For Marx, famously, religion was the 'opium of the people': a cultural phenomenon that served to blind people to their 'real' needs. For him, religion in the form of sets of ideas or institutional structures ultimately served the needs of the ruling class in society. While Marx did not carry out systematic analyses of religion in the manner of Weber or Durkheim, his views have been influential and have helped to shape the anti-clericalism of many socialist movements.

Contemporary sociologists have paid less attention to religion, perhaps in response to the perceived secularisation of society (see below). In the Irish context Inglis (1998a; 1998d) has successfully harnessed the work of French sociologist Pierre Bourdieu to help explain the *habitus* or 'lasting, general and adaptable way of thinking and acting in conformity with a systematic view of the world' that underpins the unique position of the Catholic Church in Irish society. It is due to the development of such a habitus that many Irish people know almost instinctively how to behave in accordance with the tenets of their religion. It is, according to Inglis (1998a, p.11), 'embodied in the home, school and church [and] produces specific Catholic ways of being religious and ethical'. Furthermore, Bourdieu's concept of 'cultural capital', helps to show how being a 'good Catholic' in Irish society can translate into success at school, in the workplace, in business and political life and in the broader society.

Inglis's study of the nature of Catholicism remains the only systematic sociological study of contemporary religious experience in Ireland. It draws predominantly on the theoretical insights of Weber and Bourdieu to attempt to explain the still remarkable position of the Catholic Church in modern Irish society. For Inglis, the development of the modern institutional Catholic Church in Ireland has been a key element of the modernisation of Irish society — linked in the period since the Famine to both the emergence of a particular pattern of rural social structure and to the contemporary Irish form of the welfare state. He emphasises the role of women in the church, in particular as mothers, and traces the recent decline in church influence, which he puts down to a number of factors including the changing economic and social role of women and the growing influence of the media. A number of the themes delineated by Inglis are explored in the remainder of this chapter.

## RELIGION IN IRELAND: FROM 'TRADITIONAL' TO 'MODERN'

In 1987, Inglis, in the first edition of his book *Moral monopoly: The Catholic Church in modern Irish society*, was able to say that Ireland was a particularly religious country: 'one of the first impressions of the country that marks it out as different from other Western societies is that the [Catholic] Church is a strong and active force in everyday life' (p.1). In the same vein O'Toole (1998, p.66) remarks that 'when it comes to belief in the existence of the soul, in life after death, in heaven, in prayer, the Irish score so much higher in surveys than the rest of the developed world as to seem not part of that world at all.' We can ask why, and how, has religion acquired such a central role in Irish social life?

With its tag as 'the island of saints and scholars' there has been a perception that in some ways Irish people are naturally religious. Inglis (1987, p.1) remarks that it is 'as if the Irish have always been a holy and religious people who are devoted to the Catholic Church'. Similarly there have long been notions that as a Celtic people, the Irish have some sort of affinity with superstition, spirituality, magic and religious belief. We now see this view reiterated in much New Age writing and practice related to Celtic mythology (see, for example, Fay, 1997, pp.173–88). Sociological and historical analysis show that there was nothing natural or inevitable about the development of religious beliefs, practices and institutions in Ireland; rather, these can be understood as the outcome of many complex social factors.

There is within sociological thinking a tendency to see the development of Irish religion as reflecting a move from a 'traditional', highly devotional society to a 'modern', increasingly secularised one. But the modernisation approach may tend to oversimplify this process. In reality, the nature of religious belief and practice in Ireland has been very dynamic over the last two centuries and more, and its development has certainly not been unidirectional. For example, it was only with the rise of the Catholic middle-class in the late nineteenth century that Mass attendance grew from its mid-century rate of approximately 35 per cent to its turn-of-the-century level of 90 per cent (Miller, cited in Akenson, 1991, p.139). And, as we shall see later in this chapter, levels and styles of religious practice are continuing to change.

The picture that emerges from historical and sociological analysis is more complicated than a simple conception of modernisation would allow. For example, many of what may now be regarded as traditional aspects of Catholic Church practice were introduced quite recently, in the period from the end of the nineteenth century to the 1950s. Furthermore, much of what is now seen as modern or even post-modern in evolving religious practice, may represent a return to much older patterns of behaviour.

For example, historians of religion in Ireland highlight the existence of a 'folk religion', developed over a millennium, that pre-existed the development of the modern institutional churches as we recognise them today. In many respects, such as low attendance at formal religious events, a smaller gap between priests and people and a less centralised and dogmatic faith, this folk religion was closer to how many people see the modern churches developing. Some critics of contemporary religion, such as Kirby (1984, p.66), celebrate what they see as this more *authentic* expression of Irish spirituality:

A more authentic, gentle, tolerant and yet demanding faith was lived by (our) ancestors which had a deeply developed social conscience, a healthy anti-clericalism and a complete absence of puritanism and prudery when it came to sexual matters.

Kirby suggests that the language of this pre-Famine folk religion reflected a more spiritual consciousness than that embodied in the 'stylised and sentimental prayer forms' associated with contemporary practice. It also embraced, he claims, a developed social conscience that expressed itself in everyday behaviour, for example, in respect for the poor and in a form of social organisation that appears to approach a form of primitive communism or communitarianism.

Many explanations have been suggested for the almost unequalled growth in power of the Catholic Church in Ireland in the period between the Famine and the 1980s, and the parallel growth in other organised religions (the Church of Ireland and Presbyterianism in particular) through much of the same period. There has been a great deal written on this topic, and space precludes an extensive discussion here. Historians and sociologists (see Kirby, 1984, pp.55–64; Akenson, 1991, pp.139–43; Fahey, 1994; Inglis, 1998a, pp.102–28; Keogh, 1998, pp.88–114) suggest a range of key factors (listed in Figure 12.1), some of which, it must be noted, can appear to be contradictory.

## Figure 12.1 Factors affecting the development of the churches in post-Famine Ireland

- the decline of the landless cottier class (where older alternative belief systems were prevalent) due to the development of new land tenure arrangements before, during and after the Famine
- the nationalist political movement towards development of a separate national identity, where increasingly 'Irish' came to be equated with 'Catholic'
- the rationalisation of Irish society with increasing urbanisation and integration into a 'modern' and Anglophone society
- the growth of religious belief and practice as a response to rapid social change
- as part of the 'civilising process' in Western Europe, the increasing 'respectability' and 'gentling' of Irish society accompanied by the growth of moral discipline
- the successful centralisation and bureaucratisation of the various churches into more efficient administrative organisations
- from a class analysis perspective, the growth of religion suited both the British Empire and the Irish ruling class — as a distraction from class struggle and as a means of disciplining and controlling the working population.

The Catholic Church that very successfully developed in nineteenth-century Ireland went on to wield extensive power in the newly independent state until very recently, as succinctly described by O'Toole (1998, p.70):

> The groundwork laid down in the nineteenth century was the basis for the Church's triumph in independent Ireland. Once there was an Irish state, it became the effective arbiter of social legislation, having a ban on divorce inserted into the Constitution, encouraging the introduction of draconian censorship of books and films, delaying the legalisation of artificial contraception until 1979, retaining largely unquestioned control over schools and hospitals funded by the taxpayer, resisting the slow development of a welfare state.

It is common for critics to draw a pen picture of the 'traditional' (Catholic) Church in Ireland. This image is usually located somewhere around the 1950s — often seen as the heyday of the Catholic Church in Irish life, and often coinciding with the remembered childhood of the author in question. The 1920s to the 1950s has been identified as the age when 'devotional Catholicism' peaked and it saw the popularisation of practices such as pilgrimages to Marian shrines, the building of grottoes, the practice of Novenas and the development of sodalities (MacCurtain, 1997, p.247). It was also the time when the institutional church in Ireland was perhaps at its most influential.

Thus, Kirby (1984, p.15) contrasts the early 1980s with a previous era when Ireland was 'a stagnant society, presided over by a repressive and sexually obsessed church, from which the young had to flee if they were to find any space to explore and satisfy their own needs'. Similarly, Inglis (1998a, pp.1–2) contrasts the situation in Ireland today with the memory of his own childhood devotions. As we have seen, the churches did have significant ideological and social power in this period.

There has certainly been a sea change in the nature and position of all the churches in Irish society in recent decades. The turning point is usually identified as the early 1960s, when change in the churches at the global level, as manifested, for example, in Vatican 2, combined with a period of unprecedented economic growth in Ireland and a new era of openness to international investment and influence. Kirby (1984, p.19) suggests that the new prosperity and growth in the country contributed to a new optimism for the future and a critique of the familiar institutions of Irish life, including the Catholic Church. Inglis (1998a, pp.231–8) identifies the media — not least RTÉ's *Late Late Show* — as a major instrument of modernisation and stimulus of change in the church.

## RELIGION, IDENTITY AND SECTARIANISM

The religious affiliation of the population of the Republic of Ireland is overwhelmingly Roman Catholic (at 94 per cent). Only about 1 per cent of Mac

Gréil's (1996) late 1980s sample described themselves as having 'no religion', while less than 5 per cent came from other Christian denominations. The historical changes in the proportions of the population claiming membership of the different Christian religions is shown in Figure 12.2.

The decline in the relative and absolute number of Protestants in the Republic has been traced to a number of causes, including (Inglis, 1998a, pp.18–20):

- the return of British bureaucrats and servicemen and their families to Britain after Irish independence
- sectarianism
- lower rates of fertility among non-Catholics
- the establishment of a theocratic Catholic Irish state
- the operation of the *Ne Temere* decree in relation to 'mixed' marriages that forced parents to bring up all children as Catholics.

## Figure 12.2 Numbers of Catholics and Protestants in Ireland

### Figure 12.2a The Protestant population

| Year | Population | No information on religion | All Protestants[1] number | per cent | Church of Ireland[2] number | per cent |
|------|-----------|------------|--------|----------|--------|----------|
| 1861 | 4,402,514 | — | 468,939 | 10.7 | 372,723 | 8.5 |
| 1871 | 4,053,187 | — | 436,531 | 10.8 | 338,719 | 8.4 |
| 1881 | 3,870,020 | — | 404,688 | 10.5 | 317,576 | 8.2 |
| 1891 | 3,468,694 | — | 369,691 | 10.7 | 286,804 | 8.3 |
| 1901 | 3,221,823 | — | 343,552 | 10.7 | 264,264 | 8.2 |
| 1911 | 3,139,688 | — | 327,179 | 10.4 | 249,535 | 7.9 |
| 1926 | 2,971,992 | — | 220,723 | 7.4 | 164,215 | 5.5 |
| 1936 | 2,968,420 | — | 194,500 | 6.6 | 145,030 | 4.9 |
| 1946 | 2,955,107 | — | 169,074 | 5.7 | 124,829 | 4.2 |
| 1961 | 2,818,341 | 5,625 | 144,868 | 5.2 | 104,016 | 3.7 |
| 1971 | 2,978,248 | 46,648 | 125,685 | 4.3 | 97,739 | 3.3 |
| 1981 | 3,443,405 | 71,983 | 126,156 | 3.7 | 95,339 | 2.8 |
| 1991 | 3,525,719 | 99,704 | 111,699 | 3.2 | 89,187 | 2.5 |

**Notes**

1 Total non-Roman Catholic population excluding those refusing to state their religion, those claiming no religion and adherents of non-Christian faiths, where these are identifiable. In 1991, the figure for 'no information' includes those listing their religion as 'Christian'.

2 For 1991, the Church of Ireland figure includes those describing themselves as 'Protestants'.

(*Source*: Inglis, 1998a, p.19)

**Figure 12.2b The Catholic population**

|                       | 1861 % | 1911 % | 1936 % | 1961 % | 1981 % | 1991 % |
|-----------------------|--------|--------|--------|--------|--------|--------|
| Northern Ireland      | 41.0   | 39.5   | 33.5   | 34.9   | 38.0*  | 38.4   |
| Republic of Ireland   | 89.4   | 89.6   | 93.5   | 94.9   | 93.0   | 91.6   |
| All Ireland           | 78.1   | 75.3   | 75.4   | 74.7   | 76.8   | 75.0   |
| Number in thousands   | 5,768  | 4,391  | 4,248  | 4,243  | 4,925  | 5,123  |

Adapted from Walsh, 1970, p.7 and Censuses of Population 1981 and 1991 (Ireland and Northern Ireland).

* estimated figure
(*Source*: Coakley, 1998b, p.89)

In addition the lack of growth of alternative religious denominations may be partly due to the paucity, until recently, of significant inward migration into Ireland. This may change as immigration from a broader range of sources becomes an established feature of Irish society. Mac Gréil (1996) suggests that the low proportion of the population describing themselves as of 'no religion' indicates the importance of religion as part of the Irish person's self-identity. Sociologists generally agree that religion does have the capacity to be a strong indicator of personal, community and national belonging, as has been the case in Ireland.

Akenson (1991, p.xi) claims that 'the cultural differences between Protestants and Catholics are so central to modern Irish history that to evade them leaves a great black hole in the nation's story.' As he points out, the perceived 'fact' of difference between the two is taken for granted, in relation to both the Irish living in Ireland and the Irish diaspora. But it has also been agreed that the differences cannot be explained in terms of faith or belief alone (Akenson, 1991, p.12):

> For at least a century and a quarter it has been commonplace for observers of Irish life to note that the differences between Protestants and Catholics in Ireland have nothing to do with religion *per se* and everything to do with divergent cultural traditions or with economic discrimination.

In other words, the relationship between religion and identity in Ireland has been, and remains, a complex one.

From its earliest days, the independent Irish state began to define its people, through the state apparatus and official discourses, in terms of 'Catholic' and 'non-Catholic'. This dichotomy has always been attractive to commentators on Irish social issues. As Akenson points out, such contrasts 'were easily drawn in the nineteenth and early twentieth centuries and this was especially prevalent because it was an age that was given to thinking about cultural differences in racial terms' (1991, p.10; see also Gibbons, 1996, pp.149–63). Religious difference has become a central theme in thinking and writing about Irish history and contemporary society, not least because of the continuing conflict in the North of the country.

Akenson's study of the historical differences between Irish Catholics and Protestants has gone a long way towards debunking many of the myths that have arisen about the two communities — both within Ireland itself and among the ethnic Irish of Australasia, North America and Britain. He focuses on a number of key areas where historians and sociologists have theoretically tied religion to other aspects of social life, specifically in relation to economic involvement, family size and structure and matters of sexuality and gender.

Akenson reports (1991, p.26) that differences in relation to family size emerged late and that present-day variations in family structure began from very small differences that emerged in the nineteenth and early twentieth centuries. Furthermore, there is evidence that the clergy of both religious groupings had similar attitudes to sexual morality; indeed, 'the image of the late nineteenth-century Catholic priest out beating the hedge rows for courting couples has become such a dominant motif that one forgets that the Protestant clergy had methods of enforcing sexual morality [for example, public shaming] that would have made the Catholic priests envious' (Akenson, 1991, p.36). Overall, based on available historical evidence, Akenson (1991, p.108) is led to conclude that, despite strong beliefs in Irish society about the social repercussions of Protestantism and Catholicism, there is:

> no empirically verifiable evidence that cultural factors caused a differentiation between the two religions on major social and economic axes. Neither in family structure, nor in economic behaviour, nor the treatment of women was there any compelling evidence for major differences, and, in some instances, there was positive evidence of fundamental similarities. What differences there were in these matters were much more plausibly ascribed to class than to culture.

Given these similarities, the interesting questions then are: how and why were the two groups so clearly differentiated? McVeigh (1995) argues that this process of differentiation can best be brought under the term 'sectarianism'. This is the process, familiar to nearly all Irish people, whereby religious differences are noted — through picking up clues from names, accent, school attended, sports played — then evaluated and sometimes acted upon in a way that is discriminatory.

The historical background of settler colonialism was obviously of key importance in the emergence of sectarianism: 'the triumph of the Protestant Reformation in England and its failure in Ireland meant that religion became the key signifier between settler and native — especially as second and third generation English and Scots planters became increasingly "Irish"'(McVeigh,

1995, p.626). By the nineteenth century, religion, politics and identity were inextricably linked in Ireland. As a result, non-sectarian politics such as that espoused by James Connolly became the exception that proved the rule.

Sectarianism — like racism — must be seen in structural terms not in terms of individual pathology. In other words, it is a quality of Irish society as much as of 'prejudiced' individuals. It has provided a means of institutionalising inequality and conservatism north and south of the border. The blatant forms of sectarianism in the North have been reflected in the South by a 'pluralist theocracy' (McVeigh, 1995, p.632) that recognised and entrenched religious difference. All major religious groups were explicitly recognised in Article 44 of the 1937 Constitution and they had high levels of control over 'their own' institutions, such as schools, hospitals and charities.

Sectarianism is about identity in the broadest sense of the term (McVeigh, 1995, p.627):

> Sectarian labels are about more than religion . . . they approximate more to notions of ethnicity — involving nationality, politics, culture, 'race', and boundary maintenance as much as faith and religious organisation. Religious identity . . . remains the main signifier of ethnic difference in Ireland.

But these identities are complex: what makes an 'Ulster Catholic' or an 'Irish Protestant'? Religious conviction and organisation is an important part of the story but what makes a Protestant a 'Protestant', a Catholic a 'Catholic' and a Jew a 'Jew' is determined by the interaction of historical, religious, social, cultural and political factors (Poole, 1997). Religion has operated in Irish society as an ethnic and cultural marker not necessarily related to beliefs or practices. Thus, suggests Akenson, 'it mattered not if an individual entered his church only to be baptised and to be buried, the life he lived between these two signal events was, in the eyes of those with whom he dealt, the life of either a Protestant or a Catholic' (1991, p.129).

Religious boundaries are both self-defined and other-defined. Each identity provides a positive evaluation of its own characteristics, plus a negative denunciation of the other side's: we're not like that lot! (Akenson, 1991, p.133). 'Otherness' was, and is, created and re-created through practices like endogamous marriage (marrying within the group, and discouragement of 'mixed' marriages) and segregated or 'denominational' education. It has only been by keeping themselves segregated in family life and by separating the young that it has been possible for religious communities — in Ireland as elsewhere — to develop and perpetuate unique world views and, at the same time, sometimes grossly inaccurate views of each other.

The harsh reality of sectarianism in the North is familiar to all. In the Republic, sectarianism was perhaps most vivid during the 1920s (Akenson, 1991, p.4):

Mostly a rural affair, it consisted of hectoring, intimidating, burning and murdering isolated Protestants, most, but not all, of whom were owners of small town businesses or of relatively large farms . . . between early December 1922 and late March 1923 192 houses belonging to the Protestant minority in southern Ireland were destroyed. An outcome of the sectarian atmosphere that accompanied the establishment of the state was a reduction in the number of Protestants from 327,000 in 1911 to 221,000 in 1926.

It is also true that the sense of physical threat felt by Protestants in the South rapidly diminished as the state became more securely established. There was also some evidence of anti-Semitism in Ireland, particularly during the early part of the twentieth century (Keogh, 1998) but its extent and meaning remains a matter for debate.

Kirby (1984, p.52) suggests that the Catholic Church hierarchy, in its attitudes to issues such as desegregated education and 'mixed' marriages has continued to actively contribute to sectarianism, despite a rhetorical commitment to ecumenism. But in many ways the enthusiasm for division was shared by both 'sides' — each jealously guarding its own institutions, from boy scouts to schools and hospitals.

## RELIGION, POWER AND SOCIAL INEQUALITY

Religion is always intertwined with structures of social inequality (Restivo, 1991, p.154):

For the upper classes, it was a social activity intertwined with political ideologies and alliances, and a tool of oppression. For the lower classes, religion was a source of hope and release from the trials and uncertainties of everyday life. For the middle classes it was a source of rules about appropriate demeanour and deference.

There is a strong link in all societies between religion and power, including *political power*. The unity of religious and political power begins to decline in more technologically advanced and complex societies but the connections remain important, not least in Irish society. Religion has continued to be drawn upon by secular leaders in Ireland for legitimation and administrative organisation. Religious personnel continue to be involved in political activity to shore up their own hierocratic power.

In Ireland, the exercise of church power has taken place through ideological power (the power of belief systems), through the control of resources (land, property, health and education systems) and, it is increasingly being revealed, through coercive physical power (usually described today as 'abuse'). There has been relatively little attention paid in contemporary Ireland to these facets of power wielded by the churches: an element of the more general lack of critical analysis of religion alluded to earlier. Nic Ghiolla Phádraig (1995, p.597) has gone so far as to argue that the 'liberal critique of the church' serves to divert attention from other more important issues relating to inequality, such as the distribution of wealth. Pioneering work by Whyte (1971; 1980) analysed the often close relationship between church and state in independent Ireland, while more recently Inglis (1987; 1998a) has usefully drawn attention to the vast institutional power and resources the Catholic Church retains to this day.

## Gender and religion

Macionis and Plummer (1998, p.508) point out:

> All world religions are patriarchal. They have male gods at the centre of their cosmologies; favour men to be their officials on earth; and frequently devise ways of excluding women both from church and society. Many more recent sects and cults that are emerging seem to keep this patriarchal order.

Recent times have seen some change, most notably in Reform Judaism and most of the Protestant Churches (O'Connor, 1998, p.64). Some smaller groups, such as the Quakers, have always exhibited a high degree of equality of ministry (Wigham, 1992, p.53). The Roman Catholic and Eastern Orthodox faiths still strongly resist any moves towards equality, while the Anglican Church has seen deep divisions in some countries over the issue — especially in Australia and England.

O'Connor (1998) reminds us that most analyses of the position of women in Irish society ascribe a strong causal element to the structure and nature of the churches, especially the Catholic Church. O'Dowd (1989, pp.13–21) has outlined some of the key aspects of the evolving relationship between women and the churches in post-independence Ireland. He argues that 'to some degree all the churches shared an image of women's proper role, seeing it as familial, self-sacrificing and altruistic in the practical sense' (1989, p.13). In Catholicism, the Marian cult, which idealised motherhood while abjuring all manifestations of female sexuality, held sway. Catholic social teaching emphasised 'the family ideal, the family wage, and the natural role of woman as mother and home-maker'. This viewpoint is outlined at length in Inglis's (1998a, pp.178–200) discussion of the special role of the mother in the development of Irish Catholicism. The Protestant religions were more inclined to focus on the father as the senior figure in an economic and spiritual partnership.

O'Dowd (1989) lists a number of ways that legislation in the Free State put into practice elements of Catholic social teaching and this was accompanied by a range of other 'campaigns' and social initiatives, often (if not exclusively) aimed at women, for example, the campaigns against birth control or 'jazz dancing'. It can also be argued that the political-commercial-religious elite in Ireland has been a very male-dominated one and that this is reinforced by the existence of exclusively male elite schools and an exclusively male religious hierarchy.

The relationship between gender and religion in Ireland is not a simple one: while undoubtedly patriarchal, the churches did provide opportunities and support for women when there were few other avenues (Fahey, 1987). By 1941, one out of every 400 women in Ireland was entering a convent (cited in MacCurtain, 1997, p.248). Religious life was one of the only ways that women could access positions of power or responsibility in Irish society, for example, in further education or in management positions within the fields of education, social welfare and health. There was a contradictoriness in this position, well expressed by MacCurtain (1997, p.252):

> The image of the nun in midcentury Ireland (and elsewhere) was that of a docile and submissive figure clad in a black or white or blue sweep of garment with a medieval headdress who rarely raised her voice or eyes. Yet these same women were major players in church–state relations below the official level of the Catholic hierarchy. Owners and matrons of the main hospital systems in the country, they were entrusted by the state with the state's industrial schools and orphanages and with the responsibility of implementing the state's fragile and largely underdeveloped welfare policy.

At the level of the individual household and family, Inglis analyses in detail the role of the Irish (rural) mother in the development of the Catholic Church. His contention (1998a, p.199) is that:

> The domination and control of women by the Church, and the necessity for women to ally themselves with that dominating power if they themselves were to have any power, led to their high level of marital fertility which, in turn, created the need for postponed marriage, permanent celibacy and emigration among their children. These practices were encouraged by the mother in the home through a devotion to the Church, a rigorous sexual morality, and a physical and emotional distance from her children. It is this scenario, reenacted over the generations, that is the essence of the dialectical relationship of power between the church and family in modern Ireland.

This summarises fairly neatly Inglis's argument that the alliance of otherwise powerless mothers and the ever more powerful institutional church was the basis for the modernisation of Irish rural life and thus Irish society. The ascetic and constrained lifestyle enforced by a holy alliance of mothers and priests provided, according to Inglis's analysis, the conditions under which Irish property relations, occupational structure and demographic patterns altered in the post-Famine period. While Inglis's argument is fascinating, it is the case that similar discourses of femininity, rationalisation and control emerged in other societies where Catholicism was less influential, for example, early twentieth-century Australia (Reiger, 1985). Like Weber's suggestion of the link between Protestantism and the emergence of capitalism, Inglis's analysis of maternal power has the capacity to provoke interesting sociological analyses.

What of future relationships between gender and religion in Ireland? O'Connor (1998, p.67) suggests it is likely that religious institutions will maintain much of their current dominance, especially through their control of education; their linkages with middle-class religious pressure groups; and also inasmuch as they 'provide moral validation for the unpaid love and labour of the majority of Irish married women'. She also points to tensions, for example, in the gulf between Catholic Church teaching on birth control (a stern No) and Irish women's use of contraception (an enthusiastic Yes!). Similarly, increasing criticism is being voiced of the patriarchal nature of the church and the exclusion of women from any meaningful position in the church hierarchy.

Inglis (1998a, p.199) suggests that once women were able to access alternative sources of power through the workplace and public life (from the 1960s on) they were increasingly freed from the ideological power of the church. Gender issues have also been crucial in providing a site for oppositional discourses in relation to the church, in particular around matters of gender roles, reproduction and sexuality. While oppositional discourses to the hegemony of religion in Ireland have been few, Nic Ghiolla Phádraig (1995, p.598) suggests that *feminism* has been an important critical force, for example, through its central involvement in the various contraceptive rights, abortion and divorce campaigns.

## IDEOLOGICAL CONTROL AND INSTITUTIONAL POWER

The extent of ideological control was and is reinforced by the churches' control of institutions such as education, health and social welfare and the generation of 'expert knowledge' such as medical discourses on childbirth or social studies discourses on attitudinal change.

A political discourse that focused on national identity based on difference from 'Protestant England' (and to a lesser extent Protestant Northern Ireland) helped to solidify the ideological control of Catholicism. There has been little organised (or even disorganised) anti-clericalism, unlike in France or Italy, for example. This has also been linked to the failure of left-wing politics to develop in Ireland (Mair, 1994, p.404). This contributed to the phenomenal institutional power of the church in Ireland. As Fintan O'Toole has remarked (1998, p.67):

An Irish person was, and is, likely to be born in a Catholic hospital, educated at Catholic schools, married in a Catholic church, have children named by a priest, be counselled by Catholic marriage advisors if the marriage runs into trouble, be dried out in Catholic clinics for the treatment of alcoholism if he or she develops a drink problem, be operated on in Catholic hospitals, and be buried by Catholic rites.

O'Toole is describing the 'cradle to grave' welfare system that was developed by the churches, particularly by the Catholic Church, in Ireland during the nineteenth and twentieth centuries. The historical development of welfare institutions, and thus many of the service-delivery aspects of the Irish welfare state, is intrinsically tied up with the expanding role of the churches in Irish social life during this period. Indeed O'Toole suggests (1998, p.65) that in the Republic the Catholic Church became a 'surrogate state'. And, as Akenson (1991, p.109) points out, the institutions of the different churches were also an expression of their self-perceptions: they 'crystallised in social practice what the Irish people believed to be the proper relationship between persons of differing Christian denominations. The institutional structures were the mechanisms whereby the Irish-Catholic and Irish-Protestant people kept themselves apart from one another.'

Historically, the Protestant Churches had been involved in a number of philanthropic, educational and health care institutions. After the repeal of the penal laws, and during the nineteenth and twentieth centuries, the Catholic Church became increasingly involved in a wide range of institutions from hospitals (for example, St Vincent's Hospital, Dublin) to homes for 'unmarried mothers' (the Magdalen Laundries), elite boarding schools (Glenstal Abbey) and borstals and residential homes for young people (for example, Letterfrack). The rapid growth of involvement in these institutions was facilitated by the large numbers of men and women entering the religious life (Kirby, 1984, p.56). This suited the state as religious labour was cheap or free, and the capital costs were met by fundraising from the flock and through 'dowries' brought in by the middle-class religious (MacCurtain, 1997, p.248)

For example, in education, a marriage of convenience was entered into between the emerging Irish state and the Catholic religious orders who already controlled significant elements of the education system. The existing denominational, single-sex schools provided a fertile ground for recruitment to the ranks of the religious, teaching costs were kept low through non-payment of full wages to religious staff and the school provided the sort of product desired by the state — young people schooled in orderliness, discipline, obedience and self-control (MacCurtain, 1997, p.249). The church offered the state continuity and stability and in return sought its support for continuity and stability in its own work (Nic Ghiolla Phádraig, 1995, p.609).

Though the operation of many religious institutions has now been opened up to critical examination, at the time of their operation there was little questioning of church control of welfare and educational institutions. As Nic Ghiolla Phádraig (1995, p.601) suggests, 'belief in the altruism of the religious running them and the fear of challenging the church together with ignorance of conditions and the inmates' lack of powerful connections isolated them from public scrutiny.' In the last two decades there has been an intense critique of such bodies, in line with trends in other Western countries. The critique has taken many forms, from films such as *Our Boys* and TV series such as *States of fear*, to government reports (Madonna House) and statements by ex-'clients' themselves. The overall result has been a shift in the public perception of religious institutions in general.

More recent times have seen a decline of religious involvement in public institutions. The causes have been various but, as well as the exposure of abuses of power mentioned above, have included the sharp decline in vocations, especially in the religious orders; changes in church teaching about welfare and the role of the state (it had argued for the principle of 'subsidiarity', that the state should not undertake any functions that could be fulfilled by individuals or the local community — see Curry, 1998, p.10); the expansion of the state itself and its penetration into social affairs; and an increased demand for the professionalisation of services. Overall, Nic Ghiolla Phádraig (1995, p.617) argues that there has been a decline in the institutional power of the Roman Catholic Church in Ireland:

> There are many spheres of Irish life over which the church has little or no influence. The mass media are the church's main competitors in the interpretation of Irish society. Public administration is outside the church's influence. The leading sector in Irish society and the one to which state policies are increasingly moulded is that of business and finance and transnational capitalism. Here again the church is inexpert and a nonplayer. There has been a growing distance between bishops and politicians with regard to social policy and family law.

Nic Ghiolla Phádraig points out that the very structures of the church are reflective of inequality: both through their hierarchical nature that centralises power, and their almost total exclusion of women from positions of power. So, despite the existence of 'a very clear radical movement' in the church (expressed most clearly in CORI), it has functioned to re-create the existing structures of inequality in Ireland. Nic Ghiolla Phádraig (1995, p.598) suggests that in Ireland the modern institutional church and the modern nation state developed simultaneously and 'gestated in mutual interdependence during most of the nineteenth century and into the twentieth'. The taken-for-granted intertwining of state and Catholic discourse was not threatened until the expansionist and consumerist economic policies of the 1960s.

## EDUCATION

According to John Curry (1998, p.72) 'the influence of the churches (especially Catholic) on the development of the [education] system is profound.' The churches retain to this day a central role in education in the Republic of Ireland, and this is recognised and supported by the state through funding and the ceding of organisational control to religious bodies. There are few other developed countries where explicitly religious schools are supported to such an extent. A number of sociologists see the religious control of education as the key to broader church power.

Schools are a major site of religious socialisation: operated through control over staffing, language, symbols, curriculum, physical environment and 'ethos'. Elite religious schools provide an analogous institution to the British 'public school' and are a source of intake for the professions, politics and business, while other schools (for example, those run by the Christian Brothers and the Ursuline and Presentation Sisters) aim to provide education for the children of middle-class and working-class families.

As in other institutional areas, the overt influence of the churches over education is waning, largely through a virtual drying up of the supply of religious to teach in or to manage church-owned schools. This was one of the reasons for the successful development of second-level community schools, despite Catholic Church objections (Curry, 1998, p.88). The church still attempts to operate as gatekeeper to the teaching profession at second level but does not have the same extreme level of influence as at primary level (where *all* teacher training is still controlled by religious bodies). There is also increasing (though grudging) government support for multi-denominational primary schools, of which there are now sixteen in the country (*Irish Times*, 10 July 1998), and Irish-language *gaelscoileanna* which are less directly under religious control. Another phenomenon is the significant number of Catholics attending elite Protestant-identified secondary schools such as the High School and Alexandra College in Dublin, or Newtown in Waterford (a Quaker school).

## SECULARISATION

Secularisation is of concern to all the churches in Ireland. According to the Moderator of the Presbyterian Church in Ireland, Dr Harry Allen, speaking in 1998, Dublin is now 'one of the most secular cities in Europe, where vast numbers of people, especially those under 40, have no significant church connection' (*Irish Times*, 3 June 1998).

Secularisation has been defined (by Berger, as cited in Hornsby-Smith and Whelan, 1994, p.8) as 'the process by which sectors of society and culture are removed from the domination of religious institutions and symbols'. In its broadest sense it refers to the increasing separation of the profane and the sacred, and the gradual downgrading of the latter, that has taken place since the development of agricultural societies. It suggests a 'disenchantment' of society (Weber's term): a process whereby the spiritual and the supernatural come to play a lesser role in people's lives and may be replaced by more rational and scientific modes of thinking and expression. It is also often taken to refer to the decline of religious institutions in public life, for example, a reduction in the political power of the churches and a decline in the status and prestige of religious figures. And in terms closer to the contemporary common-sense understanding of the concept, it can relate to a decline in participation in formal and informal religious activities, such as weekly attendance at Mass or daily prayer.

It has long been suggested that in all these senses, Ireland is a secularising society, particularly as it has also been seen to be a modernising one. But as we have already noted in this chapter, religious belief, identity and practice are very complex entities; as a consequence, any attempt to 'measure' the extent of secularisation of Irish society is fraught with both epistemological and methodological difficulty.

The key analysis of secularisation from the quantitative point of view is found in the work of Hornsby-Smith and Whelan (Hornsby-Smith, 1994; Hornsby-Smith and Whelan, 1994). This can be supplemented by reference to the increasing quantity of survey data (of varying quality and reliability) that has emerged in recent years. Ireland, due to its rapid economic and social change, is said by Hornsby-Smith and Whelan (1994, p.8) to provide 'a particularly interesting test case for the generally hypothesised relationship between industrialisation, modernisation and religious transformation'.

Hornsby-Smith and Whelan suggest (1994, p.5) that, at the beginning of the 1980s, 'on the wide range of indicators considered, both parts of Ireland were far less secularised than any of the countries of western Europe, although there was evidence that generational change might be reducing the differences.' O'Toole, writing in 1995, was able to suggest that Ireland remained 'exceptionally religious by the standards of the western world' (1998, p.66). There is evidence that there may have been some change even since then, though inevitably the published sociological analysis lags behind the events somewhat.

Sociologists have linked secularisation to the 'decline of community' and to urbanisation, education, the changing nature of work, social mobility and individualism. Hornsby-Smith and Whelan aimed to test these hypotheses. They point out, 'all these variables serve as proxies for the length and type of exposure to particular kinds of experiences that reinforce or retard the development of meaning systems . . . for a Christian world view' (1994, p.9). But they are also highly critical of any notion that there is an inevitable or automatic link between secularisation and processes of social and economic change such as industrialisation and urbanisation.

The relationship between social change and religious activity is indeed a complex one. Many commentators have observed that rapid social change in itself makes the certainty offered by established religions *more* attractive, as Coulter (1997, p.295) suggests in her analysis of the 1995 divorce referendum campaign:

As Irish society changes — with the grip of religion weakening, the growth in male unemployment, the rise in female employment, and the fundamental shift in sexual mores and attitudes towards personal rights and liberties — a huge vacuum appears at the level of public policy and official ideology. At the moment the only thing that appears to fill it is the consumer-driven ideology of Western capitalism, with its lack of concern for the vulnerable in society and its insensitivity to the social solidarity that holds society together. The divorce debate, and the high 'No' vote recorded, showed the deep unease that exists with this vision of the future and the widespread desire to stem its advance.

The same writer — and many others — responded in a similar vein to the (for some) unexpectedly high vote received by Rosemary Scallon (Dana) in the 1997 Presidential election.

## Religious attitudes

UCD Professor of Politics Brigid Laffan argues that Ireland is not secularising as rapidly as might appear (*Irish Times*, 16 September 1997). She suggests that while attitudes have changed considerably, changes in religious practice have not been as dramatic. Laffan suggests there has been a change in the role of religion in Irish life. She argues that the Roman Catholic Church in Ireland has lost its 'moral monopoly' and that individual Catholics now want and expect to make up their own minds about matters of private sexual morality.

One of the main sources of information we have on religious beliefs and attitudes in Ireland is the survey data reported by Mac Gréil (1996). When asked if they saw their religious upbringing as a 'hindrance', very few of Mac Gréil's respondents said they did. But the importance of religion in one's upbringing appears to have become far less marked since 1972/73. Mac Gréil suggests that there may be 'changes in the place of religion in the socialisation of the young . . . the religiosity of the homes and of the schools may be modifying somewhat'. He concludes that 'any rise in secularism in primary socialisation will inevitably result in a reduction in the perceived importance of religion in the growth and development of the person.'

However, over 85 per cent of Mac Gréil's sample said they felt 'extremely' (25 per cent) or 'somewhat' (60 per cent) close to God, leading him to comment, once again, on the 'strong religious ethos of the population'. This may be compared with the UK where only 21 per cent say they have no doubts about existence of God, and 26 per cent do not believe in God or do not know if He exists (Macionis and Plummer, 1997, p.517).

According to an *Irish Times*/Market Research Bureau of Ireland (MRBI) opinion poll carried out in late 1997 (*Irish Times*, 12 November 1997) only a fifth of Catholics follow the teaching of their church when it comes to making 'serious moral decisions', compared to 78 per cent who 'follow their own conscience'. This latter figure rises to 92 per cent for eighteen- to thirty-four-year-olds. More than half of the people surveyed by MRBI disagreed to varying extents on the church's attitude to major moral and canonical issues, including divorce, contraception, priestly celibacy and women priests.

## Religious practice

Another dominant strand in thinking and writing about the process of secularisation has been to focus on indicators of formal religious activity. Like attitudinal data, such indicators are attractive to positivistic approaches (see Chapter 2) and lend themselves to statistical measurement and manipulation.

Mac Gréil's work *Prejudice in Ireland revisited* (1996) examines trends in religious practice in Ireland over the period from 1972/73 to 1988/89 as measured by his surveys. He points out that any attempt to measure religiosity is necessarily limited and selective. For example, 'church membership', according to Mac Gréil, may be measured according to: participation in religious activity; commitment to religious beliefs and norms; acceptance by co-believers; and formal registration of membership. His own study aimed to measure only the first two of these factors. He suggests that 'levels of participation in Mass and in the Sacraments are generally accepted as basic measures of active [Catholic] Church membership'. At a deeper or more exacting level, 'various forms of pastoral and evangelising activity' are also important criteria.

Mac Gréil's research has been complemented by that undertaken for the European Values project (Whelan, 1994) and by opinion polls undertaken by bodies such as the MRBI for media organisations and for the churches themselves. Taken together, the data indicates fairly rapid and accelerating changes in religious practices; but these processes vary considerably in terms of the sociological variables of location, class, gender and age.

Surveys show that weekly mass attendance has declined from 87 per cent of Catholics, to around 60 per cent in the period 1981 to 1998 (Figure 12.3). These levels may be compared to those of Australia: 37 per cent in 1981 (Waters and Crook, 1993, p.381) and a European average of 30 per cent (O'Connor, 1998, p.61). The highest levels of Mass attendance are found in Connaught/Ulster and the lowest among those brought up in Dublin. In Mac Gréil's opinion, urbanisation (especially residence in Dublin) is the strongest factor causing decline in church attendance. He suggests — in line with other analysts of secularisation from Durkheim onwards — that this may be due to a 'lack of community' in the city, though offers no evidence to support this.

Prayer remains a popular activity, with nearly 40 per cent of people claiming to pray several times a day, and only 10 per cent praying less than once a week. Mac Gréil suggests that 'the practice of prayer on a regular basis must indicate a strong

## Figure 12.3 Weekly mass attendance in the Republic of Ireland 1981–1998

| Year | % | Comments | Source |
|------|-----|----------|--------|
| 1998 | 94 | older people | Survey of Diocese of Cashel and Emly published in *Irish Times* |
| 1998 | 92 | people over 65 | MRBI poll for *Irish Times* |
| 1981 | 87 | all people | European Values Survey |
| 1998 | 87 | Connacht/Ulster people | MRBI poll for *Irish Times* |
| 1990 | 85 | all people | European Values Survey |
| 1988/89 | 82 | all people | Mac Gréil (1996) |
| 1998 | 66 | all people | MRBI poll for *Irish Times* |
| 1998 | 60 | people 18–34 | Survey of Diocese of Cashel and Emly published in *Irish Times* |
| 1998 | 60 | all people | RTE Prime Time poll |
| 1998 | 50 | Dubliners | MRBI poll for *Irish Times* |
| 1998 | 41 | 18–24 yr olds | MRBI poll for *Irish Times* |
| 1990 | 40 | urban unemployed | European Values Survey |

degree of belief'. The least likely to pray are those that are most educated and most urbanised. Mac Gréil surmises that there may be a decline in occasions like the family rosary or regular family prayers. This view is supported by Archbishop Dermot Clifford (*Irish Times*, 5 November 1998) who suggests that 'family prayer would seem to be the victim of the modern age: television, telephones and the pace of life has squeezed out the family rosary.'

Confession has sharply declined as a religious activity, with over a tenth of Mac Gréil's respondents saying they never went. The MRBI figures show an even more precipitous decline in this activity. Mac Gréil suggests that this reflects a substantial change in the nature of Catholicism in Ireland that 'merits serious theological and pastoral examination'. There has also been some decline in what Inglis calls the 'magical' aspects of Catholicism: the use of religious medals, holy water, pilgrimages and retreats.

The least religious people, according to Mac Gréil, are those that are either tertiary educated or have incomplete secondary education, work in non-manual jobs, are Dublin-born, and are single males aged twenty-one to thirty-five. Conversely, the most religious people are primary-educated, well-off Connaught/ Ulster widows aged over 51. In fact widows are so religious that Mac Gréil (1996, p.182) suggests that 'the religious practice of widowed respondents approaches that of those living a "regular life" in religious orders.'

Vocations have experienced a sharp decline in Ireland, as in the rest of Western Europe. The number of students training for the priesthood in the seminaries in Maynooth, Dublin, Thurles, Waterford and Carlow was about 220 in 1998. Two decades previously there were 600 studying at Maynooth alone (see Figure 12.4). However, as Mac Gréil points out, this is not due to parental resistance: the vast majority of his respondents would welcome their child becoming a nun or priest (presumably safe in the knowledge that — like being an astronaut — it is extremely unlikely to occur!).

## Figure 12.4 Numbers entering Maynooth seminary

| Year | No. | Year | No. |
|------|-----|------|-----|
| 1996 | 18 | 1992 | <40 |
| 1995 | 26 | 1991 | 51 |
| 1994 | 37 | 1988 | 61 |
| 1993 | 40 | 1986 | 76 |

(*Source: Irish Times*, 11 September 1996)

## THE DISENCHANTMENT OF THE (IRISH) WORLD?

In Ireland the immediate danger to faith is not unbelief but shallow faith . . . the danger is that religion will be reduced to a minor leisure time activity, a convention retained but only on the margins of life, something devoid of challenge or depth. (An Irish priest cited in Kirby, 1984, p.37.)

A number of reasons for the decline in religious practice in Ireland has been suggested. One may be a general convergence with European and Western behaviour: figures are even lower for other Catholic countries like France, Spain and Italy. Second, the number and frequency of high-profile church-related scandals, while by no means unique to Ireland, have without doubt had a negative effect on the Catholic Church. These have ranged from the Bishop Eamon Casey case in 1992 to the numerous cases of sexual and physical abuse in church-run institutions, as well as individual cases of sexual and financial abuse. Third, the media has operated as a supplier of alternative value systems and also as an alternative way to pass time and socialise.

In 1984, Kirby was already seeing evidence that a 'major crisis' faced the Catholic Church. It had 'not yet awakened to the major challenge that faces it if it is to find any significant role for itself in the fast-changing Ireland now taking shape' (1984, p.10). It was, for him, a church that was unsure of what message it should preach and one that relied too much on a largely irrelevant set of principles and priorities. In asking *Is Irish Catholicism dying?* Kirby suggested that the secularising trend had been accentuated by a rupture between church and people, contributed to by the very organisational success of the church itself. The forms of the 'modern' Irish Catholic Church have actively contributed to this disenchantment: 'where the old was intimate with God and saw his hand in the things of the world, the new was stylised and sentimental encouraging a divorce between things spiritual and material' (Kirby, 1984, p.66). In 1978, a Working Party of the Catholic bishops had concluded that, 'for many the practice of religion is more a matter of law/routine/social pressure, rather than a result of intellectual or personal conviction' (Kirby, 1984, p.35). Does this mean that for many in Ireland religion has become a meaningless, ritualised practice?

Drawing on his interpretation of what was happening in other Catholic countries, Kirby argued for an activist role for the churches, with a shift in focus from policing private morality to one of public intervention in issues of public policy, such as poverty, overseas aid and ethics. It would challenge social and economic inequality and draw on the approaches of liberation theology in the developing world (1984, pp.74–83). He called for greater involvement by the laity, partly as a response to the decline in vocations, but also as 'the Church has little hope of addressing itself to the needs of the new generation of Irish people until it facilitates the laity to become involved at all levels of Church life' (1984, p.38). Harking back to the folk religion of earlier Ireland, he saw the desirable shape of the church as 'a community of ordinary Christians exploring their faith in ways which challenge them to a more socially committed life and a simplicity of lifestyle' (1984, p.13). This would find organisational expression in 'basic Christian communities' (1984, p.88), a direction echoed by other church writers such as Owen O'Sullivan (1997). Writing over a decade later, O'Toole sees a similar trajectory for the church, one where 'the Irish church in the year 2000 will look remarkably like what it was in 1800 — a focus for a relaxed but deep spirituality in which the broad culture rather than devotional and behavioural rules is what matters (1998, p.75).

The alternative for these critics is to follow the route of the churches in other Western European societies and to 'adapt to a liberal society tacitly agreeing to provide religious services for a largely apathetic people' (Kirby, 1984, p.14). It has been suggested that many European societies are now witnessing the emergence of 'civil religion' (Bellah, 1967) or a 'social church' where people seek and use religious values and symbols without the social commitment involved — often referred to (pejoratively) in Ireland as 'à la carte religion'. For example, a former Moderator of the Presbyterian Church, Dr Allen, reported critically on 'social baptisms' among Spanish Anglicans, 'where families, suitably dressed, arrive at the church door, take photographs, and then proceed to the hotel for a meal, without ever going into the church. This also happens at confirmation time. They keep the custom but refuse the commitment' (*Irish Times*, 3 June 1998). There is little evidence yet whether such practices are becoming widespread in Irish society.

## THE FUTURE OF RELIGION?

There is much evidence that periods of rapid change lead to a greater level of religious activity. While economic, social and technological change has the capacity to undermine religiosity, for some, religious belief and practice provide a framework for responding to change. Given that there is evidence of rapid social and economic change in contemporary Ireland, how might the churches and religious practice change in the future?

This is a challenge that has been taken up in various ways by the churches in Ireland. In their attempts to respond to the threat of secularisation they have attempted to make themselves more relevant and in touch by involving themselves more in social and political issues, embracing the media and changing their practices. This may help to attract more people but it also risks blurring the sacred and profane, and demystifying the nature of religion. As Taylor (1989, p.3) points out, for religious regimes whose power and authority depends to some extent on the effectiveness of symbol and ritual, this can be a serious problem. Once the mystery has gone, what exactly is left?

One possible direction is a shift towards mysticism and New Age religions, such as a rediscovery of paganism (Fay, 1997). As the established churches become disenchanted and lose much of their mystery, perhaps there will be a greater attraction to more sect-like religious communities, and charismatic leaders may find favour over bureaucratic ones. Macionis and Plummer, (1998, p.522) report that it is estimated there may be as many as 20,000 new religious groupings in Europe alone. There is a possibility that such developments will embrace Ireland.

Catholicism and some of the other mainstream churches have at times incorporated mystical and personalised practices associated with the 'charismatic renewal' that borrow much from the evangelistic sects (Szuchewycz, 1989). The Catholic charismatic movement peaked in Ireland in the late 1970s. There is little information on the development of minority religions or cults in Ireland (but see Coulter, 1984) though public concern about them seems to have diminished compared to previous decades.

Another direction that the churches may take, which is of importance in countries like the United States and Australia, is to take a key role in the debate over emerging ethical dilemmas related to technological and social development. Many people are concerned about issues such as biotechnology, cloning, the human genome project, medical ethics, reproductive technology and the general direction of the development of scientific knowledge. At this stage, the churches have contributed little to the minimal public debate on these issues in Ireland. Similarly, there is a lot of concern about the effects of economic growth, particularly as it may lead to greater social inequality and a generally less caring society. There has been more of a response in Ireland to these issues, particularly through bodies like CORI, and the rhetoric of equality and social justice informs much of the language of the contemporary church at grass-roots level.

Multiculturalism is an issue that is only beginning to emerge in Ireland, though it has been of importance in the Western world in terms of religious change. For example, in the UK the most rapidly growing religions include those associated with immigrant populations, such as the Muslim and Hindu religions. Largely as a result of migration, around 3 per cent of the European population now identify themselves as Islamic (Macionis and Plummer, 1998, p.517).

A recent event that stimulated much debate about the nature of religious experience in the West, including in Ireland, was the remarkable global response to the death of Diana, the Princess of Wales. Again, this event raised the issue of what constitutes a religion, sociologically speaking. Boer (Re:Public, 1997, p.81) relates the death of Diana to the concept of civil religion — the process whereby there is a:

> dispersal of religious and mythic functions from the conventional religious institutions and into culture itself. In this process various bodies and institutions took on religious and quasi-religious functions that attempted to fulfil some of the religious needs that were no longer supplied by religious institutions.

It has been suggested that shopping and sport (Inglis, 1998c; Coakley, 1998a) are perhaps among the new religions, suffused as they are with symbols, rituals and sacred sites.

Boer suggests that 'civil religion as a global phenomenon has been creeping, perhaps a little more slowly than other dimensions of culture, into the global arena, particularly through a global media that is able to transmit and present iconic figures to a world-wide audience.' Such iconic figures include Nelson Mandela, Mother Teresa, and Diana: described as (perhaps the first) 'civil religious saint'. The death of the latter two in the same week of 1997 only served to mutually reinforce their 'saintly' status. As McPhillips (Re:Public, 1997, p.88) suggests, 'there is little doubt that Diana's qualities of attentive motherhood, service to the poor and sick, personal frailty, innocence and humility have already become imbricated in a discourse of saintliness and even divinity.' If this is indeed the case, it is easy to see how her death had strong reverberations within Irish Catholicism, where the image of the saintly Mary/mother figure is so powerful (Inglis, 1998a, pp.178–200).

Furthermore, as McPhillips further points out, the public response to Diana's death saw a (re)merging of the sacred and the secular. The funeral service itself combined elements of religion at its most formal, with celebrity schmaltz (via

Elton John) and high emotion. The presence of sacred symbols was accompanied and outweighed by more prosaic and profane symbols, such as teddy bears, scribbled notes and ribbons. In effect it represented a combining of culture and faith, the sacred and the profane that harked back to earlier religious forms, not dissimilar to those called for by critics like Kirby.

The response to Diana's death also highlights the extent to which, as revealed by the sociological research in Ireland, 'religion' is becoming far more a matter of *personal* fulfilment and salvation. As McPhillips suggests, 'Diana's great redemptive action was that in the heroic act of connecting up the damaged parts of her self, she held out to all of us the possibility of becoming divine through achieving selfhood' (Re:Public, 1997, p.91). In Ireland, as elsewhere, perhaps it was this aspect of her life and death that appeared to touch upon such a powerful public chord.

# 13
# Community, space and citizenship

Community is a popular word in Ireland. We like to think of our society as made up of communities and permeated by a spirit of community. Public discussions assume that communities are good and desirable forms of social organisation. Those without a community are said to lead impoverished lives or believed to be neither stable nor reliable members of society. Leaders of church and state favour community responses to social problems like poverty, unemployment and crime. Local residents combine to defend the interests of their community against outsiders, whether property developers, road engineers, or Travellers. Health professionals, media personalities and educators claim to serve the community. Our communality is part of our image of Irishness, reflected in literature, media and politics. So we would expect *community* to be a core concept in Irish sociology.

Interestingly, it seems not to be a core concept in contemporary British (or perhaps more accurately, English) sociology. It does not feature in Giddens's widely used textbook *Sociology* (1993), nor in a number of recent English texts. For a time, more than two decades ago, debates about the concept of community and about research into communities did engage the attention of a number of English sociologists (Bell and Newby, 1971; 1974), but the interest was temporary and exceptional. British accounts of 'community studies' describe research undertaken in Ireland, Wales and Scotland, rather than England (Wright, 1992, pp.196–8; McCrone, 1992; Day, 1998). They encourage us to see 'community' as part of the structure and culture of Celtic rather than Anglo-Saxon societies — or perhaps to recognise that British perceptions of the Celtic fringe identify it as a place where community-based social relationships are stronger and more influential.

This reminds us that societies understand and represent themselves in different ways — which is why (as we remarked at the start of this book) sociology texts, despite their implicit claims to be universal, are never simply transferable across societal boundaries. If Irish society is often represented as a society of communities, British society has understood itself as a *class* society. This does not mean, of course, that either representation is necessarily true: class divisions are as significant in Irish society as they are across Europe (see Chapter 6), but it does suggest that even if an English sociology can ignore the topic of community, an Irish sociology should not.

There is a widespread belief, fostered by sociologists, that class divisions are typical of modern, industrialised or capitalist societies, and that an increase in the significance of class parallels a decline in the importance of community. Community is linked with the pre-modern and the 'traditional', while modern societies are characterised by the *loss of community*. People respond in a variety of ways to this loss. For some the apparent disappearance of community is a source of regret, even of fear. They believe that people need community, and that the shortcomings of modern life such as high rates of crime and mental disorder are attributable to its decline. For others, the collapse of community is an essential stage in the growth of human freedom; it liberates us from intrusive social control and stultifying conformity. They reject attempts to re-create the social forms of the past in order to solve the problems of the present. Our ideas about community thus reflect an implicit thesis about *progress* or *regress*; they express our emotional and evaluative responses to social change.

This chapter outlines some of the ways that sociologists have defined community, and how they have used it to address a number of sociological issues. Early in the history of the discipline, the concept of community became entangled with rurality; this has shaped our thought not only about society and social change but also about *space*. Here we trace descriptions of community in Irish sociology that seek to connect rural life, tradition and community; and urban life, modernity and the loss of community. And we examine sociological critiques of community and community development and also of community studies as a method of research.

Community is increasingly being linked with the concept of citizenship. Thus, we take a brief look at the rekindling of interest in community expressed as *communitarianism*. Communitarian theorists share many interests with the classical sociologists who first made community a central theme: concerns about citizenship and political participation, about the relationship between the individual and society, and about the need to strengthen civil society in a world that has become increasingly abstracted and globalised and beyond the control of the ordinary, everyday, 'non-expert' actor.

## THE CONCEPT OF COMMUNITY

What do people mean by 'community'? In the mid-1950s an American sociologist (Hillery, 1955) set out to examine how his colleagues had defined and used the concept of community in order to find agreed definition or common usage. He counted over ninety definitions and concluded, tongue-in-cheek, that the only common element was that they were all 'about people'. We will not try to add another definition to the list, but will instead suggest why the term tends to cause such confusion.

Community is commonly used in two different ways: to refer to *place* (as in 'the local community') or to refer to a *type of relationship* (some prefer to call this 'communality', or even 'communion'). Many of our uses of community refer to a particular geographical location. We use phrases like 'the Tallaght community', or 'the community of Corofin' or 'the Gaeltacht community west of Galway'. It would usually make little difference if we were to substitute 'population' or 'people' for 'community' in such phrases — all these words refer to people who happen to live within a demarcated territory whose boundaries have been established according to the administrative systems of the state (for example, a townland) or the church (a parish).

In choosing to use 'community' we imply that there are some social, as well as spatial, features that hold people together and allow them to be thought of as a social unit. Community is most often used to refer to territorial areas that are fairly *small* in scale — small enough for most people to know, or know a bit about, each other; and small enough for the area to be a source of shared identity for its inhabitants. When we refer to a small location as a 'community' we imply that the people who live there know each other and share a sense of being part of a defined social group — of course, this may not actually be true.

At this point 'community as place' starts to overlap with 'community as relationship'. In this second sense, what moulds an aggregate of individuals into a community is that there is among them a special sense of identity — a 'communion' or 'communality' of spirit that derives from feelings of shared interests and position in society (it is no surprise that the words 'communion' and 'community' share a common linguistic root). When we refer to a local group as a community, we suggest that there is agreement or consensus to the extent that we can refer to 'the community' itself as an entity over and above its members, with its own opinions, history, aspirations and needs.

It is easy to slip from, on the one hand, calling a place a community into, on the other, attributing to its *inhabitants* a particular identity and set of social relationships. But it is also possible to talk of a community in a social sense without tying it to any space at all. People may have feelings of shared identity as members of a community that has no common geographical base, such as professional and occupational groupings (the academic community, the business community), religious denominations (the Methodist community) or groups who share a common lifestyle interest (the arts community; the Internet community). This helps to make community a complex and confusing concept, in both sociological theory and everyday usage.

A third element in the idea of community is that it refers to relationships between people that are informal and multidimensional. Community relationships depend on people having considerable knowledge about each others' lives and on being able to take for granted, in the absence of such knowledge, that the attitudes, beliefs and experiences of others are probably very like our own. Relationships 'outside the community' are then seen as the opposite: impersonal, formal, specific in their goals and lacking in emotional content. In Parsons's terms, they are instrumental rather than affective. State institutions are often taken as the most extreme example of formal organisation or association. For Weber (see Chapter 4), state institutions operate not on shared meanings and values but on clear and explicit rules and principles, usually codified into laws and regulations. State employees are expected to relate to the public in an instrumental way, unaffected by emotional reactions or private interest. This might suggest that the social relationships that give rise to our feelings of shared identity and group belonging are only found at the level of community, not in relation to the formal, rationalised state.

These ideas encourage us to think about society, and about social and historical change, in terms of pairs of linked antitheses: in the case of community as place, it is usually 'rural' versus 'urban', and in the case of community as relationship, 'community' versus 'the state'. Much sociological discussion of community puts forward the claim that modern society is hostile or inimical to the survival of community. Such a claim is very difficult to assess, for it admixes two ideas that really need to be examined separately: that *locality* is no longer an important source of shared identity for people today; and that in modern society *any* sense of shared identity with others is increasingly difficult to achieve.

## Sociology and community

Lee and Newby (1983) suggest that when we look at how sociological thought developed at the end of the nineteenth century we can identify two somewhat different sociological problems where ideas about community are implicated. The first is Durkheim's concern to foster *moral individualism*: a type of relationship between the individual and society that will encourage individual autonomy but one that will not collapse into egocentrism as societies differentiate and become more complex. For Durkheim, the advancing division of labour might, if not carefully managed, leave individuals with no sense of moral obligation to any social group or collectivity. Community, in the sense of a collectivity that can provide individuals with a sense of shared identity and mutual dependence and a basis to act for the common good is, for him, something that will always remain an important issue for civil society.

The other way that community constitute a sociological problem derives from the concern that industrialisation encouraged new types of social relationships that suppressed or even destroyed human communality. This concern is particularly associated with the German writer Tönnies (see Chapter 1). Both sociological problems are responses to the profound social and cultural changes that result from industrialisation. But where Tönnies' ideas have underpinned a modernisation thesis that assumes the decline of community to be a key 'fact' about the modern world, Durkheim reminds us of humans' *need* for community. For Durkheim, community is something that constantly reappears or is re-created in social life, albeit in new and not always immediately recognisable forms.

We return to a discussion of Durkheim's sociological problem later in the chapter when we examine the recent rise of communitarianism. Until recently, sociological understandings of community were most influenced by the problem presented by Tönnies, whom Lee and Newby (1983, p.31) see as a major contributor to 'an important tradition in sociology . . . founded in a critique of the dehumanising effects of industrial capitalism'. Tönnies believed that urban industrial society was not a continuation of the past but a rupture with it that brought heavy costs in its wake. To elaborate this argument he constructed a distinction between two types of social relationships, represented as polar opposites, labelling them (in German) *Gemeinschaft* and *Gesellschaft* or, as generally translated, communal and associational.

In the pre-industrial world, Tönnies argued, most of the relationships that engaged people were intimate, face-to-face, enduring and based on detailed knowledge of the other people involved, their biography and their place in local society. But with the rise of industrial capitalism such communal types of relationship were replaced by impersonal, contractual, calculative or instrumentally rational ones, based on a limited knowledge of the personal circumstances of others, and on formalised rules for associating with those with whom we may have only distant, partial or transient contact. We learn to know about others only what we need to know, in order to achieve our ends. This led Tönnies to ask if the development of industrial capitalist modernity should be thought of as progress at all.

For Tönnies the concepts of *Gemeinschaft* and *Gesellschaft* did not identify particular social groups, but articulated how industrial society had altered the basis of social relationships and rendered them less personal and emotional and, therefore, less human. But sociologists later took up his historical critique in ways that substantially changed it. First, they assimilated it into the armoury of modernisation theory to help detail the process — seen as positive — whereby 'traditional' societies give way to 'modern' ones. Second, they turned Tönnies' analysis of changing relationships across time into an analysis of contrasting relationships across *space*. *Gemeinschaft*, or community, became associated with rural space, while *Gesellschaft* was associated with urbanity.

Tönnies' contemporary Georg Simmel (see Chapter 1) had already started to develop a pathbreaking analysis of urban life. Simmel depicted city living as the essential condition for the development of relationships based on impersonality, rational calculation and alienation; but also as the basis of creativity. The city-dweller's experience of constantly having to manage relationships with strangers or with large-scale, bureaucratic institutions typically produces, Simmel suggested, reserve, defensiveness and a lack of curiosity in interpersonal dealings. Equally, the experience of having constantly to engage with others whose interest in you is transient and world-weary produces creative and innovatory, if often exaggerated, strategies for making an impact through the presentation of self. Unfortunately the sophistication of Simmel's insights into the urban condition largely failed to inspire subsequent sociologists. Captured by an ideology that equated the city with the modern and progressive and relegated rural society to the backward and traditional, they took for granted that community was linked to 'the rural way of life' while urban living meant a loss of community. Community came to define, simultaneously, a vanished pre-industrial world and a vanishing traditional/rural world.

## Community and space

The association of community with rurality has continued to distort and confuse sociological understandings of both. The idea that 'urban' and 'rural' stand for opposed cultural worlds where relationships carry quite different meanings implied that we could describe a typically urban way of life and contrast this with a typically rural way of life. In practice this has been impossible. Sociologists were encouraged to assume that this division of society could have some theoretical or scientific significance, but the proof has persistently eluded them. In Chapter 11 we suggested that it may be more useful to see the rural/urban split as part of a type of cultural politics rather than as a reference to a social reality. But sociologists in Ireland and elsewhere have repeatedly tried to develop a rural sociology and an urban sociology as if these specialisms had a real basis; they have then foundered while trying to establish exactly what it is that constitutes 'the rural' or 'the urban' and what differentiates one from the other. Although cultural difference has not been the only basis used to distinguish between urban and rural, it has been the most enduring and widely used (Mormont, 1990).

One version of the cultural argument sought to connect the presence or absence of community in local social relationships with the scale and density of a physical settlement pattern. Rural and urban settlement patterns seem very different: one involves intensive use of space to carry a dense concentration of people, the other distributes a small population sparsely over a large spatial area — so why should this not explain differences in culture? The 1930s Chicago sociologist Louis Wirth argued that the way of life characteristic of modern cities is the result of a fundamental rupture between humans and nature produced by the large population size, heavy population density and the extreme heterogeneity of people living in urban settings. He suggested that it was not natural for people to live in these sorts of conditions (note the association here of 'natural' with less crowded rural living) and in response people had to develop an intensely artificial — or 'civilised' — mode of living that had much to do with an awareness of differentiation (racial, religious, occupational) and with managing relations with strangers. The urban way stems from urban demography, while in rural populations awareness of differentiation is minimal and relationships are patterned by community or the assumption of a shared identity, history and culture.

That overcrowding or dense population is specific to urban areas can be challenged: Irish history provides much evidence of 'congestion' in rural districts, and the concept of 'rural slum' was often applied to nineteenth-century British villages. But more importantly Wirth's approach rests on a belief that physical location and associated demographic characteristics have a profound effect on social and cultural relationships. This idea continues to arouse much interest and debate. While most sociologists reject such a spatial or physical determinism — the idea that people are *caused* to act in certain ways by the physical conditions in which they live — the idea is readily accepted by architects and criminologists. For example, the pioneers of the 'garden city' ideal in Britain, architects Raymond Unwin (1863–1940) and Barry Parker (1867–1947) believed that through the creation of 'low density housing with green belts and separate industrial and agricultural areas' you could re-create the pre-modern community and reduce the stresses and conflicts of urban industrial life (Morris and Morton, 1998, pp.60, 61). This idea was taken up in Britain in communities such as the Cadbury company's Bournville settlement and similar 'garden cities' in Australia and the United States. Architects and town planners in Dublin to this day struggle to find the best way to design corporation estates so that they will produce 'a community' (Bartley, 1999).

But sociologists tend to be unhappy with explanations that ignore the meanings that people attach to their surroundings and which are an important influence on action. To design a suburban environment in opposition to the physical shape of the decaying inner city, so as to reduce teenage vandalism, will fail if adolescent boys find this sort of environment boring and alienating. But while most sociologists would be sceptical that spatial location determines human social relations, many are prepared to admit it may be an influential factor.

The idea that you could locate an 'urban way of life' and distinguish it sharply from a 'rural way of life' was rapidly undermined as empirical research began to show that most places fall somewhere between the two and exhibit a mix of rural and urban characteristics. The notion of a *rural–urban continuum* was introduced in the 1950s as a way to evade this difficulty and attained some popularity among sociologists. It suggested that places in society are not strictly rural or urban, but fall on a continuum of 'more or less' rural or urban. Thus, any given place can be described in terms of its characteristic relationship patterns and, to the extent that these can be said to be 'more communal' or 'more associational', placed on the continuum.

But this idea soon attracted criticism. At an empirical level, a succession of studies described city-centre neighbourhoods that had precisely the 'community' characteristics ascribed to the most rural types of settlement. Young and Willmott's 1957 study *Family and kinship in east London*, for example, depicted Bethnal Green as a stable, homogeneous community where family, kin and neighbours remained important and enduring elements of people's lives. Places like these came to be known as urban villages. The challenge to the rural–urban continuum was compounded further by research that indicated that the countryside way of life was increasingly 'associational' as growing numbers of rural locations became sites for commuter villages and dormitory suburbs.

In addition, the theoretical basis of the rural–urban continuum lost its appeal in the face of critiques of modernisation theory and its assumption of convergence towards a single type of society. The continuum concept represented little more than a spatial version of the modernisation approach. It assumed, without investigation, that modern societies experienced a homogenisation of space, whereby the differences between rural and urban locations would eventually dissolve and all spaces would carry the same culture, way of life, social experiences and symbolic meanings. And, if urban experience was the essence of modernity, the rural, that is, the traditional, was doomed ultimately to fade away.

## Disentangling community from space

Is it possible to find a way to talk about the rural and the urban that does not rely on the presence or absence of a communal culture? Two theoretical attempts to resolve these issues have helped breathe some new life into what had become a rather stale and static debate. The first was developed in the 1970s and became known as the 'new urban sociology'. Its leading figures, particularly Manuel Castells and the social geographer David Harvey, produced a radically new perspective on the urban. They argued that we cannot understand a contemporary city by only researching social relationships within the city itself. What has to be investigated is the nature of capitalist development in the society as a whole and the involvement of the state in managing this. Cities, they said, are a spatial expression of how the state manages the collective consumption needs of different groups in society so as to sustain a particular development strategy. A strategy of industrial development by foreign capital, for example, may depend on the availability of cheap labour; but workers may only accept low wages if they have low housing costs. This requires state intervention in housing provision, such as the construction of housing estates or apartment complexes, and the concentration of low income groups within them (the government of Singapore has been particularly active in this direction). From this perspective, urbanism or *urban settlement forms* are treated as an effect rather than a cause — the result of capitalist development strategies on a national or even global level. McKeown's (1986) discussion of the production and consumption of urban areas is an interesting Irish example of the sort of research that this approach has encouraged, while Davis's (1990) analysis of the development of the city of Los Angeles is perhaps the classic in this field.

At first this new theoretical perspective seemed to offer a firm foundation for developing a new and distinctive urban sociology, but its end result has been to once again undermine rural–urban distinctions. If cities are the product of how the state and the market allocate consumption goods like housing, parks, education and transport facilities between different social classes, there seems no reason why we cannot apply the same analysis to rural areas. Indeed, if what we want to do is explain the total spatial form of society, including the uneven distribution of population between different locations and the uneven distribution of jobs and facilities, then there is a strong case for arguing that this should be addressed *as a totality*, and not through two separate subdisciplines — one that addresses rural localities while the other focuses on urban ones.

Another way to approach the rural–urban contrast also developed, based on an analysis of work and production rather than the spatial allocation of consumption goods. Growing out of rural sociology, this approach sought to identify as rural those areas that were monopolised or dominated by agricultural work, while industry was assumed to be mainly located in cities and towns. Agriculture was a form of work and production that appeared to differ in some interesting respects from typical capitalist industry. For example, while urban industries typically employed large workforces of several hundred or more, even the very large commercial farmers in the richest grain-growing areas of Europe, such as south-east England, rarely employed more than twenty farm labourers. The relations between boss and labourer tended to be more personalised and in some respects more oppressive than the impersonal contractual relations found in urban factories (Newby *et al.*, 1978). But most farming throughout Europe continues to use little or no employed labour, relying heavily on what can be supplied by the farm family itself. This form of production — family farming — seems to be a distinctive feature of late capitalist society that reinforces a wide range of other social differences between urban and rural areas.

While farm enterprises were being transformed by technological changes from the 1950s on, this was much more advanced in some lines of production (dairying, cereal growing) than others (cattle rearing). In general, farming still relies far more on natural production processes (the action of the sun in transmitting energy to crops, seasonal changes necessary for crop growth) than urban industrial production does. Perhaps most importantly, the relationship between farming and space, in the form of farmland, was argued to be quite different from that between urban industry and space. This was put forward as the main explanation for the visible differences between rural and urban areas such as population density. Urban industrialists can intensify production and expand output without greatly increasing the land area (the factory site, for example) in which production is carried out; farmers, by and large, can only expand production by increasing the area of land that they farm. In this sense, land is a basic element of agricultural production in a way that it is not in industry. Land therefore has an importance in the rural social structure that is quite specific to rural areas; the rural class structure is shaped around land ownership and access to land and has a different form from class structures in urban industrial settings (Buttel and Newby, 1980; Marsden *et al.*, 1993).

In summary, this perspective claimed that, while agriculture and industry are both found in advanced capitalist societies, they are very different in their developmental histories and in their effects on social structures and spatial patterns. This approach also challenges the 'convergence' assumptions built into modernisation theory. It draws our attention to the fact that, under capitalism, the organisation of different forms of work and the social relations involved in them do not necessarily become increasingly similar. In some cases they actually become *less* alike. If this is true of agricultural compared to industrial work, then there may be good reason for saying that rural life is generally different from urban life and should be studied separately.

This approach came close — in the 1970s and 1980s — to transforming rural sociology into a sociology of agriculture and food production (Buttel and Newby, 1980). It stimulated much interesting research in these areas, often concerned to discover the distinctive development paths we might expect agriculture to follow and the varying development experiences of societies with a large agricultural sector and those almost entirely urban and industrial. A notable feature of this research is its rejection of any assumption that agriculture is a backward or less modern branch of contemporary work than urban industry. It does not see the industrialisation of food production as bringing rural areas closer to a universal industrial norm. Rather, it argues that how capitalist industry takes hold of food production differs in very critical ways from how it has taken over the production of most other goods. Difference, not backwardness, is the key idea.

However, trying to redefine 'rural' and 'urban' as 'agricultural' and 'industrial', respectively, also brings difficulties. A rural area today may well contain more non-farm workers than farmers, so it is hard to justify treating rural as if it equated to agricultural. Industries now commonly locate in rural areas, and the future of such areas is more likely to be shaped by global industrial or tourism trends than by the prosperity or otherwise of agriculture. The control that farmers used to have over rural land is being contested by tourist, mining, forestry and other interests, for which the countryside is also a source of exploitable resources. As greater numbers of rural dwellers now commute to work in towns, some rural areas no longer support *any* production, neither industrial nor agricultural, but are locations for *consumption*, whether of housing, scenery or unpolluted air. The distinctive relationship with space as land that used to characterise agriculture may also be dissolving, at least in some instances. In some lines of farming, technological change now allows farmers to expand production without expanding land area. New food production systems such as hydroponic vegetable growing, along with feedlot production of cattle and 'battery' production of pigs and poultry have to an extent turned farming into a set of activities that, were it not for environmental and planning regulations, could probably be carried out just as well in the city.

## The eclipse of community

In Chapter 1, we characterised sociology as the study of modern society and suggested that for many sociologists an important aspect of modernisation is urbanisation. Under the influence of Tönnies and Simmel, the expansion of cities tended to be equated with the growth of impersonal, formal or contractual relationships between people. These replaced the multi-stranded, face-to-face relationships found in small-scale and rural settlements. Thus developed an enduring tradition of thought that superimposed a series of binary oppositions: modernity versus tradition; large-scale versus small-scale; impersonal versus intimate; city life versus rural community. Within this conceptual framework, the development of modernity went hand in hand with the loss or 'eclipse' of community (Stein, 1964).

But to say that community is eclipsed by modernity can mean a number of things. One is what we might call the *eclipse of communality* thesis. If community refers primarily to a type of relationship between people, then this argument proposes that modern individuals find it very hard to establish authentic and intimate relationships with others or to develop a secure sense of identity, and that this was not such a problem in the past, in less modern societies. Certainly many sociologists would agree that individuals in modern society experience problems with identity. Those aspects of personal identity that used to be preordained by membership of social groups and institutions are now increasingly open to individual choice. We may now choose our religion, nationality, family membership, even (with some difficulty) our gender. As such identities can increasingly be selected, constructed and manipulated, it seems to become harder to accept them as being authentic. Yet paradoxically, these same conditions increase the concern about and search for an authentic identity in modern society. Thus, while communality becomes less available to people in modern society, the quest for community intensifies. So we might argue that the development of modernity does not lead to the eclipse of community but to its opposite — a greater valuing of what community might represent.

A second concern is with the contemporary *eclipse of locality*. This combines a number of strands of thought. One is that attachment to local place, and its significance for one's social identity, declines in modern society. Modern social identities are constructed from universalistic categories such as gender, occupation, profession or social class. That you happen to come from Cork or Dublin, or from the Northside or the Southside, has decreasing relevance for how you think about yourself and how others treat you. Indeed, modernisation theory suggests that an essential condition of industrialisation is that people lose such particularistic attachments to a specific local place and, as a consequence, they become spatially and socially mobile, prepared to move to wherever their labour is required. This contributes to the process of nation-building, where identification with the whole territory of the state replaces identification with the specific locality where you were born or raised.

This assumption — that as societies develop, the significance of local differences decline — has been strongly challenged within sociology. For example, dependency theory predicts that economic development *heightens* differences across societies and increasingly differentiates regions and localities, depending on how they are incorporated into the international division of labour. The experience of rural development in Ireland seems to support the dependency position. Rather than an even urbanisation of rural Ireland, there has been an increasing polarisation between east and west (Commins, 1996) and between areas that have specialised in large-scale commercial farming and those where agriculture has declined and has been replaced by industrial and service sector employment. Territorial boundaries may be redrawn in the process of development, but do not disappear (Tovey, 1985). Locality and territoriality continue to play a part in social organisation and people continue to see their own locality as a basis for collective identification, even collective action.

Whether locality is declining as a source of identity and attachment in contemporary society is an empirical question that needs further research. Many people today live in a place they have few positive feelings about or even dislike intensely. This reminds us that it is important not to confuse residence in an area with living in a community. However, this may also have been true for earlier societies — perhaps even more so when escape from a disliked locality was even less of an option for most people then than it is now.

When people talk of the eclipse of locality, they may be claiming that in the contemporary world, local societies can no longer be regarded as self-contained or isolated from the rest of society. In the past, perhaps, it made more sense to think of society as made up of a series of discrete subsocieties, each with its own social and territorial boundaries. We often think of the past as a time when most of people's interactions were with their kin and neighbours, within a circumscribed space. Their lives were lived out within the overlapping social boundaries of the local parish, the catchment area for the local school and shops and the local labour market. Again, this may not be true: while in some previous historical periods people did live in fairly immobile societies, there have been many societies long characterised by large-scale movement of populations — whether as individual migrants or as displaced groups.

Today our daily lives are conducted across a greatly enlarged space, made possible by continual developments in the technology of transport and communications — from the telephone to cheap air travel. In both rural and urban areas today, we cannot assume that local people have lives that are independent of the wider society. Arensberg and Kimball claimed in the 1930s that the small farmers of Co. Clare were largely independent of the national agricultural economy because most of what they produced was consumed within their own households. That may or may not have been accurate then, but it would be difficult today to find farmers in any part of Ireland who were not tied into national or international economic systems. Typically they sell their farm output to large food processing companies and buy their fertiliser, machinery and other farm inputs from TNCs operating on a global scale (see Chapter 3).

The relationships that engage most people in modern society are spread out over a much larger territorial area than in the past. But this is also related to people's class position and income level. In both rural and urban settings, the lives of people from working-class or low-income backgrounds still tend to be conducted within quite constrained spatial boundaries, while it is primarily the middle class and the affluent who are able to escape from the constraints of locality when they wish (Bartley, 1999, pp.242–3). In some of its senses, then, community may be experienced by some social groups in Ireland more than others, and the thesis about eclipse of community may not apply equally to different social groups.

A third argument relates to the *eclipse of local autonomy*. When Stein coined the phrase 'eclipse of community' in the mid-1960s, he was mainly concerned with the spatial distribution of *power*. He argued that throughout the previous century local autonomy enjoyed by small American communities had steadily been eroded, resulting in a concentration of power in the state and federal 'centre'. Such centralisation was a result of urbanisation, industrialisation and bureaucratisation, which had combined to reduce the capacity of local decision-making institutions (local government agencies, local education committees and health boards, local parish organisations) to determine their own affairs.

This echoes the argument outlined above, that modernisation destroys the closed and self-contained nature of local communities, but it stresses the importance of their relations with the state. We noted earlier that the Irish state makes frequent use of the concept of community to address the Irish public, and it often appeals for co-operation between state and community as a way of solving pressing national problems. Yet Stein suggests that it is the centralised, bureaucratic state that is mainly *responsible* for destroying community, by removing local institutions' power to take independent action.

## COMMUNITY IN IRISH SOCIOLOGY AND IRISH SOCIETY

There is a long tradition of ethnographic research on communities in Ireland, much of it concentrated on rural areas and 'perhaps unduly concentrated on peripheral and island communities in the West of Ireland' (Curtin, 1996, p.252). The best known of these, indeed the archetypal account of the Irish community, was by the American anthropologists Arensberg and Kimball, who spent two years in the early 1930s living in and studying a rural area of Co. Clare. Their work gave rise to a number of publications, among them the celebrated *Family and community in Ireland* (1940).

The study area was quite remote — a good distance from the market town of Ennistymon — and was inhabited predominantly by small farmers. Arensberg and Kimball's description of small farming in the locality emphasised its familial nature. They showed how the fortunes of the farm enterprise were entwined with the survival of the family on the land and how the relationships of family members were also those of boss and workers within an enterprise. But they also emphasised how this type of farming gave rise to, and relied upon, particular sorts of local relationships outside the immediate family. Individual farm households, which independently met their own needs by working their privately owned land, were drawn into relationships at the local level through two community institutions: *kinship* (many of the households in the area were related by marriage) and the practice known as *cooring* (the exchange of labour between households, either routinely, or at particular points of the year, such as haymaking, when labour needs were high).

According to Arensberg and Kimball, both these institutions reflected the strong value that local culture placed on the obligations of neighbourliness. The institutions tended also to have a similar effect at local level: they continually reproduced a level of equality between the different farm households in the local area and prevented any from falling into severe poverty or debt, or from becoming particularly wealthy. For Arensberg and Kimball, then, rural life in the 1930s was strongly shaped by the local community and the feelings of mutual identification, mutual dependence and collective solidarity to which it gave rise.

Although Arensberg and Kimball's research methodology and their conclusions have, over the years, been heavily critiqued, their image of the typical rural Irish community has retained its potency. Three features have had particular force. First, Arensberg and Kimball frequently refer to the isolation, remoteness and self-containment of the local area, reinforcing the idea that the people there constituted a naturally distinct and boundaried local society. Local households are shown as economically isolated from the rest of Ireland as, even though they were part of a country-wide system of cattle production, much of their farming was to meet their own consumption needs. The people are also depicted as culturally distinctive from those living in the more anglicised eastern counties. Second, the account tends to emphasise the similarities between households and local residents much more than the differences between them. For example, there are few non-farming households in the locality; and there are no big variations in the size of local farms. Though there were both big and small farmers in Ireland at the time, Arensberg and Kimball suggest that each tended to be found in different localities, and thus in different communities.

Third, in a local economy of this sort there are many occasions for conflict, such as between father/farm boss and sons/farm labourers, between family members around inheritance, or between households over ownership of land, but the strongest impression in the study is of agreement and harmony. This image of rural community — self-contained and separate from 'society in general', homogeneous, bound together by local institutions and characterised by co-operation and consensus — continues to dominate contemporary 'community' discourse in Ireland. It permeates public belief about what Irish society was like in the past and what, ideally, it should be like today.

Curtin (1988, p.77) has argued that Arensberg and Kimball did not entirely ignore conflict, but for 'theoretical and methodological reasons' were more interested in exploring social harmony, stability and integration. The problem was in how their research was taken up by others: 'for long, the generally uncritical acceptance of their account . . . discouraged the discovery and analysis of conflicts of interests as normal social structural features of rural communities.' Most subsequent sociological and anthropological studies of Irish rural communities have ignored conflict; strange, perhaps, given the broader interest — especially among anthropologists — in issues such as informal dispute-resolution in small-scale societies. Explanations for the maintenance of social order in rural Irish communities have, in their appeal to qualities of 'nativism' and 'primitivism', tended to produce a rather misleading image of social harmony. Similarly, much attention has been focused on the role of the Catholic Church. This has led researchers to exaggerate the Catholic moral virtues embodied in the Irish family and community. Where local disputes have been studied (Leyton, 1966, Messenger, 1969) they have generally been treated 'as events almost separate from the general pattern of social relationships' or 'dysfunctional elements of a taken-for-granted social order' (Curtin, 1988, p.78).

A potential source of dissimilarity, difference and conflict within communities is that of *gender*. Arensberg and Kimball largely sidestep this phenomenon: while recognising the very different lives led by women and men in rural Ireland, they treat gender roles as complementary and mutually reinforcing. Brody, in a later (1973) study of a western small-farm area, depicted men and women as living in virtually separate communities, so different were their life experiences, identities and aspirations. According to Brody, the local institutions at the core of the rural community were the shop and the pub. Those whose social life revolved around the shop were most marginal to the 'traditional' community: young single women expecting to emigrate, and older married women who — despite active involvement in farm work — were not regarded as having any particular farming skills or knowledge. The frequenters of the pub were men identified with the agricultural life of the area, mainly older farm owners, but also some younger expectant heirs. Thus, suggested Brody (1973, p.164), 'the one place outside the home which people regularly visit thus identifies their relationship to the community.' Indeed, for young men to visit the shop rather than the pub was an indication that they were seeking an identity outside the local farming community and were highly likely to emigrate in the near future.

Rural Ireland had undergone a process of urbanisation since the time of Arensberg and Kimball's visit. At the time of Brody's work, the younger generation in the countryside had adopted an urban view that saw little to value or conserve in rural life. As a result, those left behind in rural areas had become profoundly demoralised. Brody, like so many sociologists before him, linked urbanisation to a weakening in the bonds of community. He noted the decline of co-operation or *cooring* in farmwork, the new isolation of local households from each other, the growth of individualism among the young and the increasing emphasis on self and self-realisation against the claims of community membership. For Brody, modern life or, as he calls it, 'urban capitalism', tolled the death-knell of community — an image that resonates in Curtin's (1988, pp.82–3) vivid description of an atomised rural life pervaded by an absence of community:

> Households in the villages are intensely private and neighbours seldom visit. On a journey through the area on a winter's night, one sees each house distinguished by the flashing television screen. On entering a house, one finds individuals or families alone. Indeed people are unsure how to handle the unexpected visitor. 'Pure' social calls have little meaning and one is expected to state one's business at the door. People do not like to be caught unaware by a caller and indeed callers seldom catch occupiers unaware. In many houses, the front door is rarely used, which means that one has to go round the house. Barking dogs give advance warning and delay the visitor. On reaching the back door, the impression is of an intensely private order being invaded.

## Community action and the ideology of community

While the eclipse of community thesis has had considerable support from Irish research into rural communities, a number of studies have examined the discourse of community and how it is produced, used and appealed to by specific social actors. This approach suggests that, however the communities themselves are regarded, a *rhetoric of community* is alive and well in Ireland and is persistently and frequently reproduced in public debates and discussions. A number of writers have sought to explain the persistence of this rhetoric in instrumental terms. They emphasise its usefulness to powerful groups in Irish society, including the state and its agents. They argue that evocations of community, and of what the community wants and needs, can be an effective way to legitimise the actions of those in power, and to minimise challenges from those disadvantaged as a result.

Harris's (1984) anthropological study of industrial development in North Mayo offers this type of account. The development was a product of globalisation and the new international division of labour: encouraged by the IDA, two branch plants of multinational companies located in the area and proceeded to dominate the local economy with regard to employment provision. This produced some important changes in the local society, not least a large growth in the number of women working outside the home since the factories mainly sought female workers. In addition, the industrial development benefited some locals more than others, bringing most benefits to those who were property-owners or entrepreneurs who could sell land or other commodities to the new factories or could profit from the increased spending power in the area.

Harris argues that the coming of transnational capital to Ireland severely challenges a view of Irish nationhood that sees a self-contained economy as an essential part of the nation. Economic globalisation fractures the unity of the national economy: local areas may become more oriented to the global horizon of the TNC than to other localities within Ireland. As the reality of 'the nation' becomes ephemeral and change becomes ubiquitous, it becomes necessary to find an alternative source of collective identity. Community provides just such an alternative.

It is within this context that Harris explains the uses of community in North Mayo. The management of the new firms, the state (via the IDA) and members of the local bourgeoisie represented the industrialisation process to local people as a way to help the whole local community. Harris argues that this strategy to create a local consensus around economic development does not equally favour everyone in the community; indeed, when overt conflict arose, local leaders responded by redefining the boundaries of the community. For example, when fitters in one of the factories took unofficial strike action in pursuit of union recognition, the factory threatened to withdraw its operations from Ireland if they did not return to work. This led the local Community Council to intervene and demand that the men should go back to work or leave the area. According to Harris (1984, p.163):

'troublemakers working against the interests of the community' were not welcome. The fitters, who might well be seen as part of the local 'community' by virtue of their residence in the town, were thus defined out of the community until such time as they submitted to the local consensus.

O'Carroll (1985, p.147) suggests that organisations such as Community Councils, who claim to 'represent the community', are in effect a local extension of the state. When people claim to be community leaders, this encourages others to think that behind them there is 'a solidly united community with whom they have close ties, share a common value system and over whom they can exercise authority'. For O'Carroll, that type of community no longer exists. In reality most community or similar voluntary organisations are set up with the encouragement or at the instigation of the state; those who emerge as community leaders at the head of such organisations are as likely to owe their position to the operations of the state as to any sort of community franchise.

Irish state and other agencies most commonly use the term 'community' in connection with aspects of service-delivery, for example, in the areas of welfare, health, education or development. Thus, community services are generally not organised by the local community on the basis of a diagnosis its own needs, but are nearly always services delivered to residents in a locality. Community policing is a case in point; it refers not to policing by the community of itself, but to policing by the state, delivered to those living in a particular area with the co-operation of local organisations such as residents' associations. The use of 'community', according to O'Carroll, is a rhetorical flourish. It obscures the fact that the state does no more than deliver services to the Irish population on a *territorial* basis — by geographical locality, rather than by gender, class or age. Its primary purpose is to confer legitimacy on state activities. In North Mayo, as discussed by Harris, it maintains an appearance of agreement around a development process that might otherwise be recognised as a source of increasing social inequality. In the case of community policing, it helps to maintain support for localised state intervention in support of social order.

O'Carroll (1998) uses a similar framework to look at the Blood Transfusion Service Board (BTSB) in Ireland. In Ireland, he notes, blood donation is surrounded by a 'community ethos': it is organised on the principle that it should be a free gift between strangers, not a market exchange as in the United States. But the transfusion service has not always worked to benefit the community in Ireland. When the system broke down in the case of the Hepatitis C scandal, the BTSB made recourse to the community principle, in order to 'prevent change and ignore uncertainty while failing to minimise the risk of infection' (1998, p.113). Thus the BTSB, O'Carroll suggests, prioritised maintaining 'public confidence' over securing the safety of the public who used its services.

## Community action

If the state and other powerful agents in Irish society can invoke an ideology of community in order to get certain things done, can ordinary residents in a locality not do so too? And if the state enjoys enhanced legitimacy from using a rhetoric of community, might this not also be true of local actors and groups? As suggested earlier, there is reason to expect that spatial inequality, in a globalised society, is as much a part of people's everyday experience as other inequalities. Thus, much collective action in Irish society appeals to community rather than to, say, class or gender. This 'urge towards community' has a long history in Ireland, going back at least to the self-help strategies of Muintir na Tíre in the 1930s. Moreover, as Curtin (1996, p.268) points out, the idea that community-based groups could help to tackle problems of rural poverty and disadvantage is neither novel nor peculiar to Ireland. As an approach it was sponsored both by the US government and by development agencies associated with the United Nations as a way to respond to the problems of rural areas in Asia, Africa and Latin America.

Community mobilisation or action may, as Harris argues, be a way for advantaged groups to work with the state to maintain their local dominance. But it may also take the form of a mobilisation *against* the state, in particular against the appropriation of power from the local level as Stein highlights. The two approaches to community action have been usefully typified as *integrationist* and *oppositional* (Curtin and Varley, 1995). The former tendency can be seen, for example, in the work of Muintir na Tíre and its structure of Community Councils. Curtin and Varley (1995, p.379) see this organisation as remarkable for its 'all-together' ideology. It has an ability to project itself as concerned only with the 'common good' and to transcend divisions of class, party, gender, religion or even space. This allows it to claim to speak for the locality as a whole and that all locals stand to benefit from its activities. The strategy of the Community Councils is to try to build partnership ties with the state and to work through established political networks using traditional political methods such as lobbying.

The oppositional tendency, on the other hand, found its expression in the 'social action' elements of the first EC-funded anti-poverty programme in the 1970s (Curtin and Varley, 1995, p.380). The programme adopted a view of community that focused on disadvantaged categories *within* localities, such as low-income farmers or women with no independent source of income. It did not emphasise a partnership with the state; indeed, it argued that the state actively helped to underpin structures of disadvantage, and that redistribution of wealth and power would require struggle, confrontation and consciousness-raising tactics — including confrontation with the state and its agencies.

The two approaches to community action are thus distinguished by their attitude towards the state: is it part of the solution, or part of the problem? But analysts of community action have also noted that the Irish state's orientation to community development groups has varied over time. Until the 1980s, it saw such groups as having no more than a marginal contribution to make to local social service provision and as largely irrelevant to economic development. But since then the community sector has come to be constituted as a significant actor in its own right, certainly in policy discourse if not in the political process itself. The change is visible, for example, in the development of the FÁS community enterprise programme (CEP), the Third EC Programme to Combat Poverty, and a series of mainly EU-inspired 'area-based development programmes' since the late 1980s. These have included the Forum programme in Connemara; the PAUL project in Limerick; the Pilot Programme for Integrated Rural Development, the LEADER I and II programmes, and the establishment of 38 locally based partnership companies and numerous other 'partnership' organisations (Geddes, 1998, pp.56–60). These institutional mechanisms have helped to place terms like 'partnership' and 'participation' at the centre of contemporary development discourse both in Ireland and in the international sphere (Share and Curley, 1997; Sabel, 1996). They are evidence of an attempt by national and EU institutions to 'institute a formal structure of co-operation between the state and local actors' (Curtin and Varley, 1995, p.383).

What may be distinctive and interesting about the current phase of community development is how it has been driven by state agencies. A number of critics (Curtin and Varley, 1995; Community Workers' Co-operative (CWC), 1996) have argued that state interests, as much as any 'bottom-up' demands from the community, have elevated 'community' to a prominent policy position. We can thus ask: why has the Irish state now become interested in fostering this model of community development, and what are the implications for local development groups? Here we might note the failure of the state, for the 1980s and much of the 1990s, to respond effectively to the issue of unemployment, in particular the collapse of agricultural employment and long-term unemployment in urban 'black spots'. Its response, spurred by the availability of targeted EU funds, was to develop a discourse of 'co-responsibility' for economic growth. Stimulation of the economy, and to a certain extent provision of services, was now a job for both state and community.

One of the most significant implications of this approach has been the decline of oppositional tendencies in community action and the triumph of the *integrationist* approach. Curtin (1996, p.268) suggests that 'playing according to the rules of this new game may mean that empowerment of the poor is now to be achieved not through protest and conflict with power-holders, but through consensus-based partnerships.' Groups that are not included in the local coalition of community and state agencies may find themselves excluded from local development strategies. But for those groups that are included, the experience may be unsatisfactory. The activity open to the partnerships may reflect the availability of funding rather than a commitment to ideals of community development (CWC, 1996). The responsibilities that the partnerships and constituent voluntary groups take on may be very burdensome. Another problem is that the development strategies that evolve from local partnerships generally fail to be integrated effectively into regional or national planning. Finally, despite a growing rhetoric of 'participation' in development policy discourse in Ireland, many elite groups remain hostile to the idea of participatory democracy. Hostility appears particularly entrenched within sectors of the civil service, which has been pervaded (Commins, 1985) by a 'technocratic or managerialist ethos' that often conflicts with the democratic and participative ideals of community groups. Crowley and Watt (1992; see also Rolston, 1991) argue that the state's interest in entering into partnership with community groups derives mainly from its interest in maintaining control over the economy — 'partnership' community development strategies, where control of funding remains in the hand of the state, enhance its control over local economic activity.

So, is the oppositional tendency in community activism completely dead? The legacy of Fr. McDyer's mobilisation in Glencolmcille (Tucker, 1987) — which challenged the Irish state's core assumptions about the nature of development — may linger on in movements like the Campaign for the West. But examples of opposition today are more often found in single-issue campaigns, for example, against hospital closures or the erection of mobile phone masts. The focus of such campaigns tends to be on resisting the impact of national planning strategies on a specific locality, rather than attacking the strategies themselves. Yet the distinction is not clear-cut. Curtin and Varley highlight examples of how local women's groups may understand themselves to be community-based and to that extent integrationist, even while using local relationships as an opportunity to forward feminist principles and forms of social analysis.

There have been instances since the late 1970s where local communities have vigorously resisted the introduction of certain sorts of industrial production, such as the opposition by residents of Killeagh, Co. Cork, to the siting in their locality of a Merrill Dow chemicals plant (Peace, 1993; Tovey, 1993). At stake in such struggles is the principle that how local resources should be used (and the meaning of development itself) should be determined by local people, not by the central state or by the IDA. Thus, the integrationist and oppositional tendencies can be linked together in particular campaigns in complex ways. There are times, then, when we might want to argue that an ideology of community is being used to empower local groups and institutions rather than to disempower them. But it always remains important to investigate *which* local people and local institutions are being included and which are being excluded, whenever 'community' is evoked.

## RE-CREATING COMMUNITY

Irish sociologists may increasingly treat the concept of community with suspicion, but elsewhere there has been a marked resurgence of interest in it. This is linked to a new political and philosophical movement known as *communitarianism* (Crow and Allen, 1994), which claims affinities with a range of attempts 'on the ground' to build 'inclusive communities'. These include various forms of community politics at the local level, EU initiatives to create various forms of membership groups that cross national borders, and the United Nation's 'Local Agenda 21'.

Communitarians define their activities as 'the politics of building inclusive communities' (Tam, 1998). Such communities are based on the citizen as the central agent, and their power relations are organised in such a way as to enable universal participation, not excluding any members. Communitarians emphasise that they are not trying to go backwards to create some idealised pre-industrial community, but to develop new principles for organising social, economic and political life. They see similarities between their movement and the co-operative movement of the nineteenth century (which in Ireland led to the establishment of co-operative creameries and other food processing organisations, and to the Credit Union movement). They believe that 'co-operative communities', which respect and care for all their members, are necessary for social well-being and that social and political progress depends on finding 'a third way' between right and left, or between individualism and authoritarianism.

Communitarianism is a movement that identifies, and then tries to address, three sets of problems in contemporary society:

- the collapse or threatened collapse of collective forms of identity
- the decline of trust in 'experts' and other authorities
- the problem of citizenship.

Groups, organisations and other types of collectivities are failing to supply people with a stable sense of identity to counter the individualism generated by a world organised around market competition. Communitarians look to Durkheim as someone who contributed to the development of 'a communitarian form of liberalism' in opposition to the individualistic liberalism that threatens to destroy social solidarity (Tam, 1998, p.3). Building on Durkheim's ideas, the American sociologist Amitai Etzioni, one of the best known of contemporary communitarian theorists, defines the objective of the communitarian movement as to 'provide the social bonds that sustain the moral voice, but at the same time avoid tight networks that suppress pluralism and dissent' (1995, p.122).

The re-creation of community is also put forward as a solution to the loss of trust in authority that is said to typify late modern societies. O'Carroll, commenting on the involvement of the BTSB in the spread of Hepatitis C, remarks that 'until the disclosures of the blood tribunal, the level of trust in blood in Ireland remained quite high . . . post-tribunal Ireland will be a fundamentally different Ireland precisely because it will be characterised by a shift from trust in experts and public institutions to the calculation of risk involved in participation in them' (1998, p.114). Peillon argues that crises of trust, in the church, in medical institutions and in food, is rapidly propelling Ireland towards the state that Giddens has termed 'high modernity'. For Peillon (1998, p.118), Irish society illustrates Giddens's thesis that a change in trust is central to the transformation of modern societies:

> In traditional societies, trust follows the network of face-to-face relations, those of community, kinship or friendship. One trusts what is familiar and this trust is sustained by traditional rules and personal loyalty. The development of the industrial society has brought about what [Giddens] calls *simple modernity*, in which trust has become more impersonal. Every day one trusts the technical competence of other people, the expertise of those who possess the relevant specialised knowledge. Today, whole populations are learning that experts disagree with each other and have no monopoly of truth. The unreliability of the expert-systems has created the real possibility of a generalised collapse of trust, and has ushered in another stage of modernity: that of *high modernity* in which we still depend on abstract and expert systems but we are now responsible for the expertise we choose to trust.

The communitarian idea of inclusive communities is an attempt to address and resolve the issue of loss of trust. But — in a quite post-modern way — it does not attempt to restate the traditional authority of the expert, but calls for the creation of a form of community life that allows for open and public debate between experts and ordinary citizens (Tam, 1998, p.7):

> Any claim about what is to be accepted as true can only be validated under conditions of co-operative enquiry . . . questions about what collective action is to be taken for the common good are not to be left to political elites who are rarely answerable to their fellow citizens . . . or [left to] to individuals in the marketplace.

Communitarianism tries to redevelop what Habermas has called 'the public sphere', an arena of open debate in which, ideally, all citizens, as reasoning beings, can participate on equal terms and all authorities can be called on to justify, through reasonable debate, their authoritative pronouncements.

The concept of *citizenship* is central to communitarian thought. To many writers on community, particularly those more sceptical of it, citizenship and community are conceptions of the individual/society relationship that, at best, pass each other without touching or, at worst, are actively hostile to each other. But for communitarians the development of community is also the development of citizenship. They call for a form of civil society that exhibits three characteristics (Tam, 1998, p.197). Citizens should:

- take responsibility for values that go beyond themselves (for example, volunteering to care for others)
- work together as equals in voluntary and community groups to achieve together what they cannot achieve alone
- provide a 'third force' to balance state and market activities.

Community, in this context, does not refer to a social entity with a local place or distinctive culture, but to a way of acting in society and of relating to others that can be inscribed in the organisational principles that govern every institution in society, from the family to the firm (Tam, 1998, p.219). Community is then what gives civil society its civility.

## The critique of communitarianism

Communitarianism makes a brave attempt to reconstruct the idea of community so that it can be located within radical democratic politics. But many commentators are not convinced. Curtin (1996, pp.249–50) reminds us of the perennially ambiguous nature of the concept:

> In the left-populist perspective, community is best understood as expanding participatory democracy, providing for more direct forms of government,

decentralised decision-making and even political and economic equality . . . [but] community . . . is also much in favour with the conservative political tradition. Here, however, the emphasis is on the notion of community as common good, on public-spirited individuals with respect for the rights of others, on authority and order and on reducing civil society's dependence on the state. . . . Community is a symbolic construct capable of invoking for all its supporters the positive notion of communality and sharing, but also presenting the possibility of being subjected, in each case, to particular meanings.

Critics of communitarianism tend to see in it a conservative movement that masquerades as radical. They claim, for instance, that the communitarian view of citizenship emphasises the obligations of the individual to the community at the expense of the rights of the individual against community controls.

American sociologist and political activist Richard Sennett, in *The fall of public man*, argued that attempts to establish 'real communities' should be recognised as 'a tyranny of intimacy' that converted 'claustrophobia into an ethical principle' (1977, p.310). Sennett was highly sceptical of the move towards localism in political practice and sociological thinking, driven by a nostalgic belief that a more 'intimate scale' of public relationships would change the nature of a system of international power that was ever-expanding. For communitarians (Sennett, 1977, p.339):

Community becomes a weapon against society, whose great vice is now seen to be its impersonality. But a community of power can only be an illusion in a society like that of the industrial West, one in which stability has been achieved by a progressive extension to the international scale of structures of economic control. . . . The result is that the forces of domination or inequality remain unchallenged.

Communitarians have been accused of being complacent about traditional social arrangements, failing to recognise their intolerance or capacities for repression. For feminist theorist Iris Marion Young (1990, p.300), communitarianism favours 'unity over difference, immediacy over mediation, sympathy over recognition of the limits of one's understanding of others from their point of view'. She suggests that communitarianism ignores how communities can make illegitimate moral claims on their members. Many find the 'paradigm communities' that communitarians invoke — family, neighbourhood, nation — particularly troubling in this respect. Young argues that such communities can never be genuinely inclusive. Their identity always depends on the exclusion of some people, since 'any definition of what members have in common necessarily implies some form of closure against "outsiders"' (Day, 1998, p.235). Her own position is to advocate 'a politics of difference' not a politics of community, one that recognises the extent of heterogeneity and particularity of individuals that can never be exhausted by collective categorisation. In a reversal of Simmel, Young idealises the sort of relationship that can be 'experienced between strangers in the life of the city' (Day, 1998, p.235). Indeed, our discussion has traced a full circle: community is opposed to (post-)modernity as rural is to urban.

When, in the late nineteenth century, Tönnies started a debate on community, it was in an attempt to raise serious questions about what he saw as the destructive impact of modern industrial society on the human spirit. The debate that has recently been regenerated by the communitarian movement also questions the impact of late or post-modern society on individuals and on their relations with larger collectivities. How can we develop a sense of social identity if not through membership in larger communities? Are certain sorts of communal bonds — a sense of pride in an identity that is shared with others — necessary if we are to exercise public-spirited commitments? Will a growing ethos of self-fulfilment destroy 'the traditional community ties that are necessary for active citizenship' (Lichterman, 1996, p.1)?

Lichterman argues that contemporary culture encourages the idea that one's own individuality has inherent — even supreme — value. This orientation, which he terms 'personalism', upholds (1996, p.6, [italics added]):

> a personal self that lives with ambivalence towards, and often in tension with, the institutional or communal standards that surround it . . . personalism does not necessarily deny the existence of communities surrounding and shaping the self, but it accentuates an individualised relationship to any such communities. In contrast with a political identity that is defined by membership in a local, national, or global polity, a traditional religious identity that gets realised in a fellowship of believers, or a communal identity that develops in relation to a specific community, the personal self gets developed by *reflecting on individual biography, by establishing one's own individuality amidst an array of cultural, religious, or political authorities.*

Lichterman's discussion suggests that community, far from being an uninteresting or outdated concept for a late modern sociology, is as central as ever. But sociology needs to rethink the questions it has usually asked about community. If late modern society is moving towards a form of identity that is personalised rather than collectively shared, how can we be encouraged to practice personalised political commitments? And what social and political forms of communality can best help us to do so?

## POSTSCRIPT: COMMUNITY STUDIES AS SOCIOLOGICAL METHOD

It can be said of Arensberg and Kimball's work that, although it purports to offer a general view of rural society and community in Ireland, it is no more than a study of a very specific and possibly rather unique place: two townlands in the hinterland of Ennis. It may be illegitimate to generalise from that specific place to wider social conditions, but it is open to question (Wilson, 1984; Gibbon, 1973) as to whether this is what the American anthropologists were intending. Arguably they were more interested in testing a particular social theory in a specific location — Clare is where they happened to find themselves. It would be fairer to say that generations of Irish sociologists have read Arensberg and Kimball's work *as if* it were about (rural) Ireland in general, rather than being a study of a particular place and time.

However, the idea that you can study a society by studying individual communities has a long, if contentious, history within sociology. Ethnographic research in a spatially defined area — the community studies method — has attracted sociologists who aspire to a mode of research that is perhaps more holistic and qualitative and can better capture the complexities of people's life experiences. Curtin (1996, p.251) makes the point that, while official statistics and surveys can provide useful information in relation to social structure and socio-economic conditions, they cannot reveal the more subtle aspects of life that manifest as people carry out their everyday tasks and as local social relationships are created and re-created. An ethnographic or community studies approach, he suggests, can 'go a long way towards filling the gaps in our knowledge of local social experience'.

But the community studies approach has attracted much criticism. The severest complaints concern the possibility of generalising the findings within an individual community to the broader society. Community studies researchers have often tried to argue that life in the community they studied was 'at once distinct and unique, but also representative' (Day, 1998, p.237) but critics deny this possibility. Studying a series of communities, they claim, cannot generate cumulative knowledge about society but only a succession of interesting but unrelated slice-of-life portraits. Bell and Newby refer to 'that bane of community studies, non-comparability of data' (1971, p.140), while Harper says that community studies exhibit 'a complete absence of common framework or theoretical position, indeed most of these studies lack an individual theoretical position and this severely questions their contribution to the general theme of rural life' (1989, p.165).

According to Crow and Allen (1994), as the community studies approach does not produce work that is cumulative, it is not easily incorporated into the mainstream of social theory and analysis. There is a strong feeling among critics that 'whatever their individual merits, the various studies do not display enough continuity and comparability to allow useful generalisation, of the kind that has been regarded widely as the end goal of the social sciences' (Day, 1998, p.233). Analyses of individual communities may have value as *case studies* that may illustrate a larger theme (such as rural modernisation) or suggest possible new lines of exploration and add, as Day says, 'some richness of observation to the sociologist's diet' (1998, p.234). But they may be no more than, as Glass (1966) somewhat contemptuously suggests, the sociologist's inadequate substitute for the novel.

A second criticism of community studies relates to how they portray the community. Wright (1992, p.202) suggests that this tends to be in an ahistorical vein with a focus on equilibrium and order within the community and being unable to explain social change. Similar critiques have been made of Arensberg and Kimball's work (Gibbon, 1973). Day (1998) indicates that this sort of criticism has become standard. Community studies are said to represent communities as if they were clearly defined, their boundaries well known and understood, and without ambiguity as to who is inside or outside the community. They are said to represent communities as if they were always small-scale and characterised by consistent, coherent sets of relationships that behave 'in a system-like way to maintain the status quo and resist external pressures for change.' In other words, communities tend to be portrayed, within community studies, as devoid of structurally based conflicts and to persist largely unchanged over time. How telling these sorts of criticisms are may be open to question. While it is true that many studies, particularly those of rural communities, have tended to produce limited accounts of community life, it could be argued that this reflects the theoretical ideas that underpin the research as much as the research methodology.

Within the small body of community studies in Ireland, one work stands out as having a more interesting and challenging set of theoretical premises: the work of Australian anthropologist/sociologist Chris Eipper, who carried out a study of the town of Bantry in the early 1980s, published in 1986 as *The ruling trinity*. Eipper aims to reinterpret 'the conceptual parameters' of community studies. He argues that the 'local level' cannot be analysed in isolation from national and international 'levels', nor be treated as a micro-system within a larger society or social system. Community and society are in his view not separate or separable systems: to research a local community is but one way to develop an understanding of social life. It can provide us with some valuable insights but cannot in any way give us a complete picture of reality.

Eipper's primary interest is in the analysis of class dynamics as these influence the reproduction of power and consciousness in Irish society (see Chapter 6 for further discussion). His work is an exploration of the class character of the relationship between the 'ruling trinity' of church, state and business. He argues that these relationships occur both locally and nationally and can, in fact, *must* be studied in both settings. Eipper thus explicitly rejects the idea, so often conveyed in community studies, that class is something external to — even an intrusion into — the local community. For him, class relations in Ireland and especially those between state, church and business have been forged and exert their influence simultaneously at local and national levels.

Eipper's is a study of 'development' in Bantry. It documents the arrival of the transnational company Gulf Oil and traces its impact on pre-existing power relationships in the town, particularly economic (between local employers and their labour forces) but also the social, political and ideological forms of power. It examines the involvement of state agencies, such as the IDA, and other national actors in managing the economic process at the local level. Eipper examines both how international capitalist forces and economic trends were dealt with locally, but also how they shaped the locality itself. Thus, he tries to escape the tendency in many community studies to treat macro-level structures as if they were no more than contextualising constraints on micro-level interaction patterns.

From this perspective, community studies offer an opportunity to sociologists interested in class and power relations in society that most other research methodologies miss: 'how to analyse class as it is lived in a specific social habitat' (Eipper, 1986, p.7). All of us, Eipper suggests, experience class power in our everyday lives in two ways: as impersonal power, exercised over us by functionaries who are acting as the representatives or agents of remote or abstracted organisations; and as personal power, exercised over us by people acting 'in their own right' and in face-to-face, multidimensional contacts. How we respond to each of these processes influences and constrains our capacity to respond to the other. If we accept the personal authority of the local big employer, we may find it less easy to reject the power of the business class in general to determine Ireland's economic and social destiny. On the other hand, to undermine the personal authority of employers at the local level may generate resistance to the broader structuring of power characteristic of capitalist society. Owners of businesses in Bantry, politicians, civil servants, clergy and lay functionaries, Eipper suggests, literally 'personified' the reproduction of a Catholic-nationalist corporatist state in Ireland. Through their own activities as members of local society, they contributed both to reproducing and changing the character of the national ruling bloc.

Though Eipper is rather unclear as to whether Bantry is a 'locality' or a 'community', his emphasis on change, power, conflict, division and opposition, and on the study of local life as a way to better explain the structures of the broader society, suggest that a community studies methodology retains much value. Community, though a much maligned term in global sociology, may continue to provide a way to better understand the complexities of Irish society and everyday life.

# 14
# Media

In their book *Australian television and international mediascapes* Cunningham and Jacka state that (1996, p.3):

> The last ten years have seen profound changes in television cultures of many countries. Technological innovation, industrial realignments and changes in regulatory philosophy have transformed a collection of comparatively self-contained systems into one of increasingly international patterns of ownership and increasingly global flows of programming.

Why open this chapter with a quote from a book about *Australian* television? First, it concisely identifies some of the key technological and industrial trends that are shaping the contemporary mass media; expansion on these themes will form an important element of this chapter. Second, we believe a link with Australian experience might be apt for at least some of the following reasons. Australia and Ireland are at opposite and possibly peripheral ends of a transnational, English-language media globe. But each has a media and cultural influence that significantly outweighs its political or economic position, from *Neighbours* to *Riverdance* to U2 and the BeeGees. Each is intimately incorporated in each other's media industry: Australian content forms a significant element of Irish TV programming; the Irish-based company Independent News and Media controls the bulk of Australia's non-metropolitan newspaper industry, and is a significant media player in that country.

Both countries are being increasingly penetrated by global media organisations and forms. For example, in each, a commercial television station (TV3 in Ireland/Network 10 in Australia) is controlled by the same Canadian company, Canwest. At the same time, both are doing a bit of global expansion of their own: Australia into South-east Asia and the South Pacific; Ireland into South Africa and New Zealand, for example. Each nation has identified the so-called 'content industries', from tourism to film-making and fashion, as key drivers of economic growth and employment, and has developed state policies in support of these. Crucially, in each country there is much concern about issues of media influence, ownership and control, new technologies, and national cultural identity.

In both Ireland and Australia, as in the whole of the developed world, the mass media have become ubiquitous, pervasive and a part of our existence that is taken for granted. As the French sociologist Sorlin (1994, p.17) remarks: 'there is no immunity against the media. Even people who never read a newspaper and have no television set are surrounded by messages, be it only advertisements stuck on walls.' We routinely make use of the media in every aspect of our lives: the radio provides company as we start the day; our trip around the supermarket is accompanied by piped music and advertising; we spend many hours in front of the TV set as it carries signals from cable, video, DVD or computer game console; we look to newspapers, magazines, books, CD-ROMs or the World Wide Web for information on any topic we wish; CDs or tapes provide background music as we work or socialise or travel.

In some ways it is impossible to separate out 'the media' as a discrete entity within our society. Many of the issues and aspects of social life we have discussed in this book are permeated by the technologies and processes of the media. For example, our knowledge and understanding of crime is almost entirely determined by the media; the political process takes place largely through the newspapers, radio and television; our notion of ourselves as a modern society is expressed through advertising imagery, film and video and popular music; even the contours of class and inequality are reflected in the choices we make (and can make) about what sorts of films to watch, books to read, radio stations to listen to or newspapers to purchase.

It is possible to apply a sociological imagination and critically examine the history, nature and development of media *institutions*, as organisations that pursue particular ends, from the creation of a national identity to the maximisation of profit. We can also analyse the content of media *messages*, whether they have obvious meanings that lie on the surface, or deeper, structural patterns that reveal themselves only through systematic processing and theorising. Furthermore, we can look at how people, as *audiences*, consume the media, and how they make their own sense of what they see on the screen, or read from the page, or hear on the dancefloor.

## SOCIOLOGY AND THE STUDY OF THE MEDIA

Despite how the mass media have insinuated themselves into every aspect of our daily lives, sociologists have perhaps paid them less attention than they might. There may be a number of reasons for this comparative neglect. First, sociologists have until recently tended to pay comparatively little attention to private aspects of everyday life, such as domestic work, food preparation and consumption, or everyday leisure activities. There has tended to be more emphasis on public aspects of modern society which were seen to be more important, such as work, politics and education. The mass media, as a part of life that is largely private, domestic and mundane, especially in terms of its consumption, have been victims of this emphasis.

Second, the mass media have been neglected in academic study as they fall on the wrong side of the high culture/popular culture divide. Apart from what is sometimes seen to be the more 'serious' side of the media (news, current affairs, politics and — because of its links with business and propaganda — advertising), the bulk of media output — soap operas, romance novels, chat shows, pop music — has tended to be viewed as trivial and unworthy of academic attention. There is also a strong gender division here. It is no coincidence that the media forms listed above are those that have tended to be consumed by, and associated with, a female audience.

Third, the mass media are very much a creation of two forces — technology and economics — that have tended to be neglected by sociologists, though with some notable exceptions. Sociologists, especially within the European tradition, have been demonstrably uncomfortable with analysing the commercial world of the media, except in critical terms; they are far more comfortable with the world of public service broadcasting. Similarly, and again with some important exceptions, sociologists have not examined in great detail the technological basis of our modern society. They tend to be more at home with texts (other people's and their own) than with machines, buildings or technological systems.

Finally, into the vacuum left by sociology, the analysis of the media has been largely taken over by other cognate disciplines, such as media studies, communications and cultural studies. The work in these areas draws inspiration as much from literary theory, philosophy and psychology as from sociological writers. In the United States, for example, the discipline of communications is heavily dominated by psychology while in Europe philosophy and literary criticism have provided much of the language for analysing the media. Given the well-established modes of criticism and analysis within these relatively new disciplines and inter-disciplinary fields, does sociology have anything distinctive to contribute to an understanding of the media?

We would argue that it is important to maintain a sociological dimension to studies of the media and that this can provide a useful complement to other approaches. In particular, sociologists can help to look at how people create, use and interpret the media; in this way they can balance analyses that tend to focus very much on the media as text, such as those derived from literary and film theory. Sociologists can make use of social theories and categorisations to examine how media processes are underpinned by relationships of power and inequality. According to Mary Kelly and Barbara O'Connor (1997, p.1), in one of the few published collections of sociological analyses of the Irish media, 'access to and mode of participation in [media] cultures are structured and limited by social class, by gender, by ethnicity, by location in space, and by generation.' Sociological analyses can also help us to understand how people use and interpret the media —

how television, cinema, radio and other media forms are integrated into the textures of everyday life.

Given the ubiquity and pervasiveness of the media, there are many ways that they could be studied and analysed. In this chapter we have chosen to follow a fairly conventional approach, in essence derived from mechanical concepts of the communication process. In this model (S→M→R) a Sender transmits a Message to a Receiver. In sociological terms we can think of these three elements as:

- the *producer* of the media message
- the message itself (or *text*)
- the *audience* for the message.

In reality, the process of communication is far more complex than this model suggests (see Sless, 1986) and engineering metaphors have not always been particularly helpful in understanding the human communication process but, for our purposes, it is useful to organise our survey of the media in this way.

Before looking at these three aspects in some detail, we start with a brief review of theoretical approaches to the media. We follow this with an overview of the development of the mass media in Ireland. In particular, we focus on the media in relation to the issues that have formed a key theme of this book: the experience of modernity and questions about the nature of development in Ireland. We then consider the three aspects of production, texts and audiences. This is followed by an examination of some significant sociological and social policy issues in relation to the Irish media; and we conclude with a discussion of how the media and communications industries may develop in the future, and what the sociological implications of such developments might be.

## THEORETICAL MODELS FOR UNDERSTANDING THE MEDIA

There are very many theoretical models for understanding how the mass media 'work', which range from communication theories derived from engineering, to psychological and psychoanalytic models and a wide range of sociological theories that mirror the dominant perspectives within sociology. With limited space here we briefly outline some main points but for an exhaustive but accessible discussion of the numerous approaches, see McQuail (1994).

Functionalist sociological approaches to the analysis of the media tend to have much in common with the dominant perspectives in psychology. They aim to describe and understand what it is that people, and society, 'get out of' the media; in other words, what functions the media performs. In psychology this is known as the *uses and gratifications approach*. For functionalist sociology, the media have a broad range of functions in society. These include a *surveillance* function, whereby the media allow us to know what is going on around us, everything from the price of bread to the latest situation in the Balkans; and a *status conferral* function, whereby the media reflect high status individuals and groups in society, from Princess Diana to the latest Lotto winner. The media also function to help *apply social norms*, partly through direct provision of information (for example, stop smoking campaigns) but also through the negative portrayal and censure of deviance, such as overeating or robbing banks. This is part of the media's broad function of the *transmission of culture*. This ranges from the socialisation of children (for example, through television programmes such as *Sesame Street*) to the maintenance and passing on of national heritage (Irish-language programmes and films like *Michael Collins*). Finally, the media have been seen to have a *narcotising* function (or dysfunction) — they can flood society with too much information, thereby making it difficult for people to agree on norms and values or to know how best to act (Macionis and Plummer, 1998, p.587).

Criticisms of the functionalist approach and many of the psychological theories of the media centre on the fact that they tend to be highly descriptive. They are good at categorising and listing various effects and uses of the media. However, they are not very useful as a way to understand the crucial dimensions of power, conflict and inequality in relation to the media, nor are they very useful for understanding change. More critical approaches to the media have tended to dominate sociological work in the area, particularly those derived from Marxist and feminist perspectives. A key issue is the *political economy* of the media — in other words, who owns and controls the media institutions; how are media companies integrated into other forms of capitalist enterprise; and what are the relationships of power involved? A second focus is on the content of the media, especially in terms of *ideology*. How does the media provide a distorted or biased view of the world, and why might this be the case? Sometimes there is an attempt to link the two concerns: to show how particular patterns of media ownership and control lead to the dissemination of particular messages, but this is notoriously difficult to demonstrate. Furthermore, Marxist approaches to the media have paid little attention to audiences, that is, how media messages are consumed and interpreted. Much of the impetus towards an audience-focused study of the media has come from feminist research.

One of the first targets of the second wave feminist movement which emerged after the late 1950s was the mass media. In key texts of the women's movement, such as Betty Friedan's *The feminine mystique* (1963) and Germaine Greer's *The female eunuch* (1971), the imagery of advertising, and of women's magazines, in particular, was condemned. The use of blatant sexual imagery and demeaning images of women as barely intelligent 'housewives' has been a target of criticism and critique — a tradition that has continued in books such as Naomi Wolf's *The beauty myth* (1991). The subsequent rise of academic feminism within communication/media studies and sociology has seen a sustained critique not only of the media themselves but also of the paradigms, methodologies and concepts within which the media have been analysed. In particular, feminists have sharply critiqued the supposedly 'value-free' approach of much functionalist and psychological analysis. Similarly, they have criticised critical and Marxist approaches for their gender blindness. In their methodological and theoretical preference for qualitative approaches to research, feminist media analysts have brought new light to previously neglected areas of the media, such as audiences and education, and have given academic respectability to the study of previously derided aspects of the media such as the soap opera, the romance novel, pop (as opposed to rock) music and daytime radio and TV. There has been an interest in how the media are intertwined with other aspects of everyday life, such as eating, self-esteem and domestic relationships within families. Frequently, in feminist analyses of the media, there is an explicit attempt to link into broader questions of female oppression, discourses of power and dominant sexist ideologies.

As in other areas of sociological investigation, the particular theoretical lens that is used will determine, to a large extent, the knowledge that is generated. In sociological studies of the media we can perhaps discern a pattern where a fascination with the power of technology has given way to a highly critical stance, to be in turn replaced by an acknowledgement of the complexity and diversity of the phenomenon being studied. This reflects how new media technologies themselves are received with various combinations of enthusiasm and fear, before they either fade away (CB radio, skywriting) or are assimilated into the textures that are taken for granted in everyday life. The challenge for sociologists, then, is to analyse the place of the media in social life, without ascribing them a greater influence than they might merit.

## THE MEDIA AND NATIONAL DEVELOPMENT

The development of the media in Ireland has been very much tied up with the emergence of the nation state and with the 'identity' of that nation. The state has occupied an influential role in the development of the Irish media, for example, in relation to broadcasting policy. During the nineteenth century, newspapers were actively mobilised in support of nationalist and unionist politics; in the early part of this century, radio was central to the formulation of the newly independent state; film has been mobilised as a carrier of messages about national identity; and since the 1960s television has been seen as an overarching symbol and carrier of modernity. More recently, policy-makers have identified the Internet as a way of responding to the opportunities of an increasingly globalised world. Ireland is not unique in the fostering of such overt linkages: the media have been closely linked to the development of the state in societies as diverse as Nazi Germany, the emerging island nations of the South Pacific and developing economies such as Malaysia.

Despite this central role, the Irish state has not maintained direct control over the media in the manner that has been evident in many emerging nations. Rather, as Hazelkorn suggests, state policy towards the media has 'mimicked economic policy generally: the state filling the vacuum, promoting, regulating and deregulating sections for pragmatic never ideological reasons and in ways always beneficial to private interests' (1996, p.29). As long as private enterprise has been able to reflect the dominant ideological tenor of the country, the state has been prepared to allow it free rein. The government has become involved in the media industries only when there has been little capacity or enthusiasm in the private sector to participate. Then it has done so in ways that have ensured benefits flow to private business people and other powerful groups.

Pervading many of the debates about the mass media has been the issue of domination by outside forces and the extent to which the Irish media can, or should, be a means of fostering, developing or reflecting a distinctively Irish culture. A central concept has been that now known as cultural imperialism. Concern about the influence of British and American cultural products — particularly mass media products such as magazines, films, TV and radio programmes and popular music — has been long standing. It formed part of the early debates over the establishment of a national radio service (McLoone, 1991) and was revisited in the 'Rainbow Coalition' government's Green Paper on Broadcasting in 1995 (Department of Arts, Culture and the Gaeltacht, 1995, pp.132–6).

There is evidence that the early days of the Irish state saw a strong ideological element to media policy. The development of aspects of the media, for example, some newspapers and radio and to some extent film, were tied to particular ideas about national identity and culture. In this regard the emerging Irish state was no different to others in Europe and more recently countries such as Singapore and Malaysia that have been attempting to 'build' their nation. As in many countries, the relationship between state and media has also involved religious bodies, and Inglis (1998a) has stressed the powerful influence of the Catholic Church, especially in relation to issues of censorship. It is argued by many writers that for much of its history, the Irish mass media focused on the creation of a particular view of national, religious and cultural identity, one that has only been challenged with the advent of television and, more especially, exposure to media messages from outside the country. For many analysts (for example, Laffan and O'Donnell, 1998, p.173), the media have been part of the modernisation of Irish society and culture — in particular, a shift from 'a relatively homogenous, closed, Catholic culture' to 'an open, pluralist, culture today' based not on a single fixed identity but on a multiplicity of identities.

The early days of the Irish mass media saw a desire to break free from British cultural domination. This motive was one of those underpinning the foundation of the now-defunct *Irish Press* newspaper. In the 1920s Thomas O'Rahilly, a leading Catholic spokesman, asserted that 'in matters of the spirit we are becoming more and more England's slaves'. Publicity seeking support for the launch of the *Irish Press* claimed that 'the Irish people were in a condition of mental bondage, purchasing from their British former masters practically all the material which sustained their minds' (Curran, 1996, pp.8–12). Similarly, the foundation of Radio

Éireann was based at least partly on a desire to escape the influence of British music hall entertainment. But as Brian Fallon suggests (1998, p.11), the process by which elements of 'culture' are used and appropriated are complex and not necessarily amenable to direction from the state or other powerful societal forces such as the churches:

> Ireland, badly in need of a developing national culture of her own, was hopelessly outgunned by external forces — mainly commercial — over which her leaders had little control, and few institutions or public bodies knew how to combat these forces effectively. Well-meaning but backward-looking people might call Jazz 'jungle music', and Radio Éireann for a while held out against it, yet that did not stop the young from buying or listening to jazz records. If officialdom was hostile to swing music and the like, it was a simple matter to switch to the BBC Home Service and listen to Henry Hall. The clergy might storm from their pulpits on Sundays against the 'pagan' English yellow press, yet in nearby streets — sometimes, even, just outside the church gates — those same newspapers were on sale and doing a brisk trade. As for the popular cinema, it was of course subject to censorship, but in no way could it be banned; it was a source of state revenue, and arguably it kept young people out of worse places, such as pubs.

Kelly and Rolston (1995, p.563) suggest that the Irish media have had to tread a fine line between seeking 'to represent the existing socio-cultural worlds' within Irish society, and reproducing a particular version of cultural and national identity. They argue that the broadcasting media have been particularly successful in elaborating and developing a specific sense of Irish national identity without endangering social solidarity or losing touch with large sections of their listenership. But the elaboration has been 'within relatively narrow confines . . . defined by class, gender and elite interests within Irish society and by the existing consensus which favours these groups' (1995, p.576). Thus, RTÉ reflects a picture of the Irish as a homogeneous people that live in family households; are largely uninterested in intellectual debate or in high culture; share interests in sport, current affairs and a limited range of 'traditional' and popular forms of music; and are fond of chat. For Kelly and Rolston (1995, p.570) 'the united phalanx of nation, state and church, reproduced on radio, did not encourage the development of alternative cultural practices or of a class-based cultural critique. On the contrary, the all-encompassing concept of nation functioned to hide class differences, as well as those based on gender.'

Other factors have also helped to shape the particular form and content of the Irish media. Fintan O'Toole suggests that emigration has been very important in shaping the expression of Irish culture in general (see also Chapter 5). He argues that it 'simplified the representations of Irish experience and made it possible to imagine Ireland as a cultural monolith' (1997, p.163) — generally, a Catholic, rural one. As a result, some of the, for O'Toole, most crucial media and cultural representations of Irish identity were produced within the media and culture of another society: the United States. For example, acute expressions of aspects of Irishness were found in the films of John Ford and the plays of Eugene O'Neill. In the meantime, according to O'Toole (1997, p.164) 'in the silence left by emigration, the aesthetics of emptiness took hold. Empty wilderness is seen as innately more noble than ordinary urban existence.' The focus on rural life and culture, to the virtual exclusion of urban experience, has permeated Irish media products from *The Kennedys of Castleross* (radio soap), *The Riordans* (TV soap) to *Ryan's Daughter* (feature film) and the best-selling books of Alice Taylor (for example, *To the school through the fields*). While RTÉ had its long-running TV soap *Tolka Row*, there was little other popular depiction of urban Ireland on either the large or small screens until *The Commitments* (feature film), *Fair City* (TV soap) and the videos of U2.

It is undeniable that the media have had an important part to play in the development of an Irish identity. Yet they have also been important in linking that identity to others in complex and sometimes contradictory ways. Thus, while the Irish media institutions have been an important element in the development of an indigenous 'Irish' culture, the same institutions can also be seen to have played an important role in the integration of Irish culture into a broader Anglo-American culture and its particular vision of 'modernity' which has become dominant in the years since the Second World War. The influence of this global culture is often seen in terms of *cultural imperialism*.

## The media and cultural imperialism

Cultural imperialism is a concept that has come to prominence in the post-war period, particularly in the context of discussions about the media and their relationship to development and modernisation (see Chapter 3). The pre-eminence of Anglo-American media forms, from action movies and soap operas to advertising, has raised concerns about the effects that global (usually understood as Anglo-American) culture may have on local or indigenous cultures, especially in peripheral or semi-peripheral countries such as Ireland, Malaysia or Australia. There are concerns that the world's cultural diversity could diminish (much as there are concerns about eco-diversity of animal and plant species) and that the result will be a homogeneous global culture. An optimistic view of this process is that the intensification of contacts and communications across cultural boundaries will produce a cultural melting pot from which may emerge a new global culture that is an amalgam of elements of the separate cultures it replaces. A more pessimistic, and more widespread view, is that the dominant Anglo-American culture may usurp the role of other cultural forms and become *the* worldwide culture.

Cultural imperialists take the latter, pessimistic view. They argue (for example, Sklair, 1995, p.151) that the culture of powerful countries is imposed on weaker countries in an exploitative way. Powerful First World countries have the capacity to impose their values and beliefs not only on poor Third World countries but also on wealthy industrialised countries such as Canada, Australia and Ireland. Global culture is then not the outcome of equal participation by all of the world's cultures but the result of dominant societies' imposition on other cultures and societies. While this thesis has focused on a whole range of cultural forms, from management theories to forms of wedding ceremony, the mass media are seen as the key channel for cultural imperialism (Street, 1997, p.75).

An influential proponent of the media imperialism thesis has been the American dependency theorist (see Chapter 3) Herbert Schiller. During the 1970s his work created considerable interest in many countries, including Ireland, as people began to express concern about the extent to which 'foreign' media was displacing local or national indigenous media. He argued (1979, p.23) that transnational media groups (these would now include companies such as Sony, Philips, Viacom, Bertelsmann, Disney, News International, Reuters) should be seen as agents for 'the promotion, protection and extension of the modern world system and its leading component, the MNC [multinational corporation], in particular'. Global media work to open up, create and deliver global markets to other multinational corporations and through the manipulation of mass media audiences, transform these into loyal consumers of the products of the TNCs.

Though Schiller writes about transnational media corporations and dominance of the media by core areas of the world, it is primarily the US-based media TNCs he has in mind and which his theories have been most used to critique. 'Proving' the cultural imperialism thesis has been understood primarily as a matter of documenting the ownership of the global mass media and the origins of their content. If in a given society the media are found to be largely owned by US-based TNCs and/or if their content is found to originate primarily in America, this is seen as evidence for media and cultural imperialism. A world media system characterised by cultural imperialism will be found to be markedly asymmetrical; it will contain far more information flows from the centre to the periphery than the other way round — people in the periphery come to know a lot about the culture of the centre society but centre societies learn virtually nothing about the periphery. Moreover different peripheries will learn very little about each other. For example, in recent conflicts between Rwanda and Zaire, letters to the press in South Africa complained that while the South African media focused on news of entertainer Michael Jackson and President Clinton, it said little about what was happening in another part of Africa. Similarly, it could be said that in Ireland we know more about the weather in the United States, than we do about the politics of Denmark or Austria.

Schiller's approach stimulated much research that established the overwhelming extent to which the world media were penetrated by American-owned corporations and American cultural content. In the case of broadcasting, it suggested that global media flows were controlled predominantly by American and European TNCs, with formidable barriers facing outsiders who might try to gain entry to the system (Sklair, 1995, p.161). TNCs can 'dump' their products on Third world countries, including news items and programmes, while the flow of news from poor to rich countries remains very restricted. A study of international television flows in the early 1980s found large amounts of imported, mainly US, entertainment programmes in most of the sixty-nine countries surveyed, especially at prime time periods when advertising revenue is at its highest. Not surprisingly, it also concluded that 'no socialist Third World country programmes were ever shown on prime time US television' (Sklair, 1995, p.162). Indeed, apart from some British costume dramas, very little 'foreign' programming is shown on US TV at all.

Schiller's ideas prompted some research (Fahy, 1978) in Ireland that revealed the state of media dependency. As early as the 1940s three-quarters of all feature films screened in Ireland came from the United States, and a further fifth from Britain. The Irish experience was not very different from other European countries at the same time, where the proportions of American films screened ranged from 80 per cent in Belgium to 67 per cent in Spain. Even in countries that had their own film industries, like Britain and Italy, around two-thirds of all films screened were imported from America. In relation to TV, Fahy noted that in 1976, 59 per cent of RTÉ transmission time was made up of imported programmes, mainly sourced from the United States and the UK. Conversely, imported material made up only 2 per cent and 13 per cent respectively of United States and UK domestic TV schedules. In addition, of course, many (over 45 per cent) Irish TV viewers also had access at that time to a range of domestic British TV channels.

Data for radio and for newspaper readership appeared more hopeful. RTÉ radio had 73 per cent of the audience compared to, for example, 11 per cent for BBC Radio 2. RTÉ material was reported to be overwhelmingly Irish-sourced, though this may have concealed the real origin of programming, for example, most music material was recorded outside Ireland by non-Irish artists. Readership of Irish newspapers was also high — about two-thirds of adults claimed to see an Irish daily fairly regularly and about 88 per cent claimed to read an Irish Sunday paper. This compared with up to 12 per cent seeing English daily papers and about 40 per cent reading an English Sunday paper on a regular basis. Once again, this may conceal the real sources of information. Like all newspapers, the Irish press is heavily dependent on overseas-based news agencies, such as Associated Press (AP) and Reuters, for a very large proportion of news material. According to Fahy, Ireland was probably even more dependent on news agency sources than other small European countries due to the small number of foreign correspondents retained by Irish media companies.

Things have changed considerably since Fahy's research, but the direction of change is not easy to capture. A small but increasingly significant film industry has developed in Ireland, though the flow of material into cinemas that is not Irish or

Anglo-American has probably declined. Multi-channel television, with a great many more channels than in the 1970s, is now available to most Irish viewers and this increase contains a greater choice of Irish-based stations, with the recent launch of TV3 and TG4. The strength of Irish newspaper reading and radio listenership appears to be in decline, though again the field has been reinvigorated to a certain extent by new outlets, for example, *The Sunday Business Post* and expanding local and community radio, as well as a new national station in *Today FM*. There has also been a boom in magazine publishing. The material used in radio programmes appears to have a higher Irish content than before as Irish performers have gained international prominence and distribution. In addition, the use of Irish foreign correspondents by newspapers and broadcasting news departments, in preference to the transnational news agencies, has increased.

It is difficult to be conclusive about the nature or extent of cultural domination in today's complex global mediascape. Ireland is saturated with media images derived from other cultures, as is the case for nearly all societies. Yet there remains a vigorous local media discourse, with strong and consistent audiences for indigenous products such as national and local newspapers, local radio and Irish-produced TV programmes. Furthermore, Irish audiences may have the capacity to interpret media messages from a range of sources through their own interpretative frameworks (see below). O'Toole (1997, p.171) suggests (pessimistically), 'for a generation that grew up on American television shows, America will always be interwoven with memories of an Irish homeland and an Irish childhood.' But it will always be the case that how Irish children (and adults) interpret *Charlie's Angels*, *The Simpsons* or *Dawson's Creek* has at least the potential to be very different to the meanings derived in California. Furthermore, analysts of the Irish media now have to contend with a new factor: the undoubted success of some Irish media products within the global mediascape. Media images, products or ideas are no longer (if they ever were) tied to national boundaries. Thus, as Fintan O'Toole (1997, p.175) states:

> In the 1990s America and Ireland represent not opposites, not a dialogue of modernity and tradition, but a continual intertwining in which far from Ireland being the past and America being the future, America can constitute Ireland's past and Ireland can invent America's future . . . when young Irish people [U2's *Rattle and Hum*] can best embody an American dream, and young Americans can best represent Irish tradition to the world [*Riverdance*] we are dealing not with anything so simple as cultural domination or even so rational as cultural exchange, but with something obsessive, repetitive, continually unfinished . . . we are dealing with the ways in which the notion of America itself is an Irish invention, the notion of Ireland an American invention.

How then are we to interpret the success of U2 and Boyzone, the Irish soccer team, *Riverdance* and Roddy Doyle on the global stage? Has this led to an increased national confidence and strengthened national identity, or has Irish culture been undermined by globalisation, understood as Anglo-American media imperialism?

## DEVELOPMENT OF MASS MEDIA INSTITUTIONS IN IRELAND

The mass media embrace a very broad range of institutions and activities, content and audiences. Traditionally, perhaps, they are seen to refer to newspapers, magazines, film, radio and TV. They may also expand to include book publishing; the recorded music industry; numerous aspects of advertising; video, computer games and arcades; theme parks and, most recently, online services, CD ROMs and DVD. In this section we examine very briefly some aspects of the development of three main areas of the Irish media: newspapers, radio and television, as these are the ones that have been given most attention by historians and sociologists. The potential for further research into the Irish media is great.

### Newspapers

As a mass medium, newspapers have had a long history in Ireland, with the first newspaper being published in 1649, and the oldest in continuous publication being the Belfast *Newsletter*, founded in 1737 (Oram, 1993, pp.53, 105). The development of newspapers has been intertwined with social and political struggle. For much of their history newspapers have been associated with particular political groupings or positions, or have reflected the concerns of economic and social interests. But, like virtually all other mass media in Ireland, the press is dependent on advertising, with at least of 43 per cent of its income coming from this source (Rapple, 1997, p.70). More recently they have attempted to broaden their commercial appeal in response to competition from magazines, radio, TV and now online information services. But the market continues to be highly segmented, with particular newspapers targeting, for example, well-off business people while others define their readership in terms of local communities.

An interesting example of the development of newspapers in relation to their social context is found in the now-defunct *Irish Press* newspaper group. The *Irish Press* was founded specifically as communications medium for the Fianna Fáil party — in the face of hostility from existing papers — and was 'central to [the party's] struggle for hegemony in the early 1930s' (Curran, 1996, p.8). The interests behind the paper were a complex mix of American supporters of the party, prominent members of the Irish bourgeoisie, local party organisations and activists and the leadership of the party itself, in particular Eamon de Valera. There was also tacit support from the Catholic Church, and the party used the church's campaign against popular British newspapers as a way to assist development of the *Irish Press*.

According to Curran (1996, p.13) the *Irish Press* was a populist paper. In other words, it 'represented "the people" as a political category with interests separate and distinct from the pro-metropolitan interests of the "elite" in power'. It sought to channel working-class radicalism towards the Fianna Fáil party. In line with dominant Catholic thinking of the time, it presented rural culture as the 'authentic culture of the people'. It also had an early emphasis on and consciousness of the dependency of the news media on the news agencies of the core countries, in this case Britain, and pursued an anti-imperialist line. Thus, 'the guidelines for sub-editors reflected a conscious determination to align the press with anti-imperialist and revolutionary movements elsewhere in the world, even to the extent of giving limited sympathy to the Soviet Union' (Curran, 1996, p.15).

As the independent Irish state developed, the *Irish Press* continued to reflect the position of Fianna Fáil, which was to become the dominant political force in the state. It attempted to appeal to the same coalition of interests as did the party: a sometimes uneasy mixture of small farmers, the urban working class, indigenous industrialists and the nationalist political position. To many it reflected the voice of 'official' Ireland, with support for nationalist politics, the Catholic Church, rural life, the Irish language and private property. Its eventual decline, while probably as much to do with financial and business intrigues, has been broadly interpreted as symptomatic of the break-up of the discourse of 'official Ireland'.

Ireland, despite the domination of the Independent News and Media group (see below), has a flourishing newspaper culture. At the national level, readers have access to a broad range of views from Irish and imported newspapers. There is also a strong local newspaper industry; local newspapers are very much tied to locale, with close coverage of affairs in specific parishes and neighbourhoods. Local newspaper publishers have been very assiduous in providing local coverage, with 'editionalising' to reflect particular markets in different areas or suburbs.

## Radio

Radio was also perceived as a very important medium in the nation-building process. The national service was launched as 2RN in Ireland in 1926. According to Hazelkorn (1996, p.28) it was (like Australia's ABC) consciously modelled on the BBC formula for public service broadcasting. It was part of the civil service and was seen as a vehicle for promoting national sovereignty and cultural/religious identity. According to a historian of Irish broadcasting (Gorham (1967), cited in McLoone, 1991, p.4), Irish radio was:

expected not merely to reflect every aspect of national activity, but to create activities which did not exist. It was expected to revive the speaking of Irish; to keep people on the farms; to sell goods of all kinds from sausages to sweep tickets; to provide a living and a career for writers and musicians; to re-unite the Irish people at home with those overseas; to end partition.

According to Kelly and Rolston (1995) Radio Éireann had a 'symbiotic' relationship with both the Catholic Church and the Gaelic Athletic Association (GAA), two of the more powerful institutions in the new state. Broadcasts of religious and sporting events helped to build radio audiences and also increased the influence of the institutions concerned. Radio was important in the preservation and subsequent repopularisation of Irish traditional music and also, in the 1940s and 1950s, for the development of Irish drama, with broadcasts of new plays by writers such as Brendan Behan, Austin Clarke and James Plunkett (Fallon, 1998, p.147). RTÉ now serves a diversified and differentiated audience, in conjunction with local and national privately owned stations.

Since the late 1970s the dominant position of RTÉ has been challenged by these commercial radio stations, particularly at the local level. Independent radio was legalised in 1989, in the face of concerted opposition from the national broadcaster, after over a decade of almost unfettered activity by pirate radio stations that developed a loyal local listenership. Despite early financial and programming problems with stations such as Capital (Dublin) and national stations Century and Radio Ireland (now Today FM), plus the removal of a license from a Limerick station, local radio now appears to be in a very healthy state, with twenty-one stations licensed as of July 1999, and in many areas it commands a higher listenership than RTÉ Radio 1 (*Irish Times*, 20 July 1999).

## Television

Television arrived in Ireland at 7pm on New Year's Eve 1961 though, for a short period prior to that, some enthusiasts on the east coast were able to pick up British TV signals (Tobin, 1996, p.63). RTÉ was set up under the Broadcasting Act 1960, which not only established the television service, but removed broadcasting as a whole from the direct control of the Department of Posts and Telegraphs. By 1966, 85 per cent of Irish homes had a television set (Sheehan, 1998, p.138).

The development of television in Ireland has been very important in relation to debates about modernity. In the 1960s a national TV network, like a national airline, became a very important symbol of development. In this regard, Ireland was no different to other similar European countries, such as Norway, that adopted TV at a similar time (Macionis and Plummer, 1998, p.586). Hazelkorn (1996, p.28) describes how TV in Ireland has been associated with modernising tendencies:

The arrival of Radio Telefís Éireann in 1960 coincided with a phenomenal growth rate of economic change, transforming Ireland within a decade from an agricultural to an industrial society. Over the decades it has powerfully challenged traditional cultural forms and vented the aspiration of an emergent middle class, whose allegiances are increasingly attuned to continental Europe, undermining the primacy of the countryside in national life.

For Inglis (1998a, p.92), similarly, television was a key instrument of modernisation. It 'brought the sophisticated, glossy image of urban life into the heartland of rural Ireland. It provided a constant reminder of what most Irish people were not'. For him, it was also instrumental in bringing about the gradual decline in the power and authority of the Catholic Church: 'the social process where moral discourse was limited to what was taught in the school, read in the occasional newspaper, heard on the radio and from the pulpit every Sunday, was changed by the little box which appeared in the corner of Irish homes' (1998a, p.93).

As in many countries (for example, Australia) the early days of TV saw domination by (and concern about) American programming, from *Mr Ed* to *The Fugitive* but, gradually, home-produced material became more popular, as the country developed the infrastructure and personnel necessary to create it. RTÉ came to produce an impressive amount of drama and other programming that often attempted to relate directly to the social changes that were taking place in Irish society (Sheehan, 1987). Of particular importance were debates over economic development and the liberalisation of family law (Kelly and Rolston, 1995, p.574). Ultimately RTÉ was a commercial service, dependent on advertising, and this inevitably limited its ability to push beyond the limits of popular taste. Inglis (1998a, p.232) sees this commercial element as very important and links the development of television to the expansion of advertising and the creation of a consumer society in Ireland.

We have provided a very sketchy outline of some of the media development in Ireland. Each media form, of course, has its own detailed and complex history. In the three forms mentioned here, we can see a common involvement in issues of national identity. Such debates tend to be most intense in the period around and shortly after the introduction of a new medium, when provision is likely to be limited and the state is most involved. As the medium becomes more ubiquitous and as commercial considerations become more dominant, the medium often tends to become taken for granted. Few people, except for 'moral entrepreneurs' and perhaps media studies academics, get very worked up about what is on TV in Ireland today; radio is virtually ignored; and the most voluble public discourse is reserved for the new mass medium: the Internet.

## MEDIA PRODUCTION

As mentioned at the opening of the previous section, the diversity of media forms makes it very difficult to generalise. This applies also to the processes and institutions of media production. Each form, whether TV, newspapers or recorded music, has its own organisational and institutional processes and forms and also specific technologies and occupational roles. For example, it is impossible to discuss together the work of journalists and sound engineers, without a comprehensive understanding of the newspaper and music industries.

Yet there are important commonalities about the processes that shape the various forms of media production. As media forms become established, there emerge institutional, industrial and regulatory processes that strongly influence the day-to-day production of media messages. A large media organisation like RTÉ or the *Irish Times* is in many ways like any other large bureaucratic organisation. The production of the evening TV news or an edition of a newspaper is the outcome of the work of many people, organised in an occupational structure where routines, work practices, bodies of knowledge and forms of technology that help to structure the final product are often taken for granted. In addition, there are legal controls and limitations, such as those presented by Ireland's powerful defamation laws. At times, the structure and nature of the ownership and control of media organisations may have an important influence. It may be hard to demonstrate the personal intervention of a media tycoon like Rupert Murdoch or Tony O'Reilly, yet the particular company policies, management styles and individual preferences of media owners can shape the nature of the media product. We look briefly here at two aspects of the media production process: media ownership and the role of technology.

A feature of media ownership across the world is the *convergence* of formerly separate companies into large media conglomerates. Some of the names of these conglomerates are also familiar global brands, such as Sony, Disney and Philips; others may be less well known in the public arena (Viacom, Bertelsmann, Cisco). The business pages of the press are full of stories of takeovers and mergers, as formerly nationally based companies like Eircom, Disney or Bertelsmann seek out 'strategic partners', joint venture opportunities or are involved in takeover bids.

The convergence of media production operates at two important levels. On the one hand, there is the coming together of previously disparate companies into giant business conglomerates. A media conglomerate will typically embrace interests in the production, distribution and/or marketing of some or all of the following: film; video; TV; recorded music; book, magazine and newspaper publishing; business information and consultancy; satellite services; computer software and perhaps consumer electronics, toys or theme parks. Thus, it is now unsurprising for a particular media product — such as Madonna or *Star Wars* — to be produced and distributed through multiple arms of the same global conglomerate.

The convergence at the business level has been facilitated by technological convergence, especially through the development of *digital technologies*. Digitisation means that formerly separate technologies, such as computers, photocopiers, telephones and TVs, can now 'talk' to each other and, increasingly, can be combined to form new products. Similarly, digital production and recording has broken down the boundaries that previously existed between film, television, music or computer software. Any of these is now easily convertible into another, and new entities such as digital movies, computer games and the Internet are entirely new types of media that could not exist a short time ago.

There is considerable debate over the effects of the changes that have taken place. Critics argue that convergence may have similar effects to cultural imperialism; indeed, the two processes are often seen to go hand in hand. For example, the linkage of Eircom with strategic partners in Europe serves to reduce the capacity of the Irish people to control their 'own' telecommunication and media industry. Convergence is linked to the marketisation of the media industries, with a perceived reduction in the public service ethos that has typified European (and Irish) broadcasting.

On the other hand, it is possible to see how the processes of industrial and technological convergence can 'open up' the media. The emergence of giant conglomerates and the decline in the monopoly public service organisations may provide space for the development of smaller, 'niche' players in the interstices of the mega-media corporations. In Ireland, for example, there has been a huge expansion in the number of independent production companies in the TV, film and audio-visual fields. Furthermore, the digitisation and miniaturisation of production technology means that people can now make videos, publish books or produce music recordings, and even distribute them, without the need for a large production infrastructure like a record company, publishing house or film studio. Partly as a consequence of such technological change, but also due to financial pressures, public service broadcasters like RTÉ (and the new TG4 service) are increasingly acting as facilitators and *publishers* of programming, with their core production activities being stripped back to such activities as news and current affairs.

## Media ownership in Ireland

In Ireland, as elsewhere, newspapers and magazines are increasingly owned by large conglomerates, often with numerous other interests in areas such as the food industry or other branches of the entertainment industry. Furthermore, in Ireland, unlike in the United States and Australia, there is no specific legislation in place to control media ownership. However, little research has been carried out in Ireland into media ownership or the impact of cross-media ownership (where a company has interests, say, in newspapers, TV and telecommunications). Concern has been expressed from time to time about these issues and other effects of media monopoly such as political interference and below-cost selling of newspapers.

In Ireland, the public media sector has been dominated by RTÉ, embracing TV, radio, teletext, the *RTÉ Guide* and, until 1999, cable television distribution. The indigenous media player in the private sector is the Independent News and Media group. It has a dominant position in the Irish newspaper industry, accounting for two-thirds of all Irish newspaper sales daily and a large proportion of Sunday newspaper sales. It owns the highest selling daily newspaper, the *Irish Independent*, plus the *Sunday Independent*, *Evening Herald* and *Sunday World*. It has a 50 per cent share in the biggest selling tabloid newspaper, the *Star* and a 24.9 per cent share in the *Sunday Tribune*. It also owns ten regional weekly newspapers (including the *Kerryman* and the *People* newspapers) and through its sister company, Princes Holdings (a joint venture with US telecom giant, TCI), controls the country's second biggest cable TV operation (*Irish Times*, 13 January 1998, p.12) and a major Internet company, Internet Ireland/Unison.ie.

The company is also a global media player with interests on three continents. It has a 13,500-strong workforce. It is a major newspaper-owner in South Africa (with 11 titles) and in New Zealand. It is one of the largest regional newspapers companies in Australia and dominates the Queensland regional market. Across the world it has more than 160 titles. In the early 1990s it made an unsuccessful bid to purchase Australia's primary publisher of 'quality' newspapers, Fairfax. It also has broadcasting interests in New Zealand and Australia, where it has substantial radio interests in partnership with the US group, Clear. In 1998 it sold a highly successful billboard company in France, and it has one of the largest outdoor advertising companies in Australia.

## Changes in media production

The technology of production has always been very important to an understanding of the media. Media institutions have frequently been open to rapid technological and industrial change, especially the broadcast media and the music industry. Change has perhaps been slower in book publishing and newspapers, due to different sorts of markets and, in newspapers, union resistance. But recently new text-processing and printing technologies have also brought significant change to these areas. Such changes are not just a matter of technological evolution. Typically they are tied up with conflicts over power. The titanic battles between Rupert Murdoch and the British newspaper unions were linked with issues of technological change as much as union strength. In Ireland there has been a history of conflict over technology in the main public media organisation, RTÉ.

In Ireland as elsewhere, public service broadcasters have been affected by the developments in broadcasting and communications technology. Partly as a result of such changes, partly as a response to increased competition in a less regulated environment, they have been forced to adopt the methods of commercial broadcasters, including new technologies and work practices. According to Hazelkorn, who has studied the changes in work practices in RTÉ, digital technology, in particular, has broken down the demarcations between journalistic, presenter and engineering skills. Some positions have been largely eliminated (sound operators, lighting electricians) while new areas have opened up, for example, for IT experts and multi-skilled engineers. Some jobs have been 'reskilled' — journalists, for example, are now more directly involved in the presentation/publishing process.

Overall, 'RTÉ has used a combination of early retirement, redeployment, retraining and alterations to staffing structures to effect the necessary cost efficiencies required by increased demands of competition and commercialisation' (Hazelkorn, 1996, p.33). With casualisation and flexibilisation of the workforce, more people can now make more programmes more easily. The changes have had differential gender effects. As in the newspaper industry, women have disproportionately benefited from the changes, with greater job loss in male-dominated 'craft' areas, like electrical work, and expansion on the 'creative' and administrative side, such as research. These changes have broad implications for media in general. Hazelkorn (1996, p.37) highlights in particular the development of the 'independent production sector' as a key outcome. Increasing proportions of the output of public service broadcasters is undertaken by such companies. They are especially good at producing the relatively cheap and flexible 'infotainment' programmes (cookery shows, house and holiday programmes, entertainment news) which are currently so much a staple of TV programming.

## MEDIA TEXTS

There are many ways to interpret and analyse media texts (Berger (1992) and Thompson (1990) provide excellent guides). Many of the methods, while adopted in full or partially by sociologists of the media, derive from the disciplines of literary theory, philosophy or psychoanalysis/psychology, and may be difficult to reconcile or combine with objective sociological knowledge of media institutions and audiences. Of particular influence has been the *semiotic approach* (Barthes, 1973) which attempts to interpret the media as a series of 'signs' that may relate in various ways to an underlying 'reality'. A more positivist approach is that of *content analysis* which ultimately involves categorising and counting various aspects of media messages, for example, how many and what sort of ads on RTÉ TV feature a female voice-over? Other approaches to textual analysis may focus on questions of *ideology* — how particular sets of signs, symbols and textual elements relate to broader issues of *power* in society; or on questions of *genre* — how does a particular TV show or magazine story fit in with the expectations that the audience has developed from previous exposure to similar media products? Here we look at three examples of textual analysis of Irish media forms: Sheehan's analysis of Irish TV drama; Barton's analysis of the Irish 'heritage' film; and Keohane's analysis of the music of the Pogues. While these do not reflect all the approaches outlined above, these examples have been selected as they each relate to some of the broader questions of development and identity discussed elsewhere in the book.

## Television

Sheehan (1987) has carried out an extensive analysis of Irish television drama for the period from the launch of RTÉ in 1961 to the mid-1980s. Her aim (1987, p.6) is to develop 'an analysis of Irish television drama in terms of the underlying meaning of the stories being told and the emerging patterns of meaning, within the larger patterns of indigenous and imported television and within the development of Irish social history'. Sheehan's analysis comes very much from the point of view of literary criticism (1987, p.55). For example, she makes little attempt to understand the position of audiences, apart from some references to RTÉ's own audience research panel. She has little time for much of 'popular' television product, which she regards as 'aesthetically and psychologically immature, but by no means ideologically innocent' (1987, p.63).

Despite her elitist position, and her perfunctory dismissal of alternative interpretations (see Banks, 1990), Sheehan's is an interesting and valuable overview of the surprisingly large amount of TV drama produced by RTÉ. In current television schedules the individual TV play or, indeed, the mini-series of three to six episodes, is almost extinct; but during the 1960s and 70s in particular, television drama was a very important cultural form, and series such as *The Spike* (1978) and individual plays such as *The Ballroom of Romance* (1982) had a great social and cultural impact.

Sheehan draws on a number of approaches that typify much sociological analysis of media texts. She draws on the analysis of *myth* to explain why TV drama in general is important and attractive to audiences, and why it tends to follow certain forms. She overtly places her analysis of Irish TV drama within two main frames: the economic and social development of Ireland within the global economy; and the institutional structures of RTÉ as an organisation. For her, the restructuring of capital, as seen in the development of the information economy, is central to an understanding of how RTÉ drama output changed over the period. In addition she details the conflicts within RTÉ, which culminated in the late 1960s, over managerial control and the issue of cultural imperialism. The decline of a critical voice that was prepared to examine the changes taking place as Ireland modernised was linked to both these processes. In the later stages, international co-productions, with output aimed specifically at the international audience, shaped the sorts of topics that could be dramatised. In particular there was a strong emphasis on relatively non-controversial costume and historical drama.

## Film

Unlike Sheehan, Barton (writing a decade later, in 1997) draws explicitly on the theoretical basis of post-modernism to analyse recent developments in Irish film, in particular what she terms 'Irish heritage cinema'. Her analysis is stimulated by the release of what became the most popular (in Ireland) Irish-made film of all time, Neil Jordan's *Michael Collins*. Barton draws our attention to two implications that a post-modern sensibility towards film can produce. On the one hand, post-modernism in film involves drawing upon various images of the past to create a feeling of nostalgia, much as advertisements for Levi's jeans have drawn on images and music of the 1950s and 1960s. But, by playing around with technique, post-modern film can also draw attention to the *constructedness* of historical narratives — unlike realist cinema, which naturalises history. Unfortunately for Barton, the heritage film tends to follow the first of these approaches, thus producing a sanitised product for a global media market.

As in much of the film of Australia and Britain, there has been a strong emphasis in Irish cinema on historical and period drama — defined by Barton as 'heritage cinema'. The popularity of such films on the global stage (and of Hollywood films such as *Dances with Wolves* or *Fried Green Tomatoes at the Whistle Stop Café*) is based on the 'universal mood of nostalgia'. Irish heritage films reflect 'an "imaginary" past, a kind of glorious Celtic never-never land' — part of a 'desire to mobilise Irish myth in an international culture' (Barton, 1997, p.43). Film-maker Orla Walsh refers to this as the BBC image of Ireland: 'a fairy-tale Ireland, an *Into the West* kind of thing' (Sullivan, 1997, p.35). According to Barton such cinema does little to challenge conventional forms of storytelling; rather; it is conservative in structure and form, and politically and thematically cautious.

For Barton, the emphasis on the past may mean not having to deal with current issues. Citing the post-modernist theorist Jameson, she suggests that 'nostalgia for the past is often an unwillingness to come to terms with the present; in a society in which the reporting of child abuse, murder and marital violence is now a daily occurrence, there is a good argument for retreating into an imaginary state of grace, "the deliberate substitution of the pastiche, and imitation of past styles for the impossible invention of adequate contemporary or post-contemporary ones"' (1997, p.43).

Such conservatism may relate to the new imperatives guiding the arts in Ireland: 'the "theming" of Ireland' seen in the production of 'Irish pubs', heritage centres, Eurovision song contests and advertising geared towards tourists and potential investors. The desire to present the country as 'primitive and edenic' is closely linked to how the country is 'sold' by Bord Fáilte to tourists, through 'superb scenic landscapes; a quiet island with a relaxed pace of life; a distinctive heritage and culture; an absence of mass tourism; a friendly welcoming, convivial people; and a green, unspoiled environment' (Sheerin, 1998, p.45)

According to Barton (1997, pp.50–51) the rural romanticism and apoliticism of the heritage films is aimed at the '[British] Sunday evening television audience, the *Ballykissangel* viewer'. Such films are 'marked by a nostalgia for the past, for pastoral innocence; many of them are actually set in the past, the remainder are set in a rural Ireland which bears few traces of modernity'. A similar point could be made in relation to two box-office successes of the late 1990s that post-dated Barton's analysis: *In my Father's House* and *A Love Divided*.

## Music

Recorded music has possibly been Ireland's most successful popular cultural export and we can easily highlight the international success of acts as diverse as traditional group The Chieftains and DJ David Holmes. A number of writers (for example, O'Connor, 1991) have suggested that music reflects in a particularly acute way questions of Irish culture and identity. Cork-based sociologist Kieran Keohane has analysed the music of the band The Pogues in terms of how it expresses particular aspects of Ireland's post-modern and globalised position. For Keohane, the music of The Pogues, a band that grew directly out of the Irish diaspora, is a 'pastiche' of styles and places, an example of the interface of the global and the traditional, and combines in a unique style elements of the folk tradition with punk. The content of the music is similarly complex, 'loaded with historical references and images which are carefully pieced together and linked to contemporary experiences, lending coherence and historical sense to the culture of the diaspora' (Keohane, 1997, p.296). In this way, the music of the Pogues illuminates the historical legacy of emigration, not in the romantic way that much historiography or heritage cinema does, but in its full complexity. Keohane argues (1997, p.297), 'the Pogues' pastiche is more than simply a historically-informed text relating past with present. It is, more importantly, a medium and a device which subjects history and experience to a thoroughgoing radical critical examination.' Thus, it challenges not only romantic images of Ireland — unlike, say, the music of another band of the diaspora, the Saw Doctors — but also the mythical images of the metropolises of the core countries: it reveals the 'underside' of New York, Frankfurt and London, and how these global cities have been (and are still) built at least partly on immigrant and exploited Irish labour.

Sheehan, Barton and Keohane have each analysed aspects of the Irish media in relation to issues of national identity, globalisation and the 'proper' relationship between the media and the society it does (or does not) reflect. These remain key issues in relation to the media in Ireland, pervading both industry policies, for example, the 1995 Green Paper on Broadcasting, and critical responses. There are many who feel (as do all the above critics, to varying degrees) that the increasing globalisation of media production and distribution is a threat to our ability to tell 'our own' stories. The tendency, when producing for an international marketplace, is to provide what is attractive and non-controversial. But media producers will often respond, in the face of such criticism, that 'this is what the audience wants'. It is to audiences, then, that we now turn.

## MEDIA AUDIENCES

Consideration of the media process indicates how important a knowledge of the audience is. We may claim that the producer of a media message has a certain intention or that a text has specific overt or covert meanings; but how people themselves interpret and understand media messages is of crucial importance if we are concerned about, say, the effects of the media, or how the media form a part of people's everyday lives.

Furthermore, the audience has been shown to be very important in the development of the media. Technologically oriented stories about the development of radio, television or other mass media tend to focus very much on the invention of the technology and its gradual development and dissemination into society. But as Sorlin (1994, pp.47–55) has shown, the audience is a significant part of the media development process. Thus, the audience for mass newspapers was built on a pre-existing market for news-sheets, privately circulated newsletters and so on; similarly, the development of the radio industry was greatly assisted by a community of amateur enthusiasts. More recently the Internet industry was largely developed by a community of computer programmers and individual users, who helped to develop browser software, search engines and other applications, that were subsequently picked up and commercialised by major companies.

In recent years there has been a growth in the theoretical and practical importance of sociological audience research. This research has been driven by a number of concerns, especially those related to power (Kelly and O'Connor, 1997, p.3). They include:

- What is the power of the media relative to that of the audience; in other words, to what extent does the media itself determine how it is interpreted?
- How is interpretation and use of the media shaped by aspects of cultural identity, such ethnicity, age, class or gender?
- What are the responsibilities, if any, of the media to its audience(s)?

### Researching audiences

All media companies are intensely interested in the topic of audiences. After all, as many critics have pointed out, the key role of the media institution is to *sell audiences to advertisers*. The company needs to know the size of its audience, its composition and nature (often seen in terms of consumers with particular levels of spending power) and, increasingly, *how* the audience consumes the product. Highly sophisticated methods of researching audiences have been developed by international companies, such as Nielsen, incorporating technology, for example, 'people meters' that measure exactly who is watching what and when on the TV screen. The technology is being continually developed, to enable it, for example, to track people's purchases (via packaging bar codes) and to link these to demographic categories and to particular advertising campaigns.

While demographics have been the main interest of the commercial media, psychological studies of the audience have dominated academic research in the area. As well as the uses and gratifications approach that has attempted to define and measure why people consume the media, there has also been a focus on the effects of the mass media, often on those perceived to be more susceptible to its messages, particularly children. Within this tradition there has been a great deal of interest in the issues of violence, health and welfare and, more recently, sexist imagery. Much of the research has been carried out using experimental techniques and questionnaires.

The most recent approach to audience research has been that based on the notion of the viewer or reader of the media as an interpreter of messages within a social environment, rather than a person with a particular mental orientation or a consumer within a demographic group. This approach often focuses on the 'fan' — the dedicated user of specific media products, such as comic books, *Star Trek* or romantic fiction. The methodology of research is usually ethnographic, in the sense that the researcher tries to get close to the experience of media consumption, and to enter the world of the media consumer. The data gathered is often rich and complex, though inevitably difficult to generalise to larger groups of media users. The interest in ethnographic and socially situated research reflects something of how we typically use the media: often less as a series of individual media events, but more as a continuous *flow* of messages, images and information, into which we may dip in and out during the day with varying degrees of attention (this point was first made by the British Marxist critic Raymond Williams). This aspect is vividly expressed by Sorlin (1994, p.43):

> The reception of the media, especially those that are broadcast, is akin to situations we experience daily, for instance at work, or when we are driving: moments of relaxation, of dispersed attention are interrupted by sudden tensions. Except when they read or watch very seriously, people are content to pick up a few segments from a continuous flow. But what has been absorbed, however partial it is, will be reused in other circumstances, in friendly conversations, at parties, in meetings at work and, likewise, the successive moments of the conversation with friends or colleagues will, alternatively, be exciting and cool. Information borrowed from the media and daily concerns will constantly overlap.

The concept of *mass* media implies a large and relatively undifferentiated audience. It is very much tied in to the development of the technologies of newspaper publishing, cinema, radio and, above all, television: technologies that have compressed time and space in such a way that very large numbers of people (up to several billion for events like the soccer World Cup) can experience the same messages and images at virtually the same moment. But to a certain extent the 'mass media audience' is a fiction, brought into being through the process of talking about, measuring or analysing it. In reality, people experience the media alone, in close domestic and family environments or in relatively small public groups. The media is thus, as Sorlin has suggested, inevitably linked with other aspects of our everyday social interaction.

Until relatively recently, sociologists and other academic analysts of the media — in Ireland as elsewhere — had tended to neglect the study of audiences, preferring to focus on media texts or, to a lesser extent, production processes and structures. There may be a number of reasons for this. First, it is far more difficult to research audiences. Media are above all *mass* media, consumed by very large numbers of people; but much of this consumption takes place in the domestic arena (generally the sitting room of the private home). To study audiences then requires that researchers gain access to a significant number of private spaces for an extended period of time. This is expensive and time consuming; it is far easier to focus research activity on a collection of video tapes or newspaper cuttings that can be easily and relatively cheaply analysed in the researcher's office!

Second, while media companies or their agents (market researchers, ratings companies) collect vast amounts of detailed information on audiences, this information is commercially very valuable and sensitive. Media companies are loathe to hand over even historical data to academic researchers, except for a very high fee. Third, and perhaps most crucially, the lack of audience research reflects some of the dominant concerns within sociology as a whole which we outlined in the first section of this book. As we have seen, sociology has been oriented towards the 'public' world of work, power and social issues. It has tended until recently to ignore or at least play down aspects of everyday life, including the domestic arena and popular culture. The mundane everyday activities of watching TV, listening to pop records and reading newspapers have often been seen as relatively unimportant. It is really only with the influence of feminist sociology that the audience has come to assume the same level of importance as media institutions and the production of media texts.

A good example of the type of audience research that reflects such concerns is that of the British researcher Marie Gillespie, who has studied how television is part of the lives of a group of London Punjabi teenagers. She argues (1995, p.205) that 'TV talk, though it may seem esoteric and trivial, is an important form of self-narration and a major collective resource through which identities are negotiated.' In other words, how people think about, respond to and talk with others about what they see on TV makes up a part of their process of defining themselves and others. Given that people may spend more time watching TV every week than going to work, or being with family members, this is hardly surprising.

Gillespie's research is part of a group of studies that has shown how people across the world are able to make sense of global media products in their own ways.

For example, Ang (1985) has studied how the US soap, *Dallas*, was watched by a group of women in the Netherlands; Gripsrud (1995) has traced the reception of another US soap, *Dynasty*, in Norway, while Miller (1992) examined how the people of Trinidad made their own use and interpretations of the US daytime soap, *The Young and the Restless*. Such detailed and culturally integrated consideration of audiences can address issues such as the extent to which indigenous or local cultures are 'undermined' by media, as the cultural imperialist argument would suggest. Gillespie finds that far from being a threat to British-Asian culture, programmes like the Australian soap, *Neighbours* — extremely popular among the young people she studied — are integrated into people's own lives in new and unexpected ways that help them make sense of their own lives and everyday cultural experiences.

Similarly, Kelly and O'Connor (1997, p.8), in their overview of Irish audience studies, report that they reveal 'the enduring vitality of subcultural identities, in particular those of class, gender and ethnicity'. Audience research can reveal evidence of resistance to powerful media messages; of viewers and readers that can create alternative, even subversive, readings that are 'against the grain of the text'; of those that can gain 'unofficial pleasures' from the media: not what the producers or programmers had in mind!

## Audience research in Ireland

For both theoretical and practical reasons, sociological audience research in Ireland has adopted a qualitative methodology, as opposed to the quantitative methods used by the media industry or the experimental methods favoured by psychologists. Qualitative audience research, according to Kelly and O'Connor (1997, p.3) can 'explore the rich cultural terrain at the interface between media, power and subcultural discourses and identities'. It (1997, p.4):

> requires in-depth analysis of the responses of (usually) a small number of individuals or groups to media texts, and an interpretation of these responses in the light of the socially situated culture or lifeworld of the viewer . . . although one of the limitations of this approach is the care needed in generalising findings to the population in general, the advantage is the access it offers to the local and everyday cultures and frames of reference which ordinary people bring to their reading of media texts.

In *Media audiences in Ireland*, Kelly and O'Connor (1997) provide a good overview of recent academic audience research, though 'qualitative research' has been interpreted as open-ended or semi-structured interviews with people *about* their media use; there is little evidence of observational or participative studies that attempt to establish *in situ* how people use the media in their ordinary everyday environment. Underpinning many of the studies is a concern with *power*: who has it — the audience or the media institutions? Is there a 'dominant ideology' at work, basically leading people to think in particular ways, or does the notion of the 'active audience' make more sense: where people can take what they wish from the media and interpret it in their own ways, even in an oppositional fashion? Kelly and O'Connor (1997, p.10) conclude that both these tendencies are apparent:

> The media confirm the ideological and symbolic power of some powerful and high status groups while weakening and disorganising those with little power. And yet it is possible for the latter to use the media creatively for their own psychological, pleasurable and cultural purposes. However the pleasures of the text can be highly seductive and hide the symbolic power of the media to confirm the status quo, in particular perhaps by its ignoring of voices and cultures 'from below' and its non-articulation of alternative and radical perspectives.

Three examples from Kelly and O'Connor's collection reveal different aspects of the power relationship between audiences and media institutions. They are briefly outlined here, in relation to the three questions about power raised above.

Media analysts have long had a concern with the power of the media relative to that of the audience, particularly in relation to those audiences perceived as 'vulnerable'. The greatest concern has been expressed in relation to the child audience. Margaret Gunning's research, carried out in 1995 and reported in 1997, focused on the response of a group of Dublin school children to their favourite programmes, *Baywatch* and *Den TV*. She aimed to focus on the *pleasures* of TV, rather than more negative aspects, and drew not only on sociological methods but on more psychoanalytically based theories derived from film studies, especially those that related to the pleasures of looking.

Gunning found that children have good knowledge of the constructedness of television shows, indeed, 'one of their greatest pleasures was in the deconstruction of the programme in terms of the set and the physical make-up of the characters' (1997, p.263). They enjoyed a recognition of the more 'subversive' meanings in *Den TV* and enjoyed the 'act of looking' in *Baywatch*. Overall, Gunning found the relationship between children and TV 'empowering', in contrast to some popular and academic conceptions. The children, she concluded, 'showed an ability to play around with the messages of the medium, whether in the form of playful imitation, or in the exhibition of their powers as critics in the deconstruction of its artificiality' (1997, p.266). As a result, she argues that debates on children and television must take into consideration the views of the audience, that is, the children themselves, who are not passive pawns of the TV industry.

The recognition that different audiences, and sections of audiences, can derive alternative meanings from media products is one of the key themes of recent audience research. It is now taken for granted that interpretation and use of the media is shaped by aspects of cultural identity, such ethnicity, age, class or gender. In a study carried out in the mid 1980s, O'Connor analysed the responses of groups of people to a 1982 TV drama (*The Ballroom of Romance*) in terms of class and gender, and the intersection between the two. Responses to the film were shaped by the groups' differing genre preferences and the perceived relevance of the film (O'Connor, 1997, p.83):

> The full significance of the film for each group included not only their interpretation of specific scenes and sequences, but also their response to the film in terms of the pleasure which it afforded and the perceived relevance to their own lives. Because they inhabited different kinds of discourses and had access to different cultural competences, the viewing situation was framed in ways which differentially influenced the pleasures and meanings of the text. Or to put it another way, the groups had different ways of seeing the film based on different kinds of enjoyment, different levels of emotional involvement, and different points of engagement with the text.

The responses were complex, but it was apparent that, for example, men and women interpreted the film in different ways and derived various meanings from it. Men tended to focus more on the informational level — as an indication of what rural Ireland was like in the 1950s — whereas women had a more emotional response. There was also a difference in the response of working-class and middle-class viewers. Furthermore, a number of different patterns became apparent as determined by the intersection of gender *and* class.

Finally, there is a question as to whether, given the (limited) power that the media hold over the creation and dissemination of meanings, they have any responsibility to their audience(s)? This issue is linked closely to the concept of the 'public sphere' developed by the German social theorist Jürgen Habermas (see Chapter 15). For Habermas the public sphere was a place for discussion oriented towards the common good, untainted by commercial or governmental interests. The ideal location of the public sphere was, for Habermas, the coffee shops and salons of eighteenth-century Europe. The question can be asked whether the modern mass media allow — or should allow — such a space for disinterested public debate.

This is a topic that is addressed in Sara O'Sullivan's analysis of RTÉ 2FM's *Gerry Ryan Show* (GRS). She suggests (1997, p.167) that talk radio, of the sort found on the GRS, 'provides a rare opportunity for Irish audiences to participate in mass mediated debate and discussion'. She asks whether the show can be seen as part of the public sphere — or is it no more than entertainment, attracting listeners for RTÉ to sell to its advertisers? Might it have a democratic function, allowing for the raising of important issues or the influence of public opinion? An additional issue that is of great interest, given the success of TV shows like *Oprah*, is the significance of the public discussion of what were formerly seen as 'private' matters, for example, sexuality, domestic relationships and personal opinions. This may be of particular importance in the Irish context, where so many recent political and social debates (over abortion, divorce, sexuality, child abuse and so on) relate to what might be seen as the world of the 'private'.

O'Sullivan identifies four types of call to the GRS which she terms:

- expressive
- exhibitionist
- service encounter
- troubles telling.

People call in to express views, to seek help, to offer support or to get things off their chests. She concludes that while the show allows for these sorts of expression, it does not encourage critical discussion of social and political issues. One reason is that access to the show is controlled by RTÉ staff: 'this control on participation makes it difficult to see how the show might have a contribution to make to the public sphere, where, in theory at least, access should be open to all' (1997, p.177). Ultimately, the GRS is about entertainment, and this key production value shapes what can be discussed (and how). Nevertheless, the GRS has dealt with serious issues such as child abuse and domestic violence and O'Sullivan suggests that it 'offers a space in the public sphere where matters of public concern may be discussed with others in similar situations' (1997, p.178). It provides a form of self-help for at least some listeners. While there is a concern that radio phone-in shows encourage talk at the expense of action, O'Sullivan concludes that 'calling the show is an important social activity, and . . . this form of participation might have consequences for Irish society, as well as for individual callers' (1997, p.185).

Audience research carried out in Ireland has uncovered similar data to that in other societies:

- People's responses to the media are complex.
- The media form an important part of people's lives but do not dominate it, as is sometimes feared by critics.
- People seek out what they enjoy in the media, use it to provide pleasure, a sense of belonging, company and something to talk about with their friends and workmates.
- What the media offer in terms of information is often limited and skewed. If people do not have alternative sources of data on a topic, the media will often provide their only information.

## MEDIA AND THE PUBLIC SPHERE

This final point is one that has been of great concern to sociological analysts of the media: to what extent do media messages provide people with information and ideas that can help them to exert greater control over their own lives. In other words, are the media a threat to individual freedom and the public good? As we have seen, the media are often interpreted in terms of their position in the 'public sphere'. As the media become increasingly pervasive within social life, their role as an arena of symbolic struggle is seen to become more important.

A number of writers have argued that the media have come to replace other institutions, such as religion, education and the medical profession, as the locus of social knowledge and 'expertise'. The American writer Margaret Morse (1998, p.9) suggests that:

> Social institutions of family, education, politics, religion, and the economy — once the matrix for enunciating, conveying, interpreting, and enacting narratives stored in print or in local and familial memory — have converged to some degree or other with the media. The television is virtual baby-sitter, matchmaker, educator, (non)site of electoral, legislative and executive political events, a judicial body, a church, and a mall. Electronic neighbors, hosts, announcers, instructors, performers, and communicators of all kinds now share the interpersonal tasks of presenting and narrating culture with 'real' parents, teachers, actors, politicians, ministers and . . . salespeople.

A similar point is made by Inglis in his discussion of the declining influence of the Catholic Church in Ireland. He suggests (1998a, p.233) that 'the symbolic domination of the Church in the public sphere' has been replaced by the world of 'journalists, commentators, producers and spin-doctors'. Indeed, he goes so far as to argue that in Ireland the media now *are* the public sphere. If this is indeed the case, what do the media have to say about the sorts of public issues that we have discussed in this book; the things that are of interest to sociologists?

Devereux (1997, p.231) suggests that coverage of social problems such as poverty in the Irish media is meagre. But he also points out that it is important to examine how social issues are constructed and presented in 'fictional' programming such as soap operas, especially as there is evidence of increasing overlap and blurring of boundaries, between 'fictional' and 'non-fictional' programming. As part of a broader analysis of the Irish media (reported in Devereux, 1998), Devereux examined the treatment of social issues in the popular Irish rural TV soap, *Glenroe*. He concludes that the creators of the show 'conform to the wider institutional shyness of challenging the television audience vis-à-vis poverty and social problems' (1997, p.232). *Glenroe* depends on humour and strong characterisation as major elements of its attraction and differs from other soaps that focus far more on 'social issues' — including its own predecessor *The Riordans* (see Sheehan, 1987, pp.128–35; pp.158–62). As a consequence *Glenroe* attempts to reflect reality in a 'comforting' way and 'at a safe distance' (1997, p.235). Production staff express fears about alienating the audience of a top-rating programme. The show's 'over-emphasis on the lives and experiences of the rural middle class as its choice of central characters ensures that *Glenroe's* plots and storylines only occasionally touch upon problems of a social kind' (1997, p.239).

The programme-makers claim to be non-ideological in their treatment of issues and to specifically avoid 'preaching' to the audience. But Devereux argues (1997, p.235) that:

> *Glenroe's* limited account of the lives of some of those who make up the Irish poor conforms to the more general shortcomings in RTÉ's portrayal of poverty, which is as a result of the fact that the television station reproduces a predominantly liberal framework in its coverage of poverty and other social issues. In either its refusal to acknowledge the existence of the unequal social structure or in the often circumscribed ways in which it tells poverty stories it is patently ideological. It is ideological because it helps to maintain unequal power relationships through either the refusal to challenge the basis of such relationships or indeed to suggest possible alternatives. It is also ideological because it treats inequality in a 'taken-for-granted' fashion and thus contributes to the reification of poverty and inequality.

In *Glenroe* the 'solutions' to social problems are seen to lie in personal, individual acts of kindness, tolerance or 'good deeds'. Problems of class and inequality become family or community problems: not structural ones that stem from the nature of Irish society itself. This applies to groups such as Travellers and the long-term unemployed whom, while present within the narratives of the show, are marginal in relation to the central, middle-class, characters.

*Glenroe* is unexceptional in its treatment of social problems and issues, though Devereux points out that other soaps (for example, *Brookside* in the UK) have made greater efforts to reflect 'reality'. In Australia similar charges have been laid against *Neighbours* and *Home and Away*. The apparent movement away from social issues may reflect the changing nature of the medium of television. As we have suggested above, the medium of television, like pop music and video, has become comprehensively domesticated. These are entertainment media that are taken for granted and which form an integral part of everyday life. It is not clear whether it now makes sense to think of them as constituting 'the public sphere' in the manner suggested by Habermas. It may be that this role has moved on to other, newer media, in particular those emerging in the convergence of broadcasting, publishing, computing and domestic technology; in other words, digital television, 'smart homes' and online communications. It is with a brief consideration of these emerging technologies that we conclude this chapter.

## MEDIA AND THE FUTURE

What are the consequences for Irish society and identity of an increasingly globalised media and cultural sphere? How will the penetration of digital information technologies into every aspect of our lives, from cars to computers and mobile phones, affect the social interactions and processes we have discussed throughout the book? These are issues for the sociologists of the future to analyse, but it may be possible to point to the directions of some trends.

Convergence — in both its technological and institutional senses — means that the barriers that separated 'the media' from other aspects of social life are becoming increasingly meaningless. At the institutional level in Ireland we have witnessed the joining together of an electricity utility (the ESB) and a foreign communications company (BT) in a joint venture (Ocean) to provide telephony services to businesses and Internet services to the public. Such links between companies from previously separate business sectors are becoming common. In 1999 the Irish public made a huge investment in the shares of Telecom Éireann (now Eircom), a company that is internationalising and has expanded its operations into the Internet sector. The share issue may be seen a step towards breaking down private/public divisions within Irish society, and while such share issues leave the institutions of power largely untouched (and indeed may serve to increase the existing power of the wealthy), expanded share ownership may have implications for political attitudes or behaviour.

Not surprisingly the sociological approach offers both optimistic and pessimistic scenarios. The Irish government's Green Paper on Broadcasting of 1995, while specifically concerned with radio and television, outlined these in a vivid fashion (Department of Arts, Culture and the Gaeltacht, 1995, p.131):

> [Broadcasting] can be a motor of modernisation, cultural innovation, social transformation, even democratisation. It can cultivate a healthy public sphere in which national self-confidence flourishes and is oriented towards the future as a set of challenges to be met in a progressive way. It can critically interrogate a nation's history, culture and identity and offer a vantage point for the renewal of that heritage. But broadcasting can also be a threat, pitting profit motive against collective rights, deterritorialised imperialism against minority cultural needs. It can disfigure us politically, homogenise us linguistically, and depress our inclination for cultural expression.

There are many critics who are pessimistic about the directions that media ownership and deregulation are taking. A leader of the Communication Workers' Union, David Begg (1997, p.66), suggests that it is ironic that deregulation of the media and communications industry, rather than creating competition, has led to the 'creation of cartels of large multinationals'. He is sceptical that these giant conglomerates can be controlled in any way by democratic forces.

There are also more fundamental concerns about how the media are affecting social life. Morse (1998, p.4) points to a system of human interaction completely mediated through electronic technology:

Today, virtual sex on an electronic chatline or the arrival by mail of a cubic zirconia ring ordered by phone from a home shopping channel are complex chains of exchange between images, symbols, bodies, objects, and money that are ultimately based on the instant transportability and the ease of processing images and digital information.

For Morse, while television may offer people a 'shared culture' of 'unifying experiences' and even a degree of 'interaction', such features only appear desirable because the medium itself has helped to undermine these aspects of social life.

Morse, like Helena Sheehan (see above) are both, in different ways, convinced of the centrality of storytelling in the maintenance of culture. For Sheehan, the television is largely a neutral channel through which stories and messages flow. Morse is far more interested in — and worried about — the implications for culture of giving over the power of storytelling to machines. For her, the TV is only an interim technology. It is in computer networks that the process reaches its conclusion: 'it is left to the genres of cyberculture to develop the full implications of the impression of being immersed *inside* a virtual world' (1998, p.4) — where the 'you' of the television's address becomes the 'I' of the computer/user.

While many analysts of the media see the trend towards globalisation in negative terms, there are those who see it in a much more optimistic light. For some, the technocratic future offers the potential for increased democracy and human interaction, for greater knowledge of the world and of each other, and for more liberating ways of doing business and work. New media forms, such as the Internet, that are not 'owned' by any single company or nation, are seen as an alternative to cultural imperialism and globalisation, offering perhaps the potential for a *new internationalism*. A compelling example is the Internet-supported international campaign to defeat the World Trade Organisation's Multilateral Agreement on Investment (MAI), a planned treaty favouring TNCs that would have impacted severely on all the non-core economies of the world. The campaign against the MAI started in the United States, but was very effectively diffused across the world through the media, including the Internet.

Ireland is perceived as a particularly favoured location within this new world order. After all, the communications industry is the defining industry of the twenty-first century. Ireland is a country with a well-educated workforce that speaks English, the language of the global media. It has a rich cultural heritage that it can draw upon to generate attractive media products, like *Riverdance*, films, festivals and online content that can tap into the market offered by the huge Irish diaspora. The challenge is to create the right conditions and to grasp the opportunity.

At the start of this chapter we referred to the developing international mediascape that embraces non-core countries such as Australia and Ireland. In a sense the *mediascape* is a developing 'shared culture'. We can ask what kind of culture is it? Is it a homogeneous Anglo-American imperial culture that Irish people will inevitably become submerged in, or does it provide the opportunity for Irish people to insert their particular cultural nuances into a developing global sensibility? Given the dual processes of globalisation and specialisation/ fragmentation that are taking place in the media and allied industries, this is a very difficult question to answer. You are encouraged to engage critically with the media that surround you, even as you read this chapter, and to think about your own response to this challenge.

15

# New social movements

Recent chapters of this book have focused on culture and cultural processes in Irish society and have drawn our attention to how Irish culture may be changing. In Chapter 11 we introduced the concept of cultural politics to emphasise that culture is not only learnt in childhood socialisation or inherited from past generations, but may also be drawn on as a resource, invoked and redefined by social groups as they struggle to achieve social status and to realise aspirations and interests. In Chapter 13 we introduced the idea that group identities can be considered part of culture, and that people mobilise themselves to act, or are mobilised by others, on the basis of identities such as community, class or gender.

In this chapter we aim to develop these ideas through a focus on the sociology of *new social movements* (referred to in this chapter as NSMs). This has been one of the fastest growing areas of sociological research in recent years. NSMs interest sociologists as they seem to reflect new ideas about how to 'do politics' or bring about social change. It is widely claimed that in contemporary Irish society people have become apathetic about politics and lack interest in or respect for those who commit themselves to political activity. But the strength of social movements in contemporary Irish society, from community development to environmentalism, and from feminism to Rural Resettlement, suggests that it is the conventional, institutionalised form of party politics that people are apathetic about, and that many actively seek other ways to become involved in shaping Irish society. In this chapter we suggest how this development may be linked to cultural and structural changes within late modern societies. We suggest that the study of NSMs can reveal much to us about the nature of modern society in general, and specifically of Irish society.

## THE SOCIOLOGY OF NEW SOCIAL MOVEMENTS

Why are sociologists now so interested in NSMs? One reason is that there appears to have been a strong increase in such new forms of collective political action across the world since the late 1950s. Collective popular action — such as the Solidarity movement in Poland — was a major element in the extraordinary fall of communism in Eastern Europe at the end of the 1980s. Prior to this, the emergence of the greens in Europe (especially Germany) during the early 1980s, the global anti-Apartheid movement of the 1970s and the student and peace movements of the 1960s had played a major role in societal changes. These events and experiences suggest that there has been a striking shift in how political action and change occur in late modern society. This might reflect other social and cultural changes, including in the nature of democracy itself. Certainly, in labelling these as 'new' social movements, sociologists suggest they are closely connected with features of contemporary society that mark it out from earlier periods of modernity.

If today's social movements are 'new', how do they relate to 'old' ones? The classic 'old' social movement that most sociologists have in mind is the labour movement that developed in the nineteenth century as a response to the onset of capitalist industrialisation. Many would regard this as the first modern social movement, as Tilly (cited in Scott, 1992) points out:

> People have, to be sure, banded together more or less self-consciously for the pursuit of common ends since the beginning of history. The nineteenth century, however, saw the rise of the social movement in the sense of a set of people who voluntarily and deliberately committed themselves to a shared identity, a unifying belief, a common programme, and a collective struggle to realise that programme.

The workers' movements were clearly class-based. In Tilly's view they emerged as class became the major dimension of social inequality in the early period of industrialisation. A feature of NSMs, then, is that they are *not* class-based. Even if most of their membership is drawn from a particular social class, their demands and goals are not confined to the interests of that class. The social identities through which they interpret society are more likely to be based on gender, age or ethnic/cultural identity. Furthermore the 'newness' of such social movements compared to more traditional ones is defined, according to Goldblatt (1996, p.137):

> not only in terms of the obvious differences in goals and aspirations, but also of their site of political operation (civil society and culture over the state and politics), organisational structure (open, fluid and participatory), social composition (aligned along non-class cleavages), motivations to participation (morally and ideally as opposed to interest-based politics), unconventional forms of political activity (direct action, symbolic protest, mobilisation of public opinion) and core aspects of their ideological positions.

This is a very tightly packed list and we try below to examine its contents and explore some of their implications. For the moment, we note three important aspects of NSMs. The first has to do with how people are attracted to them and what they expect of their members. An NSM is more likely to have a loose organisational form that allows people to largely define their own degree of participation; and less likely to rely on the creation of formal hierarchies and defined official positions. The second is that NSMs tend to act and express themselves politically in ways that differ strongly from the conventional political behaviour of established parties, interest groups and lobby organisations. This difference stems at least partly from the fact that NSMs are less concerned to change political structures than to alter people's everyday culture and consciousness. The third is that NSMs are less concerned to achieve power or realise material improvements for a particular sectional group (as, say, a trade union may be) and more concerned with universal values and ideals. All these claims, as we see below, have been disputed, both as a general account of what NSMs are like and as applied to specific examples of such movements. But they retain the potential to illuminate features of contemporary society and particularly its political and cultural practices.

Sociologists have started to debate and research NSMs as a striking aspect of contemporary social life. But the sociological interest in NSMs is also driven by an intellectual and theoretical curiosity. So, while they have sought to describe and explain a new aspect of modernity, sociologists have also developed a range of theoretical explanations to try to account for this phenomenon. The theoretical discourse around NSMs has had two major expressions: rather crudely these have been labelled the European and the American approaches. We open our discussion of NSMs with a brief outline of these.

## EUROPEAN PERSPECTIVES ON NSMS

### Habermas, critical theory and new social movements

European sociological interest in NSMs stems from a desire to identify agents of *social transformation* — particularly those actors who can bring about radical and emancipatory change in what is often seen to be an unequal, unjust and socially or culturally destructive modern society. Many theorists have been interested in NSMs in the hope that they might replace earlier class-based movements as agents of social change and might succeed, where those had failed, in overthrowing or transforming capitalist society.

Of particular influence has been the German sociologist and philosopher Jurgen Habermas. Habermas is one of the 'critical theorists' within German sociology that has sought to carry forward Marx's theoretical analyses of capitalist society by taking into account major changes in advanced capitalism unforeseen by the nineteenth-century theorist. For example, Marx expected that, as capitalism advanced, economic crises such as stock market crashes, depression and large-scale unemployment would intensify and inevitably precipitate revolutionary political change. Generally speaking, this did not occur, and critical theorists have stressed the extraordinary capacity of modern capitalism to contain and deal with such crises, without having to change itself in any radical way. Where Marx believed that capitalist exploitation would so impoverish the working class that it would ultimately force through revolutionary change, critical theorists have emphasised how capitalism has been able to 'buy off' the threat of working class political mobilisation, by a process of gradual but continual improvement in material standards of living and an integration of workers into an expanding consumerism.

As a critical theorist, Habermas has developed an analysis of late modern society that includes a deep interest in NSMs: could the youth, peace and ecology movements, for example, all prominent in Germany over the last three decades, be the collective forces to inherit the task of emancipating society? Habermas's (1987) analysis of contemporary society persuades him that NSMs are an outcome of and are now integral to the social structure of late capitalism. They may therefore be expected to play a significant role in helping it to change.

Habermas's analysis of late modernity owes much to Weber, perhaps even more than to Marx. He emphasises the idea that in modernity, the 'life-world' is increasingly subjected to 'colonisation' by the 'social system'. Life-world here means the sphere of everyday, immediate social experiences of individuals, their face-to-face relations with others particularly in the intimate domains of family, kinship and friendship. It is a world where we relate to others as people with minds and selves. When we communicate with others, we are constantly oriented towards the establishment of mutual understanding and, if possible, agreement. The social system is the external, impersonal world of institutions and formal role-relationships, particularly economic and political ones, that are organised through hierarchies of power and authority. Institutions operate on the basis of instrumental reason: they seek the most efficient means to achieve their goals, and this usually involves forms of domination and coercion — people are treated merely as objects and means to ends.

Following Weber, Habermas sees modern society as being characterised by a continuous expansion of instrumental rationality and is afraid that this is reaching the point where it threatens to take over relationships within the life-world — interpersonal relationships are becoming increasingly calculative and impersonal. The emergence of NSMs, then, can be seen as a response by the life-world to the threat of colonisation by instrumental reason. NSMs are movements 'to defend the life-world'. This explains why they possess some distinctive features when compared to earlier, more conventional class-based movements. In particular, it explains why they are typically less concerned with the instrumental pursuit of material goals and interests and more interested in finding new ways of living, of relating to others, of exploring identities and developing the self.

# Touraine, social movements and post-industrial society

The French sociologist Alain Touraine has also investigated the relationship between social movements and their social context. He has been described (Scott, 1992) as a 'structuralist' as he suggests that social movements are determined by social conditions such as the class structure. He identifies two types of society where social movements are important:

- industrial society, where the main productive activity and source of social power is in manufacturing
- post-industrial society, where it is the production of knowledge, and the power derived from it, that is most important.

Since, Touraine argues, these types of society are structurally quite different, the social movements found in each will also vary.

Industrial societies give rise to industrial or workers' movements (Touraine, 1982) that develop around struggles in the sphere of work. These usually focus their demands on the state, for example, in demanding access to economic decision-making. As they succeed in their claims, they increasingly become part of the system of government and therefore less identifiable as social movements (see our discussion of corporatism in Chapter 4). In post-industrial society new movements emerge that are no longer concerned with the workplace or with accessing state power. They develop in civil society (the realm of social life that is neither primarily economic nor primarily political) and are mainly concerned with defending it against the state. In post-industrial society, according to Touraine, those who wield power are not the owners of material production resources but the controllers of knowledge — science, technology and the media. NSMs in post-industrial society aim to defend those subordinated to technological or knowledge control, that is, all ordinary citizens whose lives are governed by the decisions of a knowledge elite. They seek not to become part of that elite but to defend culture and civil society against it, so they are less concerned to organise themselves into effective lobbies or interest groups along conventional political lines and more interested in developing alternative lifestyles and ways to relate to knowledge and technology. Though following a different route, Touraine reaches much the same conclusion as Habermas: NSMs are qualitatively different from earlier social movements in both their ideology and forms of activity. At the same time, they play a similarly important role as mobilisers of collective action against the forces of societal domination and coercion.

While this account of NSMs is necessarily abstract, derived from a view about the nature of post-industrial society, Touraine (1983) has made a detailed study of the anti-nuclear movement in France and through this seeks to demonstrate the applicability of his model. Both the anti-nuclear and the ecology movements can be seen as expressions of resistance against the concentration of certain types of knowledge in state hands, and against the use of knowledge for purposes that threaten 'all citizens' and not just a certain section or class in society. Neither is 'political' in the sense of seeking access to state decision-making or of taking over state power. Touraine suggests that when these movements do become politicised, as in the formation of green parties, this is a deviation from their real nature and an indication of their failure — a point of view that has, understandably, been controversial.

## AMERICAN PERSPECTIVES ON NSMS

From the European perspective, NSMs are characteristically treated as harbingers of the future, not an attempt to escape into a romanticised past. They are seen as a response to critical issues in modernity, around contemporary forms of social organisation and ways of life, that moves us towards new types of society and social relationships. This interpretation is in striking contrast to that of functionalists, such as Smelser (1962), who see oppositional social movements as indicative of a problem or failing in the social system — evidence of social strain. This view assumes that those who take part in such movements are rejecting the present in favour of the past: they are traditionalists who want to reconstruct pre-modern social conditions and relationships. There is a presumption that if whatever is malfunctioning in the system can be repaired, the strains that cause social movements to develop will be removed and the movements themselves will fade away.

Recent American work on social movements has moved from functionalism towards an approach known as *resource mobilisation theory* (RMT). RMT treats social movements as organisations and asks how they obtain the resources they need to function effectively. The main resource needed by a social movement is mobilisation itself: the emergence of large numbers of people who agree with the movement's ideas and aspirations and who are prepared to support it and take part in its campaigns. From this perspective, the main question that social movement researchers should pose about any particular movement is: how does it succeed in securing those resources? The answer will differ according to the movement and society being studied. Each has to be examined in its own right, without presuppositions about the sort of movement it might be.

If the European approach to NSMs has been characterised by 'grand theorising', the American approach has leaned in the opposite direction, emphasising the collection of data within a relatively restricted conceptual framework. But this does not mean it is without theoretical assumptions. One assumption is that social movements can be addressed as examples of *social organisation*: answers to questions about social movements are to be found in an analysis of one or more movement organisations, and how they generate attention, enthusiasm and support among target audiences, rather than, as is the case from the European perspective, an analysis of the broader society.

Thus, an RMT approach to the study of the environmental movement in Ireland would entail a study of the various organisations involved, such as Greenpeace and the Green Party on one side and An Taisce, the Irish Wildbird Conservancy and the Heritage Council on the other. The RMT approach has its advantages. If we can assume that the membership of the movement coincides with the membership of these organisations and that movement activities coincide with the organisations' activities, then we have a relatively clear picture of the boundaries and characteristics of our object of study. But to limit the concept of social movement so severely can mean we end up identifying it only with its formal, hierarchical, organisational structures. This leaves out all the fluid, unorganised, localised occasions in everyday life where the values and goals of the movement are put into practice. If Irish people, though not members of such organisations, start to recycle household waste, would we not want to include them in a study of Irish environmentalism?

A second major assumption of the RMT approach is that people are essentially rational and so participate in social movements for instrumental reasons. It sees social movements as being most likely to mobilise people: when they aim at goals that are in the interest of many; when they clearly articulate these goals; and when they can convince people that a social movement is the best way to realise them. If the movement or organisation fails on any of these criteria, people will not recognise that their interests are at stake, or will favour other organisational forms, such as lobby groups or political parties, at the expense of the social movement. RMT does not distinguish between social movements and other forms of collective organisation. They are points on the same spectrum. People can move from one to another on the basis of a rational decision about which is more likely to be effective. There is a clear contrast here with the European approach to social movements, which sees them as a specific and unique type of collective action that requires theoretical interpretation.

It is unlikely that the RMT assumption about the instrumental rationality of movement participants stands up. Mobilisation as members or participants in social movements may stem from instrumental grounds, but this alone is unlikely to fully explain people's actions. I may discover a movement that looks likely to achieve something in my interest (say, a movement to increase the salaries and social standing of sociologists in Ireland), but if I can see that it will succeed without my participation, then I need not take part. Others can make the running for me. If everyone thought like that, nobody would ever become involved. So it seems that a movement that can successfully mobilise support has to appeal to more than a person's rational understanding of their own best interest. If this was true of early social movements like the labour movement, which attempted to realise the interests of a specific section of society, then it seems even more likely to be true of NSMs that claim to speak for 'all the people'. For example, it may be in the interest of humanity as a whole to consume and waste less and conserve resources for the future; but for each individual in the present generation, to reduce present consumption levels may be to go against immediate self-interest. Thus, if people are to be mobilised by the ecological message, it must touch on something other than their instrumental reason.

Any account of how NSMs successfully mobilise resources must reflect how they appeal to a range of concerns: about identity; about new ideas and their practical expression; and about the rejection of conventional values and lifestyles. Indeed it can be argued that to treat NSMs as if they were a means to something else is to mistake their nature. Melucci (1989) suggests that people participate in NSMs and their activities as an end in itself: as a symbolic expression of dissent from the dominant culture. This may be why, for example, green activists do not necessarily choose the most 'efficient' way to organise to achieve a goal, if efficiency means adopting hierarchical or undemocratic structures of leadership or decision-making.

## Synthesis

Recent discussions of NSMs have tended to integrate elements from both the European and American perspectives. Supporters of RMT have recognised not only the capacity of social movements to realise political objectives and instrumental goals but also the significance of the movements themselves as sources of cultural change and new symbolic meanings in society. Indeed, one of the most important achievements of NSMs, as Scott (1992, p.157) points out, is to redefine 'politics'. For example, they highlight new issues that the state should concern itself with, such as waste recycling, and others that it should withdraw from, such as censorship. Writers from the European tradition now recognise that the social structural or ideological characteristics of societies are not sufficient to explain the emergence and development of specific NSMs. They recognise that it is also important to examine the organisational factors emphasised by RMT, such as resources and concrete social and political contexts.

## EXPLAINING SOCIAL MOVEMENTS

Why have NSMs and new forms of protest and opposition become such a significant feature of contemporary societies? There are three dominant explanations:

- post-materialism
- the idea of a 'new' middle class
- the argument that an important political shift in developed societies has provided space for new forms of political mobilisation and action.

## The post-materialist thesis

The post-materialist thesis is associated with Inglehart (1977) who claimed that his large-scale attitude research (mainly among Americans) revealed that social values were, for some social groups, shifting from 'materialist' to 'post-materialist'. The main social group concerned was the young, well-educated generation that had grown into affluence and stability after the Second World War. This group was less preoccupied with career advancement and the acquisition of wealth and more interested in the overriding goal of 'self-fulfilment'. Inglehart suggests that the growth of social protest movements since the late 1960s can be explained by generational change and the experience of affluence. At least among the highly educated, increased affluence has apparently led to an interest in 'non-material' forms of fulfilment that relate to social relationships, autonomy and self-realisation. This point reflects Touraine's concept of post-industrialism: the phase of modernity associated with the growth of higher education, expansion of the service sector and increased affluence.

## The new middle class thesis

The post-industrialist thesis also underpins the second explanation for growth in NSMs — the new middle class thesis. It is suggested that changes in the class structure of developed societies in recent decades have inverted the relationship between class position and social unrest — these days it is not the industrial working class that joins in protest movements but the well-educated and professionally oriented middle class. Why should this be so? Post-industrialist theorists claim that late modern society is experiencing the emergence of a new middle class. Whereas the 'old' middle class based its position on the ownership of material wealth, the new middle class is made up primarily of 'knowledge workers', whose power derives from control of specialist or expert knowledge. In their working lives these workers may find themselves in conflict with members of the old middle class who are their employers. Knowledge workers aspire to significant autonomy in their work but the conventional employer still tries to control the workforce tightly. The employer wants to make a profit, whereas the new-middle-class employee is interested in the use of knowledge for its own sake. Many members of the 'knowledge class' work as professionals in public sector employment. They also experience conflict between their desire for self-direction and the bureaucratic controls that the state seeks to enforce.

Some advocates of this thesis (see Maheu, 1995) suggest that the new middle class is the agent for a new round of class struggle, where it will challenge the 'old' class of entrepreneurs and managers. It is suggested that in this struggle the working class will play a conservative part, supporting the old class. This approach then sees NSMs as primarily *class-based*, like the old social movements. Others are less convinced of this and suggest that the new middle class tends to provide strong support for single-issue movements (such as the anti-nuclear or Third World solidarity movements), but is not generally oppositional.

## The political thesis

The third explanation for the growth of NSMs focuses less on changes in social structures or values and more on the political arena. In many developed societies political parties have sought to shed their identification with particular classes or interest groups to become 'catch-all' parties (the British Labour Party under Tony Blair being a prime example). As a result, the social controls that political parties have traditionally exercised over their supporters are reduced, leaving citizens free to take up new political goals and new ways to engage in politics. At the same time, new forms of corporatist relations (see Chapter 4) have developed between powerful interest groups and the state, so consolidating power in the hands of elites. The policy-making process becomes less accountable to the general public, increasing levels of alienation and resistance among those excluded from it, particularly the well-educated, professionalised, middle ranks of workers. They are then more likely to reject existing forms of political involvement and to seek or invent new ones outside the conventional party-political system.

## Giddens, emancipatory politics and life politics

British sociologist Anthony Giddens suggests an approach to NSMs that integrates most of the ideas we have discussed. He argues that late modern society is characterised by the development of a new type of *life politics* — a politics of the self — in contrast to the older *emancipatory politics* — a politics of resistance to exploitation, inequality and oppression (1991, p.211). The latter includes political movements that aim to free people from the residues of the past (in the shape of tradition) or from current inequalities of power and domination. It tends to mobilise those who already enjoy a degree of emancipation to work to remove such conditions from society in general. An emancipatory politics is thus, according to Giddens, a politics of 'others'. The mobilising principle common to all forms of emancipatory politics is a belief in individual autonomy as the greatest good. To free people from subjection to constraint and domination is to enable them to exercise autonomous control over their own lives and destinies. It is a characteristic assumption of modernity that this is a good thing. But emancipatory political movements say little about how people should use their autonomy; this is where life politics has something to offer.

If emancipatory politics is a politics of others, life politics is a politics of the self. Giddens describes it variously as a politics of choice, a politics of lifestyle, and a politics of self-actualisation. The emergence of such a politics, he argues, is a sign that societies are reaching the stage of 'high' or 'late' modernity, where most, if not all, members of the society enjoy freedom from material constraints, such as poverty and hunger, and from domination by other social classes or groups. The aim of life politics is to develop an ethics around the issue of 'how should we live?' (1991, p.215). One of its most interesting effects is to make the processes of 'doing politics' as important an issue as the outcomes. How we organise ourselves to protest is as important as whether or not we achieve specific goals. Giddens borrows from feminism the phrase 'the personal is political' to express this idea: our everyday life is intimately connected with how society is organised, and our everyday processes of identity construction and interpersonal relationships form the basis for wider social organisation.

In a sense, we have now come back to where we started, with Habermas and the idea that NSMs are 'movements to defend the life-world'. For Giddens it is not so much that the life-world needs defending in late modernity, but that it needs to be expanded, developed and authenticated. We could say that NSMs are movements to add meaning to lives that have achieved a certain level of material comfort and legal freedom but lack a sense of authenticity and personal worth.

## NEW SOCIAL MOVEMENTS AND IRISH SOCIETY

In the remainder of this chapter we draw on the ideas outlined above to examine the experience of NSMs in Irish society. We discuss three examples here and in Chapter 17 we focus on a fourth, the environmental movement. In two of these cases (the women's and environmental movements) studies exist that draw explicitly on social movement theories to understand the Irish experience. In the other two (Catholic fundamentalism, Irish Travellers), the claim that we are dealing with an NSM at all may be contested; they have not yet been examined within this framework by Irish sociologists.

Discussing these cases helps us to learn more about Irish society. To what extent do explanations for the emergence of NSMs, such as the thesis of the 'new middle class', apply to a late developing, peripheral or dependent society like Ireland? Are new movements here a response to or shaped by indigenous Irish conditions, or are they more an example of cultural imperialism or external 'modernising' input into Irish culture? At the same time, to discuss particular examples of Irish movements allows us to explore further the concept of NSM and the theories and assumptions that lie behind it.

### The women's movement

Nearly all writers on NSMs point to a limited number of concrete examples: usually youth, student and peace movements, the ecology movement and the women's movement. The women's movement is generally regarded as an example of a 'classic' NSM. It has also been of great importance to developments in Irish society over the past four decades at least and no sociology of Ireland can ignore it. Some recent studies of the Irish women's movement (Mahon, 1995; Connolly, 1996; see also Galligan, 1998a) explicitly make use of the concepts and ideas of social movement theorists. Here we briefly examine the contrasting accounts presented by Mahon and Connolly.

Each writer agrees with Dahlerup (1986): the women's movement is a conscious, deliberate attempt to collectivise in order to bring about social change — with a focus on the political system as the target and with a key resource in the commitment and active participation of its members. Thus, each invokes a resource mobilisation perspective on the Irish women's movement. Connolly's analysis generally remains within this perspective. She treats the women's movement primarily as a set of social movement *organisations* and asks how they mobilised resources and ultimately achieved a degree of institutionalisation within the Irish political system (Galligan, 1998a, takes a similar approach). Mahon's discussion moves fairly quickly to circumstances outside of the women's movement and its constituent organisations; she emphasises the movement's wider social, economic and political context.

Each writer raises questions about characterising the women's movement in Ireland as a new social movement. Connolly argues strongly that it is not historically 'new'; we can trace the women's movement lineage back to the 1850s. She makes no theoretical distinction between 'old' and 'new' social movements nor does she adopt Giddens's distinction between emancipatory and lifestyle movements. As a result, Connolly may overstress the instrumental rationality and politicisation of the Irish and the international women's movements and underemphasise their symbolic or non-conventional methods of protest; she treats these as a result of exclusion from conventional institutional sources of power (1996, p.45). Other writers (for example, Oakley and Mitchell, 1998) have suggested that the international women's movement has embraced elements of both political activism and concerns about personal identity — that is, both emancipatory politics and life politics.

Another issue relates to the origins of the Irish women's movement: is it an indigenous phenomenon or, as opponents have sometimes labelled it, a cultural import? For Connolly, the Irish women's movement is 'organically' part of a global women's movement, but must also be recognised as Irish. We can only explain its resurgence in the 1970s by recognising that throughout the preceding fifty years or so — a period not at all conducive to feminist political success — a committed cadre of Irish feminists kept the movement alive. This group helped to form and maintain 'inter-movement networks' that provided a basis for organisation and mobilisation when the atmosphere once again became supportive. For Connolly, to say that the movement is distinctively Irish is to say that it is not *new*. This is a central finding of her research, and she argues that earlier research had overemphasised the significance for the contemporary Irish women's movement of external factors, such as the international Civil Rights and anti-Vietnam movements of the 1960s (1996, p.47).

Mahon also recognises earlier feminist movements but highlights the novel characteristics of the present one by referring to it as second wave feminism — 'an international phenomenon' that emerged in the United States and Northern Europe in the late 1960s and early 1970s (1995, p.677). What was internationalised, in her account, was not just the ideology of women's liberation but also the social structural conditions that enabled mobilisation to succeed among women exposed to it. She emphasises, in particular, the entry of large numbers of relatively well-educated women into the labour market. Such women usually entered jobs that were poorly paid or less satisfying than those that men, without necessarily better qualifications, held. From these conditions emerged feelings of relative deprivation that provided fertile ground for recruitment by the developing women's liberation movement.

Thus, the conditions faced by women in Ireland who were not part of the older established women's networks, but who were to become mobilised in the movement in the 1960s and 1970s, becomes an important part of the explanation. The Irish economy at that time was not the same as that of the post-war United States. As a late industrialising economy, Ireland offered few opportunities for industrial work for women. There was no critical labour shortage in the 1970s and 1980s to draw women into labour force participation. Indeed, state policies such as the public sector marriage bar discouraged women from aspiring to work outside the home. For Mahon what created fertile ground for an Irish mobilisation around feminist issues was: in the 1970s, the 'modernising influence' of EEC accession; in the 1980s, progressive changes in Irish women's education and labour force participation; and in the 1980s and 1990s, 'resistance to the EC's modernising influences' on the issues of divorce and abortion.

Mahon suggests, in summary, that once the structural conditions existed for the emergence of a women's movement, it developed more or less automatically. This is a common assumption in relation to NSMs that Connolly questions. Following RMT, she introduces the organisational resource issue as a major variable that intervenes between structural conditions and mobilisation. But Connolly has little to say about the structural changes in Irish society that Mahon sees as so relevant. While tracing the important links between earlier women's groups and the second wave feminist movement, Galligan (1998a, p.57) also stresses the close parallels between the development of the Irish women's movement and those in other Western countries such as Britain, Spain, Greece and the United States, for example, in the issues addressed by feminist groups and the issues that led to conflicts and splits within them.

The Irish feminist movement thus provides a good example of how varying social movement theories can produce different interpretations of reality. It also helps to bring into an Irish context some other issues that concern NSM theorists.

For example, it questions how we define success for a social movement like the Irish women's movement. Does it reside in incorporation and institutionalisation within the boundaries of 'conventional' interest-group politics? Or does it reside in the achievement of changes in lifestyles and the establishment of 'submerged networks' that make up the wider social movement? It also poses the question: how significant has the women's movement been in Ireland as a 'modernising' influence? The next case may shed further light on this question.

## Catholic fundamentalism

In April 1981 an organisation came into existence that was to have a major and divisive impact on Irish society for at least the next ten years. This was the Pro-Life Amendment Campaign (PLAC), set up with the aim of having an amendment inserted into the Irish Constitution that would formally guarantee the absolute right to life of the human embryo from the point of conception. The background to this demand was the rapidly increasing availability of abortion in many European countries and, in particular, its recent legalisation in 'traditionally Catholic countries such as Italy and Spain' (Inglis, 1998a, p.83). PLAC succeeded in having the amendment carried in the Referendum of 1983 after a bitter and divisive referendum campaign. In 1986 the strength of newly reorganised Catholic fundamentalism revealed itself again with the defeat of a referendum to amend the Constitution to allow for divorce legislation.

Further details on the activities of Catholic fundamentalists over the period can be found in Inglis (1998a), O'Reilly (1992) and Hug (1999). We are less interested here in describing the events that took place than in developing an explanation for them — specifically one that is framed by the debates over NSMs. Both Connolly (1996) and Mahon (1995) regard the emergence or resurgence of Catholic fundamentalism as one of the major events that has shaped the Irish women's movement over the past decade. Connolly argues that it was a significant force that pushed Irish feminists towards more mainstream activities and organisations during the 1980s, encouraging them in particular to use the courts as an arena to struggle for women's rights. Catholic fundamentalism thus helped, argues Connolly, to make the Irish women's movement into a less radical, more diffuse and more institutionalised social movement (1996, p.68).

Mahon (1995) emphasises the divisive impact that the formation of the Society for the Protection of the Unborn Child (SPUC) and later PLAC had on the women's movement and how subsequent campaigns helped to mobilise women into taking a more active part in the debates, on both sides. To that extent, Mahon suggests that the clash between the women's movement and a revived Catholic fundamentalism empowered women generally, even while it helped to destroy the idea of a single 'women's movement' that could articulate values that all women, by virtue of their gender, could agree on.

How can we understand the social impact of Catholic fundamentalism in Irish society during the 1980s and early 1990s? We suggest here that one useful way to understand it is to treat it as an example of an NSM. This is not the orthodox viewpoint, which treats Catholic fundamentalism as an inherent part of Irish society that occasionally becomes more vocal and politicised. Thus, while the women's movement has generally been interpreted as a (new) social movement, Catholic fundamentalism is painted in as the ubiquitous background against which Irish women have had to struggle for equality (Connolly refers to the anti-abortion campaign as 'a counter-right movement' (1996, p.63), but does not develop the idea further).

This prompts the question: is there something about how NSMs have been sociologically defined that prevents us from recognising religious fundamentalist movements as movements? Can a model of an NSM that has been developed to study movements like the women's, peace or environmental movements, make any sense at all of right-wing or conservative movements? We return to this question later to help us explore and develop the definition of an NSM. But we can also ask: why define Catholic fundamentalism as a social movement at all? What difference would it make to our understanding of Irish society — and of the role of religion and religious institutions in Ireland during the 1980s and early 1990s — to conceptualise the rise of religious fundamentalism in this way?

Journalist Emily O'Reilly (1992) has written a detailed account of the many and varied organisational forms, tactics and strategies used by the Catholic right in Ireland during this period. She interprets the phenomenon very largely as the achievement of a single individual, John O'Reilly (presumably no relation), 'a little-known state employee' who 'hijacked this country's social legislation for almost two decades' (1992, p.7) through his 'machinations on behalf of the conservative Catholic lobby' (1992, p.16). According to her, John O'Reilly was involved or instrumental in setting up a succession of Catholic fundamentalist organisations from the Irish Family League to PLAC, from SPUC to Family Solidarity, and including the Anti-Divorce Campaign of the mid-1980s and the second pro-life campaign of the early 1990s. In particular, she claims, John O'Reilly is a member of and has made maximum use of the organisational resources of the Knights of St. Columbanus, 'a patriarchal, secretive, Catholic, fundamentalist network of individual men who seek to exert power and influence through infiltration of hostile groups and organisations, anonymous lobbying, and the targeting of individuals hostile to their orthodoxy' (1992, p.20). O'Reilly quotes from a paper written by John O'Reilly in 1988 in which he argued that the Knights were particularly well placed to exercise secret influence over the direction of Irish society's development since 'an organisation or a group is never more powerful than when it influences events without itself being regarded as the initiator' (1992, p.29). Emily O'Reilly traces the concealed hand of the Knights within most of the Catholic fundamentalist organisations set up during the period, in particular PLAC. But behind the Knights we always find this single individual — John O'Reilly.

By contrast to this account of the remarkable influence of a committed individual, UCD sociologist Tom Inglis treats of the public morality campaigns of the 1970s to 1990s (contraception, divorce, abortion, homosexuality, sex education) as a consequence of the activities of the Catholic hierarchy or of the Catholic Church as a whole. Though he concedes that it was only towards the end of the 1983 pro-life campaign 'that the clerical resources of the Church began to be used fully' (1998a, p.84), he nevertheless claims that an analysis of the campaign shows that 'the hierarchy used the full organisation of the Church to urge the laity to remain loyal to its teachings and to incorporate these into the political framework of the country' (1998a, p.87). In relation to the 1986 divorce referendum, despite describing 'the anti-divorce lobby' as 'not formally linked to the Church' he concludes that 'the referendum demonstrated the continuing ability of the hierarchy to set limits to the political sphere in Irish society' (1998a, p.90). Inglis's account is part of the dominant public discourse in relation to these events: that the Catholic Church continued to claim the right to exert power and influence over Irish society. The only difference was that, due to changes in circumstances and social values, it did so through relatively autonomous organisations of lay Catholics rather than directly through the church hierarchy.

Both these explanations — one individualistic, the other institutionalist — are highly conspiratorial accounts of social change, where appearances are deceptive and hidden interests work covertly behind organisational fronts. When dealing with a religious institution like the Catholic Church, this conspiratorialism is hard to accept. It implies that the church membership or *laity* plays no part except as pawns of the hierarchy or the Knights: they must be dupes who cannot see they are being manipulated, or their religious devotion is spurious and a product only of indoctrination, coercion, opportunism or laziness. This is where an NSM approach may be useful. From the point of view of NSM theorists, social change is not the result of a conspiracy and those involved are not the unwitting dupes of conspirators. We are encouraged to take participants in NSMs seriously as competent and committed actors, even if their goals are antipathetic or alien to us.

An NSM approach also raises important challenges to standard interpretations of the power of Catholicism in contemporary Irish society. While we discussed the position of religion in Irish society in some detail in Chapter 12, here we wish to revisit some of the more influential interpretations of religion in Irish society that have been produced by sociologists, and ask how these might relate to our suggestion that Catholic fundamentalism should be treated as a social movement.

The first writer we examine, very briefly, is Tony Fahey, author of a broad range of sociological papers on Catholicism and Irish society. In his (1992a) paper, 'Catholicism in Ireland', Fahey's primary concern is with secularisation: how well has modernisation theory predicted the progress (or otherwise) towards secularism in Irish society? He suggests that although recent data on the falling numbers of Catholic clerical and religious personnel working in Ireland might indicate fairly strong secularisation tendencies, when placed in a broader historical perspective this conclusion could be quite misleading. Fahey suggests that the numbers of recruits to the church in the late nineteenth and early twentieth centuries was abnormally high. This was a remarkable period of Catholic resurgence and reconstruction in the years after the Famine. Since the 1960s there has been an inevitable return to more normal and 'sustainable' levels (1992a, p.308).

By so treating change in the church, Fahey creates the impression that we are witnessing a process of Irish society 'normalising or renormalising itself'. This obscures the fact that church influence in social affairs was the focus of sustained mobilisations and struggles throughout the 1970s and 1980s. For example, Fahey does not refer to the part played by the women's movement in challenging Catholic teaching, particularly in areas to do with family relationships and the control of fertility. To that extent, Connolly's complaint that 'the centrality of the women's movement to the rapid pace of *social change* in Ireland has not been adequately demonstrated by mainstream sociology' (1996, p.44) seems justified. But in ignoring the challenges to the church during this period, Fahey also ignores the possibility that movements to *defend* it against secularising pressures also developed. The only 'activists' he recognises in recent Irish Catholicism are those 'church groups taking a leading role in highlighting problems of poverty and social justice in Irish society . . . providing a dynamism of sorts in the shape of a new, poverty-centred oppositional role for the church' (1992a, p.311). This helps to buttress the assumption, which we question further below, that social movements are inherently oppositional and on the side of the weak, excluded or powerless.

We should also note that for Fahey — and he is by no means alone in this — 'Catholicism in Ireland' refers first and foremost to the institutional church and its members (priests, nuns, monks, brothers) and only in a quite limited way to the laity. He justifies this position by arguing that the resurgence and reconstruction of the nineteenth-century church was primarily focused on the institutional church and left little room for lay activity to develop. The new 'strongly devotional Catholic culture' that did emerge among the laity was, he says, strongly oriented to and dependent on church ritual, and he suggests that lay religious behaviour remains quite ritualised — 'for many adherents, their religion is not a very profound thing' (1992a, p.311). It is not surprising, then, that Fahey does not consider the possibility that a strong force in securing 'continuity' for Catholicism in Ireland in recent years might have been the emergence of a lay Catholic social movement.

This may encourage us to ask why lay Catholics, in contemporary Ireland, would continue to support their church. A possible answer is offered by two other analyses of the position of the contemporary church: Inglis (1998a) and Nic Ghiolla Phádraig (1995). Each answers in terms of *power*: the power of the church over its lay members. We suggest that an NSM perspective might have produced a rather different understanding of power to those offered.

Nic Ghiolla Phádraig, like Fahey, disputes the relevance for Ireland of the secularisation thesis. She suggests that 'the greatest puzzle facing sociologists examining religion in Ireland [is] its continuing strength' (1995, p.594) and offers as a solution an analysis of the church in terms of its power over Irish society. She suggests that Irish Catholics continue to practice their religion and to support their church's political positions because the church has some power to compel them to do so. Nic Ghiolla Phádraig argues that this power derives from two key sources: ideological control and control of significant material, organisational and human resources.

Nic Ghiolla Phádraig pays little attention to the Catholic laity. She notes the presence in Irish Catholicism of 'a very clear radical movement' (1995, p.613) which is critical of the institutional church, and talks about the contribution the church makes to the reproduction of inequality in Irish society. But in both cases her discussion focuses almost entirely on the actions of priests and members of religious orders. Only belatedly does she raise the possibility that the activities of lay Catholics may also be important for sociologists to examine, suggesting that the current decline in religious vocations may be opening a gap that could be filled by greater lay involvement. She notes, significantly, that this may have happened as lay Catholics have 'been . . . taking the lead on political matters such as the campaign against divorce and abortion' (1995, p.616). But she does not develop this point in relation to her overall thesis about the power of the Catholic Church.

In terms of power, how should we interpret this involvement by the laity? Is it evidence for a decline in the power of the religious institution or, on the contrary, evidence for a resurgence and regrowth in that power? This leads us to ask how we should define the Catholic Church itself: does it consist only of the hierarchy, priests and religious, or does it also incorporate the laity. If the laity are indeed part of the church, how does the church exercise power over this part of its own institution?

The issue of power is also central to Inglis's (1987; 1998a) work. Inglis argues that the Catholic Church should be recognised as a 'power bloc' in Irish society, and refers to similar 'power resources' (ideological authority, organisational strength) as those cited by Nic Ghiolla Phádraig. But Inglis pays far more attention to the position of the Catholic laity. He does not believe that Irish lay Catholics are coerced, compelled or manipulated into supporting their church, but insists that as rational, self-interested people they have something to gain from their membership. Since the church is a power bloc, participation allows ordinary Irish people access to some power for themselves, whether in the form of occupational advancement, material wealth, or social prestige and the respect of their fellow-citizens. Inglis (1987, p.64) is quite explicit about his view of human nature, saying that people's involvement in society:

presupposes a more fundamental, calculated and selfish struggle to get their own way. Even when people appear to be acting on the basis of a non-rational commitment to a norm such as 'love thy neighbour as thyself', their actions can be understood as an attempt to gain a more immediate goal such as the moral respect of others.

This is a rather pessimistic view of human nature that ignores the possibility that people can act in support of values and ideals, not just their interests. Inglis seems to back away from this perspective as he develops his argument further; ultimately his analysis reflects two contradictory understandings of power and its exercise. One is the *zero-sum* theory of power, where power over another involves no more than coercion and control. The other is the *non-zero-sum* theory of power, where power is a relationship between two parties where each has something to gain: the 'powerless' party has co-operation to offer, and may gain some reward — and some power — from compliance. The latter approach to power may apply in particular to legitimate power, based on a level of agreement and used to some degree for the common good rather than for selfish sectional interests. Weber tells us that these are the most stable, successful and durable forms of power, because subordinates do not experience their obedience as bowing to compulsion; rather they feel that in obeying they increase their own capacities to live the way they want.

Inglis's analysis moves ambiguously between these two concepts of power. Sometimes he presents the church as supremely powerful, coercing a powerless laity; at other times he suggests that in complying with, supporting, or even trying to expand the power of the church lay Catholics can expand their own power and their capacity to realise their interests. In discussing the 1983 pro-life campaign he says that it was 'from the beginning a lay Catholic movement which attained the full support of the Church. The issue . . . was whether the Constitution should be changed to reflect the interests of this lay Catholic pressure group and the Church as a whole' (1998a, p.87). But he follows this almost immediately with an analysis of the referendum campaign that presents it as a matter of pressure, from the institutional church, on the state and individual lay Catholics, to accept that its teachings on abortion should enter Irish law.

A similar ambiguity can be seen in Inglis's discussion (1998a, pp.88–91) of the 1986 divorce campaign. We might conclude that he rejects the zero-sum approach to power, recognising that there are ways that membership in a powerful church and obedience to its rules can be empowering for the laity; but in the end he is unwilling to treat the church as in any sense a 'legitimate authority' in Irish society. To put this another way, Inglis is one of the few sociologists writing on Irish religion to recognise the importance of treating the laity as more than simply dupes of the church — and that must be regarded as a major advance. However, ultimately, his approach is not as effective as it could have been as he does not pay enough attention to differences among the laity — neither to those who experience membership in the church as empowering, nor to those who do not.

How does this relate to our attempt to connect religious fundamentalism to NSM theory? If we think of what happened in the 1980s and early 1990s as the emergence of a religious social movement, we can be alert to issues of power, and of lay membership of the church, in rather different ways. In particular, we can think of the laity, at least certain sections of it, as more actively involved with their religion and more committed to specific values and ideological world views than most commentators appear to recognise. We must stop thinking that it is only 'the church' that resists secularisation, for example, by trying to tighten its coercive and manipulative grip over a relatively passive lay membership. The laity may also resist secularisation and may even outflank the institutionalised church in how it does so.

This may lead us to reconsider the power of the Catholic Church in Irish society. It now appears not to be dependent on the passive obedience of the laity but perhaps more on the active work of lay members as they repair and redevelop the vulnerable power resources of the church as an institution. As both Inglis and Nic Ghiolla Phádraig point out, powerful groups or institutions in society stay in power because they possess both material and ideological resources. But ideological control is never static, it must constantly be re-created and reproduced in the face of threats and challenges. The fundamentalist campaigns of the last twenty years can be seen as mobilisations by certain sections of the Irish Catholic laity to defend and promote a world view and a set of values. The concept of social movement offers a useful way to understand the practices and strategies involved. Sociologists of religion in Ireland should perhaps refocus their attention away from the single social movement organisation — the institutional church — and broaden it to encompass the wider social movement, including significant groups of lay members.

Can we legitimately talk of a religious movement in terms of NSM theory? Perhaps not if religious beliefs and affiliations are no more than vestiges of the pre-modern stage of social development. But this only makes sense if we assume that modernisation implies secularisation and the triumph of reason and science over faith and theology. It may be time to re-examine this idea, particularly in the light of Giddens's suggestion that late modernity is accompanied by the emergence of life politics movements that attempt to give meaning and purpose to individual lives. If Giddens is right, should we expect a resurgence of religion in late modernity, rather than its disappearance? And is this more likely to generate 'new religions' (such as Scientology) that spring directly from the struggle to make sense of contemporary experience and the self, rather than to appear as a movement by an established religion to retain its ideological and material power base in society?

NSM theorising may lead us to make distinctions between 'new' and 'old' movements that are too rigid. The Catholic fundamentalist movement in Ireland suggests that 'traditional' ideas can be transformed as they are brought into play in new circumstances; they can indeed become part of a late modern politics of choice and lifestyle (we can perhaps see parallels here with the trajectory of the Irish language).

A more serious barrier to acceptance of Catholic fundamentalism as an NSM lies in the genealogy of the term itself. We have seen how in Europe the NSM concept has been directly linked to a progressive politics and philosophy through its treatment in the works of Habermas and Touraine. It is hard to see Catholic fundamentalism as progressive in this sense. If we term it an NSM, does this open up the category to *any* social movement — the French National Front, for example? For the RMT perspective, this is not an issue, as it does not involve any evaluation of the nature of a social movement. Should social movements be studied simply as organisations, or is it necessary to link them to specific theories about societal change? We will try to develop these issues further with our final case study.

## The Irish Travellers' movement

Roman Catholics remain a majority group in Irish society and this colours any assessment of a social movement that pursues their interests. On the other hand, Travellers are one of the most significant minority groups in Irish society. With Ireland's increasing religious, political, cultural and sexual diversity, greater attention is now being paid to the experiences and human rights of minority groups. The pressure to adapt to diversity is exerted both from within elements of the majority — not least sections of the state — but also from minority groups. One of the most significant sources is the Traveller movement: does this make it a new social movement and, if so, what are the implications of NSM theory for an understanding of the changing position of Travellers in Irish life?

One view suggests that there has been an increased tolerance of diversity within Irish society, and that Travellers have benefited from this. This optimistic view would point to expanded educational provision, the role of the media, EU membership, foreign travel and a general improvement in living standards as positive factors. According to this view, greater tolerance of diversity is another mark of a successfully modernising society. A more pessimistic view of the position of Travellers in Irish society would draw attention to the increasing *intolerance* of diversity in Ireland, as indicated in the racist response to refugees, asylum seekers, New Age Travellers and any others who display 'visible difference' (Pollack, 1999; McVeigh, 1998; Kuhling, 1998). It would stress the continuing difficulties experienced by Travellers in gaining basic human rights and how legal and bureaucratic structures help to maintain an institutional structure of discrimination.

Generally missing from either the positive or negative accounts is any recognition of how Travellers themselves, as a social movement, have helped to shape their incorporation into modernity. By and large, recent sociological research on issues related to Travellers in Ireland has paid little direct attention to this aspect of their lives. For example, McCann *et al.* (1994), a major volume on the topic, focuses on the emergence of new understandings of Travellers as a social group within social science and policy discourses, rather than within the Travelling community itself.

It is widely recognised that there has been a radical transformation of how the position of Travellers has been interpreted over the past twenty-five years: from a subgroup of the poor, or subculture (see Chapter 11), to a distinct ethnic group. According to McCann *et al.* (1994, p.xi) 'the concept [of ethnicity] has radical implications for the study of Irish Travellers because it approaches Traveller culture as distinct and valuable in its own right with its own historical path of development, rather than as a short-term adaptation to poverty or marginality.' It has also, they claim, encouraged major changes in policy towards Travellers, identifying 'the need for policies which respect cultural differences, rather than ones which seek to erode them in the name of the settled community's image of "social improvement" or its administrative convenience' (1994, p.xii).

The claim that Irish Travellers constitute a distinct ethnic group is controversial within academic research. Where Ní Shúinéar (1994) argues strongly for recognising Travellers as a distinct ethnic group, McLoughlin (1994) responds just as strongly that this is not a useful or productive way to understand their experience. We pause briefly here to discuss how *ethnicity* has been conceptualised in these debates and suggest that an NSM approach could add important dimensions to our understanding of social change in this area.

For Ní Shúinéar ethnicity is a matter of possession of objective social and cultural characteristics that can be used as criteria to decide, in relation to any social group, whether it is an 'ethnic group' or not. The main characteristics are:

- biological self-perpetuation
- racial difference
- shared fundamental cultural values and cultural difference
- social separation from other groups
- the presence of language barriers
- hostility or antipathy between the group and members of other groups.

In her view, Irish Travellers can be shown to exhibit all of these and thus 'meet all the objective scientific criteria of an ethnic group' (1994, p.54).

There is an alternative way to understand ethnicity that has received attention from sociologists and anthropologists. It focuses on the *subjective* dimensions of ethnic group membership rather than on an objective possession of racial or cultural characteristics. Here, ethnicity resides:

- in the belief by members of a social group that they are culturally distinctive and different to outsiders

- in their willingness to find symbolic markers of that difference (for example, food habits, religion, forms of dress, language) and to emphasise their significance
- in their willingness to organise relationships with outsiders so that a kind of 'group boundary' is preserved and reproduced.

McLoughlin (1994) treats ethnicity not as a set of objective characteristics but as a *claim* that groups make about themselves or about others. Claiming to be an ethnic group is, in her view, part of a larger social and political agenda. Instead of asking: does this group really meet the objective criteria that constitute ethnicity? we should ask: does it help this group's situation to be pursuing this agenda — to 'play the ethnic card' — rather than some other one?

We may clarify the debate further if we briefly shift from thinking about ethnicity to a related phenomenon: national identity. The system of national identities that we know today emerged during the nineteenth century with the universal growth of nationalism (see Chapter 11). Nationalism is best understood as a social movement attached to a clear social and political agenda. We can also distinguish between nationalism and nationality: the latter refers to cultural or social differences that exist between groups (such as language), while the former refers to social movements that claim equality of status and self-determination for groups that feel themselves to be distinct.

By analogy it might be useful to use the term 'ethnicism' to talk about how groups make claims based on cultural difference and 'ethnicity' to refer to observable cultural differences. But we would have to recognise (where neither McLoughlin nor Ní Shúinéar do) that there is no necessary correlation between the two: a group can seek to establish its cultural worth even if it does not appear to possess anything that clearly distinguishes it culturally from others; and conversely groups that may be culturally very distinctive may not embark on an ethnicist movement at all.

This discussion suggests that the debate around Travellers' ethnicity is to a degree misplaced. It may be more useful to study how an ethnicist movement has arisen among Travellers in recent years and how this has profoundly affected both Travellers themselves and policy-makers and members of Irish society more generally. We can investigate whether this change in the Traveller discourse has been of benefit. For example, has the shift from a 'culture of poverty' discourse towards ethnicity helped to empower Travellers themselves?

The Dublin Travellers' Education and Development Group (DTEDG) should be regarded as a very significant organisation in terms of the development of ethnicism within the Travellers' movement. It developed in the early 1980s as an organisation that involved equally both settled people (mainly social workers or researchers with a professional interest in Travellers) and Travellers. This signalled a major difference from previous bodies, such as the National Council for Travelling People, which had been set up by and included only settled people and which worked *for* rather than *with* Travellers. John O'Connell (1992, p.7), Director of the DTEDG, described this difference:

> When we formally established the DTEDG in 1985 we acknowledged Travellers as an ethnic group. We decided that any work with Travellers should support their right to retain and develop their identity . . . We also wanted to offer our skills in support of Travellers in their struggle for justice and acceptance in Irish society.

Gmelch, an anthropologist who has written extensively on Traveller culture, has focused on the development of a Traveller ethnicity that can be traced back to the 1880s (Gmelch and Gmelch, 1976). She has documented (Gmelch, 1989) in particular the growing politicisation and mobilisation among Travellers during the 1980s. An important step was the establishment in 1984 of the organisation Mincéir Misli — significant because it was a Traveller-run organisation and also because it used for its title Gammon or Shelta words, signalling to the world at large for perhaps the first time that Irish Travellers saw themselves as a distinctive ethnic group that counted possession of a distinct language as a central symbol of this distinctiveness (see Binchy, 1994; Ó Baoill, 1994).

Gmelch's account of Mincéir Misli suggests that it closely resembles many NSM organisations in the multi-faceted nature of its analysis of Travellers' problems and of possible solutions to them. It has acted variously as a political lobby for Travellers' rights, a training ground for movement spokespeople, a contact point for group members and a cultural agency (publisher, film-maker) intervening in the perceptions of Travellers held both by Travellers themselves and by members of the settled society.

Although language has emerged as a significant marker of ethnicity for Travellers, a more significant symbol that summarises and captures for them their essential identity and difference from other groups in Irish society is *nomadism*. There is a certain irony in this, given Gmelch's suggestion that the emergence of ethnicism among Irish Travellers is linked to their transformation from a predominantly rural, mobile group in the 1960s to a substantially urban, 'immobile' group in the late 1980s.

Gmelch argues that the experience of urban migration (by 1981 over a quarter of all Traveller families were based in Dublin) has been a particularly important factor for the emergence of the Traveller movement. It contributed to a situation where settled people's anger and hostility towards Travellers greatly increased, which in turn helped to politicise Travellers themselves. It also helped to create the conditions under which collective mobilisation of Travellers was made easier. Urbanisation gave Travellers 'the logistical ability' to organise themselves (Gmelch, 1989, p.309) and, in the forging of an explicit group identity that followed, nomadism or at least the cultural transmission of 'a nomadic mindset' from one generation of Travellers to the next has become their most important distinctive attribute. Stimulating this development has been the growth of contacts between Irish Travellers and Traveller and Gypsy organisations elsewhere in Europe, also engaged in creating ethnic identity systems to symbolise their own distinctiveness.

We suggested earlier that an NSM perspective on the situation of Irish Travellers might be useful. In particular, it helps us to recognise that Travellers have been actively involved in a movement for recognition as an ethnic group and that this claim is not only a result of changes in thinking or practice among policy-makers, community workers or academic researchers. But considering the Irish Travellers' movement as an ethnicist social movement does lead us to the question: how has social research and theorising among professionals helped to produce this new phenomenon? And has sociology actively contributed to social change?

The 'culture of poverty' approach to interpreting their situation, first developed by McCarthy (1971), profoundly influenced how ordinary Irish people thought about Travellers and helped to shape the policies that were introduced to deal with 'the itinerant problem' during the 1970s. McCarthy has since rejected this approach and admitted that it 'has done them a great disservice in so far as the theory has been used by certain people to discredit Travellers and to negate their separate cultural identity' (1994, p.128). Although the development of a different theoretical approach to Travellers, based on the idea of a distinct ethnicity, has been in part a result of the fact that Travellers have become more vocal and that researchers have begun to listen, it is also clear that outside professionals and intellectuals have contributed in no small way to the elaboration of ethnic identity and ethnicist claims that Travellers have experienced.

O'Connell (1992) documents how researchers and community workers who operate with conceptions of Travellers as a culturally oppressed (not simply economically marginalised) group were involved in running workshops and consciousness-raising courses with Travellers in the early to mid-1980s. McCann et al. (1994) also indicate the extent of dialogue between researchers and Travellers around the concept of ethnicity. To a certain extent concepts of cultural oppression and ethnicity were already gaining currency among sociologists and social activists in Ireland as a way of understanding social exclusion and marginalisation in general, before they were specifically used to understand the situation of Travellers. The role of intellectuals both from within and outside social movements in developing movement ideas and practices is an issue that has generated much interesting sociological research in recent times. We mention it here to show that sociology itself, inasmuch as it helps to develop conceptual tools, has a potential role in bringing about social change.

## SOCIOLOGY AND THE STUDY OF SOCIAL MOVEMENTS

We started this chapter by asking: why should sociologists be interested in NSMs? To end, we turn that question around and ask: what does the recent growth in sociological interest in NSMs tell us about the development of sociology itself? The development of a burgeoning NSM literature does suggest some profound changes in the discipline of sociology. In particular, it indicates a shift away from *structural* types of analysis towards an interest in *action* and *agency* — a desire to identify those social actors that actively bring about or resist change.

For some sociologists this is a victory for Weberianism over Marxism. Marx suggested that capitalist society produced two opposing classes with an *objective* reality: we can explain why people act in certain ways by drawing attention to their class membership. Weber agreed that we can deduce a certain class structure from an examination of the organisation of capitalist society, but this may reveal little of what happens in terms of struggles for power and social honour and about dominant ideas and values. For Weber, this requires an analysis of *subjective* reality: whether people recognise themselves as a class, or perhaps another sort of collectivity such as an ethnic, religious or occupational one. It is only then that we can identify the significant agents of modern society.

It would be wrong to overemphasise the differences between Weber and Marx on this point. Each sought to address the fact that, to paraphrase Marx, it is people who make history but they do not choose the circumstances in which they do so. Sociologists have always had to deal with the dilemma of structure and agency (see Chapter 6) — what weight to give to the external and unchosen social circumstances that shape our action, and to the voluntary meaning-creating and choice-making activities of individual or collective actors. The current focus on NSMs suggests that sociological theorising has moved towards the agency side of the equation, without wanting to entirely abandon structure.

What we have termed the European perspective on social movements has tended towards a more structural interpretation of NSMs whereas the dominant American perspective is more action- or agency-oriented. Hence the European insistence that NSMs are of structural importance to modern (late capitalist, post-industrial, post-materialist) society, and so should be studied by sociology; American research lacks such a rationale. As European researchers increasingly emphasise the symbolic creativity and cultural innovation of NSMs, they move towards a position that recognises the limited value of structural analysis. Increasingly, the movements have to be regarded as the *source* of (new) social structure, rather than simply the product of it. Social cleavages, including class cleavages, can be seen to emerge from the ideological and political struggles of the movements rather than just being part of a determinant social structure. In the second part of this chapter we looked at some cases that may benefit from a social movements analysis. We hope this may illustrate how this approach can open up issues to do with agency in Irish society and focus on the active participation of Irish people in creating their own distinctive social world.

# Part IV

A post-modern society?

# Introduction

Throughout this book, we have emphasised the links between the evolution of sociology and the parallel development of modernity. If there has been such a thing as the 'project of modernity', sociology has been very much part of it. It has sought to come to grips with perhaps the most rapid and far-reaching change in history, as human beings have adapted to urban living, routinised industrial employment, diminishing networks of kin and new experiences of time, movement and space. Much of our discussion has focused on the notions of development and modernity and has questioned how such terms and concepts have been applied to Irish society. We have tried to resist the tendency to submerge the Irish experience within a generic view of 'Western development', and to emphasise that the Irish experience is not merely 'deviant', but may have something to say about how we conceptualise and analyse social change.

If the nineteenth and the first half of the twentieth centuries were about the global spread of modernity, at least since the 1960s there has been an argument that we are now entering a new historical epoch: *post-modernity*. This is the time of 'post- . . . ': post-modern; post-industrial; post-capitalist; post-Fordist . . . ; each refers to a feeling that we are entering a new era and thus leaving something behind. Perhaps less clear is whether post-modernism refers to a way of being, a way of thinking about being, or both. We do not intend to delve into the genealogy or archaeology of the concept of post-modernity here. Rather, we will briefly signal some of the issues developed in the concluding part of the book.

If post-modernism is a way of being, there seems to be some agreement on what that might mean. A post-modern world is perhaps above all a world where *information* is the fundamental resource. Information is seen to underpin new forms of economy (in particular, so-called service industries such as finance, tourism and education); new types of relationships (those mediated through the mass media or the Internet) and new types of wealth and power (as in Foucault's couplet, power/knowledge, where each helps to constitute the other). Post-modernism is also about the compression of time and space, as the world of speed and mobility comes to dominate our social interactions and relationships.

The facilitator of the information age is *technology*, in particular, the technologies of communication and information — computer networks, jet travel, satellites, silicon chips. There tends to be a strong element of technological determinism in thinking about post-modernism. In the same way that the steel/coal/rail/electricity complex 'created' the world of modernity, post-modernism is seen to be at least partly the outcome of computers and allied technologies.

Post-modernism is also the age of *reflexivity*, a term we introduced in Part I. It is quintessentially a self-conscious and knowing age, whether expressed as an obsession with body and image; an increasingly self-referential mass media; or a sceptical and tentative social studies that is increasingly aware of its own implication in relations of domination and uncertain of the validity of its procedures and ideas. In post-modernism we may *know*, but we also know how *and* why we know and why we might not.

This leads us to the second position — that post-modernism is not really so much about changes in the real world, but in how we talk about and analyse that world. Here the key concept is the collapse in the validity of what are termed 'totalising narratives'; in other words, those types of knowledge that seek, and claim, to offer answers to the 'big' questions about our lives and society. The totalising, or grand, narrative is very much associated with modernity, where first the global religions, then the sciences, then Marxism and functionalism, and perhaps latterly economics, have provided an overarching framework for people to make sense of their society and lives.

In post-modernism, faith in grand narratives has declined as they collapse under their own contradictions. There has been a shift towards the local, the specific and the contextualised. We can only know what is happening in the here and now in relation to the particular object that we are studying for the moment. We can not generalise, for to do so is to do violence to the diversity of experiences and identities. Indeed, we can no longer assume that 'identity' is unified and singular. Post-modernism asserts that our identities are multiple; constituted through language (especially, for example, by the powerful discourses of the media, the law and medicine) and intimately related to and shaped by the circumstances that surround us.

Much of this is very threatening to sociological thought and practice. First, it challenges sociology's claims to be a grand narrative, and it is certainly the case that the broad theoretical schemas of functionalism and Marxism have fallen into disfavour. At their peak they claimed to be able to explain everything from art to sexuality: now they have often been replaced with eclectic theoretical approaches that may equally draw upon literary theory or psychoanalysis as on the categories of class, gender or ethnicity. Second, with post-modernism has come a suspicion of positivism, indeed, of evidence in general. So much of post-modern theorising depends on language and the play of language. Sociologists are far less inclined now to go out 'into the field'; they are often more interested in the analysis of documents, the deconstruction of visual imagery or the mining of a small number of in-depth interviews. Large-scale scientific survey research still goes on, but is rarely seen to have anything exciting to say at a theoretical or conceptual level. Third, the very concepts of society and nation, which we have seen to be so central to the sociological enterprise, have increasingly been called into question. Ex-British Prime Minister Margaret Thatcher's celebrated remark that 'there is no such thing as society' captured the post-modern mood, if not its politics. National borders dissolve into transnational entities like the EU or the North Atlantic Free Trade Area (NAFTA), while simultaneously populations fragment into consumer groupings, ethnic enclaves and gated communities. The result, for post-modernists, is a world that is constantly in flux and impossible to pin down, whether by sociologists or anyone else.

It is from within such a context that we look back and trace some of the recent developments in Irish society that might help us to think through this putative new state of affairs. We have chosen to focus on three areas that we feel have much to tell us about how our society might be changing, and that reflect some of the developments within the field of sociology itself, as it seeks to come to terms with the (possible) new era.

The first two — consumption and environmentalism — to some extent mark the shift, both within the economy and within sociological interest, from *production* to *consumption*. If nothing else, the age of post-modernity is defined through its practices of consumption. It is the time when shopping has become the Western world's major leisure activity and when the shopping centre, as suggested in an earlier chapter, has become the new cathedral. But consumption is not without its costs and, we argue, it has been a stimulus towards a politics and an ethos of environmentalism that has become one of the contemporary world's most significant aspects. Finally, we examine the phenomenon of globalisation. Does it make sense any more to talk of a sociology of Ireland as we have claimed for this volume? Or do the dual forces of transnational economics and global culture render such concepts and projects anachronous? We are sure that the arguments we make in the final chapters will leave as many questions for the future as answers — at least we hope so.

# 16
# Consumption

What is consumption, and why is it of interest to sociology? Consumption refers to how we use material objects, though the term also includes the use of services like having a haircut or going to the doctor and of facilities like transportation systems or landscapes. Consumption is a central part of everyday life. It has a great deal to do with how we meet our material needs but includes much more, as this chapter will reveal. How we consume goods and services makes up much of what we conceptualise as culture; for in consuming goods and services we consume culture and we also create and re-create it.

Given the key significance of consumption in our lives, the attention accorded to it by sociologists has been remarkably limited. While the term 'consumer society' has long been used to describe modern, capitalist society, its analysis has been left to economists and psychologists rather than to social theorists. But within the last decade a sociology of consumption has begun to establish itself. This is linked to a renewed interest, among sociologists in general, in culture and processes of cultural change that is replacing earlier preoccupations with social structure and structural processes. It is also connected with a growing interest in the sociology of young people and youth culture. Young people are in some senses the archetypal consumers of contemporary society, not only because they often have more disposable income than other groups, but also because the link between consumption and the construction of identity seems to be particularly evident in their consuming behaviour.

## THEORETICAL ANTECEDENTS

As we have stressed throughout this book, sociology developed historically as the study of modernity. This renders the lack of interest in consumption particularly odd as, for many people, increased consumption is the distinguishing feature of modern society. We can find a reason, perhaps, in how the early sociologists structured the understanding of modernity. The inheritance of Marxism is particularly important here for, in spite of Marx's emphasis on a materialist approach to history, he focused predominantly on just one aspect of the production and exchange of goods: that of production. While he saw capitalism as a system that encouraged people to consume and to 'fetishise' commodities, he helped to divert sociological attention away from consumption by arguing that the inevitable tendency of capitalism was towards the 'immiseration' of increasing numbers of working people, to the extent that this would provoke a socialist revolution.

Marx suggested that by the time capitalism had become fully established in the world the experience of the working class would generally be one of such reduced consumption that they would be unable even to buy the bare necessities of food and clothing, let alone the more optional goods from which a lifestyle and personal identity might be created. As far as the developed world is concerned, at least, this prediction has turned out to be wrong; but it meant that Marxist sociologists were relatively uninterested in, or unprepared to examine, the expansion of working-class consumption that took place.

Weber also helped, in a different way, to direct sociological attention away from the place of consumption in modern society. He argued that the development of capitalism was significantly shaped by the emergence, in early modern Europe, of a particular type of Protestantism (see Chapter 12), which he called 'ascetic Protestantism' to emphasise its stress on self-denial. Ascetic Protestants were committed to an ethic of hard work and success in their working lives, but saw this as a way to honour God, not to acquire a luxurious lifestyle. This encouraged Protestant businessmen to accumulate large amounts of capital that they reinvested in their businesses rather than spending it on themselves; many became wealthy capitalist producers but nevertheless lived domestic lives of frugality or, at best, modest comfort. The success of these businessmen encouraged others to follow their example. Weber thus provides a fascinating explanation for the growth in early modern Europe of a 'culture of capitalism' that, in promoting dedication to work and entrepreneurial success, substantially accounted for the spread of capitalism as an economic system. But he did not explain how, as capitalism developed and matured, the ascetic ethic of the early capitalists came to be replaced by the contemporary acceptance of consumption, or what we might call an ethic of consumption.

We commence this chapter, then, with an examination of how an interest in consumption has developed in recent sociology, despite the preoccupations of the founders of the discipline. We examine Veblen's early discussion of consumption, which continues to influence contemporary approaches, and the sorts of questions posed by the sociology of consumption. We are also concerned with how a sociology of consumption might be relevant to understanding Irish society. Although there has been research in Ireland on aspects of culture, and on attitudes to commodities like food and drink, or the landscape, a sociology of consumption is only beginning to develop. But we should not take for granted that the history of consumption or its significance in everyday life have been the same in Ireland as, for example, in Britain, where most of the work in this field has been done to date. An Irish sociology of consumption may help to question theories that have emerged from the core countries, and may also suggest new perspectives on the nature of social change and modernisation in Irish society.

Some of the most powerful critiques of consumption and its place in modern societies have been generated by the environmental movement. A key contributor to sociological debates that has emerged from this tradition is André Gorz, whose arguments we examine at the end of this chapter. For Gorz the degradation of the environment is linked not just to how, in developed capitalist society, we organise production, but also to the unsustainable way that we manage consumption. The challenge that faces contemporary environmentalism is to somehow reverse the trend of capitalist development, that has seen a continuous expansion in consumption levels and in the desire for consumption across the world.

There are links, then, between this chapter and the next, which deals specifically with environmentalism. Both topics raise questions about the further development of society and of sociology itself. If sociology grew originally out of a set of Enlightenment beliefs — in progress, the advance of reason and science — is there a sense that these new concerns are helping to undermine those beliefs? Are they pushing us towards a new type of sociology — perhaps a 'post-modern sociology' for post-modern times?

## FROM LEISURE CLASSES TO MASS SOCIETY

We noted earlier that Weber associates capitalist development with the repression of the desire to consume, rather than its expansion. In response Campbell (1987) aims to develop a theory to explain the parallel revolution in consumption. He initially confronts the question: why do we need an explanation at all? Surely it is natural to human beings to consume and all that can hold them back is a lack of resources? Even if modern patterns of consumption satisfy more than basic needs, have there not always been examples of greed and extreme desire for material possessions, in all societies? If so, then there is nothing peculiar about the place of consumption in modern societies.

Campbell argues that there is something significant to be explained. The behaviour of modern consumers is rather mysterious, in two ways. First, in the apparent limitlessness and insatiability of contemporary wants and of contemporary consumption: 'rarely can an inhabitant of modern society, no matter how privileged or wealthy, declare that there is nothing that they want. . . . It is a central fact of modern consumer behaviour that the gap between wanting and getting never actually closes' (1987, pp.37–8).

Second, as well as being continually renewed and re-created, wants are continually extinguished: 'a natural corollary of endless wanting is the high rate of product (and hence want) obsolescence' (1987, p.38). As a result, modern society is 'symbolised at least as much by the mountains of rubbish, the garage and jumble sales, the columns of advertisements of second-hand goods for sale and the second-hand car lots, as it is by the ubiquitous propaganda on behalf of new goods' (1987, pp.38–9). Although we take these phenomena for granted, they are historically neither normal nor natural. In pre-industrial societies, consumption was governed by custom and tradition that set limits to the possible range of wants a person would have, though these were socially variable. We therefore need to explain how the specific pattern of consumption found in modern, industrialised societies developed and how it is maintained. Campbell surveys three theories of consumption in his search for an adequate explanation, and we now briefly review these.

The first approach he terms *instinctivist*. This explanation — familiar from economics — suggests a biologically based desire to consume. Human wants are seen to be inherent and 'triggered off' by goods that enter the individual's environment. Humans are thought to have a 'latent demand' for goods that is unleashed when new goods come onto the market. A problem with this approach is that it is unable to distinguish between biological *needs* (food, warmth, sex) and culturally mediated *wants* (diamonds, fast cars, Playstations). Nor can it explain how wants vary across societies or over time. In particular, it cannot address Campbell's point that we can rapidly 'stop wanting' what are still perfectly usable — and to others, still desirable — consumer goods.

The second approach Campbell calls *manipulationist*. This sees consumers as compelled to develop wants by outside agents, particularly advertisers. This approach does not endow consumers with a pre-given capacity to seek out specific goods or satisfactions; rather, it treats them as passive objects of external influences. Campbell believes this approach overstates the power of others, even of advertisers, to create wants. While he does not wish to suggest we have *instinctive* wants that are independent of outside influences, he argues that we should not ignore the range of other cultural influences (churches, government agencies, kinship networks, family and friends) that help to shape our consumer behaviour. Much research suggests that consumers are not passive recipients of advertisements, they can actively discriminate between and evaluate the messages they receive. They can do this because they live in a world that has already been given meaning by their culture. Advertisers may try to exploit 'the desires and dreams of the consumer' (1987, p.47) but they do not create these in the first place, or at least, not in a cultural vacuum. It seems more plausible to say that what producers and advertisers try to manipulate are not the wants of consumers so much as the symbolic meanings that consumers attach to goods and products.

This idea is central to the third perspective identified by Campbell, which derives from the work of Thorstein Veblen (we can call this approach *Veblenist*). Veblen, remembered today chiefly for his book, *The theory of the leisure class* (1925), and his phrase 'conspicuous consumption', was an American sociologist who studied the 'new rich' in late nineteenth-century America. He was particularly interested in the processes whereby this group sought to gain social acceptance among more established elites. He argued that, among the wealthy, acts of consumption were a way to display, signal or lay claim to social status, as they reflected the level of wealth that the consumer possessed. Veblen suggested that commodities not only satisfy wants or needs, but also function as ways to convey meanings about oneself to others. Thus, acts of consumption are themselves signs or symbols; they belong to the cultural realm as much as to the economic.

While Veblen's own development of this idea was perhaps somewhat simplistic it has been very fruitful for more recent work on consumption. Veblen assumed that human beings are motivated above all else by the desire for 'emulation', that is, to compete with others in displays of wealth and prestige. He also assumed that the only significant cultural message contained in a commodity was its price: in purchasing a commodity a consumer is primarily sending the message to others, 'see how rich I am, that I can afford this!' But as Campbell points out, consumption goods also carry other meanings, particularly about taste and style, and these may have little to do with price. The overriding concern with price, and with 'conspicuous consumption', may be peculiar to newly wealthy groups that have acquired a new social position that they need to validate; but it may not be so important for those whose status is secure or who have no particular interest in upward social mobility.

Does Veblen explain for us why modern consumption has the character of restless insatiability? There is a partial explanation, perhaps, in his claim that humans strive constantly to emulate those higher up the status ladder than themselves. They must therefore be constantly prepared to change their consumption habits and styles. Those they emulate must also constantly invent new lifestyles or fashions in order to maintain their superiority. Thus, suggests one writer, 'drinking champagne or malt whiskey, once the preserve of the aristocracy, has moved down the social status ladder in this century, so that the upper echelons either cease to drink those drinks, or consume more exclusive and expensive vintages' (Bocock, 1992, p.127). This may explain the restless nature of modern consumption among those at or near the top of the social hierarchy, but it does not explain a significant feature of modern consumerism — that concern with consumption and style is now widespread across the *mass* of the population.

We develop this issue further in the next section. We end here by noting that Campbell does not support any of the perspectives outlined above. In his view, patterns of consumption can only be explained in relation to cultural movements that present as valuable and intelligible certain ways of behaving, while others are seen to be bizarre or irrational. The cultural movement that he sees as responsible for presenting modern consumer behaviour as the only good way to respond to commodities is the Romantic movement of the early nineteenth century. It was, for Campbell, this movement that introduced a new 'consumer ethic' into developing capitalist society.

# MASS CONSUMERISM AND THE AFFLUENT WORKER

Early sociological work on consumption, such as Veblen's, focused on the upper classes. It was not until the mid-twentieth century that sociologists began to ask questions about consumption behaviour among the industrial working class. They then tended to be primarily concerned with one question: does the rising standard of living and the increased availability of consumer goods, associated with industrial capitalism, lead to a blurring of class divisions within industrialised societies? Put more bluntly, do workers who experience affluence become more like middle-class people? The question was prompted in particular by the post-war boom in the British economy that led to rising wage levels for industrial workers, especially skilled workers in new industries. Compared with workers in the older, heavy industries like coal-mining and ship-building, it appeared that workers in the new industries turning out mass consumer durables were not only better off but seemed to be the forerunners of a new type of employee who no longer fitted easily into the traditional view of the industrial working class.

A major British study of such workers (Goldthorpe et al., 1968–9) set out to explore this question. It found that there were differences in lifestyle and consumption behaviour between workers in the old and new industries. The 'affluent workers' tended to be more home-centred, spent less time with other men in traditionally male pursuits such as football or the pub, were interested in spending money on the home (house decorating, domestic gadgets) and generally had at least one car in the household. But the authors of the study were not prepared to infer from this that 'affluent workers' were becoming more middle class. Their instrumental orientation towards work as a way to finance consumption, rather than as a source of personal satisfaction, had more in common with other members of the working class than with the middle class. What seemed to be happening was the emergence of a *mass consumer society* in Britain, where consumption patterns were being generalised across social classes rather than being sharply differentiated along class lines.

Such differences in lifestyle and consumption patterns were closely linked to the economic conditions in Britain at the time. They did not necessarily last into the 1970s and 1980s. Decline in older heavy industries such as steel-making, ship-building and coal-mining reduced the ranks of the 'traditional working class' and, in some regions of the country, led to reduced affluence, even in households where people worked in the newer industries. This helped to push consumption patterns back towards meeting basic needs. But it is probably fair to say that the experience since the 1970s of the majority of people in developed capitalist societies has been one of gradually increasing affluence. The relatively well-paid who could make choices about consumption began to take for granted that their jobs could provide enough income not just to live, but to support a relatively affluent lifestyle (Bocock, 1992, p.133):

This marked a move from the primary source of identity being based upon the paid work role a person performed, to identities being constructed around lifestyles and patterns of consumption. . . . The mode of consumption changed from one concerned primarily with basic material provision . . . to a mode concerned more with the status value and symbolic meaning of the commodity purchased.

'Conspicuous consumption' was moving down the status hierarchy as societies became more industrialised.

## CONSUMERISM AND CONSUMPTION IN IRELAND

This account of changing consumption patterns and meanings is based on the post-war pattern of economic development experienced by core capitalist countries such as the UK, the United States and Germany. Given the very different pattern of economic and social development in Ireland in this period, we would expect the Irish experience of consumerism to be rather different. There was no post-war development of large-scale consumer good manufacturers in Ireland. When a manufacturing industry did develop in Ireland during and after the 1970s, it was generally oriented to export markets.

Consumption processes in Ireland thus need to be understood in the context of the uneven development of global capitalism. This unevenness applies as much to the spread of modern consumption patterns as it does to the diffusion of modern capitalist economic relations. Dependency theory has provided a useful way to understand the processes of uneven development (see Chapter 3) and has been extensively used by sociologists to explain the Irish experience of development (O'Hearn, 1998). But dependency theory largely concerns itself with how capitalism has developed in Ireland as a structure of production, and has little to say about how our position as a post-colonial or late developing semi-peripheral society in Europe may have shaped our practices or values in relation to consumption.

The dependency perspective suggests that incorporation into the sphere of multinational capitalism increases social divisions within the incorporated society. Penetration of TNCs into the economy creates a local elite of business people and others who help to manage or who supply professional or financial services to the TNC subsidiaries. This elite can enjoy a level of consumption not far below that of equivalent groups in core societies and, because of its cross-national contacts and networks, it may be very ready to adopt 'conspicuous consumption' values or to emulate international colleague groups in lifestyle and purchasing behaviours. At the same time, dependent development re-creates and expands a marginalised sector of society, condemned to poverty and exclusion from discretionary consumption. This analysis is very general and raises as many questions as it answers if we try to apply it to Ireland. The connections between dependency and consumption are generally discussed in the context of relations between the First and Third Worlds. They ignore uneven development *within* the First World, or the presence of semi-peripheral societies with distinctive historical trajectories on the margins of developed cores.

The nature of dependency analysis makes it difficult to account in any way for the consumption experience of the majority of the population in a society such as Ireland, that is, those who are neither part of the internationalising elite nor of the socially and economically excluded. Nor does it help us to trace the specific effects of trends such as increasing urbanisation. Sociologists have tended to see a close association between consumption and urban settings. Cities are seen as particularly conducive to consumerism as they provide the best opportunities to obtain desired goods and services and also for displays of status associated with consumption choices. Urbanisation in turn is linked to capitalist development and industrialisation. Thus, less developed countries, with more rural populations, should be slower to develop modern consumption practices. Though Ireland remains more 'rural' than many other European societies, Dublin and a number of other cities do have long histories in relation to consumption, including a history of change and fashion. It is wrong to assume that consumerism is a very new feature of Irish society.

One way to improve the usefulness of the dependency perspective is to investigate the specific nature of dependent consumerism. Sklair (1995, p.148) suggests an adequate understanding of modernisation requires an examination of two aspects of change: the first is a society's *transition to producerism*, the increased mobilisation of its people to work more productively. The second is a society's *transition to consumerism*, the increase in material consumption associated with a mass consumerist society. Dependent societies, it is argued, have less control over the management of their economy than do core societies. Similarly, we could say that dependent societies are less able to manage their own consumption behaviour. But what would this mean? — that they are less able to act to protect local consumption values, or to promote local cultural products and items? that they are more vulnerable to external evaluations of the status and prestige that stem from the consumption of certain goods, and so would have less confidence in indigenous status systems?

There is no reason that the development of consumerism should mirror that of producerism. We can suggest four possible combinations, that may identify different types of society within a core — periphery framework. The core societies of the world are high-producer/high-consumer societies; many 'underdeveloped' African and Asian countries are low-producer/low-consumer societies. Between these are two further possibilities: low-producer/high-consumer societies (perhaps in a process of decline from a former core position but continuing to finance a high standard of living from past colonial relationships); and high-producer/low-consumer societies, which put resources into the development of industry and capital, but institutionalise low wages. Sklair terms this last combination 'ascetic developmentalism' and suggests that China reflected this approach at least up to the mid-1980s. The concept negates the modernisationist argument that the low levels of consumption found in less-developed countries are the result of 'traditional' norms and constraints. The absence of mass consumerism in a society may not indicate poverty or a lack of economic resources, but it can reflect a specific ideological or cultural evaluation of consumption.

The concept of ascetic developmentalism captures rather well the era of economic self-sufficiency introduced in Ireland by the Fianna Fáil governments of the 1930s, 1940s and 1950s. While these governments urged restraint on consumption as part of a deliberate development strategy, it was also clearly more than that. The image of a lifestyle of modest comfort, combined with hard but healthy manual work, assumed the status of a distinctively Irish ideal. Limiting consumption was part of a broader strategy to establish cultural as well as economic and political independence from Britain, along with attempts to revive the Irish language and develop distinctively Irish dress codes. If British society was thoroughly urbanised, then it was the lifestyle of the frugal but relatively secure small farmer that was to symbolise Irish identity. If British society was characterised by materialism and consumerism, then Irish society would develop in the opposite way, through an emphasis on spirituality and non-material enjoyments.

For many Irish people ascetic developmentalism continued to dominate life into the 1960s, 1970s and even the 1980s. Taxation policies (high taxes on labour, low taxes on land and capital) and generous support for TNCs left much of the Irish workforce with relatively modest increases in their standard of living, despite continually rising levels of productivity at work and even despite increasing wages. But until the 1980s, restraints on consumption could retain some validity as a marker of Irishness; it is only relatively recently that the ideological legitimation for them was stripped of any conviction.

We have few sociological studies of consumerism as it is experienced in everyday Irish life. The ethnography of French anthropologist Hervé Varenne (1993), based on ten months of living with his family in Ballinteer, Dublin 16, during the mid-1980s, is a source of partial but fascinating data. Based on participant observation of daily suburban life the Varennes draw a number of conclusions about the people they see around them. 'Greenhill' as they call their area, hovers ambiguously between successful middle class and struggling working class. It is difficult to decide whether the inhabitants have escaped poverty and small-town provincialism to realise a dream of social mobility, or whether they have 'traded the rich community life of small rural villages or dense urban neighbourhoods for isolation, loneliness, a kind of metaphoric death in an inauthentic world of rootless consumerism' (1993, p.102). 'The debate grinds on' Varenne adds, 'among the people of Greenhill themselves as the lawns get mowed, flowers planted, new carpeting put down and last but not least, mortgages get paid and new housing estates sprout up in the fields up the hill and down the road.'

What emerges clearly from Varenne's account is that the new consumerism of this type of life is not fully accepted by everyone and remains a source of confusion, guilt and defensiveness to many. As one of his respondents remarks (Meg Fleming, in Varenne, 1993, pp.115–16):

> There are a lot of women that haven't time for just sitting down with a child. I find in modern day, today, in Dublin especially, of course I haven't any views of anywhere else, because I haven't lived anywhere else, that they just really concentrate on the house. They have this idea of the perfect house but, I mean, my house is just a home as far as I am concerned. But you have this perfect house, carpet, furniture, fridge, washing machine, everything has to be there and number one child arrives when all this is done. This is the new, this is definitely, I am sure it's everywhere, whereas we did it all the other way. We had six children and never thought about the consequences. . . . Which would you prefer: wake up and say "I've got a pain". You go to hospital and they tell you you have cancer? Or would you prefer to sit at home with a carpet you don't like? Which I don't like. A day will come when you can replace it. Don't rush it.

## CONSUMPTION AND CLASS

A central issue that has emerged in the sociology of consumption (already revealed in the work of Goldthorpe *et al.* (1968–9), discussed earlier) is the relationship between consumption and social class. Sociologists — and even more particularly, market researchers — have generally assumed that social class determines consumption patterns, or at any rate that if we know what occupational, educational and income bracket a person fits into we can fairly accurately estimate the consumer behaviour they will display.

Is class the main factor that shapes consumption patterns, or are there more significant divisions along other social lines such as gender, ethnicity or age? We mentioned earlier that the sociology of consumption has generally assumed that the modernisation process involves a move from low to high consumption levels, and that modern society is often conceptualised as a mass consumption society. A 'mass society' does not display marked differentiation between social classes, so one would expect only minor differences in relation to consumption patterns. Most people will watch the same television programmes, drive similar cars, dress their children in similar clothes, and so on. Studying consumption patterns in society then can be one way to examine how significant class differences remain for explaining social behaviour.

The relationship between class and consumption can also be reversed. Instead of asking if class determines consumption, we can ask whether consumption practices are part of what shapes and determines class position — the question asked by Goldthorpe *et al.* (1968–9). Most sociologists would now argue that differences in consumption may be as important as those in occupation or economic position in shaping the stratification system. To continue thinking in terms of class stratification in modern societies — even using that term in its broadest sense to include both economic and cultural meanings — we need to integrate discussions of consumption with those about class. Veblen has offered us one way to do this with his argument that consumption practices are used to signal and intensify class differences through an emphasis on variations in lifestyle and 'taste'. Later, we will see how the French sociologist Bourdieu has integrated this idea into an analysis of stratification in modern French society.

First, we need to discuss further the argument that in a modern 'mass' society consumption varies significantly by social class, and that class remains a very important cause of differences in consumer behaviour. Until the 1980s it was commonplace for researchers or advertisers to assume that the best way to understand consumer behaviour was to link it to a class analysis, distinguishing between classes on the basis of a combination of income level and occupation (Bocock, 1992, pp.134–5). Income level was assumed to correspond fairly closely with occupation, with the highest class (managers, administrators or professional workers) regarded as having the most disposable income and the lowest class (those relying on state benefits, casual workers) seen as having the least.

In practice, income (usually household income) appeared to correlate closely with the amount people spent on different consumption categories each week — food, housing, transport — and therefore how much surplus income they could spend on other goods, such as consumer durables (TVs, washing machines, CD players) or luxury items (holidays, restaurant meals or wine). Bocock tells us that in Britain in the late 1980s, very clear patterns in relation to the consumption of a number of consumer durables were found across households from the highest to the lowest class. It was particularly clear in relation to luxury items like dishwashers (just under one-third of high professional and managerial households possessed one, compared to 1 per cent of unskilled manual households) and PCs (around 40 per cent at the top, down to 14 per cent at the bottom). On the other hand, 98 per cent of all households, regardless of class position, had a TV set and there was little variance across classes in the proportion owning a VCR. Consumption of some goods had become 'mass', then, in Britain by this time, yet there were still large gaps between classes in terms of other goods. Whether this can tell us much about class processes in British society or not, it does clearly reveal the depth of income inequalities that continues to be part of British society.

What about Ireland? Research by the Combat Poverty Agency (Murphy-Lawless, 1992) suggests that similar differences exist here. A 1992 study compared the weekly spending patterns of two household types, one with an income of £200 to £250 per week, described as an 'average' family, and the other relying on unemployment payments. After paying for food and fuel, housing and transport, the 'average' family had 37 per cent of its income left over while the other family had 34 per cent. Out of this surplus each family spent about the same proportion on consumer durables and other goods (10 to 11 per cent). The family on unemployment payments spent a higher proportion of its income (but a lower absolute amount) on drink and tobacco than the 'average' family, but the 'average' family spent a much higher proportion on clothing, shoes and services of various kinds (mainly related to leisure and recreation, such as going to the cinema or out for a meal, getting clothes dry cleaned or hair cut, caring for a family pet). Neither family could be described as high consumers; even the 'average' family had very little surplus income after standard items in the family budget, such as professional haircuts, were accounted for. But they did have more than the other family, as one might expect, and used it on different forms of consumption.

Categorising class in terms, primarily, of income and, secondly, of occupation, seemed to work quite well, until recently, as a way to predict consumption patterns in different societies. Some lifestyle differences were also evident, particularly at the higher end of the social class system between, for example, professional people on one side and managerial or business personnel on the other, that produced some differences in consumer behaviour, but these were relatively slight and appeared to be declining in importance as educational qualifications expanded and access to older professional jobs became more open.

Studies of food consumption patterns from a wide range of European countries suggest links between social class and the sort of food that is eaten (Mennell *et al.*, 1992; Warde and Tomlinson, 1995). An interesting aspect is the apparent influence of conceptions of healthiness of food on consumption patterns by class (and by gender). Most studies indicate that the diet eaten by upper-middle- and middle-class households usually corresponds closely to whatever is 'the nutritionally approved orthodoxy of the day' (Mennell *et al.*, 1992, p.54). In the 1980s when health experts urged people to reduce their intake of salt, sugar and saturated fats and to increase their intake of fibre, 'so a class-gradient is observed in the use of items such as skimmed milk, vegetables and brown bread' (1992, p.54). Higher income groups are more likely to eat fresh fruit and vegetables (Warde and Tomlinson, 1995, p.248) and, indeed, the proportion of people who are vegetarian is highest in the middle class. Working-class people tend to eat more animal fat than upper class households and use tinned or frozen rather than fresh vegetables; they also are more likely to fry food than to bake or grill it. It would be patronising — and decidedly unsociological — to assume from this that working-class diets are based on ignorance or lack of interest in health. Rather, the factors that determine food choices are complex, as stressed by Warde and Tomlinson (1995, p.252):

The possible range of motivations behind differential food expenditure is large. It could be the result of concern with status or health, or it might be a matter of style and fashion, or one literally of taste, or it might be a consequence of long-learned and deeply entrenched preferences developed in childhood.

Notwithstanding the complexities involved, Warde and Tomlinson draw attention to the remarkable strength of the association between class and food preferences, suggesting that even a study of an 'aggregated grocery bill' has quite strong predictive power in relation to class. But again, the connection between class and food preference may be highly complex (Warde and Tomlinson, 1995, p.253):

> There are several possibilities, for instance: occupational community and communication between colleagues; level of education, a process wherein obtaining credentials coincides with the learning of other cultural practices; the nature of differential scheduling of the working day between different occupations, involving eating out during working hours, or levels of class self-recruitment.

It would therefore be a mistake to jump to conclusions or judgements about such consumption patterns.

## CLASS AND OTHER SOCIAL CATEGORISATIONS

Bocock (1992, p.138) argues that by the 1980s some market researchers (who seem to have been ahead of sociologists) were becoming dissatisfied with the results to be gained from using conventional class categories for consumers. They began to find that better predictions derived from the use of age-based categorisations — young adult, middle-aged, older people — instead of or as well as class. The idea that difference in lifestyle is found not only between classes but also within them, particularly between different age groups, began to attract sociological attention.

Among sociologists this connected with a long established interest in subcultures (see Chapter 11), particularly in the youth subcultures that had emerged since the 1950s. A striking feature of youth subcultures has been how they have been marked by internal divisions (mods versus rockers, hippies versus punks) that bear a relationship to social class (rockers were working class, mods were lower middle class or in non-manual occupations) but are always expressed through differences in consumption styles: in clothing, haircuts, music, transport, use of leisure time. At the other end of the scale, there has been a growing recognition of the distinctiveness, in terms of both disposable income and consumption patterns, of older people (Bocock, 1992, p.141). This recognition is sometimes expressed through the concept of 'the Third Age'. It reflects the 'greying of society' that most Western societies (Ireland is an exception — see Chapter 5) are now experiencing. This has created a larger stratum of older people with reasonably good incomes (due to improved pensions) and considerable leisure to spend on consumption. It has also produced a certain awareness among older people themselves that they constitute a separate social group with distinctive interests and tastes.

Age is not the only categorisation that is widely used to understand consumer behaviour: gender is increasingly recognised as very significant. In a sense this has always been recognised by market researchers and advertisers but until recently their analysis of consumption in the general population was based on a narrow conception of the typical household which contained a typical nuclear family characterised by a simple division of labour. Adult male(s) were primarily concerned with providing the household income, while adult female(s) managed the disposal of that income. In other words, women controlled the consumption behaviour of households while men were seen as relatively marginal to the process. This image was underpinned by a model of the typical modern family as made up of a husband employed in paid work outside the home and a wife engaged only in domestic duties. It is mirrored in the 1986 Irish Consumer Research report *The Irish housewife — A portrait*. The housewife is the key target for business because she manages and negotiates household consumption, though ultimately her capacity to spend is limited by her husband's capacity to earn, that is, by his class position.

More recently gender has come to be recognised as a factor that is highly relevant to shaping lifestyle, and hence consumption. To some extent this reflects the decline of the 'typical household', the emergence of an increasing number of single-person households, and of women as individuals who work and consume in their own right. It also reflects the growing recognition of the involvement in consumption by men (Bocock, 1992, p.142):

> Young men with reasonably well-paid jobs, or with a disposable income as a result of living with parents, were the first major target group in the youth market in the 1960s. However, as patterns of consumption and relative affluence have spread in the 1980s, older groups of men have become targets for consumption by advertisers.

As more women are drawn into the paid labour market, more men are opting to, or finding that they have to, share in the tasks of managing household consumption (McKeown *et al.*, 1999). At the same time, increases in family breakdown and divorce mean that increasing numbers of older and often relatively affluent men are establishing their own independent households and consumption patterns to go with this.

While the purchasing power of consumers continues to be largely determined by their occupation and economic position, it is increasingly clear that class in this restricted sense cannot provide a full explanation of how people use that power, or whether they use it at all. Between the capacity to consume an item and its consumption there intervenes a range of factors to do with taste, style and aspiration that may be more strongly influenced by age or gender than by class. This point has two important implications: first, social stratification is a more complex phenomenon than economistic accounts of social class have been able to reveal. Second, an adequate understanding of social stratification will have to integrate conventional class divisions with those associated with distinctive 'cultures of consumption' linked to gender, age, occupational status and quite possibly region, national identity and ethnicity. Since economic class does not determine all significant divisions in society, including divisions in consumption behaviour, we need to develop theories of class that can incorporate more than one dimension of stratification.

## CONSUMPTION, DISTINCTION AND IDENTITY

The work of Weber may help. As we saw in Chapter 6, Weber distinguished between class and status as independent outcomes of the distribution of power in society. While he defined class primarily in terms of material resources or educational credentials, he related social status to the degree of social respect or esteem that people are accorded within society due to their social group membership. Status groups may be based on ethnicity, religion or profession, or may simply be groups that display a particularly valued lifestyle. For Weber most of the conflicts around inequality in modern society were the result of rivalry and competition between status groups, rather than between classes. Subsequent discussion of his ideas has generally focused on ethnic or professional status groups, but Weber's inclusion of 'styles of life' suggests that groups that are differentiated by patterns of consumption are also relevant to social stratification.

A problem with Weber's analysis is that having pointed out to us that status differences do not necessarily coincide with class differences, he offers little help in rejoining the two to construct a coherent picture of differentiation in modern society. But the challenge of reintegrating patterns of consumption into a theory of social class has been taken up by Pierre Bourdieu. Bourdieu starts from a Marxist position on class and locates the cause of social inequality in the social structure, especially the economic structure. But he adds to this a quite Weberian concern to understand differences between groups in terms of status.

Bourdieu's main work on this topic is *Distinction: A social critique of the judgement of taste* (1984), based on 1970s research into stratification in French society. One of Bourdieu's main purposes is to establish that 'taste' is not a purely individual or idiosyncratic quality, but is socially derived and socially utilised. Bourdieu says that the exercise of taste, as evidenced in patterns of consumption, is the main way that social groups distinguish themselves from one another. Here he is echoing ideas we have already seen in Veblen, but in emphasising the making of distinctions Bourdieu suggests that a focus just on conspicuous consumption is too crude to express the complexities of the stratification process.

Both Marx and Weber link class position to the ownership of capital. One of Bourdieu's major contributions has been to distinguish between two different types of capital that people may own — the traditional concept of economic capital, and his own concept of *symbolic* or *cultural* capital. While economic capital refers to material wealth, embedded in property, stocks, shares and money, cultural capital refers primarily to the various forms of intellectual resources that exist in society. These range from particular educational qualifications to the capacity to appreciate, critique or create new cultural forms and objects. Social groups differ, not only in the access they have to these sorts of capital but also in the extent that they esteem or aspire to either. Society is characterised by continual struggle, not just between groups in a stratification system but also over the stratifying mechanisms themselves — over whether knowledge or wealth, taste or property, should be dominant in differentiating individuals and groups and arranging them in a hierarchy of value.

Bourdieu is in no doubt that making distinctions along these lines is an important part of maintaining social inequality. They are part of how dominant groups try to retain their position. This process has necessarily become increasingly subtle and sophisticated in an era when consumption has become democratised and access to valued lifestyles and their material trappings appears to be open to broader sections of the population. Bourdieu's perspective, it should be noted, remains essentially structuralist: society is organised around the distribution of economic and cultural capital and the structural position an individual occupies greatly influences their capacity to choose between and adopt alternative lifestyles.

But Bourdieu is also emphasising that individuals are not entirely determined by structures. People respond to and act on the symbolic meanings attached to different commodities and different patterns of consumption, and develop beliefs and aspirations based on these meanings that are relatively independent of their structural position in society. Thus, in consuming, or in exercising taste in consumption, people create and establish differences between social groups, rather than simply expressing them. Thus, Bourdieu's work reveals to us how shopping reproduces society — or rather, how the act of choosing to purchase one consumption item instead of another contributes to the validation, or the disconfirmation, of a social structure based on status hierarchy. Whether Bourdieu can ultimately combine a structuralist emphasis with an image of the consumer as a creative and relatively autonomous actor is still much debated. But he has firmly established the issue of taste in the contemporary sociology of consumption, and other sociologists have adopted and developed this theme, particularly to see how taste and style are used by individuals to establish or create a specific personal identity. In this development, some essential parts of Bourdieu's approach have apparently been abandoned.

For Bourdieu, judgements of taste in consumption are part of the learned and acquired habits of groups in different locations within the social class structure.

They are also ways to create distinctions of status and to reproduce status stratifications within society; in other words, to create and reproduce social structure. But other writers have argued that in contemporary society consumption patterns have become so disconnected from class divisions that they constitute a virtually autonomous source of social differentiation and identity. With the advent of relative affluence for large sections of society, consumption has become a matter not just of meeting needs and securing material comforts but of lifestyle. This term connotes individuality, self-expression and self-consciousness in matters of style: 'one's body, clothes, speech, leisure pastimes, eating and drinking preferences, home, car, choices of holidays etc. are to be regarded as indicators of the individuality of taste and sense of style of the owner/consumer' (Featherstone, 1987, p.55). Society, it is argued, has now moved beyond the 'mass consumption' stage of the 1950s and 1960s; the emphasis in today's marketplace is not on providing consumer durables at affordable prices and standardised quality, but on providing the consumer with *choice*. The choices that consumers make are now central to their self-construction of a distinct social and personal identity.

Why the change? Post-Fordist arguments start from an analysis of change within industry (Kumar, 1995). New technologies and production methods emphasise flexibility in the use of labour and materials. In the area of marketing, strategies rely on the generation of brand loyalties and the establishment of minor, surface differences between essentially similar products. This gives industry a leading role in encouraging consumers to seek identity in differentiated consumption. But it tends to portray the consumer as a passive receiver of new products and marketing strategies. Other researchers argue that consumers themselves play an active, and sometimes uncontrollable or unpredictable, part in making decisions about consumption, and that they do this because they approach consumption primarily or increasingly as a matter of identity-construction (Lash and Urry, 1994).

Why should consumption be taking on such an important role in developed societies? One answer is that as a result of passing through the 'mass society' stage, we now live in a world where established class or status group differences have become blurred or have disappeared, so that they are no longer available as a source of personal identity. In a world characterised increasingly by what Giddens calls 'life politics' (Chapter 18), identity has to be sought and located in other arenas. Another answer goes back to Marx's analysis of the development of capitalism itself, and particularly to his suggestion that capitalism tends to devalue the experience of work. It deskills workers, removes any elements of craftsmanship from their working lives and allows them to be treated by employers as little more than commodities themselves, to be bought and sold on the labour market. The expansion of capitalism makes productive work an increasingly unsatisfactory source of personal identity. While work relationships are highly inegalitarian and constraining for most people, the marketplace becomes increasingly the place where people can experience themselves as free and equal citizens. Through exercising choice in our consumption practices we feel ourselves to be free; free to reconstruct what we 'really' are outside of the controls and constraints of work. Thus, there has been a shift in society 'from the primary source of identity being based upon the paid work role a person performed to identities being constructed around lifestyles and patterns of consumption' (Bocock, 1992, p.133; see also Baumann, 1991)).

We are now far removed from the explanation for modern consumerism that Campbell labelled 'instinctivist'. Far from seeing consumption as a way to meet a pre-existent human need, we see it as a form of symbolic communication, where meanings about identity and outlook on life are exchanged with others. Developing this idea, French sociologist Jean Baudrillard has insisted that we should understand consumption, in contemporary society, as primarily the consumption of symbols or meanings. In consuming meanings, moreover, we *become* these meanings. Identity, Baudrillard says, does not exist outside of or before consumption, it is constructed in consumption.

A T-shirt declares: 'I shop, therefore I am.' Shopping has become the second most important leisure activity in the United States , after watching TV (itself a form of preparatory shopping). This has stimulated much sociological interest in the development of the shopping mall — according to Langman (1992, p.43), 'the signifying and celebrating edifice' of consumer culture in the contemporary world. Renegotiation of 'shopping' from the satisfaction of basic needs in a local marketplace to a form of mass entertainment has been seen by others as one of the greatest achievements of modern capitalism.

Langman suggests that contemporary, that is, late capitalist and post-modern, society is best described as 'amusement society'. Leisure is now central to the experience of selfhood, and shopping the pivotal leisure activity. Shopping malls are physically designed to promote various forms of loitering, parading and strolling as part of the consumption experience. Most discussions of contemporary shopping practices emphasise the part played by strolling, browsing and 'grazing'. As the shopping mall becomes a leisure centre, those who visit it are likely to spend much of their time gazing on the goods on display and fantasising about them as much as actually buying. As this redefined concept of shopping is transmitted around the world as part of a developing global capitalism, it is argued, increasingly, populations of countries that have not experienced affluence are drawn into the fantasising mode as well. The post-modern understanding of consumption thus has implications far beyond the affluent elites of the world who can afford to purchase. At the same time, both overtly (through store detectives and security guards) and covertly (through physical layout and closed circuit TV), the mall or department store is not open to everyone; it excludes the very poor and those with no capacity or inclination to buy.

Attractive as the theories of Baudrillard and followers are, we must remember that the degree of affluence in a society and its distribution across classes still constrains the extent to which shopping and the shopping experience can provide a new source of individual identity. We may also question whether it is true that in late modern or post-modern society individuals lack a strong sense of identity and are therefore free (or forced, depending on your point of view) to construct one through consumption. In most developed societies, even if class is less salient than before, people still derive significant personal identities from where they live, and their cultural, ethnic and familial ties. In Chapter 15 we have seen how modern Irish society has been characterised by the emergence of social movements that offer identities based in ethnicity, religious ideology and gender. Among certain social groups across the world identity may have come to depend very heavily on the exercise of consumer choice, but it would be a mistake to assume that this provides the only model towards which the rest of the world is inexorably moving.

At the same time, we should note how central consumption has become to the social and cultural life of many or most societies in the world. We now examine some critiques of modern consumerism, particularly from within the ecological movement. While we may find much in these critiques to be morally persuasive, we need to ask ourselves what chance they have of succeeding in bringing about a fundamental alteration in contemporary social behaviour if it has become so crucially organised around consumption.

## THE ECOLOGICAL CRITIQUE OF CAPITALISM

The culture of developed capitalism is often criticised for its consumerist emphasis. As Campbell reminds us, all human beings consume, but modern 'consumer culture' seems to be preoccupied with consuming almost to the point of obsession. But what is wrong with consumerism?

Tomlinson (1991) suggests that most standard criticisms depict modern consumerism as essentially immoral. Its immorality takes the form primarily of selfishness: the argument is that the preoccupation with buying and owning things renders people less concerned with the needs of others. Indeed, there are linguistic connections between the economic meaning of consumption and its older medical usage: both are linked to wasting and dissipation (Williams, 1976; du Gay et al., 1997, p.88). While this may be true at an individual level, Tomlinson warns us against assuming that a consumer culture necessarily encourages selfishness or dissipation more than any other sort of culture. Records of people living in famine or near-famine conditions show that these can generate attitudes and behaviour towards possessions that those living in the developed capitalist world would find unconscionably selfish (Turnbuler, 1974). For Tomlinson, it is impossible to find evidence to prove that any culture, affluent or deprived, produces more or less 'general selfishness' in people.

Moral objections to consumerism are often based on an explicit or implicit religious commitment to spirituality as the highest value. They are objections to materialism as much as to consumption, and express the belief that it is wrong to attach greater importance to the satisfaction of bodily needs than spiritual ones. While most of us might agree with this it is still important to note that what is expressed is not an empirical judgement about the effects of a consumer culture but a claim about how we should live. Another moral criticism objects to the hypocrisy of society in using notions of free choice and free expression of identity to underpin contemporary uses of consumer goods: 'if we think we are free when our choices have in fact been consciously constructed for us, then this is a dangerous illusion of freedom' (Tomlinson, 1990, p.13). This is close to the perspective that Campbell defined as manipulationist; it sees consumer culture as something that turns human beings into uncritical recipients of the meanings and messages advertisers have attached to commodities. Writers like Baudrillard, for example, who celebrate how people use consumption to creatively construct personal identity are criticised from this point of view for fostering what is essentially an illusion.

Since the 1970s a rather different form of criticism of modern consumption has gained widespread currency. This is often called 'the ecological critique' as it combines a concern about the social consequences of consumption with concern about its environmental consequences. Problems of waste, pollution, and the depletion of physical resources have been brought into the argument. Put at its simplest, the ecological critique says that contemporary consumerism in the developed world is neither socially just nor environmentally sustainable. To continue with it into the future is to let ourselves slide into a crisis the consequences of which may be catastrophic for human life on earth.

Many of those influenced by this critique have concentrated primarily on the consequences of continued high consumption levels for the physical world. They often leave out the consequences for society in terms of continued human misery. One writer whose ideas have been influential within the green movement in Europe, and who integrates both dimensions of concern, is André Gorz. Gorz was a member of the French intellectual left (a supporter but not a member of the French Communist Party) during the 1960s, but from the 1970s began to detach himself increasingly from conventional socialist politics, believing that the new problems being generated by the developed capitalist era demanded new solutions. In *Farewell to the working class* (1981), Gorz asks who might be the harbingers of the new society that needs to be created, since it is increasingly obvious that the working class can no longer play this role; not only has it been incorporated into the affluent society and its pursuit of consumption, it is not even through the transformation of work and work relationships (as Marx had predicted) that society is going to be transformed.

Rather, for Gorz, the only possible way forward for society now is to abolish paid work, or at least to reduce it to the minimum necessary to maintain a reasonable standard of welfare. Believing that late capitalist society is moving towards a post-industrial form, Gorz argues that new developments in technology are creating the conditions under which people can work less and still enjoy a good standard of living. The problem is that these new technologies are being harnessed to strategies to make people do more work — for longer hours — in pursuit of ever-rising goals of consumption.

For Gorz, contemporary capitalist society is in a state of crisis. In itself this insight is not new but how Gorz develops it may be. The causes of the crisis are economic and environmental; but these feed into the political sphere so that it becomes increasingly difficult for conventional politics to find a way to manage the crisis. The economic aspect of the crisis primarily concerns the failure of economic growth to solve problems of poverty and marginalisation, both within developed societies and within the underdeveloped regions of the world. Gorz argues that strategies for continuous economic growth are not a solution to poverty and inequality, but tend to exacerbate them. Continual economic growth also severely damages the physical environment. Like many other environmentalist thinkers Gorz believes that the earth has to be recognised as finite in its 'carrying capacities' — neither natural resources, nor the capacity to absorb waste and pollution, are inexhaustible. However, it is not only capitalist production processes that are responsible for environmental degradation and poverty, Gorz argues, but the type of consumption that is characteristic of capitalism is also responsible. Solving the crisis therefore requires a radical transformation of both production *and* consumption.

How does capitalist consumption contribute to increasing poverty? In developing this idea Gorz makes a number of interesting suggestions. The first concerns the economic crises that capitalism experiences. As capitalism expands across broader sections of the globe, he argues, individual capitalist entrepreneurs face increased competition and are less able to realise a profit from production. In trying to deal with this problem capitalists encourage forms of consumption that intensify the pressure on an already overextended environment. They turn to built-in product obsolescence and the production of disposable items and of items that cannot be repaired. This stimulates a drive towards increased consumption that exacerbates economic divisions.

Second, Gorz identifies three features of consumption that ensure the persistence of global poverty despite continual increases in aggregate levels of consumption. *Detrimental appropriation* refers to how in capitalist societies resources that are abundant tend to be monopolised by a minority, producing an artificial scarcity of consumption goods. The famine in nineteenth-century Ireland is a classic example of artificial scarcity, in that sufficient food was being produced in the country to feed the population but much of it was owned by a minority who continued to export it for profit. Similar cases have been documented in more recent famines in Third World countries. Another example is urban building land, where a shortage of land for social housing is often the result of monopolisation of this resource by large capitalist interests. *Exclusive access* is Gorz's term for how some goods and services depend for their value on restricted access. Possession of a private beach is an example; its value would be substantially reduced if new legislation opened it up to public use and enjoyment. A more crucial example is private transport — the fewer cars there are on the road, the more value accrues to the owner of a car as a means of transport, whereas if roads are crammed with traffic the value of owning a car may become doubtful. Finally, *distinctive consumption* develops some of Veblen's arguments. Gorz suggests that much of the increase in aggregate consumption revealed by statistics derives from an increase in the consumption of products that have a high exchange value because of their prestige rather than their benefit to human welfare, for example, jewellery, air travel, private swimming pools, gold-plated bath taps and other luxury items. What appears from statistical records to be a steadily rising standard of living in industrial capitalist societies is in fact only a steady rise in expensive or conspicuous consumption.

The model of development that contemporary capitalism has adopted, which assumes that all problems and needs can be answered by stimulating individual consumption (even when the needs are collective and would be better addressed collectively) is a major part of the problem. Gorz refers in particular to how developed societies organise the provision of housing, transport and health care. Individual solutions to collective problems are more expensive, but also increasingly ineffectual, and as a result societies end up consuming an increasing proportion of the wealth they produce in an attempt to reproduce existing standards of living. Economic growth is fuelled by continual increases in the level of consumption, especially private consumption, but the benefits of such increases in terms of improvements in the quality of life continually diminish. Inevitably this bears hardest on the poorest sections of society and increases their impoverishment. But it also contributes to the depletion and exhaustion of resources in the natural world on which we depend for our well-being: construction materials, energy resources and unpolluted air and water.

The problem of reproduction of poverty is thus inseparable from the problem of environmental degradation. To achieve an environmentally and socially sustainable future depends heavily on our capacity to transform the nature of consumption in the developed capitalist world. The strategy Gorz suggests for doing this is to alter our system of values so that we begin to see leisure and free time as more important than the commodities we can buy from putting in longer and longer hours of work. The drive towards continual economic growth destroys not only the environment but also our human capacity to enjoy and use free time and to meet our own needs in the process. At the moment free time and self-determined activities that are outside paid working hours and are enjoyed and encouraged for precisely that reason are under continual pressure to be converted into the consumption of commodities.

It is the dominant cultural understandings of wealth and of well-being that need to be transformed, as these lie behind the pressure for unsustainable economic growth. But who might lead a movement for such a transformation — for the abolition of consumption-driven work and its replacement with more leisure and self-provisioning? It is unlikely to be the industrial working class, since its identity and ideology is still crucially linked to the world of work. If such a movement comes at all, Gorz suggests, it may come from those who are already marginalised from work — the unemployed and socially excluded, many of whom have found ways to live and to meet their needs outside of the formal economy.

Gorz's analysis also provides a way to understand how global economic relations contribute to environmental degradation and increased poverty in Third World countries. Most analyses of these issues point to the importation of developed capitalist methods of production into Third World countries as the main problem. In Gorz's view the key problem is the standard of consumption demanded by First World populations which leads us to treat the people and the environment of less developed countries as mere resources to be exploited for our own use and enjoyment. In this context the adoption by growing numbers of Third World or ex-socialist countries of the capitalist model of an affluent, consumption-oriented lifestyle is a disastrous development. It cannot resolve problems of poverty within these societies but increases the pressures on an environment already made fragile by the consumption practices of the developed world. Only a switch to practices of sustainable consumption, which must take place first and foremost in the developed world, can help to resolve the threat of environmental and social disaster in the world as a whole.

In attacking the idea that problems of poverty and inequality can be solved by encouraging more growth, Gorz is not alone. A number of environmental economists and green theorists are now putting forward similar arguments. Douthwaite, an economist, has constructed a 'no growth' scenario (1992) for Irish future development to replace what he sees as our current obsessive and unhealthy focus on growth. He offers a reinterpretation of the 'self-sufficiency' development strategy pursued by de Valera and the first Fianna Fáil administration (suggested earlier as a possible example of ascetic developmentalism) in the context of contemporary environmental thought. For Douthwaite, that early attempt at independent development foreshadowed the type of strategy for sustainability that is going to have to be adopted everywhere if we are to avoid environmental catastrophe in the future.

We mentioned earlier that Gorz's work has had a wide influence on European green thought. It would be wrong to suggest that his ideas are unchallenged; he has critics both outside and within the green movement, not least over the question of whether people must reduce their consumption levels to avoid environmental and social disaster. While some environmentalists agree with Gorz, there has been a growing movement in recent years in favour of *changing* consumption rather than reducing it — to persuade people to change from buying products that damage the environment to products that are established as environmentally safe. This is often called green consumerism. While from Gorz's point of view it would be nonsensical to suggest that we can save the environment through consumption of commodities, supporters of green consumerism see this as a perfectly sensible, if partial, solution. In the next chapter we examine the environmentalist movement itself in more detail. One of the questions we ask is whether Irish environmentalism should be understood as a movement against capitalist development, or as part of the growth of consumption and consumerism that characterises late capitalist society.

# 17

# *Environmentalism*

It is entirely possible that when the history of the twentieth century is finally written, the single most important social movement of the period will be judged to be environmentalism. (Robert Nisbet, *Prejudices: A philosophical dictionary*, p.101)

If the growth of consumerism is one of the most striking features of contemporary society, another is the rise of environmentalism as a critical response. In this chapter we look more closely at environmentalism: at the sorts of concerns and ways of thinking that have characterised the environmental movement internationally and in Ireland. We ask what recent environmental disputes and conflicts can tell us about the sort of society we are, or are becoming, and conclude with a brief discussion of the implications of these emergent concerns, not only for society but also for sociology.

While there are those that would disagree with Nisbet (above) and suggest that the women's movement has perhaps been more influential, few sociologists would dispute the proposition that environmentalism is one of the key social forces of our time. Yet it has really only existed in its modern form for some thirty years. Its origins are in the early 1960s, when a new environmental consciousness began to take hold, first among natural scientists and researchers, then in the public imagination. The emerging environmental movement was strongly influenced by a number of popular scientific books, the best known being Rachel Carson's *The silent spring* (1962). As these were taken up in the media, the significance of the natural world and of human intervention in it became a topic for widespread public debate.

During the late 1960s and early 1970s public awareness and concern began to manifest itself in new organisational forms. Long-established environmental organisations, such as (in the UK) the Royal Society for the Protection of Birds or (in Ireland) An Taisce were joined by many new organisations. These generally had a different sort of membership — younger, middle rather than upper class, urban rather than rural, possessing what Bourdieu calls symbolic capital as part of the new 'knowledge class' of late capitalist society. They also tended to differ in their organisational activities, usually being more activist and ready to take part in protest demonstrations and media campaigns rather than engaging in private lobbying of government and influential politicians, as the older organisations did. In some countries, such as West Germany and The Netherlands, the 'new left' mobilisations of the late 1960s came to incorporate environmental issues and the developing discourse of ecology was influenced by left-wing ideas, though in other countries this was much less the case. This was a particularly crucial period, it is often claimed, for the development of an ecological perspective and world view. Although it spanned less than a decade, it was a time when the new environmental protest groups were most creatively engaged in working out what would become the central themes in environmental knowledge, philosophy and concern.

During the 1970s the environmental movement grew rapidly — particularly in North America, some European countries and Australasia. Some of the struggles and protests in which environmental groups became involved, such as those against the building of nuclear power stations in a number of European countries, attracted worldwide attention and helped to generate more resources and recruits for environmental organisations. The period was also characterised by the 'greening' of government policy debates and discourses: 'by this time, environmental issues had become generally recognised political and social problems; they commanded the attention of governments and industry, as well as activists and the mass media' (Jamison *et al.*, 1990, p.10). As a result of their success, environmental organisations began to find themselves enlisted by governments in the search for practical solutions. What had previously been oppositional, protest organisations, against any participation in conventional politics, had to find ways to accommodate established institutions. In many countries the environmental movement became fragmented as a result, particularly over the issue of whether green activists should form themselves into a political party and look for an electoral mandate, or whether they should remain outside the political arena and work to change the personal awareness and behaviour of individuals instead.

This debate became a key theme in the 1980s, and into the 1990s when a range of other internal conflicts and disagreements within the movement have also become more evident. In a sense, this simply means that environmentalism has become normalised. As environmental awareness and concern have come to play a more dominant role in state policies and in general public debate, differences of opinion about how problems should be tackled and about the ethical and scientific bases of various approaches are almost inevitably going to lead to new forms of organisational mobilisation and action. Indeed, just as countries that did not divide politically along a left — right axis in terms of economic policies have often been regarded as less modern societies, so today the presence of a strong environmental movement and of publicly expressed environmental concern is widely assumed to be a feature of the more developed societies. We are familiar with this in Ireland, where our level of environmental awareness is often taken as an indicator of how much (or how little) we have 'become modern'.

The above short history suggests that the environmental movement embraces many different political positions and strands of thought. However, here we cover briefly just two ways to categorise green movements that are fairly widely used in the literature: the distinction between deep and shallow ecology, and the distinction between radical ecologists and conservationists.

## Deep and shallow greens

The first point to note here is that 'deep' is a term that some green groups have claimed for themselves, in order to suggest that the approach of other groups is too shallow to bring about effective change. But some social theorists, especially Marxists, consider the ideas of the deep greens themselves to be quite superficial, at any rate in terms of their understanding of society and social structures. Deep ecologists are characterised by two features (Naess, 1997):

- a belief that there is no valid difference or separation between 'human beings' and 'the rest of nature'
- a commitment to a spiritual rather than a scientific orientation to nature.

Deep ecology is thus concerned about the fate of the earth as a total system, rather than of individual elements within it such as the human species. This total system — nature — is something to be revered by humans, who should try to understand its workings, through intuitive or mystical means, in order to adapt to and co-operate with it, instead of using an aggressive scientific perspective to dominate and manipulate parts of the system in the human interest. The Gaian philosophy is probably one of the best-known examples of this way of thinking.

Shallow, or sometimes light, greens often accept elements of the deep ecology perspective, but combine a reverence for and desire to conserve nature with a belief that political intervention is essential if we are to address and control the root causes of environmental degradation, generally identified as human ignorance, greed and social wastefulness. This implies a rejection of the deep ecologists' subordination of humans to the wider system in which they live; instead, human action in the world remains the key to progress, and this includes both political intervention and the continued use of science to solve problems — even those that science earlier helped to create. This can be termed a human-centred rather than nature-centred form of environmentalism. One of its clearest expressions is the 'limits to growth' thesis, which conceptualises the natural world as a set of resources for meeting human needs and absorbing human waste, and argues that we cannot take for granted that these resources are unlimited. It is in the human interest to identify the limits (for example, the level of population that the planet can carry) and then to take steps to ensure we remain within them.

# Radical ecologists and conservationists

Cutting across the deep/shallow division is another: radical ecologists and conservationists. The distinction refers to the extent of social and political change thought necessary to resolve and reverse the problems of the natural environment. Radical environmentalists believe that environmental degradation is the outcome not just of aspects of human behaviour like ignorance, greed or carelessness, but of the particular forms of social organisation and social relationships found in the developed capitalist world: the pressure exerted by multinational capital on natural and social resources over increasing areas of the globe; the technocratic rationality that dominates contemporary capitalist society; and the hierarchical and oppressive authority relationships that persist in work places, educational institutions and families — these are ultimately the causes of the destructive way we behave towards our natural environment. Radical ecologists are clearly influenced by Marxist analyses of capitalism, but differ crucially in rejecting the Marxist belief in continued economic growth as the key to progress, as we saw in our discussion of the writer André Gorz in Chapter 16.

By contrast, conservationists tend to believe in the capacity of the existing social system to manage environmental problems without having to change very much or alternatively do not hold any detailed social and political theories. In the former case, they characteristically adopt the positions referred to as green consumerists or green capitalists. They argue that either capitalist entrepreneurs, or consumers, or both, as rational individuals, will come to recognise that it is in their best interest to insist on organising production in ways that do the least damage to nature. Some who adopt this position claim that capitalist industrialists already recognise that avoidance of waste and pollution actually increases profits, so need no further incentive to move to cleaner forms of production. Others argue that a careful adjustment to tax and market systems, such as energy taxes or 'polluter pays' charges, can provide compelling incentives for cleaner industry, while remaining within the capitalist market system. Similarly, green consumerists argue that if consumers refuse to buy products that are not environmentally friendly, then capitalist businessmen will quickly stop producing them. A well-known and well-publicised example of both green capitalism and green consumerism is the Body Shop company, a British-founded chain of cosmetics outlets that has spread across much of the developed world and has made substantial profits from marketing products that are not tested on animals and are claimed to be less depleting of natural resources and less polluting than other cosmetics.

Both pro-capitalist and politically indifferent greens tend to share a belief that environmental change means starting with change at the level of *individual* knowledge, attitudes and behaviour. They see education and regulation as the main ways to achieve this, and look to the state as a central source of support in both cases. Education is seen as preferable, as it provides individuals with enlightened self-interest, but some regulation by the state is also required as some social groups are thought to be particularly resistant to persuasion and education. By contrast, radical ecologists see the state as a major part of the problem. It is the state's commitment to and support for capitalist enterprise that encourages the continuing development of environmentally destructive forms of technology, such as opencast mining or nuclear power. Radical ecological organisations thus tend to remain primarily protest and oppositional organisations outside the sphere of state policy formation. They seem to have diminished in importance in the past decade, whereas non-radical groups have been able to establish themselves as advisors, consultants and educators on behalf of the state.

## WHY ENVIRONMENTALISM NOW?

Later in this chapter we examine the environmental movement in Ireland in the light of these distinctions and ask what sort of social movement it is and what impact it may be having on Irish society. But first we briefly discuss a question that is particularly central for sociologists, although probably not for most environmentalists: why has environmentalism developed on such an international scale now? What is it about the contemporary period that has given rise to such strongly felt concerns about environmental damage and danger, shared by apparently very diverse social groups and across a range of societies and cultures?

An obvious answer is that environmental concern has developed in response to increasing environmental destruction. As more people have become aware of how urban industrial society has polluted and degraded the natural environment, the air we breathe and the water we drink, and the habitats of numerous animal and plant species, more are starting to voice their anger and opposition. In other words, the dangerous condition that the physical environment is now in is sufficient reason for people to mobilise to protect and conserve it.

But there are some reasons to doubt this explanation. The countries where environmental movements are most strongly organised are not necessarily those that are experiencing the greatest environmental damage (compare, for example, environmental conditions in northern Europe with those in oil-rich regions of Nigeria); and those involved in environmental protests tend to be drawn from particular social classes and groups, not necessarily those who face the greatest environmental risks (usually the urban working class or rural poor). Many people are concerned about environmental problems of which they have no direct experience (for example, whaling) or that they cannot directly perceive for themselves but must rely on science to tell them about (the hole in the ozone layer). Thus, in taking up environmental issues people are not simply responding to 'facts' about the physical environment.

Durkheim stresses that social events and phenomena should always be explained in terms of *social* causes. Since the environmental movement is a social phenomenon, to explain its existence we should examine the social context in which it has developed, and its social consequences. We cannot simply point to physical changes: acid rain, high levels of nitrates in water, the disappearance of the corncrake or the last remnants of unspoilt countryside in Europe. But if we reject the physical explanation, what social explanations might be plausible? We look here at one possibility — and return to the issue again at the end of the chapter.

## Environmental organisations as moral entrepreneurs

This argument has been developed particularly by Stephen Yearley, though he has since (1995) moved away from it somewhat. It is developed in detail in *The Green case* (1991) and has stimulated considerable discussion. In this study, Yearley suggests that a good way to explain why environmental organisations and pressure groups have recently become so significant can be derived from the study of social problems in general. Why is it that, at a particular point in time, some issues figure prominently on society's list of 'things that have to be dealt with', and others are hardly visible? Quite often, the public prominence of a problem bears little relationship to its actual severity; for example, studies of public panics about crime and deviance suggest they are just as likely to occur when official crime statistics are declining as when they are increasing (see Chapter 10); or that the public may 'panic' about one type of activity (say, taking Ecstasy) that can be much less dangerous than another (say, drinking alcohol). An important factor in such cases is the activities of individuals or groups who, for whatever reason, have decided to organise a crusade in relation to a particular issue.

Sociologists have termed such people moral entrepreneurs. Although their concerns are moral rather than business ones, such people have much in common with business entrepreneurs: they take risks in launching their product on the market; they are good at identifying ways to sell the product; and they are prepared to invest their personal status, as well as their own and others' resources, in the promotional campaign. The global organisation Greenpeace fits well into this entrepreneurial model, though we might be less sure about organisations such as An Taisce or the Irish Wildbird Conservancy. But Yearley's general point is that a considerable part of the prominence now enjoyed by environmental issues is a result of the promotional, lobbying and organisational activities carried out by environmental protection organisations. This implies that the environmental concern we find in any society today is significantly shaped by the nature and characteristics of environmental organisations, that is, the sort of membership they appeal to; their relationships with government and the media; the sources of their funds; and what sort of paid or unpaid staff they recruit.

Yearley's has been called a *social constructionist* approach: instead of treating public concern about the environment as a reflection of physical processes, he draws our attention to the active part played by environmental agencies as they construct public perceptions of environmental problems. This helps us to understand some features about public concern, for example, its rather selective focus of attention. The threatened extinction of a species of beetle or spider generally draws much less public attention than that of a bird or a whale. We could explain this on the grounds that where environmental organisations are very dependent on the public for support and funds, they are most likely to take up the cause of the more appealing endangered natural species. Conversely, organisations that have easy access to private or public funds can afford to worry more about threats to the survival of organisms that are scientifically important but not visually attractive — but then these organisations probably play a smaller part in shaping public environmental awareness.

The social background of an organisation's membership may also help to explain why it tries to awaken interest in some issues but not others. The Irish Georgian Society, for example, is a good example of a moral entrepreneur organisation that was very active in promoting public concern about developments in the Irish urban environment in the 1970s, such as the destruction in south inner-city Dublin of Georgian houses to make way for modern office blocks. But the Society largely ignored other developments in relation to the built environment, such as the urban redevelopment that was undertaken to house those moved out of the north inner-city into new suburban estates. We could relate this selective interest in Dublin's architectural problems to the class position and, perhaps, the Anglo-Irish cultural identity of leading members in the Society.

Environmental organisations also differ in their relationships to and the use they make of the work of scientists, physical planners, economists and other professionals; in their readiness to work with party politicians; and in their interest in becoming a political organisation. They also vary in the extent they think it important to make connections between the emergence of significant problems in the natural environment and trends within contemporary society. Differences like these affect the world view within which they talk about the environment, environmental problems and environmental solutions. In turn these specific world views are conveyed to the wider public through the promotional and campaigning activities of the major organisations.

The social constructivist perspective is very useful for developing a sociological account of contemporary environmentalism. But it may also have the effect (as in Yearley, 1995) of encouraging us to over-focus on formally constituted environmental organisations such as Greenpeace, the World Wildlife Fund, and so on, and we may thus lose sight of an essential feature of modern environmentalism: that it is not just a series of formal organisations but a *social movement*. To develop this point further we now look in some detail at the Irish experience of environmentalism.

# ENVIRONMENTALISM IN IRELAND

Environmentalism in Ireland exhibits a range of richly varied forms. It includes at one end of the spectrum variants of deep ecology such as the beliefs of Celtic religion revivalists, New Age Travellers and the growing Wicca movement, with, at the other end, scientists and other environmental professionals employed in the Environmental Protection Agency and Dúchas. It also encompasses eco-warriors and tree-lovers; local activists involved in one-off battles over forms of economic development proposed for their localities (from chemical factories to fishfarms); long-established residents' associations and leisure and sporting organisations that lobby the state to protect their local areas and amenities; political activists in the Green Party; and spokespersons for the leading environmental organisations who shade over, at times, into the official state policy-making community.

Yet this rich texturing of the Irish environmental movement is not at all evident from most public or academic discussion, and particularly not from how politicians, state policy-makers and policy advisors speak about it. Within Irish environmentalism, then, there are evidently conflicts about who is to be included as a legitimate environmental voice and who is not; who is on the 'lunatic fringe' and who is mainstream. As sociologists, whenever we write or speak about the environmental movement in Ireland we need to remind ourselves of the contested status of the object of our analysis.

The history of environmentalism in Ireland is similarly contested. Most discussions open with the claim that environmental awareness has come late to Irish society, compared with our more advanced European colleagues. Thus, Coyle (1994, p.63) remarks that 'attitude surveys during the 1980s revealed Ireland to be consistently at or near the bottom of the league in terms of concern for the environment, especially when the issue was a trade-off between economic growth and environmental protection'. This late development is usually ascribed to one or both of two causes:

- the generally low level, until quite recently, of *cultural modernisation* in Irish society, a result of our native traditionalism and isolation from Britain and the European core
- our low level of *economic development*, which meant not only that job creation was seen as the over-riding priority until well into the 1980s, but also that the Irish environment thus fortuitously escaped the extensive degradation of rapid industrial growth, meaning that there was, until recently, little environmental damage for Irish people to be concerned about.

In opposition to the received wisdom, Baker (1990) has pointed out that ecological movements emerged on the Irish scene as early as the 1960s, at much the same time as in other European countries. She also argues that activism was significantly shaped and strengthened by the Irish experience of being an economically peripheral region of Europe, subject to specific patterns of economic relations with the developed world and particular cultural concerns as a result of colonial domination. The early environmentalism that emerged in Ireland reflected radical environmentalism (see above). Even if it was confined to a small minority of the population, it contrasted markedly with the conservationist and state-oriented form of environmentalism that now dominates the Irish scene. This movement away from radicalism is fairly characteristic of the general trajectory of European environmentalism, so we may conclude that there is nothing particularly backward or different about the Irish experience.

Baker links the emergence of ecological politics in Ireland to the period of rapid economic change and industrialisation of the 1960s and early 1970s. This process helped to stimulate a range of new social movements in Ireland, most notably the feminist movement. For Baker (1990, p.53) the most significant of the early ecological movements was the anti-nuclear movement, which emerged in the 1970s in response to the state's decision to use nuclear power to generate electricity. This decision was supported by all main political groups at the time, including (with some internal conflict) Labour and Fine Gael. Moreover, the announcement that a nuclear power station was to be built at Carnsore Point in Wexford was also, initially, greeted with enthusiasm by local people. But by 1973, local resistance had started to crystallise as local activists formed themselves into a Nuclear Safety Association and started to make contact with Irish branches of Friends of the Earth (founded in Dublin in 1974) and a range of other groups in what was to become an expanding anti-nuclear national coalition. Baker reports (1990, p.55) 'the bulk of the anti-nuclear campaign . . . was conducted within the context of loosely woven, informal and locally based campaign groups. These numbered at one point approximately 102 separate groups and operated throughout Ireland.'

By the time of the first Carnsore protest festival in 1978, the campaign was attracting widespread support from young people across Ireland, especially from third-level students, and from groups in the United States, France and Italy. In 1979 Fianna Fáil set up an Interdepartmental Committee to re-examine the case for nuclear energy in Ireland and in the following year it was announced that the Carnsore plan had been 'postponed'. As it subsequently emerged, the nuclear energy option had been abandoned at this point by all the main political parties. The anti-nuclear campaign in Ireland thus turned out in the end to be more successful than a number of others, notably those in the European core countries of France and Britain. It seems that the success of the Irish movement was in many respects attributable to its ability to draw on and exploit aspects of that 'traditional culture' (in particular, the religiosity of Irish people and their commitment to international peace and neutrality) that many commentators later were to claim held back the development of a 'modern' attitude to the environment in Ireland.

Tovey (1992b; 1993) argues that commentators on Irish environmentalism, especially those within certain strands of the environmental movement, have not only forgotten about this early radical manifestation but tend also to ignore other historical dimensions. She argues that we should recognise two distinct environmentalisms in Ireland which have different histories and social locations, and which express different and even opposed interpretations of Irish development. She suggests we call one of these *official* environmentalism, as it is led primarily by environmental experts from a range of academic disciplines (planners, economists, agriculturists, chemists, botanists, zoologists) who usually work through the established environmental organisations. A significant number work in the public sector, directly or indirectly employed by the state.

The other strand Tovey labels *populist* environmentalism as it represents a relatively independent movement of dissent, by ordinary people working at the local level, from the dominant ideologies of modernisation, development and growth. Populist environmentalism reflects the activities of a different set of organisations, such as the community development movement in rural Ireland, and its activists may not necessarily see themselves as environmentalists (though they are increasingly likely to claim this label as it becomes more politically legitimate). Tovey links populist environmentalism to local communities' experiences of economic underdevelopment, rather than to cultural modernisation; thus it may be seen as a more direct descendant of Baker's 'early ecological politics' in Ireland than the official variant.

As well as noting the varied history of Irish environmentalism, we can look at some of the main social or political factors that helped to shape it. Two can be picked out in particular — one external and one internal: the growing importance placed by the EU Commission on implementing environmental legislation; and the change in urban — rural relationships within Ireland.

Membership of the EU has obliged Irish governments to introduce a wide array of environmental initiatives. The evidence suggests that the Irish government has accepted the obligation and responded quite proactively to European environmental concern (Coyle, 1994). A series of EU directives in areas such as air and water pollution and wildlife protection have been incorporated into Irish law or framed as government regulations. In 1990 the Environment Information Service (ENFO) was established, followed by the Environmental Policy Research Centre within the ESRI which was to examine economic aspects of environmental policy. In 1993 the Environmental Protection Agency was established, and the National Development Plan 1994–1999 contained an entire chapter on the 'environmental situation', a substantial increase on the previous Plan (Coyle, 1994, p.65).

In Coyle's view, these initiatives partly reflect the government's desire for us to show ourselves to be 'good Europeans', but are also an attempt to capitalise on the shift in European tastes towards green consumption, especially in the areas of food and tourism. A consequence of this activity has been to greatly expand the occupational opportunities available to environmental professionals in Ireland, beyond the traditional niches within third-level education and the public service. There are now many more public service jobs (including in local government) and independent environmental consultants increasingly find work in monitoring, advising and recommending strategies for environmental management under the new environmental regime. Those groups active in environmental organisations and campaigns, and most in favour of expanding state intervention in environmental regulation in Ireland, are members of the new 'knowledge class', arguably the class most likely to benefit from such expansion.

A second important factor that has shaped Irish environmentalism is the changing urban — rural relationship. Urbanisation has meant more than just an increase in the proportion of the population living in towns and cities rather than in small villages or the open countryside. It has included changes in the balance of political power between agrarian and industrial interests, and an increasing dominance of urban-based cultural practices and assumptions over rural ones. Brody (1973) interpreted what was happening to the west of Ireland during the 1950s and 1960s as a process of rural *demoralisation* in that the skills, values and way of life of country people were increasingly perceived by rural dwellers themselves to be worthless, as they began to internalise dominant urban cultural positions. During the 1970s and 1980s, profound changes in Irish agriculture and agribusiness helped to weaken the political strength of farmers as the numbers engaged in commercial food production contracted steadily and as their interests began to take a back seat within the policy-making process to those of the food industry. These changes have contributed to a significant change in our perceptions of what the Irish countryside is for, and how it should be managed (Tovey, 1994).

Until quite recently it was widely taken for granted that farmers had the prior right to determine the use of rural land, and this was reflected in, for example, the exemptions from planning permission allowed to certain kinds of agricultural development. While most Irish people also took for granted that they had a right of access to farm land for recreational purposes, this was subject to common-sense rules about not interfering with agricultural production, and it was the farmers, as the land-owners and food producers, who were seen as the natural managers of the countryside. But in the last decade these assumptions have been challenged. Urban-based conservationists, recreational groups and tourism interests have begun to make claims on the Irish countryside that undermine and attack the management role previously accorded to farmers.

Coinciding with the economic and political retreat of agriculture, the emergence of new sets of interests in relation to land has opened up a new debate about the future of rural Ireland (McGrath, 1996). Increasingly dominant in this debate is the claim that rural Ireland must be managed and regulated in the interests of the urban population. This tends to mean that the availability of rural space for leisure, recreation and education is increasingly given priority over the use of rural land to produce food. This is not true of all areas but is particularly evident in relation to large tracts of the west and north-west where any belief that small farms can be viable food-producing enterprises has been more or less abandoned. Similar arguments exist in relation to areas of the country where landscape and recreational values are high and where farming is still relatively small-scale and capital-extensive. The recent government/EU-sponsored programme for Rural Environment Protection Scheme (REPS), for example, has been concentrated particularly on these sorts of areas. It encourages farmers to think of themselves increasingly not as food producers but as environmental conservationists working on behalf of an increasingly urbanised Irish society (Tovey, 1997).

'Conservationist' environmentalism, as we previously suggested, tends to find itself in opposition to 'radical' ecological movements. It is generally 'deep' rather than 'social' ('shallow') in its prioritising of the needs of nature over those of human beings. It does not locate environmental problems within an analysis of societal development, but sees them as the outcome of individual human failings such as greed or carelessness. It looks for solutions, not in a transformation of society, but in keeping human intervention in nature to the barest possible minimum level. The dominant trend in current Irish environmentalism, at least of the 'official' variety, is now towards conservation and the identification and preservation of 'our natural heritage'. How do we explain this particular preoccupation?

Some writers see it as the profoundly conservative (in the political sense) response of a society that has experienced traumatic or demoralising changes in its sense of national identity. In relation to British experience, Hewison (1987) argues that the rise of a 'heritage industry' feeds on and encourages a nostalgia for the past when Britain was an imperial power and its culture was globally dominant. As a historian, he is very critical of the misleading version of the past that he claims is generated through the heritage industry's packaging of nostalgia. He is also concerned about the snobbishness, lack of faith or interest in contemporary popular culture, and the right-wing political stance that he detects within it. We might feel this to be a harsh judgement on the growth of a heritage movement in Ireland, while noticing how well that movement has successfully rehabilitated similar social icons for the Irish past, for example, in the focus on conserving the Irish 'great house'. Are there any grounds to suppose that Irish national identity has recently undergone similar traumatic changes to the British one? It could be argued that since the late 1960s all the conventional symbols of Irishness — Catholicism, rurality, communality, possession of a distinct language — have been systematically stripped of their value and legitimacy, necessitating a new version of our identity and a revaluation of our past. But the search for heritage in Ireland has also produced new populist versions of history, as people have come to value the traces — implements, buildings, clothing, emigrants' letters — left by ordinary Irish people in their passing through previous centuries.

It may also be that the rise of conservationist concerns and the preoccupation with heritage, natural and built, is a reflection of how consumption and consumerism have become drivers of contemporary Irish society. Within modern consumer society, we suggested in Chapter 16, people find a sense of personal identity less in their work roles or productive activities than in their consumption behaviour. Tourism, like shopping, has become a defining activity of late modern society. We visit and consume heritage sites, interpretive centres, recreational amenities, nature. The past and the physical world are turned into commodities that can be purchased and consumed by the tourist, who does not have to be a visitor from another country but can be anyone who spends time gazing at and enjoying in a detached way signs of the lives of others. Forms of tourism help us to signal to others and confirm to ourselves the sort of person we are, our tastes and interests and the social group we (would like to) belong to.

The rise of conservationist environmentalism in Ireland can thus be interpreted as a further indication of how 'developed' Irish society has become. We can understand environmental conflicts as struggles between those who want to use nature for productive purposes — to exploit natural resources — and those who wish to consume nature for personal satisfaction or as part of their social identity. To so link the rise of environmentalism in Ireland to the rise of consumerism is rather ironic, given that European environmental and ecological thinkers like Gorz have identified consumerism as a major *cause* of environmental degradation. Given its embeddedness in late modern social life, a reduction in consumption as a solution to environmental destruction now seems unlikely. Whether a change in how we consume — such as consuming nature by appreciating it — may present a solution, remains to be seen.

## POSTSCRIPT: A NEW SOCIOLOGY FOR AN ECOLOGICAL AGE?

Recent research interest in the area of consumption is part of a broader movement away from *structure* and towards a focus on *action* and *process*. We see this in how research and theorising on consumption has fed into sociological accounts of social class. In trying to explain variations in consumer behaviour across social groups, theorists like Bourdieu have recognised that purely structuralist accounts of class are no longer tenable. While some connections remain between class position and consumer practices, we must recognise that people are not automatically prompted by their class background to consume in specific ways. People also use specific forms of consumption as a strategy to achieve, claim or maintain a particular class position. The image of the individual as a self-conscious, strategic social actor who responds to images of self and identity is supported by much of the sociology of consumption.

The interest in consumption and consumerism is moving sociology in a direction that is different from, but connects with, earlier interests within the discipline. The implications of ecology and environmentalism are perhaps more challenging. Some writers go so far as to warn that once sociologists start to take on environmental issues in a serious way, they may find the enterprise of sociology itself cannot be continued — unless extraordinary changes occur in the fundamental assumptions of the discipline. The threat of environmental catastrophe is forcing profound changes, they argue, in our conventional political and economic rationality. Why should sociology expect to be immune?

The argument may be overstated but there are at least three ways that it can be developed further. The first concerns how and whether sociology can take into account *physical* as well as social causes and impacts on the social world. The second concerns the boundaries of *society*: as we become more aware of the rights of non-human animals, do we need to rethink our conception of society to include them, or some of them? And the third concerns the nature and status of *science*, as it is increasingly challenged by the growing environmental risks that result from its application.

The issue of physical impact reprises our earlier discussion about the social constructionist perspective, where environmental concerns are best understood as the product of moral entrepreneurs. This approach implies that public concern is not generated primarily from a recognition of potentially catastrophic changes in the natural world, and that it does not really matter — from a sociological point of view — whether such changes are 'real' or not. Some sociologists find themselves unable to accept such a conclusion: thus Martell (1994, p.124) finds problems with Yearley's social constructionist approach. Martell does not believe that environmental problems can simply be manufactured by organisations who want to manipulate public morality — they must have a physical or scientific base or they would be quickly discounted by the public or challenged by the many groups and organisations with a reason to oppose environmentalism. A study of how and why environmental problems become socially defined as problems is useful, certainly, but 'ought to complement rather than be counterpoised to explanations based on the objective existence of environmental problems'. More recently Yearley has come closer to this position, noting that the 'marketing' role undertaken by environmental agencies is only one factor in a situation that must also include 'the state of the environment itself' (1995, p.657).

But sociology is not very well equipped to build 'the state of the physical environment' into its perspectives and theories. It is a discipline concerned with the study of the *social* world. In its early decades its practitioners worked hard to establish the difference between social and physical reality and to establish that quite different sciences are needed for the study of each. Durkheim, for example, insisted that social processes and events should always be explained by *social* causes, not psychological or physical ones. The development of sociology in the century or so since Durkheim elaborated this view has been predominantly in line with this approach: it explains the social by means of the social. Thus, while early theories of crime sought physical or psychological causes, a sociological approach has concentrated on analysing the social processes through which people become defined as criminal (see Chapter 10). Similarly, while early discussions of gender focused on physical difference, contemporary sociologists are generally very unwilling to concede that men's and women's biological or physical attributes determine or explain their social roles or position in society (see Chapter 8). Sociology has progressively defined its reality as a purely social reality, in that physical systems and environments play virtually no part other than to provide the context for social relations and actions. If sociologists now have to accept that changes in the physical world have major consequences for the organisation of social life, perhaps even for its survival, the nature of the discipline itself may have to be reconsidered.

The second way that environmentalism challenges sociology relates to the boundaries of society. Though not true for all environmentalists, there has been a strong drive by some, certainly within deep ecology, to rethink the position that human beings have traditionally accorded to other animals. Such philosophies reject the anthropocentric view that humans are separate from and superior to the rest of nature, and therefore entitled to use it, its physical resources and animal species, as mere objects for their own satisfaction. Even those who do not embrace deep ecology have been led by their interest in the operations of nature in general to reconsider their attitude to animals and to the suffering that humans cause to them. Considerable efforts have been made by environmental philosophers (Singer, 1997) to establish a theory of 'animals rights' that, while it recognises the inability of animals to claim such rights for themselves, finds ways to argue that they should still be accorded some level of rights.

Sociologists have investigated how the different social settings in which we encounter animals lead us to define animals differently: from 'almost human' in some settings (the family sitting-room) to 'almost a material object' in others (the scientific laboratory) — even when we are dealing with the same type of animal (a dog) in each setting. This has encouraged the idea that there is nothing intrinsic to animals that means they should be treated as if they merited no respect or consideration. To the extent that we agree to accord animals certain rights, or recognise human obligations towards them, we define them as part of the social community. This opens up the possibility that the boundaries of 'society', the fundamental entity studied by sociology, need to be redrawn so as to include at least some animal species. Even if we do not consider that interactions between animals are part of 'our' society, we might want to include aspects of human — animal interaction.

The third way that the encounter with environmentalism may prove profoundly unsettling for sociology is in relation to the connections between sociology and modernity. As a child of the Enlightenment, sociology's development was shaped by beliefs and assumptions that were at the core of modernity itself — in particular, the belief in progress, science and rationality. The rise of environmentalism has fundamentally challenged each of these tenets. The discovery that the advance of civilisation and prosperity in much of the world directly contributes to environmental damage that may threaten the viability of human life on earth, if not the earth itself, makes it very hard to maintain a belief that the history of humankind is a history of progress. Environmentalism has revealed to many the integral role in environmental damage that has been played by science itself and by the use of scientific knowledge to control the material world. Even if we still need science to identify the damage for us, and perhaps to offer remedies, the authority of science and the credibility of scientists have been among the most obvious victims of the rise of environmentalism. Finally, environmentalism poses questions about our capacity to act to solve environmental problems, or our capacity to identify and activate a rational strategy to deal with environmental risks. Within the movement worldwide, there is a strong if minority strand that no longer believes that normal methods of political intervention can solve the problems. For these environmentalists, the solution has to be found elsewhere, at the level of the personal and, in terms of a personal conversion, to absolutely transform the way we live. The well-springs for this are not rationality, but emotions, values or religious mysticism.

Rejection of progress as a grand narrative of history; rejection of a blind faith in science; a preference for emotionally and value-based forms of action over rational strategic forms — these are all commonly said to be features of the post-modern culture that is emerging as we transit the millennia. The encounter with environmentalism might thus lead towards a post-modern sociology. What would such a sociology be like? We can hypothesise that it would be a sociology that is most concerned with the local and immediate, and then only in a provisional way, that distrusts the idea that we can produce any overarching explanation for social development. It would be a sociology that prefers qualitative methods of research, perhaps, and that sees itself as closer to history, anthropology or cultural studies, than to the economic or natural sciences. It would be a sociology of human beings as not just minds but also bodies, multidimensional creatures shaped as much by non-rational wants and desires as by their capacities for intentional, planned action. But in the end, would such a sociology help us to understand post-modernity, or would it merely reflect it?

# 18
# *Ireland goes global?*

Since the 1980s, the idea of globalisation and the emergence of a global system has attracted increasing attention from sociologists. But is this idea really new? Many sociologists, especially those working in the area of development studies, have been using similar perspectives for considerably longer than this, certainly since the emergence of dependency theory in the 1960s as an alternative to the modernisation approach. As we have emphasised throughout this book, sociologists attempting to understand Irish society and its particular pattern of development have necessarily had to work with an analysis of international or global change, given the Irish experience of colonialism and later incorporation into transnational economic links. As O'Hearn (1992, p.17) suggests, such changes must be understood as 'representations of global cyclical processes'. What can we now add through a discussion of globalisation and social change?

This chapter proposes that a number of new ideas can be usefully developed. First, we would suggest that analyses of Irish dependent development within a global system by O'Hearn and others have tended to be rather one-dimensional. They tend to focus on the economic level only and have little to say about political or cultural impacts of globalisation. But such aspects cannot simply be read off from economic processes; they must be discussed and analysed in their own right. Second, the extent and manner of Ireland's incorporation into a wider international or global system needs to be treated as something that changes over time. It is widely suggested that in recent decades the world has become globalised in ways that are both quantitatively and qualitatively new. Thus, earlier approaches, influenced by dependency theory, may need to be replaced by new theories of globalisation.

Third, the term 'globalisation' is increasingly used in sociology to refer not just to new processes and relationships that are making the economies — and perhaps also the political and legal systems — of different societies more integrated, but also to a subjective change, broadly experienced. This is a change in mindset, or in the sense of collective identity, that is variously expressed when people start to think of themselves as world citizens, global consumers or participants in a world culture. We can think, for example, of the recent rise of 'world music' as a label for a range of ethnically varied indigenous musics — including traditional Irish music — that constitutes an organised totality from which the music fan in contemporary Ireland can select. As recently as ten years ago, traditional Irish music was thought of as belonging to and understandable only as part of national Irish culture. Now it is a globalised entity.

This chapter focuses, therefore, on globalisation as a political and cultural issue, rather than an economic one. In these contexts, it aims to raise questions about globalisation as a subjective experience as well as the objective processes that are thought to be involved. The subjective impacts include not only the impacts on citizens and on cultural audiences, but also on sociologists. We end the chapter, and the book as a whole, with a brief discussion of how globalisation is transforming some of the core concepts and assumptions about society and, in particular, the path to modernity of those societies, like Ireland, that were previously assumed to be peripheral or even deviant in relation to world history.

## WHAT IS GLOBALISATION?

Robertson (1987) suggests that we think of globalisation as referring to the process or processes whereby the world becomes 'a single place'. This means that globalisation perspectives are not just about an increase in the intensity and impact of relationships between societies or nation states, which we might call *internationalisation*; they are also about how such relationships are helping to contribute to a new sort of world characterised by *transnational* institutions and relationships.

How have sociologists come to recognise that a single world is emerging at this time? We can identify two different positions. One is that recognition of 'the global' is a natural outcome of an analysis of modernity. Globalisation is then simply part of the process of becoming modern, or of the transition to late modernity. In the second case, globalisation is associated with post-modernity. A global world is then seen as more than just the world wide expansion of modern institutions, characteristics and relationships across the boundaries of the developed world. It is something qualitatively new, that may radically transform our experience and understanding of society and social life. We start by developing the first position and will return to the second one later in this section.

We started this book with a suggestion that 'classical' sociology offers us three distinctive, and not always compatible, ways to understand the modern world. One, associated particularly with Durkheim, treats modernity as largely coterminous with *industrialisation* and an advanced division of labour, linked to the growth of industrial technologies and associated forms of work organisation. A second we take from Marx: the central and most significant feature of the modern world is that it is a *capitalist* world — the capitalist form of economic organisation and relationships, inherently exploitative and unjust, explains the important features of modern society such as its class divisions and its ideological forms. The third perspective is associated with the work of Weber, who suggests that the development of the modern world is significantly shaped by the unfolding of *rationality*, or dependence on instrumental reason, as the key feature of modern social action and institutions. Weber's work can be extended to suggest that modern societies tend to converge in culture and way of life as they are increasingly permeated by rational principles.

Each of these accounts of modernity can be developed to explain why late modern society is globalised. For example, industrialisation theorists argue that modern industrialism has a 'universalising imperative' (McGrew, 1992, p.82). This is often expressed through the idea of technological determinism: once the technology associated with industrial methods of production is introduced into a society it inevitably leads to profound rearrangements on the social, cultural and even political level in that society. In a more contemporary version of this argument the transformative capacity of technology is now so great that it has moved us from industrial into post-industrial society. The latter is based on the use and production of knowledge rather than material resources. Society has undergone the Third Industrial Revolution and has been profoundly transformed by the development of new forms of communications or information technology, in particular the computer and electonic communication networks.

A feature of this new technology is that it can connect workers and work activities across infinite expanses of space. The technology of post-industrialism — the jet, the Internet, orbiting satellites — tends to erase distance and to shift human social activities from the places and spaces where they were previously carried out. The internal logic of technological development that has brought about the move from industrial to post-industrial society is now facilitating interconnectedness across the world — an essential basis for the emergence of globalisation. From this standpoint, a globalisation perspective is simply a recognition of the increasing connectedness and interdependence across space that is enabling work, production, communication, recreation and culture routinely to transcend the boundaries of the locality, region and nation state.

Analyses of modern society as capitalist society produce a rather different evaluation of globalisation. One of the best-known protagonists of this perspective is Wallerstein (1983), who argues that we live in a single world system — the capitalist world system. The driving force that underpins it is the relentless search for profit and, though it contains a varied range of cultures and political forms, it is characterised by a single international division of labour. The capitalist world system is structured around unequal relationships between core, semi-peripheral and peripheral areas, each of which provides distinctive functions for the system as a whole. The material conditions of societies, social groups and households are ultimately determined by the position their locality holds in the world system. Sklair has also developed an account of globalisation as driven by the dynamics of capitalism (1995) which we discuss further below.

A key way that these accounts of globalisation differ from those of industrialisation theorists is their emphasis on the *unevenness* of capitalist expansion across the world, whereas industrial or technological determinist theories tend to emphasise the homogenising experience of globalisation. Wallerstein emphasises unevenness when he focuses on the international division of labour between core and peripheral areas and regions, as does Sklair when he writes (1995, p.7) that:

> The global system is marked by very great asymmetry. The most important economic, political and cultural-ideological goods that circulate around the globe tend to be owned and/or controlled by small groups in a relatively small number of countries. Until recently it was both convenient and accurate to use the term 'Western' to describe this asymmetry.

Capitalism can thus be seen, in this global stage of its development, as reproducing on a world scale the inequalities between spaces and between social groups that previously characterised its expansion across local or national societies.

Theories of globalisation that emphasise either technological developments that overcome the barriers of physical distance or economic practices associated with capitalism have generally tended to neglect the issue of *culture*. Yet many people are very concerned about culture when they think of the processes whereby 'the world is becoming a single place'. The central assumption of modernisation theorists, largely unchallenged until quite recently, was that globalisation is accompanied by cultural homogenisation or the expansion across the world of a particular type of culture associated initially with the West (Street, 1997). This is a culture that is oriented to control, planning, management and intervention in the social and physical worlds through the use of rational — legal principles and scientifically based knowledge. Global culture is thus expected to be the same as the culture of modernity, but on a larger scale. Modernisation theorists expected it to incorporate elites from less-developed parts of the world and to spread from there to encompass the mass of the population in those societies, eventually bringing about a global mass culture. In turn, this was predicted to have political effects at the global level, as it diluted people's commitments to particularistic forms of identity such as those provided by the locality, the ethnic group and the nation (see Chapter 11). It was hoped to replace these with universalistic categories of identity that would provide the basis for the emergence of global politics or even a global state.

We return to the issue of culture and globalisation later in this chapter. For the moment we wish to emphasise how, in each of the perspectives outlined above, globalisation tends to be understood as an extension of existing processes within modern society. What we are offered as models of a global world are essentially little more than those of modern society, expanded to a global level. Is this all that globalisation means, or should the concept be alerting us to the emergence of something that is qualitatively new? We need to ask ourselves 'whether humanity is witnessing the unfolding of a new historical epoch . . . or alternatively whether the present 'phase' of globalisation simply conceals a renewed strengthening of the existing structures of western modernity' (McGrew, 1992, p.63). One area that might provide some pointers is that of the nation state, and its fate in the context of the UN, EU, NAFTA and the North Atlantic Treaty Organisation (NATO); we turn to this issue in the next section.

## GLOBALISATION AND THE STATE

Of major interest to theorists of globalisation is its likely impact on the contemporary political order. The political order found in late modernity is usually described as an international political system constituted from nation states and their relationships with each other. The question about the effects of globalisation is then a question about the nation state: is globalisation strengthening this form of political organisation and helping to secure its survival over time? or is it, conversely, undermining the nation state and contributing to the emergence of a new global political order that will take a quite different form?

In Chapter 4 we pointed out that while the term 'nation state' is widely used by sociologists, it can be both confusing and misleading. It suggests that every state corresponds exactly to its nation as the entity it represents and governs. The experience of Ireland and of most nation states is that a happy coincidence of state and nation has historically been the exception rather than the rule. We therefore describe the modern world political order simply as one of 'states', while recognising that they generally claim to rule over a nation and typically engage in attempts to build a single nation, as a routine part of governance strategies. The question of how globalisation affects the state is of particular interest to Irish people as we live in a semi-peripheral region of a global system; and because as a post-colonial society the national identity constructed around Irish statehood is still relatively underdeveloped and unstable.

Irish society shares with other peripheral societies a need for political institutions that can act to some degree independently of economic ones and can influence the effects that global economic changes have on the local population. As we have argued throughout, peripheral economies tend to be incorporated into international economic processes and relationships on terms that benefit the core more than the periphery. Capitalist development has a tendency to promote the centralisation of wealth, production, technological innovation and skilled labour, drawing these into the core regions and out of the peripheries. If a peripheral society is to have any hope of avoiding this fate, it can only be through active political intervention into market processes. The state is the most likely political institution to aspire to that role. Even if it cannot alter international economic processes, it can still play a significant domestic role in managing their impact on the population, for example, by equalising the costs across social groups or shielding the weaker groups from harsh exposure. If globalisation encourages the destruction of the national state, can we assume it will be replaced by some other political form — perhaps a world state, or a regional political formation like the EU — that would fulfil a similar function?

Although states are at least partly the product of nations or of national movements aspiring to and demanding self-government, they also play a very important part in creating 'the nation': in the construction of ideas about national identity; in the representation of natural boundaries of membership; and in creating social solidarities based on loyalty to the state as the nation's guardian. Nation-building in this sense has been one of the principal activities of the Irish state since 1922 and it seems clear that in engaging in this, Irish state agents were well aware of the particular difficulties associated with a post-colonial situation, where stereotypes of national worth had to be almost entirely reversed, and reasons found for people to switch their political allegiances. We could say that, in this sense, the Irish state was an active participant in the construction of a new particularistic culture and world view for Irish people which, whatever its disadvantages, did provide a rationale for at least *some* people to continue to live in, work for and invest in the survival of an underdeveloped, peripheral country with a low standard of living. If globalisation destroys the national state, is any other political entity likely to be engaged in a similar project of cultural construction? Will there be any reason left for Irish people to accord priority to the 'imagined community' of Ireland? Could any form of nationalism survive the demise of the nation state and if so, what would it be like?

Most contributors to the debate on globalisation seem to agree that it weakens or destroys the national state. McGrew (1992, p.87) summarises their arguments: '[globalisation is seen as] compromising four critical aspects of the modern nation state: its competence; its form; its autonomy; and ultimately, its authority or legitimacy.' If states can no longer meet the demands of their citizens for economic growth or security without engaging in collaboration with other agencies, such as other states, or TNCs in particular, this seems to suggest that they have lost much of their *competence*. To make any impact on world events, states today have to participate increasingly in international organisations, such as the UN, which have taken over some of their functions with regard to managing and regulating individuals and their activities. This seems to indicate that the national state is changing its *form*.

The points given above suggest a decline in the capacity of states to act in an *autonomous* way, not only outside their own territorial boundaries but also within them. The range of policy spaces or issue areas within which the national state can define its own strategies, and take independent action to implement them, is decreasing, and while this is clearest in the economic and financial areas it extends increasingly into other areas, such as use of airwaves for national broadcasting, decisions about deployment and equipping of military personnel, or even decisions on how to manage gender differentiation in the labour market. Finally, if states have lost competence, have parted with some of their former functions and powers to international agencies and have lost a capacity to act autonomously in formulating policy, they must also be losing *authority and legitimacy*. Ineffective governments cannot expect obedience and loyalty from citizens who will soon come to perceive them as illegitimate and useless political forms.

Those most convinced by these arguments tend to understand globalisation in terms of the second of the three positions we outlined earlier, that is, as referring primarily to the global spread of capitalism. Often, as Marxists, they are not particularly sympathetic to, or concerned about, the survival of national states in any case. Their position is associated with theorists from Western Europe or from other highly developed areas of the world — where most of the current changes to state forms are taking place — rather than from less developed regions, where aspirations to national statehood and the idealisation of this political form as the normal form for a modern society remain much stronger.

There are some European theorists who are far less convinced that the national state is inevitably disappearing. One of the best known is the British sociologist Michael Mann and we will briefly discuss some of his ideas here. Mann (1990) has suggested that we can identify four main theses about globalisation and its political impacts, and that each of these needs to be considered separately before we can draw any general conclusions:

1   Globalisation primarily means *capitalism*, and global capitalism undermines the power and the authority of the national or local state.
2   There are other aspects of globalisation — particularly the globalisation of *environmental risk* — that create situations where the national state is no longer competent to handle affairs.
3   Globalisation is a process of economic restructuring that has *diverse cultural impacts* — it fragments existing social groupings and identities, and constructs new ones without local or territorial reference; the identity associated with the nation and hence the nation state collapses in the face of new collective identities.
4   Globalisation is a process that affects not just economics, or culture, but also the distribution of *power*. In terms of a global power system, national states are no longer the dominant actors. They have not been so in the recent past, and there is no reason to assume they will be in the future either.

We develop each of these points further below, concentrating particularly on the first as it is is probably the most widely shared within the globalisation literature.

## Global capitalism and the state

Does the global expansion of capitalism threaten to destroy the national state? For Sklair (1995), the critical feature of global capitalism is that the territorial organisation of production no longer corresponds to the territorial boundaries of the state. In a globalised capitalist system, production and exchange are organised transnationally, and the impetus for further capitalist expansion and development is located in the transnational rather than the national arena.

The clearest example of this is to be found in the activities of TNCs. They forge new divisions of labour, new financial arrangements and new trading agreements across state boundaries in order to take advantage of economic opportunities wherever, politically, they may arise. Yet it has been pointed out that TNCs still lean heavily on their 'home states' for support and for the political power that these can make available, for example, US-based TNCs have been strongly supported by US Federal and state governments. While in some cases TNCs treat political divisions across space as irrelevant to their activities, in other cases they recognise the significant services that the state can provide for them, such as the management of local labour markets, the supply of infrastructure or the provision of tax concessions and other financial benefits. Hamelink (1993) suggests that TNCs form *symbiotic* relationships with the states where they locate, both strengthening the state and using it to empower themselves in significant ways.

We might conclude that capitalism today is not fully globalised, but quite mixed, involving combinations of transnational, national, and regional operations. This very unevenness, which is linked to the continuing existence and inter-ventionist powers of the national state, is indeed one of the main sources of profit open to any capital that can be mobile across state boundaries. This would suggest there are strong reasons for assuming the national state will continue to exist and to be a significant political form in late modern capitalism.

Sklair has put forward a second argument for believing that global capitalism undermines the national state. This focuses on the issue of 'actors' in the global capitalist system rather than on structural forces. He asks, quite simply, who is the most significant or most powerful actor that can shape what happens in the contemporary world economy? And he answers that who or whatever it is, it is not the state. In his view this is a strong indicator that we no longer operate in an 'international' capitalist system but in one that is 'transnationalised' or globalised. The key actor in the global system, for Sklair, is a *global capitalist class* — one that 'unquestionably dictates economic transnational practices, and is the most important single force in the struggle to dominate political and cultural-ideological transnational practices' (1995, p.8).

This class is still in the process of formation, as is the global system in which it acts. It is made up of: executives in TNCs; 'globalising bureaucrats'; politicians and professionals who support and legitimate global capitalist strategies; and certain sorts of consumerist elites, working in the media or as dealers in global consumer goods. These are the people who, to put it crudely, we might say now rule the world. They come, Sklair says, from diverse national origins but share a global outlook and a conception of themselves as 'citizens of the world'. They have also increasingly emerged as an elite social network, as a result of similar education and career experiences (particularly, attending one of a set of elite US business schools) and developing similar lifestyle and consumption patterns.

Since this global capitalist class is neither fully developed nor coherent, we might wonder about its capacity to act collectively and in a single-minded way to further global capitalist interests. But Sklair raises important questions about the capacity of states, as local *political* actors, to exercise any significant power in a global capitalist economy. There are two further issues that need to be considered here: first, it is probably wrong to assume that processes that diminish or undermine the state affect *all* national states with equal force and in similar ways. McGrew, for example, points out that 'advanced capitalist states may have greater autonomy in the global system than peripheral states, whilst the US has greater autonomy in some domains (eg military) than in others (eg financial). Propositions suggesting the general erosion of state autonomy in the face of increasing globalisation therefore demand considerable qualification' (1992, p.91).

We might add that the claim that states in a globalised capitalist system have little competence or autonomy may well overstate the amount they possessed in the past. Certainly, people in peripheral or dependent societies have already been aware for a long time that their states can do little, in an autonomous way, to develop their own economies or to protect their own particularistic cultures. Is the change that is being emphasised now only that core societies are starting to experience what peripheral societies already know? Are theories about the declining power and authority of the modern nation state emanating most strongly from sociologists that work in those societies whose states were previously dominant world powers but which have now lost this position, such as Britain?

We may put this another way: perhaps one of the most useful contributions of a global perspective is that it broadens the range of social and political experiences that can now be seen as normal. The experiences of the periphery, which were regarded in the past as deviant and as attributable to the fact that such societies were neither fully modern nor fully competent and independent states, may now start to be seen as normal and as representing one of the many ways that modernity is experienced in a differentiated, uneven, global capitalist system.

Although states may lose effectiveness and competence in a globalised capitalist world, this does not necessarily mean that loss of legitimacy immediately follows. In fact this seems a rather narrow understanding of the bases on which social groups may accord legitimacy to a political institution. It is quite often suggested that Irish society would run much more effectively (or efficiently) if it were governed directly from Brussels, but this is not widely perceived as a serious reason to abolish the Irish state. It may well be true that with the increasing globalisation of capitalism, the decisions that crucially affect our economic and cultural futures are made more and more by agencies other than the state, whether we recognise this or not. But whether that will ultimately produce a withdrawal of compliance from the state by citizens remains very much open to debate.

# Other forms of globalisation

The second point that Mann noted was essentially about environmental developments, and it adds a further dimension to our discussion of environmentalism in Chapter 17. Many writers on environmental problems make the point that this is one of the few genuinely global issues (Yearley, 1996). This usually involves one or both of two separate claims: first, the risks and dangers that result from damage to the environment do not just affect some parts of the world or some social groups or classes — they threaten all of humanity; second, although environmental damage may originate in one country or region of the world, it characteristically spreads beyond these local boundaries fairly quickly. We might think here of acid rain, for example, or the Chernobyl nuclear disaster. On acid rain, Yearley comments that 'acidic gases can travel a great distance in the atmosphere before they are brought down in rain; consequently, the countries affected were not always the ones believed to be responsible for causing the pollution' (1991, p.42). Environmental campaigners in Scandinavian countries were already concerned about the damage that acid rain generated from coal-burning power stations was doing to their trees in the 1970s. But the main countries that were causing the problem, the UK and West Germany, did not notice any great damage for another decade at least and were very unwilling to accept any connection between their domestic methods of producing energy and the death of trees in another country. In Ireland, we have been very aware of the dangers to our sheep and lamb production, for example, posed by a nuclear explosion thousands of kilometres away in Belorussia.

Environmental problems, then, are increasingly recognised as global threats, and it is increasingly accepted that they can only be managed through some form of global co-operation and action. This has been a basis for further social and political globalisation. For example, it has encouraged the emergence of international networks of environmental activitists and of transnational environmental organisations like Greenpeace, and it has contributed to the formation of a global 'knowledge class' of leading scientists working on environmental indicators. It also appears to underpin the growth of global or supranational regulatory bodies like the United Nations Environmental Programme (UNEP), or the International Union for the Conservation of Nature (IUCN) — though some more cynical commentators suggest the relationship may be the other way round, and that the reason that we now believe environmental problems to be global ones is that agencies exist that have a vested interest in stressing this point. But however we interpret it, it is undeniable that the emergence of environmental risk as a new category of threat facing human beings is a further indication of limits on the power and competence of the modern national state.

Are environmental issues unique in this respect, or can we think of other issues that are 'global' in the same way? If there are no others, we may be doubtful about the impact of environmental risk on its own as a force for change in the global political order. Ultimately, too, we need to consider whether a world organised in some way other than around relations between national states could necessarily handle environmental problems any better. Even if environmental damage crosses state borders, it may still be important not to lose sight of the need to act locally as well as globally. Environmental destruction may have transnational consequences but it often has national causes, and it may be that the national state will remain the most effective agency to address and remove the causes of risk.

## Globalisation and collective identities

Mann's third issue has to do with the impact of a globalised world system on collectivisation and on social identities as a basis for this. This reminds us again of how far globalisation implies *restructuring*. Global capitalism is not just a process of straightforward incorporation of ever more of the world's territory into capitalist relations. It involves profound changes within the world capitalist system, as some areas of the world, and some localities within these, and some social groups, are incorporated into the system and others that were previously within it are organised out of it. The experience of many inner-city urban areas over recent decades in the more developed parts of the world is a good example of this. They have undergone a shift from being a core location for important heavy industries to being a location for holding a reserve army of labour as heavy industry has lost ground to light industry, and light industries relocated into suburban, small-town or rural settings. If we carry the idea of restructuring far enough we can reach the point where, as McGrew says, 'within the same state, community and street, there will be those whose lives are deeply implicated in and tied to this new "transnational capitalism", and many others who are either its victims or who exist on its margins' (1992, p.79).

Many theorists argue that this restructuring weakens the state as it gives rise to new identities based on far more *localised* commonalities — local experiences of industrialisation or de-industrialisation, shared ethnic or racial categorisations, and shared experiences of social, cultural or political exclusion. Much discussion of the new social movements found in core societies (see Chapter 15) portrays these as movements by social groups that have been excluded or marginalised by the process of restructuring, and who have responded to the experience by seeking to affirm and validate new sources of identity that help to explain why their experiences have differed from others. This sort of argument has been used, in particular, to explain 'new' ethnic movements in Europe, such as the movement for Turkish cultural and ethnic recognition in Germany.

Do such movements, and the new politics of identity associated with them, necessarily threaten or undermine the national state as a legitimate regulator of social life and as an 'official' source of collective identity? Ethnic politics, it is true, have sometimes led to the fragmentation of existing states, but often the result is the establishment of at least two more nation states to replace the fragmented one (eg the re-division of Czechoslovakia into separate Czech and Slovak Republics). We might expect similar outcomes from contemporary territorial secessionist movements such as the Scottish Nationalist movement, which is less easily categorised as an 'ethnic' movement. With other types of identity politics the impact on national collective identity may be less obvious.

Mann addresses the issue of gender and sexuality as a source of identity, in this context. One way that global restructuring may transform collective identity is by heightening the significance of gender identity as opposed to, for example, national identity. The social movements and political pressure groups that have built up around gender issues do tend to have a strong international or transnational dimension, though as we saw in Chapter 15 when discussing the women's movement in Ireland, they are also strongly shaped by the history, politics and social structure of the particular societies in which they operate. Moreover, such groups are usually strongly oriented to bringing about political changes, not just changes in cultural practices or ideas. Since it is at the level of the national state that political change is mainly achieved, through legislation and regulation, Mann suggests that this may be a case where transnational identity politics can reinvigorate national politics and can strongly influence citizens' perceptions of the national state as a legitimate ruler (depending, of course, on how the state responds to group demands).

## Globalisation and power

The last of the four issues we outlined at the start of this section is connected with what might be called trends in *geopolitics*. Are these contributing to the emergence of a transformed political order in which the national state no longer plays a central role? Those who believe they are often point to the declining recourse to, or declining effectiveness of, military violence and war as a means to resolve international political conflicts. Giddens (1985) has identified the use of military violence as one of the four main institutional complexes that constitute the modern nation state, and this argument largely conforms with his position. It suggests that to the extent that war has ceased to be the preferred way of dealing with problems between states — or even an option, given our current nuclear capacity to destroy everything in destroying our enemies — states are ceasing to have much relevance as international actors and have also suffered a clear loss in functions and in competence.

To think that wars have become less frequent and violence decreased in recent decades may be to project a Western European experience onto the world at large and to ignore, for example, the huge loss of life in conflicts in Iran, Iraq, Rwanda, Ethiopia and many other developing countries. As importantly perhaps, as Mann has pointed out, the key geopolitical actors of some decades ago, when war was still widely regarded as an acceptable option among Western states, were not national states at all, but are better described as empires. During much of the twentieth century it was not the European national state but the European colonial empire (British, Spanish, Dutch, Belgian or even Russian) that dominated geopolitics; and the wars fought during this period were primarily wars between imperial rivals. Since the Second World War, geopolitics was dominated by US-led NATO and its cold-war relations with the USSR, followed more recently by the development of a broader Western Atlantic military space, again dominated by the United States, and primarily confronting what is often described as 'the Arab world'.

The important geopolitical actors during this period, then, have not been national states, nor even international groupings of such states, but power blocs based on control of military resources. In Chapter 4 we suggested that one of the most lasting definitions of what constitutes a state is Weber's argument that states are institutions that can claim a legitimate monopoly on the use of violence. If we think of the contemporary world political order along these lines we may agree that neither earlier in this century, nor now, has it been nation states as such that have monopolised violence; it has always been supranational political entities that have tried to do so. Moreover, a number of writers suggest now that the expansion of pooled means of violence at the transnational level is being paralleled by a fragmentation of the means of violence at the sub-national level, as both political and criminal groups across national states develop their own 'private' or illegal armies, as, for example, in Colombia or Mozambique. What this may indicate is that there is a process of *political restructuring* going on, in terms of ownership of power, to some extent comparable to the economic restructuring processes discussed above.

What can we conclude then about the impact of globalising processes on the national state and the world political order associated with it? First, perhaps, that the issues are still very open. There are at least three possible outcomes of political globalisation that can be identified, and little clear reason as yet to decide which is most likely to be realised. National states may remain as key elements in the world political order (suggesting that the world may be becoming more international but not necessarily more global). Or intensifying international relationships may eventually prompt the establishment of some sort of *global state* that may resemble present national states but on a larger scale. Or the end result will be some totally new forms of governance, probably quite unlike anything we have experienced so far.

Second, we might conclude that globalisation is not a simple or one-dimensional pattern of change, but is in fact extremely complex. Rather than thinking of globalisation as a movement towards a new pattern of social, economic and political relationships, it may be better to follow McGrew (1992, p.65) in seeing it as a process whereby 'human interaction, interconnectedness and awareness are reconstituting the world as a single social space'. What is attractive about this approach is that it shifts our focus — away from the external changes taking place in the modern world and towards a study of how we experience and interpret that world. This suggests that a critical factor in the whole globalisation process, which we have not yet discussed, is culture.

## GLOBALISATION AND CULTURE

Because of our history of emigration over several centuries (see Chapter 5), being Irish has always meant in some sense living in a global society. But it is only in recent years that this has become a matter of self-conscious recognition among Irish people, giving rise, for example, to demands for the vote for Irish people living abroad and to the development of a more inclusive sense of Irish identity that the diaspora could identify with. The emergence of a globalised Irish identity seems to be bound up with a contrary process — a fragmentation of Irish national identity into localised identities of class, gender, language, religion or region. Some sociologists argue that these developments are inextricably intertwined in a process of 'glocalisation'.

A global sense of Irishness helps to highlight the diversity of localised ways in which one can be Irish (gay-Irish, Black-Irish, Mayo-Irish, Boston-Irish); at the same time the local identities that come to replace national ones are often more universal or universalisable and encourage the growth of global identifications (for example, being a woman in a patriarchal society or being a member of a minority language group in an English-speaking world may come to be more significant for understanding one's identity than simply 'being Irish'). Globalisation and localisation can thus be mutually reinforcing processes.

How we evaluate the impact of globalisation on identity depends very much on how we assess its impact on culture. Discussions of the cultural impact of globalisation have been dominated by one issue in particular: the issue of cultural homogenisation or standardisation. This means, essentially, that as societies with their associated cultures become increasingly incorporated into a single global system, the cultural differences between them are eroded and we are gradually faced with a single global culture.

The idea that cultures are becoming homogenised or are increasingly indistinguishable from one another is widely shared across different groups in Irish society — it is by no means only a preoccupation of sociologists. By and large, it is regarded as something to be regretted, lamented or if possible resisted, though if instead of talking of cultural homogenisation we talked of the 'spread of civilisation' across the world, we might get a rather different response. As we noted earlier, supporters of modernisation theory take for granted that the process of modernisation includes a process of cultural change that brings developing societies closer to the culture of the developed societies; they also take for granted that this is a civilising process and is therefore to be welcomed. Yet nearly everyone dislikes the prospect of cultural homogenisation.

What is it that is supposed to be becoming homogenised in the cultural globalisation process? The examples that people focus on cover a wide range — from cultural artefacts like domestic furnishings, architecture, or TV shows; to cultural practices such as child-rearing, wedding ceremonies or the management of the 'mad' and the 'bad'; through to language, ideas and meanings, and even to collective identities. Most people respond rapidly to visible features of daily life, such as the spread of McDonald's fast food stores, or the appearance of similar shops and products in identically designed shopping malls across the globe. The wide range of possibilities that we may have in mind about 'world culture' is precisely what makes the issue so complex and hard to assess. Another difficulty is the range of ways that the cultural homogenisation argument is articulated. The next section briefly explores some examples and arguments that sociologists have offered in this field.

## THE GLOBAL CULTURE-IDEOLOGY OF CONSUMERISM

Sklair argues that a central feature of the emergent global communication system is that it has increased the opportunities for 'hegemonic control on a global scale' by the supporters of capitalism out of all proportion compared to the past (1995, p.85). By 'hegemonic control' he means control of society through control of its dominant ideas. The unprecedented increase during the 1980s in the scale and scope of electronic media communications has allowed a small group of TNCs 'the potential for distribution of messages on a scale never before achieved' (1995, p.86). The huge expansion of the communications system has not provided a real channel for alternative views — quite the opposite: 'the central messages are still, and more powerfully, those of the capitalist global system' (1995, p.85).

Sklair explains how the media can perform many functions for global capitalism. Not only do they speed up the circulation of goods through advertising, leading to larger profits, but they act as socialisation agencies for the dominant ideology — which Sklair labels 'the culture-ideology of consumerism'. They can inculcate it into people from an early age. He cites research, for example, that shows that the average young North American has been exposed to more than 300,000 television commercials by the age of 16. At the heart of this socialisation process is a systematic blurring of the boundaries between information, entertainment, and promotion of products; the result is that all of the media and all of their products are transformed into 'opportunities to sell ideas, values, products, in short a consumerist world view' (1995, p.88).

Sklair is aware of the dominant position that the US media hold within the global system, but differs from theorists of cultural imperialism such as Schiller (see Chapter 14) in arguing that the national origin of media contents, and national ownership of media organisations, is not really of great significance. Sklair believes that the global media operate not on behalf of American consumerist culture specifically, but on behalf of global capitalism. The problem is not cultural imperialism but the ideology of consumerism that underpins the global expansion of capitalism and that renders all cultures ultimately the same. This means that the global media can continue to homogenise culture even when they are operating with media communications that are entirely indigenous or 'national' in content. Irish radio record programmes today may use more recordings of Irish artists and Irish musical compositions than formerly, but in Sklair's view this changes nothing since the message of these cultural products is the same as that of the American or UK produced material that was dominant in earlier years. Both offer the same culture-ideology since both are products of a global capitalist system that reaches into every sphere of life.

Another version of a similar thesis can be found in Ritzer (1993; 1996) who coined the term 'the McDonaldisation of society' to capture the multifarious contemporary processes of global cultural standardisation. Ritzer suggests that we can see the McDonald's formula for running a successful global fast food business (specifically, with the emphasis on predictability, so that the customer knows exactly what to expect in terms of menu, taste, service, decor and price no matter what part of the world they happen to be in) as one of the best examples of what Weber called formal rationalisation. A key feature of contemporary capitalist society, Weber suggests, is that it searches for ever more efficient instruments to realise profit, one of which is to pursue economies of scale through standardisation and homogenisation. Globalisation, in this instance, can be understood simply as the further expansion of capitalist rationality. And since Weber argued that processes of formal rationalisation spread eventually into all spheres of modern society, this helps to explain why the routinisation and standardisation of industrial output 'should increasingly be found in many other spheres — not only production, but also leisure, culture, education, religion and politics' (Kumar, 1995, p.189)

## CRITIQUING THE CULTURAL HOMOGENISATION THESIS

Standardisation, or homogenisation, is not the only process shaping a globalised world. Earlier we saw that processes of globalisation accompany and seem to be entwined with processes of localisation. In terms of cultural products and cultural consumption, while one important trend is towards standardisation, another appears to be towards diversification. Kumar comments, for example, on how large producers and retailers in the food industry 'have pursued a two-pronged strategy of the "globalisation of tastes" together with the provision of specialised "exotic" foods from all over the world. McDonald's on the one hand; Safeways on the other' (1995, p.61). He suggests that we can see this as part of a strategy of transnational capitalism as it seeks to realise the most effective mix of economies not just of scale but also of 'scope' — that is, to reach as much of the consumer market as possible and indeed to create consumer demand where it does not already exist.

But arguments like these are vulnerable to the same sorts of criticism as were made — as we saw in Chapter 16 — against analyses of consumption that treat the consumer as a mere object for manipulation, and the arguments of media audience analysts outlined in Chapter 14. Schiller's theory of cultural imperialism in particular has been criticised on these grounds. He uses a dependency perspective to describe the growth of a US-dominant transnational media system, but treats this system essentially as an *economic* system, without paying much attention to the *cultural* dimension of the media. He assumes that if media audiences are exposed to a barrage of messages that convey the importance, desirability and modernity of an American-inspired consumer lifestyle, they will automatically internalise these messages and act them out. This treats audiences as no more than passive consumers of media products and ignores the question of *how* people read, understand and respond to the content that the media presents to them. But as we saw in Chapter 14, research on media audiences shows that they are far more active, complex and critically aware in their readings than the theorists of media imperialism have allowed. As Kumar remarks: 'to eat at McDonald's is not necessarily to be McDonaldised' (1995, p.194).

Schiller's thesis, it could be argued, is not really about cultural imperialism at all (only economic imperialism) since it does not address the defining feature of culture which is that it is about the transmission of and response to *meanings*. But this criticism seems even more germane to Sklair's approach: without sustained research, how can we know what meanings are transmitted in Irish, American or any other national form of popular music, for example? More crucially, even if the songs all transmit the same message, how can we know without research whether the audience receives this message at all, or hears it and responds to it in a critical and detached way? Should we not start with the assumption that people are more active and creative in responding to cultural items and artefacts, perhaps especially to 'foreign' ones, than Sklair seems to envisage?

## Clarifying culture

Some interesting contributions to the debate have been made by the Swedish anthropologist Ulf Hannerz (1990; 1991). Hannerz is in no doubt that cultural imperialism theorists are right about the one-sided and uneven nature of global communication flows between centres and peripheries. But he is much less convinced (1991, p.109) that the outcome must inevitably be cultural homogenisation:

'a quick look at the world today' may afford this 'master scenario' a certain intrinsic plausibility; it may seem like a mere continuation of present trends. It has of course, the great advantage of simplicity. And it is dramatic. There is the sense of fatefulness, the prediction of the inevitable loss of large parts of the combined heritage of humanity.

But none of this necessarily makes it true.

Hannerz suggests that if we are to develop the argument any further we must clarify what we mean by culture. Then we need to identify the different frameworks in which cultural flows take place and are managed and organised. Culture, he suggests, is a flow of meanings between people; and takes place within four particularly important frameworks:

- the market
- the state
- everyday 'forms of life'
- social movements.

We need to discover whether all of these frameworks encourage cultural change to go in the same direction, towards homogeneity, or whether some may offer opportunities for cultural autonomy and resistence to dependency in peripheral societies. This would allow us to break down and critique the cultural homogenisation thesis.

Those who believe in cultural homogenisation as the outcome of globalisation, Hannerz argues, recognise only the *market* as the framework within which cultural flows are organised. They largely ignore the other three although these can also be very significant. For example, the management of meanings and flows is one of the most important things done by the contemporary *state*. States are involved in organising culture and cultural processes for their citizens for a number of reasons — to develop them as members of a nation as well as citizens of the state; to manage the differences between groups that have a bearing on their being slotted into positions in the occupational or other social hierarchies; to provide citizens with what we might call cultural welfare, that is, with cultural products thought to exemplify high standards of intellectual or aesthetic quality; and so on. We can see from this that state involvement in cultural processes can encourage homogenisation (clarifying and supporting the national culture) *and* differentiation. It may also, through its attempts at cultural welfare, provide citizens with tools they can use to develop self-conscious and self-aware stances towards themselves and their own cultural world, as a basic precondition for autonomous cultural growth.

The *form of life* framework may well be the most important. It involves 'the everyday practicalities of production and reproduction, activities going on in work places, domestic settings, neighbourhoods' (1991, p.113). Here there are no formal authorities and no specialists in the production and dissemination of meaning; the cultural processes are diffuse and uncentred, shaped mainly by people's everyday experiences as they participate in local and international divisions of labour. Since they are less subject to attempts at management from the centre, there is more room for cultural autonomy and innovation. This is also true, finally, of *social movements* as arenas for the development and transmission of cultural meanings.

Although movements exist against a background of globalisation, as we saw earlier in this chapter, they are often not fully integrated and organised on a global basis, leaving more space for free play of local and national meanings.

Why distinguish these different frameworks? Hannerz says it is the inter-relationships between them that shape 'how the periphery is drawn into world culture, now and in the future' (1991, p.116); yet each framework differs substantially from the others in the extent to which it fosters centralisation and homogenisation, or decentralisation and differentiation. Peripheral states, on one hand, often engage in active resistance to too much free flow of information or free movement of cultural meanings; the maintenance of cultural distinctiveness is often essential to the continued legitimacy of the state (a good example is the highly interventionist media and cultural policy of Singapore). On the other hand, the forms of state found in peripheral societies (for example, nation states) are themselves largely based on ideas that have been diffused transnationally from the more developed world; and peripheral states are large-scale importers of culture from the centre, not just in relation to media products, as noted already, but also when they introduce, for example, national educational systems and meritocratic ideologies, concepts of time-keeping at work, private property rights and individual responsibility before the law. Even the market, understood by cultural homogenisation theorists to be the major force for global homo-genisation, can be involved in promoting differentiation in the periphery, for example, in searching for niche products, especially in popular culture areas like music, to meet the constantly changing consumerist demands of the centre: 'let us observe that much of what the entrepreneurs of popular culture in the Third World are doing these days involves carving out such niches. . . . Nobody with any experience of West African urban life can fail to be impressed with the constantly changing variety of popular music — highlife, juju, Afrobeat, apala, or whatever' (1991, p.119).

In Nigeria, Hannerz points out, imported material in cinemas or on television appears quite frequently but seems to be much less attractive to Nigerian people now than it was in the past, and it draws little attention or involvement from them, compared to locally produced sitcoms. In Australia, similarly, locally produced TV has dominated the ratings since the 1970s (Cunningham and Turner, 1997). Luke Gibbons emphasises that in recent decades the media programmes that proved most challenging for Irish audiences (because they were also most involving) have been Irish-based; even when they were heavily influenced by imported formats (1996, p.4). Local cultural entrepreneurs involved in organising such new cultural items may lack material resources, but what they possess is local knowledge, which is less available to the culture businesses at the centre of the global system (could Hollywood have invented *Riverdance*?). They know their territory, they are competent in its cultural practices and sensitive to its meanings, and this derives primarily from their involvement in the local forms of life.

For such reasons, Hannerz suggests, we may find that a theory of *cultural maturation* better describes how peripheries are drawn into global cultural processes than a theory of cultural homogenisation. What he means by this is that the periphery 'takes its time reshaping metropolitan culture to its own specifications' (1991, p.124). At first, cultural forms imported from the centre seem to remain unaffected by their contact with indigenous items and to dominate and threaten to replace local or peripheral forms. But later, as they begin to interact with elements in the peripheral culture they begin to be altered by it; their position on the cultural market comes to be set, in effect, from within the periphery and its forms of life, not from without. Hannerz believes that this is the main source of the creativity found in the popular music culture of West Africa, for example: 'local cultural entrepreneurs have gradually mastered the alien cultural forms which reach them through the transnational commodity flow and in other ways, taking them apart, tampering and tinkering with them in such a way that the resulting new forms are more responsive to, and at the same time in part outgrowths of, local everyday life' (1991, p.124). The peripheral culture should never be seen, then, as defenseless; it is a place where 'locally evolving alternatives to imports are available, and where there are people at hand to keep performing innovative acts of cultural brokerage' (1991, p.125). It is a place where global cultural forms are typically reconstructed and indigenised, often in unexpected ways: as Gurnah (1995, p.123) asks of the Zanzibari enthusiasm for 1950s pop, 'why did Africans choose to be part of this global culture and so passionately love — of all people — Jim Reeves? In order to be "modernized"? Hardly.'

## Creole cultures?

If we accept Hannerz's view, we have to accept that cultural distinctiveness while it still survives is not so absolute as it was in the past (and it was never entirely absolute). It is becoming a matter of degree. Moreover, cultural differences are likely to be found increasingly *within* societies, not just between them, since they grow out of interactions with local and differentiated forms of life. Interestingly, Hannerz suggests that the capacity of societies or localities to respond creatively to imported cultural forms may well depend to a considerable extent on the economic conditions within the periphery: the better off people are, the more likely they are to exercise creativity and to resist cultural colonisation from the core. Paradoxically then, cultural difference may depend on involvement in the world economic system rather than on isolation from it.

Hannerz suggests that a useful term to describe the impact of cumulative interactions between core and peripheral cultures is *creolisation*, a term borrowed from linguistics. Creolisation 'suggests that cultures, like languages, can be intrinsically of mixed origin, rather than historically pure and homogeneous. It clashes conspicuously . . . with received assumptions about culture coming out of nineteenth-century European nationalism. And the similarities between "creole" and "create" are not fortuitous' (1991, p.127).

Creole cultures result as people actively make their own syntheses out of the foreign and the indigenous. So while in some important respects the amount of cultural diversity and differentiation in the world *is* diminishing with globalisation and cultural imperialism, it is also important to recognise that new, if creolised, cultures and cultural products emerge as a result of globalisation. We should also notice that cultural differences at the local level within state societies may become increasingly apparent as states become less able to enforce their nation-building scenarios and as local areas are integrated in differing ways into global economic and cultural systems. It does not take much imagination to see how the reconstruction of dominant Western cultural forms in this way has taken place in Ireland — from *The Riordans* and *The Late Late Show* as Irish takes on global TV forms, to Irish Country and Western to American Confederate flags at Páirc uí Caoimh. It seems implausible to suggest that these cultural forms are any less Irish than those regarded as somehow more indigenous or authentic.

## GLOBALISATION AND SOCIOLOGY

According to McGrew, globalisation 'strikes at many of the orthodoxies of social science' (1992, p.64). It raises questions about some of sociology's 'foundational concepts' — especially the concepts of society and of the nation state — that emerged at the birth of the discipline in the nineteenth century and still hold a privileged position in the language of contemporary sociology. McGrew points out that, from the beginning, sociology set out to study 'modern society'. But this was understood to be a cohesive, boundaried, integrated social system and so became virtually indistinguishable from the territorially boundaried national state. 'Society' was studied, effectively, as a series of 'national societies', and it was the development and destiny of such national societies that sociology sought to explain.

But for McGrew, as the world becomes more globalised, and as national boundaries are penetrated and transcended by multiple transnational connections and exchanges, to continue to focus on the destiny of 'national societies' becomes harder and harder to defend. If globalisation is 'reconstituting the world as one place', he suggests, sociology may need to redefine its project away from society as the social embodiment of the national state and refocus instead on the emerging world society if it is to continue to make sense of the contemporary human condition.

Globalisation, McGrew argues, must also make us confront again and re-think the idea of post-modernity. We ended Chapter 17 by asking if a post-modern sociology could help us in any way to understand the post-modern social world. McGrew suggests that perhaps it cannot. The discovery of the significance of globalisation implies, he suggests, that we need to be able to produce valid accounts of universal phenomena, whereas post-modern theory argues that only particularistic accounts of the experience of the here and now can have validity. Globalisation seems to suggest the presence in world society of some universal socio-economic processes and perhaps of some universal cultural ones as well. To McGrew it is ironic that 'at the very moment sociology encounters the possibility of a "world society", it is gripped by the discourse of post-modernity which denies the plausibility of any universal truths or knowledge through which such an emerging "global social formation" might be comprehended' (1992, p.64).

If 'society' is to be removed from its central position in the vocabulary of modern sociology, what could replace it? At first sight post-modernism seems to offer an intriguing answer to this question: 'nothing'. Post-modernist theorists suggest that the human world is 'irreducibly pluralistic' (Bauman, 1991, p.35). It is split up into a multitude of self-managing units and sites that are not assembled in any sort of order, either hierarchical or horizontal. To understand such a world we must avoid *imposing* an external order on it by using totalising concepts such as 'society'. Instead, we must accept it as an essentially incoherent world. In studying it we must resist the temptation to assume that the accounts we produce of particular situated social episodes or events have any more general application.

McGrew emphasises that we cannot begin to understand the process of globalisation unless we assume that there are some universal processes in operation that are, if not uniting all of humanity, at least transforming relationships between people in very significant ways. They may be universal processes that generate difference, not sameness, but they can still be treated as universal. We might conclude from this that post-modernism is also doomed to be a victim of globalisation, alongside the conventional modernist conception of society (1992, p.98). But if we are to return to the Enlightenment project of producing a 'science' of social life, it cannot be with the same concepts and terminology as before. Instead of taking 'national societies' as the primary units of sociology we will have to develop 'a sociology of one world' that recognises that 'global processes are now partly constitutive of social reality everywhere' (Archer, quoted in McGrew, 1992, p.98).

There is a third way that globalisation might be seen to strike at the heart of the orthodoxies of social science. This is through its transformation of the 'normativities' that characterised Enlightenment sociology (Euromosaic, 1996): globalisation might help to transform the world through the way it helps to *normalise* the experience of the periphery, and to rescue it from the perception of deviance. The 'modern' core experience can no longer be seen as the only civilised or fully human experience of reality.

Our discussion in this chapter suggests two ways that this might happen. One has to do with the impact of globalisation on the state. We have heightened our awareness of the modern state's lack of autonomy and competence within a globalising world, and its continual struggle to maintain legitimacy in the eyes of its citizens. But what is now presented to us as an experience of the national state in the period of globalisation has *already* been the experience of peripheral societies and their states for a long period of time. What in the past was assumed to be a deviation from the norm, where the norm was that of the independent, self-governing, autonomous state, has now become the standard.

Similarly with culture. The exotic, quaint cultures and traditions associated by core societies with peripheral and especially post-colonial societies are beginning to emerge as attractive examples of cultural diversity, and as saleable commodities on global cultural and tourism markets, just as core or 'normal' states with their unified and civilised cultures are fragmenting into cultural diversity. We might say that ethnicity has been rediscovered to be a normal part of human social life. For a society like Ireland, and for sociologists studying it, this in the end may turn out to be the most important and the most profound of the transformations that globalisation is bringing about.

McGrew's suggestion that in a globalised world sociology should abandon its concern with national societies is not accepted by everyone. An eloquent defence of an alternative has been made by Bryan Turner (1990, p.343):

Since its formal inception in the first half of the nineteenth century, sociology has been, generally implicitly, located in a tension or contradition between a science of particular nation states and a science of global or universal processes. It developed ambiguously as a science of the specific societies of the industrial world and as a science of humanity. Although the vocabulary of sociology is typically couched at a sufficiently abstract level to suggest that it is a science of universal social processes . . . in practice sociology has been developed to explain and understand local or national destinies. . . .

Paradoxically we might argue that the greater the sociologist, the more local the purpose, namely that sociology developed by brilliant insights into concrete issues of local capitalistic development. . . . Since the modern world is itself subject to the contradictory tensions of globalisation and localisation, secularisation and fundamentalisation, of modernisation and post-modernisation, we should expect to see these contradictions reflected in the conceptual apparatus of sociology itself.

We hope that this book has taken at least the first steps towards explaining an Irish 'local or national destiny', while not losing sight of the destiny of humanity.

# References

Åberg, A.
(1999)
'Modern nature? Images of nature and rurality in Swedish cinema'. Paper to European Rural Sociological Society conference, Lund.

Akenson, D.
(1991)
*Small differences: Irish Catholics and Irish Protestants, 1815–1922.* Montreal and Kingston: McGill-Queen's University Press/ Dublin: Gill & Macmillan.

Allen, K.
(1997)
*Fianna Fáil and Irish Labour: 1926 to the present.* London: Pluto.

Allen, K.
(1999)
'The Celtic Tiger, inequality and social partnership'. *Administration* 47(2). pp.31–55.

Allen, M.
(1998)
*The bitter word: Ireland's job famine and its aftermath.* Dublin: Poolbeg.

Altman, D.
(1999)
'The globalisation of sex'. *Age* (Melbourne) 14 July.

Anderson, B.
(1983)
*Imagined communities: Reflections on the origin and spread of nationalism.* London: Verso.

Ang, I.
(1985)
*Watching Dallas: Soap opera and the melodramatic imagination.* London: Methuen.

Aniagolu, C.
(1997)
'Being black in Ireland' in E. Crowley and J. Mac Laughlin (eds) *Under the belly of the tiger: Class, race identity and culture in the global Ireland.* Dublin: Irish Reporter.

Anthias, F.
(1999)
'Theorising identity, difference and social divisions' in M. O'Brien, S. Penna and C. Hay (eds) *Theorising modernity.* London: Longman.

Arensberg, C.    *Family and community in Ireland*. Cambridge (Mass.): Harvard
and S. Kimball    University Press.
(1940)

Atkinson, A.    'Poverty in Ireland and anti-poverty strategy: A European
(1997)    perspective' in A. Gray (ed.) *International perspectives on the Irish
economy*. Dublin: Indecon.

Bail, K. (ed.)    *DIY feminism*. Sydney: Allen and Unwin.
(1996)

Baines, S.    'Promises and perils of home computing: gender and the
(1992)    'technologization' of distance learning' in Granite (ed.) *NICTs
and the changing nature of the domestic*. Amsterdam: SISWO.

Baker, J.    'Studying equality'. *Imprints* 2(1). pp.57–71.
(1997)

Baker, S.    'The evolution of the Irish ecology movement' in W. Rudig (ed.)
(1990)    *Green politics I*. Rotterdam: Erasmus University Press.

Banks, M.    'Irish television and society'. *Media, culture and society* 12.
(1990)    pp.403–407.

Barth, F.    *Ethnic groups and boundaries: The social organisation of cultural
(1969)    difference*. London: Allen and Unwin.

Barthes, R.    *Mythologies*. St Alban's: Paladin.
(1973)

Bartley, B.    'Spatial planning and poverty in North Clondalkin' in D.
(1999)    Pringle, J. Walsh and M. Hennessy (eds) *Poor people, poor places:
A geography of poverty and deprivation in Ireland*. Dublin: Oak
Tree/Geographical Society of Ireland.

Barton, R.    'From history to heritage: some recent developments in Irish
(1997)    cinema'. *The Irish Review* 21, pp.41–56.

Bauman, Z.    *Intimations of postmodernity*. London: Routledge.
(1991)

Bauman, Z.    *Life in fragments: Essays in postmodern morality*. Oxford: Blackwell.
(1995)

Baxter, J.,
M. Emmison,
J. Western and
M. Western (eds)
(1991)

*Class analysis and contemporary Australia*. Melbourne: Macmillan.

Bayley, D.
(1991)

*Forces of order: Policing modern Japan*. Berkeley: University of California Press.

Beale, J.
(1986)

*Women in Ireland: Voices of change*. Basingstoke: Macmillan.

Beck, U.
(1992)

*Risk society: Towards a new modernity*. London: Sage.

Begg, D.
(1997)

'The danger posed to democracy posed by the new media monopolies' in D. Kiberd (ed.) *Media in Ireland: The search for diversity*. Dublin: Open Air.

Bell, C, and
H. Newby
(1971)

*Community studies: An introduction to the sociology of the local community*. London: Allen and Unwin.

Bell, C, and
H. Newby (eds)
(1974)

*The sociology of community: A selection of readings*. London: Cass.

Bellah, R.
(1967)

'Civil religion in America'. *Daedalus* Winter. pp.1–19.

Berger, A.
(1992)

*Media research techniques*. Beverly Hills: Sage.

Bibby, A.
(1996)

*Trade unions and telework*. Report produced for International Trade Secretariat FIET.
[http://www.eclipse.co.uk/pens/bibby/fietrpt.html]

Binchy, A.
(1994)

'Travellers' language: a sociolinguistic perspective' in M. McCann, S. Ó Síocháin and J. Ruane (eds) *Irish Travellers: Culture and ethnicity*. Belfast: Institute of Irish Studies, Queen's University Belfast, for the Anthropological Association of Ireland.

Blaxter, M.
(1995)

'What is health?' in B. Davey, A. Gray and C. Seale (eds) *Health and disease: A reader*. Buckingham: Open University Press.

Bocock, R.          'Consumption and lifestyles' in R. Bocock and K. Thompson
(1992)             (eds) *Social and cultural forms of modernity*. Cambridge: Polity
                    Press/Open University.

Bocock, R. and     *Religion and ideology*. Manchester: Manchester University Press/
K. Thompson         Open University.
(eds)
(1985)

Bonanno, A.,        *From Columbus to ConAgra: The globalization of agriculture and
L. Busch,           food*. Kansas: University Press of Kansas.
W. Friedland,
L. Gouveia and
E. Mingione (eds)
(1994)

Bonner, K.          Review of P. Clancy *et al*. (eds) *Irish society: Sociological
(1996)             perspectives* in *Irish Journal of Sociology* 6. pp.212–20.

Boston             *Our bodies, ourselves: A book by and for women*. Boston: Boston
Women's             Women's Health Book Collective.
Health Book
Collective
(1973)

Bourdieu, P.        *Distinction: A social critique of the judgement of taste*. London:
(1984)             Routledge and Kegan Paul.

Bourdieu, P.        'What makes a social class? On the theoretical and practical
(1987)             existence of groups'. *Berkeley Journal of Sociology* 32. pp.1–17.

Box, S.            *Crime, power and mystification*. London: Tavistock.
(1983)

Boylan, T.          'Rural industrialisation and rural poverty' in C. Curtin *et al*.
(1996)             (eds) *Poverty in rural Ireland*. Dublin: Oak Tree.

Boylan, T. and     *Political economy and colonial Ireland: The propagation and ideological
T. Foley            function of economic discourse in the nineteenth century*. London:
(1992)             Routledge and Kegan Paul.

Bradley, A. and    *Gender and sexuality in modern Ireland*. Amherst: University of
M. Valiulis (eds)  Massachusetts Press.
(1997)

Breathnach, P. (1985)    'Rural industrialisation in the West of Ireland' in M. Healey and B. Ilbery (eds) *The industrialisation of the countryside*. Norwich: Geo.

Breathnach, P. (1993)    'Women's employment and peripheralisation: The case of Ireland's branch plant economy', *Geoforum* 24(1). pp.19–29.

Breen, R., D. Hannan, D. Rottman and C. Whelan (1990)    *Understanding contemporary Ireland: State, class and development in the Republic of Ireland*. London: Macmillan.

Breen, R. and D. Rottman (1985)    *Crime victimisation in the Republic of Ireland*. Dublin: Economic and Social Research Institute. [Paper no. 121].

Breen, R. and C. Whelan (1996)    *Social mobility and social class in Ireland*. Dublin: Gill & Macmillan.

Breen, R. and C. Whelan (1999)    'Social mobility in Ireland: a comparative analysis' in A. Heath, R. Breen, and C. Whelan (eds) *Ireland North and South: Perspectives from social science*. Oxford: Oxford.

Brett, D. (1996)    *The construction of heritage*. Cork: Cork University Press.

Brody, H. (1973)    *Inishkillane*. London: Allen Lane.

Buckley, M. (1997)    'Sitting on your politics: the Irish among the British and the women among the Irish' in J. Mac Laughlin (ed.) *Location and dislocation in contemporary Irish society: Emigration and Irish identities*. Cork: Cork University Press.

Bunton, R. (1998)    'Inequalities in late-modern health care' in A. Petersen and C. Waddell (eds) *Health matters: A sociology of illness prevention and care*. Buckingham: Open University Press.

Buttel, F. and H. Newby (eds) (1980)    *The rural sociology of the advanced societies*. Montclair: Allenheld Osmun.

Byrne, A. and    *Women and Irish society: A sociological reader.* Belfast: Beyond
Leonard M. (eds)  the Pale.
(1997)

Calhoun, C.     'Social theory and the public sphere' in B. Turner (ed.) *The*
(1996)        *Blackwell companion to social theory.* Oxford: Blackwell.

Callan, T. and   *Measuring trends in poverty over time.* Dublin: Economic and
B. Nolan       Social Research Institute [Working paper no. 7].
(1988)

Callan, T. and   'Poverty and policy' in S. Healy and B. Reynolds (eds)
B. Nolan       *Social policy in Ireland.* Dublin: Oak Tree.
(1998)

Callan, T.,     *Poverty in the 1990s: Evidence from the Living in Ireland survey.*
B. Nolan,      Dublin: Oak Tree.
B. Whelan,
C. Whelan and
J. Williams
(1996)

Campbell, C. '   *The romantic ethic and the spirit of modern consumerism.* Oxford:
(1987)        Blackwell.

Carey, M.      'Women in non-traditional employment in Northern Ireland: a
(1997)        marginalised form of femininity' in A Byrne and M. Leonard
             (eds) *Women in Irish society: A sociological reader.* Belfast:
             Beyond the Pale.

Castles, S.     *The age of migration: International population movements in the*
and M. Miller    *modern world.* Basingstoke: Macmillan.
(1993)

Clancy, P.      *Participation in higher education: A national survey.* Dublin: Higher
(1982)        Education Authority.

Clancy, P.      *Who goes to college? A second survey of participation in higher*
(1988)        *education.* Dublin: Higher Education Authority.

Clancy, P.      'Education in the Republic of Ireland: the project of modernity?'
(1995a)       in P. Clancy *et al.* (eds) *Irish society: Sociological perspectives.*
             Dublin: Institute of Public Administration in association with
             the Sociological Association of Ireland.

Clancy, P.
(1995b)
*Access to college: Patterns of continuity and change.* Dublin: Higher Education Authority.

Clark, J. and
M. Diani (eds)
(1996)
*Alain Touraine.* London: Falmer.

Cleary, A.
(1997)
'Gender differences in mental health in Ireland' in A. Cleary and M. Treacy (eds) *The sociology of health and illness in Ireland.* Dublin: University College Dublin Press.

Cleary, A. and
M. Treacy
(1997)
*The sociology of health and illness in Ireland.* Dublin: University College Dublin Press.

Cloke, P. and
N. Thrift
(1990)
'Class and change in rural Britain' in T. Marsden, P. Lowe and S. Whatmore (eds) *Critical perspectives on rural change.* London: Fulton.

Coakley, Jay
(1998)
'Sports and religion: is it a promising combination?' in *Sport in society: Issues and controversies.* Boston: McGraw-Hill.

Coakley, John
(1998)
'Religion, ethnic identity and the Protestant minority in the Republic' in W. Crotty and D. Schmitt (eds) *Ireland and the politics of change.* London: Longman.

Cockburn, C.
(1983)
*Brothers: Male dominance and technological change.* London: Pluto.

Coleman, D.
(1992)
'The demographic transition in Ireland in international context' in J. Goldthorpe and C. Whelan (eds) *The development of industrial society in Ireland.* Oxford: Oxford University Press/ The British Academy.

Collins, C. and
E. Shelley
(1997)
'Social class differences in lifestyle and health characteristics in Ireland' in A. Cleary and M. Treacy (eds) *The sociology of health and illness in Ireland.* Dublin: University College Dublin Press.

Commins, P.
(1985)
'Rural community development — approaches and issues'. *Social Studies* 8. pp.165–78.

Commins, P.
(1995)
'The European Community and the Irish rural economy' in P. Clancy *et al.* (eds) *Irish Society: Sociological perspectives.* Dublin: Institute of Public Administration in association with the Sociological Association of Ireland.

Commins, P.     'Agricultural production and the future of small-scale farming'
(1996)          in C. Curtin *et al.* (eds) *Poverty in rural Ireland*. Dublin: Oak Tree.

Commins, P.         *Developing the rural economy — problems, programmes and*
and M.J. Keane     *prospects.* Report no. 97. Dublin: National Economic and
(1994)              Social Council.

Commission on   *Consultative process: Background document.* Dublin: Stationery
the Points      Office. [http://www.irlgov.ie/educ/comm.htm]
System
(1999)

Connell, R.     *Teachers' work.* Sydney: Allen and Unwin.
(1985)

Connell, R.     *Gender and power: Society, the person and sexual politics.* Sydney:
(1987)          Allen and Unwin.

Connell, R.,        *Making the difference: Schools, family and social division.* Sydney:
D. Ashendon,        Allen and Unwin.
S. Kessler and
G. Dowsett
(1982)

Connell, R. and *Class structure in Australian history.* Melbourne: Longman Cheshire.
T. Irving
(1980)

Connolly, B.    'Women in community education and development —
(1997)          liberation or domestication?' in A. Byrne and M. Leonard
                (eds) *Women and Irish society: A sociological reader.* Belfast:
                Beyond the Pale.

Connolly, L.    'The women's movement in Ireland 1970–1995 — a social
(1996)          movements analysis'. *Irish Journal of Feminist Studies* 1 (1).
                pp.43–77.

Connor, S.      'Welcome to your new body'. *Independent on Sunday* 21 March.
(1999)          p18.

Corcoran, M.    'Informalization of metropolitan labour forces: the case of Irish
(1991)          immigrant in the New York construction industry'. *Irish Journal
                of Sociology* 1. pp.31–51.

Corcoran, M.    *Irish illegals: Transients between two societies.* Westport,
(1993)          CT/London: Greenwood.

Corcoran, M.    'Heroes of the diaspora?' in M. Peillon and E. Slater (eds)
(1998)          *Encounters with modern Ireland.* Dublin: Institute of Public
                Administration.

Coulter, C.     *Are religious cults dangerous?* Cork: Mercier.
(1984)

Coulter, C.     *The hidden tradition: Feminism, women and nationalism in Ireland.*
(1993)          Cork: Cork University Press.

Coulter, C.     '"Hello divorce, goodbye Daddy" Women, gender and the
(1997)          divorce debate' in A. Bradley and M. Valiulis (eds) *Gender and
                sexuality in modern Ireland.* Amherst: University of Massachusetts
                Press.

Courtney, D.    'Demographic structure and change in the Republic of Ireland
(1995)          and Northern Ireland' in P. Clancy *et al.* (eds) *Irish society:
                Sociological perspectives.* Dublin: Institute of Public Administration
                in association with the Sociological Association of Ireland.

Courtney, D.    'The quantification of Irish migration'. Paper to conference *The
(1997)          scattering: Ireland and the Irish diaspora: A comparative perspective.*
                Irish Centre for Migration Studies, University College Cork,
                September.

Courtney, D.    'A quantification of Irish migration with particular reference to
(2000)          the 1980s and 1990s' in A. Bielenberg (ed.) *The Irish diaspora.*
                Essex: Addison Wesley Longman.

Coyle, C.       'Administrative capacity and the implementation of EU
(1994)          environmental policy in Ireland' in S. Baker *et al.* (eds)
                *Protecting the periphery.* Ilford: Cass.

Crompton, R.    *Class and stratification: An introduction to current debates.*
(1998)          Cambridge: Polity.

Crotty, R.      *The cattle crisis and the small farmer.* Mullingar: National Land
(1974)          League.

Crotty, R.        'Modernisation and land reform: real or cosmetic, the Irish case'.
(1983)            *Journal of Peasant Studies* 11 (1) pp.101–16.

Crotty, R.        *Ireland in crisis: a study in capitalist colonial undevelopment.* Dingle:
(1986)            Brandon.

Crow, G. and      *Community life: An introduction to local social relations.* London:
G. Allen          Harvester Wheatsheaf.
(1994)

Crowley, E.       'Making a difference? Female employment and multinationals in
(1997)            the Republic of Ireland' in A. Byrne and M. Leonard (eds)
                  *Women and Irish society: A sociological reader.* Belfast: Beyond the
                  Pale.

Crowley, N.       'Local communities and power' in T. Caherty *et al.* (eds) *Is
and P. Watt       Ireland a third world country?* Belfast: Beyond the Pale.
(1992)

Cuff, E.,         *Perspectives in sociology.* London: Routledge.
W. Sharrock
and D. Francis
(1998)

Cullen, L.        *An economic history of Ireland since 1600.* London: Batsford.
(1987)

Cullen, M.        *Girls don't do honours: Irish women in education in the 19th and
(1987)            20th centuries.* Dublin: Women's Education Bureau.

Cullen, P.        'Immigration to Ireland reaches record levels'. *Irish Times* 30
(1997)            October.

Cunningham, S.    *Australian television and international mediascapes.* Cambridge:
and E. Jacka      Cambridge University Press.
(1996)

Cunningham, S.    *The media in Australia: Industries, texts, audiences.* Sydney:
and G. Turner     Allen and Unwin.
(ed.)
(1997)

Curran, C.
(1996)
'Fianna Fáil and the origins of the Irish Press'. *Irish Communications Review* 6: pp.7–17.

Curry, J.
(1998)
*Irish social services*. Dublin: Institute of Public Administration.

Curtin, C.
(1988)
'Social order, interpersonal relations and disputes in a West of Ireland community' in M. Tomlinson, T. Varley and C. McCullagh (eds) *Whose law and order? Aspects of crime and social control in Irish society*. Belfast: Sociological Association of Ireland.

Curtin, C.
(1996)
'Back to the future? Communities and rural poverty' in C. Curtin et al. (eds) *Poverty in rural Ireland*. Dublin: Oak Tree.

Curtin, C.,
T. Haase and
H. Tovey
(eds)
(1996)
*Poverty in rural Ireland: A political economy perspective*. Dublin: Oak Tree.

Curtin, C. and
C. Ryan
(1989)
'Clubs, pubs and private houses in a Clare town' in C. Curtin and T. Wilson (eds) *Ireland from below*. Galway University Press.

Curtin, C. and
T. Varley
(1995)
'Community action and the state' in P. Clancy et al. (eds) *Irish society: Sociological perspectives*. Dublin: Institute of Public Administration.

Curtin, C. and
T. Wilson
(1989)
*Ireland from below: Social change and local communities*. Galway: Galway University Press.

CWC
[Community
Workers
Cooperative]
(1996)
*Partnership in action: The role of community development and partnership in Ireland*. Galway: Community Workers Cooperative.

Dahlerup, D.
(1986)
*The new women's movement: Feminism and political power in Europe and the USA*. London: Sage.

Daly, M.          *The spirit of earnest inquiry: The Statistical and Social Inquiry*
(1997)            *Society of Ireland 1847–1997.* Dublin: Institute of Public
                  Administration.

Daly, M.          'The Statistical and Social Inquiry Society of Ireland' in
(1998)            K. Kennedy (ed.) *From famine to feast: economic and social change
                  in Ireland 1847–1997.* Dublin: Institute of Public Administration.

Daniel, A.        'Trust and medical authority' in A. Petersen and C. Waddell
(1998)            (eds) *Health matters: A sociology of illness, prevention and care.*
                  Buckingham: Open University Press.

Davies, B.        *Frogs and snails and feminist tales: Preschool children and gender.*
(1990)            Sydney: Allen and Unwin.

Davis, A. and     *States of health: Health and illness in Australia.* Sydney:
J. George         Harper Collins.
(1993)

Davis, M.         *City of quartz: Excavating the future in Los Angeles.* London:
(1990)            Verso.

Day, G.           'A community of communities? Similarity and difference in
(1998)            Welsh rural community studies'. *Economic and Social Review*
                  29(3). pp.233–58.

Delaney, E.       'State, politics and demography: The case of Irish emigration,
(1998)            1921–71'. *Irish Political Studies* 13, pp.25–49.

Delanty, G.       'Beyond the nation-state: national identity and citizenship in a
(1996)            multicultural society. A response to Rex'. *Sociological Research
                  Online* 1(3). [http://www.socresonline.org.uk/1/3/1.html]

Department of     *Active or passive? Broadcasting in the future tense.*
Arts, Culture     [Green paper on broadcasting]. Dublin: Stationery Office.
and the
Gaeltacht
(1995)

Department of     *Investment in education. Report of the survey team appointed by the
Education         Minister for Education in October, 1962.* Dublin: Stationery
(1965)            Office.

Department of Education and Science (1998)
*Adult education in an era of lifelong learning* (Green paper on adult education). Dublin: Stationery Office. [http://www.irlgov.ie/educ/pdfs/adultedu.pdf]

Department of Equality, Justice and Law Reform (1997)
*Ireland's combined 2nd and 3rd reports under the UN convention on the elimination of all forms of discrimination against women.* Dublin: Stationery Office.

Department of Health (1994)
*Shaping a healthier future: A strategy for effective healthcare in the 1990s.* Dublin: Department of Health.

Deutsch, K. (1966)
*Nationalism and social communication.* Michigan: MIT Press.

Devereux, E. (1997)
'The theatre of reassurance? Glenroe, its audience and the coverage of social problems' in M. Kelly and B. O'Connor (eds) *Media audiences in Ireland.: Power and cultural identity.* Dublin: University College Dublin Press.

Devereux, E. (1998)
*Devils and angels: Television, ideology and the coverage of poverty.* Luton: University of Luton Press.

Devine, F. (1997)
*Social class in America and Britain.* Edinburgh: Edinburgh University Press.

Devlin, J. (1997)
'The state of health in Ireland' in J. Robins (ed.) *Reflections on health: Commemorating fifty years of the Department of Health 1947–1997.* Dublin: Department of Health.

Doak, R. (1998)
'(De)constructing Irishness in the 1990s — the Gaelic Athletic Association and cultural nationalist discourse reconsidered'. *Irish Journal of Sociology* 8. pp.25–48.

Doorley, P. (1998)
'Health status' in E. McAuliffe and L. Joyce (eds) *A healthier future? Managing healthcare in Ireland.* Dublin: Institute of Public Administration.

Dore, R. (1987)
*Taking Japan seriously.* Stanford: Stanford University Press.

Douthwaite, R. (1992)    *The growth illusion*. Dublin: Lilliput.

Downes, D. (1992)    'The case for going Dutch: the lessons of post-war penal policy'. *The Political Quarterly* 63 (1). pp.12–24.

Drudy, P. (1995)    'From protectionism to enterprise: A review of Irish industrial policy' in A. Burke (ed.) *Enterprise and the Irish economy*. Dublin: Oak Tree.

Drudy, S. (1991)    'Developments in the sociology of education in Ireland 1966–1991'. *Irish Journal of Sociology* 1 pp.107–127.

Drudy, S. and K. Lynch (1993)    *Schools and society in Ireland*. Dublin: Gill & Macmillan.

du Gay, P., S. Hall, L. Janes, H. Mackay and K. Negus (1997)    *Doing cultural studies: The story of the Sony Walkman*. London: Sage/Open University.

Durkheim, E. (1964)    *The rules of sociological method*. New York: The Free Press.

Dwyer, M. and P. Taaffe (1998)    'Nursing in 21st century Ireland: Opportunities for transformation' in A. Leahy and M. Wiley (eds) *The Irish health system in the 21st century*. Dublin: Oak Tree.

Edley, N. and M. Wetherell (1995)    *Men in perspective: Practice, power and identity*. London: Prentice Hall.

Edmondson, R. (1997)    'Older people and life-course construction' in A. Cleary and M. Treacy (eds) *The sociology of health and illness in Ireland*. Dublin: University College Dublin Press.

Eipper, C. (1986)    *The ruling trinity — A community study of church, state and business in Ireland*. Aldershot: Gower.

Etzioni, A. (1995)    *The spirit of community*. London: Fontana.

Euromosaic (1996)
*The production and reproduction of the minority language groups in the European Union*. Luxembourg: European Commission.

Fagan, G. (1995)
*Culture, politics and Irish school dropouts*. Westport CT/London: Bergin and Garvey.

Fahey, T. (1987)
'Nuns in the Catholic Church in Ireland in the nineteenth century' in M. Cullen (ed.) *Girls don't do honours: Irish women in education in the 19th and 20th centuries*. Dublin: Women's Education Bureau.

Fahey, T. (1992a)
'Catholicism in Ireland' in P. Clancy, M. Kelly, J. Wiatr and R. Zoltaniecki (eds) *Ireland and Poland: Comparative perspectives*. Dublin: Department of Sociology, University College Dublin.

Fahey, T. (1992b)
'State, family and compulsory schooling in Ireland'. *Economic and Social Review* 23(4). pp.369–95.

Fahey, T. (1994)
'Catholicism and industrial society in Ireland' in J. Goldthorpe and C. Whelan (eds) *The development of industrial society in Ireland*. Oxford: Oxford University Press/The British Academy.

Fahey, T. (1998a)
'Progress or decline? Demographic change in political context' in W. Crotty and D. Schmitt (eds) *Ireland and the politics of change*. London/New York: Longman.

Fahey, T. (1998b)
'Housing and social exclusion' in S. Healy and B. Reynolds (eds) *Social policy in Ireland: Principles, practice and problems*. Dublin: Oak Tree.

Fahey, T. and J. Fitzgerald (1997)
*Welfare implications of demographic trends*. Dublin: Oak Tree/Combat Poverty Agency.

Fahy, P. (1978)
Dependency in the Irish mass communications system (an exploratory study). Unpublished paper read at the Sociological Association of Ireland Conference, Cork.

Fallon, B. (1998)
*An age of innocence: Irish culture 1930–1960*. Dublin: Gill & Macmillan.

Fay, I. (1997)
*Beyond belief: A mind-blowing pilgrimage through religious Ireland*. Dublin: Hot Press Books.

Featherstone, M.    'Lifestyle and consumer culture'. *Theory, Culture and Society*
(1987)              4(1). pp.55–70.

Featherstone, M.    Travel, migration and images of social life' in W. Gungwu
(1997)              (ed.) *Global history and migrations*. Boulder: Westview.

Forbairt            *Ireland: the digital age, the internet*. Dublin: National Software
(1996)              Directorate, Forbairt. [http://www.nsd.ie/inflitdi.html]

Foucault, M.        *The birth of the clinic: An archaeology of medical perception*. New
(1973)              York: Vintage.

Foucault, M.        *The history of sexuality. Vol 1. A introduction*. New York: Vintage.
(1980)

Fox, N.             'Postmodernism and 'health' ' in A. Petersen and C. Waddell
(1998)              (eds) *Health matters: A sociology of illness, prevention and care*.
                    Buckingham: Open University Press.

Frank A.            'The development of underdevelopment'. *Monthly Review*,
(1967)              September. pp.17–30.

Furedi, F.          *Population and development: A critical introduction*. Cambridge:
(1997)              Polity.

Galligan, Y.        *Women and politics in contemporary Ireland*. London: Pinter.
(1998a)

Galligan, Y.        'The changing role of women' in W. Crotty and D. Schmitt
(1998b)             (eds) *Ireland and the politics of change*. London/New York:
                    Longman.

Game, A. and        *Gender at work*. Sydney: Allen and Unwin.
R. Pringle
(1983)

Garda Siochána,     *Annual Report on crime for 1996*. Dublin: Stationery Office.
An
(1997)

Garvin, T.          'Theory, culture and Fianna Fáil — a review' in M. Kelly *et al.*
(1982)              (eds) *Power, conflict and inequality*. Dublin: Turoe.

Garvin, T.
(1998)
'Patriots and republicans: an Irish evolution' in W. Crotty and D. Schmitt (eds) *Ireland and the politics of change*. London/New York: Longman.

Geary, R.
(1951)
'Irish economic development since the Treaty'. *Studies* Vol. Xl. No. 160. pp.399–419.

Geddes, M.
(1998)
*Local partnership: A successful strategy for social cohesion?* Dublin: European Foundation for the Improvement of Living and Working Conditions.

Gellner, E.
(1983)
*Nations and nationalism*. Oxford: Blackwell.

Gibbon, P.
(1973)
'Arensberg and Kimball revisited'. *Economy and Society* 4. pp.479–98.

Gibbons, L.
(1996)
*Transformations in Irish culture*. Cork: Cork University Press.

Giddens, A.
(1985)
*The nation-state and violence*. Cambridge: Polity Press.

Giddens, A.
(1991)
*Modernity and self-identity — Self and society in the late modern age*. Cambridge: Polity.

Giddens, A.
(1993)
*Sociology*. Cambridge: Polity Press.

Gillespie, M.
(1995)
*Television, ethnicity and cultural change*. London: Routledge.

Glass, R.
(1966)
*Conflict in society*. London: Churchill.

Gmelch, G.
and S. Gmelch
(1976)
'The emergence of an ethnic group'. *Anthropological Quarterly* 49. pp.225–38.

Gmelch, S.
(1989)
'From poverty subculture to political lobby: the Traveller Rights movement in Ireland' in C. Curtin and T. Wilson (eds) *Ireland from below: Social change and local communities*. Galway: Galway University Press.

Goldblatt, D. (1996)    *Social theory and the environment.* Cambridge: Polity.

Goldthorpe, J.H. and others (1996)    (1968–9) *The affluent worker in the class structure.* 3 vols. Cambridge: Cambridge University Press.

Goldthorpe, J.H. and C.T. Whelan (eds) (1992)    *The development of industrial society in Ireland.* Oxford: Oxford University Press.

Gorz, A.    *Ecology as politics.* London: Pluto.

Gorz, A. (1981)    *Farewell to the working class.* London: Pluto.

Gould, S. (1997)    *The mismeasure of man.* Harmondsworth: Penguin.

Gray, B. (1997)    'Unmasking Irishness: Irish women, the Irish nation and the Irish diaspora' in J. Mac Laughlin (ed.) *Location and dislocation in contemporary Irish society: Emigration and Irish identities.* Cork: Cork University Press.

Gripsrud, J. (1995)    *The Dynasty years: Hollywood television and critical media studies.* London: Routledge.

Guinnane, T. (1997)    *The vanishing Irish: Households, migration and the rural economy in Ireland, 1850–1914.* Princeton: Princeton University Press.

Guiomard, C. (1995)    *The Irish disease — and how to cure it. Common sense economics for a competitive world.* Dublin: Oak Tree.

Gungwu, W. (ed.) (1997)    *Global history and migrations.* Boulder: Westview.

Gunning, M. (1997)    'Children and television pleasure' in M. Kelly and B. O'Connor (eds) *Media audiences in Ireland: Power and cultural identity.* Dublin: University College Dublin Press.

Gurnah, A. (1995)    'Elvis in Zanzibar' in A. Scott (ed.) *The limits of globalization.* London/New York: Routledge.

Habermas, J.       'Life-forms, morality and the task of the philosopher' in P. Dews
(1987)             (ed.) *Autonomy and solidarity — Interviews with Jurgen Habermas.*
                   London: Verso.

Hamelink, C.       'Globalisation and national sovereignty' in K. Nordernstreng
(1993)             and H. Schiller (eds) *Beyond national sovereignty: International
                   communication in the 1990s.* Norwood NJ: Ablex.

Hanlon, G.         'The emigration of Irish accountants: economic restructuring
(1991)             and producer services in the periphery'. *Irish Journal of Sociology*
                   1. pp.52–65.

Hannan, D.         'The significance of small-scale landholders in Ireland's
and P. Commins     socio-economic transformation' in J. Goldthorpe and
(1992)             C. Whelan (eds): *The development of industrial society in Ireland.*
                   Oxford: Oxford University Press/The British Academy.

Hannan, D. and     *Traditional families? From culturally prescribed to negotiated*
L. Katsiaouni      *roles in farm families.* Dublin: Economic and Social Research
(1977)             Institute.

Hannan, D.,        *Trading qualifications for jobs: Overeducation and the Irish labour*
B. McCabe and      *market.* Dublin: Oak Tree/ Economic and Social Research Institute.
S. McCoy.
(1998)

Hannan, D.,        *Coeducation and gender equality: Exam performance, stress and*
E. Smyth,          *personal development.* Dublin: Oak Tree/ Economic and Social
J. McCullagh,      Research Institute.
R. O'Leary,
D. McMahon
(1996)

Hannan, D. and     'Dependency, status group claims and ethnic identity' in
H. Tovey           A. Spencer (ed.) *Dependency: Social, political, cultural.*
(1978)             Proceedings of the 5th Annual Conference of the Sociological
                   Association of Ireland. Belfast: Queen's University of Belfast.

Hannerz, U.        'Cosmopolitans and locals in world culture' in M. Featherstone
(1990)             (ed.) Global culture: Nationalism, globalisation and modernity.
                   London: Sage.

Hannerz, U.        'Scenarios for peripheral cultures' in A. King (ed.) *Culture,*
(1991)             *globalisation and the world system.* Basingstoke: Macmillan.

Hardiman, N.
(1998)
'Inequality and the representation of interests' in W. Crotty and D. Schmitt (eds) *Ireland and the politics of change*. London/New York: Longman.

Herper, S.
(1989)
'The British rural community: an overview of perspectives'. *Journal of Rural Studies* 5(2) 161–84.

Harris, L.
(1983)
'Industrialisation, women and working class politics in the West of Ireland'. *Capital and Class* 19. pp.110–17.

Harris, L.
(1984)
'Class, community and sexual divisions in North Mayo' in C. Curtin *et al.* (eds) *Culture and ideology in Ireland*. Galway: Galway University Press.

Harris, L.
(1989)
'Women's responses to multinationals in Co. Mayo' in D. Elson and R. Pearson (eds) *Women's employment and multinationals in Europe*. London: Macmillan.

Haughton, J.
(1995)
'The historical background' in O'Hagan, J. (ed.) *The economy of Ireland*. Dublin: Gill & Macmillan.

Haughton, J.
(1998)
'The dynamics of economic change' in W. Crotty and D. Schmitt (eds) *Ireland and the politics of change*. London/New York: Longman.

Hayes, M.
(1990)
'Migratory birds and roundy heads' in R. Kearney (ed.) *Migrations: The Irish at home and abroad*. Dublin: Wolfhound.

Hayles, N.
(1995)
'The life cycle of cyborgs' in C. Hay (ed.) *The cyborg handbook*. London: Routledge.

Hazelkorn, E.
(1991)
'British labour and Irish capital: evidence from the 1980s' in Galway Labour History Group (ed.) *The emigrant experience: Papers presented at the second annual Mary Murray Weekend seminar*. Galway: Galway Labour History Group.

Hazelkorn, E.
(1996)
'New technologies and changing work practices in the media industry: the case of Ireland'. *Irish Communications Review* 6: pp.28–38.

Heath, A. and M. Savage
(1995)
'Political alignments within the middle classes, 1972–89' in T. Butler and M. Savage (eds) *Social change and the middle classes*. London: University College London Press.

Hederman
O'Brien, M.
(1998)
'Healthcare — the context' in E. McAuliffe and L. Joyce (eds)
*A healthier future? Managing healthcare in Ireland.* Dublin:
Institute of Public Administration.

Heidensohn, F.
and M. Farrell
(eds)
(1991)
*Crime in Europe.* London: Routledge.

Heidensohn, F.
(1989)
*Crime and society.* London: Macmillan.

Hettne, B.
(1990)
*Development theory and the three worlds.* Harlow: Longman.

Hewison, R.
(1987)
*The heritage industry: Britain in a climate of decline.* London:
Methuen.

Hillery, G.
(1955)
'Definitions of community: areas of agreement'. *Rural Sociology*
20(2). pp.111–23.

Hindley, R.
(1990)
*The death of the Irish Language: A qualified obituary.* London:
Routledge.

Hobsbawm, E.
(1990)
*Nations and nationalism since 1780.* Cambridge: Cambridge
University Press.

Hodgins, M.
and C. Kelleher
(1997)
'Health and well-being in social care workers'. *Women's Studies*
*Review* 5. pp.37–48.

Hoggart, K.,
H. Buller and
R. Black
(1995)
*Rural Europe: Identity and change.* London: Arnold.

Hornsby-Smith,
M.
(1994)
'Social and religious transformation in Ireland: A case of
secularisation?' in J. Goldthorpe and C. Whelan (eds) *The*
*development of industrial society in Ireland* Oxford: Oxford
University Press/The British Academy.

Hornsby-Smith,
M. and
Whelan, C.
(1994)
'Religious and moral values' in C. Whelan (ed.) *Values and social*
*change in Ireland.* Dublin: Gill & Macmillan.

Hout, M. and J. Jackson (1986) 'Dimensions of occupational mobility in the Republic of Ireland'. *European Sociological Review* 2 pp.114–37.

Hug, C. (1999) *The politics of sexual morality in Ireland.* London: Macmillan.

Humphreys, A. (1966) *The new Dubliners: Urbanisation and the Irish family.* London: Routledge and Kegan Paul.

Huws, U., N. Jagger and S. O'Regan (1999) *Teleworking and globalisation.* IES Report 358. Brighton: Institute for Employment Studies.

Hyde, A. (1997) 'The medicalisation of childbearing norms: Encounters between unmarried pregnant women and medical personnel in an Irish context' in A. Cleary and M. Treacy (eds) *The sociology of health and illness in Ireland.* Dublin: University College Dublin Press.

Industrial Development Authority (1999) Industry sectors — pharmaceuticals IDA website sectors [http:www.idaireland.com/isph.html/]

Illich, I. (1976) *Limits to medicine.* London: Marion Boyars.

Inglehart, R. (1977) *The silent revolution: Changing values and political styles among western publics.* Princeton: Princeton University Press.

Inglis, T. (1987) *Moral monopoly: The Catholic church in modern Irish society.* Dublin: Gill & Macmillan.

Inglis, T. (1998a) *Moral monopoly: The Rise and Fall of the Catholic church in modern Ireland.* Dublin: University College Dublin Press.

Inglis, T. (1998b) *Lessons in Irish sexuality.* Dublin: University College Dublin Press.

Inglis, T. (1998c) 'A religious frenzy' in M. Peillon and E. Slater (eds) *Encounters with modern Ireland.* Dublin: Institute of Public Administration.

Inglis, T.
(1998d)
'Foucault, Bourdieu and the field of Irish sexuality'. *Irish Journal of Sociology* 7. pp.5–28.

Inglis, T.
(1998e)
'From sexual repression to liberation?' In M. Peillon and E. Slater (eds) *Encounters with modern Ireland*. Dublin: Institute of Public Administration.

Jackson, J.
(1987)
'Social science in Ireland'. *International Social Science Journal*, 112.

Jackson, J.
(1998)
*Social science in Ireland*. Unpublished paper for the Sociology Department, Trinity College Dublin.

Jackson, J. and
U. Barry
(1989)
'Women's employment and multinationals in the Republic of Ireland: the creation of a new female labour force' in D. Elson and R. Pearson (eds) *Women's employment and multinationals in Europe*. London: Macmillan.

Jacobsen, B.
(1988)
*Beating the ladykillers: Women and smoking*. London: Gollancz.

Jacobson, D.
(1989)
'Theorising Irish industrialisation: the case of the motor industry.' *Science and Society* 53 (2). pp.165–91.

Jamison, A.
et al. (1990)
*The making of the new environmental consciousness*. Edinburgh: Edinburgh University Press.

Jamrozik, A.
(1991)
*Class, inequality and the state*. Melbourne: Macmillan.

Jenkins, E.
(1999)
*Tongue first: Adventures in physical culture*. London: Virago.

Kane, E.
(1996)
'The power of paradigms: social science and intellectual contributions to public discourse in Ireland' in L. O'Dowd (ed.) *On intellectuals and intellectual life in Ireland*. Belfast: Institute of Irish Studies/Royal Irish Academy.

Kearney, R. (ed.)
(1990)
*Migrations: The Irish at home and abroad*. Dublin: Wolfhound.

Keating, P. and
D. Desmond
(1993)
*Culture and capitalism in contemporary Ireland*. Aldershot: Avebury.

Kellaghan, T. (1989)    'Research, evaluation and policy' in D. Mulcahy and D. O'Sullivan (eds) *Irish educational policy: Process and substance.* Dublin: Institute of Public Administration.

Kelleher, C. (1997)    'Preface'. *Women's Studies Review* 5. pp.vii–viii.

Kelly, M. and B. O'Connor (eds) (1997)    *Media audiences in Ireland.: Power and cultural identity.* Dublin: University College Dublin Press.

Kelly, M. and B. Rolston (1995)    'Broadcasting in Ireland — issues of national identity and censorship' in P. Clancy *et al.* (eds) *Irish society — Sociological perspectives.* Dublin: Institute of Public Administration.

Kennedy, K. (ed.) (1998)    *From famine to feast: Economic and social change in Ireland 1847–1997.* Dublin: Institute of Public Administration.

Kennedy, P. (1997)    'A comparative study of maternity entitlements in Northern Ireland and the Republic of Ireland in the 1990s' in A. Byrne and M. Leonard (eds) *Women and Irish society: A sociological reader.* Belfast: Beyond the Pale.

Kenny, M. (1997)    'Who are they, who are we? Education and Travellers' in E. Crowley and J. Mac Laughlin (eds) *Under the belly of the tiger: Class, race, identity and culture in the global Ireland.* Dublin: Irish Reporter.

Keogh, D. (1998)    *Jews in twentieth century Ireland: Refugees, anti-semitism and the Holocaust.* Cork: Cork University Press.

Keohane, K. (1997)    'Traditionalism and homelessness in contemporary Irish music' in J. Mac Laughlin (ed.) *Location and dislocation in contemporary Irish society: Emigration and Irish identities.* Cork University Press.

Kerbo, H. and M. Inoue (1990)    *Deviant behaviour.* Washington: Taylor and Francis.

Kirby, P. (1984)    *Is Irish Catholicism dying?* Cork: Mercier.

Kirby, P.
(1997)

*Poverty amid plenty: World and Irish development reconsidered.*
Dublin: Gill & Macmillan/Trócaire.

Kirkham, G.
(1990)

'The origins of mass emigration from Ireland' in R. Kearney (ed.)
*Migrations: The Irish at home and abroad.* Dublin: Wolfhound.

Komito, L.
(1984)

'Irish clientelism: a reappraisal'. *Economic and Social Review*
15(3). pp.173–94.

Kuhling, C.
(1998)

'New Age Travellers on Cool mountain' in M. Peillon and
E. Slater (eds) *Encounters with modern Ireland.* Dublin: Institute
of Public Administration.

Kumar, K.
(1995)

*From post-industrial to post-modern society.* Oxford: Blackwell.

Laffan, B. and
R. O'Donnell
(1998)

'Ireland and the growth of international governance' in
W. Crotty and D. Schmitt (eds) *Ireland and the politics of change.*
London/New York: Longman.

Langer, J.
(1992)

*Emerging sociology: An international perspective.* Aldershot:
Avebury.

Langman, L.
(1992)

'Neon cages — shopping for subjectivity' in R. Shields (ed.)
*Lifestyle shopping: The subject of consumption.* London: Routledge.

Language
Planning
Advisory
Committee
(1986)

*Irish in the education system.* Dublin: Bord na Gaeilge.

Language
Planning
Advisory
Committee
(1988)

*The Irish language in a changing society — Shaping the future.*
Dublin: Bord na Gaeilge.

Lash, S. and
J. Urry
(1994)

*Economies of signs and space.* London: Sage.

Leane, M. and
E. Kiely
(1997)

'Single lone motherhood — reality versus rhetoric' in A. Byrne
and M. Leonard (eds) *Women and Irish society: A sociological
reader.* Belfast: Beyond the Pale.

Lee, D. and
H. Newby
(1983)
*The problem of sociology*. London: Hutchinson.

Lee, D. and
B. Turner (eds)
(1996)
*Conflicts about class: Debating inequality in late industrialism*.
London: Longman.

Lee, J.
(1989)
*Ireland 1912–1985: Politics and society*. Cambridge: Cambridge
University Press.

Leeuwis, C.
(1989)
*Marginalisation misunderstood: Different patterns of farm
development in the west of Ireland*. Wageningen: Wageningen
Agricultural University.

Lennon, M.,
M. McAdam
and J. O'Brien
(1988)
*Across the water: Irish women's lives in Britain*. London: Virago.

Lentin, R.
(1993)
'Feminist research methodologies'. *Irish Journal of Sociology* 3.
pp.119–38.

Lentin, R.
(1998)
'"Irishness", the 1937 Constitution, and citizenship: a gender
and ethnicity view'. *Irish Journal of Sociology* 8. pp.5–24.

Lentin, R.
(1999)
'Racializing our Dark Rosaleen: feminism, citizenship, racism,
antisemitism'. *Women's Studies Review* 6. pp.1–17.

Leonard, M.
(1997)
'Women caring and sharing in Belfast' in A. Byrne and
M. Leonard (eds) *Women and Irish society: A sociological reader*.
Belfast: Beyond the Pale.

Leyton, E.
(1966)
'Conscious models and dispute regulation in an Ulster village'.
*Man* [new series] 1. pp.534–42.

Lichterman, P.
(1996)
*The search for political community (American activists reinventing
commitment)*. Cambridge: Cambridge University Press.

Lincoln, C.
(1993)
'City of culture — Dublin and the discovery of urban heritage'
in B. O'Connor and M. Cronin (eds) *Tourism in Ireland: A
critical analysis*. Cork: Cork University Press.

Lumby, C. (1997)
Bad girls: The media, sex and feminism in the 90s. Sydney: Allen and Unwin.

Lynch, C. (1997)
'Literacy is a human right: an adult underclass returns to education' in E. Crowley and J. Mac Laughlin (eds) Under the belly of the tiger: Class, race, identity and culture in the global Ireland. Dublin: Irish Reporter.

Lynch, K. (1987)
'Dominant ideologies in Irish educational thought: consensualism, essentialism and meritocratic individualism'. Economic and Social Review 18(2). pp.101–22.

Lynch, K. (1999a)
Equality in education. Dublin: Gill & Macmillan.

Lynch, K. (1999b)
'Equality studies, the academy and the role of research in emancipatory social change'. Economic and Social Review 30(1). pp.41–69.

Lynch, K. and C. O'Riordan (1999)
'Inequality in higher education: a study of social class barriers' in K. Lynch Equality in education. Dublin: Gill & Macmillan.

Lynch, K. and E. McLaughlin (1995)
'Caring labour and love labour' in P. Clancy et al. (eds) Irish society: Sociological perspectives. Dublin: Institute of Public Administration.

Mac Gréil, M. (1996)
Prejudice in Ireland revisited. Maynooth: Survey and Research Unit, Department of Social Studies, NUI Maynooth.

Mac Laughlin, J. (1994)
Ireland: The emigrant nursery and the world economy. Cork: Cork University Press.

Mac Laughlin, J. (1997a)
Location and dislocation in contemporary Irish society: Emigration and Irish identities. Cork: Cork University Press.

Mac Laughlin, J. (1997b)
'Ireland in the global economy: an end to a distinct nation?' in E. Crowley and J. Mac Laughlin (eds) Under the belly of the tiger: Class, race, identity and culture in the global Ireland. Dublin: Irish Reporter.

MacCurtain, M.    'Godly burden: The Catholic sisterhoods in twentieth-century
(1997)           Ireland' in A. Bradley and M. Valiulis (eds) *Gender and
                 sexuality in modern Ireland*. Amherst: University of
                 Massachusetts Press.

MacFarlane, A.   'The changing role of women as health workers in Ireland.'
(1997)           *Women's Studies Review* 5. pp.18–36.

Macionis, J.     *Sociology: A global introduction*. London: Prentice Hall.
and
K. Plummer
(1998)

Maguire, A.      'The accidental immigrant' in I. O'Carroll and E. Collins (eds)
(1995)           *Lesbian and gay visions of Ireland: Towards the twenty-first century*.
                 London: Cassell.

Maheu, L.        *Social movements and social classes*. London: Sage.
(ed.)
(1995)

Mahon, E.        'Feminist research: a reply to Lentin'. *Irish Journal of Sociology* 4.
(1994)           pp.165–9.

Mahon, E.        'From democracy to femocracy: the women's movement in the
(1995)           Republic of Ireland' in P. Clancy *et al.* (eds) *Irish society:
                 Sociological perspectives*. Dublin: Institute of Public
                 Administration/Sociological Association of Ireland.

Mahon, E.        'The development of a health policy for women' in J. Robins
(1997)           (ed.) *Reflections on health: Commemorating fifty years of the
                 Department of Health 1947–1997*. Dublin: Department of Health.

Mair, P.         'Explaining the absence of class politics in Ireland' in J.
(1994)           Goldthorpe and C. Whelan (eds) *The development of industrial
                 society in Ireland* Oxford: Oxford University Press/The British
                 Academy.

Mann, M. (ed.)   *The rise and decline of the nation state*. Oxford: Blackwell.
(1990)

Marsden, T.,      *Constructing the countryside*. London: UCL Press.
J. Murdoch,
P. Lowe,
R. Munton and
A. Flynn
(1993)

Marshall, G.      'Outclassed by our critics?'. *Sociology* 24(2). pp.255–67.
and D. Rose
(1990)

Martell, L.       *Ecology and society*. Cambridge: Polity.
(1994)

May, T.           *Social research — Issues, methods and processes*. Buckingham:
(1997)            Open University Press.

McAuliffe, E.     *A healthier future? Managing healthcare in Ireland*. Dublin: Institute
and L. Joyce      of Public Administration.
(eds) (1998)

McBrierty, V.     *Ireland and the knowledge economy: The new techno-academic
and R. Kinsella   paradigm*. Dublin: Oak Tree.
(1998)

McCann, M.,       *Irish Travellers: Culture and ethnicity*. Belfast: Institute of Irish
S. Ó Síocháin     Studies, Queen's University Belfast, for the Anthropological
and J. Ruane      Association of Ireland.
(eds)
(1994)

McCarthy, G.      'Nursing and the health services' in J. Robins (ed.) *Reflections on
(1997)            health: Commemorating fifty years of the Department of Health
                  1947–1997*. Dublin: Department of Health.

McCarthy, P.      *Itineracy and poverty: A study in the subculture of poverty*. MA
(1971)            thesis. University College, Dublin.

McCarthy, P.      'The sub-culture of poverty reconsidered' in McCann, M.,
(1994)            S. Ó Síocháin and J. Ruane (eds) *Irish Travellers: Culture and
                  ethnicity*. Belfast: Institute of Irish Studies, Queen's University
                  Belfast, for the Anthropological Association of Ireland.

McCrone, D.    *Understanding Scotland — The sociology of a stateless nation.*
(1992)    London: Routledge.

McCullagh, C.    'Deviance and crime in the Republic of Ireland' in P. Clancy
(1986)    *et al.* (eds): *Ireland: A sociological profile.* Dublin: Institute of
Public Administration.

McCullagh, C.    'Getting the criminals we want — the social production of the
(1995)    criminal population' in P. Clancy *et al.* (eds) *Irish society:*
*Sociological perspectives.* Dublin: Institute of Public Administration.

McCullagh, C.    *Crime in Ireland: A sociological introduction.* Cork: Cork
(1996)    University Press.

McDonnell, O.    'Ethical and social implications of technology in medicine: new
(1997)    possibilities and new dilemmas' in A. Cleary and M. Treacy
(eds) *The sociology of health and illness in Ireland.* Dublin:
University College Dublin Press.

McGrath, B.    'Environmentalism and property rights: the Mullaghmore
(1996)    Interpretive Centre dispute'. *Irish Journal of Sociology* 6.
pp.25–47.

McGrew, A.    'A global society?' in S. Hall, D. Held and A. McGrew (eds)
(1992)    *Modernity and its futures.* Cambridge: Open University/Polity.

McKeown, K.    'Urbanisation in the Republic of Ireland — a conflict approach'
(1986)    in P. Clancy *et al.* (eds): *Ireland: A sociological profile.* Dublin:
Institute of Public Administration.

McKeown, K.,    *Changing fathers? Fatherhood and family life in modern Ireland.*
H. Ferguson    Cork: Collins.
and D. Rooney
(1999)

McKevitt, D.    'Irish healthcare policy' in E. McAuliffe and L. Joyce (eds) *A*
(1998)    *healthier future? Managing healthcare in Ireland.* Dublin: Institute
of Public Administration.

McLoone, M.    *Cultural identity and broadcasting in Ireland: Local issues, global*
(ed.)    *perspectives.* Belfast: Institute of Irish Studies, Queen's University.
(1991)

McLoughlin, D. (1994)    'Ethnicity and Irish Travellers: reflections on Ní Shúinéar' in M. McCann, S. Ó Síocháin and J. Ruane (eds) *Irish Travellers: Culture and ethnicity*. Belfast: Institute of Irish Studies, Queen's University Belfast, for the Anthropological Association of Ireland.

McQuail, D. (1994)    *Mass communication theory*. London: Sage.

McSorley, C. (1997)    *School absenteeism in Clondalkin: Causes and responses*. Clondalkin: Clondalkin Partnership.

McVeigh, A. (1997)    'Screening for straights: aspects of entrance policy at a gay disco'. *Irish Journal of Sociology* 7. pp.77–98.

McVeigh, R. (1995)    'Cherishing the children of the nation unequally: sectarianism in Ireland' in P. Clancy *et al.* (eds) *Irish society: Sociological perspectives*. Dublin: Institute of Public Administration.

McVeigh, R. (1998)    'Irish Travellers and the logic of genocide' in M. Peillon and E. Slater (eds) *Encounters with modern Ireland*. Dublin: Institute of Public Administration.

Melucci, A. (1989)    *Nomads of the present*. London: Hutchinson Radius.

Mennell, S., A. Murcott and A. Van Otterloo (1992)    *The sociology of food: Eating, diet and culture*. London: Sage.

Merchant, C. (1980)    *The death of nature: Women, ecology and the scientific revolution*. San Francisco: Harper Collins.

Messenger, J. (1969)    *Inis Beag: Isle of Ireland*. New York: Holt, Rinehart and Winston.

Millar, R. (1998)    'Worklife mobility typologies as background to current class position — a research note'. *Economic and Social Review* 29(3). pp.259–84.

Millen, D. (1997)    'Some methodological and epistemological issues raised by doing feminist research on non-feminist women'. *Sociological Research Online* 2(3) [http://www.socresonline.org.uk/socresonline/2/3/3.html]

Miller, D.          'The Young and the Restless in Trinidad: a case of the
(1992)             local and  global in mass consumption' in R. Silverstone
                   and E. Hirsch (eds) Consuming technologies.
                   London: Routledge.

Mills C. Wright    The sociological imagination. Harmondsworth: Penguin.
(1970)

Moane, G.          'Lesbian politics and community' in A. Byrne and M. Leonard
(1997)             (eds) Women and Irish society: A sociological reader. Belfast:
                   Beyond the Pale.

Mormont, M.        'Who is rural? Or, how to be rural: towards a sociology of the
(1990)             rural' in T. Marsden, P. Lowe and S. Whatmore (eds) Rural
                   restructuring. London: Fulton.

Morris, A. and     Locality, community and nation. Abingdon: Hodder and
G. Morton          Stoughton.
(1998)

Morris, J.         'Inequalities in health: ten years and a little further on' in
(1995)             B. Davey, A. Gray and C. Seale (eds) Health and disease: A
                   reader. Buckingham: Open University Press.

Morse, M.          Virtualities: Television, media art, and cyberculture. Bloomington
(1998)             and Indianapolis: Indiana University Press.

Murphy-            The adequacy of income and family expenditure. Dublin: Combat
Lawless, J.        Poverty Agency.
(1992)

Murray, P.         'Health services review 1998'. Administration 47(2). p.268.
(1999)

Naess, A.          'Sustainable development and the deep ecology movement' in
(1997)             S. Baker, M. Kousis, D. Richardson and S. Young (eds) The
                   politics of sustainable development. London/New York: Routledge.

Nash, C.           'Embodied Irishness: gender, sexuality and Irish identities' in
(1997)             B. Graham (ed.) In search of Ireland: A cultural geography.
                   London: Routledge.

Nettleton, S. and J. Watson (1998)    *The body in everyday life*. London: Routledge.

Newby, H., C. Bell, D. Rose and P. Saunders (1978)    *Property, paternalism and power*. London: Hutchinson.

Nic Ghiolla Phádraig, M. (1995)    'The power of the Catholic Church in the Republic of Ireland' in P. Clancy *et al*. (eds) *Irish society: Sociological perspectives*. Dublin: Institute of Public Administration.

Nisbet, R. (1982)    *Prejudices: A philosophical dictionary*. Cambridge (Mass): Harvard University Press.

Ní Shúinéar, S. (1994)    'Irish Travellers, ethnicity and the origins question' in M. McCann, S. Ó Síocháin and J. Ruane (eds) *Irish Travellers: Culture and ethnicity*. Belfast: Institute of Irish Studies, Queen's University Belfast, for the Anthropological Association of Ireland.

Nolan, B. (1999)    'Income inequality in Ireland'. *Administration* 47(2) pp.78–90.

Nolan, B. and C. Whelan (1997)    'Unemployment and health' in A. Cleary and M. Treacy (eds) *The sociology of health and illness in Ireland*. Dublin: University College Dublin Press.

Ó Baoill, D. (1994)    'Travellers' Cant — language or register?' in M. McCann, S. Ó Síocháin and J. Ruane (eds) *Irish Travellers: Culture and ethnicity*. Belfast: Institute of Irish Studies, Queen's University Belfast, for the Anthropological Association of Ireland.

Ó Buachalla, S. (1974)    'Permanent education in the Irish context'. *Studies* Winter. pp.355–65.

O'Carroll, I. and E. Collins (eds) (1995)    *Lesbian and gay visions of Ireland: Towards the twenty-first century*. London: Cassell.

O'Carroll, J.      'Community programmes and the traditional view of
(1985)             community'. *Social Studies* 8(3/4). pp.137–48.

O'Carroll, J.      'Blood' in M. Peillon and E. Slater (eds) *Encounters with modern*
(1998)             *Ireland*. Dublin: Institute of Public Administration.

O'Connell, J.      'Working with Irish Travellers' in DTEDG File. *Irish Travellers:*
(1992)             *New analysis and new initiatives* (originally 1989). Dublin: Pavee
                   Point.

O'Connor, B.       'Gender, class and television viewing: audience response to the
(1997)             *Ballroom of Romance*' in M. Kelly and B. O'Connor (eds)
                   *Media audiences in Ireland: Power and cultural identity*. Dublin:
                   University College Dublin Press.

O'Connor, N.       *Bringing it all back home: The influence of Irish music*. London:
(1991)             BBC.

O'Connor, P.       *Emerging voices: Women in contemporary Irish society*. Dublin:
(1998)             Institute of Public Administration.

O'Donnell, I.      'Criminal justice review 1998'. *Administration* 47 (2). pp.175–211.
(1999)

O'Donovan, O.      'The plan for women's health and the politics of knowledge: A
(1997a)            brief commentary'. *Women's Studies Review* 5. pp.159–62.

O'Donovan, O.      'Contesting concepts of care: The case of the home help service
(1997b)            in Ireland' in A. Cleary and M. Treacy (eds) *The sociology of*
                   *health and illness in Ireland*. Dublin: University College Dublin
                   Press.

O'Donovan, O.      'Industrial development and rural women in Ireland' in
and C. Curtin      T. Varley, T. Boylan and M. Cuddy (eds) *Rural crisis: perspectives*
(1991)             *on Irish rural development*. Galway: Centre for Development
                   Studies, University College Galway.

O'Dowd, L.         *The state of social science research in Ireland*. Dublin: Royal Irish
(1988)             Academy.

O'Dowd, L.         'Church, state and women: The aftermath of partition' in
(1989)             C. Curtin, P. Jackson and B. O'Connor (eds) *Gender in Irish*
                   *society*. Galway: Galway University Press.

O'Dowd, L.    'The states of Ireland: some reflections on research'. *Irish Journal*
(1991)        *of Sociology* 1. pp.96–106.

O'Dowd, L.    'State legitimacy and nationalism in Ireland' in P. Clancy,
(1992)        M. Kelly, J. Wiatr and R. Zoltaniecki (eds) *Ireland and Poland:
              Comparative perspectives*. Dublin: Department of Sociology,
              University College Dublin.

O'Dowd, L. (ed.) *On intellectuals and intellectual life in Ireland*. Belfast: Institute of
(1996)        Irish Studies/Royal Irish Academy.

O'Dowd, M. and *Chattel, servant or citizen: Women's status in church, state and
S. Wichert (eds) society*. Belfast: Institute of Irish Studies, Queen's University
(1995)        Belfast.

Ó Drisceoil, D. 'Jews and other undesirables: anti-semitism in neutral Ireland
(1997)        during the Second World War' in E. Crowley and J. Mac
              Laughlin (eds) *Under the belly of the tiger: Class, race, identity and
              culture in the global Ireland*. Dublin: Irish Reporter.

O'Hara, P.    *Partners in production: Women, farm and family in Ireland*. New
(1998)        York and Oxford: Berghahn.

O'Hara, T.    'Current structure of the Irish health care system — setting the
(1998)        context' in A. Leahy and M. Wiley (eds) *The Irish health system
              in the 21st century*. Dublin: Oak Tree.

O'Hearn, D.   *Putting Ireland in a global context*. Occasional Papers Series 8.
(1992)        Cork: University College Cork, Department of Sociology.

O'Hearn, D.   *Inside the Celtic Tiger: The Irish economy and the Asian model*.
(1998)        London: Pluto.

O'Mahony, P.  *Crime and punishment in Ireland*. Dublin: Round Hall.
(1993)

O'Malley, E.  'Industrialisation in Ireland' in P. Clancy *et al.* (eds) *Ireland and
(1992)        Poland — Comparative perspectives*. Dublin: University College
              Dublin.

O'Neill, C.   *Telling it like it is*. Dublin: Combat Poverty Agency.
(1992)

O'Reilly, C.      'The Irish language — litmus test for equality? Competing
(1996)           discourses of identity, parity of esteem and the Peace Process'.
                 *Irish Journal of Sociology* 6. pp.154–78.

O'Reilly, E.      *Masterminds of the right.* Dublin: Attic.
(1992)

Ó Riagáin, P.     'Bilingualism in Ireland 1973–1983: an overview of national
(1988)           sociolinguistic surveys'. *International Journal of the Sociology of
                 Language* 70. pp.29–51.

Ó Riagáin, P.     *Language policy and social reproduction in Ireland 1893–1993.*
(1997)           Oxford: Oxford.

O'Shea, D.        'A particular problem in the East . . .' In A. Leahy and M. Wiley
(1998)           (eds) *The Irish health system in the 21st century.* Dublin: Oak Tree.

O'Sullivan, D.    'The ideational base of Irish educational policy' in D. Mulcahy
(1989)           and D. O'Sullivan (eds) *Irish educational policy: Process and
                 substance.* Dublin: Institute of Public Administration.

O'Sullivan, D.    'Shaping educational debate: a case study and an interpretation'.
(1992)           *Economic and Social Review* 23(4). pp.423–38.

O'Sullivan, O.    *The silent schism: Renewal of Catholic Spirit and structures.*
(1997)           Dublin: Gill & Macmillan.

O'Sullivan, S.    '"The Ryanline is now open . . . " Talk radio and the public
(1997)           sphere' in M. Kelly and B. O'Connor (eds) *Media audiences in
                 Ireland: Power and cultural identity.* Dublin: University College
                 Dublin Press.

O'Toole, F.       *Meanwhile back at the ranch: The politics of Irish beef.* London:
(1995)           Vintage.

O'Toole, F.       'The ex-isle of Erin: Emigration and Irish culture' in J. Mac
(1997)           Laughlin (ed.) *Location and dislocation in contemporary Irish
                 society: Emigration and Irish identities.* Cork: Cork University
                 Press.

O'Toole, F.       *The lie of the land.* Dublin: New Island.
(1998)

Oakley, A.
(1998)

'A brief history of gender' in A. Oakley and J. Mitchell (eds) *Who's afraid of feminism: Seeing through the backlash.* Harmondsworth: Penguin.

Oakley, A. and
J. Mitchell
(eds)
(1998)

*Who's afraid of feminism: Seeing through the backlash.* Harmondsworth: Penguin.

OECD
(1997)

*Education at a glance: OECD indicators.* Paris: OECD.

Offer, A.
(1981)

*Property and politics.1870–1914: Landownership, law, ideology and urban development in England.* Cambridge: Cambridge University Press.

Oram, H.
(1993)

*Paper tigers: Stories of Irish newspapers by the people who make them.* Belfast: Appletree/RTÉ.

Owens, M.
(1992)

'Women in rural development: a hit or miss affair'. *Womens Studies Centre Review* 1. pp.15–19.

Parker, L.
(1993)

'Rising crime rates and the role of police in the Czech Republic'. *Police Studies* 16 (2). pp.39–42.

Peace, A.
(1993)

'Environmental protest, bureaucratic closure: the politics of discourse in rural Ireland' in K. Milton (ed.) *Environmentalism — The view from anthropology.* London: Routledge.

Peillon, M.
(1982)

*Contemporary Irish society: An introduction.* Dublin: Gill & Macmillan.

Peillon, M.
(1992)

'State and society in the Republic of Ireland' in P. Clancy *et al.* (eds) *Ireland and Poland — Comparative perspectives.* Dublin: University College Dublin.

Peillon, M.
(1995)

'Interest group and the state' in P. Clancy *et al.* (eds) *Irish Society: Sociological perspectives.* Dublin: Institute of Public Administration in association with the Sociological Association of Ireland.

Peillon, M.          'Community of distrust' in M. Peillon and E. Slater (eds)
(1998)               *Encounters with modern Ireland*. Dublin: Institute of Public
                     Administration.

Peillon, M. and  *Encounters with modern Ireland*. Dublin: Institute of Public
E. Slater            Administration.
(eds)
(1998)

Petitt, L.           'A construction site queered: 'gay' images in new Irish cinema'.
(1999)               *Cineaste* 24(2/3) pp.61–3.

Pollack, A.          'An invitation to racism? Irish daily newspaper coverage of the
(1999)               refugee issue' in D. Kiberd (ed.) *Media in Ireland: The search for
                     ethical journalism*. Dublin: Open Air.

Poole, M.            'In search of ethnicity in Ireland' in B. Graham (ed.) *In search of
(1997)               Ireland: A cultural geography*. London: Routledge.

Porter, S.           'Why should nurses bother with sociology?' in A. Cleary and
(1997)               M. Treacy (eds) *The sociology of health and illness in Ireland*.
                     Dublin: University College Dublin Press.

Power, R. and    *The national farm survey 1992*. Dublin: Rural Economy Research
M. Roche             Centre, Teagasc.
(1993)

Pringle, D.,         *Poor people, poor places: A geography of poverty and deprivation in
J. Walsh and         Ireland*. Dublin: Oak Tree/Geographical Society of Ireland.
M. Hennessey
(eds) (1999)

Rapple, C.           'Ownership, standards, diversity: a way forward' in D. Kiberd
(1997)               (ed.) *Media in Ireland: The search for diversity*. Dublin: Open Air.

Re:public (ed.)  *Planet Diana: Cultural studies and global mourning*. Sydney:
(1997)               Research Centre in Intercommunal Studies, University of
                     Western Sydney, Nepean.

Reiger, K.           *The disenchantment of the home: Modernizing the Australian family
(1985)               1880–1940*. Melbourne: Oxford.

Restivo, S.          *The sociological worldview*. Oxford: Blackwell.
(1991)

Rex, J.          'National identity in the democratic multi-cultural state'.
(1996)           *Sociological Research Online* 1(2).
                 [http://www.socresonline.org.uk/1/2/1.html]

Richards, W.     'Behind closed doors: Homeworkers in Ireland' in A. Byrne and
(1997)           M. Leonard (eds) *Women and Irish society: A sociological reader.*
                 Belfast:BeyondthePale.

Ritzer, G.       *The McDonaldisation of society: An investigation into the changing*
(1993)           *character of contemporary social life.* London: Pine Forge.

Ritzer, G.       *The McDonaldization of society.* [revised ed.] Thousand Oaks CA:
(1996)           Pine Forge.

Robertson, A.    *Beyond the family: The social organization of human reproduction.*
(1991)           Oxford: Polity.

Robertson, R.    'Globalisation and societal modernisation: a note on Japan and
(1987)           Japanese religion'. *Sociological Analysis* 46. pp.35–42.

Robins, J. (ed.) *Reflections on health: Commemorating fifty years of the Department*
(1997)           *of Health 1947–1997.* Dublin: Department of Health.

Rolston, B.      'Voluntary sector funding'. *Scope* 130. pp.10–12.
(1991)

Rose, K.         'The tenderness of the peoples' in I. O'Carroll and E. Collins
(1995)           (eds) *Lesbian and gay visions of Ireland: Towards the twenty-first*
                 *century.* London: Cassell.

Rostow W.        *The stages of economic growth.* Cambridge: Cambridge University
(1960)           Press.

Rottman, D.      *The criminal justice system: Policy and performance.* Dublin:
(1984)           National Economic and Social Council.

Rottman, D.,     *The Distribution of income in the Republic of Ireland: A study in*
D. Hannan,       *social class and family-cycle inequalities.* Dublin: Economic and
N. Hardiman      Social Research Institute.
and M. Wiley
(1982)

Ryan, A.
(1997)
'Gender discourses in school social relations' in Byrne, A. and Leonard M. (eds) *Women and Irish society: A sociological reader.* Belfast: Beyond the Pale.

Ryan, L.
(1990)
'Irish emigration to Britain since World War 2' in R. Kearney (ed.) *Migrations: The Irish at home and abroad.* Dublin: Wolfhound.

Sacks, P.
(1976)
*Donegal mafia: An Irish political machine.* New Haven: Yale University Press.

Sabel, C.
(1996)
*Ireland: Local partnerships and social innovation.* Paris: OECD.

Saris, A.
(1997)
'The asylum in Ireland: A brief institutional history and some local effects.' In A. Cleary and M. Treacy (eds) *The sociology of health and illness in Ireland.* Dublin: University College Dublin Press.

Saunders, P.
and P. Harris
(1990)
'Privatism and the consumer'. *Sociology* 24(1). pp.57–75.

Savage, M.
(1995)
'Class analysis and social research' in T. Butler and M. Savage (eds) *Social change and the middle classes.* London: UCL.

Savage, R.
(1996)
*Irish television: The political and social origins.* Cork: Cork University Press.

Schaffer, K.
(1988)
*Women and the bush: Forces of desire in the Australian cultural tradition.* Melbourne: Cambridge University Press.

Schiller, H.
(1979)
'Transnational media and national development' in K. Nordenstreng and H. Schiller (eds) *National sovereignty and international communication.* Norwood NJ: Ablex.

Scott, A.
(1992)
'Political culture and social movements' in J. Allen, P. Braham and P. Lewis (eds) *Political and economic forms of modernity.* Cambridge: Open University Press/Polity.

Scott, A.
(1997)
'Introduction — globalization: social process or political rhetoric?' in A. Scott (ed.) *The limits of globalization: Cases and arguments.* London: Routledge.

Sennett, R.
(1977)
*The fall of public man*. Cambridge: Cambridge University Press.

Share, P. and
H. Curley
(1997)
'Partnership and rural development: possibilities and pitfalls for Australia'. Paper presented to Rural Australia Beyond 2000 Conference, Wagga Wagga.

Shaughnessy, L.
(1997)
'Female genital mutilation: beyond mutilating mothers and foreign feminists'. *Women's Studies Review* 5. pp.123–34.

Sheehan, H.
(1987)
*Irish television drama: A society and its stories*. Dublin: Radio Telefís Éireann.

Sheehan, J.
(1979)
'Education and society in Ireland, 1945–1970' in J. Lee (ed.) *Ireland: 1945–70*. Dublin: Gill & Macmillan.

Sheerin, E.
(1998)
'Heritage centres' in M. Peillon and E. Slater (eds) *Encounters with modern Ireland*. Dublin: Institute of Public Administration.

Shortall, S.
(1997)
'Women, farming and access to land'. *Irish Journal of Sociology* 7. pp.111–18.

Silke, D. and
G. Whyte
(1999)
'Social security review 1998'. *Administration* 47(2) pp.135–74.

Silverman, M.
(1989)
'"A labouring man's daughter": constructing "respectability" in South Kilkenny' in C. Curtin and T. Wilson (eds) *Ireland from below*. Galway University Press.

Silverman, M.
(1993)
'An urban place in rural Ireland: an historical ethnography of domination, 1841–1989' in C. Curtin, H. Donnan and M. Wilson (eds) *Irish urban cultures*. Belfast: Institute of Irish Studies, Queen's University.

Simmel, G.
(1971)
*Georg Simmel on individuality and social forms*. [D. Levine, ed). Chicago: University of Chicago Press.

Singer, P.
(1997)
*Animal liberation*. London: Pimlico.

Skeldon, R.
(1997)
'Of migration, great cities and markets: Global systems of development' in W. Gungwu (ed.) *Global history and migrations*. Boulder: Westview.

Sklair, L.
(1995)
*Sociology of the global system*. London/New York: Prentice Hall/Harvester Wheatsheaf.

Slater, E.
(1993)
'Contested terrain: differing interpretations of Co. Wicklow's landscape'. *Irish Journal of Sociology* 3. pp.23–55.

Sless, D.
(1986)
*In search of semiotics*. London: Croom Helm.

Slowey, M.
(1987)
'Education for domestication or liberation? Women's involvement in adult education' in M. Cullen (ed.) *Girls don't do honours: Irish women in education in the 19th and 20th centuries*. Dublin: Women's Education Bureau.

Smelser, N.
(1962)
*Theory of collective behaviour*. London: Routledge and Kogan Page.

Smith, A.
(1986)
*The ethnic origins of nations*. Oxford: Blackwell.

Smyth, E.
(1997)
'Labour market structures and women's employment in the Republic of Ireland' in A. Byrne and M. Leonard (eds) *Women and Irish society: A sociological reader*. Belfast: Beyond the Pale.

Smyth, E.
(1999)
*Do schools differ? Academic and personal development among pupils in the second-level sector*. Dublin: Oak Tree/ Economic and Social Research Institute.

Smyth, E. and
Hannan, D.
(1997)
'Girls and coeducation in the Republic of Ireland' in Byrne, A. and Leonard M. (eds) *Women and Irish society: A sociological reader*. Belfast: Beyond the Pale.

Sorlin, P.
(1994)
*Mass media*. London: Routledge. [Key ideas series].

Stein, M.
(1964)
*The eclipse of community*. New York: Harper and Rowe.

Street, J.
(1997)
'"Across the universe" — the limits of global popular culture' in A. Scott (ed.) *The limits of globalization*. London/New York: Routledge.

Sullivan, M. (1997)    'The Visit, incarceration and film by women in Northern Ireland: an interview with Orla Walsh'. The Irish Review 21, pp.29–40.

Sutherland, E. (1961)    [1949] White collar crime. New York: Holt, Rinehart and Winston.

Sweeney, P. (1998)    The Celtic tiger: Ireland's economic miracle explained. Dublin: Oak Tree.

Swingewood, A. (1984)    A short history of sociological thought. Basingstoke: Macmillan.

Symes, D. and T. Marsden (1983)    'Complementary roles and asymmetrical lives: farmers' wives in a large farm environment'. Sociologia Ruralis 23(3/4).

Szasz, T. (1961)    The myth of mental illness: Foundations of a theory of personal conduct. New York: Harper and Rowe.

Szuchewycz, B. (1989)    '"The growth is in the silence": The meanings of silence in the Irish Catholic charismatic movement' in C. Curtin and T. Wilson (eds) Ireland from below: Social change and local communities. Galway: Galway University Press.

Tam, H. (1998)    Communitarianism: A new agenda for politics and citizenship. London: Macmillan.

Tannam, M. (1999)    'At home from abroad: the experiences of some migrant women in Ireland'. Women's Studies Review 6. pp.19–32.

Taylor, L. (1989)    'The mission: An anthropological view of an Irish religious occasion' in C. Curtin and T. Wilson (eds) Ireland from below: Social change and local communities. Galway: Galway University Press.

Theweleit, K. (1987)    Male fantasies vol. 1: Women, floods, bodies and history. Cambridge: Polity.

Theweleit, K. (1989)    Male fantasies vol. 2: Male bodies: Psychoanalyzing the white terror. Cambridge: Polity.

Thompson, E.P.  *The making of the English working class*. Harmondsworth: Penguin.
(1968)

Thompson, J.  *Studies in the theory of ideology*. Cambridge: Polity.
(1984)

Thompson, J.  *Ideology and modern culture*. Cambridge: Polity.
(1990)

Tobin, F.  *The best of decades; Ireland in the 1960s*. Dublin: Gill &
(1996)  Macmillan.

Tomlinson, A.  'Introduction: consumer culture and the aura of the commodity'
(1990)  in A. Tomlinson (ed.) *Consumption, identity and style*. London:
Routledge.

Tomlinson, J.  *Cultural imperialism*. London: Pinter.
(1991)

Torode, B.  'What you see is what you get?' *Economic and Social Review* 30(1)
(1999)  pp.91–107.

Touraine, A.  *The voice and the eye*. Cambridge: Cambridge University Press.
(1982)

Touraine, A.  *Anti-nuclear protest: The opposition to nuclear energy in France*.
(1983)  Cambridge: Cambridge University Press.

Tovey, H.  'Milking the farmer? Modernisation and marginalisation in Irish
(1982)  dairy farming' in M. Kelly *et al*. (eds) *Power, conflict and
inequality*. Dublin: Turoe.

Tovey, H.  '"Local community": in defence of a much-criticised concept'.
(1985)  *Social Studies* 8(3/4). pp.149–64.

Tovey, H.  '"Of cabbages and kings": restructuring in the Irish food
(1991)  industry'. *Economic and Social Review* 22 (4). pp.333–50.

Tovey, H.  'Rural sociology in Ireland: a review'. *Irish Journal of Sociology* 2.
(1992a)  pp.96–121.

Tovey, H.
(1992b)
'Environmentalism in Ireland — modernity and identity' in
P. Clancy, M. Kelly, J. Wiatr and R. Zoltaniecki (eds) Ireland and
Poland: Comparative perspectives. Dublin: Department of
Sociology, University College Dublin.

Tovey, H.
(1993)
'Environmentalism in Ireland — two versions of development
and modernity'. International Sociology 8 (4). pp.413–30.

Tovey, H.
(1994)
'Rural management, public discourses and the farmer as
environmental actor' in D. Symes and A. Jansen (eds)
Agricultural restructuring and rural change in Europe. Wageningen:
Wageningen Agricultural University.

Tovey, H.
(1997)
'Food, environmentalism and rural sociology: on the organic
farming movement in Ireland'. Sociologia Ruralis 37(1). pp.21–37.

Tovey, H.
(1999)
'Rural poverty — a political economy perspective', in D. Pringle,
J. Walsh and M. Hennessey (eds) Poor people, poor places: A
geography of poverty and deprivation in Ireland. Dublin: Oak
Tree/Geographical Society of Ireland.

Tovey, H.,
D. Hannan and
H. Abramson
(1989)
Why Irish? A sociological interpretation of Irish national identity
and the Irish language. Dublin: Bord na Gaeilge.

Townsend, P.
and N. Davidson
(eds)
(1982)
Inequalities in health: The Black Report. Harmondsworth: Penguin.

Tucker, V.
(1987)
'State and community: a case study of Glencolumbcille' in
C. Curtin and T. Wilson (eds) Ireland from below: Social change
and local communities. Galway: Galway University Press.

Tucker, V.
(1997)
'From biomedicine to holistic health' in A. Cleary and
M. Treacy (eds) The sociology of health and illness in Ireland.
Dublin: University College Dublin Press.

Tucker, V.
(1999)
'The myth of development' in R. Munck and D. O'Hearn (eds)
Critial development theory — Contribution to a new paradigm.
London: Zed books.

Turnbull, C.
(1974)

*The mountain people.* London: Picador.

Turner, B. (ed.)
(1990)

*Theories of modernity and postmodernity.* London: Sage.

Turner, B.
(1996)

'Introduction' in B. Turner (ed.): *The Blackwell companion to social theory.* Oxford: Blackwell.

TWG
(1995)

[Technical Working Group] *Interim report to the Steering Committee on the Future of Higher Education.* Dublin: Higher Education Authority.

Vandergeest, P.
(1996)

'Real villages: national narratives of rural development' in E. DuPuis and P. Vandergeest (eds) *Creating the countryside.* Philadelphia: Temple University Press.

Varenne, H.
(1993)

'Dublin 16: accounts of suburban lives' in C. Curtin, H. Donnan and T. Wilson (eds) *Irish urban cultures.* Belfast: Institute of Irish Studies, Queen's University.

Veblen, T.
(1925)

*The theory of the leisure class: An economic study of institutions.* London: Allen and Unwin.

Wagner, P.
(1994)

*A sociology of modernity: Liberty and discipline.* London/New York: Routledge.

Walklate, S.
(1995)

*Gender and crime: An introduction.* London: Prentice Hall/Harvester Wheatsheaf.

Wallerstein, I.
(1983)

*Historical capitalism.* London: Verso.

Walsh, B.
(1970)

*Religion and demographic behaviour in Ireland.* Dublin: Economic and Social Research Institute paper 55. p.7.

Walter, N.
(1998)

*The new feminism.* London: Little, Brown.

Warde, A. and
M. Tomlinson
(1995)

'Taste among the middle classes, 1968–88' in T. Butler and M. Savage (eds) *Social change and the middle classes.* London: UCL.

Waters, M. and    *Sociology one*. Melbourne: Longman Cheshire.
R. Crook
(1993)

Weber, E.    *Peasants into Frenchmen*. Stanford: Stanford University Press.
(1976)

Weber, M.    *The Protestant ethic and the spirit of capitalism*. [Trans.
(1970)    Talcott Parsons]. London: Unwin.
[1920]

Weeks, J.    *Sex, politics and society: The regulation of sexuality since 1800*.
(1989)    London: Longman.

Whelan, C.    *Values and social change in Ireland*. Dublin: Gill & Macmillan.
(1994)

Whelan, C.    'Class transformation and social mobility in the Republic of
(1995)    Ireland' in P. Clancy *et al.* (eds) *Irish society: Sociological
    perspectives*. Dublin: Institute of Public Administration in
    association with the Sociological Association of Ireland.

Whelan, C. and    'Marriage and the family' in C. Whelan (ed.) *Values and social
T. Fahey    change in Ireland*. Dublin: Gill & Macmillan.
(1994)

Whelan, C. and    *Social mobility in the Republic of Ireland: A comparative perspective*.
B. Whelan    Dublin: Economic and Social Research Institute.
(1984)

Whyte, J.    *Church and state in modern Ireland 1923–1970*. Dublin: Gill &
(1971)    Macmillan.

Whyte, J.    'Church, state and society, 1950–70' in J. Lee (ed.) *Ireland:
(1979)    1945–70*. Dublin: Gill & Macmillan.

Whyte, J.    *Church and state in modern Ireland 1923–1979*. Dublin: Gill &
(1980)    Macmillan.

Wickham, J.    'Dependence and state structure: foreign firms and industrial
(1983)    policy in the Republic of Ireland' in O. Holl (ed.) *Small states in
    Europe and dependence*. Vienna: Austrian Institute for
    International Affairs.

Wickham, J. (1986)   'Industrialisation, work and unemployment' in P. Clancy *et al.* (eds): *Ireland — A sociological profile*. Dublin: Institute of Public Administration/Sociological Association of Ireland.

Wickham, J. (1997)   'Where is Ireland in the Global Information Society?' *Economic and Social Review* 28 (3)

Wickham, J. (1998)   'An intelligent island?' in M. Peillon and E. Slater (eds) *Encounters with modern Ireland*. Dublin: Institute of Public Administration.

Wigham, M. (1992)   *The Irish Quakers: A short history of the Religious Society of Friends in Ireland*. Dublin: Historical Committee of the Religious Society of Friends in Ireland.

Wiley, M. and B. Merriman (1996)   *Women and health care in Ireland: Knowledge, attitudes and behaviour*. Dublin: Oak Tree.

Wilkinson, R. (1996)   *Unhealthy societies: The afflictions of inequality*. London: Routledge.

Williams, R. (1976)   *Keywords: A vocabulary of culture and society*. London: Fontana.

Williams, R.   'The health legacy of emigration: the Irish in Britain and (1996) elsewhere'. *Irish Journal of Sociology* 6. pp.56–78.

Willis, P. (1977)   *Learning to labour: How working class kids get working class jobs*. Farnborough: Saxon House.

Wilson, T. (1984)   'From Clare to the Common Market — perspectives in Irish ethnography'. *Anthropological Quarterly* 57. pp.1–15.

Wolf, N. (1991)   *The beauty myth*. London: Vintage.

Wong, S. and J. Salaff (1998)   'Network capital'. *British Journal of Sociology* 49(3). pp.358–74.

Woolgar, S. (1988)    *Science: The very idea.* Chichester: Horwood/London and New York: Tavistock.

Wright, Erik Olin (1989)    *The debate on classes.* London: Verso.

Wright, S. (1992)    'Image and analysis: new directions in community studies' in B. Short (ed.) *The English rural community: Image and analysis.* Cambridge: Cambridge University Press.

Yearley, S. (1991)    *The Green case.* London: Routledge.

Yearley, S. (1995)    'The social shaping of the environmental movement in Ireland' in P. Clancy, S. Drudy, K. Lynch and L. O'Dowd (eds) *Irish society: Sociological perspectives.* Dublin: Institute of Public Administration in association with the Sociological Association of Ireland.

Yearley, S. (1996)    *Sociology, environmentalism, globalisation.* London: Sage.

Young, I. (1990)    'The ideal of community and the politics of difference' in L. Nicholson (ed.) *Feminism/postmodernism.* London: Routledge.

Young, M. and P. Willmott (1957)    *Family and kinship in east London.* London: Routledge and Kegan Paul.

# Index